THE DINKA HISTORY

THE ANCIENTS OF SUDAN FROM ABUK AND GARANG AT CREATION TO THE PRESENT DAY DINKA 2015

Lewis Anei Madut-Kueendit

Dr. Madhel Malek Agei's Bull, Marial, from the Apuk-Jurwiir area of Thiet, Tonj. A mighty symbol of the Dinka traditional leadership.

The publisher wishes to acknowledge and thank Dr. Douglas H. Johnson for his invaluable help and support for Africa World Books and its mission of preserving and promoting African cultural and literary traditions and history. Dr. Johnson and fellow historians have been instrumental in ensuring that African people remain connected to their past and their identity. Africa World Books is proud to carry on this mission.

Copyright © 2011 Lewis Anei Madut-Kueendit
Edited by Cheryl Battridge AE

ISBN (Paperback): 9780994363138

First published in 2011 by Mignic Technologies

The contents of this historical work have been presented in such a way that there is some repetition in the information that is relevant to several topics or sub-topics to allow ease of cross-referencing for the reader.

No part of this publication may be reproduced, stored in a retrieval system, or transmitted, in any form, or by any means, electronic, mechanical, photocopying, recording or otherwise, without the prior permission of the publishers.

This book is sold subject to the conditions that it shall not, by way of trade or otherwise, be lent, re-sold, hired out or otherwise circulated without the publisher's prior consent in any form of binding or cover other than in which it is published and without a similar condition including the condition being imposed on the subsequent purchaser.

Cover design, typesetting and layout: Africa World Books
Unit 3, 57 Frobisher St, Osborne Park, WA 6017
P.O. Box 1106 Osborne Park, WA 6916

"The biggest weapon in any cultural contest is to orient your people to know their origin and their culture."

DEDICATION

This book is written in memory of my late father, Madut-Kuendit, whose great deeds in Awan-Parek territory continue to earn us respect in the eyes of the Awan community. His personality cult inspired me to put his name down to record for posterity. I owe him respect and identification for founding for us such a strong family foundation after our family line was badly thinned out by the infamous slave trade era of the bygone Turkiyya with its succeeding Mahdia, two slave trade periods of more than seventy years in Sudan. I also dedicate this book to him for taking me to school. My great mother, Luac Akɛɛn Buk, was the cause of my father's pride in me. I also dedicate this book to her. The two made me to be what I later came to be in real life. My family line must continue to venerate them for eternity.

Fig 1: Showing Paramount chief Dhor Ariik Mawien. Paramount chief Dhor Ariik Mawien started as executive chief of Lou-Mawien territory in 1971 when he succeeded his elder brother, Ring Ariik, who died in a helicopter accident. Great Dhor Ariik currently aged 87, soon became paramount court president for Akop regional court, a position he held until the SPLM/A (Sudan peoples' liberation movement/army) decentralisation policy of 2003 created four more peoples' regional courts in his Akop sub-region of Tonj. (Akop is an area comprised of the territories of Lou-Mawien, also called Lou-Ariik, Kongöör, Apuk- PadƆc, Awan-Parek and Lou-Paher. It is a region of the Rek Dinka. Akop is located north east of today's Tonj North county in Warrap state.) Great Dhor Ariik, however, continued as court president for his Lou-Mawien territory, a position from

which the president of the government of South Sudan gave him the honorary title of paramount traditional leader for Warrap state as well as for the entire Bahr el Ghazal region in 2009. He succeeded his elder brother as previously mentioned, Ring Ariik Mawien, who took over from his father Ariik Mawien the Great, paramount court president and traditional leader Dhor Ariik became one of the few longest serving traditional chiefs in the whole of Bahr el Ghazal, coming from one of the most noted holy clans among the Dinka. Great Dhor Ariik is also known as the greatest Spear Master of the century in the whole of the Dinka traditional society in the Bhar el Ghazal region.

Fig 2 (opposite): Map of ancient Northern Sudan showing the Butana steppe areas which were lived in by the Jaang ancestral community before coming to Matemma and Khartoum areas in 360-90AD

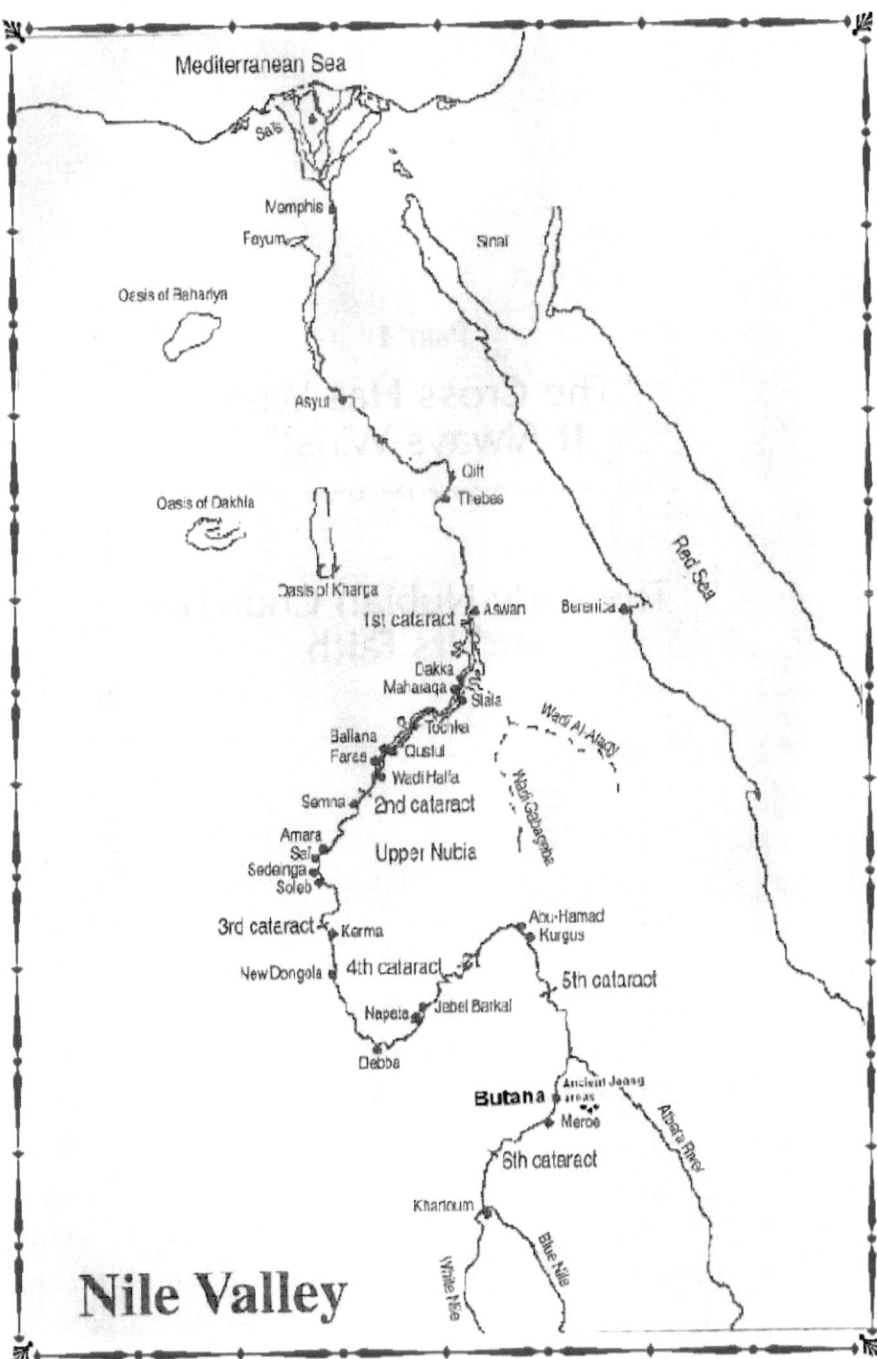

Fig 3: Showing the author in his office in 2006 when he was governor of Warrap state. Ustaz Lewis Anei Madut-Kuendit is the first writer to write a book on the history of his Dinka people, a renowned and comprehensive classic which tells of the origin and historical evolution of today's biggest nationality in the Republic of South Sudan. The book came to the fore at the right time when his people have just finished with the first major project, the national liberation and creation of a nation state. This masterpiece work and series of public lectures and talk shows that dominated Juba television screens and other media outlets in Juba have popularised him as a writer of consequence and a man deeply loved by his Dinka people.

Fig 4: Showing a Rek Dinka girl leading a display song bull for her brother (behind the bull). Photo taken: 1952, Tonj.

ACKNOWLEDGEMENTS

It has not been an easy task for me to embark on writing this marathon work on the history of the Dinka people to whom I belong. This explains why the book took many years, from 1979 when I started the research, up to 2011. First and foremost I appreciate my determined effort and persistence despite Sudan worldwide noted upheavals caused by the more than two decades of civil war of liberation in Southern Sudan during my research times.

However, from this outset I must admit that I am personally accountable for the errors and contents of this historical reconstruction of the history of my Dinka people. This is because it was me alone who conducted the research work, collected the data material and sat to piece together those material data obtained from the Dinka and from some of the Nilotic and other Sudanese peoples as well as from those documentaries on creation, on the world flood of Noah, on prehistory, on ancient and on the Mediaeval peoples.

I am, however, thankful to so many people who in one way or another contributed to the making of this book. First and foremost my gratitude goes to my former lecturers, the late Ustaz Lazarus Leek Mawut and the late Dr Domasio Dut Majak, both of the University of Juba. The two lecturers are next to my father in this regard for they contributed greatly in shaping my initial inclinations for history. Their prosperous lectures, advice and inspiration allowed me to undertake this field which was not touched one day by any Dinka scholar and gave me the impetus to pursue the writing of this book. They deserve my appreciation and thanks.

Next is the adept chronicler Captain Kɔng-Mayardit Dau Agɔth whose invaluable information about some of the Upper Nile Dinka communities added more impetus for the author to proceed ahead, as the history of Upper Nile Dinka is so invaluable for the Dinka of Bahr el Ghazal region, who are barred off from their brethren in the Upper Nile by the big Nile and its large swamp marshes since they left the Upper Nile region nearly seven hundred years ago. My thanks to Captain Kɔng-Mayardit has no limits.

Apart from Captain Kɔng-Mayardit there are three former commissioners of Tonj, Cuɛibɛt and Rumbek Counties: Brigadier Charles Kuol Deng Kuol, General John Lat Zakaria and General Paul Macuɛi Malok, three Dinka liberation struggle authorities who wholeheartedly facilitated my research activities in their respective Dinka counties during the SPLM/A liberation years. More importantly they supervised and supported workshops, seminars and symposiums that brought many leading Dinka intellectuals, chiefs and other community traditional leaders and elders to add and evaluate my collected data material. Next is my friend and colleague Captain Dut Makoi Kuok, who was, at the time, the headmaster of the historic Rumbek secondary school. He and his wife Acitgiɛr Nɔk Marial Buɔɔt availed the use of his residence and the use of that big historical school for my research purposes.

HE Engineer Chol Tɔŋ Mayay, Governor of Lakes state, Mr Cirillo Chol Mayuɔm of the SPLM Information Department, Lakes state SPLM secretariat, Ustaz Gɔɔr Dhaal of Rumbek education office and Dr Peter Mahal of UNICEF, among many others, also gave invaluable support for my research activities among the Lakes state Dinka communities in Rumbek. These friends and colleagues deserve recorded thanks and appreciation for the invaluable support and encouragement they gave to me in Rumbek during my research time there.

But what can I say of the members of my family? Ajäk Bol Madut, Balanga Citjang Duör, Margret Adut Manyuɔl and the young daughter of mine, Kuei Anei Kuendit!? These wives of mine deserve thanks, for not only did they preserve all those heaps of collected data material in their homes at the time of war in Southern Sudan and after the war, but they were also supportive, encouraging and confident about the entire book project. I used my family resources to the point of selling my family cows over the years in order to pay for the research costs, transport from place to place, varied computer typesetting and the huge editing, printing and publication costs. I really owe them many thanks. I give a special word of thanks to Kuei Anei Kuendit in whom I have belief she can further my name in her lifetime as I did for my father.

Many thanks to my computerists Mariah Kayanja of Mignic Technologies (U) Limited, Mrs Tabitha Karimi Silas of Destiny Image Enterprise, Hurlingham shopping centre, Nairobi, Kenya and Mrs Mary of Creative Media Printing and Advertising, Juba, South Sudan. I thank these three among many for their special commitment to organise with me the massive research data and manuscript into this book.

My thanks also go to our big uncle of the Southern Sudanese people – the Governor of the Central Bank of South Sudan, Uncle Elijah Malok Alɛɛng. I am thanking him for his invaluable contribution and for finding time to open my Dinka history symposium held in Rumbek secondary school in 2003. The Ministry of Higher Education, Science and Technology in the government of the Republic of South Sudan and Mr Yol Luol Koor, the Executive Director at the office of the President of the Republic, takes the sum total of my thanks and appreciation for the support they offered, thus enabling the first printing and publishing of this book in its first edition in 2011.

However, this acknowledgement cannot close without expressing my sincere gratitude and thanks to Mr Peter Deng of Africa World Books in Australia and Miss Cheryl Bettridge, AE, president of the Society of Editors in Western Australia. I thank the two for their concern and the critical editorial work they did for this second edition of my book. Their uncountable communication on the editorial work with me from that faraway country cannot be forgotten.

Finally, I must value and appreciate the young scholar from my area, Mr Emmanuel Monychol Akop. I thank him for his expert preface to the second edition which he wrote after a critical read of the book. I finally give sincere appreciation and thanks to my Dinka community in Australia for the great concern which they showed for their history book up to the launch day. I thank everyone for contributing to the making of this book about the Dinka people.

TABLE OF CONTENTS

Dedication	*v*
Acknowledgements	*xiii*
Preface to the First Edition	*xxvii*
Preface to the Second Edition	*xxxvii*
Abbreviations	*xlv*
A Guide to the Dinka Alphabet, Letters, and Pronunciation	*xlvii*
Introduction	*li*

Chapter One: Who Are The Dinka?

The Dinka Physical Features	1
Who are the Dinka?	10
Bulls	42
The Dinka Defence System	47
Evolution of the Dinka Names	48
Jiëëng and Jääng	51
Muɔnyjäng	52
Jenge or Zenge	63
Dinka	64

Dinka Social Classifications	66
The Dinka Age-Set System	80
Family ɣöt Thok or Mac-Thok	83
Lineage (Wäär Or Gɔl)	84
Clan (Dhiëth)	85
Section (Baai)	87
Territory (Wut – Also Called Baai)	87
Sub-Tribe	88
Tribe	89
Dinka Lands, Economy and Their Ways of Life	90
Dinka Settlement Mode	94
Dinka Demography and Population Status	103

Chapter Two: The Dinka Rural Setting

Dinka Material Culture	115
Dinka Traditional Homemaking	119
Dinka Home Furnishings	122
Dinka Traditional Dress and Decoration	127
Dinka Rural Work and War Implements	131
The Dinka Dietary System	134
Dinka Fattening and Fattening Season	135
Harvesting, Threshing and Storage of Food Produce	140

Chapter Three: Dinka Months, Seasons and Weather Cycle of the Year (The Dinka Calendar)

Dinka Months and Seasons	144
Sub-Seasons	145
Gärnhom: The Dinka Physical Initiation to Manhood	163
Celestial Bodies and Their Impact on the Dinka World	171

Chapter Four: Dinka National Communities

Introduction	183
Bahr El Ghazal Dinka Communities:	184
Rek Dinka Tribe	184
Social Configuration of the Rek Dinka:	
The Kuei Territorial Sections of the Rek	196
Kuei Sections in Awiel East and Awiel South	199
More about the Lith Community of Rek	201
Further Background Story of Lith	208
The Battle of Ayuomlual	210
The Battle of the Wife of Buonglek at Angääc	214
How the Rek Made its Migration into Bahr El Ghazal	217
The Kuei Component of Rek and its Sections	218
Sections of Kuei	218
The Famine of 1658AD in the Awan Area	238
Family Genealogical Descent of Sub-Chief Gai	
Aleeng and Dr John Garang:	241
The Dispute Between Wol-Adhieu and Loŋaar Ayuueel	244
Lith Section Of The Rek	253
Territorial Configuration of the Lith Section Of The Rek:	255
Gïr Component of The Rek	256
Current Areas Of The Gïr Section of the Rek	262
The Agaar Dinka Tribe	263
Social Configuration of the Agaar Dinka	273
Malual Dinka	275
The Pajok Section of Malual Dinka	278
The Palieupiny Sections of Malual	281
Luacjang Dinka	282
Factors that Kept the Luac Population in Check	292
Territorial and Administrative Configuration of	
The Luac Dinka	293
Gok Dinka and its Sections	295

The Battle of Kurnyuuk 306
The Battle of Barantök: 308
The Battle of Wär-Adeet: 308
Territorial and Social Composition of the Gok
    Dinka Community 313
Kiec Dinka 314
Social Administrative and Territorial Composition
    of Kiec Dinka 318
Aliap Dinka and its Sections 319
Social and Territorial Composition of Aliap Dinka
    (Aliap Dinka And Its Sections) 327
Atuöt Dinka 330
Twic Dinka of Bahr El Ghazal 331
The Beginning of Twic Dinka 333
The Emergence of the Community Name Twic from Kuac 334
Separation of the Twic into Two 338
How the Twic went away from Luacjang 342
Original Inhabitants of Present Twic Land 344
Territorial and Administrative Composition of the Twic
    In Bahr El Ghazal 346
Twic Dinka Sections by Payams 347
The Ngok Dinka of Abyei 347
Ruweng Migration to the Western Upper Nile 352
Upper Nile Dinka Communities 356

Chapter Five: Dinka Cattle

The Dinka Cattle Complex 376
Dinka Cattle Vocabulary and Metaphorical Association 382
Dinka Cattle Colour Imagery 392
Castration and Non-Castration of Bulls 400
Ox-Names for Dinka Cattle Owners 403
Dinka Idioms (Maany) are Linked to Cattle 404

Song Interpretation	498
Dinka Personal Names and the Cattle	413
Cattle and Sacrifice Making	419
Bulls as Sacrificial Objects	421

Chapter Six:
The Social Institution Called Marriage Or Thiëëk

Introduction	425
Types and Ways To Marry Among the Dinka	433
Dinka Customary Marriage	434
Division of Dowry Cattle and the Issue of Aruëth	445
Kueth Nya or the Taking of The Bride to Her New Home	452
Gem Nya or the Handing Over of the Bride	453
Marriage Through Betrothal, Called 'Luny Kɔu', and 'Mek' or Choice	455
Marriage Through Elopement; Jötjöt	457
Marriage Through Impregnation	460
Marriage by Choice from The Girl's Side	461
Marriage Through Abduction	462
Ghost Marriage	463
Levirate Marriage	467
Sororate Marriage	471
Dissolution Of Marriage or Divorce	474
Gross Indecency	477

Chapter Seven:
The Origin Of The Dinka People (An Ethnographical Survey)

Introduction	486
The Beginning of Things	490
Dinka Creation Myths	491
The First Dispute with Nhialic	496
The Dinka First Parents After their Quarrel with Nhialic	498

The Children of Abuk and Garaŋ	499
Garaŋ's Division of Roles to His Sons	504
The Panthou Creation Area: Its Extent And Ecology	506
Climatic Conditions After Creation to the Time of Noi's Flood	509
People of the First Millennium after Creation	510
Manhacuuk in the 3rd to 4th Millennium After Creation	517
The Pestle Story and God's Withdrawal to the Sky	520
The Dinka Version of the Human Suffering Before The Flood of Noi	525
The World Flood of Noi According to the Dinka (Its Point of Eruption, Extent and Time)	527
The Historic Ark of Noi	531
The Flood's Point of Eruption, Extent and Time	535
After the Flood as The Dinka Know it	540
The Dinka Parent Stem	540
Introduction	540
Dinka Knowledge of the Post-Flood Period	542
The Tower of Babel and the Dinka	547
The Confusion of Languages	552
Dinka Pre-Ancient Forebears went to Mongolia, China And Southwest Asia	553
Are Dinka And Nuers Descendants of Jacob or are they not?	556
From Jiel In Canaan to Ajaang in Ancient Wawat	557
Egypt and the Dinka Forebears	559
The Era of Oppression	563
The Pharaoh of Oppression	565
The Biblical Exodus According to the Dinka	566
The Plagues or Disasters	569
An Eyewitness to the Disaster	572
The Disaster by Blood	573

The Disaster on Domestic Animals	573
Destruction by Storm	574
Destruction by Locusts	574
Destruction Through Darkness	575
The Final Night of Death	575
The Pharaoh of the Exodus and His Fate in Dinka Mythology	576
The Abiel Faction Comes to the Wawat Region in Ancient Northern Sudan	578
(The Coming of the Dinka Ancestors to Ancient Northern Sudan)	578

Chapter Eight:
A Lineage From Primordial Chaldeans Becomes Jääng And Nuers In Sudan, Dongola Region

Dinka Forebears and their Routes of Entry Into Ancient Northern Sudan	583
The Story Of Mayuääl	590
Jieldit and his Faction Joins the Jääng in Wawat	596
Kush Kingdom and the Dinka Ancestors	600
The Shift From Napata to Meroe	604
Ancient Geography of Meroe	606
The Beginning of the Decline of Kush Kingdom	608
The Fall of Meroe and the Final Dispersal of the Blacks	609
Burial System Of The Meroites and Today's Dinka Burials	611
Jääng After the Fall of Meroe	612
Luo and Nuer Migration to Khartoum after the Fall of Meroe	614
Reasons for the Jääng Move to the Khartoum Region from a Tbarai Shendi Areas	618

Chapter Nine:
The Jääng Migration from the Khartoum Region to Blue and Upper Niles

Introduction	620
Jääng First Contact with the Arabs (The Story Of Awalad Abbas)	622
Jaang Settlement Areas in Khartoum	625
Luo-Funj and Burun Migration Away from the Khartoum Region	627
Nuers' Migration from the Khartoum Region to Western Upper Nile In Southern Sudan	629
Jääng Migration from The Khartoum Area to Northern Upper Nile In Southern Sudan	630
The Blue Nile Route Column	632
The White Nile Route Column	634
Luo Resistance to Jaang Migration Into Northern Upper Nile	636
Jääng Migration From Kurmuk to Southern Upper Nile	640
Nuer-Jääng Myth of Origin	641
Basin Ecology of the Jääng Settlement Areas before they Migrated To Bahr El Ghazal	650
Upper Nile Geography in Mediaeval Times	651

Chapter Ten:
The Jääng Migration To Bahr El Ghazal

Introduction	652
Exploration Surveys into Bahr El Ghazal	653
The Departure Plan and the Debate Before the Takeoff To Bahr El Ghazal	655
Leadership Quarrels and Rites on the Riverbank Before Crossing the Nile	656
Problems Encountered During the Crossing Moments	657
Events after Crossing to the West Bank (Encampment Locations)	662

The Jaang Migratory Waves Into The Bahr El
    Ghazal Interior From The Ajäk Area Of Today's
    Yirol West County   669

Chapter Eleven:
Slavery, Slave Trade And The Dinka People
Introduction   673
Turco-Egyptian Colonisation of Sudan   674
Slave Trade and the Dinka   674
Background to Slavery   676
The Beginning of the Slavery of the Turkiya In Sudan   679
The Coming of the Slave Trade to the Bahr El
    Ghazal Dinka Areas   685
Slave Trade Routes and their Network in Dinka Lands   687
Great Lual Ngor Slave Kingdom at Axerdit
    in the Apuk-Giir Area of Nyarmong   693
Mahdia and Slave Trade in Dinka Lands   696
Ngok Dinka Support to the Mahdists' Movement   697
Malual Dinka Support for the Mahdists' Movement
Some Dinka Chiefs are Descendants of
    Slave Traders' Agents   711
The Anglo-Egyptian Era and the Dinka (1898-1956)   715
Abolition of the Slave Trade in Dinka Lands   715

Bibliography   *717*

PREFACE TO THE FIRST EDITION

The idea that led to the writing of a history book on my Dinka people started in 1979. That idea was moulded one day in a conversation I had with my late father, Madut-Kuendit. That conversation took place in our more than 400-year- old village of Tharakon in Awan-Parek area of Jur-Bol section where I come from. The day was 23 December that year. From Tonj town where I was working as a medical assistant I went to my home area to visit my old father in the village, a distance of about eighty miles north of Tonj town. One evening I sat beside him in the courtyard of the homestead of one of his junior wives, Aẋok Arop Dök, a woman he married after my mother in the early sixties. Stepmother Aẋok came from the Patɛk clan people in the neighbouring Lou-Ariik territory. I sat by the old father to record the historical saga of our Payii clan. This was the initial purpose of my visit to him.

As the most elderly Spear Master[1] of his territory at the time I saw him as the appropriate cultural custodian to tell the ancient saga of

---

[1] Madut-Kuendit was the most senior Spear Master in his Awan Parek territory at the time of the interview. He was about ninety years old or above when he was being interviewed by the son. Spear Master in Dinka is a religious holy man in the community.

our clan, the community history of our area and perhaps to tell me something about Rek Dinka. By then the old father was a renowned community liege, a government member of our natives' court and a traditional omda² of Awan territory. He was a member representing his community in the traditional court of the Akop region of the then Tonj district. Being also a spiritual leader of his family, clan and community, what the Dinka people call Bäny-Bith, he was also the Godfather of his territorial Age-group known in Awan-Parek territory as Mabior-Kuendit.

Surprisingly enough the old omda became a genius in Dinka oral history. He made a fascinating account and presentation which enthralled the son. He thus instilled into the son a kind of unquenchable urge to attempt writing about the entire Dinka history as a nationality. From then the idea to equip oneself with the necessary instruments for approaching this untapped field about the Dinka people started to come into mind. The Dinka nationality, whose ethnic origin has never been tackled by any historian, was now to become a challenge for the old man's son. The idea to research into Dinka roots of origin and to write a book of this kind therefore began to take shape. From that useful conversation the son was given the impetus towards the idea and all aspects of thought and actions were thus geared towards this desire. This, becoming a burning desire, later became the principal reason for going back to school and for shifting from being a student of sciences to become a student of Arts during my Rumbek secondary school days (1981 to 1983). In 1984, the idea succeeded to shape my decision to get matriculated to the faculty of education–arts section at the University of Juba, where I was to get specialisations in history and literature, two disciplines found to be the necessary weapons for a writing mission in history as conceived from the old man

---

2   Omda is an Arabic word for a community headman. The title denotes a legal, administrative and socio-religious figure in a Sudanese concept.

since 1979. Thus the book grew out of that original idea to know about the family history of my clan, an idea that since then has been kept cultivated and in the course of my time was able to nurse itself into me wanting to become a writer and write about people's roots of origin.

That feeling was later deepened when at the University of Juba I met two college lecturers of history – Ustaz Lazerus Leek Mawut and Dr Damasio Dut Majak. The two lecturers truly gave me what I wanted from the university. They sharpened my desire for history as a discipline. Professor of literature Taban Lo Lyong also gave me additional impetus and skills for constructive and creative writing through literature. Literature as a discipline was to equip me with writing skills as I wanted a strong basis in the English language to tackle the history of my people. Very few know how to read and write Dinka language and English language is the official language in South Sudan, at least for the time being. I was therefore obliged to write the history of my people in a foreign language as it is the official language of my country today.

I offer this book primarily as a contribution to the promotion of my Dinka culture; and although the work is on the Dinka people, it also attempts to shed light on all the Nilotic peoples. Besides, the book is hoped to help readers to form a picture about the true ancient peoples of Sudan, especially the Nilotic ancient communities of the Sudan who with the Dinka have been in Sudan for quite a number of centuries, even before the rise of the Kush Kingdom that gloriously lived on the African continent for well over a thousand years since it started in the 8th century BC. The Ministry of education in South Sudan will certainly benefit our schools and universities through this history book.

Of course one of the tasks of an historian is to make others know of his people. An historian also has a duty to orient his people to know their origin and be committed to their culture and therefore know their history. I therefore felt and took it as a duty upon myself to trace and reconstruct the obscure history of my nationality which has continued to exhibit a culture so rich, a culture that has been providing Sudan, especially Southern Sudan, with such values and feats that are very well appreciated in this country and the world at large.

This ethnographical survey is the first attempt to tackle the ethnic origins and history of the Dinka people, a field which has since long been viewed by even the early generations of the Dinka educated elites as a mystery to attempt to tackle. This fear has either been due to lack of documentary evidence, lack of willpower or lack of opportunity to undertake such a difficult task. Our Dinka roots of origin has been so long a cherished wish of the Dinka educated elites, who have been craving to have their history written. It is hoped that the book will address the curriculum needs of our schools in South Sudan, particularly for the Dinka children. This is in addition to answering the general readership wishing to be informed about the Dinka despite the turbulent times in which the author had to carry out the intricate research work and also answer for the patriotic demand to contribute to the process of national liberation as a war combatant in the battlefields and, at times, act as a teacher to students behind the war fronts in the SPLM/A liberated areas. The desire to accomplish the task, however, kept on persistently to its final conclusion like this.

Despite those difficulties the author was able to painstakingly wander in many parts of the Dinka land, conducting intensive research work among Dinka rural communities in the Upper Nile up to Renk at the extreme end of the Upper Nile. The author had to also wander in Bahr el Ghazal areas up to Awiel sub-region at the extreme end of Bahr el Ghazal in the true northwest of the country.

Although the author hails from the Rek Dinka heartland of Tonj, the research activity as explained above carried him to many areas of the Dinka. For instance, I had to go to the northern Upper Nile region to collect historical data material among the Abialang, Nyiel,

Ageer and the Dongjol Dinka communities. Areas such as Twic-East and Bor including those Dinka areas in central Upper Nile as well as Dinka sections in the Yirol area in eastern Lakes state in Bahr el Ghazal were all strenuously covered. Those places were covered in a matter of a decade. Such research activities were also conducted among Gok and Agaar Dinka in Lakes state. Symposiums, workshops and panels to prove the relevancy of the collected data material were done in Rumbek, Cueibet, Thiet and many other places in central Bahr el Ghazal. Rek, Twic, Luacjang and the large Malual Dinka in northern Bahr el Ghazal were also covered, including Ngok Dinka of Abyei.

Over 500 Dinka elders in their seventies, eighties, nineties and even those in their hundreds and above were asked to give their oral accounts through research interviews and questionnaires. Many of those elders interviewed across Dinka lands were those who had survived the test of time and remained as cultural custodians of the traditions and history of their respective communities and families, clans and indeed the history of the entire Dinka nationality as heard from their fathers, mothers and senior relatives, including grandfathers. The data material so far collected and finally reconstructed like this was also shared by the author with some historical and anthropological circles, research experts[3], some of the metropolitan Dinka in Sudan and also with the diaspora Dinka.

After this strenuous effort, covering a period of three decades (1979 – 2011), the author finally sat out to launch this work into publication as a first edition. The book is now in its second edition. It is updated, expanded and revised. Four chapters have been added to the original seven chapters to make eleven chapters. This was done

---

3   John Ryles of the Rift Valley Institute was one such renowned research expert and writer who shared the data material and primary manuscript with the author in Rumbek, UNICEF compound, 2004. John Ryles gave very useful guidance.

on the request of our Dinka readers. In the view of the author this book can be an authentic testimony or proof to the long casual belief by the Dinka people that their ancestors came from Northern Sudan and from the Middle East, and while the book attempts to uncover the long history of resistance against external domination that has for all times come from the Northern Sudan corridor, it primarily seeks to address the issue of Dinka origin and identity in the context of Sudan cultural and ethnic setup.

Although the present day Dinka are about eighty percent a non-literate society, they have been very successful in preserving an oral history rooted in their long migrations from the Middle East to Egypt, to Northern Sudan and to their present settlement areas in the Republic of South Sudan where they are firmly and finally rooted and apparently never to go any further south like their ancient and Mediaeval forebears have done across the ages.

The Dinka of today will never be pushed any further south by whatever power unless by the eminent reason of population explosion, and since very little about them was recorded, firstly by colonial authorities and then by Christian missionary writers, as found in what was left as colonial archives which were mostly administrative reports on chiefs and on Dinka resistance to the condominium rule, much remained to be the work of the enlightened members of the Dinka community.

Except for one colonial administrator, Godfrey Lienhardt, who tackled only the religious aspect of the Dinka and Fr Neble, who attempted to translate Rek Dinka words into English, nothing touching history and roots has ever been documented about the Dinka. This work seeks to differ with those cursory approaches for a number of reasons: in the first place, the research work so far done had an added value as the author had chosen to approach Dinka nationality in a rather holistic manner. The book is tackling the Dinka people historically, anthropologically and socio-economically. This is because the author had the advantage of being an Indigenous intellectual who has personally shared in his people's history and culture as well as in his people's struggle for freedom. Being in his early sixties the author is also in an advantageous position to interpret his own culture. Secondly, the wars of liberation struggle between North and South Sudan since the departure of the Anglo-Egyptian colonialists in 1956 has made it difficult for outside researchers to have access to areas of Southern Sudan which have for so long been war theatres. Since 1956 to the time of the publication of this book much has happened to shape the popular consciousness among Southern Sudanese to write their own histories such as this.

Beside political conditions in Sudan which sought to limit the access of foreign scholars, and due to the impact of this long tradition of more than fifty years of wars, Southern Sudanese local communities have become so sensitive and wary about discussing such matters as their history with outsiders, and their own sons and daughters were those in a better position to overcome those obstacles. Above all a history whose data material is largely dependent on oral traditions and on oral accounts collectable from a non-literate community, such a history can only be succinctly delved into and accurately interpreted by scholars from within the very culture. This is, however, not to suggest that thorough foreign scientific research programs in peaceful times cannot yield better outcomes. On the whole, the exigency to undertake this marathon project was dictated by the expedience to obtain historical data from the rapidly disappearing age; however, the work so far done does not purport to be the final truth about the Dinka people. Nonetheless it will certainly be the first documented attempt to bring the past to link with the present. Apart from the Dinka, it will also be a reference book on most of our ancient Sudanese communities and, above all on the Nilotic peoples.

On the whole, the book seeks to tackle the Dinka people from their remotest prehistoric beginnings, from what they know as their antediluvian cradle land. It tries to tackle the Dinka, right at their pre-ancestral formative stages, from their antediluvian times to the early post-flood periods and down to the prehistoric development and grouping of man after the ecumenical flood of Noah (Noi). The book tries to trace the Dinka all the way from Panthou. This is the Dinka creation spot where Abuk, the Dinka first mother of mankind, and Garang (Garaŋ), the Dinka first human male being to be created on earth, were created by *Nhialic*, the Dinka word for God.

Attempt has been made to trace the Dinka remotest forebears of the antediluvian times through to those of the flood of Noi's time up to the post-flood era. The book goes on tracing the Dinka primordial ancestors, from the Sumer or Mesopotamian region where man first gathered at Shinnar. Dinka knowledge of the Babel tower and the universal flood of Noah is testified by their very accurate oral accounts. Using their mythical and legendary stories the book vividly traces the Dinka ancestral movements from Mesopotamia (present Iraq) to China and Mongolia regions, to the southwest Asian region of today's Yemen and Saudia.

Moving to the land of Canaan (today's Palestine and Israel) and to Egypt the story then heads to the northern end of ancient Northern Sudan in the region of Wawat where ancient Dinka forebears came during the Biblical Exodus time. When they came they landed and settled among the black communities – the descendants of Ham who many centuries BC migrated out of Egypt for various reasons and settled in those northern parts of the present Northern state of Sudan. That region of Wawat covered the areas of the then known blacks' principalities of Wawat and Yam. The book also explains how the Dinka forebears helped those Indigenous black communities to form the most impressive and enduring Kush Kingdom that gloriously lived on the African continent for more than a millennium, starting from about 750 BC to 350 AD when the Kush Kingdom collapsed and disappeared altogether at the hands of the nearby Ethiopian ancient kingdom of Axum.

The book also traces the Dinka society from their ancient times of Kush Kingdom to their clear emergence as a fulminant fighting community in the northern region of Sudan prior to their coming to Khartoum. It also explains how they acquired their generic name Jaang, to later become Jieng and Muonyjang. The name Jaang came into being after their movement from Napata-Dongola area and from Al Alaif region to Meroe and later to Atbara or the Butana steppe areas, then to Al-Matemma up to Al Banaga area from where they proceeded to Jarjar (present Omdurman), Jeily, Khartoum, Patihap, Jebel Aulia and Soba, areas which now make the present Khartoum state.

The book gives an account of the physical and human reasons behind such a long phenomenon of centuries of southward migration from the Middle East to Egypt, then to ancient far Northern Sudan. The book also tackles Dinka composition, their territorial setting and their way of life during the Mediaeval Ages to the present modern era. It also touches on their status during the Turco-Egyptian colonial era of the heinous slave trade and its succeeding Mahdia period and the Anglo-Egyptian era of 1898 to 1956.

All these chronological accounts are done through those inscrutable vistas and pathos of historical epochs. It was done by sieving from those great heaps of epic, religious and antique songs that allude to even the pre-flood world of the society descended from Abuk and Garang. While the book powerfully sheds light on the Dinka roots of identity as it essentially focuses on the Dinka, it also touches on other Sudanese communities, especially the Nilotic societies that have been with the Dinka since many centuries BC up to the present 21st century. It is hoped that the book will stimulate debate and perhaps spark renewed interest for much more scientific research. I am especially happy that at long last the much cherished and long awaited Dinka history book has now come out, foremost for my Dinka community and also the Nilotes in general and the rest of the Sudanese and the ecumenical readership.

PREFACE TO THE SECOND EDITION

People who write about their culture have a mission to preserve the culture and educate the people about how good their culture is. They work to weed out things alien to their culture. They are cultural custodians. They help their people to avoid things that were once abhorred and which are now commonplace. For example, among the Dinka lie telling, gossip making, begging, malice, theft, prostitution and so on was not a common phenomenon. Within Dinka society a young man or woman associated with such things as mentioned above will never marry or have social privileges. His or her loose tongue, malice or any of those antisocial acts will affect his or her children and descendants.

Culture is power. That is why it often leads to lack of understanding, conflict and suppression among communities, nations and peoples. The burning of books containing other people's views, the incarceration of writers and artists and the destruction of cultural heritage sites are some of the actions usually done in expression of cultural intolerance. Actions like these illustrate how deeply people fear the power of culture. Culture and its activities make people resilient. Culture enables us to preserve peoples' stories for future generations.

Mr Lewis Anei Madut-Kuendit probably had those things in his mind when he sat down to write '*The Dinka history: From Abuk and Garang at creation to the present day Dinka*'. He is a South Sudanese academician who is in love with the written word. He calls himself the man between the old and the new generation, a middle man who must connect the old, the past, the new and the ones to come. The middle man's role has prompted him to quickly capture and write his people's history.

His Dinka history book, which consists of chapters about his people's culture, was widely received and recognised by the Dinka elites as their true history and culture. When it first appeared in its first edition in 2011 it was immediately recognised as reflecting his Dinka people, who number about five million, in a complex and wide distribution along both sides of the White Nile River between the Northern Sudanese Kotsi region of Jebellein and the Gemeiza area near Juba in the Central Equatoria state of South Sudan.

Mr Lewis Anei Madut-Kuendit is a true example of a Dinka man enriched with two cultures. He has undergone all of the Dinka Indigenous education system. He underwent all the traditional initiation rites and other social and physical or practical activities which make a Dinka man a fully grown up man according to the Dinka concept about man. By western concepts and standards with regard to what constitutes an educated man Lewis Anei holds a university first division Bachelor's degree in education where he majored in literature and history. Mr Lewis Anei Madut-Kuendit currently serves as a national cultural advisor at the Ministry of Culture, Youth and Sports. He was the first appointed governor for his Warrap state. Prior to becoming a governor he had served as a secondary school teacher where he careered as a headmaster in several secondary schools in the country. Mr Lewis Anei also served in the army as a soldier up to the rank of captain during the liberation days in his country. This is besides having served in several local government positions in

Warrap state, first as an administrator and secondly as commissioner for his Tonj North county. He hails from the Awan-Parek section of the Akop sub-region of Tonj North county.

'The Dinka history…', his first elaborate masterpiece, vividly expresses who the Dinka people are, and although he later wrote a second book on his people's religion, the book expresses their understanding of God, their economic and judicial systems and the entire Dinka social setup.

Apart from explaining his people and their way of life, the author may have solved some political questions. For example, his research done more than twenty years ago shows that Dinka people believe their original ancestors, Garang and Abuk, were created by the creator at Panthou, the creation spot for the Dinka people.

While opening up the Dinka and their way of life for the world to see, Mr Lewis Anei's ability to identify and documentarily preserve the richness of the Dinka Culture is indubitable. When one tries to alienate through vague translation, words which form the basis of a people's philosophy, it becomes difficult to fully comprehend the message, but Mr Lewis Anei seriously took care of this. He writes the word in Dinka and then explains it in English.

Some attempts has always been made by some African writers to translate key word or words from their languages into a foreign language (English, German, French, Portuguese, etc) but all have failed as they tend to miss the deeper meaning and essence of the words, and sometimes, they place the word out of its cultural or social context. Key words in a language are the essence of any language. It is the word or words that make the Dinka person re-live his or her past, and while these words are creating a sense of feeling at home for an Indigenous Dinka reader, the non-Dinka who will read this book will be in touch with the Dinka culture through these preserved words in the mother tongue but clearly defined in the alien language.

Mr Lewis Anei has cleverly escaped this failure which betrays many African writers. When the author requested me to write a preface to the second edition of this Dinka history book I saw in it a trap, smartly laid down for me by a very serious writer from a generation far above me. Mr Lewis Anei seems to tell the younger generation of the Dinka through me that, by instructing one of their own generation to provide an appraisal to a book written about the past and the way of life of their society to which they have very scanty information, he was telling them to undergo a march onto a high mountain top. By so doing he had truly asked all of us to focus and cherish our culture and promote it.

Mr Lewis Anei appears very serious when he talks about the need to safeguard South Sudanese cultures within South Sudan and among South Sudanese in diaspora. He is a man in love with his culture. This is evidently portrayed by his association with a wide range of Dinka communities. He knows Dinka history, customs, norms and beliefs. On a number of occasions he has said that customs, norms, values, virtues and beliefs are the sources of enlightenment and that anybody who does not know his people's culture is like a tree without roots. He lamented his inadequate knowledge about other cultures and says he writes only about the Dinka culture because it is the only one he knows and it is the very culture into which he was bred and groomed into an adult.

As the leading Dinka writer who has put into the written word a comprehensive history and analysis of his community and its way of life, Mr Lewis Anei Madut-Kuendit has taken his society as a worthy project, striving to enlighten his other South Sudanese communities and the world at large to understand who the Dinka people are. Through this, Mr Lewis Anei believes his non-Dinka South Sudanese may find certain shared commonalities which can form the basis for a South Sudanese national identity. In this way he will have contributed towards the national efforts to eradicate tribalism and other backward attitudes which emanate from tribal chauvinism. In South

Sudan many people still think about their own tribes because they do not know that other tribes and cultures do exist and are equally important or, at least, they share certain values, virtues and norms. Those shared cultural ingredients are important in the creation of mutual understanding and social harmony between the people in South Sudan and any people anywhere in the world.

Culture is the people and people are the culture. A people without a culture is like a tiny boat violently pushed into a deep blue sea without a rower guiding it. Continued long wars of liberation have interrupted normal life in South Sudan. Many people left South Sudan during war times to stay in foreign lands as refugees, Diasporians or to study abroad. Because of this, those born outside or who grew in those alien environs did not have the chance to undergo cultural rituals and initiation rites which are concrete prerequisites to build cultural insights in an adult member of the society. A large population of our today's youngsters therefore became totally alien to their own people and culture. As we move away from our own culture we become disadvantaged by the cultural gap created by war and as we begin to want to shy away from our own ancestral culture and seem to enjoy the exotic cultures acquired from outside our society, we therefore become out of context and outlandish as we come back home, and as we become so, we begin to see our own people's culture as a trap or as some kind of a chain that has tied us down. Worst of all, we begin to see culture and the knowledge of it as a sign of backwardness. We are or have become a generation who go to dot com… and see things of the past as outdated and outmoded, and as we do so we abandon our own culture and our identity and we become adopted into the cultural identity of those who are committed to their people's culture and identity. Many communities were assimilated in this way.

Yes, we are a new generation, the dot com generation who say we are supposed to be free; the French philosopher says, "Man is free but he is in chains everywhere".

Budding writer as I am, I feel small to undertake such a challenging task to provide a preface to a compelling work such as this. There are among the Dinka great academia poets and writers who are capable of writing a graphic preface with the sense of authority, but having been asked and duly trusted with this immense work of history, I saw in it a call to take pride in my culture and in my people. I felt the importance of having to contribute to the preservation of my culture in such a rapidly decaying society.

I saw in it an opportunity to regenerate interest in my culture and to make a call to other South Sudanese people to learn about me through this great book and to also reflect and take chances to write about their cultures and people, so we can uplift our own unique culture as a nation and use the knowledge of each other to create harmony between us. It is through the knowledge of each other that respect is compelled and trust built.

If we know who we are we can weed away tribalism and build in nationalist sentiments. It is when we learn about each that we can say, "Oh dear, we are the same people after all…", and we can achieve this through making cultures known to each other by means of the written word, like in this book.

Mr Lewis Anei Madut's book is a call to come to our senses in this post war South Sudan that had just been born but came face to face with advancing modernity and technology. During war time our morality had greatly been put to the test by so many trials and tribulations. For instance, poverty brought stealing, begging and adultery, things which the Dinka had earlier abhorred as most anti-social practices.

Reading the Dinka history book, my joy in the re-lived past became insurmountable. Looking around, however, I quickly find that we are lost, especially amongst the urban Dinka girls, young ladies and boys. A lot of the Dinka urban boys have become niggers. Urban Dinka girls and women have decided to bleach their beautiful dark brown and smooth skins. Significantly it was degrading and a taboo in the past to see a Dinka girl exchanging sex for money! In the past and until today among the rural Dinka, sex was and continues to be something sacred, reserved for procreation. Right now, the Dinka girls and Dinka young ladies, the pride and wealth of the Dinka society, are seen in Juba, Kampala and Nairobi streets, New York and Australian cities, selling themselves for a few dollars and panties!

This book and its cultural import is an elder's call to the younger generation of the Dinka to come back to live in the way people used to live and to safeguard their culture. Since good cultural norms and values are universal, it is also a call to the South Sudanese youth of our time and future to respect who they are and what they stand for. The book is an ultimate must to be read by anyone interested in who the Dinka people are and what they do or believe in, good or bad. The book can serve as an inspiration to future writers who are interested in making other nationalities understand their own people and their way of life.

Emmanuel Monychol Akop
Editor-in-chief
The Juba Telegraph News Daily
Juba, South Sudan

ABBREVIATIONS

SPLM/A: Sudan peoples' liberation movement/army
Omda: An Arab word for a community leader
Ganun: An Arabic word for law
BC: Before the birth of Jesus Christ
AD: After the birth of Jesus Christ
Deut: Deuteronomy
Ch: Chapter
ECS: Episcopal church of Sudan
V: Verse
FM: Francis Mading
Dr: Doctor of philosophy
DC: District of Columbia
USA: United States of America
Ibid: In the same book above; repeat
A/cdr: Alternate commander
Cdr: Commander
KUP: Khartoum University Press
Gen: Genesis
Kms: Kilometres
Mt: Mountain

KCB: Karen Central Bureau
Ex: Exodus
Pl: Plural
Vol: Volume
SANU: Serbian academy of sciences and arts (Srpska akademija nauka i umetnosti)

A GUIDE TO THE DINKA ALPHABET LETTERS AND PRONUNCIATION

Dinka people have a language which at its general level is homogenous because all the Dinka communities do hear themselves. Yet Dinka language displays more than one dialect. This Dinka language is called *Thoŋ Muɔnyjäŋ*. Some call it *Thuɔŋjäŋ*. The ongoing linguistic research has formally classified this Dinka language into six broad dialect groups, each of which could be fit to have its own translation, although a major plan to unify Dinka dialects into one cannot be ruled out in the near future. This is important if the Dinka people would like to raise their language to a *lingua franca* level and to be an official national language in South Sudan. Rek Dinka dialect or speech form is regarded by linguists as the '*Southern Dinka dialect family*', spoken in central Bahr el Ghazal by what are known as the Rek language cluster. These are the Rek Dinka people of Tonj, Gogrial and Awiel plus Waau people of Chief Majɔk Majɔk in Western Bahr el Ghazal state. This Rek dialect group is also known as the 'K' group for they use the letter 'K' for certain words and names, for example, Kuin, Kiir, Kiec, Makiir, etc.

The second dialect family is what are called the '*northwestern Dinka dialect group*'. This dialect cluster covers the Ruweng cultural group of the Padang Dinka. It consists of Pan-Ru and Alor Dinka communities of Biemnhom and Panriɛŋ counties in the western Upper Nile region. This dialect group also includes Ngok Dinka of Abyei. The third is the '*south-central dialect group*', which is comprised of Aliap, Kiec, Agaar and Gok Dinka communities in Lake state. This dialect cluster is also known as the '*Agaar dialect group*'. They also constitute what are called the 'C' Group among the Dinka. They call Kuin as Cuin, Kiir as Ciir, Makiir as Machiir, etc. The fourth is the *southeastern Dinka dialect group*' consisting of those Dinka communities of Twic, Bor, Hol and Nyarweng. This dialect cluster is also known as the '*Bor dialect group*'. The fifth is the '*northeastern dialect group*' consisting of those Dinka communities which are Thoi, Rut, Paweny, Ngok of Lual Yak on the Sobat, Luac Aköök Yiɛu of Khor Fluth, Dongjol, Ageer, Nyiel and Abialang people of Renk county. This dialect group is also known as the *Dongjol dialect cluster*'. Together with the *northwestern dialect group* they are sometimes regarded as the 'Padang dialect group'. 'Atuöt', which is a combination of Nuer and Dinka speech forms, makes the sixth dialect group. That of the Malual Dinka is part of the 'Rek dialect cluster'.

Rek Dinka dialect seems to have been the original Jieng language for it still preserves archaic words of the ancient and Mediaeval forebears. It is also very melodious, good in inflection and easy to pronounce. Rek dialect is euphemic, polite in its tone and approach. It is not offensive but it is full of symbolism, imageries and it effectively conveys Dinka lore and fine tuned speech. This is in addition to its connotative ability with words that display more than one level and meaning.

Despite some noted deficiencies in clarity and specificity of its orthography, the below guideline is a fairly standardised Dinka pronunciation matrix across the various Dinka dialects. Dinka languages have up to seventy alphabets. It has double vowels which express the extended or long sounds common to all the Dinka vocalisations. Breathy vowels are there to also determine meaning. Two dots called diphthongs are usually placed on some vowels to convey breathy articulation (e.g.: ä, ë, ɛ̈, ï and ö). Yet to be resolved with clear cut solution by the linguists is the issue of tone which has no system developed as yet.

DINKA CONSONANTS

'G'. In Dinka alphabet 'g' is used as in 'gain', not as in 'George'. e.g. Gak, Gok, Goat etc.

'C'. The letter 'c' in Dinka is pronounced as 'ch' as in 'Church' and 'Churchill' and not as in 'crock' or 'clock', 'crak', etc. As such, 'Ciec' is pronounced by Lakes state Dinka communities as 'Chiech' and 'Nhialic' in all Dinka dialects is pronounced as 'Nhialich'. Rek Dinka people use 'K' to pronounce 'Ciec' as 'Kiec'.

'Ny'.   These two letters are combined and pronounced as in the Dinka word *'Nya'* meaning 'Girl' in English. Thus, 'Bäny' in Dinka which is 'Chief' in English is pronounced 'Bäny' with a slight opening of the mouth and the tongue not pressing on the roof of the mouth.

'Dh, Th, Nh'. These combinations are pronounced with the top of the tongue pressed more firmly against the teeth than it is in English.

Special Dinka letters that are added to the Roman Alphabets are pronounced thus:

'ŋ' is pronounced like 'ng' as in 'singing', 'linking', 'blinking'… etc. In this book, we invariably used 'ŋ' in place of 'ng' and vice versa as in Garang to also appear as Garaŋ. Ngor will also appear as ŋor, Ngok as ŋok and so forth.

'ɛ, ɛ́, ɛ̈':. This Dinka special type of the English 'e' is pronounced like the 'a' in 'bat', 'cat', etc. A diphthong strip used on the ε helps to differentiate this form of breathy ε from the ordinary ε and the one with two diphthongs. It can differentiate kεεk (an opening) from kέέk (quarrel).

Final consonants are often softened in pronunciation:

A final 'c' sounds somewhat like 'j', 'k' somewhat like 'g' and 't' somewhat like 'd'.

The tendency to slur the final consonant is mostly found in the Bor dialect group. A special Dinka Vowel 'ɔ' used in place of 'o' is necessitated to bring meaning where the sound of 'o' cannot convey what a Dinka person means. E.g. Lɔr, meaning 'roll it' or 'go' and cɔr which means 'blind', etc. The letter 'X' is used in place of 'H', e.g. Xöt, meaning house, 'Xɔk', meaning cows, etc.

In this book an attempt has been made to give the meaning or the English equivalent of a word as the word occurs in Dinka. A Dinka word is either put in bold in italic, in brackets or as a footnote which is provided to further clarify the meaning to ease reading and understanding for our non-Dinka readers of this book. Breathy vowels such as ä, á, é,ë, ε̈, έ, ö, ï .... etc. are used to assist pronunciation and meaning.

INTRODUCTION

"May it be my privilege to have been the first Dinka to document his people's history as this, so that I am regarded as the first authority on Dinka history and when I leave this world, the foundation which I laid remains as a reference for eternity."

PART 1

This introduction seeks to introduce the reader to the main themes of the book by historical epochs and phases. It is a continuation of the preface. It gives a synopsis of the various stages of the Dinka ancestral development and migratory movements, details of which will come under each chapter and phase.

As the book covers an immensely long period of time going far into those inscrutable prehistoric and primordial periods of human history, it has been found convenient to divide the whole book into four broad periods, the first of these being the mythical period, which is regarded by the rural Dinka as the time of the Beginning of things. This time is that period extending from those primordial times of the antediluvian eras of the human first parents at creation and the society that descended from them prior to the devastating flood of Noah. This was an otherwise difficult period which caused many years of research work. Dinka religious epic and hymnal songs, creation and religious mythologies, ancient tales and legends have all been of great help in discussing this period. Dinka knowledge of the pre-flood world of the society that descended from Abuk and Garang was of significant help during the research for this period.

The second (the post-flood, the period pre-ancient times) in our division of time length in this book) covers those peoples and times after the flood of Noah – that antediluvian figure which the Dinka oral accounts clearly present as Noi. For this period attempt is made to trace Dinka remotest ancestors across and through the mitosal cobwebs of human development. The research work anchored Dinka people at one of the three sons of Noi. In so doing the author was able to determine the Dinka racial root. From the mass of books on prehistory and the ancient world prior to that time when man made his human gigantic leap from primitive farmers and geographic wanderers to an organised and settled urban life, we came out with the origin of the Dinka people. Through this we descended to the era when man organised himself into governing systems called kingdoms or civilisations that started from Sumer in today's Iraq. From all this a picture of the Dinka forebears has been constructed.

By the strength of those primordial accounts this second period is made to also tackle the Babel tower's community and times in Babylonia when Nhialic (God) confused man into many languages. This second phase also gives light and clues as to the direction taken by those who later became Dinka ancestors after the Babel tower dispersal from that Babylonian settlement. During this phase the reader is to know that Dinka primordial ancestors first took to the Far East, to the areas that are today's Mongolia and China, then to southwest Asia, the region which is today's Yemen and Saudia, before they went back to Babylonia as a people known as Chaldeans.

This is the time when the would-be Dinka clear ancestor Jiel (Abraham) came to the land of Canaan to become the father for the Arabs (through Ismael), the Dinka, the Nuers and Israelites through Jacob, whom the Dinka people know as Riɛl (Gen.Ch.32. V 24-32), and Esau, who is the Dinka Mayuääl.

Data material for this period has largely come from the rich Dinka mythological tales and classic songs presently used in religious and ritual occasions, songs usually sung by those infested by spirits, clans' genies and gods called Jak. Those sources greatly enriched this period. Great wealth of information for this period has also come from written sources on prehistory, the post antediluvian era.

The third period covered by the book is the era regarded by historians as the antiquity- the time when Dinka remotest ancestors could be discernibly traced to a widely known ancestor by the name of Jiel, whom Dinka traditions considers as an historic patriarch from a region that tends to point at southern Mesopotamia, present Iraq.

During the early parts of this third phase in world history, Dinka ancestors are believed to have participated in the great primordial transhumant migrations which gave rise to the present human and racial ecumenical distribution. This period also covers the epochs in which Dinka primordial ancestors migrated from lower Mesopotamia to the land of Canaan and later to the Land of Rip[4], the Dinka ancient name for Egypt. This third period also tries to tackle the four centuries that Dinka forebears spent in Egypt up to the time of the Biblical Exodus, which is the time when the great Abiɛl made his southward migration to Elephantine Island, about Aswan in Upper Egypt. They then moved to Wawat areas in the far northern limits of the ancient Northern Sudan.

This phase also covers ancient Jaang subsequent participation in

---

4   The Dongjol Northern Dinka sections of Ageer, Nyiel and Abialang in Upper Nile state have songs which give the name of Rip for ancient Eygpt.

the establishment of the Kush Kingdom in present Northern Sudan. The Kush Kingdom started from the time when Egypt's power slipped into decline at the close of the Egyptian new kingdom period, that is, during the 11th century BC. This is the time when the blacks' chiefs of the then vassal principalities of Egypt that were Wawat, Irtjet, Satju, Medja, Kaw and Yam, principalities that lived in the now Berber-Shendi reach, shook off the yoke of Egypt's colonialisation or influence and became kings of their own[5]. This is the time when those blacks, today's Nilotic communities, began to select their kings from their hereditary ruling families, but, in about the 8th century BC, a king of Jaang ancestry by the name of Kacke, came into power and under this Kacke (presented by historians as Kashta) the Kush Kingdom was able to acquire control of Upper (i.e. Southern) Egypt and under his son Piɛng (hear him in Dinka) the whole of Egypt was under Kush control (750-719 BC). Piɛng ruled that vast area from what is now Abu Hamed in present Northern Sudan to the Nile Delta in Lower Egypt.

Although the Assyrians later captured Egypt in 671 BC and pushed our people back under another Jaang King-Tharxakua (fight for our cattle), Kush Kingdom continued in the middle Nile to complete its known thousand years.

This third period also covers the Dinka ancestors and the ancestors of the present Nilotic black communities who lived together with those Dinka ancestors during an intermediate period of the ancient era known as the Iron Age. This is the time when the Dinka forebears and their contemporary black communities of the Napatan period were forced to move out of Napata and its S-shaped Nile bend region to Meroe, following the defeat of King Tatun Amon in 661 BC. These were the forces of King Esarhaddon who came

---

5   Dr. John Garang de Mabior's speech at Nyayo Stadium,(2005), Nairobi, Kenya.

from Assyria. This period also describes those events when Dinka ancestors became a fulminantly fighting tribe and had acquired their generic societal name – Jaang. It also covers that time length of three centuries AD when Jaang finally moved in the last parts of the 3rd century AD from Meroe. This is the time when Jaang moved from present Matemma and from the confluent area of Takkaze which is today's Atbara River area to the Khartoum region.

In that century after the fall of Meroe, Jaang ancestral society had reached those areas extending from the region of the 6th cataract to Jarjar (present Omdurman), Sheinab (present Khartoum) peninsula and Jeily as well as Tiaptiap, the current Patihap Township in Omudurman. They also extended to as far as those areas including present sections of Khartoum, which are current Jebel Aulia and Soba. Here, in those areas, Dinka ancestors completed the first half of the 4th century AD. For a period of about 150 years since the destruction of Meroe, Dinka ancestors lived in the Shendi–Matemma and Khartoum region. They were not, however, among those communities who replaced the main Nile region, people who became the heirs of the bygone Kush Kingdom. By the time of the emergence of Nubian Christian Kingdoms of Nobatia, Makuria and Alodia or Alwa, Jaang and their Nilotic brethrens had already come to the Upper Nile region.

The fourth and the last stage of our division of this book covers the era known as the Middle Ages, also called Mediaeval Ages, a period that commenced from about AD 1000 to the time of the Turco-Egyptian conquest of the Sudan which started in 1821. During the first quarter of this Middle Ages, Dinka ancient society was badly locked up in a number of decades of internecine wars of resistance from the already settled Nilotic black communities in what is now the northern Upper Nile area of the present Renk-Jelhak-Jebellein and Kosti and their surrounding areas. Those Nilotic communities preceded Jaang from the Khartoum area about half a century earlier.

They wanted to forestall Jaang southward migration as Jaang was abandoning the desert and the violent menace then prevalent in the Khartoum area. That violent menace was coming from the tribes of Eastern and Western Sudan which replaced the former Kush Kingdom region on the main Nile before Khartoum.[6]

By the early parts of the Middle Ages the Dinka, still known then as Jaang, had become even more of a fulminantly fighting community. They had at this time succeeded to displace those original inhabitants of the Northern and central Upper Nile Basin areas up to AD 1000. At this time, Dinka Mediaeval forebears had reached the southern Upper Nile. From that period onward they became firmly settled up to the time when the middle Nile valley people were affected by the then known great epidemics such as smallpox and cholera when large sections of Jaang Mediaeval society decided to migrate to the west of the White Nile in a huge migration exodus, crossing at the present Shambe shore on the spots of Anyɔɔp and Kɔrcök and going into the deep interior parts of the tropical African forest region now called Bahr el Ghazal. They came to this area by the first quarter of 1300 AD. By the last quarter of the Middle Ages Dinka society in the two regions of Bahr el Ghazal and Upper Nile had firmly settled for well over 400 years after they fought their one hundred years' wars of their conquest of the Bahr el Ghazal- 1340 to 1820 AD.

PART II

Having now made the preceding periodisation and synoptic appraisal of each of those four stages of our historical epochs to be covered by the book, this remaining part of our introduction will

---

6   Basil Davidson, The growth of African civilisations, East and Central Africa to the late 19th century, Longman groups Ltd, p. 80

deal with what could be regarded as the descriptive ethnography which is still part of the prelude or introduction to the book. The book in its details by chapters and phases will discuss Dinka historical evolution and their relationship with the Jews and the rest of the Nilotic communities in Sudan and in Africa.

As the book will be the first major attempt on Dinka national history authored by a writer who has personally shared in his peoples' rich oral history, this part of the introduction and the preface and the first opening chapter, when all are read together, will give clues on the Dinka origin and their development into a tribe. This is before chapter seven could put an end to the question of the origin of the Dinka people. Dinka present national dimensions in the country are provided by chapter four and as can be observed from the preface, much effort has been made to trace the Dinka origin from the great mythical aura, the very source of humanity, from the remotest human beginning according to the Dinka knowledge of man on earth from creation through to their foreseeable ancestors who came to Sudan during those ancient times. In addition the book tackles the routes used by those ancient Jaang ancestors when they started to come to Sudan.

Attempts have also been made to highlight on all the Dinka people from their historical perspective in both Upper Nile and Bahr el Ghazal regions. It is by this down-to-earth approach that the book was able to tackle that aura of a mystery which had since long sought to envelope into obscurity the ethnic origin of the Dinka people.

Although Dinka history has been so long a coveted area of study by many Dinka intellectuals, opportunity did not lend itself to them for reasons attributed to the pursuit of other community higher goals such as national liberation and the quest for freedom. Presently at hand came the national exigence for the current Dinka educated population, mostly the young generation who are apparently losing contact with their roots, their history, culture and heritage, to have their national history given to them. The preface and this introduction at hand are prepared as the beginning of the national history of the Dinka people.

Before closing this introductory presentation mention has to be made on the previous premise which has for so long been professed that true history and one which is supported by empirical scientific facts. This premise has been found to hold no water. It is found to be anomalous by modern science. Ethnography or ethno-history has come to be a scientifically accepted branch of anthropology concerned with the reconstruction of the histories of non-literate peoples using oral techniques. When used for various national groups ethno-history was found to have had remarkable success. In the past people erroneously believed to have no history in the conventional sense have now come to have their histories written using oral traditions. Oral tradition is a product of myths, legends and tales of even primordial origin. All are known to make oral traditions of any given society and peoples from the very beginning of time.

Myths, legends and tales are essential sources with which anthropologists and historians have always been able to successfully reconstruct the anthropological and historical past of races. Oral tradition data has therefore been one principal source from which much of this work has come. In a cursory touch, myth can be seen as usually a story that originated in the primordial times, sometimes dating far back into the inscrutable past and always concerned with the early history of a people and natural events. It is also about how the world began. Legend, for its part, can be described as a story from the past, a story which tends to relate the glorious deeds of significant persons in a family genealogy and when told as tales in the course of time, becomes legendary and may become mythical in the course of many centuries. Historians trace the sources of legends and compute the epochs and times of their occurrence and are thus able to construct historical chronologies.

Dinka mythologies, legends and epic songs contain tales about the beginning of things. Dinka is a community endowed with an in-depth concern for history and has instinctive memory power and acumen that let it remember even the remotest events going as far as even the flood of the Biblical Noah and beyond. Before the advent of science and the Darwin theory of evolution, myths and legends have been the foundations of life and the timeless cradle of all the early religions from which life shaped itself. Accordingly, members of a given society appear to be unconcerned about their historical and heroic saga of their nations, of mankind, of their classical past and, indeed, of the mythologies and tales handed down to them from their ancestors. Such people can also become unconcerned with posterity and cannot as such make good leaders for their people and nations.

The history of any given society can only be authentic if and when material information about that society or people is delved out of the primordial times of the beginning of things from which myth has its home and from which the original norms governing mankind and forms of life are derived. And if that is so, then the study of the Dinka must seek to dig into those primordial times, into those inscrutable vistas beyond prehistory, neatening together those dotted fragments of popular traditions that have been handed down throughout the ages in the form of tales, legends and myths. It was having done it this way that the book came to suffice as a historical documentary for the Dinka, a documentary which will certainly be good for the rest of the research efforts that might follow in this field of study.

Furthermore, those historical vistas and epochs covered were astutely researched and accurately focused to illuminate the very roots and parent stems for the Dinka people. Each stage of Dinka societal descent from within the long and complicated cobweb has been given serious concern, a lot of research effort has been placed on the genealogical undulations which stemmed from within the various clusters of mankind called races. The research tried to also trace as far as the three sons of the Biblical Noah of the famous ecumenical flood which purged the world of the first population of mankind who descended from either the first human primates as the Darwinists would suggest, or who descended from the creation of first humans known by the Dinka as Garang and Abuk, the first couple of mankind.

While the Jews and the ancient Near Eastern peoples were able to remember some features, places, cities, events, experiences and names of individuals who were earliest members of the human race, the antediluvian society that lived on earth between the time of creation and the flood of Noah (Gen.Ch36 V 7-9), Dinka people in South Sudan also present an oral literature with fascinating similarities and parallels with those of the antediluvians, the early Sumerians, the Babylonians, the Akkadians, Assyrians and the Hebrew myths and epic stories between creation and the world flood of Noah.

PART III

Our discourse of myths, legends and tales as useful sources for data material for writing the history of the Dinka people as discussed in part II above leads us to our tackling of the Dinka people in the context of mankind in general. Thus, as the Dinka are part of mankind, it is imperative at this outset to have a brief look into the story of man. Mankind, which the Dinka call *manhacuuk,* is in general a family of many branches and the Dinka know they belong to one of those branches of manhacuuk. Their origin as they put it is no doubt part of that inscrutable long history of man and the universe. Many historians, especially the evolutionists, tend to suggest that history of man could be traced back to the time of the geological age known as the Pleistocene epoch.

This is the time some 65 million years ago when in the Cenozoic era the first primates appeared on land[7]. By gradual evolutionary development, primitive humans of the Old Stone Age period, ranging from 3 000 000 to 100 000 years ago, appeared on land. This evolution continued through the Pleistocene epoch, then to the Middle Stone Age period from 100 000 to 20 000 years ago, to the Neolithic or new Stone Age period which lasted from 20 000 to 15 000 years ago. During this time man fully developed into his present state and had become what evolutionists call Homo Sapiens – man who had moved out from old Stone Age practices to the advanced use of metals such as silver, bronze and iron to make tools and weapons and organised himself into his present advanced social and political organisation.[8]

That being the evolutionists' concept about how man came into his present shape over millions of years, the religious people markedly came to differ with this view. They believe man was created by God. They consider man to have come into existence through a divine act, right from the time of God's creation of the world. Apart from the evolutionists' theory and that of the people of the Bible and Quran, Dinka people have their own version of the story of mankind, a version which is definite. Their concept of the universe and its existence, however, have affinity with the creation theory of the Middle Eastern peoples. The claim by the Dinka to have emanated from that Middle Eastern culture during those remote prehistoric times therefore finds support and authenticity, right from this cradle point of human concept about the coming into being of the universe. Dinka people believe in the creation theory. 'Dinka religion: their belief system' (2013), a book by the same author, critically explains how Nhialic created man and the universe.

---

[7]   David Crystal, 'The Geological Time Scale' (in) the Cambridge Encyclopaedia, 4th edn, C.U.P, London (2000), p. 1223

[8]   JA Kapiyo & A Owino, The evolving world, a history and government course, Form One Secondary, O.U.P, Kenya (1996), p. 122

Throughout the ages, individuals, communities or peoples have tried to explain how they came into existence. The explanation is given through oral traditions from myths and legends handed down by ancestors. The Dinka people believe that man and the universe were created by Nhialic – the creator. To them, man and the universe did not just come from nowhere or from nothing. They were from the divine work of Nhialic.

From their rich mythological traditions, Dinka society came to know their original grandparents were created by Nhialic and their ancestors were therefore part of that great prehistoric culture of man. They know their first parents did not come by evolution as the Darwinists would have us understand. They know mankind came into existence through the divine creation by God. They also know they came from the Middle East. Dinka exact origin has since been a serious matter of concern for the Sudanese and foreign writers of history. There have been attempts to postulate where and when Dinka founding ancestors first came into existence, but those social anthropologists – be they Arabs, Europeans or Sudanese writers, on Southern Sudanese found themselves faced with the dilemma of how to pinpoint or proceed for the exact origin of the Dinka people, although they tended to present various theories and hypotheses.

Failing to go up to the exact point, those writers overtly agreed to only say that 'Dinka ancestors were part of the Nile valley peoples from antiquity'. They therefore conclude that Dinka people are but a branch of the Nilotic race. This conclusion is partly true in that Dinka forebears have been among the Nilotes since antiquity and that Dinka people have stayed in Sudan for well over 5000 years to the time of the writing of this book, and so by that very long association and stay, they have become Nilotics. They are therefore a people of the Nilotic race.

As far as Sudan is concerned, there is nothing that can be known by the Sudanese in Sudan without the Dinka side of the story. This is because Dinka people were among the early communities who came to Sudan much earlier than some of the communities, such as the Arabs who came to Sudan only in the 7th century AD. Dinka ancestors came to Sudan before the establishment of the Kush Kingdom, which came into existence about 1000 years before the birth of Jesus Christ. The exact time of the Dinka ancestral arrival into Sudan is discussed in chapter eight of this book, but the fact is that Dinka society had lived in Sudan for such a long period of time, from many centuries BC to the present day.

To use some of the views of Professor Yusuf Fadl Hassan, historians, unlike narrators and chroniclers, do not merely endeavour to relate events and describe situations. They principally and more importantly analyse and explain events and times. This analysis and explanation is not a cursory or perfunctory exercise. It entails chronological account making, involving logical, coherent and systematic ordering of facts and historical events so that relations between them are construed or seen with causes and consequences identified. Besides this role, historians do analyse phenomena and explain events in an objective manner, giving due consideration to all relevant facts of the situation being described. This is irrespective of whether those facts or parts of them do or do not contradict the historian's own inclinations, however, should the historian's interest in his work be grounded on national, racial or political stereotype and biased prejudice, he can, for instance, say without fear that the Beja people in Eastern Sudan were of Arab descent.[9] In this way objectivity and dispassionate considerations, which should be the ultimate weapons of a professional writer of history, are abjectly compromised!

Again, we are all aware that such basic norms pertinent to impartial works of history "are always hard to achieve in practice" – says

---

9   Yusuf Fadl Hassan, The Arabs and the Sudan. Edinburgh University Press, (1967), p. 36

M. Abdel Rahman in his 'Theories and Hypothesis' (in) *The Writings concerning Southern Sudan* ... (1986). This is true because all writers are humans and when they deal with human situations – past or present, it becomes difficult for them to help being involved and because of national, racial or political prejudice, it becomes difficult if not impossible for an historian to write with some kind of detachment similar to that with which natural scientists approach physical sciences.

Yusuf Fadl in his *The Arabs and the Sudan* (1967) admits that national, political, ethnic or racial prejudices not only affect judgement or interpretation of facts, they also influence identification of basic data, selection and recognition of which are regarded as relevant facts.

Such a vast country as Sudan with peoples of diverse cultures, religious and racial complexities, objectivity and dispassionate detachment was bound to suffer a great deal in the writings of both ancient and modern history of the Sudan; and since Sudanese professional writers on Sudan history have predominantly been Muslims and Arabs from Northern Sudan, it was therefore not surprising to find that those scholars failed to prepare a well balanced and comprehensive history of the country, a fact which greatly contributed to lack of harmony and trust between the two parts of Sudan, North and South. A complete blackout was made of the role played by Southern Sudan in the ancient and modern history leading to the making of the modern and independent Sudan.

Nevertheless, and for reasons of objectivity, certain factors acting as hindrances for those writers may be accepted: the language barrier, lack of documentary sources and above all, the obscurity of oral tradition for most of the history writers hailing from different racial and religious origins. These factors were there as some of the hindrances. Such factors may have made an insurmountable inability to write an overall Sudanese history. But, despite this defence, some Northern Sudanese historians have been very deliberate in their stereotypical determination to either diminish or completely deny the early presence and role of the early and modern Southern Sudanese communities. They were blindly in favour of the Arab racial presence and role which they say the Arabs played in Sudan. They were doing this so as to project Arabism as the dominant culture in Sudan.

In a wholesale attempt to deny even the large Dinka society which has been in Northern Sudan for thousands of years before the recent coming of the Arabs into Sudan in 642 AD, Professor Mohd Omer Bashir blatantly argues that, 'the Southern tribes have no more claim to be the original people of Sudan than the Arab tribes who emigrated to the north from Saudi Arabia and Egypt'.[10] It is understandable that similar ways exist in the writings, theories and hypotheses of even the finest and most distinguished thinkers such as Shakespeare and many others. Writers are not immune to powerful and reasonable criticism and since this is even true of the authors of such monumental works of universal value and of enduring interest, it could be less difficult to discern writings of virtual propagandists who are only engaged in an overt justification of their culture and political points of view to which they were personally and actively involved, not merely as spectators and observers, but as participants and beneficiaries.

In line with the above mentality, Northern Sudanese scholars advanced a number of perfunctory theories and hypotheses about the Dinka origin. They did not bother to go deeply to trace the origin of the Dinka. This book will put to an end the dilemma of where the Dinka people originated and where they came from as well as when they came to Sudan. That being so, we are to start saying there are many theories advanced by different historians about the origin of the Dinka, but for the purpose of this book, only two of those theories will be discussed.

---

10   Mohd Omer Bashir

CONTEMPORARY WRITERS' THEORY

Scholars of Sudanese history from Sudan and abroad made several attempts to postulate the origin of the Dinka people. However, perhaps for reasons highlighted above, these historians sought to dive into the shallows of history and perfunctorily claimed that Dinka ancestors just emerged in the region west of the Upper Nile, suggesting the present Bahr el Ghazal region! Others talk of the present Lake No area, believing the Dinka to have come there in about AD 1000 from Kapoeta-Lake Turkana-Imatong Mountain Triangle region where they believed them to have lived with the rest of the other Nilotics up to C. 3000 BC.[11]

The view of this book on the two hypotheses takes the first as a mere conjecture and therefore a naught as the Dinka people only appeared in the South after the 4th century AD when they came from Northern Sudan. Kenneth Okeny's hypotheses, however, have a little grain of truth in them although he did not make sufficient effort to separate the Dinka from the Nilo-Hamitic groups of the Nilotic societies whom he might be referring to in his book. The Nilo-Hamites must have come to that region much earlier or, according to some other traditions, were pushed there by the Dinka society which came from the Khartoum region at about the end of the 4th century AD. The Dinka found the Luo groups and those Nilo-Hamites already entrenched in the Upper Nile region. Kenneth's postulation may be true of the Nilo-Hamites and perhaps the Luo tribes who started to move into that region upon the arrival of Jaang (Dinka ancestors) from Khartoum. The Dinka and their closest kinsmen, the Nuers, never reached Kapoeta-Imatong areas since their southward migration from the Khartoum region. However, at the wake of the Dinka

---

11   Kenneth Okeny, 'The political history of Southern Sudan', (in) The role of Southern Sudanese people in the development of modern Sudan, K.U.P., (1986), p. 36

migration from Jonglei areas to Bahr el Ghazal in 1340 AD, when they vacated the south-central Upper Nile areas, those Jaang sections which decided to remain in this part of Upper Nile became overwhelmed by the Nuers who have just moved in from Bentiu areas in western Upper Nile. It is true that parts of those Jaang sections which remained in Upper Nile moved further south along the Nile as to reach those areas of Eastern Equatoria, but their migratory limit did not go beyond the present Bilnyang or the now Baria territory south east of Juba town. Some of the east bank Dinka popular tales in Upper Nile seem to indicate their ancestors later came back from Bilnyang area. The Dongjol dialect speaking Dinka sections, in particular, have accounts suggesting their return from Bilnyang area back to their present abodes north of Malakal up to the Renk area in the northern Upper Nile state.[12]

---

12   From research interview by the author with Paramount chief John Gaijang Awuol of the Paweny Dinka of Atar and SPLA A/cdr Nyong Deng Nyong from Abialang Dinka people of Renk, 2003.

CHAPTER ONE: WHO ARE THE DINKA?

THE DINKA PHYSICAL FEATURES

Although Dinka people are similar in many respects to their other Nilotic groupings in South Sudan, Kenya and Uganda, Nilotic groups such as the Nuers and, to some extent, the Luo, Dinka people are physically noticed as being essentially different from the rest of the Nilotics except for the Nuers with whom they have one remote common ancestry.

The Dinka, the Nuers and the Luo, in contrast to the rest of the black Africans, are well-built and are generally of good skin texture. They are a very tall, proud and regal-looking people with a redolent attitude to foreign ways. Until recently the Nuers were regarded by non-Dinka communities in South Sudan as a mere branch of the Dinka and for that reason they were called *Dinka-Nuers* by non-Nilotic South Sudanese. The Dinka and the Nuers have smooth skins and are taller than all the Africans, however, Dinka people, in contrast to the Nuers, are much taller. The Dinka are the tallest people in Sudan and are amongst the tallest in the world. Their people have long been noted for their exceptional height. Very many of their men have huge stature. Some tall Dinka people go to more than six feet in height. But there is one exceptional case of Manute Bol from the Twic Dinka of Warrap state who went beyond seven feet.

Manute Bol is a 21st century example of an extraordinary human being towering above the rest of the world. He is 7 ft and 7 inches tall. His parents were also of extraordinary stature. The mother was 6 ft and 10 inches tall while his father was 6 ft and 8 inches tall. But Manute's grandfather was taller than Manute himself. He was 7 ft and 10 inches tall! While Manute is a rail-thin figure in physique, his grandfather was a massive tower. Manute stormed the world basketball tournaments for the last two decades. He scored 1 559 points for the NBI (Northwest basketball institute) in the US during his basketball lifetime. He made money for himself and for the NBI.[13]

This tallness of the Dinka may be hereditary, environmental, dietary or all three. Their daily intake of several high protein foods such as milk, meat and fish, taken right from childhood may be taken into account. As described under Dinka lands, economy and their ways of life, Dinka environment is largely a swampland made of vast tracts of savannah plain with little strips of wooded forest lands mostly found in Bahr el Ghazal. Almost the whole of the Upper Nile and many areas in Bahr el Ghazal are mostly made of shrub forests, and according to science, humans found in such an environment with few trees and savannah plain, in type are always tall and slim.

Dinka scalp hair is black, short, crinklier and mostly shingled. The majority of the men wear beards with a moustache. They have a semi-flat nose with extraordinarily high cheekbones. Some can be seen having a rather pointed nose which is somehow shorter than the English nose. They are structurally slim. They walk with the loping

---

13   www.nwbball.com

Fig 5: Showing a 7 ft. and 7 inches Manut Bol from the Twic Dinka in Northern Warrap state, South Sudan. Manut Bol was one of the tallest human beings in the world (1962-2011)

gait of rural people accustomed to travelling barefoot. Their girls and ladies are slenderly graceful and well muscled. Most of the Dinka men have a giant physique and are macho-built.

Although Dinka people are negroid and in some cases appear aubergine black, it is perhaps because of the climatic impact of the African tropical sun which generations had been exposed to over the millennia they spent in this tropical Africa. Their primordial and ancient forebears, who did belong to early ancient waves of emigrants that came into Sudan from Egypt and from the Middle East, were of brown complexion. Prior to coming to Egypt and Sudan they were Caucasoid because they were from the brown race. Accordingly, some of the Dinka can still astonish people with their semi-brown skin texture. The majority of the Dinka men do not show visible hairs on their bare bodies, yet, with a close look, a Dinka man could be seen to have diminutive hair permeating the forelimbs and the chest as far as the belly. Dinka people with their kin, the Nuers, generally have a becoming facial shape. Few have bushy eyebrows. Unlike their Bantu counterparts who have thick and heavy tongues and stout mouths, their tongues and lips are light and well-shaped. This makes their vocalisation easy and they can pronounce any foreign word or name with ease due to the physical agility of their tongues.

Owing to the many wars of Kush Kingdom times, Dinka forebears, Jaang by then, adopted a practice of making very painful cut lines which became parallel scar marks on the head, starting from the forehead and ending at or before the occiput. This facial scarification was initially done to distinguish a Jaang person from others during battles. Jaang society from that ancient period continued with this practice through to the Mediaeval Ages and up to this modern era. During the Middle Ages the practice was made to encompass all genders, a cultural practice that is maintained by many Dinka communities to this present 21st century. This is because Dinka women and girls used to participate in battles and in wars by the side of their men or relatives, especially when the war had come to be fought at home or in the nearby neighbourhood. It was only quite recently that women and girls from Bahr el Ghazal were spared from the ordeal of this facial scarification practice. Bor and some Yirol Dinka communities still make scarification marks on the faces of their girls, but their scarification marks are neither big nor wound all over the head like those of men. They make few scars confined to the face.

Apart from easy identification in battles, Dinka people came to use these facial scarification marks as a cultural practice whereby adolescent males are initiated to maturity or manhood. It became an important cultural institution of the Dinka society and is celebrated each time when good numbers of adolescent males in a given territory are initiated to manhood. These scarification marks of identification range from the single scar line wound almost over the entire circumference of the head from the face and temples to the occiput as done by Abialang Dinka community of Renk county at the last northern end of the Upper Nile state to the four scar lines crossed to both sides of the head, starting from the forehead and ending midway between the ears and the occiput. This is the practice among Rek, Malual and Gok Dinka communities in Bahr el Ghazal region. That of Gogrial and Malual Dinka plus Gok in Cueibet county, in Western Lakes state, virtually meet between the eyebrows and also at the occiput, and, unlike all other Dinka national groups, Agaar Dinka people in the centre of Lakes state have more than four facial scar marks, a practice which is similar to that of the Nuers. They do five scar lines that start behind one ear and pass across the face in close parallel lines, ending behind the other ear. Ngok or Ruweng Dinka communities do theirs like the Agaar Dinka, but they add more scar lines, from the age of eight upwards, and these are placed closer than those of the Agaar Dinka and the Nuers.

Luacjang Dinka community in Tonj East county do their facial

Fig 6: Showing two modern Dinka girls, AtƆng Ngɛng Bol Malek from Tonj East, posing in her Dinka traditional dress, (2012) and Alɛk James Majök from Bor Dinka, a student at university (2011)

scars in the Agaar pattern, but they contend with four scar lines like the Rek Dinka and because of their proximity with Luacjang people, a small section of Rek, known as Lou-Payer in the eastern parts of Northern Tonj, they adopted the same Luacjang facial scarification pattern of four scar lines wound around the head like the one of the Nuers. It is only the speech accent which differentiates these Lou-payer people of Rek from Luacjang people.

Bor and Twic people in Jonglei state, including their neighbouring Dinka groups such as Hol, Nyarweng and Duör, are known to use an upwards v-shaped facial mark between the eyebrows. Atuöt Dinka – who would want to be known as Rel, make small discreet scarring on the face. Kiec Dinka community abandoned this facial scarification practice almost a century ago. Besides this facial scarring for identification all the rural Dinka of both sexes extract six incisor teeth between the lower canines. They do this practice at about the age of twelve or thirteen years.

The beauty of the Dinka girls is special. Most of the Dinka girls are usually slim. Some can be gracefully slender, admiringly exquisite and charmingly pretty. Their skins glow with natural beauty. A typical Dinka star girl can be metallically bronze and exceptionally elegant with well-shaped or well-spaced and gleaming upper teeth lined on the underneath by a typical black gum. For the Dinka, black gum and spacious upper teeth are marks of beauty. It is for this reason that Dinka girls are usually very expensive to marry. A Dinka bride may require more than a hundred well selected dowry cows paid to her family as her bride price. This is so particularly among the west bank Dinka and among the Bor and its neighbouring Dinka communities in southern Upper Nile region, Jonglei state. The Ngok Dinka girls of Abyei area also present such rare beauty as is described above.

Such expensive marriages for Dinka girls can be even more if, in addition, the girl happens to be from the upper social class or generally from the aristocratic or chief class. Dinka people have upper, middle and lower classes just like most world societies such as is the case in Europe and India. In any case, an average girl from an average family or from an ordinary clan may range from 40-50 cows paid as her bride price. This is on the average although marriages ranging from 30 and below can also be found, especially among the low caste and in situations where a married man is making a subsequent marriage after his first marriage had exhausted his marital contributions due to him from the family. Low bride prices of this nature can also be found in situations where the girl's virginity is spoiled through her pre-marital sex, which is uncommon and very much abhorred by Dinka society.

In Dinka society extramarital and pre-marital sex accounts for most of the violent conflicts among the Dinka communities, even today. Over-aged and illegally conceived girls do not have good marital value among the Dinka, and as most Dinka men marry more than one wife with aristocrats and cattle tycoons going up to ten or more wives, no woman without a husband or without a home can be found in Dinka land, at least in the rural countryside. All Dinka girls usually have marital opportunities and even the divorced woman could still have somebody to marry her. For this reason prostitution is not available in Dinka land. Among the rural Dinka no woman could stay unmarried except for nowadays Dinka women dwelling in the urban towns and cities where they are exposed to foreign cultures brought by western values enshrined in what are called human and women's rights. To the Dinka people fornication, adultery and prostitution are degrading and are greatly forbidden by custom in the Dinka world.

Most Dinka men are macho-built. Some appear typically gigantic, immensely huge, tall and powerfully built so that a Dinka man can appear to be seen with commanding prominence. Dinka men usually qualify as frightening warriors and it is for this that they are regarded by others as the 'warriors of the White Nile.'[14]

When Herodotus, an emeritus ancient Greek writer, visited the Kush Kingdom up to Meroe in 430 BC, he was astonished by an exceptionally tall and gigantic people he found in the kingdom. Those were the Dinka ancestors known by then as Jaang. In his own words, Herodotus described those ancient Dinka forebears as being *"...tall, huge and the most handsomest of all the people in the world"*. Herodotus also found them as cattle rearing people. He realised they only used to eat '*...roasted meat and drank nothing except milk...*'[15] Today's Dinka largely depend on milk as part of their daily food intake. They eat boiled or cooked meat from their abundant cattle or livestock and wildlife.

WHO ARE THE DINKA?

The Dinka people call themselves Jiëëŋ, (Jaaŋ) or Muonyjang. They are a South Sudanese national community who inhabit seven of the ten states of the new South Sudan Republic. They live in the Upper Nile and Bahr el Ghazal regions in South Sudan, but they are found in almost all the towns and cities in South Sudan and abroad. Dinka people are a branch of the Nilotic race in Africa and in South Sudan. They are the largest section of the Nilotic race. Dinka national community constitutes the biggest single national group in South Sudan. They are densely spread over the aforementioned two regions that are Upper Nile and Bahr el Ghazal. The disputed national population census count done in 2008 put the Dinka at nearly five million people. A proper scientific population count done in peaceful times may place the Dinka at six or seven

---

[14] John Ryle, Warriors of the White Nile: The Dinka, Time–Life Books, USA (1982)

[15] Herodotus, History, Vol. III, 430 BC

million people. They live by tribes, sections, families and clans and in large and small communal formations.

In the past, Dinka ancient forebears were among the earliest Sudanese societies who inhabited the northernmost parts of the Nile region in Sudan after Khartoum. They lived there many centuries BC, precisely in what is now the true northern state of today, between Shendi and Egypt. More than two decades of research work inside the country has shown that Dinka ancient forebears had lived in this part of the Northern region of Sudan as far back as the times of Wawat, Napata and Meroitic periods of the historic Kush Kingdom that came up and lived in present Northern Sudan beyond Khartoum since 725 BC to 350 AD.[16]

After the fall of the Kush Kingdom at Meroe in 350 AD, at the hands of the neighbouring kingdom of Axum, the Dinka ancient community slowly moved out from the Meroe area and settled in the areas that are presently Butana steppes in the Atbara-Shendi areas. They also lived in present Matemma and in Al Banaga areas before they came to the Khartoum region. After spending the last parts of the 3rd century AD in this region those forebears moved again to the areas of present Omdurman, present Jeily and the area of present Khartoum South. They extended to present Jebel Aulia and Soba townships. They also extended up to the area which is the present Buri township to the east of the confluences of the Blue and White Niles. Those Jaang forebears came to this Khartoum area when the Nubian kingdom, heir to the bygone Meroitic kingdom of Kush, had already begun in the far north from Dongola areas as far as Aswan in Upper Egypt. For nearly a century they lived in the present Khartoum state areas. They came to the Khartoum region as Jaang society, not as Jieng, Muonyjang or Dinka. Towards the end of the 4th century or the beginning of the 5th century AD, the Jaang society moved out

---

16 Stanley Burstein, (ed.) by Marks Wiener, Kush and Axum, ancient civilisations, (1998), pp. 20-29

of the Khartoum region in a final migration that brought them to the northern Upper Nile and southern Blue" Nile areas. They departed Khartoum areas in groups, driving their livestock with them.

The group that went to southern Blue Nile region up to Lake Tana areas settled in all those areas of present Kurmuk and its surrounding extremities. They had spent something less than half a century there when they decided to remigrate again to the White Nile areas of south-central Upper Nile to join the Jaang sections that parted with them to northern Upper Nile areas from Khartoum during that migration from Khartoum, the Blue Nile column of Jaang parted with the White Nile column from the Aba Island area.

The two columns of Jaang which parted to the Blue and White Nile areas from Aba Island later converged and spent several centuries along the east bank areas of the White Nile. They settled by fanning to the surrounding areas of the *Bewum* territory in present Abialang to the north west of Renk town. A group of them settled in what is now the *Giɛl* area of Abialang to the South of Renk. Large parts settled further north up to those areas such as *Kurwiir* which is the present *Jebellein* area and those areas where the holy shrine of *Ayueeldit* is presently situated. The Dinka call this shrine as *luak* (the byre) of Ayueeldit. The Arab Baggara tribes known as *Sabaah* and who now inhabit this territory call it *Khor-Ayueel* to the present day. This holy shrine area is about 40 kms north of *Jebellein* towards *Rabek* town.

Other groups settled in those areas that are now inhabited by *Akɔɔn* sections of *Abialang*. They extended into the areas which are currently inhabited by *Ageer* and *Nyiel* Dinka sections. Here, in this territory north of Malakal to Renk and to present Jebellein and to *Khor-Ayueel* area near *Rabek*, the whole of the Dinka ancestral society spent the last parts of the Iron Age or the beginning of the Mediaeval Ages.

Shortly after this time, sections of Jaang society arrived in central and southern areas of the Upper Nile Basin region, about 1000 AD. They came to those parts that are now *Pangak* Peninsula, including present *Twic* and *Bor* lands. Towards the middle of the 13th century AD large parties of them crossed the White Nile westward into a region which, in modern times, became known as *Bahr el Ghazal*. They migrated from south and central Upper Nile areas to Bahr el Ghazal in a big migratory exodus that was echoed along the whole length of the Mediaeval Nile valley and the Mediterranean world.[17] Still, they migrated as the *Jaang* tribe, but by this time they were already more than a mere tribe.

In Bahr el Ghazal, Jaang ancestral society acquired a new name, *Muonyjang*, while its sections which chose to remain in the Upper Nile region started to call themselves *Jieng,* a modified form of their ancient name Jaang. By the end of the Mediaeval Ages, those Jieng or Muonyjang finally settled as an agro-pastoral community in both regions of Bahr el Ghazal and Upper Nile.

Dinka people currently inhabit the vast stretch of land which lies in between the 12th and the 6th degrees north latitudes. From this vast expanse of land they fanned outwards from the swamplands of the central Nile Basin, covering about 150 000 square miles of land area.[18] Despite this, Dinka people still show cultural and linguistic homogeneity. Those Dinka national groups inhabiting the Upper Nile region are regarded as the *east bank Dinka* while those in Bahr el Ghazal region are sometimes call the *west bank Dinka.*

For aesthetic purposes, Dinka young folk in their typical rural countryside use a variety of things to increase their natural beauty.

---

17 This is the late Mediaeval period when the Christian or Nubian Kingdom of Makuria in Dongola was replaced by a successor kingdom of Dotawo. See Day of Devastation, Day of Contentment. The history of the Sudanese church across 2000 years by Roland Wierner, William Anderson & Andrew Wheeler, Paulines Publications Africa, Kolbe press, Nairobi, Kenya, (2000), p. 100.

18 Marc R Nikkel, Dinka Christianity, Faith in Sudan, Series No. 11, Paulines Publications Africa.

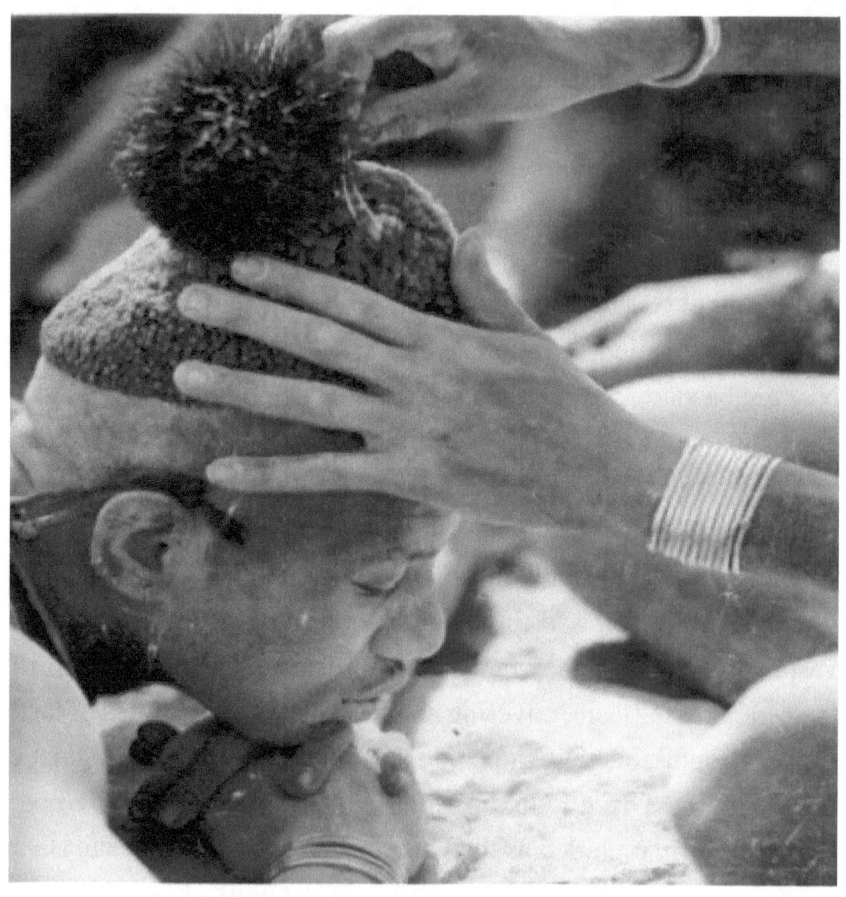

Fig 7: Showing a young Agaar man lying prone while a friend, wrist gleaming with polished brass bangles, attaches a plume of ostrich feathers to his red-dyed head curls

Their curly-shingled head hair is dyed red-brown with the ash from cow dung mixed with cow's urine. This usually turns the black hair into a brownish-shingled hair. They also adorn some parts of the body like the neck which is wound with special bead necklaces. The girls' waists are also beautified with special waist beads. See the typical Rek Dinka girl in Fig 4 of this book. The young men's foreheads are adorned with facial beads called *gaŋ*, also called *tak*, that are wound to cover part of the face and the temples above the ears. Dinka young folk also use some other dyes which they apply on their bare bodies, especially during occasions such as dance plays, annual and ritual festivals or celebrations, and also when setting out for courting to date a girl, a fiancée for marriage.

In going out to court a girl, a Dinka suitor would put on the appropriate costume, consisting of a specially organised ostrich feather called *Nɔk* in Dinka and which is fixed to a brown or red-dyed hair on the head between the back and middle parts of the head. The neck and facial beads are beautifully put and a wild cat's hide called dhök with its fine colour furs wrapped or wound on the buttocks. Then, with rhino horn or ebony rod made into a special martial club, the suitor would then take his well prepared spears and with a party of his agemates dressed in almost the same attire, he makes for the home or cattle camp of those of his fiancée to date her. Although the cattle are so integral to their economy, to their social and to their religious life, and the cow also provides them with the basic metaphors of self-understanding as well as offering them the needed aesthetic values, Dinka people do supplement their pastoral pursuits with a seasonal type of cultivation done once in a year in rainy periods known in all the Dinka lands as ker, the cultivation season.

Even with the introduction of modern innovations Dinka people continue to present themselves as a proud community with the fiercely independent spirit of a people not in need of exotic cultural values. For this reason Dinka people have been known as being very repellent to foreign ways, foreign rule and foreign religious culture that does not go with their way of life. They resisted the Euro-Christian doctrine of *one man, one wife*. Like the ancient Jews, Dinka people are highly polygamous. Chief Deng Majök from Ngok Dinka of Abyei can be cited as an example of this Dinka polygamy. He married over a hundred wives and his own children can soon make a tribe. This is like it was done by King Solomon as revealed in the Bible. The Jewish Solomon is that king who married 700 wives and had 300 concubines.

Dinka society values a man by the number of wives, children and cows he has. They marry outside their family and clan. They are an exogamous society. This system of marrying outside the family and clan is one of the factors that promotes social cohesion across the broader Dinka society. Bride wealth is paid by the groom's family as a means to finalise the marriage bond between the two clans' families. As will be detailed in chapter six under the Dinka marriage system, levirate marriage provides support for widows and their children. Dinka society is very much known for ghost, sororate and levirate types of marriages which greatly complement customary marriage. Children of co-wives are ideally raised together so that they begin to learn they are brothers and sisters. They therefore begin to identify themselves as children of one man and of one family identity right from childhood. Dinka co-wives cook for all the children of their husband although each wife has a responsibility for her own children in her own homestead. Girls learn how to cook right from the adolescent period. Dinka boys do not cook for it is not in Dinka custom for males to cook.

Girls assist their mothers in cooking. Women use clay-made pots. Boys and men depend upon girls and women for several aspects of their life. A Dinka man without a wife, a sister or strong mother finds life very miserable. It is girls and women who prepare meals for the family. It is they who milk cows for men, and milking the cows is the only duty which boys do but they don't milk cows when they are initiated to manhood. Girls and women do many things for the men, not as servants, but as an obligation from custom and tradition. Boys and men herd the cattle including sheep and goats. They construct domestic or shelter buildings such as houses, byres and other home structures. Women and girls are the ones who mobilise grass from the plains, grass with which they thatch those houses and byres constructed by men. On their part, men clear the fields during late winter, ready for cultivation. They also do fishing and periodic hunting for wild game and rodents. After boys are initiated to adulthood or to manhood, social spheres begin to overlap very little between genders. Dinka basic food is porridge which several Dinka sections call 'kuin'. The Agaar or 'C' group call it 'Cuin'. It is made from pounded durra, a type of sorghum, millet and maize grains. They eat it with broth or milk, but milk is the Dinka primary diet.

Dinka people are a very conscientious and compassionate people and are also known to be a self-contained people who greatly cherish prestige. Their value of economic individualism makes each individual and family work hard to sustain itself. Dependency is greatly abhorred in Dinka society. They are very egalitarian and capitalistic in their pursuit of life. They are a people known for moral excellence, a good ethical value that governs their daily behaviours. Dinka societies do not like bastards and illegal marriages. An illegitimate son or child is not regarded or valued by the Dinka in the same way they value legitimate sons or children (Deut. 23:2). Although Dinka people are very egalitarian and capitalistic in their pursuit of life, they show some form of socialist concept. This is because they value such things as common defence and share common property. They do certain things as a collective, things such as marriage, war and blood dia compensation to mention but a few. This proud and redolent spirit of the Dinka people is succinctly expressed in the following words of Dr. Francis Mading Deng:

"...the Dinka represent the standard of what is ideally human and therefore best. Others may have superior technology or greater wealth in monetary terms, but all things considered, Dinka land is the most beautiful, Dinka race the perfect example of creation, Dinka cattle the ideal wealth and Dinka ways the models of dignity.[19]

Dinka people do not need to be told of God as they are already aware of the presence of the creator, living above with His messengers which they call *Jak*, which is the plural form of the word Jɔk, something having the meaning of a lesser god, some of which may be *angelic beings* which God sends down to invisibly interact with mankind in His name and on his behalf. They know there is one great God.

The Dinka are a very God-fearing people. They do all their daily activities with God in the back of their minds and they hardly invoke or pronounce God unless it is greatly required by necessity. For more of Dinka religiosity and their belief in one God, see 'Dinka religion: their belief system' (2013) by the same author.

Accordingly, Dinka people highly value right against wrong. They value truth as a virtue and are blatantly opposed to lie telling which they see as injurious and demeaning. Dinka society is a strong moral based one. Dinka life is centred on humans and cattle with God overarching and about them. They are a people with high spirituality ingrained with a serene respect for their elders, for their women, their guests, their ancestral spirits in the underworld and the creator in the high. Dinka people are extremely self-conscious about their culture, about their traditional heritage, their customs and their history. They

---

19   Quoted from Marc R Nikkel's *Dinka Christianity*, 2001, p. 27, quoting from Dr Francis Mading Deng's *Tradition and Modernization: A challenge for law among the Dinka of the Sudan*, 3rd edn, Michigan, (2004)

value their culture as being of a high standard and superior to all other cultures.

Before the advent of foreign innovations, Dinka people were a very honest society with rare hospitality. They are highly generous and are a sincere people who greatly cherish honesty, trustworthiness, good reputation or pride, glory and greatness. Dinka people generally cherish bravery. They make a great effort to be recognised as heroes with valour. Because they are invincible they abhor defeat and all the demeaning attributes such as niggardliness. Rural Dinka people dislike gossiping. They demean telling of lies, capricious eating, theft, whorish sex and all those negative vices and attributes such as poverty, begging, denial of truth, wizardry, witchcraft making and fetish medicine making. They dislike all forms of fraudulent acts. They are good at fortitude and perseverance. They do not dissolve in the face of trying situations. This is why Dinka men are good in military and other armed service.

Above all, Dinka people see wit as part of intelligence. They are brave and very helpful to the needy. They love to be seen as patriotic and are ready to stand by the weak and always come out in defence for justice and the rights of others. This is why members of the Dinka society have a highly developed sense of national identity and are generally known to have national patriotic disposition. This explains why they played a major role in the country's liberation struggle. They tend to be a major element in the national army, police and other national armed units. They play an important part in the existing country's political system as many of them head South Sudan political parties. For their sheer population size, Dinka people hold a disproportionate share of the country's cabinet and the national legislature. They are rapidly becoming a major feature in almost all the towns and cities of South Sudan. They are also a big factor in business as many of them are business entrepreneurs. They operate their business throughout the country.

In the course of their history, Dinka people have absorbed many people from other communities. They therefore consist of people which they acculturised. This is because they are a nationality with very appealing characteristics that tend to attract people of other ethnic backgrounds. In fact, those in close contact with the Dinka in their rural settings tend to quickly adopt Dinka language and their ways. Some people would choose to be considered as being Dinka themselves even if their relationship with the Dinka is rather flimsy. Although Dinka people disregard women in the field of management and decision making their respect for women is exceptional.

The Dinka community greatly values wisdom and acumen and they are much inclined to accomplishing good deeds and rare feats. They are highly known for their rationale and use of common sense. They are distinguished from their kin, the Nuers, by their philosophy of *kɔŋkɔɔc* which is the Dinka word for restraint, literally meaning 'wait and let's see all aspects of the matter before acting'. *kɔŋkɔɔc* is one of the cardinal principles of the Dinka society. This *kɔŋkɔɔc* differentiates the Dinka from the Nuers whose philosophy of 'just fight and you will find the reason later', places them on the stark opposite side of rationale and common sense; and although some individuals and sections of the Dinka still show traces of *non-kɔŋkɔɔc* behaviour, Dinka society is generally very hard against irrational behaviours that are not grounded in caution, in rationale and in truth. A Dinka man or woman will always want to win a case by presenting convincing facts of his litigation.

In their value of pride, a Dinka man or woman would prepare to lose anything he or she has in order to build or protect his or her family image and name. This is because prestige as a value is one of the goals a Dinka man or woman would strive for in life. It is a value without which life has no meaning. With generosity Dinka society teaches the young against meanness or niggardliness as part of community socialisation of children. They are a hardworking society that abhors idleness and laziness. To them idleness creates dullness and poverty. They are critical, imaginative, known for their creative thinking and very good at the management of their estates. Dinka people cherish success or victory and are famous for their hospitality and friendliness. They more often than not demonstrate a high moral standard, a code of behaviour, feeding mannerism and a sense of personal dignity and integrity. Dinka society greatly emphasises greeting. They make a polite approach to people and, more importantly, to visitors and strangers. Their rules and social guidelines for behaviour are understood as being correct for everyday life. This begins with the way Dinka people greet themselves and the way they greet others. When greeting a person whom they know (an acquaintance) a Dinka person does so by giving a warm handshake. After this, they ask about each other's health and general wellbeing and about the health of their families. The Agaar Dinka say; *'Kudual'*, meaning *"Are you fine?"* But the most common greeting, particularly among the Rek Dinka, is *'Chibak!'* which means the same as *'Kudual'*. It, however, adds the meaning of *"Did you wake up well this morning?"* Bor Dinka and its affiliate Dinka communities in the same Jonglei area say *"Ci yi ruön?"* As part of the greeting etiquette, Dinka people use praise names. This is more so with men and guests. *Cibak and Kudual*, which are immediately followed by the handshake, are replied to by *'ɤɛn apuɔl guöp'* (I am fine). When a Dinka person is greeting someone with whom he/she has a personal relationship, even an acquaintance, the handshake is more prolonged than the handshake given to a casual acquaintance. Visitors to a Dinka home must be greeted by every member of the household using the handshake. This is mutually expected from the visitor(s). With foreigners the greeting accorded is also the handshake with a smile which indicates a welcome. Try to always greet a Dinka with his honorific title or surname. As a sign of respect males over the age of 60 are addressed with *Wadit,* meaning 'grandfather'. Women of the same age may be addressed as *Madit*. The title '***Wälän***' is used when greeting a person below 60 years or a man older than the one greeting him. In the Dinka world a guest is treated more importantly, lest he may carry afar the family name in disrepute.

As will be found in its details in the succeeding chapters, rural Dinka people know themselves as Muonyjang or Jieng, a name which came from their ancient name Jaang. This name, Jaang, came up in those ancient Kush Kingdom times when the name was derived from the name of one of their ancestors in history, an ancestor by the name of Ajaang, son of Deng Kuc Abiɛl. Ajaang is presented by tradition to have been a man of the times of the pre-Kush Kingdom period. By the strength of those traditions, Ajaang appears to have been born some time in the early part of the 8th century BC, before the kingdom could be established with its first capital in Napata around 900 BC. All possibilities point to the fact that Ajaang was born in the area between the first and second cataracts on the east bank area of Wawat, where the plain of Dakka is located on the mouth of Wadi Al Allagy valley, in the Darr-Toshka region.[20]

In prehistoric times and through those ancient periods down to the Mediaeval Ages Dinka ancestors have shown a transhumant character of a people who were always on the move. They made ten different types of migration in the course of history. The Dinka ancestral migration from Mesopotamia to Mongolia and China was the first. The second migration is that which brought them to southwest Asia. The third is that migration which brought our people to the land of Canaan in 2095 BC and the fourth is that of Riɛl Juöl, which brought Jaang forebears to Egypt at the end of the Old Egyptian kingdom period. The fifth was that which took Jaang ancestors by exodus from Egypt to the Wawat region in that far northern end of ancient Sudan. The sixth was that migration movement by the

---

20 5th Sudan population and housing census, 2008, priority results, Pop. census council, 26 April 2009.

THE DINKA HISTORY 23

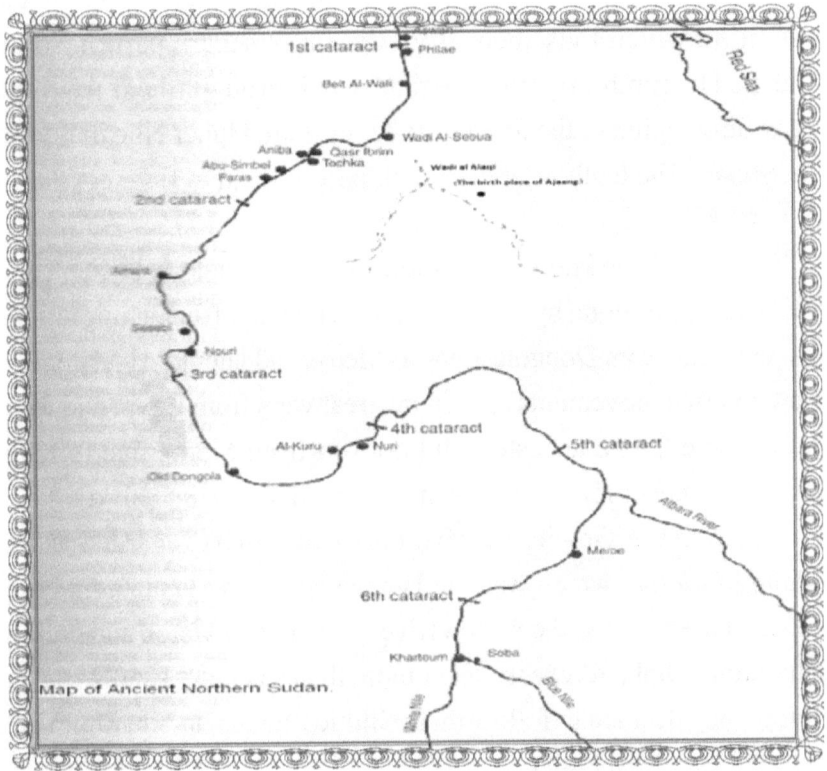

Fig 8: Map of ancient Kush Kingdom in Northern Sudan showing the birthplace of Ajaang, the founding ancestor of the Jaang (or Dinka) people

group led by Jieldit from Judaea coming by way of southwest Asia and crossing the Red Sea in 937 BC at the strait of Deire (modern Bab el-Mandab[21]), the seventh migration was that made by the Jaang ancestral community, which came from Judea and was led by Great Jök-Athurkök, the ancestor of our present Pajök clan people, who are now among the Ngok Dinka people of Abyei. The eighth is the migration which took them from the far Northern part of South Sudan. The ninth migration is that which brought them from the Khartoum region in the 5th century to northern Upper Nile in Southern Sudan. The tenth migration took part of them to Bahr el Ghazal in 1340 AD.

Those were the known migrations of the pre-historic ancient, and medieval times done by our ancestors. The rest of Jaang migrations inside Sudan from Dongola areas to Meroe and later to Al-Matemma were internal movements caused by great wars from Egypt and from Axum. The Dinka ancestors did not run from Meroe due to King Ezana's forces from Axum which destroyed Meroe in 350 AD. They remained in the vicinity of what classical writers regarded as *the island of Meroe*, which was the Butana steppes area, an area lying between the Nile and the Atbara River. In between Meroe and present Khartoum, Dinka forebears spent more than a century (350-490 AD) before they decided to follow their Nilotic brothers to Khartoum and again to Southern Sudan.

Those who remained in Meroe-Atbara areas with Jaang were a people the Dinka still remember as *Dhɔng*, a people who are the present Nuba of the mountains in the South Kordofan of today. Dinka ancient community movements in this part of Northern Sudan were relatively short migrations. They were done in search for pastures, unlike those migrations by the Luo groups who left the Meroe area in a real migratory headlong flight to the Khartoum region in the wake

---

21   The Holy Bible.

of the devastation of Meroe city by Axum. Historical artefacts from terracotta and other ancient traces indicative of the ancient Jaang society in the northern region can still be found today. These are represented by presently widespread traces of baked clay fragments, sculptures of people and other clay objects such as pottery fragments of pots known in Dinka as *Alɛɛi* and *Tony*. A lot of firing pits used by the ancient Jaang community are still found in those Northern Sudan areas between Napata and Khartoum. Those fragments date back to some 500 years BC.[22]

After leaving the present Shendi and Al Banaga areas, Jaang people came to places they renamed as Monydhurman (present Omdurman), Kar-toum, the present Khartoum, and Jeily areas, Jeily being also a Jaang name from Jieldit. There was by then a problem from the Blemmyse who are the present Beja of the Eastern Sudan, a people who had hitherto replaced the northern areas of the Nile between the fourth and second cataracts after the fall of Meroe. There was also the threat from the inland tribes from Western Sudan, a people who frequently vied for Jaang cattle on the Nile.[23]

Lack of pasture from the desert region between Atbara and Khartoum made the Jaang move to the Khartoum area. This move or migration took place in the first two decades of the 4th century AD. The other migration which took them from the Khartoum region to the southern Blue" Nile and Upper Nile regions, around the end of the 4th century AD, was largely brought about by geographical factors combined with those continued incursions from the Nobatian tribes and those from Western Sudan. These two factors were the reasons behind Jaang migration from Khartoum area to Southern Sudan.

---

22 Helen C M; Sudan: A Country Study, Washington DC; Federal Research Division of the Library of congress, (1991), p. 39

23 R Werner with W Anderson and A Wheeler, Day of devastation, day of contentment. The history of the Sudanese church across 2000 years, Paulines Publications Africa, Kolbe Press, Nairobi, Kenya (2000)

Their usual huge livestock, particularly cattle, could not withstand the desert environment that overtook the Khartoum region following the encroachment of aridity from the Great Nubian and the Sahara deserts over the past centuries.

The Jaang final departure from Northern Sudan at Khartoum to the southern Blue" Nile areas and to Southern Sudan was therefore prompted mainly by pastoral pursuits and by security dictates. At this time communities from Western Sudan had already trekked in to the northern region of Meroe and Dongola where they formed Nubia, giving rise to the Nubian kingdoms of Makuria and Nobatia. Full scale Arab occupation of that former heartland region of the blacks, which became Nubia to the north of Khartoum up to the borders with Egypt, only came after the demise of Christianity in both Egypt and Nubia in the 7th century AD.

Like was the case when Nilotic communities were dispersed from Meroe by the fatal attacks from the nearby kingdom of Axum in 350 AD, the Luo and Funj communities were again the first to leave the Khartoum region for the southern Blue" Nile and to northern Upper Nile. They preceded the Jaang community in what was to become the Nilotic march away from Northern Sudan. The Luo went away from Khartoum North some three decades before the Nuers also left the Khartoum region and went to western Upper Nile. The Nuers came and settled in the vicinity of present Koat Liech, near Bentiu, a few decades before the Jaang finally left Khartoum in 490 AD. In any case remnants of the Dinka society remained in the Gezira area to later interact with the Arabs, who in the 7th century succeeded from behind to take over the throne of the Nubian kingdom in Dongola.

Those Jaang remnants stayed up until the 17th century in the Gezira areas of the White Nile and Kosti, including Rabek as far as the area of Sennar. They only followed the rest of the Jaang in the last part of the 17th century as a result of the wars of those of

Abu Lekeleg in central Sudan.[24] Again, the subsequent migratory exodus of the Dinka people in the early part of the Middle Ages, the first quarter of the 14th century, from Upper Nile to Bahr el Ghazal, was precipitated by ecological and epidemic disease factors, among which were smallpox and cholera, epidemic diseases that affected and almost exterminated the Nile's east bank communities at the time. When they came to Bahr el Ghazal they renamed themselves Muonyjang after they defeated the original inhabitants of the region in the course of the 200 years of their wars of conquest of the Bahr el Ghazal.

By about the early decades of the 17th century AD, Dinka people in both Upper Nile and Bahr el Ghazal ceased to be a nomadic community and as they gradually settled they fully adopted agricultural practice. At this time they began to practise cattle rearing, with cultivation on equal par. When cattle diseases erupted in the Nile Basin region, including Bahr el Ghazal, and food provided other means of living, *Muonyjang* became a permanently settled community.

In the late 19th and early 20th centuries, foreign intruders, the Turco-Egyptians, followed by the Mahdists and the Anglo-Egyptians, came into Jaang lands and introduced new names for Jieng and Muonyjang: Jenge and Dinka, new names which these foreigners used at the expense of Jaang ancient and Mediaeval names.

Until future health parameters permit, Dinka people have since then disliked ironstone or plateau regions because of their cattle. They always chose flatlands rich in pasture and water. Dinka cattle, and even the goats and sheep, thrive best in flat savannah areas that are more open grassland or plains. Their livestock do not like very bushy equatorial rain forest or jungle habitats of thick forest where wild animals abound, particularly those forest areas infested by the

---

24 Mmandour Al-Mahdi, A short history of Sudan, O.U.P. (London), 1965, p. 53

tsetse fly. As people of the Nile valley they aren't used to rough and bushy equatorial jungle lands.

In the area of administration the Dinka people have since Khartoum times abandoned loyalty to one central authority. Their last experience with a single communal authority was at the time of great paramount Spear Master Dengdit, who was apparently the overall and single leader of Jaang society in the Khartoum region. According to our Dinka genealogical time chart he was Deng the 4th. Traditions are, however, disagreed over whether this was Deng, the ancestor of the Padang who descended from Jök-Athurkök, or if he was Dengdit from Payöl clan, who was taken up into heaven by the whirlwind in the Khartoum area. The third Deng, the father of Ajaang, appeared in the Wadi Al Allagy area of Wawat prior to the emergence of the Kush Kingdom.

From the end of the 4th century AD when Jaang left the Khartoum area, Dinka people evolved into a highly decentralised, segmentary and semi-independent manner of life, dividing themselves into territorial units or areas ruled then by the Spear Masters, but in this modern era they have come to be administered by government appointed chiefs vested with administrative and judicial powers, although Spear Masters still wield traditional and spiritual authority in each of the Dinka territorial units to the present day. Spear Masters still act as symbols of ancient kings who combined temporal and spiritual powers over their subjects.

Despite this decentralised pattern in their system of administration, Dinka people possess a high degree of homogeneity irrespective of some little distinctions or variations between their sub-national tribes. Dinka Agaar and its adjacent Dinka groups in eastern Bahr el Ghazal culturally stand between the east bank Dinka communities of the Upper Nile and the vast Rek Dinka in central and northwestern Bahr el Ghazal.

Rek appears to preserve Dinka culture of the ancient and Mediaeval times as it is apparently the most conservative of all the Dinka national groups, still maintaining the least diluted forms of language and traditions. Rek Dinka dialect has kept some more archaic characters and more melodious and more connotative language which is rich in inflexion and rather diplomatically polite on the general level.

The Upper Nile Dinka tribal groups, especially Bor and Twic Dinka and their neighbouring Dinka groups on the east bank of the Nile had seriously undergone considerable disruption from foreign explorers, slave traders, military and church missionaries for quite a long time due to their passage along the Nile that they became rather responsive to foreign innovations. The entire Dinka Bor, Twic and all those Dinka principalities in Jonglei state abandoned traditional African beliefs and had taken to Christianity altogether! Clans and their totemic system died out among these Dinka communities and there is no Dinka religion still being practised there. Abialang Dinka in Renk county areas bordering Nezy and Sabaah Arab Baggara are more acculturated into the nearby Arab culture and most of them have taken to Islam!

Put another way round, Bahr el Ghazal eastern Dinka living in the Lakes state pose characteristics common to the Rek Dinka in central and Northern Bahr el Ghazal. They also have characteristics of the Nile east bank Dinka. They constitute the common denominator for all the Dinka of the west and east banks of the Nile.

Among the most conservative groups outside Rek are Luac Dinka in Eastern Tonj and Twic Dinka in Northern Gogrial. Gok Dinka, west of Agaar, are particularly known for their fierce valour and hot temper nearing that of the Nuers. Abialang Dinka in Renk are known for their conceptual belief that they are the mainstream Dinka and take the entire Dinka to be a people originating from one person, their ancestor Ayueel Loŋäär as the Dinka original Spear Master from whom came the Pagong clan family tree that now permeates Dinka society in both Upper Nile and Bahr el Ghazal. Abialang Dinka believe very much in Jaang belonging to Ayueel Jiel and for this reason they use one scar mark on the forehead of their young adult males at initiation to signify the oneness of the Dinka people. Agaar for their part have a longstanding tradition in which they believe that they are the maternal uncles to most of the Bahr el Ghazal Dinka sections like Gok, Rek and Luac. To Agaar, Rek Dinka people are descendants of great Amou Marɔl, sister to Agaar Marɔl. Gok Dinka are to them the descendants of Acuɛi Marɔl and to them too, the Luac Dinka are a people of the eldest Acuɛi Marɔl.[25]

Religiously speaking Dinka people are a monotheistic society believing in one God, the creator of mankind and all things on earth and the whole universe. Dinka people are among the most religious people in the world. They have *Nhialic* as the supreme God with their Spear Master (bäny-bith) as the medium and earthly representative through whom God relates to them. The Dinka religious worldview has affinity with the great Middle East religious concepts, particularly Judaism. In a large measure, Dinka ancient and prehistoric stories and myths as well as their way of life points to the Middle Eastern ways and religious concepts. This is true because of the many similarities in the social and religious traditions and lifestyles between the Dinka and the ancient Middle Eastern peoples, especially the Jews.

As found out during the research years, Dinka people have an intuitive, unvoiced sense of kinship with the Jews. According to Salim Wilson in his '*The Ethiopian valley: the story of the people called Dinka' (1908),* "it has been surmised that prior to the exodus, some Israelites escaped from Egyptian bondage and migrated to the

---

25   This is a widely known tradition among the Dinka by this, Great MarɔlDeng Kau of the Paral clan had one son Agaar, and three daughters: (i) Amou Marɔl, (ii) Acuɛi Marɔl and (iii) the junior Acuɛi Marɔl. Agaar Marɔl, their only brother, became the founding personality for Ageer Dinka society which is now a community of so many clans and sections that make up three administrative countries which are provinces.

district of Elephantinentine" Island near Aswan...". Dinka ancient forebears were actually coming from Egypt during the exodus and are those forebears who were led by the historic Abiɛl. They temporarily settled at this Elephantine Island before coming to the Wawat area of Wadi Al Allagy in that ancient Northern Sudan. Those ancestors retained many Jewish ideals and usages which in the course of time have lost their original force and exactitude."[26]

This view by Salim Wilson is supported by Roland Werner and his colleagues when they affirmed that: *for many centuries, there has been a Jewish colony on Elephantine Island opposite Aswan and may be the knowledge of the one and only one God in contrast with the many gods of ancient Egypt, which in time encroached to the Meroe capital city of Kush Kingdom, had reached all the way to the Meroitic court through them.*[27] This Jewish community that came to Elephantine Island from Egypt were mostly the Reubenite faction of the Jacobites, among whom were great Abiɛl, the ancestor of Ajaang Deng Kuc, who led a faction of these Jacobites to Elephantine Island from Lower Egypt, the Egyptian region of Goshen then to Wawat as a group which branched out of the main body of the Biblical Exodus. Another faction of Reubenites led by Jieldit, and lineage members of Samson, later joined the Abiɛl people in this colony, centuries after the exodus, that is, in 936 BC. Other Jacobites later arrived from Judaea led by Jök-Arthurkök.

The whole of the Elephantinentine" Island colony of these Jacobites later moved to the Wawat area in Northern Sudan where they joined the black communities that came to this ancient northern region of Wawat some centuries earlier.

---

26   S Wilson, The Ethiopian valley: The story of the people called the Dinka, (C. 1908), p. 46

27   R Werner, W Anderson & A Wheeler, Day of devastation, day of contentment: the history of the Sudanese church across 2000 years, Paulines Publications, Africa, Kenya, (2000), p. 24

Those are the present Pahol groups of clans who revere the thighbone among the Dinka. The author comes from the Payii clan which is one of these Pahol groups. Those from the family faction of Samson are those who now revere the fox (awan) and the earth as their divinity totems. This fox and earth revering group of clans is known by different clan names in different Dinka lands. Some are called *Patiɔp* in Agaar land. They are known in some parts of central and Northern Bahr el Ghazal as the *Pawan, Paduɔltiɔp* and so on and so forth.

In further affirming Jaang ancestral links with the Jews a native Dinka man of today in the rural countryside would boldly tell you, "We are of one blood with those people call Israelites."[28] This, when coupled with the teeming details of similarities in the Dinka-Jewish traditional ways of life, customs and belief system, the sum total would portray some blood ties or cultural affinity at some given time in history.

Once again quoting Salim Wilson, a Dinka former slave and a Christian evangelist, he says: *"There would seem to be quite a strong dash of some blood in the Israelites and us and there is, I understand, a theory to the effect that we are an offshoot of one of the lost tribes of Israel."*[29] In his 'Nuer religion', E E Evans Pritchard considered Nuer and Dinka religions as part of the Hebrew culture when he described the Dinka and the Nuers to "have features which bring to mind the Hebrews of the Old Testament"[20].

On the social plane Dinka people are a patriarchal society, conducting their inheritance patrimonially. They are unquestiona-

---

[28] From an interview by the author with paramount elder of the Gok Dinka of the Cueibet county, Jɔk Daau Kacuɔl, dated 8-5-2002, cited as one proof of the rural Dinka knowledge of kinship with the Jews. Jɔk Daau was roughly in his eighties at the time of the interview.

[29] S Wilson, The Ethiopian valley. The story of the people called the Dinka, (1967), p. 32 20 E E Evans Pritchard, Nuer religion, (1967), p. 32

bly a patrilineal society. They place emphasis on the primogenitary right of the firstborn son. The rights of the firstborn son are almost limitless among the Dinka just like it is with the Old Testament Jews as portrayed in the Bible. As it is in the Old Testament the Dinka are to a much greater degree a polygamous people, still retaining their ancient social traditions as is visibly seen in the Bible. Read King Solomon for his many wives and concubines and see the Dinka polygamy of today. The Jews and the Dinka are the only people who practise polygamy in the world to the degree of marrying more than ten wives. The Arabs stop at four wives. African communities could go to three or five wives but very few can go further than that.

Dinka people pay only cattle as the bride's price for a dowry in marriages and since they own large herds they sometimes marry with a hundred cows or more. Some Dinka sections go up to 200 cows and more. Nowadays a Dinka girl who graduates from university can

Fig 9: Showing 150 dowry cows paid as a bride price on the author's daughter, Agom Anei, in 1998

fetch 300 cows in some Dinka places. Up to the present time, girls for marriage are as a general customary rule chosen by the family members not by the suitor, although there are some cases where a young man can, against what custom dictates upon the family, marry a girl of his own choice. The Dinka cattle dowry is paid after elaborate family negotiations involving the paternal and closest maternal kin and aunts on both sides of the suitor's parents and on the side of the bride's parents. For details about Dinka marriage see the section on the Dinka marriage system in chapter six.

The Dinka marriage system is not commercial in essence. The role of cattle paid as dowry is to legalise the new social bond between the two clans and lineages and the two families of the spouses. It is this non-commercial connotation that calls for the bride's side to pay the reverse cattle, which Bahr el Ghazal Dinka people call *Aruɛth* (plural *Aruëth*), payable to the suitor's side. Aruɛth can be better translated as 'reverse cattle or cows' when they are Aruëth. They are a number of cows paid to the suitor and his relatives in return for the cows they paid. The number of reverse cows paid in return to the bride's wealth side in a marriage differs from one Dinka tribe to another. It may even differ within a Dinka tribal sector, but if that of the Rek Dinka of Tonj North and Tonj South counties could be taken as the standard practice, then four cows are paid back to a suitor's relative or brother who paid ten cows as contribution to the marriage dowry. The four cows are paid by the girl's relative who received a share of the ten cows. Two cows are given in return for five cows received by a bride's relative and a cow for every three cows received by the bride's relative whose right of share is three cows. Those given one or two cows do not pay reverse cows which a bride relative had received during the division of the dowry cattle. A bride's relative or brother given eight cows from the dowry cattle is required to pay three cows in return. The customary practice among the Dinka is to pay reverse cows from one's own cattle rather than from the dowry cattle. Nevertheless a girl's relative, brother or father can pay the reverse cows from the dowry cattle if for any good reason he cannot pay from his own.

In the Dinka world the cow is also used as a currency, a medium of exchange. In business transactions cows are today sold for money and are exchanged or bartered for durra, goats and other articles of trade, depending on the value of that article. Like the Old Testament Jews, Dinka people do ghost marriages.[30] They marry the widows of their dead relatives and procreate children in the dead man's name, and through this the dead man's family line is maintained. The same thing is done for dead sisters or daughters, the barren and the impotent. In Dinka society a person is not severed from the family by death. He or she is known to still exist in spirit and still forms part of the family and clan. The Dinka people believe in spiritual life after death. Those who have been sinning during their lifetime are known by the Dinka to undergo spiritual death. Their spirits do not return to interact with their living family members. This is the punishment given to criminals after their physical death. This spiritual punishment presupposes the same thing held in the Christian and Islamic religious doctrines.

Apart from ghost marriage the Dinka people also do levirate marriage. In the Dinka world when a husband dies, the widow remains his wife and a legal member of the family and clan. The death of a husband does not affect the marriage. One of the husband's brothers or a near paternal relative would be chosen by the family to take care of that widow and to produce children with her in the name of her dead husband.[31] The choice of such a person is done officially by the family and a rite is done before the man takes responsibility

---

30   F Mading Deng, Tradition and Modernization, Kuch, Inc., Washington DC, (2004), pp. 138 – 140

31   Ibid

as '*Ala röt,*' the genitor. A son will be required to become a genitor to a widow for his dead father and produce children with that woman in the name of his father. That woman is not his wife. She is his dead father's wife in a social and legal sense. The son is but a genitor. The children resulting from such a marriage will be brothers and sisters to the procreator, the genitor. A Dinka son is also required to produce children with the wife of his dead father and the children so produced are called after the father, not after the biological father, whom they must regard and call a stepbrother.

When a father is too old to cohabit or do his sexual function with his junior wife, a son will be officially allowed to cohabit and produce children for his father. In Dinka custom, if a wife died before she had three children the husband would have a legal right to retrieve or recover part of his dowry cattle, leaving some cattle with his in-laws for his children orphaned by the death of their mother. Together with those children the remaining cows continue to maintain the social bond with the in-laws. There are other forms of marriage among the Dinka. They include sororate marriage whereby a daughter's son or an aunt's son is made to come and cohabit with a wife of his maternal uncle in order to produce children in the name of his dead maternal uncle. This is done only when the deceased's brothers and stepbrothers or all paternal relatives are not available.

Polygamy, levirate and ghost marriages are legitimate and are among the direct reasons for the rapid increase in the Dinka population. This population increase is, however, coupled by the constant availability of good diet because of their ever available livestock. All these nutritious foods give them high quality proteins. These are milk and meat from the cows, goat and sheep as well as from the abundant chicken and the wildlife and rodents rampantly found in the rich flora and fauna.

The Nile and its network of tributaries, streams, water ponds and pools and the territorial network of watercourses which traverses many parts of the Dinka lands all provide the Dinka with constant protein from fish and other marine creatures and plants. Those watercourses provide fish throughout the year. The Dinka are the very people described in 430 BC by the Greek writer Herodotus as being "...*the tallest and most handsomest men in the whole world.... most of them living to be a hundred and twenty years old, eating boiled flesh and had for their drinks nothing but milk...*"[32]

Dinka couples do not divorce easily. Divorce is made difficult by Dinka custom. It can only come after it has been accepted by the family, clan and the entire community, which is ultimately made to come and give their opinion through the court. Divorce between Dinka couples is allowed only after all other avenues have been exhausted by the family, clan and the entire community. In the Dinka world the primary cause of divorce has, however, always been the woman's barrenness or the death of a woman before she bore a child. The death of the husband does not cause divorce in Dinka society. Other factors that lead to divorce are usually suppressed and remedies are made to prevent divorce. The decision to accept divorce to take place involves three parties: the wife's and the husband's clans, the chief or the court and the community at large. It takes years for divorce to be accepted by the community in the traditional court of law.

Barrenness on the part of the wife is the frequent cause for divorce and if a wife commits adultery for no acceptable reason divorce is a likely outcome. Divorce can, however, come about if one of the partners poses insecurity to the other or if the woman is unbearably unruly or is found to have such a bad disease like syphilis or tuberculosis. These diseases are no longer a problem nowadays with modern medicinal remedies availed.

Dinka material wealth is embodied in their huge livestock, particu-

---

32   Herodotus, The Histories, Vol. III, C. 430 BC, in Ancient History source book: Accounts of Meroe, Kush and Axum, C. 430 – 550 BC

larly the cattle. Among the most prosperous Dinka men are those who can own up to 1000 head of cattle or more.[33] This wealth in cattle is perpetuated by the availability of girls raised through many wives whom Dinka men marry with cattle and through serious and intricate cattle management. Dinka people are able to own a lot of cows and because the cattle are so supremely important for the Dinka their life is so focused on the cattle in the cattle camps, in the villages and in the courts of law. All they say is about cattle, whether they are in a home or in the cattle camp which they call *wut*. Even when walking on a journey or between homes and villages, a Dinka man will be thinking or seen talking about a cow or his cow(s) with so and so. To the Dinka people a cow is a sacred domestic property. It is not a mere animal or a mere property. It is life, economy, prestige and a symbol of prosperity.

This Dinka obsession about cattle has resulted in some kind of community submission to the cattle and has therefore led to some form of backwardness and should be challenged by the educated Dinka elites. Alternative means to attain modern ways of living should be sought out and things like education and trade should be adopted at an intensive level.

These measures can minimise violent insecurity and constant death from conflicts over cattle among the Dinka. Keeping cows in their thousands only for marriage, prestige and for aesthetic shows should be abandoned. Cows must be kept for economic use in accordance with modern economic needs. On Dinka relations with their cows, see the *Dinka cattle complex* section in chapter five.

Virtually the only meaningful material possessions which the Dinka are able to bequeath to their children and family are their

---

33   Many Dinka people are cattle tycoons, owning more than 1000 cows. Ringthi Ariik Mawien in Lou- Ariik area, Alabek Payam, Akop sub-region of Tonj North county, is one typical example of those Dinka cattle tycoons. Dut Dut from Tonj East county area of Aköök-Teek, is another cattle tycoon in Rekland.

cherished cattle, the family and their ancestral lands and homes, lands where their cattle graze. The toch, a defined land area with a name and borders, being the most valuable possession after the cattle and the family, is another important thing, but such a possession as the toch is usually a collective possession, although certain families and clans stand to own a whole or part of a toch. There are many tochlands owned or called after certain individuals, however, such ownership is usually nominal, for things like the toch are communally shared.

To the Dinka cattle are a reflection or part of the human community. A Dinka man or woman would exist with his or her cows in such an intimate relationship just like that of man and his children. Each cow is known by name according to its gender, its colour and its markings or according to the shape of its horns. The Dinka also know their cows by their voices through the unique sound they make when they bellow. They also know their cows by their lineage and their previous owners from whom they came and are daily known, recalled and often recited in courts and in marriage negotiations. Some cows are even kept to be intimately known to the family members for generations. A given cow may be kept as a permanent family cow and its offspring usually form a cluster of lineages since they are not dispensed with in business and other usages. Payment in marriages is not done from this type of a cow and its offspring because they are not given out for any reason whatsoever. Such a cow is usually kept in the name of the clan totem which the Dinka call '*yath*'. A cow of this kind can also be accredited to the spirit (Atiëp) of one's mother, one's father, one's grandfather or an ancestor. Dinka cows know their owners and they know where they sleep. They also know all the seasons and when they should go to the toch or when they are to be released to the grazing pastures as well as when they should be brought home, away from the toch and pasture lands. Some cows are particularly preserved as cows of primal parents like Garang, Abuk,

Fig 10: Showing some of the Dinka song bulls on display. They add to the aesthetic beauty of the Dinka culture. The three bulls, Mabior, Magak and the bull in the background remained in the cattle camp for display while the rest of the cattle had been released for grazing. They will be soon released too, and will catch up with the rest of the cows in the pasture.

Dengdit, Macardit and so on. Certain cows are kept by the Dinka for family or clan divinities, *Weŋ Jɔk.*

Through such a symbiotic relationship between the Dinka and the cows, Dinka cattle are able to respond to calls upon hearing their names and bulls become even more intimate and friendly. Bulls are used as song bulls. Cows or bulls are also known by their voices which they make as they bellow. The Dinka aesthetic experiences are also possible through the cows.[34]

---

34   Marc R Nikkel, Dinka Christianity: The origin and development of Christianity among the Dinka of Sudan with special reference to the songs of

Fig 11: Showing Agaar youths dancing the Agaar dance

Among all the Nilotics, Dinka people are very well known for their rich folklore and for their use of the rich symbolism and metaphors of colour and of beauty, military feats and power. All are used through the medium of their herd, which shares history with them. For this reason Dinka women and men often bear names from the colour of their special individual ox, bull or female cow. Names such as Maker, Makur, Marial, Mabior, Malual, Ajäk, Yar, Aluɛl, Yɔm, Makuei, Akur, Kuei and so on, are given to people to recall or remember one's cow, one's ox or bull paid as a dowry cow during the marriage of one's mother.

When dancing young people, especially men, hold their arms up high above their heads, mimicking the curve of their bull's horns.

Dinka Christians, (2011), Paulines Publications Africa, Kolbe Press, Nairobi, Kenya pp. 23-28.

Dinka dance, particularly that of the Rek Dinka of Tonji and Gogrial, is the most impressive and the most organised of the Nilotes and the whole of the black Africa. The Agaar people do what they call *Dhëëŋ Nhial* in which a young man makes a very vigorous effort to leap high up above the rest who make a circle around him, singing and clapping their hands. Girls also raise their arms up and move in a circle. They all do this activity while singing and clapping their hands.

Dinka dancing songs are all imbued with rich metaphors from cows, and girls, and on great feats by them. This is in addition to the glorious deeds of their fathers, grandfathers or ancestors. In his finely groomed bull of display, the bull of particularly beautiful colour, a young Dinka man will subsume all that is pride. A bull by the colour of *Marial*[35] is the special bull of preference.

BULLS

A young Dinka man would discern all of his alter ego on his song bull, one whom he parades, singing songs that testify to the prowess and beauty which distinguishes him and the bull together. Social standing and self esteem are for the Dinka intimately linked to the ownership of cattle. Family property is also associated with cattle ownership. In the Dinka world any family or person without cows can hardly be held in esteem according to the criteria of Dinka society. From birth to death the soul of a Dinka man in his social, economic, political and spiritual experience is concerned with and sustained by his ownership of cattle. Without cows, a Dinka man can hardly marry and can't procreate children for himself for his

---

35   A bull with the colour of Marial to the Dinka is that bull with large patches of black and white colours and a red colouration on its nose. For its beauty, Marial is sometimes bought with up to ten cows. In a marriage contest the suitor whose dowry consists of Marial is likely to win the marriage.

Fig 12: Showing two different types of bulls, Mabior and Manyiel, being paraded for display as song bulls

name and for his paternal continuity. Rek Dinka people call such a person an *'abuur'*, a cattleless man whose life has no meaning in the society.

While Dinka people use cattle for ritual and religious purposes the prime use of cattle among the Dinka is for production of milk and payment of bride price. In marriages cattle are the only acceptable medium for bride price payments. After serious and elaborate discussions conducted by the two parties to the marriage and in the presence of community elders, a marriage agreement is concluded. Women can sometimes sit in marriage discussions to listen but not to express opinion for or against! Marriage discussions and the final decision is an exclusive role for men. The bride's mother cannot even be seen about during the discussion of the marriage of her daughter, let alone her opinion! After discussions and negotiations are over, a marriage agreement is arrived at and is consolidated and legalised

Fig 13: Showing three bulls which are Dinka special bulls of preference. They are three different types of the Marial bull. They are also shown for their different horns' design.

Fig 14: Showing Dinka open court sitting with an Agamloŋ, the translator, in the middle

when a down payment of the agreed number of cows is made. Paid dowry cows are transferred from both the paternal and maternal relatives of the marrying young man to those of the bride. Marriage agreement after negotiations of days, weeks, months or even years is secured and maintained by the two families and witnessed by the elders from the entire territorial community, mostly in the presence of the chief who is always from the sacred or Spear Master clan. If for any good reason the chief cannot be there, there has to be an elderly man from a renowned Spear Master clan who must have the last word for the conclusion of the marriage. This is the point at which a well known but vibrant community song is sung by both sides, a process which in essence signifies marriage conclusion and makes the spouses tied to each other as legally witnessed partners in life.

Among the Dinka the creation of children through a number of wives is the sole means by which a man may ensure continuity of his name beyond his lifetime, which approximates the concept of eternal life after death. The acquisition of cows relates to the setting up of a family large enough to perpetuate one's name after death. Raising a large family of many wives is also for one's prestige in one's lifetime as more cows and a large family qualify a person to be among the aristocratic Dinka social class. For the Dinka wealth symbolised by large numbers of wives, children and cattle promotes or maintains a man and his family to be among the upper class in the community.

For the complex and central role they play Dinka people developed a very advanced system of laws from customs and traditions to govern the circulation and management of the cattle among themselves.[36] Since Mediaeval times Dinka people were known to settle their disputes and litigations in open courts, set under a big tree for its shade and attended by everybody who wished to listen or learn community issues and history. Those open court sittings used to be presided over by a prominent Spear Master and assisted by a group of councillors who were also a group of elderly aristocrats versed in the history and social composition of the territory and adept to the background of each section, clan and family. With *Agamloŋ*, the translator or adumbrator usually seated in the middle of the court's circle and loudly repeating the statements of each speaker, litigants or disputants present arguments for their cases before the jury of elders who listen with intense attention and after thorough and elaborate comments from the audience, the jury moulds out the decision which is finally pronounced by the presiding Spear Master who was in effect the ruler of the territory on behalf of God in the high.

Such a community-based system of justice continued maintaining the social cobwebs among the Dinka, holding the society together until the advent of the Anglo-Egyptian colonialism which abolished that traditional system of judicial democracy and substituted it with a system whereby chiefs are appointed by the government to primarily implement government policies and directives among the people in their territory. These appointed Dinka chiefs have continued to settle

---

36   On this topic, see Justice John Wol Makech's Dinka customary law.

disputes and adjudicate between disputants. Nevertheless, the Dinka judicial system is still open to the present day. Public court hearings are still conducted under big tree shade and although the final verdict does come from the presiding chief, public opinion is first obtained from the members of the court and from the audience.

As was the case with those ancient Jews as described in the Bible, in the Old Testament, the Dinka system of justice gives right to even a stranger, the orphan or to a widow. *"You shall not pervert justice due to the stranger or the fatherless or widow"* (Deut. Ch. 24 V. 17). The religious or spiritual power aspect of the Spear Master in the Dinka courts of law was later removed by the British colonialists and the Dinka law court system subsequently became secular in nature. In the past adamants and society breakers of the values and norms system used to be cursed by the Spear Master or they were at worst excommunicated from the territory by the jury. Such deterrent punishments were meted out against adulterers, thieves, murderers and people proven to be wizards, however, Dinka modern secular chiefs still refer adamants to Spear Masters for swearing in attestation for or against a claim or accusation. The general welfare of the community and relationship between the living and their God, the ritual and sacred affairs in the territory, continue to remain as the domain of the Spear Masters to the present day.

THE DINKA DEFENCE SYSTEM

As far as their defence system is concerned Dinka people are generally known as a *warrior and martial society* and are for this reason referred to by John Ryle in his '*The Dinka: The warriors of the White Nile*', 1983, as "warriors of the White Nile". Dinka people have a highly developed community-based defence system in which the society is classed into Age-sets whose duty is collective defence for the territory and property of their defined polity or wut. Each

Age-set is named by a highly accepted and renowned elderly Spear Master who becomes the *Godfather* of that Age-group till all of its members fade away by death as a given generation. Each territory makes one Age-set after another in succession. Dinka Age-sets are created or named by Spear Masters, not by just an ordinary elder from the mundane clans. In this way the Dinka defence system is largely associated with Spear Masterhood. It has a religious undertone.

Dinka people are extremely martial and their history is very replete with war stories for which an individual, family, clan or wut tries to excel and make extraordinary warrior feats. Many people among the Dinka made names through wars and for this reason Dinka society is made of warrior and Spear Master clans. Through wars the Dinka people were able to acquire territories from various communities and they therefore became known as *'the lions of the Nile valley'*. This explains why they renamed themselves as Muɔnyjäng, meaning *'man of the people'*, although Muɔnyjäng can better mean a *Jääng man*.

EVOLUTION OF THE DINKA NAMES

Jiëëng, the Dinka, are not just a tribe. They are a nationality composed of twenty six large and small tribal groups. To the present day most Jiëëng or Jääng also call themselves Muɔnyjäng, particularly those in the Bahr el Ghazal region. Up to late Mediaeval times they were known as Jääng, but, by the middle of the Turco-Egyptian colonial era in Sudan (1821-1885) through the whole of the Mahdists' era (1885-1898) and the Anglo-Egyptian colonial period (1898-1956), these Jiëëng, Jääng or Muɔnyjäng came to be given different names by those outsiders and by different nationalities in Sudan. They finally came to be officially known as *Dinka* although the vast rural Dinka continue to know themselves as Muɔnyjäng or Jiëëng to the present day.

The Fertit tribal groups in the western parts of Bahr el Ghazal region and the neighbouring Baggara Arab tribes in Western Sudan, even the Baria in Central Equatoria, communities with whom the Dinka have continuous historical and geographical contacts, all came to introduce the name *Jenge* in place of Jääng, Muɔnyjäng or Jiëëng, with Fertits saying *Zenge*. All of these communities failed to pronounce Jiëng, Muɔnyjäng or Jiëng. A Western Sudanese used to say Jengai for one Jiëëng man. Jiëëng people came to dislike the Fertit, Baria and the Western Sudanese way of calling them like that. They abhorred it for the implication which is associated with such names, Jenge or Zenge, names which remind the Dinka people of the heinous slave trade era.

In later times the British colonialists came to introduce the name 'Dinka', a name with which the then Sudan metropolitan societies and the outside world came to know them to the present day. But Jieng Nilotic neighbours such as Luo and Nuer tribal groups know the society as Jaang, not as Dinka, Zenge or Jenge and although the entire rural Dinka naturally know themselves as Muɔnyjäng and Jiëëng, they nonetheless know of their ancient name *Jääng*. The name *Muɔnyjäng* is widely used by the Dinka people perhaps because it is very redolent with historical pride and because they acquired much of their present superiority complex from it.

On the whole Dinka people are called 'Muɔnyjäng'. Their Mediaeval name Jiëëng was derived from their ancient generic name 'Jaang'. In any case, much of Bahr el Ghazal Dinka prefers Dinka nationality to be known as *'Muɔnyjäng'*, but all Dinka communities would not mind if they were to re-adopt their historical name Jieng or Jääng. This is because the name Muɔnyjäng poses a gender problem as it only emphasises the male aspect, implicitly excluding the female sector of the community. Muɔnyjäng in Dinka language is masculine in meaning. It is a compound form of two words: 'Moc' means 'man' and 'Muɔny' in Muɔnyjäng is a possessive of 'Moc', and when in a compound form, 'Muɔnyjäng', it either means Jaang man or *man of the people*. This is because Jääng in Dinka means people. The name 'Jiëng' in Dinka is gender neutral, neither masculine nor feminine. Its use suggests the entire Jääng irrespective of gender, hence the choice of it.

As an antithesis to the use of the name Dinka the entire nationality in the rural countryside in Upper Nile and in Bahr el Ghazal does not know itself as Dinka as the outside world know and call them. Strange as it has come to be, the name Dinka only came into use in towns and cities from colonial times until it went into official and written literature within the country and the world at large, so much so that it became difficult for even the enlightened members of Jiëëng society to resist it. Attempts to educate Sudanese urban inhabitants to use the name Muɔnyjäng, Jääng or Jieng persistently failed over the decades. Eventually Jiëëng elites apparently acquiesced to the name 'Dinka' and a whole nationality of over five million people came to have a foreign imposed name as its official name in the country and the outside world.

Although this foreign imposed name took official precedence over the true historical names, metropolitan Jieng people came not to mind being call Dinka so long as there was no derogatory connotation implied in it. This is particularly so since it has proven unifying and has gone far and wide, however, the ongoing tide for cultural awakening may militate on Jiëëng intellectuals for a return to the original name. It is, however, not known how far this shall succeed for the Dinka to revert to Jiëëng, Muɔnyjäng or Jaang unless it be a government policy to change all foreign names such as Bahr el Ghazal, Dinka, Jebel Kunyjur, Hofrat al Nahas and so forth. Without that it is likely that the name Dinka will persist in total replacement of those ancient and Mediaeval names even among the rural Dinka.

For the purpose of this book, however, the name Dinka will continue to be invariably used in tackling Jiëëng people and their history. What now follows is the historical narrative about how Dinka people came to acquire such names in the course of their historical evolution in Sudan.

JIËËNG AND JÄÄNG

In the course of the research for this historical book on Jääng society a strong urge came up from both the rural and urban Dinka people asking for a return to their ancient true name, 'Jääng', also preferring its modified form 'Jiëëng'. But, how did this ancient name come about?

Historically the name 'Jääng' originated from the Jiëëng ancient word 'Jang', meaning people. The word 'Jääng' with a double 'ä' came up sometimes when Ajääng, the apparent common ancestor for most of the Jääng people, formed a family tree of six sons who married, and when his grandsons' and great grandsons' children married and his lines rainified by descent over a number of centuries along the main Nile region of the then Napata and Meroe centre of the blacks' civilisation between present Khartoum and Aswan in Egypt, a society which descended from Ajääng came into being. This society started to be known as *'Paan-Ajääng'*, that is, an Ajääng lineage family whose numbers increased significantly over those centuries that followed.

From around the 7th and the 8th centuries BC, Ajääng's descendants grew into a community called Jääng. They managed to increase by successful social mitosis and overtook other parallel social lineages from his direct and remote next of kin. Thus from those centuries before and after the fall of Meroe, the population of Ajääng lineages, which incorporated other Jääng agnatic sections, reached the proportion of a society which became a tribe. Clans and sections began to be clearer at this stage.

By gradual migration to the areas between Meroe and Khartoum,

Ajääng's society was already a distinctly known tribe by the name of 'Jääng'. This was up to the 3rd century AD. Their contemporary societies on the same Nile valley region of the north, the black communities, which were the Luo, Funj, Naath (our present Nuers), Mazoi (the present Mahas), Nuba, Hasa, Baryas and Blemmyse of the Red Sea littoral region, all knew them as Jaang society. Although the destruction of the Kush Kingdom at Meroe made part of Jaang society migrate up to the west coast of Africa, while part of them were driven to Axum as war captives with the rest of the blacks of the kingdom, a bulk of Jääng society moved south along the Nile to those areas between Meroe and Khartoum. By about the beginning of the 4th century AD, Jääng had come to the present Khartoum state areas. In the middle or the end of the 4th century, the Jaang society left Northern Sudan from Khartoum areas for Blue and Upper Nile areas. They later reconverged in the Upper Nile region as one Jääng. They then came to the central and southern Upper Nile areas of present Jonglei state after displacing the Luo to Eastern Equatoria and Bahr el Ghazal. Within this Jonglei state area they stayed as the Jääng tribe from the early part of the 14th century AD when some of them went to Bahr el Ghazal at the end of the first quarter of that century. They went there as Jääng. It was in the Bahr el Ghazal region that they developed a new name, 'Muɔnyjäng', as explained hereunder.

MUƆNYJÄNG

Whether by reason of pride or a historical fact, Bahr el Ghazal Dinka, with the exception of the Dinka of the Yirol sub-region, are particularly firm about calling themselves 'Muɔnyjäng' as they want to be known, in spite of the semantic segregation and the modern criticism it entails as explained earlier.

Jääng people, however, adopted this name 'Muɔnyjäng' in about the second half of the Mediaeval Ages, the heroic era when Jääng society was greatly engaged in a long period of wars of conquests, first in Upper Nile region, then in Bahr el Ghazal. During those late parts of the ancient and early Mediaeval times, Jääng society was engrossed in many wars with inhabitants of the Upper Nile Basin region, notably with the Funj, Burun, the Luo tribal groups, Bɛɛr (today's Murle) and the Nuers, then in the middle to late Mediaeval Ages, with Jur-Luɛɛl, the Bongo and the Belle tribes in Bahr el Ghazal region.

While the name Jääng was the traditional nomenclature for which they were known by their ancient and Mediaeval neighbours and by which they knew themselves, Bahr el Ghazal Dinka later succeeded to impose their celebrated name, 'Muɔnyjäng'. They used it in their daily language when referring to themselves. It was apparently an invention arising from their superiority complex and pride which they acquired from the war victories and conquests they did after their famous migratory exoduses from Khartoum in the 4th century and in Bahr el Ghazal when they went there from Upper Nile in the 14th century AD.

After crossing the River Nile at Shambe shore and other adjacent shores as they were migrating to Bahr el Ghazal, Jaang society thrust through in an array of different directions, violently landing on the Indigenous inhabitants. On leaving their first encampment locations in Ajäk land on the west bank after Shambe, they made a wedge due west, north and south, thrusting to all directions into Bahr el Ghazal's deep jungles and to all the inhabitable land areas. This was in about 1340 AD or slightly a decade after. This was in the time when a certain Dominican monk by the name of Bartholomeus from Tivoli in Italy was bishop of the Christian kingdom of Makuria in Dongola.[37]

Genealogical age computation done on those who participated in that migration of 1340 to Bahr el Ghazal, the study of the Great

---

[37] R Werner, W Anderson & A Wheeler, Day of devastation, day of contentment. The history of the Sudanese church across 2000 years

Age of epidemic outbreaks of the consummate smallpox and cholera on the Nile valley communities during the early decades of the Mediaeval Ages, all confirmed this as the time of Jääng migration to Bahr el Ghazal from the Upper Nile.[38] The migrating population of Jaang landed on those native inhabitants, coming upon them in organised and successive waves from Loŋäär's Age-sets, historically presented as 'Kiec-Manyiel', the bee.

It was the *Kiec-Manyiel Age-group* which effected the invasion of Bahr el Ghazal. Sections of Kiec-Manyiel's legions catapulted the moving exodus. Kuei, Lith and Gïr of Rek sections which were later formed did the rest of the wars in those areas that form the present Lakes state. Jaang marauding bands of youth parties from those age groups cleared any menace that laid in front, making the territory ready for an onrushing populace of the aged, women and children, driving their livestock and carrying their provisions and settling in swarms by sections and clans' formations. The unfortunate native inhabitants, overwhelmed by the fighting Jääng invaders, could only recede, retiring away in a continued retreatwith Jur-Luɛɛl later giving up its hold on Bahr el Ghazal territories and finally left in those areas that are now the Northern Bahr el Ghazal areas of Awiel, Ngok and Twic. They left Bahr el Ghazal for good in around the end of the 16th century. The last of the Jur-Luɛɛl vestige in the Abyei area, however, left in the second quarter of the 17th century when Ngok dislodged them from the area. These Jur-Luɛɛl are believed to have gone further west to the Republic of Chad in West Africa. Some of them are said to have gone further west, headlong to as far as Nigeria where they are assumed to be the present Ambororo community; however, some of the remnants of those Jur-Luɛɛl are known to have later been absorbed by the Rizzeigat and Masiriya Arab tribes that later came to the Darfur and Kordofan regions in Western Sudan. Other

---

38   30 Mediaeval Ages is the very Middle Ages which is the European period of 400 years between 1100-1500 AD

remnants of the Jur-Luɛɛl who chose not to leave the area were later encapsulated and assimilated into Muɔnyjäng throughout central and Northern Bahr el Ghazal.

The Alei section people in Ngok area of Abyei are remnants of this Jur-Luɛɛl people.[39] The Jur-Belle and Jur-col (Luo) case was, however, different from that of Jur-Luɛɛl and the Bongo. Notwithstanding the initial and later battles of resistance the Belle community and their incoming Jaang society quickly adopted a peaceful method of coexistence which started at the beginning of the 15th century. To neutralise and diffuse the initial tensions with the Belle tribe, Jaang leaders, especially the Agaars and later the Gok Dinka, whose communities directly neighboured the Belle, decided to give their girls to the Belle leaders in exchange for pieces of land for settlement and peaceful coexistence. Except for the Aliap Dinka section in the southeastern fringes of the Yirol area the present Dinka tribal sections in the Lakes region of Bahr el Ghazal acquired parts of their current territories through this peaceful social method.

'Yirol', coming from the word 'Anyirol', was the name of Lual Carbek area girl from Akot Community, then given to a water deity in an area that is now Yirol Town. This is how Yirol Town and its surrounding area acquired its name to later become the name of the entire district comprising of Ciec, Aliap and today's Yirol-West County. Great Spear Master Buöl Kuöt of the Redior clan, by then the paramount spiritual overlord for much of the Agaar Dinka, gave his daughter, Akon Buöi, to the Belle leader and the spot where Rumbek city is now situated was given to him in exchange. Buöi and his Agaar people later made Jur-Belle communities recede back into their present forest lands. They did this by tense and gradual encroachment. Great Abukuac of the Pathiöng section of Gok Dinka

---

39   From an interview with a Ngok Dinka elder, Awad Kueeth in Thiet town (2001). Ngok and Malual Dinka communities are direct neighbours with the Rizzeigat and Massiriya Arab Baggara in Western Sudan.

society also gave his daughter known by the name Aluät. He gave her to another Jur-Belle overlord from the Gwere section of Jur-Belle and was made to settle, although Gok Dinka later used physical methods to take the whole of what is now Gok land from Jur-Belle and from the Bongo.

Generally, the Jur-Belle tribe gave way to Agaar, Kiec, Aliap and Gok Dinka communities in the present Lakes state areas. The Bebui, Kidala and Morokodo sections of the Jur-Belle stepped back, further south along the present Payii River area. The Jebilieep, Sopi, Ngira and Gwere sections of the Jur-Belle tribe gradually retired southward to their present haematite stone plateau areas along the present Nam River area. They vacated those places for the Agaar section of Kuei made of Yom, Awan and Dor, sections that are present Nyang and parts of which are present Rup territories consisting of Köök and J ɔth. Those territories which were vacated by Jur-Belle for Agaar include those areas inhabited by the other sections of Kuei, comprised of Amothnhom and what is now the Aliamtooc area, east of Rumbek. Further southwest of Rumbek city, bordering Yom, Awan and Dor, areas which are currently inhabited by Pathiöng sections of Gok, were Jur-Belle sections known as Gabe, Guelo, Lori and Aranga.

Those Belle sections withdrew into the plateau forest region deeper south and further upstream to the Gul-Mar River area. The Gwere section, which had earlier inhabited all those areas which are now inhabited by the Nyang section of Agaar as far as the Gul-Mar area, also withdrew into the deeper south. The Wetu, Meri and Mandra sections of Jur-Belle to the west also gave way to the Gok sections of Ayiɛl to the southwestof Cuɛibɛt county and the Akony section in the same Gok areas of Malou-Pec Payam, west of Cuɛibɛt town. Those Belle communities withdrew upstream, away from the Gel River area to the interior areas of Puor, Kewbe and the areas of Domakija as far as the current Arua national park areas.

Having receded to that haematite stone plateau areas on the fringes of the equatorial forest parts of Bahr el Ghazal, Jur-Belle in effect vacated the mainly fertile loam soil plains and rich savannah woodland areas for the Gok to then occupy. Jur-Belle finally made sure it evaded the Jaang fatal threat by the middle of the 16th century AD.

The Bongo tribal sections, which are now of chiefs Danga Jagati, Belany and Gwoi Marɔl, lying southwest of Ayiɛl and Akony and far up the Gel River, deep into the south, also gave way. They retired away from those areas which are now inhabited by Ayiɛl, Akony and the entire *'Great no man's forest land'* of Tonj South county, an extensive forest area otherwise known as *Ror Cuɔl Akol,* translated as *the dawn-to-dusk forest*. The Bongo sections of chiefs Buguai and Awedo withdrew from all those areas which are now inhabited by the Rek sections of Thɔny and Muɔk to as far as present Tonj town and its outlying extremities. They moved further south into what is now Agugo and further to the hinterland's deep primaeval forest area, hundreds of miles into the present Zande territory of Tambura in Western Equatoria.

It took the Jaang invading society up to about the end of 1500 AD to finalise the conquest and occupation of those parts of Bahr el Ghazal they now inhabit. This is the time when they began to undertake territorial demarcation of the occupied territories as far as the northwestern end of Bahr el Ghazal borders with Western Sudan. This territorial occupation was, however, completed in the course of the 16th century.

What later followed were but isolated internal migratory zigzags by small groups, lineages and discontented individuals who made internal migrations within the region, although some sections or groups of people later returned from Bahr el Ghazal to Upper Nile, once again crossing the River Nile, back to the Upper Nile region.[40]

---

40 Awulian Section people of those of Dr John Garang are among those Jiëëng communities who remigrated back to Upper Nile from Bahr el Ghazal. They left Bahr el Ghazal at a place call Panyenlɛm cattle camp area of Jur -Lian

The Luo section, colloquially called 'Jur-col' by the Bahr el Ghazal Dinka, later chose to move to their present abodes in Bahr el Ghazal, either through some transient wars with the Dinka or by a voluntary step back to their present ironstone country, land which is haematitic in content.

Some known skirmishes with the Jääng were only those between them and the Jur-col section of Abat. The relationship between the Luo of Bahr el Ghazal and the incoming Jaang conquering society was apparently relatively cordial. The Luo people in general have been a known blacksmith community since Meroe times and when they came to Bahr el Ghazal they tended to like those areas where iron ore was random. The availability of this iron ore made the Jur-col community stick to the ironstone area, which is a relatively raised plateau land, not wanted then by the Jaang and their cattle. Besides this reason for cordial relations with the Jur-col community there was an ancient story that makes Bahr el Ghazal Luo look at the Jääng as the sons of their daughter Adeeng. Up to the beginning of the Turco-Egyptian era in Sudan, the Luo, especially the Jur-col in Bahr el Ghazal, still called the Jääng people the *'Kuadeeng'*- that is, the people of Adeeng.[41] As experts in iron smelting and blacksmithing the Jur-col, who remained in Bahr el Ghazal after the departure of Nyikang, Gilo and Nyingor, did not come into conflict with Jaang. They made sure that they kept themselves to areas not wanted by Jääng invaders.

As stated earlier, it took the Jääng society up to about the end of 1500 AD to accomplish the territorial occupation of much of those

---

section in present Awan-Parek territory in Northern Tonj. After they left Jur-Lian, they first settled at Agigim in Luacjang area of today's Tonj East. They later proceeded to the Yirol area of Kiec where they crossed the River Nile at the shore of Dhiam-Dhiam back to current Twic land in southern Upper Nile region where they finally settled as Awulian till today.

41   AJ Achile, The history of the Nile valley to the lakes, University Edinburgh, UK. (1936), pp. 186 – 190

areas they now inhabit in Bahr el Ghazal. It was at this time that the internal territorial demarcation of the acquired lands started to be effected by the great Jääng Spear Masters and warlords of the time. Division of the acquired areas into sections and territorial units continued to be carried out as new lands were acquired further on, up to the extreme north west, into those areas now inhabited by the Malual Dinka. On reaching what later became Apuökjäng, an area about Kar-Ariath in present Apuöth territory of Chief Kong Ayueel Majök of the Pariath clan in Northern Bahr el Ghazal state, the western end of the Rek migratory column divided into two:

Great Tɔng Aköt, also known as Tɔng de Rɛɛng from the Parek clan, parted in around 1560 AD from the Apuökjäng area and migrated southwest up to the Chel River area, leading the large Dinka population of Rek, consisting of over twenty different clans. Those clans now constitute what is presently known as the Palieupiny section which is further subdivided into Paliëët and Malual Buɔth-Anyaar, in all[42] consisting of over twenty different clans and presently grouped into fifteen very large executive chieftaincy areas. They occupy the east bank region of Lɔl and further from Lɔl to the west.

They also extend to the haematite ironstone country with borders as far as those western areas where they meet with the Fertit tribal group known as Kreysh and those other smaller tribes of the same Fertit to the northwest of the Wau road to Raja. Some of these Buɔth-Anyaar Dinka are now about forty miles from the central African capital town of Bangui. They also border Jur-col on their southwestern fringe on the railway line from Awiel towards Wau town.

The other branch of the wave to be later known as the *Pajök* section of the Malual Dinka remained to be led by another Spear

---

42 From an interview, September 2004, with Lt General Mark Nyipuoch Abanga, a renowned Luo political leader in Bahr el Ghazal region. Gen Mark later became governor of Western Bahr el Ghazal state at the time the author was also governor of the neighbouring state of Warrap.

Master, Great Diing Wol Lëëk, otherwise known also as Diing-Keramindïk from the Paciɛrmeth clan people of ruaal or 'sausage tree'. Keramindïk led a community of over twenty clans, which have since become many clans, consisting of (i) the Great Abiem community, now made of fourteen large chieftaincy areas and (ii) Malual-Giɛrnyaang proper which is presently made up of twenty four big chieftaincy areas.[43]

As previously mentioned those Dinka waves of invasion to the northwestern and southern parts of Awiel did not very much temper with the Luo branch of Ukuo (the Jur-col) which preceded Jääng to Bahr el Ghazal a number of centuries earlier. Those Luo groups of Ukuo came to Bahr el Ghazal from the northern Upper Nile areas of Jebellein and Jalhak. From the Jebellein area they crossed the White Nile to the west bank and by gradual movement, they finally came to settle at a place known as Ker, a location northwest of the present town of Wau, a few kilometres west of the railway line. They later moved to the present Luo homeland area, now inhabited by the Jur-col sections of Abat, Dimo and Buɔdhɔ.

Here at Ker descendants of the great Ukuo settled before the arrival of the Jääng from south-central Upper Nile. This is where the great Nyikang and his brothers Gilo, Dimo and Nyingor had the historic quarrel which split the Luo community to the present day, not in Wijpac as other sources assert. They were four sons of a certain Mol Nyandhiang. This Nyandhiang is believed to have been the one who came with a section of Luo from the northern Upper Nile area of Jebellein. Mol Nyandhiang departed the Jebellein area upon the Jaang advent from the Khartoum region. He and his people gradually moved westward through what is the current Biemnhom area of the Alor Kur Kuot Dinka through to the present Twic territory in what is

---

43 From an interview by the author with a group of chiefs from the Awiel sub-region of Bahr el Ghazal state (i) Chief Achiɛn Yöör (ii) Sub-Chief Deng Ngueel and many other elders, 12 December 2004.

currently northern Gogrial, until he arrived at that spot of Ker where he settled for generations.

When his descendants later parted after that famous quarrel, Nyikang and his two young brothers, Gilo and Nyingor, left Bahr el Ghazal to cross the River Nile on the spot later used by the returning Jääng people.

They first settled in what is now the Nyarweng Dinka area in south-central Upper Nile area. Then, they proceeded to a spot now known as Nyilual on the east bank of the Nile.

After a number of decades they proceeded to Fashoda and Akurwa where Nyikang first established the Shilluk (Collo) kingdom and from there it was subsequently moved to Fashoda where Abudhok, daughter of Nyikang, became the first queen, followed by Nyikang's son, Dak, who became the first mek[44] or king of the Shilluks.

Dimo remained in Bahr el Ghazal to become the leading founding ancestor of the Jur-col section of the Luo communities in Bahr el Ghazal. Nyingor and Gilo followed Nyikang to south-central Upper Nile. They later parted, with Gilo heading further east, where his descendants formed the Anyuak tribe while Nyingor and a group of Luo lineages went south along the Nile to become the Acholi tribe. The others went ahead to join the Luo first waves that went to Kenya and Uganda.

The Ruweng people, who later became founders of the Alor Kur Kuot Dinka in the Biemnhom area, the Ngok of Lual Yak, Paweny people of Ataar, Pan-Ru people of Panriεng and the Ngok Dinka of Abyei, recrossed the River Nile with the Ngok Dinka people of Abyei. They crossed at the Shambe shore. They went back to southern Upper Nile in about the beginning of the 15th century. From thereon they moved gradually till they again recrossed the Nile to the western regions of Panriεng and Biemnhom. They went along

---

44   Interview by the author with Lt Colonel P Omuot Anyuak Luo tribe, 24 August 2003.

with the descendants of Jök who proceeded to the Abyei area in the 17th century. This Ruweng section of Jök people was led by Great Kuol Arop Biong. The Ngok community was later joined by the Massiriya Arab Baggara, coming from the Kordofan region in the 18th century. This made the Jaang community move deeper into what has now become southern Kordofan, further northwest of the Bahr el Ghazal River area.

Within that long tradition of migration, warfare and occupation of lands, and with that vivid portrayal of marshal attributes, the Jaang people came to see themselves as being militarily superior to all those non-Jaang communities with whom they came into contact in Southern Sudan.

With that sense of invincibility from past feats vis-à-vis with those people they came into contact with, for a number of centuries since their ancestors left the Khartoum region for the Upper Nile and lastly to Bahr el Ghazal, the Jaang therefore saw themselves as the strongest of men in combat. It was within the context of this tradition that the name 'Muɔnyjäng' came up among the Jaang people. They gave this name to themselves as a way to tell of Jaang invincibility and henceforth Muɔnyjäng was used by the Bahr el Ghazal Dinka so much that it went far back to the remaining Dinka communities in the Upper Nile region where it was also adopted and invariably used together with the name Jiëëng.

Successive generations that came and passed all came to rest on the name Muɔnyjäng as a *fait accompli* name for all Jaang people, although they still had Jieeng and Jaang in their memory and in their tongue as the ancient names of the entire nationality.

JENGE OR ZENGE

The word 'Jenge', which came up in the late 19th century through to the early parts of the 20th century, was used for Muɔnyjäng, merely as an inflectional problem from those non-Nilotic Sudanese communities who could not properly pronounce the name Jiëëng, Jaang or Muɔnyjäng. Jenge or Zenge was introduced into the popular Sudanese literature by the Northern Sudanese who came to Southern Sudan to practise the slave trade during Turkiyya and Mahdia (1821–1898) in Sudan. What was domestic servitude practised throughout Africa and the rest of the world was turned into commerce in the 19th and 20th centuries in Sudan.

In the name of the Ottoman emperor from Turkey, then called the Ottoman sultan, Egypt occupied Sudan in 1821. Mohammed Ali, the Ottoman colonial ruler of Egypt and Sudan, then encouraged trade in humans in Sudan right from the very beginning of that occupation which started from Northern Sudan. By 1830s, this trade in human beings arrived into Dinka lands at its fullest scale. It came through the northwestern Upper Nile and through northwestern parts of Bahr el Ghazal, using the Fertit tribes who were easily broken up by the armies of those slave traders. They later also came through the Jur River branch of the Bahr el Ghazal River and through the river port of Meshra in Tonj North and Shambe in Yirol East. From the 1840s up to 1898, Muɔnyjäng was in great pestilence which Rek Dinka communities call 'Riäŋ Turkuk', the pestilence of the Turks. The Lakes Dinka in eastern Bahr el Ghazal call it Riäŋ Malualthith – the pestilence of the brown race, also called the Age of Malualthith. During this era, the names Jenge and 'Zenge' were derogatorily used for Muɔnyjäng. Then came the era when another new name 'Dinka' was introduced for the same Jaang, Muɔnyjäng or Jiëëng.

DINKA

While the name Muɔnyjäng was a making of Jaang people themselves – a terminology of the Mediaeval Ages, the name Jenge or Zenge, as explained above, came up during the Turco-Egyptian and the Mahdists slave trade periods (1821-1898) in Sudan.

After these periods came the Anglo-Egyptian colonial era (1898-1956) during which time the name Dinka came to be used for the same Jaang nationality and since then the new name went out, taking national and international as well as documentary dimensions that the metropolitan members of Jaang society had nothing other than to acquiesce and accept their society being known as Dinka.

But how did the name Dinka come about? Well, from accounts given by various sources, the term Dinka came to be known as a name coined by one of the British colonial administrators in Sudan during the Anglo-Egyptian condominium era. The coining of this name that came to encompass the entire nationality was made shortly after the Anglo-Egyptian reconquest of the Sudan from the Mahdists. Precisely, the word is said to have come from the name of one of the Jaang community leaders by the name of *Deng Käk* from Abialang Dinka, a Jaang community in the northern Upper Nile region of Renk.

The present village of Zahra in northern Upper Nile is believed to have been the spot where Chief *Deng Käk* is said to have had an encounter with that British colonial administrator whose name has been difficult to trace. Zahra is a village between present Jalhak and Renk. The exact date when this British colonial official coined the word Dinka is not known except that a certain Englishman who was travelling on the White Nile to Gondokoro in today's Central Equatoria did have an encounter with that community liege, Deng Käk. At one of the steamers' calling stations, apparently Geiger in the Abialang territory, the white man came across a Jaang community quite different from the Nezy Arabs and the Shilluks through which he travelled before reaching them. When he asked that community leader for his name, it is said the liege introduced himself as '*Deng Käk*'. The traveller found it difficult to pronounce Deng Käk. He therefore joined up the two names into Denka. He is said to have written it in his diary and from there on he made the rest of the foreign nationals living in Sudan, particularly those in Khartoum, use that corrupted name for the whole Jaang society in both the Upper Nile and Bahr el Ghazal.

There and then the terminology 'Denka' came into continuous usage[45] and became 'Dinka' as time went by. Some sources say it was *Stake* and *Grant* who took the name of that Deng Käk earlier than this British colonial administrator.

Grant and Stake were two British explorers who in the 1860s cruised from England to Sudan and took to the White Nile, sailing in search of the source of the White Nile. The two went as far as Masindi in Uganda of today.

All in all the new name went into official use within the then Sudan metropolis, so much so that it became difficult for even the enlightened members of the nationality to resist it. Attempts to persuade the urban dwellers in towns and cities to use the correct names, Jaang, Jieng or Muɔnyjäng, persistently failed and the new name 'Dinka' therefore flourished so much that it overrode the traditional names! Eventually the first Jaang elites acquiesced to the term Dinka which quickly became the name in official and unofficial use in towns and since then the whole society of Jiëng/Jaang or Muɔnyjäng came to have 'Dinka' as its official name for which they came to be known in Sudan and by the outside world until today!

It is unfortunate that this name 'Dinka', which had gone far and wide and which has gone into the official national and international

---

45   37 Interview by the author with Alcdr Nyong Deng Nyong from the Pabuny, Abialang Dinka section, 20 August 2003.

documentation is not known by the Jaang nationality living in the rural countryside. In their traditional setting they only know themselves either as Muɔnyjäng or Jiëng. The Luo and the Nuers in their rural countryside also know them as Jaang even to the present day. But when the new name 'Dinka' took official precedence over the traditional ancient names (Jaang, Jiëng, and Muɔnyjäng) all the elites from the Jaang society came not to mind about their nationality being called 'Dinka' since there is no derogatory connotation implied in it like the slave trade era names Jenge/Zenge and since it is all the same in unifying and had gone far and wide. Yet of late Dinka elites have come to prefer the readoption of their ancient name Jiëëng or Jääng, if not Muɔnyjäng.

DINKA SOCIAL CLASSIFICATIONS

Socially speaking Dinka people can be regarded as a multifaceted society, exhibiting different social levels and classes that are very vividly clear for a careful observer studying the Dinka from within. Dinka people in the first place are divided into two broad social lines. There are the *Kic* or the mundane Dinka folk who are members of the ordinary or non-sacred clans and who form the vast majority of the Dinka. This is on the one hand. On the other hand are those called *Monydeeng* Dinka, a group of clans who are Dinka people from the sacred clans, descended from the original holy men believed to have been accredited by the creator with the holy power infused into their souls, into their blood and into their flesh since primordial times and who now act as God's agents and intermediaries between Him and the Dinka society. These *Monydeeng* clans are found in different parts of the Dinka land. Most of the Dinka traditional chiefs have been wielding an almost dynastic authority in different Dinka lands for almost a century now. They come from this group. Although these *Monydeeng* people were very few during ancient and Mediaeval times, they have now become very many among the Dinka owing to the unmatched cattle wealth and economic, political and religious power concentrated in their hands.

These *Monydeeng* people produce what are called Spear Masters, the religious high priests who act as the proprietors of the Dinka lands and for this reason most of the territorial areas called *wuöt* are named after them. Not only are they proprietors of territorial land areas they are also the proprietors of the populations in their respective sections or areas. This is because they are what the Dinka call *Amuokwei,* meaning *preservers* of life. They are considered as the intermediaries between the creator or powers above and the community they live in. The Spear Master, called *bäny-bith* in Dinka, is a holy man or a man with spiritual powers. He is believed and seen to dispense life. He is both a *power* and a man and a spiritual representative of *Nhialic* (God) among people. Dinka people know *bäny-bith* as a carrier of life and so they call him *Amuokwei*, holder of life. They see him as a means to life. He has more of the amount of life than others. Spear Masters have in them more life than is necessary to sustain them and that is why they are able to withdraw, sustain or give life to other people.

This force or power in the Spear Masters can also be dangerous and that is why Dinka people greatly respect the *bäny-bith*. Some Dinka Spear Masters with outstanding efficacy or power potency cannot turn their heads to glance at an adversary when in full anger, lest their power might kill the adversary.[46] A word from a Dinka *bäny-bith* is known to be bitter (akec) or is effectively strong (aril) and biting, cutting and hot as hot and bitter things are biting and

---

46 Great Spear Master Kuol Ayuääl in Apuk- Padɔc territory used to make his adversaries fall to death on the instant if or when he turns to see them, and for that reason, he was surnamed as Kuol-Cieliec. That is, Kuol who does not turn to see what was behind him while angry. He lived as an undisputed paramount leader of Apuk-Padɔc during the Turkiyya.

killing. A Dinka *bäny-bith* has the power to call rain to fall or not to fall. A Dinka *bäny-bith* is a priest, but he is in effect more than the Christian priest or the Muslims' imam. He is not contrastable to the Christian ways of becoming a priest. A Dinka priest is nature-born. He prays and mediates between *Nhialic* and his people for life and for general wellbeing. The *bäny-bith* in this way is a leader of his people. In the past he was both a political and spiritual leader of his people.

As the Dinka *bäny-bith* ensures life and wellbeing for his people, he also ensures the success of his people against their life enemies. The *bäny-bith* is a preeminent figure in his society because he possesses extraordinary qualities. Dinka Spear Masters are extremely intelligent, benevolent and resolute but they can be ruthless in their decisions at times. However, on the whole they are very altruistic and priestly. As religious figures in the society they are not wicked. Their main functions can be summarised as follows:

- They pray to God for good and also for evil.
- They invocate or pray for victory for their subjects in wars.
- They sacrifice cows, mostly uncastrated bulls and uncastrated rams. They also use cocks and hens for ritual sacrifice. At times they use Kuɔljɔk (bitter cucumber) and they sprinkle people with water and spittle and libate with them for blessing.
- They cure the sick and give vitality and prosperity to their people.
- They bless the barren to bear children.
- They curse wrongdoers and bless those who do good for them and for the society.
- They settle feuds and mediate between disputants or enemies.
- They invocate to drive away dangerous animals, e.g. lions and other dangerous things of the forest and rivers. They can inhibit their danger or conversely call on those dangers to punish a wicked society.
- They call for rains when there is drought or they can call for

drought when they want to punish the community for disloyalty.
- They make offerings from their own and from community members to God for their community wellbeing.
- They heal and treat barrenness and procreation difficulties in women and men.
- They become Godfathers for the community military formations called Ric or Rem which is Age-set. Through their power of cursing, they manage and control society or individuals.
- They are lawgivers and judges for both natural and modern law.
- They are life-giving. People see them to be blessed and have their wishes approved.
- They are above and before the society and as such they command community respect. They deliver oath to the judicial obstinates.
- They represent, embody and keep the name of all the people in their society by means of grass stalks called *wal*, which the Spear Master keeps in a tight bundle. A person, whose wal or grass stalk is taken off the bundle and thrown away from the peoples' grass bundle, by a territorial Spear Master who is angry, usually dies.

Bäny-bith's potent power is more intense at his armpits, his tongue and his procreation outlet, the penis. The bitter aromatic scent is so osmic from the armpit of a true *bäny-bith* and is pungently venomous and can kill a person who for any reason happens to put their nose at the *bäny-bith*'s armpit to smell in a full scent. Part of this power also comes out through perspiration by means of the hair follicles and it is for this reason that the surroundings of a Dinka real bäny-bith always has a particular or unique smell, different from that of the rest. The spit of a *bäny-bith* is a medicine to others and can treat the sick. This is why Dinka people take the sick to a *bäny-bith* to receive his spittle.

A Dinka *bäny-bith* blesses brides at marriage for their wellbeing and for procreation. They can sometimes determine the number and type of children the spouses could have in life.

The *bäny-bith* cleanses incest and impurities which Dinka people call 'bul', a Dinka word in plural form meaning wicked deed. They generally take away (cleanse) impurities which are a result of 'bul'. Those things called bul are wicked deeds which could result into 'awiu'. Awiu is a cancerous wound resulting from a curse by another *bäny-bith*.

They propitiate God Almighty, clans' divinities called yiëth and malign gods called *Jak* to allow the couples to beget when childbearing is difficult, or for the general wellbeing of their community.

They prophesise and receive God's messages by means of dreams.

When he is made to be very angry with someone, a *bäny-bith* can call upon God or upon a malign god to kill, curse or harm that person on his behalf.

A bäny-bith does not commit crimes, lest his pieties become impure and the spiritual power goes out of him. Dinka Spear Masters are blameless because they are holy. They conjure wrongdoers and their adversaries, even to the point of death, or they can call for a misfortune to befall those adversaries and wrongdoers as a way to punish them. Some very powerful *bäny-bith* like Ayueel Loŋäär and Mayuaal in the past used to have protean ability to change form when dealing with their adversaries. Mayuaal, the founding ancestor of the Redior or ruaal revering clans, used to change in his time from human form to something else. Spear Masters also make miracles. In the past a Dinka Spear Master's body (skin) used to glow with light and can produce pied colours from his body. Great Spear Master, Akɛɛn Mathiang, from the Payii clan in the Awan-Parek area used to have speckled skin, partly yellow and partly blue-green. This was in the late 1950s. Dinka masters of spears, the holy men, auger and maintain moral levels and moral order in the society under their domain.

In the past they used to raise the dead back to life.[47] Dinka Spear Masters are potently godly and can direct or control natural forces as rains, drought, famine, diseases and other natural phenomena.

The function of the Dinka Spear Masters is summed up by the expression '*Amuokwei*', meaning they are *preservers of life*. Thus, Dinka people who come from Spear Master clans are regarded as of the *Monydeeng* or sacred clans. The word '*mony*' in *Monydeeng* is a possessive noun for *moc*, meaning *man*. It is a free morpheme in linguistic analysis. '*Deeng*' is a Dinka word for *something sacred or holy*. Thus the word *Monydeeng* means holy or sacred man.

In addition to the above description a Dinka Spear Master is usually an elderly male member from the sacred or holy clan people regarded as the special people of God, *Kɔc Nhialic*, and although a holy power called *Riŋ* can sometimes emerge or providentially be vested in a young man, a Spear Master has always been an elderly man who has been consecrated or given the holy investiture to keep the family or clan's holy spears and all other holy artefacts on behalf of the clan as the head or chief priest of the clan and the community of a given territory under his spiritual domain. *Bäny-bith* is thus a distinguished reference personality with the qualities of a holy person who is always a man of piety and who always has his community at heart.

Kic, in contrast to *Monydeeng*, is a name given to the ordinary, to the secular, to the non-sacred or to the non-holy people who constitute the majority among the Dinka, whereas *Monydeeng* is a name given to the sacred or holy people who are directly descended from Dengdit, people believed to have descended from that Deng who received the holy investiture from Garang and from God. Descend-

---

47   Mzyuaal-Cuärköö or Bänyköök used to raise the dead before he ascended up into heaven in the eyes of everybody, just like Jesus did. Kɔjɔ Kuot, the brother of Buöl Kuöt and Manyang Kuot, used to raise dead cows before he went up into the sky. Many Dinka people went up and did not return to earth.

ants of Deng-Mayuaal[48] are regarded as the ones who have continued to have holy powers over their subjects on earth. They are deemed to be rich of wisdom and can speak to God, who sometimes speaks to them through dreams.

In the quiet still of the night a Spear Master would rise up to speak to God, making pleas for the wellbeing of his people in the territory. Spear Masters are known to do this as one of their many functions. Their other main function is that they are investiture judges in their society. They deliver and manage natural justice in those areas under their domain.

They can also call for afflictions upon their adversaries. They enforce their decisions of judgement with a holy curse against non-compliance. As came above, they are also known to direct or control natural forces such as rains, droughts, famine, diseases and other natural phenomena.

In addition, they auger and maintain community moral order and they propitiate the creator, spirits of Dinka primal parents like the spirit of Garang, the spirit of Abuk and that of Dengdit. They also propitiate ancestral spirits and clan divinities as well as those lesser gods known to relate to man in the unseen world.

A Spear Master is the medium through which Dinka people give their offerings to God. They also perform rituals for a woman to beget when childbearing is difficult. Dinka Age-sets are named and fathered mostly by Spear Master clan people. The Spear Master delivers communal prayers and makes holy invocations during rituals or religious occasions or ceremonies.

On the other hand, Dinka people are again socially divided into the upper, middle and lower classes. Upper class is comprised of the Dinka aristocracy who are the ruling class, consisting of the spiritual

---

48   See Garang's division of roles among his male children and the investiture of Deng-Mayuääl with sacred functions and heir to his father (chapter 7 of this book)

lords as described above and those from the mundane clans who, in their own way, have distinguished themselves out of their ordinary status through wealth making or warrior attributes. While most of the aristocrats descend from the sacred clans who form the Dinka nobility, some of those wealthy persons from the mundane or secular clans who become cattle tycoons also qualify and are considered as part of the Dinka upper class. Some among these could also become chiefs and territories could be named after them.

Besides this upper class so described there is what could be seen as the equivalence of the European middle class. The vast majority of the Dinka fall within this social class. Those who show accepted aesthetic virtues and attributes well valued by the Dinka society at large are considered as part of this social class, people like bards, poets, positive singers and self-made people as well as successful craftsmen. These constitute this middle class. This social class forms the largest of the Dinka society. They form the populace and are the implementers of most of the Dinka communal programmes as they are mostly the fighting manpower. The warrior class made up of the mundane or *Kic* clans generally makes this class.

The third of this structural and social division is the lower class, consisting of all the people regarded as the low caste, including the typically poor and those handicapped by inheritable family diseases. Also in this social class are the witchcraft making people like the witch doctors, called *Tit* in Rek dialect, tiet when singular. These people include herbal or medicinal men. Although this category of people can be found in all parts of the Dinka land and in almost every clan due to marriages within Dinka society, their number is insignificant and therefore negligible. The lazy people and mismanagers of estates are viewed as part of this class. The Dinka people see them as social misfits.

Apart from the above divisional levels, division can also be found at the family level even between children of one mother and father.

According to the Dinka standards, children of the same parents are graded into the firstborn son called *Wendit*, the middle born son, *Wenciɛl* and the last born son called *Kun*. There may be more than Wenciɛl but there is usually one *Kun* and one *Wendit*. Daughters of one mother and father are also treated according to their right of birth. Elder daughters have particular rights over their younger sisters, rights not enjoyed by junior daughters over their elder sisters. Elder sisters have the right of a share in the distribution of the cattle dowry paid for their junior sisters who do not enjoy such rights. Junior sisters are required by social norms to respect their elder sisters whereas the junior ones only deserve affection. If the sons are more, they are grouped in twos or so. The sons are therefore treated in the family in accordance with their right of birth. However, the last born son is always associated with his mother's affairs and could sometimes enjoy those rights that are sometimes better than those of the middle born son or sons. The firstborn son is always the *heir apparent* to the leadership of the family after the father is dead. Roles are divided among the sons of one man so that the firstborn is groomed as the ultimate successor of his father and is the one usually charged with his father's family affairs. He deputises the father and could take over even before the father dies. It is the firstborn who is responsible for religious and ritual affairs, first, as an assistant to his father, and after his father's death, as the family head. With Dinka Spear Master families, it is the firstborn son who is accredited with the sacred or holy affairs to do with Dengdit and God as well as all the clan divinities and ancestral spirits. The brothers who followed him in birth only act as his assistants.

Among the Dinka, too, is what could be regarded as the mythical world in contrast to the physical world of humans or manfolk, which the Dinka call *manhacuuk*. The mythical world is the world of the dead ancestors and their spirits, the creator Nhialic, the clans' divinities known as *yiëth from the word 'yath' when singular,* and clans' gods called *Jak*, *Jɔk* when singular. These powers and spirits cast, very powerfully, on the living Dinka family and on the individuals and, indeed, the entire society as they act as participants in the Dinka living world. They are seen or comprehended as a distinct group, although forming the same world of the Dinka and occupying the higher scale in the Dinka grading of things within their intractable world.

In geographical terms, Dinka people are divided into collective territorial groupings or units and into defined tribal, sectional and cultural groups including age and Age-sets, descent and sex. There are twenty six tribal, sectional and cultural sections within Dinka nationality and within each of these broad tribal groupings are several defined geographical or territorial units called *wuöt*, *wut* when singular. Each wut is made up of its internal subdivisions, which could rightly be called sections. Each *wut* could range from 20 000 or 30 000 to 100 000 inhabitants. Each *wut* is usually administered by a chief who is nowadays assisted by four deputies. Sections are ruled by what are called sub-chiefs with the *nhom-gɔl* or gol-leader as the last administrative head at the clan level. The husband or father heads the family, assisted by the elder son and sometimes by the elder wife. In each wut are usually a number of Spear Masters.

For judicial reasons, groups of wuöt under different chiefs are grouped together into what are judicially called regional courts. Several chieftaincy areas therefore form one regional court and these huge territorial courts are treated by the government as peoples' native courts.

Such courts are headed by paramount chiefs called court presidents, most of whom come from the principal chief families and clans. They are in most cases Spear Masters themselves. Great Manyang Jɔok in Adöör land of Kiec and Dhɔr Ariik in Lou-Ariik Area in Tonj North are examples of court presidents who are also Spear Masters. These court presidents are also assisted by four members selected or elected by the communities of those polities or wuöt that they represent. These four members are also principals from distinguished families and clans. They are from the aristocratic or nobility class. Together with the court president they constitute the *grand jury* that settles disputes and problems related to cattle, marriages, adultery, theft, homicides and other litigations from the various chieftaincy areas under one judicial circuit.

In discussing Dinka social classifications mention must be made about father-son ambivalent social relationships in the family. As the man or father is obliged to look to God, his creator, sons look to their fathers as the source of their existence and support. The son in principle accepts and is expected to comply with the authority of the father for reason of fatherhood but the father-son relationship among the Dinka is not simply one of submissiveness, obedience and resignation to the father. In spite of the principle of moral ideals of filial piety to parents particularly to the fathers which Dinka people ascribe to, the relationship between a son and his father is not understood as one of dictatorship from the father with the son in compliance.[49]

On the contrary, sons in the Dinka world are often assertive and they frequently come into conflict with their fathers over a range of issues. Sons do not hesitate to urge or argue their just claims upon their fathers. In some instances conflicts of wills occur between father and son. Ownership and division of cattle in a family is one thing that frequently brings a Dinka son and his father into conflict. This is especially so during the division of the bride price dowry cattle which is the role of the father to divide the dowry cattle of his own daughter among members of the family and clan. The bride's brother or brothers at some time would want to take that role or may request more than is due to them.

Conflicts between sons and fathers sometimes occur when the

---

49   F M Deng, Tradition and Modernization, U.S.A, McNaughton & Gunn, Inc, Salina Michigan, (2004) pp. 33- 38

son feels he is grown up enough and wishes to marry. When the father refuses for his known reasons, or is wanting to keep the son longer under his own roof and under his tutelage, he would easily run into conflict with such a son. However, it is to the Dinka custom and tradition that sons must marry according to the decision of the father, which is usually backed by support from the family. Some sons could yield to their father's will while others stick to their points of view. In some instances the decision of the son prevails in the final analysis. In extreme situations a son may decide to remain dissatisfied with his lot. These are the sons who go out to openly criticise their fathers through ox-songs.[50]

Generally the son-father relationship is kept by the fact that the father is the source of the son's existence and support. This support, given by the father, demands submission on the part of the son. It entails control by the father over the son, who must be dependent upon his father for the time being. At some stage in life, a son may come to find this control, dependency and submission as irksome and therefore become anxious to detach from that control by means of a marriage, wishing to set up his own home and start his own family and lineage, for sons always hope for the day when they themselves will be known as the father of so and so, rather than to be always known only as the son of so and so. A son would hope he will one day separate, but a type of separation which does not make him separate like the separation of man from God. Notwithstanding this position of sons vis-à-vis their parents and especially to their fathers, the obligation to be within the folds of the father at whatever age is very much emphasised by Dinka society.

Those heartless children who neglect or disregard the wishes of the parents who bore them are vehemently criticised by society. Apart from the priceless begetting, the process of 'upbringing'

---

50   Ibid

which involves *caring for, feeding, protecting* and *instructing* are all included in the Dinka word *Muk*. This word *Muk*, adjectively called *Muöök*, plus the natural biological right of having begat him, in addition to the father's initial right of marriage to the mother who cost the father so much a number of cows as bride price dowry paid on her in marriage, all these in combination are what are enshrined into one single request to respect the father and to return him that 'Muöök' when the father becomes of age[42].

This son-father relationship is not the case between the father and daughter. Although Dinka girls grow in the image of their mothers owing to their close attachment to the domains of their mothers, daughters are more respectful and affectionate to their fathers than are sons to their fathers. Whereas the girl take much of the care and warmly skills from the mother, they take pride and name from the father who is the ultimate power on earth to determine who should marry her and who continue to give paternal role and services to her even after she is married. To the girl, the father is the source of her life and existence and his fatherhood overhangs her as the creator overhangs His creatures including humans.

Unlike that of the son, any bad disposition on the part of the father to his daughter can always be a bad omen for the daughter. A curse upon a daughter from the father usually has a potent implication either in that instant or can cause her not to be able to get a child in future. Daughters are disposed to giving filial respect and love to their fathers to a much higher degree than are the sons, despite their classificatory attachment to their mothers. Generally the son-father relationship is kept by the fact that the father is the source of the son's existence and support. This support given by the father demands submission on the part of the son.[51]

Because the male side is emphasised in Dinka society and matters

---

51   Ibid

to do with God are done through the father in every family, the son always remains religiously dependent upon his father. This is because it is the father who is in link with Nhialic the creator, clan divinities or *yiëth* and a chain of the spirits of his near and distant ancestors, and the whole of the unseen divine world of the powers from above and without. The son-father relationship in Dinka society is one of dependence, conjunction and opposition as was the case between man and his creator, right at the Garden of Eden as described in the Bible.

With the father and son, as it was with God and man, the son's opposition to the father is harmoniously done in the way a person in a weaker position asserts his case before a superior. The son usually expresses his opposition very cautiously for his own benefit. This is because any serious quarrel with his father could become one of the worst things a man of any age can experience.

Despite this, complete dominance of the father when the son is grown up can deny him the legitimate freedom and respect he requires to acquire for himself, for his family, his clan and also for the society at large. In situations where the son is deemed to have offended the father, he will be understood to have made disrespect to the father who is his God on earth and must be compelled to appease and propitiate him as the father does to God or to one of the divinities or ancestral spirits.

When the father dies in a Dinka family, it goes without saying that his eldest son takes over as the head of the family, assuming all of the social, legal and administrative obligations and religious responsibilities. Even when he is still alive the father is usually close to and associated with his eldest son who because of his primogenitary right was the one who married first and set up his own household, and for this reason is the first of the children to pass out of the father's control and become independent. He had the experience from his father better than the rest who were born after him.

THE DINKA AGE-SET SYSTEM

With all this said, there are as yet other social structures of importance within Dinka society. One such social structure is the grouping of the society according to *generational age*. In all the Dinka tribal groupings are found what the Dinka call **Ric** or **Rem**, which can be better called Age-set. Ric or Rem is a big and significant socio-military formation. It sometimes consists of several hundred young men depending on the size of that territory. Within one territorial unit or wut is an area having other subdivisions called sections led by sub-chiefs. An area under one chief can have a number of sub-chieftaincies, normally five or more. In this wut Age-sets are formed in succession.

There is generally one Age-set at a time in a given wut and that Age-set remains as one functional entity for ten or more years, acting as the defence unit for that territorial community after the members of the first Age-set had all married and moved away from the cattle camps and became fathers and heads of families in their homes. They can no longer effectively exercise their marshal responsibilities in the collective defence of the territory so a new group or Age-set is again created from the succeeding ages. The Age-set is given a name by its Godfather That Age-set remains to be a corporate entity for as long as all are alive.

Dinka Age-sets are usually comprised of all of the youth of the territory, whose individual ages may only be a difference of some few years between each and living as one generation. They come from all the clans, sections and families living in a territory under one chief. In former times one Age-group could come across vast territories having one name and one common defence. Nowadays Age-set is confined to one chieftaincy territory as dictated by the current population increase.

The new Age-set or Age-group begins with a community meeting of elders to designate one prominent and renowned elder from the sacred or Spear Master clans in the territory to become the father of the would-be newly created Age-set. The Godfather of the existing Age-set declares his acceptance for the need to set up an Age-set different from the one in his name.

As he was also from the sacred clan, he himself is a Spear Master like the one to name the new Age-group, who henceforth will be known as the Godfather of the would be new Age-set. Their wellbeing and prosperity including successes in wars with other territories solely depend on their Godfather designate.

After the new Godfather is designated, two things happen. The former or the existing Age-set is called upon to assemble in a huge community gathering. Members of the olden or gradually out-going Age-sets form part of the gathering. The call is made by the Godfather concerned and the whole Age-set attends in response. As described above such a gathering is territorial. It is both marshal and religious in essence and meaning in its physical content. Every member of the community is bound to attend this socio-military and religious occasion, the aged, the young, women, girls and even young children, in fact the entire territorial population attends as the younger generation from whom the new Age-set would be named on that occasion, having heard of the newly designated Godfather for their Age-group to be. On this occasion the Godfather of the existing Age-set brings forward a big uncastrated bull called 'Thɔn' in Dinka. That *Thɔn* must be a bull whose colour corresponds with the name of the Age-set earlier given by that very Godfather.

The newly designated Godfather also presents a big uncastrated bull of the colour intended to be the name for his new Age-set. In the course of an elaborate ritual celebration and cultural performances Spear Masters of the territory make their religious invocations to the ritually tethered bulls, loudly making their invocations in turns and announcing to the groups and the general public the marking of the coming into effect of the new Age-set. When the bulls have been ritually or religiously slaughtered at the height of the occasion and everybody is sprinkled with arop, the cow dung ash, libations are given to all at the occasion and each Age-set gets in to carry their Godfather, going around with him on their shoulders while the multitude follows, frenetically singing songs of the territory ranging from war songs to religious songs. With those things done for several hours, the community resumes for a full day of celebration, marked with joy and dancing, including women's hand clapping play. The bulls' meat is then divided by the concerned elders. The new Ric are then given their meat bone as their share which they will always deserve in every communally sacrificed bull in the territory.

The meat bone so named for the new Ric is sprinkled with blessed water and is libated upon by all the Spear Masters and elders at the occasion. Then it is duly given to the Godfather who gives it a final blessing with his sputum, saying his last blessing in words and presenting it to his Age-group. That new Age-group usually has one who is chosen as the steward for the group, one who becomes the group leader.

The group would then move to publicly declare ownership of that meat bone. They would take it away into the nearby forest where they would roast it and eat it in unison. Then they would return for the dance and other manly acts. Late in the afternoon, about 4 or 5 pm, the celebration would then be deemed to be over and people would disperse back to their respective villages and to the cattle camps from where they came. The Age-set will from then on be called by the name publicly given them by the Godfather. Each member of the publicly announced and celebrated Age-set would henceforth identify with his Age-set and with his Godfather.

The new Age-set acts as one unit, a fighting brigade that remains distinct, unique and corporate till its members go through to old age and gradually disappear individually by death. Throughout their lifetime this Age-set, whether as individuals or in their collective, owes to their Godfather the kind of respect which each one of them does not even give to his biological father at home. They call him father and render him services as a collective group and as individuals and they always remain on alert to respond to his summons whether in the collective or as individuals.

The author is a son of the Godfather of the *Mabior Age-set* in the Awan territory in Tonj North county. Godfather Madut-Kuendit was a successor of his uncle Ayii Mayiik who was Godfather to the *Marial Age-set*. Succeeding the Mabior Age-set of the author's father was the *Mathial Age-set* of Great Kuot Maduot of the same family lineage. The author himself belongs to the *Mathial* Age-set of his paternal uncle Kuot Maduot.

As explained earlier, the Dinka *Age-set* is usually composed of some hundreds to a thousand youths in the territory and it remains under the direct authority and command of its Godfather throughout their lifetime, but this authority is more so in war situations, in ritual celebrations and in any communal social gathering, not in legal or judicial matters which are the domains of the territorial chief, who also usually comes from the Spear Master clan. Members of each Age-set in a Dinka territory are accountable to their Godfather except for in legal or judiciary matters.

FAMILY ŸÖT THOK OR MAC-THOK

The Dinka beginning level of social classification is the family. At its starting point is the husband who brings a wife. They form a family of two people before they produce children. The father, mother and children make what the Dinka call röt thok, meaning a homestead or nuclear family. As the Dinka are a polygamous people, more wives form separate homesteads but are still part of *röt thok* which is a nuclear family; *Mac-thok* in Dinka also means the same as r̈öt thok, yet r̈öt thok has an extended meaning covering the husband, his parents, brothers and unmarried sisters in addition to his wife or wives and his children. Mac-thok in Dinka can also mean a man with his direct relatives (parents inclusive) comprised of his brothers (stepbrothers included), his paternal uncles and his father's uncles. People of one's mother are but maternal relatives or maternal kin. They are not part of the Dinka *Mac-thok* and are therefore not family members, although one's in-laws are socially members of one's family, not in a legal sense. Even brothers of one's mother are but maternal uncles and are not part of a Dinka legal family, but direct relatives of one's father are part of what the Dinka call Mac-thok.

LINEAGE (WÄÄR OR GƆL)

As Dinka people are patrilineal and follow the male line of blood relation, **Gɔl** or Kuat or Kuär become the next family level after r̈öt thok and Mac-thok. **Gɔl** has the literal meaning of a cattle hearth or a conical dung fire made in the cattle camps to smoke insects away and as a rallying place for guarding the herd in the nights. But the semantic import of **Gɔl** is that of a lineage, a descent group which is an extended level of a family. A lineage therefore is an extended family of its founding ancestor, and although a lineage continues to have the word *Paan* used still as in family, it is a bit wider in contrast to family. Lineage is a male descent line where the biological blood relation comes from one intermediate ancestor or grandfather.

CLAN (DHIËTH)

Two or more lineages make a clan, whose male members not only bear the names of their founding ancestors but they also revere or venerate one or more totemic divinities. A clan is a further extension of a lineage or lineages. A totem that binds family lineages as a clan is a nagualistic item passed down as a venerational species from the founder of a clan to his descendants as a blood- related group. That totemic item becomes a clan divinity called *yath*. All the members of that clan ascribe to it as a belief. That nagualistic item could be none other than an object, a plant or a creature with which a clan's founder has had an individual relationship in the positive so that he associates respect and identification to it. He therefore wills the venerational respect to his descendants, making them take that object, plant or creature as their protective and identificatory totemic divinity.

Clans are therefore identified by those objects that their members venerate. Both male and female born ascribe to that clan totem. Girls carry with them the strict observance of those totemic divinities or yiëth to their new families who they are married to. Her children do not observe nagualistic items from their mother's side. Her children are, however, not obliged to strictly venerate or observe those totemic divinities from their mother's side since they are required by the pater obligation to be preoccupied with those totems related to their father.

Totems and blood relations are the ones that tie all members of a clan into a strong bond and brotherhood wherever they are, even when they live in different territorial areas, sub-tribes or tribes. A Redior man or woman from the ruaal revering clan in Agaar land, for example, is a brother or sister to the one revering the same ruaal tree among the Rek, Malual, Ruweng and other Dinka national tribes. The same is true of other clans. This blood descent and totemic relations explain why most Dinka people don't marry girls from the same clans for fear of incest and procreation difficulties, which has always been the case when the spouses come from one clan. Except for Pajiɛk and Padhieu clans, all Dinka people are exogamous.

In a family, lineage or clan, names of lineage and clan ancestors are perpetuated. They are used to name children. Family lineage or clan members are easily known and identified by their ancestral names. The name of a common clan's founder is adopted by all his lineages and his name is mostly preceded by the prefix 'Pa', so that this 'Pa' is, for example, used for the clan members of 'Ker' to read 'Paker'. The Paker clan people are known as those Dinka people who have the power to identify where underground water can be found prior to digging a well. Paker people are descendants of their remotest ancestor by the name of Ker, so are the clan people of Ayii Thiek. They are Payii all over Rekland. The same is for the Parum clan people of Rum, Pakuieth clan people of Wol-Akuith, Padhieu clan people of Wol-Adhieu, Pajieng people from Ajaang, Padiangbar from Wol-Adiangbar, Pateɛk from Teek and so on and so forth.

A founding father of a clan must have not just been a mere person during his lifetime. He must have done big and positive deeds to qualify him as a family reference personality of identification for his descendants. Dinka clans have usually come from ancestors of significance during their lifetime. In most cases a clan is formed after a common ancestor has had a difference of about ten generations and above.

A clan is therefore one big social classification level for the Dinka society and despite great multiplicity of clans among the Dinka, the clan system is the strongest social tie which keeps the Dinka society in unity, and although members of a lineage and family have more and closer allegiances to the family and to the common totemic and religious descent line, the clan system provides more and more defence commitments, particularly when clan members live in one territorial area. Members of a clan are brothers and are a coherent unit of a people from one remote ancestor.

SECTION (BAAI)

Just as a clan is a combination of lineage families descending from one common ancestor, a section is an association of big, medium and small clans bound together by a strong sense of belonging, history, togetherness, unity and cooperation. Such association of clans makes a territorial section that usually rallies around one of the Spear Master's clan or lineage, which provides religious as well as administrative leadership for the section. A section may be so small as to be ruled by what the Dinka call *Bänykoor*, sub-chief in English or it can be large enough to be ruled by *Bänydit*, an executive chief. This is why a section can also be called wut. While Baai is a section or wut, it is also the Dinka name for home.

Apart from their unity of purpose, those clans making a section usually have common grazing lands such as toch, a defined land area with a name and borders, and the people in that section are ready to protect that area in a joint action against their adversaries. They usually camp together and make collective defence as well as collective attacks. That unity goes beyond physical togetherness. Their homesteads and villages are made in a cephalous way so that villagers know themselves contiguously and are ready to come together in times of need.

TERRITORY (WUT – ALSO CALLED BAAI)

A number of sections make what the Dinka people call wut, which is a historical entity under one or more executive chiefs. Present population increase and increased modern problems and their management have led to former territorial entities being decentralised to several chieftaincy areas to ease the administration of the people. A wut is a large unit consisting of sections and has the same common factors explained under a section. People within one historical area or wut have a better defence system. While a section can have its own initiates and can practise their own *Garnhom* occasion to initiate their own adolescent males to manhood, the *wut* or executive chieftaincy area, best called a territory, usually has one Age-set (Ric or Rem) at a time. That Age-set stands as the decisive military defence component of the people living in that territory. Apuk-Juwiir in the Thiet area in Tonj South county, for example, has eight historical sections with seven executive chiefs, yet it is one wut and usually goes out in one joint action. The same goes for Lou-Ariik, Apuk-Pathuɔn, Kɔŋɔɔn, Ayiɛl, Awan, Aguɔk, and so on and so forth. A Dinka tribe like Rek, Agaar or Malual, for instance, is so big to have one defence system or joint action. Malual or Agaar or Rek etc, is not Wut but is a tribe, a sub-national community.

SUB-TRIBE

In Dinka lands several territories, wuöt, form a sub-tribe which when large enough can form a sub-region under a loose confederal legal or judicial arrangement called a regional court where inter-territorial cases from different chiefs' courts are settled under one presiding traditional judge, usually called the *regional court* president. This confederation of wuöt, with independent chiefs, usually has a name, a border and usually one function, judicial, but sometimes makes administrative arrangements which may now be called payams in some places. An area called *Anan-Atak* in the Tonj East county is cited as an example of this as it is a sub-region of seven large territories including Aköök-Teek, Luackoth, Thiik and the Jalwau section of four chieftaincies, Kɔŋɔɔr, Adöör, Bäc and Pakɔɔr. Another good example is that of the Akɔp sub-region consisting of (i) Lɔu-Paher, (ii) Awan-Parek, (iii) Apuk-Padɔc, (iv) Kɔŋgoor and (v) Lɔu-Ariik. This is a sub-region of thirteen executive chieftaincy areas having five administrative payams. '*Aliamtooc-One*' and '*Aliamtooc-Two*' in Agaar land is another good case in point and so is Pakam in Rumbek North County, consisting of Niel-Niel, Manuɛr, Akɔrkɔr, Gak, Lith and Aniën. Pakam is a sub-tribe within Agaar and so is Akɔp or Anan-Atak within Rek, to mention but a few.

Dinka society is grouped up under several facets of identification and social setups, of which examples can be endlessly cited. Those regional groupings can be seen as sub-tribes.

TRIBE

As the Dinka is so large a nationality, they have found it convenient to treat themselves as tribes rather than one large community. The case of the Dinka is different from that of the Kikuyu in Kenya, Zulu in South Africa and Ausa in Nigeria. Dinka people live in two large and separate regions of the Upper Nile and Bahr el Ghazal. They are separated by the White Nile River and its sudd or swampland, which is interlaced with some tribes like the Nuers and the Shilluks in the Upper Nile region.

As covered under Dinka national tribes in chapter four, Dinka people are subdivided into twenty six large and small tribes, ten in Bahr el Ghazal and sixteen in the Upper Nile. Despite being divided into tribes Dinka people would like to be spoken of as a totality, although many Dinka do not know of the existence of other Dinka sections or tribes. Most of the Dinka tribes in the Upper Nile region are not known by Bahr el Ghazal Dinka and vice versa. A Dinka tribe is therefore an entity with one dialect, a peculiar culture, a long history of territorial togetherness and some form of defence system. Luac, Agaar, Rek, Gok, Kiec, Bor, Nyarweng, Twic, Abialang, Malual, Ngok and so on are examples of Dinka tribes.

On the whole, those are the social classification levels into which the Dinka can be placed, affording a rough understanding of the Dinka nationality to the outsider or even for a Dinka person who did not know this or who wants to know the facets into which Dinka people are constituted. Chapter four, which tackles the Dinka in their detailed geographical and administrative configurations, completes the rest as it details the Dinka, section by section.

DINKA LANDS, ECONOMY AND THEIR WAYS OF LIFE

Dinka people largely live in the centre of Southern Sudan. They are almost central to the whole of Sudan. In the Upper Nile region, Dinka people are bordered by the Shilluks to the north west. To the north east they are bordered by the Burun community of the Maban area. In the same Upper Nile they are bordered to the true west by the Nuba people of Southern Kordofan and by the Nezy and Sabaah Arab tribal sections of the Baggara at the northern limits of the northern Upper Nile region. Further north west after the Pan-Ru people of Panrieng county and Alor people of Biemnhom county the Dinka are bordered by the Massiriya Arabs who are the mainstream Arab Baggara, who inhabit much of what is geographically known as Kordofan. However, Ngok Dinka of Abyei extend a bit deeper, having borders with the Massiriya of Southern Kordofan.

In Bahr el Ghazal the Dinka are bordered to the far west by the Rizzeigat Arab Baggara of Southern Darfur and to the southwest by a group of Sudanic peoples, the Bantu tribe, communities which are collectively known as the *Fertits*. They are also bordered by a Luo tribal section which they colloquially call *Jur-col*, and in almost the same area though a bit to the south by the Bongo, and more southerly by the Zande tribe of Western Equatoria and by the Belle (Jur-Belle) people in the southern fringe of the Lakes state. They are also bordered by the same Jur-Belle of the northwestern parts of Equatoria region. Bahr el Ghazal Dinka are also bordered to the east by the Mundari tribe and by parts of the Baria tribe on both banks of Bahr el Jebel (the rocky parts of the Nile) in Central Equatoria state. To the true southeast, the Jonglei state Dinka in the Upper Nile region are bordered by the Lokoro (the Pere) people and by the Bɛɛr (or Murle) people of the Pibor district and by the Nuer-Lou people of Akobo district, as well as by the Nuers Gaajook, Gajaak and the Gaguaang of Nasir in the true eastern parts of the Upper Nile region. They are also bordered by the Lak, Thiöng and by the Gawɛɛr Nuers in Pthe anjak district in central Upper Nile.

The extent of Dinka settlement areas and their *toch* or swamps and forest lands could be roughly given at being more than the size of present Eritrea or that of many of those small West African countries. Dinka people inhabit such a vast region, lying between 12^0 and 6^0 north latitude. They live in an area which fans outwards from the swamps of the White Nile Basin. It encompasses nearly 150 000 square miles of flat savannah grassland, which dominates the terrain. It is also interspersed south and southwest with some huge and extensive forest lands. The land is also laced with rivers and streams that come to or go from the Nile River and its swamplands or toch.

Dinka territorial borders are, however, irregular and are ever expanding rather than decreasing. This fact is brought about by the Dinka large cattle and ever increasing population growth. The Dinka people inhabit this large expanse of land which extends from the Upper Nile region, where they inhabit about half of its territorial land, to the vast region of Bahr el Ghazal where they inhabit more than half of its land area. The remaining land area in Bahr el Ghazal to the southwestern fringe of an haematitic ironstone territory is where the *Luo* and the people generally known as *Fertit* live, and who in about the 12th or 13th century AD were believed to have come in to the far west of Bahr el Ghazal, in infiltrating waves from the inter-lacustrine region south of Lake Chad and from the River Chari

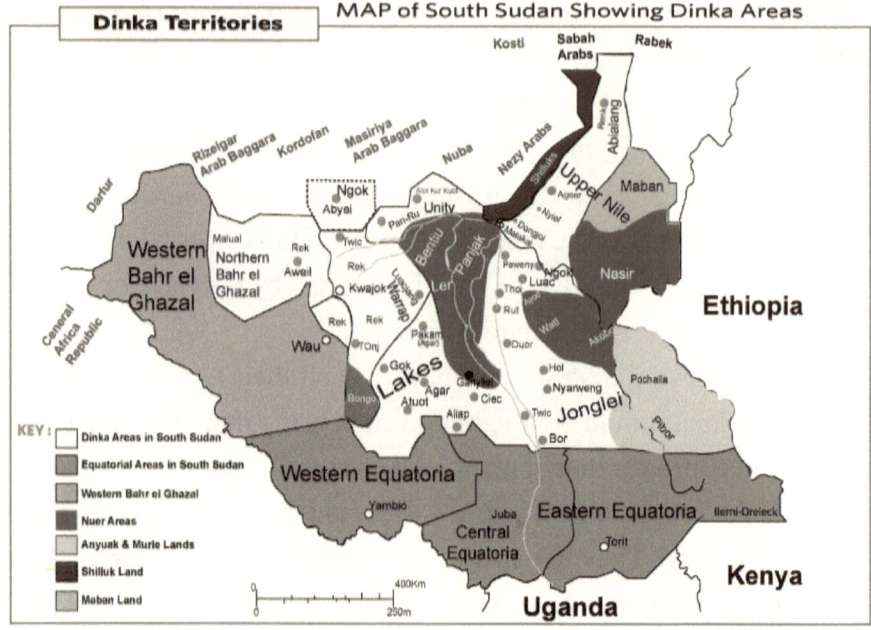

Fig 15: Showing a sketch map of South Sudan indicating the Dinka areas in white-yellow colour.

area through to the Uele Basin area.[52]

The Luo and their subdivisions in Bahr el Ghazal are also known to have come from Jebellein and Tunga region, west of present Renk. They came much earlier before the Dinka migrated from Upper Nile to Bahr el Ghazal. Part of this Luo society later returned to Upper Nile where they became the Shilluks, Anyuak and Acholi that later went to Eastern Equatoria. Other Luo group migrated further southward along the River Nile. They later settled in the Great Lakes region of Uganda. Others went to Kenya. The present Dinka-assimilated Jur-Manangɛɛr communities in Lou-Ariik in Tonj North and Apuk-Giir in Gogrial East and the Jur-Chat people in Awiel area are

---

52   Yusuf Fadl Hassan, 'Southern Sudanese and their neighbours before the colonial era', (in) The role of Southern Sudanese in the building of modern Sudan, K.U.P., (1989), pp. 21 – 22

Mediaeval remnants of the Luo. They were particularly Shilluks by origin.

Physiographically speaking, Dinka people live generally within the hot flat land ecology of Southern Sudan. They live in two of the seven ecological zones into which SDIT (1955) divided Southern Sudan. These are the central rain lands and the floodplain areas. Dinka people have good physiographic lands and agro climatic zones which makes agriculture as their mainstay second to animal husbandry[43]. Their habitats are mostly found within the tropical climatic zone of short grassland or savannah woodland suited to a mixed economy of seeds culture and pastoral activities. Rainfall or lack of it makes some places cold and others hot. In some places, the daily temperature may range from 16^0 to 29^0 C. The winds that bring most of the rains into the Dinka lands as well as to all the Nilotic areas in Upper Nile and Bahr el Ghazal, are the southeast trade winds from the Indian Ocean.[53]

Since most of the Dinka people live in the Gazelle River region, that is, Bahr el Ghazal, and in Upper Nile Basin region, where water is in abundance atmospherically, Dinka areas enjoy fairly high means of annual rainfall ranging from 400 mm in Renk territory of Abialang, Nyiel, Ageer and Dongjol Dinka communities who inhabit that semi-arid country at the extreme end of the Dinka lands in northern Upper Nile, to 1300 mm on their borders with the Zande tribe in Western Equatoria region or on their borders with Jur-Belle community in Lakes state where up to 2000 mm of rain can be recorded annually.

To the southwestern parts, between the Zande land and the Dinka of Lakes state, that is, *Bongo-Luo-Fertit ironstone territory* of thick equatorial woodland, up to more than 1000 mm of rains can be recorded annually. Generally, Dinka people inhabit those lowland basin areas between the Great East African Plateau region which

---

53   Andrew Nam Odero, Sudan livelihood characterisation of South Sudan: The use of physiographic and agro-climatic layers, (2007)

slopes down as the River Nile descends into Sudan and Egypt through Southern Sudan, and the slightly raised ironstone country southwest of the Bahr el Ghazal where live the Belle, the Luo and the Fertit tribes. Parts of the Dinka societies live on the steppes or on the central clay plain fringes where natural vegetation had either disappeared altogether or where only a few shrub-like short thorny bushes and short savannah grass exist. This type of climatic area is found right from the Dongjol, Agaar, Nyiel and Abialang Dinka areas, generally in the northern Upper Nile region.

Some of the Dinka also live in the open grassland areas or plains. Dinka people usually call this ecology 'lil', which is a flat territory with few or no trees, especially in those plains that are rather adjacent to the Nile River or its tributaries and swamplands. The majority of the Dinka of the east and west banks of the Nile live in this type of ecological belt. Those who live on the upstream of the Gazelle River also enjoy almost the same environment but those living in the swampy environs in the deep fishing areas enjoy what is relatively like a marine ecology and climate. Yet others live in the typical savannah woodland areas, in the loam, sandy, alluvial and cotton soil areas. Most of the northwestern areas of the Jonglei state are cotton soil covered by acacia trees and short shrub bushes.

DINKA SETTLEMENT MODE

In general terms Dinka people make their homes and villages on higher flood-free grounds where they utilise plains as pastures for their cattle, goats and sheep. Since they left the Khartoum area at the end of the 4th century AD, they abandoned the donkeys, camels and other desert animals. Their livestock consists only of cattle, sheep and goats.

Some of the Dinka live in areas with loam soil fit for a variety of crops including sesame, groundnuts, hard nuts and a variety of

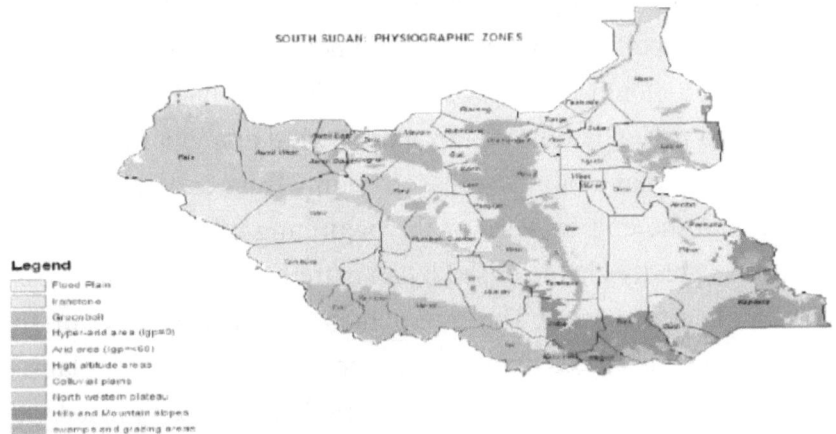

Fig 16: Showing the physiographic zones of Southern Sudan and the Dinka climatic areas

sorghum called durra. This is in addition to the bulrush millet and creeping plants such as beans, yams and pumpkins of various types. This alluvial and loam soil country is usually not flooded except on rare occasions when rains from the Great Lakes and the plateau region of East Africa become heaviest in a certain year. This is the case with central Bahr el Ghazal areas where floods from the Congo Nile water divide sometimes occur.

Like much of Southern Sudan, Dinka land is characterised by a wet period of more than two seasons of rain, which usually covers spring, summer and at times the early parts of autumn. Some years many of the Dinka areas experience extensive annual flooding of the River Nile and its tributaries. This is especially so in the east bank areas in the Upper Nile region and in those areas that are low savannah tochlands in Bahr el Ghazal region. The rain can begin sparsely towards the end of April although Dinka rains have come to begin in May each year. They become intensive from mid-May to September and fade out by late October or early November each year. Some decades ago rains in Upper Nile and Bahr el Ghazal

Dinka areas used to begin by late March. Until the 1950s the month of March was partly a rainy month. But nowadays April has started to be partly a month of the dry season period or winter months.

This wet period is followed by a dry period of about four or five months of no rain at all. Dry season begins from early November up to about the end of April or the beginning of May each year. This time is badly characterised by an extreme thirst in some areas for lack of surface water. The environment becomes harshly hot. In most of the Dinka areas that are away from the tochlands or plains, water is only obtained during this dry period of the year by means of digging wells for underground water. In some places the water table can be as deep as 100 metres or more. These months of no rain makes many people undergo a very painful experience of misery from the hot climate and thirst from lack of water and from serious efforts made in search of water for their livestock and for their domestic needs. This is the time when some parts of the Dinka environment become too hostile and harsh. Dry season is to many Dinka areas a bad omen for its very hot weather hostility and for its thirst and reduction of productive activities.

Although the wet season is better when it is contrasted with the dry winter season, it has its own disadvantages. Dry season has many diseases like meningitis, gastroenteritis of children and communicable diseases that sometimes take a great annual death toll during the dry season in most of the Dinka lands. The dry season period greatly undermines nutritional standards for the vast majority of the Dinka people due to lack of water. This dry period largely explains the nomadic character of the Dinka society. During this time the youth, as well as some of the elderly and children, move out of their settlement villages to swampy areas or toch where water and pasture abounds.

They leave their dry land cattle camps and villages and move off with their livestock to stay in the toch where they settle for the whole of the dry season till rains begin to fall back home in early May. The cattle keeping or cattle rearing folk in the toch keep their livestock on the dry season camps which are mounds or raised grounds built by ancient or bygone early Mediaeval people known as *Jur-Lueel.* Those raised grounds were built at some points along riverbanks where, in the morning hours, cattle are milked and released from their tethering pegs and herded in the nearby green pasture between or along the streams or tributaries of the Nile or swamp ponds. The youth, sometimes with the aged and women, go out to spend the day fishing. The boys and girls, for their part, also go out to search for water lilies and swamp fish which the Dinka call *apuöth,* or they wander about searching the ground for tortoises (*arou*) and digging lungfish *(luth)* from their caves. Other youth go hunting tochland game such as the lechwe antelopes (abuɔk), cob antelopes *(thïl)*, buffalo, Anyiɛr in plural *(Singular: Anyaar)* and other bigger game like elephants which the Dinka people call Akɔɔn.

In years of plenty those who spend the dry season period in the toch could really enjoy it as they eat to satiation and their health always excels in contrast to those who stay in the dry thirst of the savannah woodland or open woodland villages. Since the cows get abundant water and sufficient pasture there is usually enough milk for both children and the rest of the people in the cattle camps in the toch. The combination of milk, fish and meat at times and the variety of marine products provides high levels of protein and other dietary components. Most of the Dinka young folk always long for the dry season to come so that they can move to the toch with the cattle for this purpose. There are, however, other reasons for the youths' admiration of the dry season's life in the toch. The toch is the place for their youthhood courting of girls and is a come together place of acquaintance with the youth folk from other territories and those from distant lands. Those looking for fame through singing and other aesthetic attributes always want to be in the toch.

When rains come and water becomes available with pastures from back home, mostly in mid-May, the cattle are moved and driven back as all return to the villages in order to cultivate. This is the time of production in the year. But prior to the beginning of rains in about mid-March and early April some of the cattle rearing people would start off, returning home from the toch to help clear the fields ready for cultivation when rains of early May make people become certain of the approaching cultivation period. While cattle camp youth go home to cultivate with their people, other young men choose to remain with their cattle to enjoy what Dinka call *fattening months* during which time they drink milk and become so fat for competition with other young men from different families, clans and sections of the same wut or territory.

In economic terms the Dinka people generally lead a traditional mode of life which is a result of a mixture of the harsh environment that profoundly impinges on their way of life. During the middle months of the wet season, that is August and September, mobility is mostly through water in most of the Dinka places. This is so in those villages located in the floodland plains and in the toch" land areas as these places are particularly covered with floodwaters. During August and September up to early October, all the inter-territorial streams, swamps and ponds are usually engorged with water from the rains and the Nile River swells and surges out to cover large areas of the Dinka lands. At this time waterborne diseases, mosquitoes, wet season humidity and the usually convectional rains sometimes add up to make the rainy season another time with its own perils. Perhaps the best of all seasons for the Dinka people would be spring and autumn. Winter and summer are good for what they are, but they are the seasons in which the Dinka people feel the need for modern urban services.

While Dinka communities are pastoral agriculturists controlling vast stretches of land suitable for extensive or mechanised farming, some of the Dinka sectors are always on the move seasonally and periodically. If the plains of the more lowland areas are flooded or their pastures and fields are exhausted, they travel with their provisions and livestock to new places where settlement is possible and where plenty of good pasture for the herd is also assured. Until quite recently most Dinka did not have permanent settlement villages owing to the unreliability of their arable lands. This was, however, true of the recent past, especially among Bahr el Ghazal Dinka who kept shifting from one place to another but because they have vast stretches of land they have no land problems.

At present, cattle owning Dinka have discovered the cow to be a good source of manure and therefore soil fertility. They use the cattle, sheep and goats' dung and urine for manuring their cultivable fields. This practice has proven to give a better yield of durra and maize and is now adopted extensively, especially by the Dinka of Central Bahr el Ghazal.

Except for those living along toch lands, in the cotton or clay soil (called rɔr), those in the steppes and lowland plains, durra is the Dinka main food crop. Those in the savannah woodlands or those in the sandy soil do practise mixed farming. They cultivate a variety of sorghum – known in Sudan as durra. They cultivate groundnuts, sesame, pulses, tubers and edible climbers having underground bulbs.

Besides farming and livestock rearing, Dinka people are also good fishermen. As they are a Nilotic community since ancient times, they have lived all their time on the Nile, its swamps and its tributaries. They very well know the marine economy.

Their life has been and continues to be connected with the Nile River and its tributaries which together form the biggest swamp land they call toch. They spend part of their time each year in this swampy areas where fish abound in the various streams, ponds and rivers and much more in the small lakes that some Dinka call *baaw*. Fish is also bountiful in the toch marshes. It is also brought to the sandy or woodland homes by the inter-territorial streams and rivers coming from the *Nile-Congo water divide region* to the southwest in Bahr el Ghazal. Fish are also found in the existing natural or artificial reservoirs dug by an earlier race, the *Jur-Lueɛl,* who inhabited the region before Dinka arrival to Bahr el Ghazal in the middle of the Middle Ages. During summers and autumns, these water sources are gorged with water and fish come in through the Nile floods which connect the toch and the ponds or streams. Water sometimes comes from an upsurge of the Nile-Congo water divide that supplies much of the interior of Bahr el Ghazal. A number of rivers come to Bahr el Ghazal from the Congo upland region. This flooding during the wet seasons usually brings fish from the rivers, from the swamps and from the local lakes. They supply the upland areas with fish. Except for those living in the driest deep woody country where there are no rivers, ponds or streams, no grown up or child in Dinka land could say he or she does not know fish.

Besides, the Dinka are also good hunters of forests' wild game and are good gatherers of edible forest products like wild fruits, honey and tubers. Since early times, the Dinka people knew how to hunt wild game, rodents and other small animals and birds, all for meat. For the Dinka, hunting could be an individual activity or a collective work of a group of people, sometimes a whole Ric (Age-set). A complete village or section could go out in a joint hunting activity. This is when it involves large and wild animals like buffalos, roan antelopes *(amom)*, giraffe *(miir),* elephants *(akɔɔn)* and rhinos *(kil).* Rodents *(pl. luɔny, singular, lony)* like the canerats *(anyor),* squirrels *(alɔɔl),* the white-tailed mongoose *(kak)* and other rodents such as the porcupines *(amiyiɔk).* All those rodents could be hunted by a few individuals or by one hunter using a dog.

Before the introduction of new fruit trees such as mangoes, lemons, guava and pawpaw from Europe, from India, from the Far and Near East, the Dinka people only knew of their woodland fruit trees. Their forests are divided into three types.

The *savannah forest* is covered with grass and a few trees, mostly sycamore trees, acacia trees which are good for gum, shrub trees and other thorny bushes as well as trees that produce citrus fruits such as cuɛi which is the tamarind tree and *Amillat tree*. One of the sycamore trees called *ngaap* produces very palatable soft pig fruits as do the other sycamore types such as the red-barked or pig tree called *kuel*, which is revered as a totemic divinity tree by the Payii and Parek clan people. It also produces very palatable berries in some places.

There is *woodland savannah forest* where vegetation cover is thick with big trees and grass. This type of forest is usually full of edible fruit trees. Examples include the tamarind or *cuɛi* tree which produces a very sour or sometimes a mixture of sweet-sour flavoured fruits. Trees like *cum*, which is another fruit producing tree having sweet tasting yellowish cherries, are found mostly in Bahr el Ghazal.

Third are the big *primaeval forests* where various wild fruits can be found. These forests, which are primaeval woodland jungles, are usually the home of very wild animals and other dangerous monsters of the dark forest hades. Hunting in such inscrutable forests is only done by huge village teams or by a concerted territorial campaign, not by few or individual hunters. Some people specialise in hunting and are known in Rek dialect as *Muɔrkɔɔk*, who alone are the people who do hunt in such big forests.

In all these forest types, Dinka people also search for honey. They get it from a bee colony hanging on a tree branch or in the trees' hollows. Birds like the spurwing goose *(tuöt)*, the guinea-fowls *(wel)*, the francolin *(aweec)* and other birds known to the Dinka are also hunted for meat. Some Dinka people also eat certain edible insects like the swarming termites (yɔt) which some Dinka sections eat as a delicious pudding (a delicacy). These swarming termites are gathered from large and small anthills using fires around 8 pm in the night following an afternoon rain or a big downpour of the first rains of April or May.

Dinka economy is largely dependent on the cow although they have of late become good agriculturists after they abandoned their former nomadic nature that was dictated by the cattle needs. On the whole Dinka people are now an agro-pastoral community. They are among the hardest working people in the world. They cultivate large fields and many families usually cultivate for surplus with which they purchase more cattle and goats and sheep from those whose yields fall below subsistence quantities. With the introduction of money, cloth and other foreign products, they sell their surplus for money to buy cloth, salt and other things like medicines. Dinka economy is generally geared towards the cow as the entire society lives on cattle for milk, meat and ritual purposes, marriages and ceremonial occasions, and as propitiatory objects to the gods, divinities, family or clan totems, spirits of the bygone ancestors and parents as well as to Nhialic, the creator.

Besides production and other activities, the Dinka people create for themselves a homestead unmatched in all rural Sudan. They build a number of houses and a byre which they call *luak*, an all in one home with a clear, clean courtyard in the centre of the home. Although they make their houses from local building materials that are not concrete in the conventional western sense, their construction involves some kind of engineering work and their houses are the best in the whole of traditional Africa. Among central, western and northern parts of Bahr el Ghazal Dinka, a standard family home could comprise of, firstly the main homestead house and the girls' house if there are girls in the family. There is always the guests' house, the house for male youth, and a big byre. The wall is constructed of a mud, either made alone as a pure mud wall or made of mudded wood poles. The roof is framed with long wooden poles and thatched with grass. The houses are single circular roomed buildings whose interior sleeping floors are beautifully smoothed with a nice heath and the one entry and exit door is closed with a woven shutter known by the Rek Dinka as *athiin*. The byre, which is the biggest structure in the living compound, may last ten years before it is renewed. This is because its engineering design is superbly strong and special. The other structures (ɣöt) can go for more than five years depending on the presence or absence of the termitic ants. For detailed description of the Dinka land, their environment and activities read chapter three of this book.

DINKA DEMOGRAPHY AND POPULATION STATUS

Demographically speaking, the Dinka people are the largest single nationality in the Republic of South Sudan. They are also the biggest ethnic section of the Nilotic people in Sudan. Refer to the annexes at the end of this book for statistics. If a genuine and thorough scientific population count is carried out in the country during peace and stability time, the Dinka population may reach eight million people. The fake national population census carried out by Khartoum in 2008 before the country was split into two put the Dinka at about five million people![54] Dinka people make up more than 80% of the population of Bahr el Ghazal region where they constitute more than three of the four states of the region. Except for a less than 500 Bantu people called Bongo in the southern fringe of Tonj South county, the whole of the oil and cattle rich Warrap state is 99.9% Dinka Rek, Dinka Luac and Dinka Twic. Warrap state is located in central Bahr el Ghazal. The Northern Bahr el Ghazal state of Awiel is 99% Dinka Malual. The remaining 1% comes from a minority Luo people who have even become assimilated into Dinka Malual. The Lakes state in the east of Bahr el Ghazal is also 99% Dinka Agaar, Dinka Kiec, Dinka Gok, Dinka Atuöt and Dinka Aliap. The 1% comes

---

54   Sudan 5th population and housing census count 2008

from another Bantu people called Jur-Belle who inhabit a strip of the haematite or ironstone or plateau area, some 15 kms south of Rumbek town with Ulu as their administrative centre where the equatorial forest belt begins. Western Bahr el Ghazal state has a Dinka people called Waau of Chief Majɔk Majɔk. They are a Rek Dinka section that extends from Kuac community of Kuajök from Thar-Kueng to Wau town, the capital town of the entire Bahr el Ghazal region.

In the Upper Nile region the Dinka people constitute about half the total population of the region of three states. In Jonglei state, in south-central Upper Nile, are the Bor and Twic Dinka with a number of Dinka principalities such as Hol Dinka, Nyarweng Dinka, Paweny Dinka, Duör Dinka, Luac Dinka of Aköök Yiɛu, Rut Dinka and Ngok of Lual Yak, who inhabit the Sobat River areas up to Malakal. There is also the Thoi Dinka. In the northern Upper Nile state are the Dongjol Dinka, Nyiel Dinka, Ageer in the oilfields area and the largest Abialang Dinka community of Renk, extending to the northern end of the Republic of South Sudan, bordering the Northern Sudanese Nezy and Sabaah Arab Baggara of the Rabek and Jebellein areas.

In the Unity state of Bentiu in western Upper Nile, in the oil rich territory, are the Ruweng Dinka people of Panriɛng, also known as Ru or Pan-Ru and Alor Dinka of Chief Kur Kuot of Biemnhom county. The Ngok Dinka in the oil rich area of Abyei, a people who are historically part of the present Warrap state, live in the area of grave political contention between the Republic of South Sudan and Sudan. The Northern Sudanese call it part of its southern Kordofan and the south call it as part of Bahr el Ghazal through the Warrap state. On the whole the Dinka people make up nearly half of the population of the ten states of South Sudan.

In any case, there has not been any reliable demographic data count on the Dinka people as to all the other South Sudanese tribal communities. In spite of the 2008 national census count which put the Dinka people at nearly five million people, no accurate calculation trends have ever been documented for the monitoring of the Dinka population growth and decline, rise or distribution. The 19th century travellers' estimates on the Dinka were only casual huts counted along rivers and around army and trading centres. The 20th century figures conducted before the first national census carried out 1955|6 were based on tax payers' lists which were introduced in the 1920s and only counted the adult males capable of paying taxes to the government. The 1955/6 population census count was, however, systematic in nature in contrast to the previous colonial census counts. This is because it was the first census to employ a uniform methodology although the outcome indicated considerable variations from the previous speculative counts. In spite of the apparent uniform methodology the 1955/6 population census was all the same criticised as inaccurate.

The 1973 population census carried out in Sudan six decades later proved even less satisfactory since it was carried out before population resettlement in the south following the first civil war (1955-1972). There was great displacement of Southern Sudan communities. A big portion of South Sudan's population went to foreign lands for safety from internal civil war against the central government based in Khartoum in Northern Sudan. The Dinka people were among those who went to diaspora and into neighbouring countries of East Africa, Ethiopia and the Congo. The peace agreement of 1972 known as the 'Addis Ababa peace agreement' was made between the Northern Sudan based central government of president Ja'afar Mohd Nimeiry and the South Sudanese rebel movement, the Anya-nya One movement in 1972. The national population census was carried out only months after the signing of the peace agreement when all the refugees and internally displaced people had not completely returned home. The population count did not properly reflect Southern Sudanese communities and for this reason the results of that census count were not officially released.

The 1983 national census was again incomplete because it was conducted in the year of growing unrest and the rise of the armed resistance movement in Southern Sudan. The guerrilla activities of Anya-nya Two started largely in the Nilotic districts in both the Upper Nile and Bahr el Ghazal regions and towns. This became the SPLA in 1983. The civil unrest started in 1980 and became full scale armed movement in 1983. Any number for the Dinka or for Nilotic people based on this census count was only treated as mere conjecture. Even so, 1983 census figures were sound evidence that the population of the Dinka was underestimated in the 1955/6 population count. However, we cannot avoid picking from those figures of 1955/6, which for the first time gave some idea of the numbers of Dinka people. The enumeration used then from the court's centre corresponded roughly to internal sectional divisions of the Dinka people. However, it gives serous underestimation of the nationality, which is even more than some African countries such as Eritrea, Burundi and so forth. The 1983 population count did not even dare to indicate tribal sections, of which the Dinka are a variety of sub-national tribe groups further divided into sections inhabiting large tracts of lands and extensively occupying several provinces and districts (now counties) in the two regions of the Upper Nile and Bahr el Ghazal. The Dinka people live in more than six of the ten states of Southern Sudan in addition to the Ngok Dinka county people of Abyei. They are found in the Upper Nile state where they are the Abialang, Ngok of Lual Yak, Nyiel, Dongjol, Ageer of Paloch and Rek. In Unity state areas in western Upper Nile they are the Ruweng communities of Alor Kur Kuot and Pan-Ru. In Jonglei state they are Bor, Twic-East, Hol of Duk Padieel Nyarweng of Duk-Payueel, Ngok of Lual Yak Luac of Aköök Yiεu people of Khor Flith, Rut Paweng, Thoi, etc. In Bahr el Ghazal they are the Ngok of Abyei, Twic of Warrap state, the big Malual Dinka, the extensive Rek Luacjang, Gok, Agaar, Atuöt, Kiec and Aliap. In any case, the census count of 1983 only showed a pre-war minimum. The growth or decline of some sections or tribal groups affected by immigration plus natural decreases or increases could not be determined as will be done by one day by the South Sudanese government.

Between 1830 and 1930 AD the Dinka population, like the rest of the Southern Sudanese communities, was badly reduced by the slave trade pestilence which caused mass exportation of parts of the population taken away as slaves; inter-tribal and externally provoked warfare, war-induced famine and several outbreaks of epidemic diseases like small chickenpox and cholera, not to speak of the fatalities from the yearly malaria, all combined to cause gross reduction in the Dinka population during that period. Cholera and smallpox were usually imported to Dinka lands either from the north or from areas south of them. It was only during the last 25 years of the British rule in Sudan that control of warfare and occasional mass vaccination campaigns against those deadly communicable diseases were able to make a positive impact on population growth among the Dinka.

Apart from all these it is sometimes difficult to conduct proper statistical assessment owing to seasonal inundations, as parts of the Dinka territories are not inhabited for most of the year due to being savannah lowland. Population density calculated on the total area of a given administrative unit or district, now county, gives the impression of an informal scattering of small settlements, when in reality the inhabitable areas are limited but more densely populated. Among some Dinka settlement villages the largest permanent village can have a density of as much as 500 persons or more. This is per square mile. This population density is specifically in relation to Bahr el Ghazal Dinka areas. The type of land can also alter population distribution and therefore the population density. Areas in Dinka lands that have high population densities are those places that combine areas of flood-free land with seasonal inundated territories suitable for dry season grazing. According to SDIT4, the 1954 report on the classification of territories, the land types in the Nilotic South Sudan are (i) central rain land regions, also called rain lands, (ii) frequent flood areas and (iii) the ironstone plateau region forming part of what is described as the flood plain transition belt. It is therefore advisable not to conduct a census count in South Sudan during the rainy season. Autumn provides optimum environmental conditions for population counts of the Dinka in all the Nilotic lands as dry and rainy seasons provide difficulties to find Dinka people in their real configurations. For those population counts which show Dinka demographic and population status, see Tables I and II below.

Table I: *Showing 1955/6 and 1983 Dinka population Count*

Dinka districts	Dinka national groups or tribes	1955/6 Dinka population by areas and tribes	1983 Dinka population by areas and tribes
Renk rural council	Abialang Dinka	8,846	38,824
Melut	Paloc (Nyiel, Ageer) Dinka	13,124	21,474
Bailiet	Dongjol Dinka	19,943	57,552
	Ngok of Lual Yak Dinka	90,738	116,817
Atar	Paweny, Thoi, Rut and Luac Dinka tribal communities	16,175	19,788
Biemnhom and Panriɛng	Ruweng: Alor and Pan- Ru) Dinka	31,641	42,743
Duk-Payueel	Nyarweng Dinka	12,447	16,080

Duk-Padieet	Hol Dinka	11,058	14,940
Mading Bor	Twic Dinka	43,399	134,325
	Bor Dinka	62,231	158,815
Central Ac, Lakes (Rumbek) Western Ac, Lakes	Agar Dinka	93,064	139,281
	Gok Dinka	37,389	258,628
Eastern Ac, Lakes (Yirol)	Kiec Dinka	31,088	68,932
	Aliap Dinka	12,408	56,831
	Atuöt Dinka	58,147	92,041
Jur River district Gogrial rural council Western area council Tonj	?		
	Rek Dinka of Gogrial	107,337	229,009
	Twic Dinka of Gogrial	70,986	187,397
	Rek Dinka of Tonj	106,611	216,102
	Luac Dinka of Tonj	22,111	102,203
Awiel district	Malual Dinka	71,340	184,062
	Abiem Dinka	139,789	304,270
	Palieupiny Dinka	67,365	127,706
	Paliëët Dinka	40,736	662,356
		2,078.073	2.962.176

Table II: Showing 2008 Dinka population figures by states and counties: Sudan 5th population and housing census

S.No	State	Population	Total
1	UPPER NILE		
	Renk County	137,351	
	Baliëët County	48,010	
	Melut County: Paloch 16,215 Panhomdit 5,703 Wunamum 1,547	23,465	
	Malakal County 15% Dinka population	126,483*15= 18,972 100	
	Sub-Total		227,798+
2	JONGLEI STATE		
	Khorflus County	99,068	
	Duk County	65,588	
	Twic-East County	85,349	
	Bor South County	221,106	
	Sub-Total:		471,111+
3	UNITY STATE		
	Pariang County	82,443	
	Biemnhom County	17,012	
	Bentiu Town= 41,328 x 3 % = 3% Dinka 100 Population	1,240	
	Sub-Total		100,695+

4	WARRAP STATE		
	Abyei County	52.883# 65.790	500.000#
	Twic County	204,905	
	Gogrial West county	243,921	
	Gogrial East County	103,283	
	Tonj North county	165,222	
	Tonj East county	116,122	
	Tonj South county	86,592	
	Sub-Total		1.038.718
5	LAKES STATE		
	Cueibet County	117,755	
	Rumbek North County	43,410	
	Rumbek Centre County	153,550	
	Rumbek East County	122,832	
	Yirol West county	103,190	
	Yirol East County	67,402	
	Awerial County	47,041	
	Sub-Total		655,180+
6	NORTHERN BAHR EL GHAZAL		
	Awiel North county	129,127	
	Awiel East County	309,921	
	Awiel South County	73,806	
	Awiel West County	166,217	
	Awiel Centre County	41,827	
	Sub-Total		720,898+

7	WESTERN BAHR EL GHAZAL		
	Wau North and Wau South, 30% Dinka Population Marial Bai	151,320 ×30 % = 45,396 100 22,475	67,871+
8	CENTRAL EQUITORIAL STATE		
	Juba County 15% Dinka Population	368,436× 15% = 55,109 100	
	Yei County 10% Dinka Population	201,443×10 % = 20,144 100	20.144
	Sub-Total		75,253+
9	Diaspora Dinka including those still in Sudan		776,186[55]
	Total Population		4,123,710

Source: Statistical yearbook for Southern Sudan 2010 issued by Southern Sudan Centre for Census, Statistics and Evaluation

It is widely believed by all the enlightened Dinka people that any dedicated, well organised population census count, carried out in the Dinka areas at the right season of the year and in a time of peace and stability when all the Dinka internally displaced people, refugees and the diaspora population have come back home, could

---

55   Estimated figures according to Ministry of Foreign Affairs and International Cooperation

most likely portray the Dinka nationality at more than eight million people or something about that.

CHAPTER TWO:
THE DINKA RURAL SETTING

Dinka people are a very proud pastoral people who consider themselves as the best standard of what is ideally human. They consider themselves and want to be regarded by others as being the best humans in the world. Dr. Francis Mading Deng in his book, *'Tradition and modernization'*, unflinchingly says that the *"Dinka people represent the standard of what is ideally human and therefore best. Others may have superior technology or greater wealth in monetary terms, but all things considered, Dinka land is the most beautiful, Dinka race the perfect example of creation, Dinka cattle the ideal wealth and Dinka ways the models of dignity."*[1] The Dinka way of life, their daily, monthly and yearly activities can be best described through their homes, cattle economy, seasonal and aesthetic pursuits and through their overall cultural activities and lore.

DINKA MATERIAL CULTURE

The most important tangible material cultural assets of the Dinka in their rural setting would be their home shelters and their cattle camps, two places where all the social, martial and cultural traditions, social activities, traits and behaviours, including *dhëëŋ* which is gentlemanship, *athɛɛk* which is respect, *kɛɛc* or heroism and valour, *biökruɛɛl* or generosity and respect to social norms, are all imparted to the young ones. Different Dinka sections have, in their localities, evolved different articles of art and different homemaking styles. The common art is that of war: spears, sticks and shields. Dinka men start practising stick and spear duelling with great dexterity right from their boyhood.

As Dinka lands don't have stone and iron, their material culture is rather simple. All their homes and cattle camp structures made as shelters are made from wood, both short and long poles. Houses are, in addition to those wooden poles, constructed of grass, wattle and mud. The Dinka people are generally not good iron-workers like the *Luo (Jur-col)* who neighbour them to the southwest in Bahr el Ghazal.

In the recent past, Bahr el Ghazal Dinka people used to purchase hoes, adzes, axes and all forms of spears made from iron, all from this ironworking Luo community. During the Mediaeval and ancient times Dinka people used weapons and digging sticks fashioned from animal horns, from bones of certain animals such as giraffe scapulas and from hardwoods called *rit*, the ebony tree,

1 Dr Francis Mading Deng, *Tradition and modernization, a challenge for law among the Dinka of the Sudan*, 3rd ed, Kush Inc, Washington DC, USA, (1978), p. 70

giɛr tree and *tiit*, the mahogany tree. The absence of metal in Dinka lands must have been the reason that cultivation became a secondary practice prior to the advent of modern innovation which

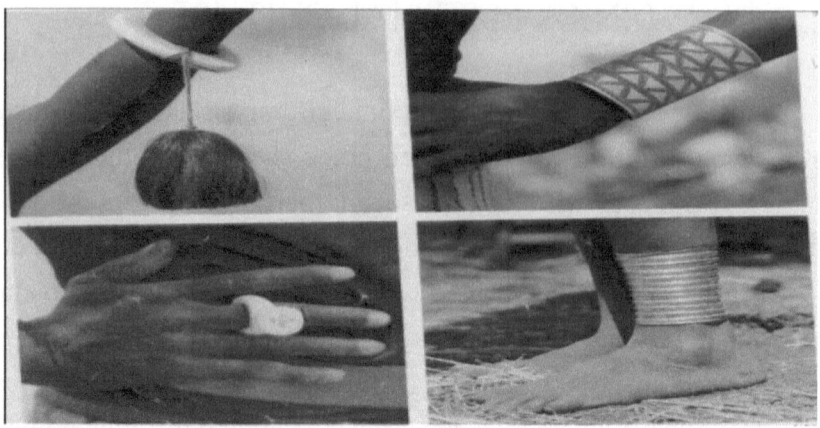

Fig 17: Showing how Dinka people wear various wristlets, armlets and anklets for decoration

is currently seeking in earnest to transform the Dinka traditional way of life. Absence of metal is certainly the reason why Dinka people became more materially dependent on their cattle even today.

A variety of items are made from metal such as wrist bracelets which they call *anhom-riaak*, copper anklets and wristlets also made from metal which Dinka people call *bäu*. There are also armlets made from iron (*wëëth*) imported from outside of the Dinka lands and these are used extensively even today. Dinka people use them for personal adornment, for making cultivation tools like hoes and for making some of the war implements such as bladed war and fishing spears. In the past great value was attached to those types of metal items. For example, ancient sacred spears called *binh löŋ* from which the Spear Masters acquired their title are believed to have long antedated the general introduction of iron into the Dinka country. Dinka use of those metal items for the aforementioned purposes, particularly the holy spears, has long been part of Dinka culture since those ancient times. The use of iron and those other metals has been, however, known to the Dinka when they were in that far end region of Northern Sudan which comprised of Wawat, Napata, Meroe and the then Sheinab areas which they came to call *Kar-toum*, the meeting place of the two streams or rivers. Those metal items were used not for construction or for any advanced technology, but for traditional warfare, cultivation and bodily adornment. Dinka metal items so described have since then formed part of the Dinka material culture.

Proud as they are, the Dinka people don't have any meaningful item within their culture which can be regarded as a permanent material culture that could last for the use of another epoch, except for their holy shrines, which are holy tombs of pyramidal structure and which are built for sainted Spear Masters.

Dinka people must therefore make serious undertakings to embark on how to put down permanent material structures, things like concrete houses, concrete school buildings, concrete health structures, permanent roads and other things of modern technology. This is possible now that Dinka land has come to have subterranean products such as oil discovered in many parts of the Dinka lands[2].

It is also possible now that Dinka people have come to adopt commerce and education as well as other modern professions at a very rapid pace and have conceived urbanisation more positively. Dinka people should therefore turn their huge cattle towards more modern use than the traditional utility for which they have been keeping them. In fact, it is the absence of any traditional or historical development or any evidence of accumulated growth and change in the Dinka cultural possessions which made the Spear Masterhood and cattle keeping as the only establishments around which Dinka religious, economic and social life was based. A variety of wooden, grass and mud made structures do not last long enough to constitute what could be classified as permanent material culture.

Fig 18: Showing a Luak frame before it is thatched with grass. The structure indicates huge force required from the men of the village. The thatched Luak structure belongs to the author in his Tharakon traditional village.

Fig 19: Showing a Dinka traditional homestead belonging to one wife

DINKA TRADITIONAL HOMEMAKING

Dinka rural homes generally consist of two or three circular wall houses, all of which are one-roomed with a wall made of short poles cut from trees and daubed with clay mud. Those houses are, however, plastered beautifully with *Tiɔmcol,* a layer of black hearth from the topsoil found at some places rich with loam soil. The muddied and plastered wall is then framed with a conical roof made of long poles cut from certain trees and thatched with a new but well organised dry yellow grass. In addition to those circular houses is usually a very commanding big house structured from the same shape and materials. The English people call it a byre or a cattle byre. The Dinka call it a *luak*. This type of structure is found in the central Rekland areas in Bahr el Ghazal and among the Ruweng people. The Agaar Dinka makes what is called *rön-nhial*, which Rek Dinka people call *Guk*, a kind of a stair house.

For the purposes of privacy and independence, Dinka men allow each wife to have her own homestead with some or all of those buildings so described. Inside the byre and at the centre of the big pork-poles, called *mëën,* is usually a dung fire called *Gɔl* which is fired and used to smoke away mosquitoes and other insects from the cows, goats and sheep during the night. Dinka houses are well constructed and beautifully plastered. Their houses and byres are neatly done and healthy to live in and are, by standard, the best in the whole of traditional

2 Most of the oil fields where petroleum for the Republic of South Sudan is currently drilled, in western and northern Upper Nile States, are located in Dinka areas of Pan-Ru and Nyiel Dinka area of Paloch. This is apart from the oil fields in Jonglei and Abyei areas and the large oil reserves discovered to underlay Warrap state areas.

Of the three houses seen above, four in some places are found among the Rek and Luac Dinka of Tonj and in all the areas of the former Gogrial district. One house is used as a guesthouse. The other one is for the girls of the home and the third is used as the master house for the wife and the husband, shared with smaller kids. The fourth is usually a granary store for the home. The byre is for milking. Milking cows, goats and sheep are kept in the luak for children who cannot go to the cattle camp during the summer season when rainy weather makes it unhealthy for them to live in the summer cattle camps as they need to avoid the usual cold from rains and the mosquitoes of the summer season. Certain Dinka communities, however, keep their children in the cattle camps despite these wet season problems.

Fig 20: Showing the Dinka holy shrines of the ancestors of the author all in Tharokon holy village in the Awan-Parek area. The tallest shrine on the right is also a shrine of the author's great grandfather, Bol Kuot Ayii of the 16th century. Next on the left is the holy shrine of Maduotdit. The third to the left is a holy shrine of his son Kuot Maduot. The one not in white is a shrine of his elder son Machara Maduot. Further left and in white is a holy shrine of Ayii Bol. Further to the left but not covered by the photographer is a shrine of those of Aköök-Matemdit, direct grandfather of the author. To the end of the picture on the left is the holy shrine of Madut-Kuendit, the father of the author.

*Fig 21: Showing a type of Dinka hön nhiel,
a traditional stair house*

Circled by those buildings is an open space of the homestead compound which Dinka people call *baai cïɛlic,* the centre of the homestead. Then there is what they call *yɔlthok,* which is the edge of the courtyard at whose margins the cultivable fields of the home begin. Women do their usual cooking work in this place *yɔlthok,* a place which could better be called the women's hearth. Women usually do their cooking in this place towards sunset and by about 6:00 or 7:00 pm, they are finished with their cooking work. Food is apportioned by the housewife into several gourd calabashes (dishes) according to the number of people in the home and is brought to the centre of the courtyard (*baai cïɛlic*) where the husband usually stays with his boys if they are at this time not in the cattle camp. People then sit on the papyrus reed mat called *yaak* or *ayiɛk* which is placed near a kindled fire made from dried up logs or wicks of wood. Here at this courtyard fire the family usually have their dinner.

Baai-cïɛlic is the central courtyard for the homestead. Although this is where all the family members spend their time before dispersing into the houses to sleep, *Baai-cïɛlic* is generally the men's courtyard part where the master of the home (father or husband) stays as the night commences. From these *baai-cïɛlic* and *yɔlthok,* respective places for men and women in the home, Dinka children get their first practical lessons in the principles of Dinka social organisation, socialisation about family ethics, norms and history, family and community legends and mythical stories as well as tales existing in the society. Before they go to the cattle camps, socialisation of children takes place in this place. This is where they are taught about society norms and customs during those early parts of the nights before they could go into the houses to sleep. Young girls who stay with their mothers at the cooking hearth and the boys who stay with their fathers at the courtyard centre are made to know their roles and functions from now on up to when they grow to become adults.

Dinka people see it as important to make their children to be familiar with their family's heritage. It is here at the courtyard that children are made to recite the names of their ancestors are made to hear and sing clan's songs in order to properly prepare his or her mind, his or her whole body and spirit to become a cultured boy or girl. Dinka people are great lovers of their traditions. Socialisation at home and in the cattle camps is very fundamental in shaping the child's outlook and it shapes the child's character, attitudes and mental horizon before he or she enters into the dynamics of the society during his or her adult life. It is from this point of childhood that Dinka children are made to now and adopt those societal values such as honest, respect to elders, integrity, generosity, courage, acumen, self–denial, patience, self- sacrifice, wisdom, patriotic dispositions, fortitude and much more of the accepted values.

DINKA HOME FURNISHINGS

By modern standards, Dinka traditional or rural home furnituring is simple. To begin with a homestead usually has two or three clay-made pots called *töny* in singular and plural form primarily used for cooking. *A töny* has a round bottom and is a somewhat narrow mouthed-shaped earthenware structure which, apart from cooking, is also used for carrying water and for keeping brewed beer. *A töny* is also used as a container for keeping water, for storing grain and for storing other things of the home. Sometimes oil or ghee from butter is kept in pots. There is also a small pot type called *agul* that is different from a *töny*. There is also another clay-made jar called *alɛɛi*. It is used as a pottery calabash. An *alɛɛi* is a large open-ended earthernware pot which Dinka people mostly use for broth when it is of the calabash size. It is also used for white stuff beer when it is made into a bigger size than that of a calabash. There is also what the Dinka people call *abuöc,* a usually big fragment from a broken pot. An *abuöc* is used by women and girls for roasting sesame and groundnuts to be pounded into a paste eaten as a pudding or used to season the broth as *kekur* in Rek dialect.

Apart from these pottery items so described above, there are other domestic items made from *kuɔt,* the gourd. It is produced by a natural creeping plant sown to produce various types, shapes and sizes of big and small oval and round bulbs as well as those of finger-like bulbs. Some are made into gourd calabashes, called *aduuk* when in plural, *aduök* when singular. The gourd calabash is used for serving all forms of food, especially grain porridge from millet, durra and maize. Gourds made into the Dinka *kec* are used for keeping cow's oil and butter. The bigger *kec*, which is called *rök* in Rek dialect, is used for storing grain, sesame or groundnuts. It is also used as a container for water.

Rök is also used as a container for keeping the Dinka traditional beer call *Muön-rer,* the white stuff, especially one which should contain beer quantity for many people as are used during celebration occasions. Some gourds of the size and shape made into milking gourd call *Ajiëp*, sometimes call *Amuj,* are used for milking cows, for keeping and for drinking milk.

Gourds are also made into what is called *jab,* a gourd structure used also for milking. Small slender types of gourds which are finger-like are bisected to become gourd spoons, which the Rek Dinka

Fig 22: Showing a Dinka pot made from clay

call *bïny-awiith* or *bïny-miëth*. The bigger types are used as scoops called *bïny-töny*.

In a Dinka home are also found certain woven items, among which are what Dinka people call *gäc,* the basket type plaited of *rieth* and used for keeping or carrying grain and other things. There is also the winnowing tray called *atac* or *atäny* made from a plaited sporobolus pyramidalis grass which the Rek Dinka call *mon.* An *atac* or *atäny* is used by women and girls for separating grain particles called *ŋeei* from flour when pounding the millet, maize or durra to be cooked into porridge, called kuin, although as mentioned earlier the Agaar people call it cuin.

There are also the *wicker cradles* which the Dinka call *adiany.* Dinka mothers use it for carrying babies on their heads when going on long journeys. It is still in use up to the present day although the Agaar Dinka woman has come to adopt a new thing called a *köndöök,* a shoulder sling carrier made from goat or sheep skin. It is designed to sling the babies on the shoulder instead of in the cradle bed or wicker cradle used on the head by the Rek and other Dinka communities. Associated with the two, *köndöök* and *adiany,* is the baby rattle, a bulb of gourd with a handle. It is called *läi* with particles of stone, durra or maize grain put into it. It is shaken by the adult or the baby or child to soothe it when it is crying.

Dinka home bedding consists of sleeping hides called *akɔt* or *biöök* from cattlehides and also from wild game skins but the one mostly used nowadays is the large reed mat called *yaak*. The Agaar people call it *ayiɛk*. It is made from papyrus reed, abundantly obtained from the toch, in the swamps or along the riverbanks. The papyrus reeds are beautifully knitted largely for people to roll over them in order to protect them from rain, cold and sometimes the blaze of the sun. Mats, *yaak* or *ayiɛk,* are particularly important for the Dinka since they are the main items used as domestic bedding.

A big log of wood is cut down from a hardwood tree which is then artisted into a mortar called *doŋ*. It is then dug into the ground somewhere at the edge of the courtyard. In Rekland *doŋ* is sometimes dug inside the byre in between the *mëën* in each home to use during rains and sometimes in the night. Each mortar usually has one or more pestle and it is used by women and girls to pound durra, maize or millet which is then cooked into porridge. Sesame and groundnuts are also pounded using the smaller mortars.

Pounding durra, millet, maize, sesame and groundnuts is an exclusive work done by women and girls, as is cooking. Men do not pound and they do not cook. Initiated adult males do not milk cows, goats or sheep. Gender division of labour is very rigid among the Dinka but couples generally help each other when need be. The exception is in these areas of cooking, pounding and milking. There is so much rigidity in these three areas that when a man is forced by a certain

Fig 23: Showing an Agaar young woman carrying her child on a köndöök

circumstance to milk the cow(s) when no one else can do it, he cannot drink the milk as it is believed that act could bring calamity to his herd. A Dinka man can cook or pound but will not eat from that food he prepared for any reason.

Roasted sesame and groundnuts are pounded into a kind of pudding or paste called *guäär* as it is called by the Rek Dinka. It is eaten alone in its paste form and is also used for broth making. A large cage or container called *adara* or *akoog*, made from woven sporobolus pyramidalis grass, is kept in every home for storing grain and other food produce such as groundnuts, maize, hardnuts and so on. There is usually more than one of this *adara*, big and smaller ones.

A type of headrest, which is a wooden structure, is used by men as a pillow. Rek Dinka people call it mageer. Others call it maŋan.

Other Dinka sections call it kuaraŋ. Beside those wooden pillows is another type, the best of all, called thööc. These wooden pillows are chipped or crafted from naturally forked branches of trees with suitable shapes. Then, there is a fighting implement called magueŋ, a type of parrying stick with a hollowed part in the middle. It is chipped in such a way as to fit the hand into it and is also used to serve as a purse or pouch for keeping some small things like a personal piece of tobacco. This is particularly so when it is from the ambatch wood called ɣör obtained from some parts of the toch or along certain riverbanks.

DINKA TRADITIONAL DRESS AND DECORATION

As for personal trinkets or dressings, women use goat and sheep skins which they clear of the hair or wool and it is very well done to wear it on the waist to cover the front parts of the thighs down to the knees, and on the back from the hip girdle down the buttocks and onto the knees up to the middle part of the legs. Those goats or sheep skins are made into an apron called *buɔɔŋ, buɔŋ* in plural. A specially fashioned apron is called *dual, duaal* in plural.

Buɔɔŋ and *dual* are skirt girdles that are decorated on their edges with particular beads of choice. They are serrated at the ends, after the knees. *Buɔŋ* are constantly worn by married women. Girls use them only during public celebrations and during dancing occasions. In the past girls used to stay nude but modernity has changed that practice. Girls of today use *jabona* which is a type of skirt from cloth. Such a dress can be seen on the girl in this picture and used to be a fashion dress for Dinka women and girls among the Rek. Dinka until today.

They still use them today during public celebrations. Such a beautiful traditional apron is made more attractive when a girl or woman

Fig 24: Showing a 1952 Rek Dinka girl in full Dinka traditional dress

applies other bodily adornment items like beads and bronze or copper bracelets, beautification items which are used as anklets, wristlets and armlets, as pictured earlier. Bead necklaces and waistlets are worn on the neck and waist.

Those worn on the waist are waistlets while earrings made from elephant tusks, copper or beads are fixed around the ear margins or to the lower tips of the ears depending on the type being used. In the past Dinka men and women used copper earrings around the whole margin of both ears for adornment. Although the use of these earrings has become outdated they are still being used by some Dinka communities in those typical rural areas where modernity is still many miles away.

The Rek Dinka girl in figure 20 above, a photo taken in 1952, is wearing a coil of whitish waist beads called *wut,* a type of bead made from ostrich eggs. She is wearing those waist beads above the hip girdle up to the navel area, covering her navel. The white coil of copper rings is worn, starting from the ankles and up almost the whole tibial length of both legs as can be seen from the picture of Atong Ngɛng Bol, holding a royal stick in figure 5, chapter one. She is that modern Dinka girl with modern artificial hair on her head, she too wears an apron decorated with beads. She wears assorted beads on the waist and on the neck are the most celebrated necklace beads called *majök*. She also wears the white slings of a bead type called *gaŋ* that hang to below the breast. It is only her long plaited hair and *brazer* (bra) cover to the breasts that distinguishes her as an urban girl. Yet Atong makes a typical Dinka lady. Her majestic appearance is in keeping with her noble background. Her grandfather, Bol Malek Jok, was the absolute ruler of the Luackoth territory until his death at a good old age in 2006. He was the paramount court president for what continues to be known as *Anan-Atak* regional court, comprised of several chieftancy areas in Tonj East county.

The girl in figure 20 is wearing other ornaments on her arms and wrists and for the purpose of the occasion which she is in, she picked a spear from among the spears of her brother, who is behind the song bull. She put a black hat on her head. She then set out, leading her brother's song bull. As can be seen, she is exhibiting the highest level of Dinka pride and beauty. This is the kind of traditional dressing known as the standard Dinka dressing by women and girls.

Men, particularly young men, wear facial beads called *gaŋ* which other Dinka people call *tak*. This is besides various types and colours of waist beads and bead necklaces. *Guɛn-jäŋ* (from the word *jääŋ*)

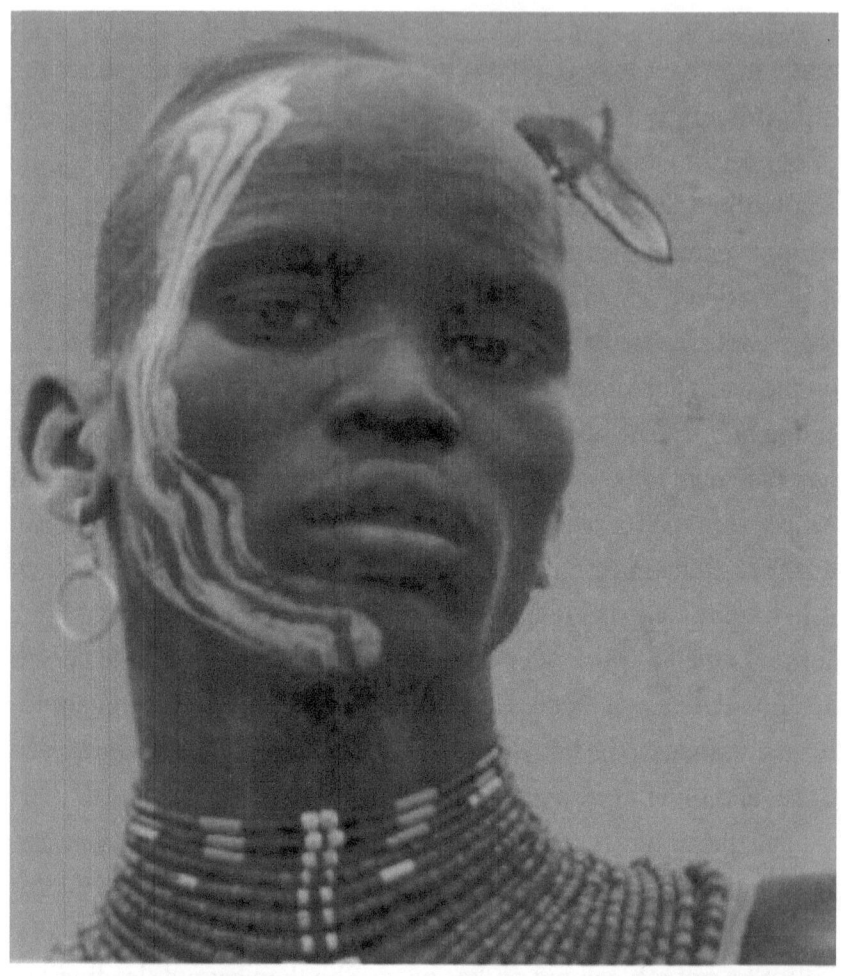

Fig 25: Showing a young Agaar Dinka man wearing guɛn-jäŋ beads on the neck with facial decoration

beads are mostly used by young men and girls from the Agaar Dinka, the Kiec Dinka, *Atuöt* (or Rel) and Aliap Dinka. Young people from Bor Dinka also prefer this *guεn-jäŋ* like the Lakes state Dinka youth folk. This Agaar Dinka young man in figure 21 who is from the Panyar section wears *guεn-jäŋ* as a bead necklace. His photo was taken in 1980 in the cattle camp by John Ryle. Indeed, the Dinka world is full of various colours of beads, worn by different age groups and for various occasions.

Although Dinka men use a garment called jalabia today, Dinka men were known to use what was known as *awäät*, a hip girdle made from woolly hides of sheep and other woolly animals. During public occasions men use *dhök*, a beautiful girdle worn on the back of the hip. *Dhök* is a woolly hide skinned out from a killed wildcat which the Rek Dinka people call *dhök*. The Yirol Dinka communities known as Aliap, Atuot and Kiec, and who reside on the west bank of the White Nile opposite the Bor people on the east bank, are particularly known for their special beads and bracelet decorations that cover almost the whole body. With modernity and foreign ways already amidst Dinka lands, rural Dinka men currently wear jalabia from the Arabs. They also wear European dresses. Complete nudity and the wearing of aprons from goats' skins are rare sights today even in the cattle camps.

DINKA RURAL WORK AND WAR IMPLEMENTS

Home tools and instruments used by men for their daily work in the home include one or two axes, adzes and a number of hoes. The number of those items depends on the number of working people in the home. All the mentioned items are made from iron by local blacksmiths. In the past, in Bahr el Ghazal, ironwork used to be the work of the ironworking Luo who used to walk the Dinka country selling those iron implements, including spears and other metal implements needed by the Dinka people, but nowadays the art has come to be known by some Dinka people who opted to specialise in ironwork. The Rek Dinka call them bël and the Lakes Dinka call them ajoŋ, ajuɔɔŋ when singular. Hoes, like spears, are made with shafts called tɔɔr into which long and straightened wooden stakes or well chipped poles are fitted for cultivation. The Rek Dinka call this long piece of chipped wood a *cit*. It is chipped and chiselled into shape and size using the adze till it becomes a long type of cultivation rod fit for the hands.

Besides this assortment of domestic items there are also fishing, hunting and war implements called spears that are of various types and use. There are generally two broad types of spears. There is what the Dinka call bith which is primarily designed as binh-mɛɛi, the fishing spear, with no sharp edges. This type of spear consists of the barbed one, with indentures which is used for fishing. It is also used in wars. It has indented serrates designed into shapes and is known by the Rek Dinka as binh-nyuɛɛth. The complete opposite type to this spear is the famous binh-löŋ, the sacred or holy spear which is a long and unbarbed or unwieldy spear used by the Dinka high priests, the Spear Masters called bäny-bith. They use it as a symbol of their office. Binh-löŋ and bäny-bith are thoroughly discussed in the book entitled 'Dinka religion: their belief system' (2013). The other type of spear is what the Dinka call tɔŋ, the bladed or sharp-edged spear. This type of spear penetrates and cuts on its sides or edges when it hits something fleshy, cuttable or penetrable. It cuts when it is used on something like meat (flesh) or something worth cutting. This type of spear has several types and shapes. There is the alɔ*l* type with somewhat curved serrates. There is also a bladed spear called *acök-kuëi,* a type of spear with serrates like the eagle's claws. There is the small and very sharp bladed spear (*maker-caak*) with serrates pointing backwards and which cannot be pulled back once it has hit through a person or animal. *Maker-caak* and *alɔl* are not pulled back once something is hit with it. There is also the *tɔŋ-alaŋ* type, the ordinary bladed spear which is mostly rinsed white.

All the spears of different types, including the holy spears, had shafts into which what the Dinka call *wai-tɔŋ* is fixed or plugged. Men do decorate those spear rods or *wai* with various colours of coils from copper and bronze metals. One man in the home or cattle camp could possess four to ten spears. He keeps them as weapons of defence, attack or assault. The spears are generally instruments of war except for the sacred spears held or kept by *bäny-bith*, the religious high priests. In the middle of the courtyard of the homestead is usually a forked wooden shrine called *roro* on which those spears are leaned during the day when they are not in use by their owner(s).

Kept by Dinka men also are thieec, wooden clubs or marshal sticks used as weapons for fighting and for defence in wars and other combat occasions. The Agaar or generally the eastern Dinka of the Lakes State call it löc in singular, läc in plural. Those who live near the toch also own simple wooden canoes called riäi in their homesteads. They use this riäi for fishing and riverine movement purposes. In each settlement may be found such public things as lɔɔr, the dance drum. Although a lɔɔr is privately owned by some individuals who made or acquired it in a settlement, a lɔɔr is generally used by everyone and is treated more or less as public property. A lɔɔr is used for a number of purposes: it is primarily used for public dance play and for information during wars. It is also used to alert and call the community on the death of a Spear Master. It is also used to notify people about dangerous animals such as lions, elephants and buffalo, to mention the most dangerous ones. Those items of the women and men so described under this chapter, the homes structures, cattle or livestock, beads and those other domestic materials makes what could be regarded as the Dinka material culture.

THE DINKA DIETARY SYSTEM

The Dinka diet largely consists of porridge called *kuin* which is the staple food of the Dinka after milk. It is called kuin by the 'K' group among the Dinka. The 'K' group are the Rek cluster. The 'C' group who are the south-central or Agaar dialect group call the porridge c*uin*. This *kuin* or *cuin* is made from pounded grain flour of durra, maize or millet and is eaten in combination with what the Rek people call *kada*. The Agaar Dinka call it *awai*. *Kada* or *awai* is what the English people call broth. Many Dinka people in their homes use this broth for porridge, but cattle keeping people mostly use milk to season their *kuin*.

Roasted or boiled meat and fish are eaten as they are available. In places near the toch or rivers, fish is constantly available. Meat is found in various ways from the abundantly available livestock, chickens, edible rodents and wild game hunted from the forests. Meat is also found from swamp creatures such as the tortoise, a*rou*, *Agaany* the monitor lizard, *nyang* the crocodile and other creatures. The beans, called *akuɛm*, of various types are also cultivated in many parts of Bahr el Ghazal. It is another edible food full of protein. Beside *akuɛm*, the Lakes state Dinka communities plant and eat a bean type called *aguɔth* which is extra-rich in protein. There is also what the Rek Dinka call *aŋeŋ*, which the Agaar people call *arɔɔl*. The groundnuts and sesame form another important diet but are of the seasoning (*kekur*) category. This *kekur* is mostly used to season the broth, pumpkins, yams and other dietary stuff. Sesame and groundnuts are eaten in their own right and are pounded into a paste of kekur or seasoner. The Rek Dinka call it *guärguär*. The groundnuts are cracked out of their kernels and eaten roasted. Some Rek people northwest of Tonj up to Gogrial and further west to Awiel eat the groundnuts unroasted! The Dinka people eat pumpkins of several types. The bigger one is known as *abudh*. Others call it *abudho*. The small type called *aɲɔny,* also *aɲɔnyjɔk*, is cooked in the same way *abudho* is cooked. Both are cooked and seasoned with groundnuts or sesame pastes and seasoned with a little salt. Beside *abudho* and *aɲɔnyjɔk* there is an edible cucumber which the Rek Dinka call *kerk-uol*. Others call it *kodho*. It is cooked in the same way *abudho* and *aɲɔny* are cooked. Dinka people also plant and eat certain tubering plants such as *amuɔn*, the yam.

DINKA FATTENING AND FATTENING SEASON

While porridge (kuin or cuin) and broth, roasted groundnuts, sesame, abuth, boiled meat and fish are among the basic daily food for the Dinka rural community, milk forms a high proportion of their daily dietary intake. This is particularly so among the young ones and the youth prior to their marriage. In the Dinka traditional world, children aged one or two are weaned from suckling their mothers using milk and only milk. Generally, Dinka children of cattle tycoons are believed to taste other forms of food only after they are several years old. Young men in the cattle camps had milk as their main food intake and it becomes the only food when they have gone out for **fattening season**, done for about three months each year. Fattening is one of the cardinal cultural practices which rural Dinka men and girls do every year. Almost every Dinka young man and girl is presumed to have gone through this fattening process several times in his or her lifetime. Fattening takes place between the end of the month of March and about the beginning or middle of the month of July each year. It is crowned by a very famous and colourful communal occasion which the Rek Dinka people call Lunybei or Agutpiny, an occasion with the meaning of communal coming together which is blended with dance and displays of girls and young men as the fattened young men are paraded before the entire gathered society.

This fattening practice begins with each family identifying or

Fig 26: Showing four very fat Rek Dinka men from the Apuk area of eastern Gogrial paraded for the auditorium to choose who the winner is

authorising their young men and girls to take a number of milking cows, which could go to ten and even more, and they are then made to move some distance away from their homes. They go and join up with the youth from other villages and those from other territories. There they begin to stay in places of absolute seclusion called fattening camps. They stay in groups, sometimes as territorial youth groups staying alone with their milking cows, boys and girls. They make small makeshift huts which they call *aduël*.

In those temporal huts where they sleep or spend the whole fattening period of three to four months, each young man stays almost immobile in his own *aduël* and the sister or boy will constantly care for him, bringing milk gourds full of milk, one after the other. Those gourds full of milk are brought in succession for him to drink for a whole day and night. The fattening young man will be required to leave no opportunity for hunger to come to him. He is encouraged to drink his milk to fill himself to the brim so that in a week's time, fatness begins to show in him. He does this while having in mind the serious competition with the other young men who are doing the same in their fattening huts and camps.

The fattening time is spent while they are aware of the *Lunybei* occasion where the fattened youth are communally seen or paraded in display and the one who is fatter than the others is pointed out by the select jury of elders and the occasion becomes his. The one chosen by the jury is therefore declared as winner and as the man of the year. The father and relatives of the declared winner become jubilantly victorious and the entire family, lineage and clan members go out in ululations for their son having won the year. Being chosen as the man of the year indicates prosperity and his family name will go out of the territory as being cattle tycoons. The prestige that goes with this victory takes a long time to fade away in the collective memory of the population in the territory. A bull is brought forth by the young man's father or brother and is ritually or publicly killed to mark that as a victory and the year is then regarded to be the year of the winner.

Before the fattest ones are paraded, Spear Masters and other influential notables appeal and invocate against any wizard who may bewitch them as they are being paraded for the purpose of selecting the winner. People with vice and ill-wish are warned or threatened through invocations. The *Agutpiny* occasion is therefore controlled by the Spear Masters against evil people. At times some young men may die as a result of too much fat in their bodies. Stories of Dinka young men who died either in the fattening huts or as they are made to walk towards the gathering place of the *Agutpiny* for the final competition occur. The young man who dies as a result of fattening is, however, deemed to have defeated the rest and is considered the man of the year. His people take pride in that and for this reason bulls are killed in celebration for him being the winner.

Fattening by milk, fattening season and its attending communal occasion, *Lunybei* or *Agutpiny*, is one of the important socio-cultural events that many Dinka communities do observe in the middle or sometimes at the beginning of the month of July each year. Rek and

Luac Dinka tribes in Bahr el Ghazal are very much noted for this social or cultural occasion. The *Lunybei* occasion is also to mark the end of the cultivation period called *ker,* the spring, and the beginning of the harvesting period call *ruël* which the English people call summer. The *Lunybei* or *Agutpiny* is a very vivid social occasion which every Dinka villager longs and hopes for and anticipates attending each year. It is called *Agutpiny* because the drum is beaten for the first time since winter and spring seasons. The drumbeat is a call that young folk who went to fatten up in seclusion places have now come out of their fattening huts and the cattle are driven towards the villages. Drums are beaten at the assembling place where a given territory is used to stage this kind of event each year. It is also called *Lunybei* because the fattened youthfolk and their cattle now come back to the community after several months of absence from their parents, relatives and community. It is an event in which the villagers, who remained to cultivate and weed, meet with their young ones who went to fatten themselves. In all the villages of the territory, women hope to one day see their sons and daughters displaying themselves for the *Agutpiny* occasion in the territory. The occasion usually demarcates between hunger and sufficiency periods when people begin to eat from their cultivated fields new produce like maize or corn, groundnuts, pumpkins, to mention but a few.

In modern times fattening season has come to be seen in the negative by the urbanised or educated Dinka elites. It is seen as an unproductive cultural practice in which the strongest members of the family, the young men and girls, take away the milking cows to a distance from family members and redundantly spend three or more useful rainy months without cultivating. They are seen to leave their parents and children, the vulnerable or the weak, virtually with no or few milking cows to support them while they must cultivate and weed the fields. These weak or the aged are the ones left to till the fields to produce food for the year. For this reason there is an inclination to outlaw this prestigious cultural practice. Although the practice encourages no productivity it does not, however, seem culturally useful to advocate outlawing such an important traditional practice which tends to encourage families to compete for sufficiency and prominence. Without the *Lunybei* occasion and fattening season in Dinka society and for the Dinka young folk, Dinka culture will lose a very important aspect of its beauty and meaning. Fattening is good for the young adults who are fast growing for it assists them to grow faster, taller and bigger. The speed of growth of the young men and girls who go for fattening is much faster compared to those who do not go for fattening.

When a cow, goat or sheep dies or is sacrificed for religious or for social purposes in the cattle camp or in the village, its meat is boiled or roasted and eaten. As explained earlier, goats' and sheep's skins provide women and girls with waist girdles call *buɔŋ*. Cattle-hides provide tethering ropes call *wiën, wiin* when in plural. They also provide sleeping skins called *akɔt* or *biöök* and other smaller utilities such as *kuɛɛr, göök, waat, adiɛɛr* and so on. The cows' urine, called *këth*, is used to disinfect the milk gourds and to curdle the milk to the Dinka taste. While the Rek Dinka use cows', goats' and sheep's urine and dung as mulch for fertilising cultivable fields goat, sheep and cattle dung is dried and used by all Dinka as dung fire, called *gɔl*. They use this *gɔl* to protect themselves and their herds from biting insects. Dinka people call those biting insects *käm* when they are many. They call it *kɔm* when singular. Dung ash called *arop* is rubbed on the body, both for decoration and as an astringent for bodily protection from flies in the day and from mosquitoes at night. Rubbing *arop* over the body is also a sign indicating that this Dinka person is actively engaged in looking after cattle and is part of his cattle's life.

HARVESTING, THRESHING AND STORAGE OF FOOD PRODUCE

In the Dinka rural countryside, the year, besides the known climatic seasons, is also divided into *puör* or cultivation season (May, June and July), *tɛm rap* and *wëc wëc* or harvest season (August, September, October, November and December), *kam* or threshing season (January and February) and *kuaar* or fields clearance season which covers the months of March and April.

As will be detailed in chapter three, Dinka people start cultivation upon the first few rains of the early or middle part of May after they cleared the fields during March and April, the field's clearance months. In the recent past the month of April was a rainy month and was therefore the month when cultivation started. The great stride of climatic change of the last three decades in the Nilotic regions of Upper Nile and Bahr el Ghazal, resulted in the month of April ceding into the dry winter season. The month of July which was the beginning month of harvest has now become the last month of the cultivation season. As weeding is regarded by the Dinka as part of cultivation activity July, which is largely a weeding month, is therefore dubbed as part of the cultivation season.

During the month of August, harvest begins in many parts of Dinka lands, especially in those areas where the soil is more of a *rup*, the sandy or loam-sandy soil where mixed farming is the case. By this time fields' groundnuts called Sudanese groundnuts (*full sudani*) start to be harvested. This is especially true of the new type of full sudani called *nyima*. Some call it *terkeka*. It is called different names in different places. Harvest of durra, called *rapjäng*, and groundnuts becomes intensive in the month of September. Most of the *rapjäng* harvesting is finished towards the end of September or beginning of October. Others can go into early November while some groundnuts and hardnuts can continue to be harvested in December, even without rains. The same is true of *aguɔth*. *The luɛɛl* variety of durra and millet is harvested in December and after. While durra harvest goes on during this rainy season, a lot of tiresome activities are incurred as durra work involves drying and accumulating on a frame which the Dinka call *kät*, *kɛɛt* in plural. Groundnuts are also dried and are finally kept in what Dinka call a*koog*. Others call it *adara*.

By about January or February, threshing of the *durra* is done. Getting durra and millet grain out of their husks, called *ayiɛl*, is one of the more difficult tasks done by the women. After the grain is isolated from the durra or millet husks, they are stored in the already prepared *adara* where they will be taken to pound for porridge making. There is virtually no month in which rural Dinka people take full rest from domestic and cattle-related work.

CHAPTER THREE: DINKA MONTHS, SEASONS AND WEATHER CYCLE OF THE YEAR (THE DINKA CALENDAR)

Every year Dinka activities are dictated by regular climatic patterns in the environment. A dry winter season of no rain makes them move to water and grazing areas from their settlement villages. They move from their permanent settlements to those swampland areas which they call toch. This toch is mostly the swamplands of the White Nile and its tributaries. It is a place where permanent buildings or homesteads are not possible because of the floods of the wet seasons. Many parts of the Dinka land usually get flooded during the wet rainy seasons, but the western Dinka lands in Bahr el Ghazal become extremely dry during the months of January to May each year, months when there are no rains. This accounts for that pattern of seasonal migration to areas near the existing rivers and swamps. Access to drinking water during this dry season becomes very difficult in many parts of Bahr el Ghazal and such seasonal movements are made as a solution to this problem. This has, however, reduced in recent years due to the international response which provided water hand pumps in many areas. Movement of people in search of drinking water has therefore been minimised for the last two decades. Accordingly, Bahr el Ghazal Dinka people found time to devote to clearing their cultivatable fields in anticipation of the rains of early May or late April each year.

Like the rest of the world's communities, the Dinka people divide the year into twelve calendar months with four major seasons as mentioned. They also divide the year into clearly marked wet and dry seasons. Their calendar of the year begins with the month when the first rains start to fall after the long spell of the hot dry season they call *mäi*. While it used to be the month of *Akɔcthi* (April), it has now become the month of *Aduöŋ* which is May. This is the time when natural life begins to come back in the villages. Water from rains becomes available.

Trees and grass begin to sprout and the entire landscape becomes green again. People who went to the toch with their livestock to spend the hostile dry season months now come back, and as family members enjoy being once again united, cultivation ushers in new life and the new year as crops begin to sprout and grow leaves while the atmosphere remains optimally cool, green and lively.

During this time of the beginning of the rainy season, uncastrated bulls, rams and cocks are sacrificed as thanksgiving offers to God for making life come back to its normality and for making the cattle and people return safely from the toch. Such sacrifices and offerings are done in almost every village and in each of these sacrifices people pray to welcome rains and the new year. Spiritual leaders call for adequate rains. They also pray for cattle and human health and for peace in the land. Because Dinka lands usually experience convectional rains with its attending thunders, Spear Masters pray for rains to come serene and calm. The wet season consists of the three months of spring called *kër* (comprised of the months of April, May and June) and the three months of summer called *ruël* (made up of the months of July, August and September).

The interim or transitional season between the wet and dry season consists of the months of autumn which Dinka people call *rut* (encompassing the months of October, November and December). The third is the dry winter season called *mäi* which is comprised of the months of January, February and March. This used to be the order of Dinka seasons until recently when climatic changes reorganised the seasons. Beginning from the early 1970s gradual climatic changes that have been happening over the many decades have made the winter season encroach into the spring season. October, which was part of *ruël*, has also become a month of autumn. April has become part of the dry season months while spring has come to begin in May each year.

DINKA MONTHS AND SEASONS:

	Winter season = mäi (dry)		2. Spring season = kër (wet)
1	January = Kol	1	May = Aduöŋ
2	February = Nyieth		June = Alɛthbor July =
3		2	Aköldit August = Bildit
4	March = Akɔcdit	3	
	April = Akɔcthi	4	
	3. Summer Season = ruël (wet)		4. Autumn Season = rut (trans)
1	September = Biɛlthi	1	November = ɣɔr Bɛkläi
2	October = Lal (rut)	2	December = Kön-Akönpiu

At the time of writing and publication of this book, April, which is *Akɔcthi*, has entirely become part of winter or the dry season months.

Rains in the Upper Nile and Bahr el Ghazal regions only come by early May. This is because of the climatic changes influenced by the aridity and desert encroachment from Northern Sudan which have long been affected by the Sahara and the Nubian Deserts. October or *Lal* has also come to be the beginning month of autumn which is the beginning month of the transitional season called *rut*. The dry season, called *mäi*, has therefore become longer than the wet season in all of the Dinka lands.

SUB-SEASONS

While the Dinka know of twelve months and four major seasons in the year, they also divide the seasons into sub-seasons. Each season is known by its months, by its weather characteristics and by what happens or by what is done during each seasonal cycle in a year. To give a clear picture of what happens in Dinka lands by seasons, by sub-seasons and by months in each year, attempt is made below to describe weather conditions, division between day and night, what happens to the topology of the land and activities dictated by each of the four seasons and their sub-seasons.

(i) The Winter Season
With this, we begin with the Dinka winter season which starts in *Kol* (January) followed by *Nyieth* (February) then comes *Akɔcdit* (March). *Kön-akönpiu* (December) is the last month of *Rut* or autumn season, that begins to come to an end when all the annual community festivals of this period have been conducted or are completed. The Dinka year continues into its eighth month known as *Kol,* which the English people call January. *Kol* is followed by the ninth month of the year called *Nyieth*, which is February. During those two winter months, the entire forest grass has dried up and is burnt. Trees have long shed their leaves and the forest land has dried up.

At this time, the new grass called *Wɛl-Nyuɔɔp,* which earlier sprouted in January or late December following the burning of the forest grass, begins to dry up for lack of dew, rains or underground water or moisture. The forests and villages remain dry at this time onward. All the nearby or territorial streams, water depressions, ponds and pools of the last wet season have all dried up and water can only be obtained through water wells dug at places where the water table can be reached several tens of metres deep into the ground! In some areas people dig deeper, up to sixty and even a hundred metres deep into the earth to be able to reach the underground water table. Stories of several diggers having died at the bottom of some deep wells due to lack of oxygen has been a known phenomenon in many parts of rural Bahr el Ghazal. Others are buried by wells which collapse on them whilst digging or clearing the bottom of the wells.

During those two months of *Kol* and *Nyieth*, women start to thresh the durra and millet grain from their husks. Storing threshed grain quantities is done at this time just as was done earlier along with other produce such as maize, groundnuts, sesame and millet. After this threshing activity some of the village people begin to set out for the toch to join the cattle already driven there by the youthfolk. Some people who are constructing new houses or *luak*, those who have newly erected mud walls in their homes, now begin putting roof frames of long poles and straws. Roofing exercise is a work done by many people. Women also begin to thatch those newly framed houses and byres. They do this with new grass which they had mobilised *(ŋeer)* and assembled into several bundles during the months of autumn. This grass mobilisation activity is a very irksome work involving grasscutting with knives and its transportation in big bundles to the villages from the grassland forests. It is a work that women must begin right from early autumn days before grass is dry or burnt away from the nearby forest.

At this time most of the livestock, particularly cattle, have been driven to the toch since the middle or the end of December. Others who have issues to solve remain behind in the villages with their cattle, still using the little but very murky waters of the village streams which have started to dry off about this time of the year. They then move to the toch in early or late January. If there are cows to be seen or heard at this time in the villages, they may be a few milking cows left to provide milk for children and the aged who cannot move to the toch. They are left in the homes to be served water from the wells during the whole of the dry season period. Very few villagers do this because it is a very tiresome duty to satisfy the cows with water from the wells, which at times dry up as the dry season reaches its zenith during the later months of winter.

Within these first two months of winter the atmosphere has already started to be hot and the sky remains dry and shows not a single cloud. Marriages should have finished in December and are no longer possible as those left to stay in the villages are mostly the nursing mothers and the aged. Most of the young men, women and children have all gone to the toch after the cattle to avoid the thirst and the hot weather of this very dry and hot winter season in the villages. At this time of the year, all other productive activities in the homes or villages cease to be seen except for the cumbersome pursuit for scarce water.

The early part of winter gradually drifts into what is typical *mäi*, the middle of the winter season. This is the month called *Akɔcdit*, also known as *Akɔc-Maper*. It is called *Akɔc-Maper* because the weather becomes very harsh, hot and dry at this time. People sweat terribly while sleeping both night and day. This is the month when the sun appears to be shining directly and powerfully as if at a close distance from the sky. Clouds, which the Dinka call *Pial* from the word *Piööl or puɔl,* now begin to appear sporadically in the sky. Cyclonic whirlwinds in the toch begin to be rampant at this time.

Back home in the villages birds begin to gather, scrambling for water in places where there are water wells. They swarm those places in search for water. Small animals such as duikers (*amuk*), gazelle (*löc* and *kɛɛth,* from the plural names *lɔɔc* and *kɛɛu*) and rodents (*luɔny, lony* in singular) of all types also suffer from thirst in the dry land forests. Those animals and rodents come to the water points during the night. Dangerous animals like lions (called *köör* in singular, *kɔr* in plural, others call it *cuär* and *ajuɔɔŋ*), hyenas called *aŋui* (*aŋuööth* in plural) and leopards, which are *kuac* (*kuëc* in plural), do also come to such places during the deep part of the night. They come there for water and they pose danger to people and to the few remaining domestic animals at these times. A lot of attention towards those animals is one of the preoccupations of the Dinka men who stay in the villages at this time.

As clouds begin to appear and gradually increase in the sky day by day, some young men begin to return to the villages to join their parents in order to clear the fields around their homes, ready for the first rains of late April or early May in preparation for cultivation. Currently the first rains begin to fall in May (*Aduöŋ*) as April has gradually become part of winter season. This part of winter when clouds begin to increase and the time of late April or early May when rains start falling is the part of winter called *Abuɔl-kër* in Rek dialect. It is followed by the time when the first heavy rains of May makes the cattle people move out of the toch and return to the villages and rains ominously begin to cease for some weeks! In this case water for the cattle can hardly be found. Dinka people call this brief but painful period *Yak-thok,* the drought-ridden period.

This is one of the difficult times when rural Dinka communities and their livestock experience acute water problems after they have been deceived by the first rains to move out of the already vacated toch. At this time there could be sufficient pastures owing to the first rains of late April or early May. During this *Yak-thok*, serious efforts are made by everybody, searching for water for the huge livestock, human consumption and domestic needs in their homes. At times it is hazardous for the youthfolk to return the cattle to the toch for several reasons. When all the cattle and people have gone away from the toch following the first rains, the toch remains desolate and very lonely for just a few people to return to it with their cattle. Moreover, flies used to unusually gather in the then vacated cattle camps of the toch, and it could be very unhealthy for the cattle and people to return to such a place where flies had swarmed almost the entire toch. Dangerous creatures of the toch are also known to replace those dry season cattle camps after man and cattle have vacated, so instead of returning with their cattle to the toch, people begin to desperately run about with their livestock from one place to another. They do this following some downpours even at some distant lands, accepting to suffer the severe thirst of this short spell of drought till real *kër* (spring season) comes in with its consecutive rains.

(ii) The Spring Season
When winter season and its very bad *Abuɔl-kër* and its succeeding *Yak-thok* comes to an end as described above, spring season comes in, in its full swing, in May. Cultivation in the villages becomes the main preoccupation in all the settlement areas. Earlier on, women had made ready the first durra seeds called *chaam* in Rek dialect. Pumpkin seeds, ladyfinger seeds, maize and groundnuts all to be sown upon the first rain or rains are the first to be prepared ready for this rain. The men on their part had earlier prepared the fields and made the hoes available with their stakes, the long and thin wooden poles called *ciit* from the singular name *cit*.

Prior to the clearance of the fields dried up cattle, goats or sheep dung had been spread over them as each household member remains in wait for the first rains. This is to fertilise the fields prior to the first rains of late April or early May. Spring is the season when the wet period begins and the bad dry and hot winter season now fades away. In today's Dinka country, *Aduöŋ* and *Alɛthbor* have become the only months of the spring season. While the community becomes engaged in cultivation, cattle that have also been returned from the toch once again form part of the homes of those families who own cattle. As the green pastures and water abound, just around homes and villages cows begin to graze to their satisfaction. They quickly become fat and milking cows begin to produce more milk for their calves and their owners. The jubilation of village children upon the fall of the first rain and the arrival of the cattle from the dry season cattle camps in the toch are among the most memorable scenes every rural Dinka person can still remember with delight when he or she comes to be in a different country or in the town. The bellowing resonance made by the bulls and cows and the insistent *oos* and *boos* of the young calves as the cattle return from pastures late in the evening also forms one of the characteristic village or rural rhythms of this spring season.

The presence of cattle in the villages at this time now gives meaning and sense of new life to the community. The bellowing of the milking cows and the *boo* cry of their calves indicate sufficiency for the home in a village where cows go about to graze nearby while the greenery of the pasture that begins right from the fields and the cool atmosphere of rains and clouds forms the beautiful scenery known of the springtime. Those are scenes that made Dr Francis Mading Deng describe Dinka land as *"...the most beautiful..."* ('*Tradition and modernization*', 1970). This cattle scene and the green landscape indicate that life has come back to normality after the miseries of the dry and hot winter season. The cattle and all their owners have now come together. The atmosphere is now so cool and water is in abundance with sufficient greenery of the village and territorial landscape.

As mentioned, the main activity of the men and their womenfolk, in addition to even the adolescent boys and girls in the homes, is cultivation at this time. People do go into their fields sometimes as early as 5 am. Some people go to the fields in the early dawn. Villagers remain working in the fields till late in the afternoon when women would then pull out and go back to the homes in order to prepare a meal, which they must cook for their husbands who they have left in the fields still cultivating! Sometimes both the husband and wife go home after midday for the husband to take rest and to return into the field at around 4 pm in order to continue cultivating until sunset, after which he would return home extremely exhausted, only to resume his work the next dawn and the cycle continues as described until the weeding period, called *puɔɔn* comes in by about the end of *Alɛthbor* or during the early part of *Aköldit*. Weeding, in some parts of the Dinka land, is largely the work of women.

Kër, the spring season, is the season when Dinka people become very busy and is the time when members of the household do the work for the rest of the year. Rains at this time intermittently begin to be heavy. They, however, come as if to allow good cultivation. While this cultivation period is happening in earnest the issue of young men and girls, having gone for fattening, forms part of the back-thought of the members of the family. Perhaps a son or two and a daughter may have gone with their milking cows and their parents would always want to hear their progress. Parents always become concerned about the competition that would soon ensue as the approaching month of July comes. July used to be the month of the famous *Lunybei* or *Agutpiny* occasion when the territory would gather to see and celebrate those who came from fattening, but climatic changes that pushed the rainy season to start in May has made *Agutpiny* take place in August. Parents cultivate while aware that the community will soon gather in *Agutpiny* to choose the young man who would win the year for having become the fattest in that year.

By the end of *Alɛthbor*, which is the month of June or the beginning of *Aköldit,* the Dinka month of July, Dinka society becomes engrossed in yet another stage of cultivation, the weeding period. The seeds that have been sown or cultivated have already germinated and are above the ground needing to be freed of weeds or grass. Weeded crops grow healthier and give good yield. The weeding period takes about two weeks or so. It takes a few more weeks for some of the crops to start ripening. This is true in those areas where the type of soil is one which allows mixed farming for crops such as groundnuts, maize and the fast ripening durra, called *chaam.*

By the middle of June before new crops are tasted or eaten, hunger becomes intensive for those households that do not have milking cows and also do not have any remaining grain surplus by this part of the year. This very bad time quickly leads to the end of *Aköldit* (July), the time when the ripened crops such as the first to be sown groundnuts, pumpkins, maize and *chaam,* are about to be tasted, but the community is waiting for the Spear Master to first do the traditionally prescribed rituals before each household is free to eat from their ripened crops. This is also about the time when the youth that have gone for fattening are close to returning for the start of the *fattening occasion* called *Lunybei* or *Agutpiny*.

The fattened youthfolk are called *aciliip* in Dinka, specifically by the Rek Dinka. The month of June and the early part of July has always been a very delicate period for Dinka society. This is the month when rains begin to be heavier, making it difficult for some women to go out of their houses to search for some edible greens which Dinka people call *wal, wäl* when singular. Those are the critical days or weeks in which the morally weak people begin to sneak out of their homes or places in the night and secretly go into the fields of their neighbours or others in order to steal from the ripened crops, a practice greatly abhorred by Dinka society. Such people who do those antisocial acts are frequently found out and usually caught. The whole society in the territory quickly becomes aware of the thief as the news usually spreads very fast. Public condemnation and negative comment makes theft the worst crime in Dinka land. Theft of this kind rarely happens in Dinka land. It is better to commit murder than to be known as a thief. Theft and adultery are crimes that spoil the reputation and prestige of not only the perpetrator but the family and lineage as a whole. At times the reputation of the entire clan is also involved, for when the clan happens to enter into dispute with another clan, this act done by its member would certainly become a fact of abuse through a song that could last long in the territory and beyond.

By about the end of July or early August ritual performances will have already been made to bless the ripened crops. This is done by the concerned Spear Masters and the community is thus permitted to eat from the ripened crops. New crops are blessed so that they do not cause *juääi* for the community. *Juääi* is a Dinka broad name for a number of ailments including fevers associated with cough, coryza, rhinitis, and so on. It includes those fevers which could nowadays be considered by medical people as malaria or fevers of unknown origin. Then, within this July, the society begins to feed from their fields' produce. Groundnuts, maize, pumpkins and other quick yielding crops form part of the initial yields which are eaten in the villages prior to harvest. In the week or two when the first yields are tasted, *Lunybei* comes in as drums are beaten and because *Lunybei* is a huge communal occasion, the community is brought all at once to a unified activity of profound significance. *Agutpiny* or *Lunybei* in this case become the first social gathering of the territory in the year since the dry winter and spring seasons. While the community comes together and goes into merrymaking as a result of *Agutpiny*, the society resilience is once again revived by the beginning of the summer (*Ruël*) season with its accompanying sufficiency.

(iii) The Summer Season (Ruël)

In the Dinka world, *Agutpiny* falls within the transition between *Kër* and *Ruël* seasons. Summer actually begins from July (*Aköldit*) and it covers the remaining two months called *Bildit* and *Biɛlthi,* which are August and September respectively. *Bildit* is the Dinka month when harvest begins in earnest. The two *bil* are generally known as the months when rains become heavy and more frequent. They are the months in which water abounds and floods begin to cover the fields in some villages situated in the plains (*lil*) and in places near swamplands. These are the months when human mobility between homes and villages is done through water. The numerous depressions of the territory begin to fill up with water and rivers start to rise and overflow their banks, flooding the low-lying land around the villages. People take their cattle into several summer or wet season cattle camps, away from villages. Youthfolk now begin the collective life of *wuön-aruɛl*, the summer cattle camps, where cattle of the territory are hemmed into those few cattle camps that are a bit above flooded grounds. Here in these summer camps a lot of community activities take place on a daily basis.

Although the summer cattle camps are owned by certain clans or by some landed gentries, or are called after their owners, cattle from different families, clans and sections are normally gathered there. Ownership of these camps is only implied. Summer cattle camps are seen to belong to the community as part of the territory. 500 to 1000 head of cattle form what the Rek Dinka call *gɔl*, a circulet camp formed by tethered cattle and for protection from rain. People and very small calves sleep or take shelter under an open-sided sturdy structure of wooden rafters which is turf-roofed overlaid with mud and is locally called *kät*. This kind of structure is made in the centre of each *gɔl*. This *gɔl* is sometimes called *kɛɛl*. One particular summer camp may consist of ten or more *kät* and one chieftaincy territory may have more than five summer camps. Due to mosquitoes and heat affecting people in their houses during this season, most of the people leave their homes in the evenings in order to spend the nights in their respective summer camps where their family and clan's cattle are kept at this time.

Back home in the settlement villages harvesting the ripened crops is the main activity during this time of summer. Girls do come back home from the cattle camps during morning hours to assist their mothers in harvesting the groundnuts from the fields and in cutting sesame and tying them on a long wooden frame which Rek Dinka call *kuïrit*. This frame is erected to dry the newly cut stalks of sesame. They also come to assist their mothers in collecting and drying the harvested durra from the fields. Girls also come home to later return to their cattle camps late in the evening with food provisions for their brothers and other people of the camp, people such as guests. In Bahr el Ghazal areas, girls are known to bring with them an assortment of food items including boiled or roasted groundnuts, cooked pumpkins, boiled maize, stalks of durra canes and much more produce to be eaten by the cattle camp people. This is the time of the year when the cattle camp people prefer homemade food in place of the milk that has been their daily intake for so long. Summer is the season of sufficiency and people are there to eat by choice between this and that food.

Young men from the cattle camps sometimes come to participate and assist their homestead people in harvesting, especially when the durra type called *rap-jäŋ* is ripened. This type of durra ripens at this time of the year. The type of soil determines the kind of durra or crop sown in some parts of Dinka land. *Lueɛl*, millet and *rap-jäŋ* are grown by the Dinka people of Bahr el Ghazal because Bahr el Ghazal Dinka inhabit those areas that are either loam, clay and sandy or a mixture of these. The Upper Nile region is mostly clay and muddy with little loam soil. The Dinka people are more coastal as the majority live near the Nile and as the region is a basin of the

Fig 27: Showing two scenes: young men sitting in a group to date young girls in the middle of them. To the back of them is a kuïrït, a frame for drying sesame. Behind the kuïrït is the green durra field of the home

big White Nile River, the territory is a low-ground regularly flooded each year. The flood leaves sufficient silt to make the land so fertile for cereal crops, but Upper Nile Dinka people do not grow millet or the *luɛɛl* type of durra. *Luɛɛl* and millet in Bahr el Ghazal are harvested during autumn, about the end of December.

As summer is the harvesting season and a period of sufficiency, it is also the time when dating becomes one of the preoccupations of the youth. This is the time when suitors and dating practitioners busy themselves with girls they admire in the cattle camps and in the villages. A lot of day and night drums beat, for dancing plays are held or are heard throughout the Dinka land at this time of the year. This is the time when suitors and applicants pay visits to the girls they want and is the time when suitors stage what the Rek Dinka call *mut*, a type of dance play occasion done by the whole territory in the name of a particular young man's fiancée. *Mut* is done during the day. It is not a dance occasion held at night.

In central Rek lands, *mut* is another dramatic social activity which, like *Agutpiny*, brings to the playground almost the entire population of the territory. Even women and the aged are attracted by various reasons to attend this *mut* occasion. Many women come with their children. The still suckling ones are even carried in their cradle beds and you will usually hear crying babies and children having rattles shaken around the playground as the dance activities go on in earnest. Young girls from different cattle camps and from different clans and sections would be seen parading themselves in running lines for the public to view them. This is one of the occasions from which some people begin to choose their fiancées or girls to later marry.

Young men in traditional attire also parade themselves. At this *mut* dancing occasion a lot of young men come with their song bulls and the whole picture is such that cannot be properly described in a foreign language like this. The occasion for crowning a king in England may pictorially simulate this kind of a scene. Those are the majestic scenes where Dinka culture is at its best. *Mut* is a whole day activity of the entire territory. It is one of the joyous socio-cultural occasions from which the young Dinka people draw many positive lessons such as the beauty viewing presented by the young girls and their young men as well as the dance styles and decorated song bulls, in addition to various artistries from the Dinka rural country. The *mut* occasion comes to an end late in the afternoon, sometimes at 5 or 6 pm. It doesn't go into the night for it is a day occasion. People disperse to their villages and cattle camps before sunset.

Even those who are not designated to marry in the year can also be seen courting the girls they admire and would also be going around cattle camps with their song bulls to draw the attention of their loved ones, about whom they are serious, after them. They also go about singing and displaying their song bulls to show they have cattle, bulls in particular. Suitors' agents and even those from unannounced applicants are usually seen going out to date girls, mostly in disguise. Agents collect secrets about those girls, about their parents and their kin. They often attract the girl's attention to love those suitors on behalf of whom they are doing the dating.

During this part of the year mature girls expect to be married. Their parents and relatives also remain on the lookout for applicants to come forward for their girls. This is the season when so many marriages are held. There are many reasons for this. This is the time when alternative food items replace cows' milk and cattle owners are able to let their milking cows go into marriages now that there are other alternative sources for food. Cattle are also very fat and healthier at this time. The majority of cows and bulls also appear fit to be paid into this or that marriage and even the old cows and bulls would appear more healthy and fit for marriage than they would appear during dry winter times.

By about the middle of this summer season several marriages begin to be officially started at the level of families. Some marriages could involve large parts of the community. Some which could go quicker are accomplished during summer, but because of elaborate procedures and discussions the majority of marriages go into autumn where they are completed before the dry season comes in. Summer and autumn are known as the best times for marriages in Dinka land. Any marriage that goes into winter or into spring is mostly postponed until next summer. Because winter splits people up very few marriages are conducted in the winter season. Spring season for its part is never a month for marriages in Dinka land. It is known for its cultivation and weeding activities. Spring is also known as a season when hunger makes people not want to dispense with their cows.

Although the climate provides humid weather during this summer season, no heat from the sun is seriously experienced as clouds and rains provide a ceiling of atmospheric canopy. This is the season of sufficiency as all the crops and fresh fruits are available. Durra stalks called *bel* in plural, *bël* when singular, provide energy from the sweet canes chewed and enjoyed by all. Durra canes (*bel*), pumpkins, groundnuts, beans, vegetables and porridge from durra, maize, millet and several other edible natural products makes summer (*ruël*) a season of sufficiency for all and even the lazy ones would just eat to satiation from what has been done by others. This is not the case when dry season months come in. Winter and spring are seasons when Dinka society experiences relative insufficiency and are the seasons in which the large sector of Dinka people experience some form of hardship, from the harsh weather and thirst of the dry season months of winter to the hard cultivation and hunger months of the spring.

Summer and autumn are Dinka friendly seasons of sufficiency, of general welfare and of many activities including the settlement of people's litigations and marriages. They are the months in which the community holds many of its collective social and cultural obligations such as religious and social occasions, occasions such as ritual offerings or ceremonies and marriages. It is even the time when friends visit. Old people begin to enjoy white stuff beer made by women for several occasions in the homes and villages, occasions ranging from ritual to social ones.

(iv) The Autumn Season (Rut)

The Dinka months of *rut* or autumn are October which they call *Lal*, November which they know as *rɔr-Bɛkläi* and the month of December which they call *Kön-AkönPiu*. Dinka *rut* season is divided into a wet part of autumn called *Anyɔɔc* and the true but rather cooler part of it. This is the time covering the month of October when rains have just ceased. It also covers that early part of November and the whole of December when the cold harmattan winds come with very cool breezes. At this time most of the Dinka land is covered with fog and dew. The atmosphere becomes foggy, forming what Dinka people call *rur* and very cold dew which they call *thäc* begins to cover the ground and the grass around. People will be seen sitting by the fireplaces at their homestead and at the courtyard edges during morning hours before the dew and fog has faded away at around 9, 10 or 11 am. This is the time when water that had earlier filled the low-lying lands, depressions (*Kɔt*), ponds (*adhuum, adhuom* when singular) and pools (*pul* in singular) begins to either percolate or recede to some nearby streams (*löl* in singular, *lɔl* in plural) and into the rivers if available in the territory. The Dinka name for a river is *agör.* Others call it *gärdit.*

At this time of the year the sun doesn't shine well and is sometimes not seen clearly until well in the afternoon. *Abuwiir*, an annual Dinka religious rite done before the water reduces from the village streams and or rivers, is held during this period of early *rut*. This is the time or month when offerings to the river gods are done in many parts of the Dinka lands, particularly in Bahr el Ghazal areas where Dinka traditional religion is still very active and strong. Whole bulls called *thön* and whole rams called *nyök-thön amɛl* are led into the nearby rivers or streams in a communal ritual or religious ceremony. Those bulls or rams are taken into the river or stream while alive and they do not come out from the waters any more. They are taken immediately by the river gods. They disappear into the water soon after their tethering ropes are given to the unseen gods, who instantly catch the rope in the river or stream. After the bull or ram is seen to have been mysteriously caught and pulled into the water by the river gods, people begin to stampede away from the river or stream and none is allowed to turn to look back! The gathering, which had been singing religious songs of the clan or of the territory, all run, racing away on the belief that the river gods may be chasing them and could catch the one who ran most slowly or the one who looked back. From the river or water stream, the bull or ram swiftly disappears into the water and does not reappear. Its bones are not even found later when the stream or river dries up. People come back to the village where they make the feast of *Abuwiir* for the whole day. Traditional beer is brewed in every homestead and villagers would now drink beer from one village and homestead to the other.

Gradually, throughout the entire Dinkaland, the green grass on the edges of the homes, village or settlement areas begins to dry up and is soon set on fire. The once wet green scene of summer begins to gradually fade away and the village surroundings begin to be clear and dry. At this time of autumn, cattle from the summer camps are moved to the villages since there are no more rains. The mosquitoes, which greatly abuse the situation of summer, now begin to disappear as water and green grass recedes. The actual *rut* now becomes the case as the harmattan cool breezes are replaced by the normal pre-winter winds, which are, however, still cool. This is the Dinka part of the autumn season in which religious festivals or celebrations are held to mark the end of the year. Sacrificial ceremonies are usually conducted in the homesteads or at the shrine or holy places.

In those religious ceremonies spiritual leaders talk to God through invocations to care for the cattle and their young folk who would be moving to the toch for water and pastures. They would appeal to God to make the Nuers across the toch mind about their own problems. This is because cattle raiding by the Nuers in the toch is a perpetual thing during the winter months. Spear Masters also invocate for dry season diseases to spare their people. This is because diseases such as meningitis and gastroenteritis in children are very much noted for their death toll among the Dinka during this dry winter season.

During this part of the year marriages are at the maximum. New houses start to be constructed. Men go out to cut short and long poles (cɔɔp) while women and girls also assist the men to mobilise mud for daubing the wattled short poles into a circular structured wall called *päny*. Cattle, that have already been made to spend their (*anyɔc*) time nearby as rains had ceased earlier, are now allowed or brought to the fields to benefit from *abuöŋ,* the new sprouts of durra green stalks that spring out of the already harvested durra in the fields. The community also becomes engaged in settling their scores before the courts. Since the month of *Lal* or October, community chiefs begin to convene communal courts' hearings to settle community cases and feuds that have been pending since the cultivation, weeding and harvesting periods. Settlement of cases used to be stopped during cultivation and harvesting seasons, except for emergency matters that have a tendency to disturb public peace and tranquillity. At this time litigants begin to go to the courts because winter will soon come and cattle will go far off to the toch.

By the middle of this *rut* season, cattle people move to their autumn cattle camp places so cattle can graze the newly sprouted green pastures called *nyuɔɔp*. This *nyuɔɔp* usually comes up after the forest grass was burnt some weeks earlier. An unexpected rain begins to fall during this time. The Rek Dinka call this *athɔrcol*. It falls shortly after the forest is burnt. This type of rain assists the new grass to sprout properly. At this time of the year many pregnant cows that gestated nine months ago begin to deliver calves. Milking cows produce more milk during this period of autumn because of the abundance of new pasture that comes up after the forest is burnt. Prior to the cattle being moved to the toch another heavy rain called *acoi-kuɔɔth* begins to fall. It is called *acoi-kuɔɔth* because it makes the thorn trees lose their thorns as that rain comes accompanied by great winds. Autumn is the season when young adolescent males are also initiated into manhood by a process called *Gärnhom*. It is done between November and the early part of December.

GÄRNHOM: THE DINKA PHYSICAL INITIATION TO MANHOOD

Initiation of matured boys who have passed their adolescence into adulthood is marked with several ceremonies and practices. But the first initiation is one in which six lower teeth are removed from every adolescent, be it a boy or girl. A girl's physiological evolution and attainment of puberty is marked by a specific rite made by women to demonstrate the girl's readiness for marriage. A ram or goat is killed and certain practices are made by women to the girl who experiences the first menstrual flow. They include *Kut Cin Mɛɛc*, a practice of applying red bean dye to the wrist to show readiness for marriage. In Dinka rural society Kut Cin Mɛɛc is one of the important ritual practices. It is a ritual performed for an adolescent girl who is at her first menstrual flow, called *Kuäc* in Dinka. Kut Cin Mɛɛc is done for such a girl by elderly women of the village. The occasion is also attended by her girlfriends. As a custom those elderly women tie some strings of red beads on her two wrists. Her head is shaved and her old beads are removed and later replaced with new ones. A ram of the red colour is slaughtered for the ceremony.

Apart from all this the girl is asked by those women to touch the slaughtered ram's blood with her hands and feet. She is then brought into the middle of a circle where those elderly women and her girl mates are standing or seated while singing and clapping. While seated in the circle a baby boy or girl is put on her lap to signify that she is going to produce children in the society.

The Kut Cin Mɛɛc ritual is done only by those elderly women whose firstborn is alive. A woman whose firstborn lived up to her old age is believed to possess good luck, supposed to come upon the young girl when she marries.

The old women then wave the girl's hands over the already kindled and slightly burning fire to warm them. This act signifies that from henceforth she can be a woman and she shall be attached to fire all the time through cooking.

After this ritual is performed, a lactating cow, preferably a heifer of red colour, is allocated to her as the only cow from which she is to drink milk. This cow becomes *Weŋ kiic*, the special cow for the girl who had her first menstrual flow.

Kut Cin Mɛɛc is then followed by another ritual called *Lɔköu* which is done by pouring anointed water on the cow and on the head, hands and shoulders of the girl in question. This performance is done only by an old Wundiör clansman.

Clan members from the Dinka Wundiör are known to be the ones accredited with the power of procreation once the girl is married. Sometimes it is an old man from the Pawutweŋ clan who is called upon to come and do this ritual of Lɔköu. The idea behind Lɔköu is for the girl to bring many dowry cows from her marriage for the benefit of her parents and family.

Pawutweŋ people, who are called Paderek in Gok and Agaar lands, are related to the cow as their nagualistic totem. Because of this they are the ones who revere (theek) the cow among the Dinka. The society has a belief with certainty that once a Pawutweŋ man is brought to perform Lɔköu to a girl who had a first menstrual flow (kuäc), that girl can be married quickly, sometimes within the same year or two. Such a girl will also be known to bring a lot of cows at her marriage, usually above the average number fetched by other girls who were not so done by a Pawutweŋ man.

The cow on which the Lɔköu ritual was performed becomes the usual cow from which the girl will continue to feed once it is lactating and the girl is in her menstrual period. In some cases or places girls can have the Lɔköu ritual done on any other lactating cow once her menstrual cycle has come. Lɔköu sometimes ceases to be done when the girl is married, but in some places the woman continues to have it done in her new family after marriage.

Facial scarification or *Gärnhom* for boys, on the other hand, is an initiation which takes place in a communal way when a good number of boys of the same age and who have passed their adolescent period are considered to have crossed the transitional period from adolescence to adulthood and have to be publicly initiated through this operation known as *Gärnhom*. It is a vivid and a dramatic event which no Dinka man in the country ever surpasses. It is a physical rite or practice that transfers the boy from adolescence to manhood. It begins with placing a request to their fathers, to their guardians and the Spear Master of the territory to permit their initiation as a group. *Gärnhom* by itself is a very painful operation from which Dinka people have come to exempt girls as it involves the cutting of parallel lines on the head, beginning from the face. In doing this *Garnhom* a very sharp knife is used by an expert who is known to initiate young adolescent males. By this operation, performed at an occasion called the *initiation rite*, very painful cut lines are made on both sides of the head, starting from the forehead between the eyebrows. The number of cut lines differs from one Dinka tribe to another.

The initiated boys in the Rek and Agaar dialects are called *Apärääk-puööl*. A single boy is *Apäräk-puöl*. This literally means the one who has just abandoned the boys' job of milking cows. In Dinka culture an adolescent who has been initiated into manhood does not do or eat certain things again during the rest of his manhood life, including the boys' duty of milking cows. Milking the cows is a work of the young boys, girls and women. According to Dinka custom, no initiated person can milk a cow, goat or sheep. It is unethical and Dinka culture is very firm on this.

As to *Gärnhom* itself, the number of horizontal parallels of cut lines on the head that later heal into scar lines can be four on both sides of the head, as is the case among the Rek, Malwal and Gok Dinka communities. The Agaar adolescent male takes six on both

Fig 28: Showing a young Agaar Dinka boy bleeding and in severe pain after he has just been brutally initiated.

sides of the head to mark him as an Agaar man. Other Dinka tribes such as the Ruweŋ cultural group, which includes the Ngɔk, Pan-Ru, Alor Kur Kuɔt and other Ruweŋ sections, make eight cut lines on both sides of the head. The Agaar Dinka, the Luac Dinka, Lɔu-Paher and the Ruweŋ Dinka people make their scar lines into a roundabout pattern that almost covers the whole circumference of the head. Both lines are, however, made not to meet at the occiput. They do theirs the Nuers' way.

The Bor Dinka group of Jonglei and Kiec have abandoned Gärnhom but Bor people do a V-shape type of scar on the forehead. Kiec does a form of discreet scars on the face, not the classical scarification done by the rest of the Dinka. The exact age when adolescent boys are initiated is not clear but it can be assumed that Dinka boys are initiated at around the age of 15 years. Initiation is done to boys when they have shown some physiological changes like pubic hair and an increase in their sexual organs, both testicles and penis. This is called *dhuel* in Rek dialect.

The rite of the *Gärnhom* occasion is only done during the autumn season after harvest. It is done in the middle of autumn, the time when the cool harmattan winds have started. It is a vivid and a dramatic event which no Dinka man in the countryside has ever chosen to miss in life. It is done as an occasion and it is one of the cultural occasions that makes a number of people gather to witness those undergoing this *Gärnhom*. Those boys who have gone into dhuel and who have obtained the consent of their principals begin to gather and when the number has noticeably grown into a sizeable number, they are allowed to go into the process of seclusion leading to initiation.

To authenticate their entry into initiation, community elders approach a known Spear Master of the area to approve their initiation as a group. Once permitted the initiates are made to undergo a period of festivities during which time they are well fed and kept in a secluded camp for about a month or so. They are required to not come back to their homes. They are not allowed to see their mothers or women. They are fed in those seclusion camps to give them good health to be able to withstand the great pain and blood loss that awaits them as they face the painful exercise of *Gärnhom*. While they remain in their seclusion camp, singing and dancing accompanies those activities to which they are subjected, activities consisting of festivities that go alongside manhood training. During the seclusion period the initiates are subjected to tough manly exercises to train them to face challenges in the near or distant future.

The initiates get exposed to very hard and sometimes harmful practices by an appointed individual valour who makes them go through mock battles as is done in real battles. They are forced into very tough experiences during their training month. All this is done to instil strength and ability to defend, attack, dodge and aim or strike. They are trained how to act bravely and make fortitude in the face of daunting and trying or painful situations. Those attributes are forcefully inculcated into them as it will soon come to be upon them to stand up to face any problem individually or as a collective. They must be trained to know how to defend the territory from foreign aggression and foreign raids on community cattle and on how they must act for the community interest.

After the seclusion and training period the initiates begin to have their heads shaped and are therefore led to a village place where they are made to sit on bare earth, sitting crossed legged in a line while singing the songs of their clans and queued up for the knifeman to do the head cutting in their turn. This is the painful *Gärnhom* operation of the cuts done on the boys' heads, cuts which are done in parallel lines as described. It is a painful operation accompanied by an acute and severe oligemic pain, followed by profuse bleeding, streaming and jutting from the painful cut lines! The author himself underwent this experience when he was initiated to manhood in 1970.

Despite the clear pain and blood that streams down the face and chest, as can be seen in the previous picture of an Agaar initiate, the initiates are required by custom to appear proud and not to show signs of a person undergoing pain. Each initiate is supposed to utter brave idiomatic expressions which Dinka people call *Maany*. Once the knifeman has finished with him, the initiate must jump up with one or a succession of his idioms to show to the audience that the experience he has just undergone was nothing to him! Parents and other relatives expect their sons to show this sign of manhood which they very much enjoy. The mere suggestion of a scream or expression of pain is enough to plunge the initiate and his family into long lasting disrepute within the community. They will be regarded as cowards forever and will get no favours from the society whatsoever. Fathers of initiates are known to jump about in praise of their sons who have shown bravery while they face that ordeal at the hands of the knifeman. A broad green *durra* leaf is then picked from a nearby durra stalk and is wound on the head to protect the cut wounds from flies. These durra leaves are changed from time to time and must remain bound to the cut wounds on the head for about a month, after which they are then removed. A woven frame called an *akuäma* is later placed on the head to keep the flies away from the scar wounds. *The akuäma* is woven in such a way that it allows air to go through the wounds to help them to cauterise, that is, to heal quickly but it still takes about two months for such wounds to heal.

The moment the knife is used to slice a line on the head and blood gushes downwards to the body, adolescence is deemed to have come to an end in the boy. The initiate becomes an adult, a man, from that moment till his death. The initiates are then made to return to their camp for proper feeding. There, they are allowed no hunger. Food of all sorts is brought to them by their mothers, sisters and at times by all the villagers. After some days from the operation day have passed the initiates are allowed to move in an organised line, passing by every village for members of the community to know that the son of so and so has become a man. They pass by the villages while singing and playing. The walking columns of Dinka initiates is a known scene which every villager and community has always witnessed. *Gärnhom* is not an annual event. It comes once in a while and may take years to be done in a given territory, depending on the availability of boys who have attained puberty and want to be initiated.

At present the majority of the educated Dinka elites in the urban towns have come to have a negative sentiment on this physical ordeal imposed on boys by custom. On several occasions the government made attempts to stop this very harmful cultural practice. But to the Dinka of the rural countryside, in the villages and in the cattle camps, *Gärnhom* continues to be a mark of honour and a proof of manhood. Even some boys sent to faraway schools come back voluntarily to receive *Gärnhom*. This is because the village and cattle camp girls usually laugh at those who have no scars of *Gärnhom* on their foreheads. They are scorned and are regarded as boys and girls feel ashamed to be seen talking to such young men who are still regarded as boys by the society. A Dinka girl in the village would find it incomprehensible to be married to an uninitiated man. For the Dinka boys themselves, *Gärnhom* makes them men. With all its trauma and disfigurations on the face or head, *Gärnhom* is the only certificate to physical maturity. According to Dinka rural boys *Gärnhom* is the only means to escape indignities of the adolescent age or boyhood. Even today boys in the villages and cattle camps are still subjected to duties and roles that make them feel like servants to their elders. They could just be beckoned and called at any time by every adult male just to send or make them labour. Boys are sometime cuffed or beaten at will whenever they are slow to please their elders. Their initiation is seen by them as the last hardship that their seniors can inflict on them, so even the fear of knife will not deflect them from their determination to become men. *Gärnhom* is a socio-cultural practice associated with the autumn season because for cauterisation of the initiation wounds it is the cool breezes of the harmattan winds of the Rut season that are required. It is also done at this time because it is the season of sufficiency, and it is the season when both the cattle and village people are in one place.

CELESTIAL BODIES AND THEIR IMPACT ON THE DINKA WORLD

1. The Moon (Pɛɛi)

The moon is called **Pɛɛi** by all the Dinka people. They know it as one big eye of Nhialic (God) with which He illuminates the universe during the night to primarily view *manhacuuk* (mankind) and his night activities. In the daytime He uses the other terribly hot eye called Akol (the sun). The moon is to the Dinka the cold benevolent eye of God. He withdraws the hot malevolent eye after the day and replaces it with Pɛɛi to give respite or rest to His earth creatures during the night. Pɛɛi shines in the nights during the lunar phase which rural Dinka call **rɛɛric.**

Pɛɛi, as the Dinka people know it, comes and goes away through a cycle of regular phases they also call Pɛɛi, the month. The moon's monthly cycle is an important tool to the Dinka, used for measuring the passage of time. The Dinka yearly calendar is synchronised to the phases of the moon. The period of days which they calculate and reckon as one Pɛɛi corresponds with 30 days, out of which are 15 days of darkness which they call *Muööthic* and the remaining 15 days of moon's light which they call rɛɛric. These 30 days of Pɛɛi are divided into a number of lunar phases. The first of these phases is that lunar time when the moon is first noticed or seen in the sky in the west at between 6 and 7 pm. It is seen low in the sky, late after sunset. This lunar time is what the Dinka people call **wilthok**. The scientists, on their part, call it a new moon or the new crescent.

Phases Of The Moon

Wilthok covers those days considered as the first quarter of the month and pɛɛi comes or appears in very thin curvature. Dinka people call this Pɛɛi-Magöt. Wilthok extends from the day of the first appearance of the moon to the time that scientists call the full

moon. It is a time or lunar period when certain things are done or are known to occur in association with this period as dictated by nature, custom and culture.

In the Dinka cultural universe the moon features prominently in art and literature. There are many clan and folktales related to the moon and the influence of the moon in human affairs continues to be a strong feature of astrology in the Dinka world. As they are known astrologers since those ancient and prehistoric times some Dinka clans have continued to revere the moon as their totemic divinity until today. Examples of these Dinka clans are those known as the **Padiangba**r who revere both the **heglig** tree and the moon. Some Dinka clans worship stars and a host of planetary or celestial bodies, including comets.

Apart from all this Dinka women who are at their menopause and mature girls, for example, are known to experience their regular monthly menstrual cycles in association with the new moon. According to the Dinka people a girl or woman whose menstrual flow did not come at wilthok is presumed to have conceived unless it is proven otherwise. On the other hand certain diseases in Dinka society such as epilepsy come as an indicator for the appearance of the new moon. Those suffering from epilepsy usually fall into epileptic fits or seizures as the new moon is or about to be seen. Epileptic attack is always an indicator for the pɛɛi being seen. The days it takes for an electro-neuronic cycle to reach the psychic lesion for an epileptic person to fall into fits are therefore known by Dinka people as being equal to the lunar cycle of 30 days to wilthok.

Besides all these Dinka people have certain occasions in relation to wilthok. One of the socio-cultural occasions done at wilthok worth citing here is the previously discussed Agutpiny, the public dance occasion held once a year to celebrate the end of the fattening period. To do the fattening Dinka youth are allowed to go to some secluded places where they make for themselves temporal makeshift camps or huts to protect themselves from rains while spending their fattening period. They are spared from cultivation which at this time is the preoccupation of every member of the community. The youth are made to take the cattle to their fattening camps with a sufficient number of milking cows in order to fatten themselves with milk. The milking cows are then milked by boys and girls into several milking gourds. Cows are milked twice a day. The fattening youths would then go in to drink the milk day and night so that they begin to grow fatter and fatter. They do this for a period of three to four months, beginning from the first rainy month of April or May each year.

Because of the element of competition before the community on the day marked as the day of Agutpiny, those young men whose fathers reared enough cows take up to ten or more milking cows so that they could become fatter than the rest to win the year as the fattest man in the territory. *Agutpiny* in Rekland used to be held at the beginning of the new moon of the month of *Akoldit* which is July, but because of the gradual weather and climatic changes that have been taking place in the Nilotic areas of South Sudan over the years, fattening celebration day has shifted to the new moon days of the month of *Bildit* which is the month of August. This is because until the 1960s the rains of the spring season used to start in late March and early April but have now changed. Rains in Dinka lands, as in all the Nilotic areas, have come to start falling in May, which is the Dinka month of Aduöŋ.

Agutpiny is a big communal occasion in which all the inhabitants of the entire territorial area do gather to celebrate for the first time since the winter and spring seasons made it difficult for the community to come together for one occasion like this. Agutpiny allows people of one polity to know themselves after having been unable to come together for maybe more than half a year. After Kon-Akönpiu (December), for all the three months of winter and the whole of spring, another three months, the community does not gather for an occasion like this.

Again, the Dinka calendar days for each month begin from the first day when the new moon is seen. The moon is therefore the reckoning satellite for calculating the monthly and yearly calendar. By way of contrast the sun and its movement provides the Dinka with the basis for determining time and days while the moon determines the days for the month, and therefore the seasons and the year.

The new moon is also associated with the time when Dinka people start to eat or taste their newly ripened crops after cultivation and slightly before harvest. It is a custom for all the Dinka to start eating from their fields' produce only at wilthok when the new moon of Biɛlthi is first seen. With the new moon the rite which precedes the tasting of the new produce is conducted by those Spear Masters accredited with the religious function to invocate away all those ailments called juääi or fevers that are always associated with the time when the community has started to eat the new produce.

Also associated with the new moon is the Dinka practice of communal beating of sleeping hides, a practice done upon seeing the new moon of the month they call **ɤorbɛkläi** which is the autumn month of November. The communal beating of the hides is done by only the women and girls. They do this in unison and in every homestead of every village in the territory. All forms of animal hides are beaten when the new moon of this month is seen. Women and girls shout their usual "Wuu Jɔk Lɔ Dor! Këräc Lɔ Tueŋ, Kepath Lor ɤa yɔu!" meaning *"Oh! You evil, go to Dor land! Bad omen, go ahead! And whatever good which is there, come towards me!"* This beating of hides goes together with those citations and is loudly said by all throughout the territory.

This is done to drive out all the evil and impurities of the wet season of spring and the summer season in particular. By this time the harmattan winds begin to blow westwards from the east and villagers do the hides' beating and the shouting of "Wuu Jɔk Lɔ Dor! Kĕrac Lor ɣa yɔu". They do this as a way to chase away those bad things that had been brought by, or which had bedevilled people during the now fading away rainy season. They say, *"Kepath lor ɣa yɔu"* as an appeal for what may be good there in Dor land to come towards them. This is so that what is good and benevolent does not go away together with the evil being chased or urged to go away. The practice is also done to welcome the new dry season of autumn and its succeeding winter.

The new moon is also linked up with certain cultural, social and religious rites and occasions. Some clans and people are known to wait for the new moon in order to conduct their rituals and sacrifices to their clans' totems, family divinities and to Nhialic. Several decisions and activities are made to wait till the new moon appears. In the wet or rainy period, especially during spring, the appearance of the new moon makes people conclude or predict the coming of rain after some spell of drought.

Again, the rural Dinka people have a belief that when the right wing, called the *young moon's arm* of the new moon, is inclined or tilted down at its first appearance, they take it as a sign of a bad omen. When they see this they expect some misfortune to happen to the community at some given time in that month or in the course of the year. However, should the left wing of the new moon appear tilted down they will rejoice, believing that there will be a misfortune to happen to their adversaries, particularly to the Arabs whom they take to be their perpetual enemies.

Rural Dinka people also have a belief that the new moon is first seen by wizards (apeth) and the cows before the rest can be able to see it when it finally appears clearly the next day. Although the cow is not understood to be a wizard, it is believed that it has some natural instincts which allow it to see some things that human beings cannot easily see with the naked eye.

People who are twins are known to regularly fall or appear sick with the appearance of the new moon. The coming of the new moon is known to show effect on the human twins who equally become unwell. For this reason, the foreheads of the twins are marked with white ash so that they do not become sick at wilthok.

Wilthok is the lunar period when Dinka people do several things, some of which have been explained above. When it first appears it comes in a thin curvature and when it reaches ɤɛɛric or full moon the Dinka people do many other things related to ɤɛɛric.

Many of the community dance occasions are done during a full moon or ɤɛɛric. Most of the travels that have to be done in the night are pended to be undertaken during a full moon. As the full moon drips into *Laciëën,* which is the last quarter of the moon's phase called old crescent, other activities which have to wait for this period are carried out.

This moon's phase called *Laciëën* is associated with some rituals that are done by some clans. Payii people, for example, do their annual religious festivals during the *Laciëën* of the month of December each year. They bring their sacrificial bulls to peg them at their religious sanctuary on the day when the moon is known or is said to have gone into *Atuur* or 'aca atuur buɔk'. Atuur is the day when the moon starts to be more difficult to see because it comes very low in the east. It is the last day of the *Laciëën.* The bulls are made to return to their cattle kraals that evening after they are invoked upon by the Spear Master and shown to God and their clan divinities that they are going to be sacrificed to Nhialic as His offerings after the day when *Muööthic* has started. The bulls are brought back to pegs the evening of the next day when the moon has formed what is called *Ajämdit.*

When the moon has on this day gone down in the east only to appear about an hour after sunset, it comes in a big red ball formation. This is what the Rek Dinka call *Ajämdit* which is the beginning day for the 15 days of night darkness, *Muööthic*. On the next day of Ajämdit bulls are sacrificed in a huge communal gathering with festivals and this takes the whole day. Dinka people barely do ritual occasions during this phase of *Muööthic*. Because of darkness due to the absence of the moon's light, rural Dinka people remain almost immobile during these nights and for this reason many activities of the night are pended for waxing and waning phases of the moon. After this comes wilthok and the monthly cycle of the moon is thus completed and repeated.

As stated the moon is well known in Dinka mythology, literature and art. There are Dinka mythologies which hold the moon as a female and the sun as a male. As mentioned earlier, some Dinka clans revere the moon as their nagualistic object. Others take it as itself a deity with a variety of functions and traditions. They worship it as such. The moon is therefore a significant satellite for the Dinka owing to its prominence in the daily life of the community.

2. The Sun: (Akol)
Dinka people have a belief that Akol shines and moves from that part of the sky far beyond where Pɛɛi is. If it were near or in the position of the moon, it would have burnt the whole universe, and because the stars are conceived to be of immense distance up in the sky, Dinka people consider the sun as being itself a star, for it is also very far from the earth. However, Dinka people think that the sun in comparison to the stars is the source of life and energy behind all worldly activities and production. Akol in the Dinka world is known as Akol-Marial.

There is a myriad of beliefs concerning the sun. Besides their scanty knowledge of it being an astrological satellite, some Dinka communities entertain a belief that it is one eye of God which He uses to brightly illuminate the universe during the day. And because of its heat Nhialic withdraws it and replaces it for the night with the moon whose ability to light the universe is assisted by a constellation of millions of stars. Akol in Dinka cosmology, literature and myths, is perceived as a male being while the moon is seen or portrayed as a female being.

There are a lot of folk tales and stories about Akol just as there are about Pɛɛi, and while the moon helps the Dinka in determining the months and seasons, Akol helps in measuring time, days and the year.

Apart from all this, Dinka people have their own way of interpreting those phenomena such as what they call 'Akol aci yɔm köök', which is a statement they use for a phenomenon that occurs at midday when the sun is overhead. When a corona ring of red surrounds the sun the Dinka people see it as a bad omen. They take it to be a sign of a big battle happening somewhere. The blood of people killed and wounded in the battle is believed to be reflected up onto the sun. The red corona ring which forms around the sun is therefore taken by the Dinka as a sign of an occurring disaster involving bloodshed.

Solar Eclipse:
Solar eclipse occurs infrequently in the Dinka world. They call it 'amion'. When it occurs, it causes total or partial darkness and it is perceived to be a disaster from Nhialic who for some reason has become so angry as to close off his eyes from people!

Bulls and rams are sacrificed to propitiate God when an eclipse occurs. A solar eclipse can be partial or total and because it rarely occurs, the Dinka people have very little literature about it.

3. Stars (Kuɛl)

Stars are known by the Dinka as those indiscrete luminates which shine from the sky during the night. They assist the moon in providing light to the universe during this time. Many of the stars are usually visible when they are not obscured by clouds or some atmospheric phenomena. Stars have been of great importance to the Dinka throughout history. They have been part of their religious practices and are used for determining seasons and times during the night. The Dinka monthly and annual calendars are influenced by the position of the stars. While there are multitudes of stars, certain stars appear prominent and brighter than others. For this reason they have acquired proper names. Some parts of the sky appear to have more stars than other parts. Star clusters and galaxies gave rise to descriptive names for a good number of stars.

Among those stars that featured to become constantly associated with certain times of the day and periods of the year are what are called *Cyer, Wet Ayuɔk-yuɔk, Wetthel Jöng* and *Atekpéi*, which is the **Milky Way galaxy** made up of many stars grooved to each other so that they appear in a continuous line or route which marks or divides the stars in the sky into half during some parts of the night. The Milky Way galaxy is clearer after midnight. The number of stars appears to increase towards one side of the sky, in the direction of the Milky Way's core.

Some of the stars are associated with particular aspects of nature and Dinka people have several myths and tales about them. Some of them represent important deities among the Dinka. Prophet Cyerdit from Twic Dinka in Bahr el Ghazal acquired his name from one of the big stars called Cyer. Stars, like *Cyer–Ayɔɔl*, assist people in determining time, particularly the one called *Cyer Bɛɛk Piny*, which appears at about 4 am. It makes travellers get up from sleep in order to start their planned journeys. It also guides those travellers towards dawn. There is also a star called *Cyer Aliim* or *Cyer Aliim Mith*. It

Fig 29: Showing how a star forming region appears at night

Fig 30: Showing the Milky Way galaxy (Atek péi)

appears at about 7 pm, low in the sky in the west. Children are shown that star and are threatened that Cyer Aliim will eat up the food if the child does not quickly eat it. Apuökpεεi also alerts people of the coming spring by the position it takes in the nights during late winter.

4. Rainbow: (Miit)

The natural phenomenon of a rainbow is known as *miit* by the Dinka people. With its very powerful visual symbolism, miit has had a very long tradition of varied interpretations by different cultures.

Strangely enough, the Dinka people take miit as a sign of an animal that lives and rises in some dry streams where it will spoil a rain that God does not want to fall, either as a means to stop its killing thunder or as a punishment to an area where He does not want rain to fall.

The rainbow, bright with those extremely beautiful colours and rather heavenly, presents itself as a mystical and intangible entity to the Dinka. It is difficult for the Dinka people to define it with clear-cut scientific explanations. Yet rainbows continue to persist as a phenomenon of a multifaceted nature. Despite its beautiful glistening colours and beautiful formation, the Dinka people fear it very greatly because they have an ambiguous perception of what it really is. They do not regard it as a benevolent phenomenon. Most Dinka say it is an animal of the type of an ass. They say it has long antennae of hair on its mouth. It pursues its human victim and while giving chase it places those antennae on the running person to suck blood out of him. The pursuing rainbow is believed to suck all the blood out of its victim until the person falls down dead.

A rainbow is therefore considered a dangerous demon that eats people and children are frightened into not looking at it when it appears in the sky. That Dinka legend which says a rainbow is an animal continues on to say that should a person chance to get the placenta of a female rainbow soon after it has given birth, that person

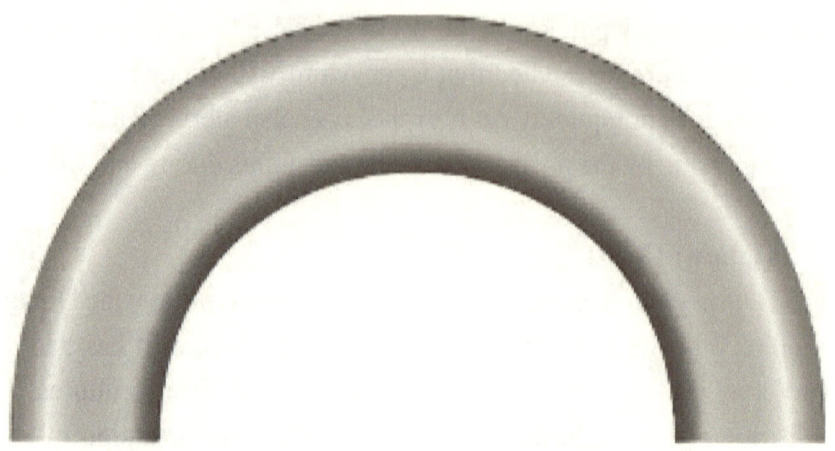

Fig 31: Showing the rainbow in its arc form

will be so rich in his lifetime. This is why there is a saying among some Dinka communities which goes as follows: **"Ci ja bi jak arɛk abi ciët ci lam miit kuany!"** meaning, "He has become so rich as if he got the placenta of a rainbow!"

CHAPTER FOUR: DINKA NATIONAL COMMUNITIES

INTRODUCTION

Dinka society generally lives in defined territorial areas which they call *Wuöt –Wut* when singular. This is unlike their ancient and Mediaeval practice when they used to settle in one large and single territorial conglomeration. Dinka people are divided into roughly twenty six tribal formations and they inhabit large tracts of land in the Upper Nile and Bahr el Ghazal regions. Owing to population increase over the last thousand years the original Jieng cultural groups have increased into full tribes that are further subdivided into sub-tribes composed of *Wuöt*. Each *Wut* is also divided into other internal patterns better called sections. Each of these *Wuöt*, sections or territorial units has a distinctive characteristic with a defined territory, a common name, a border and a rather peculiar culture and history.[56]

---

56   FM Deng, Tradition and modernization, U.S.A, Michigan (1971) pp. 3-5

In details, Dinka people have some little cultural variations although they are on the whole culturally homogeneous. In the Bahr el Ghazal region, for example, Dinka populations are so contiguous with each other that people tend to know themselves section by section. This is not the case with Dinka communities living in the Upper Nile region where the Nuers and other tribes interlace Dinka territories. However, some Dinka places in Bahr el Ghazal can be found separated by some natural boundaries such as swamps, forests, rivers or plains.

On the whole populations in each of the Dinka territories, areas, sections and sub-sections differ markedly. This is because some Dinka tribal groups are very large and populous while others are relatively small. Although the Rek Dinka tribe is apparently extensive, large and living in a continuously vast territorial extension from Tonj, Gogrial and Awiel with a population which is nearly three million people, the Padang Dinka cultural group may be the biggest among all the Dinka cultural groupings. Unfortunately, Padang Dinka live in a dispersed formation. They are scattered in different locations in the areas of Bahr el Ghazal, Upper Nile and in the Ngok area of Abyei. Padang constituents do not live in one geographical habitat as is the case with Rek, Agaar and other non-Padang Dinka tribal groupings. Dinka tribes can be shown in the following territorial and demographic configuration as they presently stand in the Upper Nile and Bahr el Ghazal regions.

BAHR EL GHAZAL DINKA COMMUNITIES: REK DINKA TRIBE

The Rek Dinka tribe is made up of three very large cultural components, *lith*, the hawk, *kuei*, the eagle and *gir*, the unsharpened bladed spear. Rek is believed to have come into being when Jaang society was yet to come to what is now the Khartoum area. The ancestors of the present *Pahöl*, the thigh bone or *call* revering clans, were the original founding family of what later became Rek.

The genesis of Rek is traceable to those ancient times when Jaang has not yet arrived in the Khartoum region. When they came to the present Khartoum-Omdurman areas, says one Dinka chronicler, Deng Tëëng, the Rek settled in what they named *Tiäptiäp,* which is the present Patihap township in Omdurman of today.

Most of the Rek Dinka clans are descendants of those who came to Sudan from Egypt, people who were led by the great Pahöl ancestor named Abiɛl from the House of Reuben, that eldest son of the Biblical Jacob. Ajaang, who became the founding father of Jaang (Dinka) society, is a great grandson of that Abiɛl.

The beginning of the name Rek can be traced to an ancient great lady by the name of Arek, daughter of an ancient Jaang liege, Jiel Loŋaar. This lady is presented by several traditions from Rek society as the grandmother of all the Pahöl people. The other intermediate Arek Loŋaar of the Mediaeval time is different from this Arek of Jiel Loŋaar. This intermediate Arek is the one who bore Tɔng-Manyangdit and Thiek Anei, two great Pahöl figures of the Mediaeval era who are widely known among Rek society as Tɔng and Thiek Arek. It is from that first great mother Arek of the Napatan period that the Rek society acquired its name, Rek. From her name came the name of the tribe of Rek.

The genesis of the Pahöl clan people can be traced in the Bible[57] and is traceable down to Abiɛl[58] who during the Biblical Exodus led a faction of the Jacobites from Lower Egypt to Elephantine Island in Upper Egypt, then to the ancient Wawat area in that extreme northern part of Northern Sudan.

As came above, Abiɛl bore a son by the name of Kuc who later

---

57 Gen.ch.32,V.24-32 for Jacob's wrestling with God : Dake's annotated reference Bible, p. 32.

58 Abiel (Abiɛl in Dinka) In Hebrew, Abiel means 'God is father' in Dinka. Abiɛl means 'God is holy', p. 1386 in 'People of the Bible of KJV (King James version) of the holy Bible'.

became the father of Deng, who bore *Ajaang* and *Manuɛr,* two historical personalities who became founders of the Jaang and Nuer communities in ancient Northern Sudan.

While in Wawat, in the Wadi Al Allagy valley area, Great Kuc bore Deng along with other sons. Deng being his firstborn son later married Arek Jiel from the Pagong clan. Pahol traditions say Arek bore Hol with Deng Kuc. Hol lived to be a great man in the early years of the rise of the Kush Kingdom. The long and short of this story of Rek evolving from this Pahöl family of Arek Jiel is that the Rek came to the Khartoum region and the Upper Nile region as a distinct community at the time of Jaang migration from the Khartoum region to Southern Sudan in 490 AD.[59] Part of the Rek went to the Blue Nile region with Gok, Agaar, going as Duör and Athööc. Athööc later became Bor Dinka.

The Rek did not go to the Upper Nile region with those communities of Jaang who later came to join the rest of Jaang in the region. Those sections of the Rek that went to the Blue Nile region later became the present Regarik people in the Karangkarang area of the southern Blue Nile. Much of the Rek came to northern Upper Nile with the bulk of Jaang from Khartoum at the time Jaang society departed from the Khartoum region to the northern Upper Nile areas.

At the time Jaang came to live in those areas in central and southern Upper Nile region, Rek society lived in those places that are now Thiöbek, Aluɛl, Agɛro and those areas which are present Abi, Guala, Paleek of Anyidi, Angakuei section areas of Athööc in present Manydeng area in Bor South. Others settled in the area known today as Pam Ayueel. Those were the takeoff settlement areas of Rek when again Jaang made yet another migration, this time to Bahr el Ghazal in 1340 AD. After crossing the River Nile at the Shambe shore of

---

59   A J Achile, *The history of the Nile valley to the lakes*, Edinburgh, (London) 1936, pp. 69 – 71.

Anyɔɔp, the Rek community encamped at present Liɛtpaciruööt in present Kiec land section of Ajäk in today's Yirol area of Adöör. From here, Rek moved to the present Payii River area where it settled for some decades. In this area, the Rek reorganised itself into three subdivisions of *Kuei*, *Lith* and *Gïr*. This is after they fought an internal war of *Ayuɔmlual*.[60] Then they moved, in around 1370 AD, to a place now known as *Amongpiny* in the present Agaar territory of the Alääp section, some 50 kms northeast of the present Rumbek city.

Towards the last part of 1300 AD, after the Jaang migratory crossing of the Nile to the west bank, the Rek came to live in the Amongpiny area and in all the areas that are the present Panyoon section in Agaar land. They also covered those areas that are today's Amothnhom, an area later settled by the Kuei section of the Agaar. This was when the Agaar community was still in the Dɔkland area of present Ganyliel, currently inhabited by the Nuers of Adɔk and Nyuong sections.

Before proceeding with the narrative account of the entire Rek, it is significant at this juncture to first render an historical explanation of why the Rek society chose to name its sectional divisions using the three names of Gïr, Kuei and Lith. The Malual component of the Rek shall later be explained as to how it came up in Bahr el Ghazal within the context of Rek.

By their very nature, the three figurative names with which the Rek Dinka tribe named its subdivisions can be understood in the context of the then existing warfare situation during that part of the Mediaeval Ages, the era when the Jaang nationality was fighting its historic wars for the conquest of lands in Upper Nile and later in Bahr el Ghazal.

1. Gïr, to begin with, is a Dinka word for a heavy and blunt metal like steel which is very strong and thick and not pliable. Any

---

60 Ayuomlual is a Dinka name of the giant turtle found during fishing occasions in some parts of the primaeval toch or swamp of the White Nile River.

sharp object or instrument cannot penetrate through it. It is repellent, stout and heavily harmful. Thus, for all of those qualities, one of the Pagak Spear Masters by the name of Akec Akol Akec[61] took 'Gïr' for naming a portion of Rek as his social and war divisional component. This name came to be used at the time when Rek society had not even arrived at the present Amongpiny area. Amongpiny, which is the Luɛɛk Payam centre at the far northern end of Rumbek Central county, is in the Aliääp section area, the area of Chief Juöl Machɔk of the Patiɔp clan people of the Pabɛɛk lineage. To further explain this historical area, Amongpiny is currently constituted with the Bɛɛr, Panyoon and Aliääp sections of Agaar into Amongpiny Payam. It borders Pagaraw Payam in the Kiec land area of Yirol, East county. It also borders the Aluak Luak area of Atuot in Yirol West to the south. It borders Pakam to the northwest. Amongpiny, through Paloch in the Panyaar section of Aliamtooc-Two is 93 miles from Rumbek through Pacong Payam. It is 55 miles northeast of Rumbek city. The area is inhabited by the Patiɔp, Redior, Pakec and other minor clans. Amongpiny is partly *Rup*, partly savannah woodland and partly a lowland plain called *Lil* which ends in swampy marshes that divide Agaar from the Nuers of Ganyliel.

Here, most of the west bank Dinka sections of Rek, Luacjang, Twic, Gok and Ruweng had either passed through it or had settled at it. Those sections which settled in this Amongpiny area had to jointly push away the original inhabitants of the territory. Those Aboriginals were the Jur-Luɛɛl and the Belle people who, until the advent of Jaang, had inhabited those areas northwest and south of this Amongpiny.

The Paröl family groups, still commemorating their great mother on par with their ancestor Hol, continued in this Amongpiny area

---

61   From an interview with chief Chol Akol Aduɔl of the Pagak clan in Thɔny area. Akec Akol was the husband of the great mother of Rek society, Amou Marɔl. Interview dated 6.12.2007

to call themselves and those with them as people of Arek. Before Jaang came to Upper Nile region, these Pahöl clan people had already made their society to be known as Rek. They had already incorporated several clans and sections to become Rek society. During the migration from Upper Nile, Pahöl people led Rek society under Great Loŋaar, Anei-Barek, Wol Kuac later to become Wol-Adhieu, Wol-Adiaŋbar and Agɔth-Cithiik. They crossed the Nile at Shambe shore and settled at Liɛtpacirööt in Ajäk area of Adöör, then to what is now Payii River area in Yirol West county of today. Then, they came and settled at Amongpiny. Agɔth–Cithiik family line later joined Luac community that moved to Rɛɛlkou with Kiec. The Pahöl section of Agɔth Cithiik rejoined Rek Section of Apuk in about the end of the 16th century, coming out from Luac when Luac split into Luackoth, Luac Adut, Luacjang and Luac-tɛɛt which later became Luac of Aköök yiɛu in the Khor Fluth area today.

Whether *Gïr* was an Age-group within Kuei or Lith or a separate Divisional component of Rek is contested by other traditions from within Rek. This makes the story of Gïr to be rather obscure, unlike that of *Kuei* and *Lith* which are very clear and straightforward. Nevertheless, such conflicting traditions which say Gïr was but an Age-set and not a section, can be valued by some still existing facts. As a matter of fact, there was something called Gïr which have partially disappeared and can only be remembered or recalled through popular sayings still existing in some parts of Rekland, sayings such as, *"yie nyan ci Gïr göök!",* meaning, "what a girl that withstood Gïr!", the essence of which is, "What a bad girl who, in spite of Gïr Age-set, has all the same remained non-conforming!", or "a girl gone through by the whole Gïr, and yet she still appears a girl despite Gïr's trampings on her!" All in all whatever it was Gïr is still known by many among the Rek Dinka as having existed and having developed during those Mediaeval centuries prior to Turkiya, perhaps developing from an Age-set to a section which was made up of an assortment of clans and from the breakaway lineages and individuals who went south from Angääc in the Jalwau area following the disastrous battle of the wife of Buonglek. This historic battle caused by the wife of Buonglek must have occurred around 1410 AD.

Gïr is also said to have been made up of the later breakaway groups of lineages and clans that also went south from Payuël in present Luackoth area to join those first groups which earlier departed from Angääc in the aftermath of the battle of the wife of Buonglek. The Rek groups or sections which went to the Payuël area after the disaster caused by the wife of Buonglek were again affected by a historic earthquake disaster of 1440 AD which caused Rek society to break up again and disperse in different directions from that Payueel area.[62] Those who ran away from Payuël and went southward also went and settled in what is now Thɔny territory which was then inhabited by a Bantu people presently known as the Bongo. Before it was to be Thɔny, the area was called Agigim, a name which must have been from the Bongo or some earlier settlers.

Some of the Gïr people and sections later went to areas that are now Muɔk of Great Chief Aköt Wut and Yar of Great Ayiɛi Cikɔm in Tonj South county after they dislodged the Bongo in those areas. Others later proceeded from the earthquake area of Panyang in Luackoth to live with Lith or Apuk people in what is now Apuk-Juwiir. Those are areas that are known to be inhabited by the Gïr section of Rek even today.

During the last years of 1300 AD when those sections of Jaang were still in the area later to become Aliääp as already described, Amongpiny acted as the Jaangs' springboard settlement of much of the west bank Dinka. It was from this Amongpiny that most of the Jaang community started to wage their wars of conquest against the

---

62 The year of this earthquake incident and that of the wife of Buonglek at Angääc were found by the computation of the genealogical descent and ages of those who were participants or witnesses of those events.

Jur-Belle tribe to the south and Jur-Lueel to the west. Bongo people were at this time inhabiting areas that are presently inhabited by the Gok Dinka and the areas which are now Thɔny, Muɔk and within and around present Tonj town up to the big forest area called *Ror Cuɔl Akol* between Malɔu-Pech in western Gok land and Tonj town. The Bongo were at this time not in close contact with any of the invading Jaang sections.

Then came the infighting between those Jaang communities that settled in the Amongpiny area. It was here at Amongpiny that Ukɔkdit, the cannibal, caused the first split among the west bank Jaang. Ukɔkdit, who became Banyolit or Chief Ku yie Köör,[63] used to turn into a lion late in the afternoons, especially at the time when cattle are coming back from pastures or from grazing and are being pegged. In the smoke usually made by the burning cow dung, Ukɔkdit would steal himself into that smoke, mingling with the returning cattle. In so doing he would capture the best gentleman of the cattle camp or the prettiest girl about to be married. Ukɔkdit would pull that victim into his makeshift hut which the Dinka people call aduël, where he would eat up the victim in hiding. This practice continued unabated until it was finally discovered one particular day. A conspiracy was then planned to kill him in a day dance occasion. His killing led to a fight. The community dispersed as a result. The Rek abandoned Amongpiny and went westward to Karɔm where they later proceeded to Angääc in today's Adöör land of Jalwau. Gok, Luac, Twic, Kiec and those sections which later became Ruweng all went to Reelkou but some of the Ukɔk's family members like Aguër Ukɔk ran eastwards from the Amongpiny until they recrossed the Nile. They gradually moved on until they finally settled at what is today's Kɔŋɔɔr section of Lith Two which is Wangulei and Pawél Payam. Descendants of Aguër Ukɔk are today the lion clan people of Chief Ajaang Duöt.

---

63   Ukɔkdit was a community liege (chief) who also turns into a lion in the right and at twilight.

Some of the Ukɔk family members left with Rek community where they are today's Palual clan people from whom came Charles Kuek Wok who himself told this story of his great great ancestor, Ukɔk-dit of Amongpiny. There was a fight between Kiek and Luac. This made Twic Dinka society move out of Rɛɛlkou and make their way to present Gok land where they temporarily settled for a number of decades after partly dislodging Jur-Belle in what is now the Pathiöng section of Gok of Abiriu Payam. They were led to this area by those great people presented by Mediaeval Twic traditions as Kuol-Alɛl from the Redior clan and Great Noi Duääng of the Pahöl clan. Twic settled in the present Gok area of the Pathiöng sections. There are places still known in Gok land today as Twic Mediaeval settlement villages, places like Rum-Twic. Noi's faction of Twic went to settle in the Karɔm and Yar-Dɔng areas in present Pagor Payam. This is before they migrated further north to be the first to pioneer the territory which is now Luacjang in present Tonj East county where they later proceeded by way of Lɔu-Paher, Apuk-Padɔc and the Jur-Lian part of Wedhou in Awan-Parek, then to Lɔu-Mawien and on until they reached their present Twic territory in northern parts of today's Warrap state. They reached there in about the middle of the 16th century.

Amongpiny have several Mediaeval stories still told among some Rek Dinka communities to the present day. Several Rek Dinka people in Tonj areas still trace their ancestors who had lived in Amongpiny before the Rek left it for their present Rekland in central and Northern Bahr el Ghazal, having moved away from what is now the Lakes state area all together.

Most of those elderly people who participated in the migratory exodus right from the Jönglei areas have died in this Amongpiny settlement area. Some managed to proceed alive, but in a very advanced old age. Great Kuol-Alɛl of Twic, for example, was buried in the Luacjang area in Tonj East after he was being carried by

Twic people when they left the present Gok area at Pagor. His big mound shrine where his remains were laid can now be found at Alɛl village in the Wun-Thuc section of Rubaar in Luacjang area, around one and a half hours walk east of Paliang town. Beside Kuol-Alɛl, Great Loŋaar, the leader of Jaang migration to Bahr el Ghazal, also succeeded to proceed with his Rek community at a very old age. He reached the Tonj area where he finally died in the present Muɔk area of Chief Aköt Wut. His big wrist bracelet that was born with his clan's founding ancestor Jieldit, a bracelet which has no opening, is now being kept by one of his family lineage known as *Paan-Agau* in the Muɔk area. It is a religious ancient relic kept as a holy artefact of the past. Loŋaar's chief opponent, Anei-Parek, died at Amongpiny, for he crossed the River Nile while he was already of age and the two decades spent between Ajäk in Yirol East and Amongpiny would have made him much older.

2. Kuei, on the other hand, is the Dinka name for the eagle. The Rek society adopted this figurative name of the eagle for its powerfulness, keen intelligence and powerful observatory eyes which see far into very great distances. Thiek Anei took *'Kuei'* as his figurative symbol for his portion of Rek society because of those qualities he saw in the eagle. He also chose the eagle for its strength and ability. Great Thiek Anei, then a renowned Spear Master and a highly respected figure from the Pahöl clan people of the thigh bone, a man whose descendants later became known as the Payii clan people, is the ancestor from whose descent line came the author.

Thiek Anei was chosen to be the head of the Kuei sector of Rek. He is presented by legends from Payii and from Rek society to have been the one accredited to give this name of Kuei to a number of clans and sections within the Rek. The giving of the name of Kuei to those sections of Rek, it is said, was ceremonised in a ritual occasion held at the present Payii River area in the decade after the historic crossing of the Nile. A cow of the colour of the eagle kuei was taken by Thiek Anei from the cattle kraal of his son Ayii Thiek ritually killed in that communal occasion. The colour symbol of the cow kuei was thus transferred figuratively to the society which since then has continued to be known as the Kuei community of Thiek Anei. Nearly seven centuries later (2011) South Sudanese people adopted this bird to be the coat of arms for their new independent country, the Republic of South Sudan. What was seen in the bird kuei by Great Thiek Anei was later seen by Southern Sudanese on the eve of their independence on 9 July, 2011 AD. The author's name comes from that Great Anei who bore Thiek.

Until that time in history, the Rek community did have two principal sacred clans, Pagong and Pahöl, whose lineage sections of Ayii Thiek later became Payii. Tɔng-Manyang, elder brother of Thiek Anei, is the founding father of the Parek clan in Awiel West. The Pahöl part of Agɔth-Cithiik later became Pakuec after his descendant Akol-Kuec. The Pahöl line of Jök became the Pajök clan in the Gogrial East areas. Other lineage factions from this Pahöl continued as Pahöl to the present day. The Redior Spear Master group were mostly within Agaar society at this time. The Patɛk Spear Master clan was yet to join Rek. The arrival of *Kɔɔk Manyang Awukdi*ääny from Bor land after Jaang had crossed the River Nile to Bahr el Ghazal later added to the list of very noted Spear Master clans among Rek society. The Pagak clan people of Agak, The Paker clan people of Ker, the Pajiɛk and the Padhieu people of Wol-Adhieu later featured in Bahr el Ghazal. The Pawutweng people of the cow also featured in Bahr el Ghazal.

Despite the ever-accepted spiritual and holy primacy of the Pagong clan people, Rek society also recognises the potency and primacy of other Spear Master clans such as Redior or Parum and Pahol who are the Payii, Parek, Pajök and Pakuec clans. Clans such as Padhieu and Pajiɛk later acquired their Spear Masterhood in Bahr el Ghazal from Great Loŋaar by an investitural transfer- not an initially inborn spirituality. The Patɛk people of the crocodile totem, who are later arrivals from among the Gajaak Nuers after Jaang had crossed to Bahr el Ghazal, have also come to show primacy in Spear Masterhood where they exist in those parts of Bahr el Ghazal, especially in places like Tonj East and Tonj North and in the Awiel and Gogrial areas where Patɛk clan people are noted for their great efficacy in cursing others, in invocations and when pleading to God for a favour. The Pagak clan people of Agak are Spear Masters responsible for the forest. They are forest masters. The Paker clan people of Ker are responsible for the underground water. The Pawutweng, called Paderek in Agaar and Gok lands, are Spear Masters whose spiritual function is centred on the cow.

The Kuei sector is currently the largest component of Rek. It begins from the Tonj sub-region in central Bahr el Ghazal where they make up about 75% of its population of three counties of Tonj East, Tonj North and Tonj South, the remaining 25% being of Lith, which is Apuk of Juwiir in Tonj South county and Apuk of Padɔc in Tonj North county, plus Luacjang in Tonj East county and the less than 5 000 non-Dinka people called Bongo in the Tonj South county.

Luackoth, Aköök-Teek, Thiik of Maɔk Makɔm and the big Jalwau made up of Kɔŋɔɔr, Bäc, Adöör and Pakɔɔr are all Kuei in Tonj East county. The whole of Lɛɛr consisting of the Ajak Chol Chan area and the big Kuac-Akeen area of Chief Mayom Akeen Köör are Kuei territories in Tonj North county. The two Lɔu territories which are Lɔu-Paɣer and the big Lɔu-Ariik also called Lɔu-Mawien in Tonj North county are sections of Kuei. The Awan-Parek area, Atok and the big Kɔŋöör area in Tonj North are populations of Kuei as is the big Noi territory of Chief Ayii Kuot plus the great Abiem area of Chief Mayar Marɛng, all in Tonj North county. Kuei became more identified with the big Nyang-Akoc Majök territory. This is how the Nyang area came to be called Kuei -Akɔc and consists of three sections, Nyang-Lurcuk, Nyang-Majök and Nyang-Lɔɔc, all in the western part of Tonj North county towards Wau from Warrap town.

In the greater Gogrial sub-region, the big Kuac-Agör consisting of eight executive chieftaincies is entirely Kuei community. The immense Aguok population made up of twelve sections is also Kuei. Nyang in Tonj North and Aguɔk in this western part of Gogrial have a claim that they are more Kuei than the other sections of Kuei. Awan Riau, also called Awan Mou, as is the big Awan Chan and the big Awan Pajok, are all Kuei in Gogrial West county. Waau people of Majɔk Majɔk found in the Marial-Baai area towards Wau city from Kuajök are also Kuei. Kuei is about 60% of the population of the Greater Gogrial sub-region of Warrap state. Twic and Apuk-Pathuɔn make the remaining 40% of Greater Gogrial population.

Kuei also covers the entire Abiem and Paliëët areas of seventeen executive chieftaincy areas in Awiel East and Awiel South counties in the Northern Bahr el Ghazal state. So big is Kuei that it constitutes two thirds of the Rek Dinka tribe. Below is Kuei in its full proportions.

SOCIAL CONFIGURATION OF THE REK DINKA: THE KUEI TERRITORIAL SECTIONS OF THE REK

1. Awan Sections:
Awan-Parek: is an area in Akɔp sub-region of Tonj North county. It is comprised of the Jur-Bol, Thöc and Ariääu executive chieftaincy sections. The author comes from the Jur-Bol section of this Awan. It also consists of the Jur-Lian section, which is composed of sections of Buɔɔng and Manoon executive chieftaincies. This Awan is currently made up of six executive chieftaincy areas.

Awan Chan: is an area in Gogrial West county. It is made up of the Rup, Ayien and Agaal-Lual executive chieftaincy sections.

Awan- Pajok: is an area in Gogrial West county and is made up of the Amuöl and Thɔn sections. President Salva Kiir Mayardit comes from this section of Awan Pajok.

Awan Mou, also called Awan Riau: is an area in Gogrial West county and is made up of the Thɔny, Thɔn and Agurpiny sections.

2. Lɛɛr sections:
Kuac-Akëën: is an area in Lɛɛr territory in the Kuanythi sub-region of Tonj North county. It is composed of the Agɔugɔu, Pagik and Pacien sections.

Ajak Chol Chan: is an area in Lɛɛr territory in Kuanythi sub-region of Tonj North County consisting of Mawaat, NÖkbiar and Madɛɛl sections.

3. Lɔu sections:
Lɔu-Paɣer: is an area in the sub-region of Akɔp in Tonj North county. It is made up of the Mathiang, Macuet, Gɔny and Matik sections.

Lɔu-Mawien, also called Lɔu-Ariik: is a highly populated area in the Akɔp territory of Tonj North county. It is composed of Bil, Manlok, Muɔc, Kuethcuär and Kɔŋdeer sections. It also consists of Juɛɛr sections of Aliaap, Jerbek and Maluil. Lɔu also includes the Paliëpiny and Jurman-Aŋɛɛr territories. The Lɔu-Ariik Area is composed of four very big executive chieftancy sections and is liable to further administrative decentralisation.

4. Anan-Atak sub-region:
Jalwau is an area in the Anan-Atak sub-region of Tonj East county. It is comprised of four executive chieftaincy areas; the Kɔŋɔɔr of Great Akuecbany Cirɔŋ Kuol, Adöör, Pakɔɔr and Bäc executive chieftaincies.

Luackoth: is an area in the Anan-Atak sub-region of Tonj East county comprised of the Awiɛn, Agurman, Buöweng and Akarau executive chieftaincy sections.

Aköök-Teek: is an area in the Anan-Atak sub-region of Tonj East county comprised of the Matik, Aliak-Liak, Midɛɛr and Manginy executive chieftaincy sections. This is the area of Chief Deng Acuil Dɔɔt.

Thiik area of Majɔk Makɔm: is an area in the Anan-Atak sub-region in Tonj East county consisting of the Anguit, Bil and Makook executive chieftaincy sections.

5. Kuanythi sub-region:

Nyang Akɔc: is an area in the Kuanythi sub-region in Tonj North county comprised of the Nyang-Lɔu, Nyang-MajÖk, Nyang-Lurcuk and Nyang-Lɔɔc executive chieftaincy sections.

Abuɔk -Ayiɔm: is an area in the Kuanythi sub-region in Tonj North county and consisting of Marial, Abiɛth or Abuɔkthi and Guac-Awan executive chieftaincy sections.

Noi Ayii Kuot Area: is an area in the Kuanythi sub-region in Tonj North county consisting of the Nokbiar, Kuanythi, Monyjooc and Alak executive chieftaincy sections. Warrap town is situated in this area of Noi.

KɔŋgÖÖr: is an area in the Akop sub-region in Tonj North county comprised of the Ming, Monyjooc, Riaŋnhom, Duör and Mathiang executive chieftaincy sections.

Atok-Buk: is an area in the Kuanythi sub-region of Tonj North county composed of the Awan-Gurwel, Atokdit and Mabior executive chieftaincy sections.

Abiem Mayar Marɛng: is a territory in the Kuanythi sub-region in Tonj North county consisting of the LiangrÖl, AkurbiÖÖk, Wun-Ameth, Agurpiny, Bor-Adök, Agutbuɔng and Liangröl-Ruup sections.

Kuac-Agor: is an area in Gogrial West county comprised of the Luk-Luk, Mathiangic, Wunkuëldit, Monyjooc, Mathiang, Dɔng, Warkɔu (1) and Warkɔu (2) executive chieftancy sections.

Waau Makuac Akec, now known as Waau Majɔk Majɔk: is an

area of four executive chieftaincy areas in the western Bahr el Ghazal state which lies between Wau town and Tharkueɛng on the way to Kuajök. It is composed of the Wau Baai of Chief Thiɛp Dhol and Marial-Baai also known as Marial–Wau of Chief Loŋaar Makuac.

Aguɔk Area: is in Gogrial West county and is comprised of the Atukuëël, Buɔth-Anyith, Marial, Wuny, Ngok-Abekyien or Ngok-Lööl, Ajak-Agör, Monydit, Pakal, Ngok-Riau, Ngok of Ayaric, Pakal-Kuööm and Pakal-Pändit executive chieftaincy sections.

KUEI SECTIONS IN AWIEL EAST AND AWIEL SOUTH

(1) The Abiem area in Awiel East County consists of the Agurpiny, Wun-Anei, Makuac, Wun-Diing, APuɔth, APuɔth-Yelker, Akanyjök, Pingdong, ɤɔu Alueeth, Duluit, Ajuet and Cimel executive chieftaincy sections.

(2) The Kuei areas in Paliëët in Awiel South county consists of the Ajak Akol Atany, Kongdeer Dut Jök, Buɔncuai, Thanybur, Akuliɛc areas and Baau or Lou executive chieftaincy sections.

All those sections so described at length make up what is the Kuei section of Rek in Tonj, Gogrial, Aweil East and Aweil South when put together. The big Malual Giɛrnyaang in Awiel North county and Malual-Buɔth Anyaar in Awiel West county are all Kuei sections of Rek.

(3) Lith, on the other hand, is a Dinka name for the hawk bird known for its deadly speed and for its stabbing attack which it makes when it suddenly lands upon its prey from just nowhere out of the sky. The hawk's distinctive voice is also powerfully threatening. Great Lerbek, a Spear Master from the Pahöl clan people of the thigh bone is said by Rek tradition to have been accredited with the right of naming a group of clans apportioned to him after Thiek Anei was given his portion that he named Kuei.

Like was done by Thiek Anei, Great Lerbek provided a cow by the colour of Lith for its symbolic colour of the hawk. Cow Lith was publicly ritualled and its colour symbolism was figuratively transferred upon that society of clans which were apportioned to him. The big liege also named his faction *Apuk*, meaning compensation, a point better explained under the **battle of Ayuomlual** which was fought in the Payii River area between his people of Lith and the Kuei people of Great Ayii Thiek. This was prior to the Rek coming to Amongpiny.

Great Lerbek's people were killed in this internal war of Rek. The war was fought in our today's Payii River area in present Kiec land. It took place some time after the historic crossing of the Nile River when people came from the Upper Nile east bank area of the current Jonglei state. Having been given the right to name and lead those groups of clans was to Great Lerbek an act of *Apuk*. It was an act of compensation to him for the misfortune done to his people in that battle caused by a quarrel over Ayuomlual, a battle which was so devastating and had to be compensated when Rek community elders apportioned him with a number of clans.

Thus the three names of Gïr, Lith and Kuei were chosen for what they symbolised. They were to be the sectional emblems for each of the three sectors of the big society of the Rek. On the forefront of the Jaang migratory exodus was this big Rek group and it was commanded by a Rek cultural hero, Great Loŋaar from the Pagong clan people of the vetiveria nigritana grass known by all the Dinka people as awaar.

The three symbolic names were to portray the Rek Dinka marshal attributes vis-à-vis other sections of the western Dinka of Bahr el Ghazal at the time. Except for Gok and Agaar who did the wars of occupation of the remaining parts of South-Central and the western areas of the present Lakes state in Bahr el Ghazal, Rek society whose forward part (the Buɔth-Anyaar) later became the fountain society for the Malual Dinka, was the Dinka invasional society which effected the conquest and occupation of the central, north and northwestern parts of the Bahr el Ghazal region from 1340 to 1600 AD.

MORE ABOUT THE LITH COMMUNITY OF REK

The Lith component of Rek is comprised of all those communities known as Apuk, be it the big Apuk-Juwiir in the Thiet area of Tonj South county, the Apuk of Padoc in Tonj North county or the large Apuk of former chief Giir Thiik, Gïr-Aɣɛclai, in what is now Gogrial East county, all in Warrap state.

Apuk-Juwiir, to begin with, is made up of two broad sections of Macuet which is itself made up of Kongdeer, Agurpiny and Aliai sections. Aliai is also made up of Aliai-Aremrap and Aliai-Buong. The second component of this Apuk is known as Maluil Chol Wol and is composed of the territories of Mangeng, Malony, Tarweng and Angol chieftaincies. Until the time of the Southern Sudan regional government policy of decentralisation in the native administration in Southern Sudan (1976) the whole of this Apuk-Juwiir territory was a large but single administrative suzerainty of Chief Malek Mathok, as it was of his father Mathok Malek and of his grandfather before his father. Chief Malek Mathok is a Parum clan man from the ruaal revering people. Ruaal is the sausage or Kigelia Ethiopia tree, the totemic divinity of the descendants of Mayuääl Banyköök. Malek Mathok, Chief Deng Aruööp Mabuɔc and Chief Malek Akuiɛn are descendants of Mayuääl who according to history is a descendant of the Jewish Esau, who is described in the Bible and is the one from whom came that intermediate descendant who became known as Mayuaal-Banyköök, whose descendants permeate the entire Bahr el Ghazal Dinka lands today.

To further clarify on this Apuk, the territory started to be known as Apuk of Bol Mel prior to the Turco-Egyptian colonial era in Sudan.

Some people used to call it Apuk of Bol-Cirial. Cirial was a surname of the same Bol Mel from the Pabuor clan people who are a cow revering people.

The territory is believed to have been first settled in the early 15th century by the Pabuor, Patiir and Padiangbar clan people. The Patiir were known until recently as people of Aguɛt Lökbaai-thoc. The Padiaŋbar, on the other hand, were known as people of Beek-Amuuk.

Some time before the Turco-Egyptian colonial period in Sudan, came one Redior clan family that broke away from the Redior mainland area of Paan Cinweer, today's family of Makuer Gol Mayen in the Agaar area of Amothnhom.

Those new arrivals, known today as the Parum clan people in Apuk-Juwiir, later emerged and among them was a prominent liege by the name of Wol Rum popularly presented by his family line as Wol-Agitjok, who greatly featured as a community leader in the slave trade pestilence era. Because he faced the menace of the slavers in defence of the Apuk people, the community gave him the leadership of the entire territory in place of the Bol-Cirial family line. Like Bol-Cirial, he was from a powerful spiritual clan.

Although Wol-Agitjok was subsequently killed in one of the battles with the Turco-Egyptian slavers, his son Malek Wol continued as the leader of Apuk. Malek Wol was also killed by the Turks and was replaced by his eldest son, Agei Malek, who immediately took over as leader of Apuk. Yet Agei Malek was also killed in a battle at Thön-Gai Spot. He was killed by the Anglo-Egyptian forces who were fighting against Apuk resistance to the Anglo-Egyptian colonial rule which was being extended to their area from Tonj.

With this, Agulet, the eldest son of Agei, decided to avoid taking over the throne. He let it go to his young stepbrother, Malek Agei. This was during the period of the second world war. Malek Agei became so famous in his time but the British colonial authorities killed him at Cuei-Ajai with one of his sub-chiefs Ayueel Baak.

The two were killed because chief Malek objected to the forceful conscription of his community youth into the military training for the second world war on the side of the British. Malek's son, Agei, took over as the chief in place of his father. He ruled Apuk up to 1953 when he decided to voluntarily resign his position and handed the throne to his brother, Mathok Malek, who ruled Apuk territory until he died in 1960. He was succeeded by his son, Malek Mathok, who reigned over Apuk until the territory was divided into two chieftaincies of Apuk, Maluil and Apuk-Macuet in 1976. The two sections of Aliai were left as sub-chieftaincy areas of Macuet. The new chieftaincy of Apuk-Muluil came out with the Spear Master Akot Makuac Akot, a descendant of the Mediaeval Bol-Cirial. The new Chief Akot Makuac comes from the Pabuor clan in the Mangeng section.

The Malony section of sub-chief Ayueel Makɛɛc, Tarweng section of sub-chief Chol Yuööt and Angol section of Paan-Görnhom were all made to constitute Apuk-Maluil under Chief Akot Makuac.

Macuet, which remained with Chief Malek Mathok, consisted of Kongdeer, Agurpiny and the two sections of Aliai-Buong and Aliai-Aremrap.

By the year 2000 Apuk-Juwiir area was again divided into several chieftaincies to ease local administration following a population increase as well as an increase in communal problems. Chief Malek Mathok was made to remain as chief for the Kongdeer section of Macuet. The clans in this section are Parum, Pakuiëth, Pagun, Pagor, Panyiɛr, Pabuor, Patiir, Patiop, Payuom and other smaller clans.

The Agurpiny section of Macuet was given over to a Pakuiëth clan man, Arop Akol Arop. Agurpiny is inhabited mainly by the Padiangbar, Pakuiëth, Pagun, Pagor and Payuom clans. There are, however, smaller clans in the same territory.

Malek Akuien Lueth became the chief for the two sections of Aliai, which is inhabited largely by the Parum, Padiangbar, Pabuor, Pagor, Pakuieth, Padolmuöt and other smaller clans.

Akot Makuac Akot remained to be chief for the Mangeng section of Apuk-Maluil. Mangeng territory is inhabited by the Pabuor, Padiangbar, Pachol, Pakot, Patiop and other small clans. Manut Baak Athian from the Pagong clan became chief for the Malony section of Apuk-Maluil which is inhabited by the Pagong, Padiangbar, Pakot, Pakuiëth, Payät Pawet and Paluet clans.

Akot Chol Yuööt from the Pakot clan became chief for the Tarweng section of Apuk-Maluil inhabited by the Pakot, Padiangbar and Parum clans.

Deng Aruööp Mabuoc from the Parum clan became chief for the Angol section of Apuk-Maluil. The main clans which inhabit the Angol section are Parum, Pawet, Pakot, Pangok, Pakuiëth and Panguet clans.

Apuk-Juwiir has four land types and is geographically made up of (i) the toch or swampland which lies on the south eastern portion of the territory. This region is highly suitable for pasture and has abundant water for animals and humans. The area borders the toch of the Thɔny community to the southeast and Luackoth community to the true east; (ii) Lil or lowland plain. This is a wet area between Bongo and Jur highlands. It is an area with silt or loam soil suitable for grain, beans and wheat production. This plain encompasses River Wanh-Alel area, the whole of Tarweng and Mangeng sections. It borders the Thɔny and Yar Ayiɛi communities to the south. This land type extends to the Malony section. (iii) is the forest land which lay east and north east of Thiet town. This is a wild forest land inhabited mostly by wild animals such as leopards, lions, hyena and outlaws who make it their home. (iv) is the sandy land which covers parts of Kongdeer, but all of Agurpiny and Aliai sections of Apuk-Macuet. It slopes westwards in a very fertile soil leading to the Luo land of the Jur-col in the extreme west. To the northwest Apuk is bordered by the Nyang section of Kuanythi and by the Kuac community of the Kuanythi region. The whole of Aliai is sandy and bordered to the northeast. Millet, durra, groundnuts, sesame and beans are grown in this land type.

Apuk-Juwiir is a large and populous area administratively constituted into Thiet, Wanhalɛl and Jak Payams. It is the biggest single community in Tonj South county today and can one day make a county of its own with Thiet as its capital town.

The other Apuk community known as Apuk of Padɔc in the Akɔp area of Tonj North county is made up of three territorial chiefdoms of Ming, Rɛɛng and Maguk sections, all under Chief Dhaal Malith Dhaal of the Pakuör clan people of the bladed spear (tɔng) and rock stone which is called kur in Dinka[13]. The Aduëët and Adɔkthök territorial sections of Chief Dut Paduɔl Mayen of the Pacuök clan is another section of this Apuk. Pacuök people are an earlier lineage branch of the Pakër clan people of water, a clan people famously known to identify the exact location of the underground water. There is then the large section called Agurpiny with another section by the name of Mayuai. The two sections are under Chief Ayäi Bol, also of the Pakër clan people of the underground water.

All of those sections of Apuk-Padɔc were until 1976 under the overall authority of Chief Bol Ayäi, as it was of his father Ayai Kuol and his grandfather Kuol Ayuääl before him. Kuol Ayuääl was the known overlord of this Apuk. He is a descendant of Kuol-Cieliec who was greatly renowned as a Spear Master of exceptional spiritual potency. Great Kuol-Cieliec in his time would make a person fall dead when he turned to face the person while angry. He was too potent to be angry with a person. He was able to make the whole Apuk of Padɔc lay prostrate in respect for him. His father was purchased in the 17th century with ten cows from the Pakër clan people in the Thiik area of Anan-Atak territory of Riaang-nhom, in present Tonj East county. This purchase was done in order for him to come to be the community saviour against a then deadly monster, a big serpent then locally known throughout Apuk-Padɔc as *Aröbö* which in the early parts of the 17th century had almost finished this Apuk people. *Aröbö* was a community threatening beast of exceptional menace and there are local stories about how that serpent used to kill people by merely coming into a glance with a person even from afar. Some people think it was a kind of dinosaur! The big snake used to rise up very high into the sky in the toch as to oversee the entire landscape and anybody who came in sight of its eyes instantly died by it merely seeing him or her. The beast did have powerful radiant eyes that saw through into the distance! Kuol-Cieliec miraculously conjured that beast to death, thereby liberating the Apuk-Padɔc community from its threat.

In later times this Apuk of Padɔc came to be known also as Apuk of Ayäi Kuol, although the toch of this Apuk continued to be invariably known as the toch of Mayen Adɛwun. At times the toch is also called the Toch of Ayäi Kuol. Ayäi Kuol, Mayen Adɛwun and Malith Dhääl, their fathers and their grandfathers before them, were great men of this Apuk in their times, beginning from the early 18th century to the end of the 20th century. Their family lines continue to rule this Apuk-Padɔc to the present time although Kuol Ayuääl's descendants still continue to have the upper hand as the spiritual overlords of the entire Apuk of Padɔc.

Then comes the big Apuk, known as Apuk-Pathuɔn, a territory which until recently was known as Apuk of Giir Thiik. It is the only Lith section in Gogrial in the whole of the former district in Bahr el Ghazal, but before the appointment of great Giir Thiik as the overall chief of this big Apuk by the British colonial administration the territory was known as Apuk of Jök Tɔng, a descendant of Great Lerbek who gave the name Lith to Apuk at the Payii River area in Yirol territory during the Jaang migration into Bahr el Ghazal.

This Apuk is made up of eight territorial chiefdoms consisting of (i) the Biöng section of Chief Madɔl Anäu Madɔl from the Pakuec clan people who revere *rol* the thigh bone as their totem; (ii) the

Nyarmong section of Chief Bul Thiik Nhomuɔt of the same Pakuec clan; (iii) the Buöyar territory of Chief Ngor Ater of the Paluɛc clan known as the people of Rap the durra, locally called Rap-Luac; (iv) the Amuuk section of the grandson of great Giir Thiik, Chief Thiik Riiny Giir of the Pakuec clan people of the same ɤol totem; (v) the Abiöör section of Chief Ngor Thiɛp Thiäng of the Paliɛcmuɔk clan people of the same ɤol totem; (vi) the Abuɔk section of Chief Thɔndit Angok Deng of the Pajök clan people of the same ɤol totem; (vii) the Adöör section of Chief Mayol Magai Agaany of the Paguer clan people of the agaany (monitor lizard) totem and finally (viii) the Jur Man-Angɛɛr section of Chief Madut Madut Deng of the Patääng clan people who revere the dog and vulture as their totemic divinities. This Apuk of great Giir Thiik is currently made up of six administrative districts called payams and is an administrative province known as Gogrial East county.

Thus, the three Apuk: Apuk-Juwiir, earlier known before Turkiyya as Apuk of Bol Mel but which in later times became known as Apuk of Malek Mathok; Apuk-Padɔc, earlier known as Apuk of Ayai Kuol, and the big Apuk-Pathuɔn known before Turkiyya as Apuk of Jök Tɔng but now known as Apuk of Giir Thiik. When taken together, the three Apuk make what is known as Lith section, the sub-cultural branch of Rek Dinka of Tonj and Gogrial sub-regions of Warrap state.

FURTHER BACKGROUND STORY OF LITH

According to accounts from Rek Dinka society in Tonj and in Gogrial, particularly in the Thiet area of Juwiir and in the area of Padɔc, a certain Mel-Agaar migrated from the Jöth section of today's Agaar tribe by about the early part of 1600 AD. He came with his cattle and family, accompanied by a number of his lineage members who settled with him among the Lith sector of Rek in what is now Patɛu village in the area of present Luackoth in

Tonj East county. Mel-Agaar came to Patɛu before Apuk divided into three. According to this tradition Mel-Agaar did have three sons: Bol Mel, Pathuɔn Mel and Padɔc Mel. Bol was the eldest son followed by Pathuon, with Padɔc as the last son.

One day at Patɛu, the Kuei community with some Gïr people began to have misgivings about Apuk over the pasture land of Patɛu. Mel-Agaar had a good herd of cattle that came with him from Agaarland. While in Patɛu he heard a rumour that the Kuei and Gïr people might attack the Apuk section people, specifically aiming at the cattle of Mel, the newcomer. There was a plan to kill his sons and take their cattle. In response Mel-Agaar decided to summon his three sons and his host people of Apuk to whom he was a guest. He intimated to them about the plan by the Kuei and Gïr people. Mel argued that he could not wait for his three sons to be killed and their cows looted asunder. He advised that his three sons go in to divide the cattle and hastily move out of the Patɛu cattle camp to some different distant lands. This was agreed in order to avoid the repeat of an earlier war between the Lith and Kuei, a war which history presents to have been very disastrous to the side of Apuk. Ayuomlual, the cause of that war, is an earlier type of giant turtle that is known to the Rek Dinka people as nhiëër.

As the story goes, Bol Mel took part of their cows and left south with a group of Apuk people and a number of clans. He later settled in what is the present Apuk-Juwiir. He particularly chose to stay in the toch part where the historic trees called ju were situated. These are the ju trees from which his Apuk section acquired its name of Apuk Ju-wiir, sometimes written as Juwiir. The territory started to be called Apuk of Bol Mel, and also as Apuk-Juwiir. This Apuk was therefore called so until recently when it became Apuk of Malek Mathok after the Turkiyya period.

Padɔc Mel, the youngest, took his lot from his father's cattle and went north from Patɛu with a number of Apuk clans. Seeking for a toch, he went as far as present tochland, around the Meshra River port area. He settled at a raised ground made by an ancient race called Luɛɛl who made it into a large mount area northeast of present Akɔp town. He settled there with his people. In time he named it Padɔc after his name. He later expanded it into a big cattle camp with the name of Padɔc. The cattle camp continues to retain that name of Padɔc to the present day. As the head of that community of clans that went with him Padɔc Mel later demarcated an area which he named Apuk of Padɔc. The territory continues to be called so until today.

The second son, Pathuɔn Mel, opted to go west with his cattle and clans that accepted to follow him. Among those who went with Pathuɔn Mel were those several lineages of Pawan, some family members from Loŋaar, Paduɔltiɔp clan people, Pagor and Pakɛu, Paciɛr who are Pakeer and the lion and wind revering clans such as Palɛɛt. Other clans such as Pagiir and Pamɛɛr, Pajiëëng and Pakiir, all went along with him as did those of Paluɛtmiir. The hippopotamus revering clans such as the Paducuek, Patir and Pakuacdiɛm, Palual, Padiaŋbar and Pakuɛny also went with him. The fire revering groups such as Pakuiëëth, Pabol and Padɛp also went as did the Ruaal-related groups. They included the Padior, Pakuin and Pabuɔl. Some lineages from the Ayii Thiek faction of the Pahöl later joined those clans there. These people later became known as the Payii in that area. Other clans and people subsequently joined after Pathuɔn had arrived in those areas that are presently called Apuk of Pathuon, which became the Great Apuk of the Gogrial East county of today. But great Jök Tɔng Lerbek continued side by side with Pathuɔn Mel as to also make the Apuk become identified with him as 'Apuk of Jök Tɔng'. Present Panɛu, Pakuec and others later joined as new sojourners from Luacjang. From Pakuec came the great Giir Thiik who emerged as the paramount chief of this Apuk during the Anglo-Egyptian condominium period.

THE BATTLE OF AYUOMLUAL

According to stories given during the research work in many parts of Reklands, there was a fishing activity by the whole Rek on the upper reach of the Payii River in what is the Kiec land of today. This event took place some years after the Jaang crossed the River Nile from the east bank region of Upper Nile. A giant turtle called *Ayuomlual* was killed during that fishing moment in the afternoon by a joint fishing party of Kuei and Lith. In the process of the killing of the turtle, it is said one of the men from the Kuei section speared it first. He realised he had struck an unusual river monster. It was immediately understood to be the giant Ayuomlual, always dangerous to kill unless by an entire fishing party. Then a man from Lith, an Apuk man, speared it second and the whole party went in and shared in its killing. After the big turtle was dead people disagreed over the ownership of the carcass and this turned into a quarrel that went on till sunset. It was, however, finally agreed that the beast be left on the riverbank as it was growing darker, the darker part of the dusk after twilight. This was on the upstream of the present Payii River. The fishing party agreed to return the next morning to flay and skin it and to divide it between them as Kuei and Lith youthfolk. Ayuomlual of our primeval swamps or Toch of the Nile region's part of the sudd is known for its immenseness. Some people say it can be as big as a hut and could be eaten by a large party of people.

When the Kuei party returned in the dawn of the next morning they found that the Apuk youth of Lith had come over during the night, eaten the whole turtle and then went away, only leaving traces of fatty debris, bony fragments and the oil-soaked ash from the fire which they had made to roast the turtle. Those were the only things found at the previous day's riverbank vicinity! The Kuei party became annoyed and their wrath led them to the cattle camps of the Apuk community only to find that the Apuk people had already departed their camps with their cattle soon after they returned from the giant turtle. The Kuei party therefore decided to follow the Apuk, running after them in pursuit, but according to the story, on the night before their departure one pregnant heifer by the colour of *Nyalek* delivered a bullock and was not able to run during the haste. Nyalek and its bullock therefore remained on the pathway, on the route. A man from Kuei called Kuëëth, trod upon the spot of that heifer Nyalek. Kuëëth took the cow and its bullock back to his kraal but as the day went by, the Kuei pursuing party failed to catch up with the running Apuk. In the afternoon they returned to their camps, very much exhausted.

Subsequently the owner of Nyalek, who realised that his cow was missing and must have remained behind, set out in search along the route from where they passed. He failed to get Nyalek after running and walking the whole length of the route they trod as they were running. For days he and his Apuk people hunted for the cow till they finally found it at the kraal of Kuëëth who refused to give it up to the owner. As the Dinka would have it, a fight took place between Kuëëth and the owner of Nyalek. The two went into a duel and after they mutually fell the whole affair was soon followed by an all out fight between the Kuei and the Apuk. In that battle of history known as the Battle of Ayoumlual the Apuk community was badly beaten to a catastrophic level. It is said some of the families were annihilated and that the battleground and the escape route were all the way littered with the fallen!

After three days of this fratricidal battle, an Apuk head man by the name of Lerbek the Great convened a gathering of the remaining Apuk people to conduct an affair of ritual battle cleansing.

He called on all sections of Lith to bring a black bull each, bulls which he had killed in the forests for vultures to feed on as a practice after a bad battle. Great Lerbek organised Apuk, telling them it was not possible for Apuk (that is, Lith) to defeat Kuei any time due to its sheer size. He asked his people, it is said, to march off further west to look for new lands, urging them not to settle or stay separate from Kuei society should the Kuei follow them west. This advice in effect was for the Lith to avoid any such fratricidal battles in the future with the Kuei community as long as the whole Rek was involved in its forward wars of occupation against Jur-Luɛɛl and the rest of the Aboriginals who inhabited the region. Great Lerbek advised that the Kuei and Lith should always share one toch or territory, but urged them to preserve the name of Apuk from becoming extinct by Kuei.

After this sermon to his Apuk community of Rek, Lerbek the Great is said to have declared he was no longer going to remain alive as the Spear Master to no people, as his people were almost finished by Kuei. Upon that declaration, Great Lerbek is said to have instantly died and was buried on the very meeting spot said to have been on the branch stream at the toch plain to the east between the present Aköt area of Agaar of Yäk and the Amongpiny area of the Aliääp section of Agaar in the far northeastern area of Rumbek.

Whether this story can be confirmed by Apuk chroniclers or not or by the lineage members of Great Lerbek who are presently among the leaders of the Apuk of Gogrial, may be immaterial at this stage so long as this legend permeates much of Rek society to the present day. As the story goes on Lerbek the Great was buried and the Apuk continued in their onward migratory move. They came and settled at Amongpiny and later at what is now known as *Karɔm*, which is an area in the present Waat section of Gok Dinka where Twic had settled some few years earlier. Here they later proceeded further to what is now Luacc" jang territory in the present eastern areas of Tonj. Then the Apuk proceeded westwards. Some few years later the Kuei community joined them, coming from the Amongpiny area from behind. From then the entire community of Rek made its slow migration till they reached what is now Adöör in the Jalwau area where they made a stopover in the areas of what is now the entire territory of Jalwau, an area presently inhabited by the Kɔŋɔɔr community of Akuecbany, the Bäc area of Chief Deng Majak Deng, the Pakɔɔr section of Chief Marial Aɣeu and the Adöör area of Chief Mabior Dau Garang. The Rek settled in this territory of Jalwau with the Angääc area in Adöör land as the central cattle camp or village. They pushed the Jur-Luɛɛl community further west, north and south as they settled in this part of eastern Tonj.

While the Rek were in this area of Jalwau, the Luacjang were still at what is now Rɛɛl-Kou, an area along the toch marshes where they briefly stayed with the Kiec and Gok communities. Kiec and parts of Gok later returned to their present location in the Yirol area. At this time also Twic had displaced the Atäk and Mut sections of Jur-Luɛɛl in what is now Luacjang territory and had settled there after they came from the present Pathiöng area of Gok in current Lakes state. The Twic in their onward move made a road-like route from Yar-Döng in present Pagor Payam. They went on all the way through Bulic-Mathiang in what is Adöör up to the areas that are present Luacjang. Traces of that Mediaeval route made by Twic can still be seen today.

THE BATTLE OF THE WIFE OF BUONGLEK AT ANGÄÄC

At Angääc in the Jalwau area another historical incident made the Rek society disperse. This was the second historical dispersal to happen to the Rek society during their forward migration in the Bahr el Ghazal region. After the battle fought by the Rek society in this spot of Angääc, part of the Kuei society took the direction of Thiik to what is now Lou-Paɣer territory. The bulk of Kuei and the whole of Lith moved to what is now the Aköök-Teek and Luackoth areas. Some of the Gïr people went south to what is today's Thɔny areas.

What happened was that a certain woman, presented by history as the wife of a certain Buonglek, or BuƆŋlek, was the cause of the battle that led to a split. She was taking a bath at a water pool in the suburb of the big Angääc cattle camp. A handsome young man from the Parum clan people of Wol-Muun came by. He was coming for a drink and did not notice the woman naked and taking a bath in the middle of the nigritana grass, awaar. She was partly hidden by awaar at the edge of that water pool. Before he could notice her the woman overtook him. She quickly and strongly caught him by the arms and tightly held him in her grip and in the struggle which ensued, as the young man wanted to rid himself out of the strange act, the woman in her malicious intention issued out a high-flown cry, wailing and calling people to come and rescue her from the man whom she loudly said had raped her by force!

In response the entire Rek folk in Angääc burst out in throngs. The devilish woman was found still wailing and tightly in full grip of a then restless young man, struggling for a way out! When her husband, Buonglek, and his people arrived, they recognised the woman to be their wife! A fight ensued in that instant as they killed the young man, whose people did not hesitate in avenging for him. The incident was enough to engulf the whole community of Rek as the young man happened to have been from the Parum section of Kuei while Buonglek was from the Pakuiëth clan people of Apuk and was therefore of the Lith section. An unestimated number of people were killed on both sides!

The battle of Angääc, or more correctly, the 'Battle of the wife of Buonglek' is a known story among the Rek Dinka in general as excerpts from the following song, sang in the late 1960s from Apuk-Padɔc can affirm:

"...Tiŋ Buɔŋlek e yindë!?
Tiŋ Buɔŋlek aci jäl wathëëi
War tɛ́ɛ́ŋ Akol, le laak wiir acuɔl.
Na wën a le laak, ke tiŋ raandë ke cath
Go lueel abartɛn
Ku du bi riööc e ɣa,
ɣɛn akë biaŋkië dɔk!
Na wën a le bɛn
Go dɔm ku kiu kiɛu,
Ci dɔm ku pɛl wuɔu
Ku bi riëëc cidöŋ wut mɛt abën
Ku tuöm tɔŋ cake liääp e tiŋ bäny
Bi manh raan rot nɔk!
Yien wic Akɔkrot bi manh raan rot nɔk!?..."

Translation:
"...What happened to the wife of Buɔŋlek!?
The wife of Buɔŋlek left in the afternoon,
When the sun was in its afternoon in order to take a bath.
And when she was taking bath, she saw a coming young man.
She then called on him to come hither!
Saying, "do not fear me! I have not removed my aprons."
When he came,
She caught him in full and strong grip and wailed!
She caught him and cried out, saying he forcefully raped her!
With that the entire manfolk of the cattle camp of Angääc burst forth!
And the battle ensued wife of! The liege, you have incited confusion,

Till human beings killed themselves the way they did! So, Akɔkrot wants men to kill each other like it was done by the wife of Buɔŋlek?"

In consequence to this battle, the Rek society parted ways a second time and dispersed in different directions. As described above, part of the Rek society went to the present area of Patɛu and what is now Wunkuel in the Aköök-Teek area. A group of clans and lineages known as Lou went headlong to what is Lou-Paɣer of today, passing through the current Thiik area. This group was led by Wol-Muun himself, father of the young man who was killed at the woman's grip. They settled at what is current Agawei and its surroundings before his descendants later proceeded to the toch region which later became the Gɔny section of Great Kuch Angui, who is himself a descendant of the very Wol-Muun. Then the bulk of Rek society went ahead, westwards in the direction of what is now Lɛɛr, Lɔɔc and Nyang, where they are currently known as Kuei of Akɔch Majök. The Cuɛitiim community and Awan sections of Kuei went to what is now called Amoldɔu in the present Aköök-Teek area due west from Angääc. With this column of Awan and Cuɛitiim were parts of Pagong lineages of Loŋaar's clan, the leader of migration to Bahr el Ghazal.

Leading this column of Amoldɔu was Great Ayii Thiek, a grandson of Anei-Barek,[64] the chief opponent of Longaar at the initial stage of the migration. Much of the Pagong clanspeople within the Rek went southward towards the present Thɔny territory. The Padiangbar people of Anei-Adiangbar went west with several other clanspeople. The rest of the story of the Rek's further migration and internal

---

64   The suffix 'Barek' after the name Anei is a Dinka word meaning 'go and bring along'. That historic Anei was the one who mobilised and urged Jaan , especially Rek, to leave the Upper Nile all at once, much against the plan and opinion of Loŋaar who wanted the conquest of Bahr el Ghazal to be first accomplished before the entire Jaang community was moved in.

zigzag by some sections, clans, lineages or individuals in Bahr el Ghazal will be told later.

HOW THE REK MADE ITS MIGRATION INTO BAHR EL GHAZAL

From the Payii River area the Rek moved to Amongpiny and further westwards and southwards to the areas now inhabited by the Amothnhom section of Agar and then to Karöm in the present Gokland area of Pagor, then to what is now Jalwau, to the Aköök-Teek and Luackoth areas in the Tonj East county of today. After several decades the Rek extended to as far as present Apuk, called the Juwiir area of Thiet Payam in Tonj South county. At the time when the Rek made that very long migratory shift to reach Jalwau from Karöm, they settled in those areas of Angääc in Adöör land in the Jalwau area of today. Here the Rek uprooted the original inhabitants of the area whom they still remember as 'Jur-Luɛɛl'. After a decade or more the Rek society proceeded west out of this Angääc area, following the split from the disastrous battle caused by the wife of BuƆŋlek, a story earlier explained. They came and settled in the areas that are present Aköök-Teek territory as far as the present Luackoth areas. Famous in those settlement areas are those historical sites such as Patɛu, AmoldƆu, Wunkuel and Luang-Luil, all in the area of present Aköök-Teek and the village areas of Luackoth such as Panyang, Payuel and the big woodland areas of the Ngircuk, Wajabak and Yungcuk cattle camps.[65] Here, the Rek made a further push on the Jur-Luɛɛl people who continued to withdraw westwards in flight, leaving much of their livestock with the incoming Rek fighting hordes.

---

65   Such Mediaeval cattle camps still carry such names in the Luackoth territory today.

However, by the time the Rek society came to the area of Jalwau, Gïr was an associate of Lith and in combination Gïr and Lith were able to stand on equal par with the Kuei component in terms of population.

THE KUEI COMPONENT OF REK AND ITS SECTIONS

SECTIONS OF KUEI

Kɔŋɔɔr, meaning forerunner, is this section of the Kuei which later remained in this vicinity of Jalwau, where they continued to be the present day Kɔŋɔɔr people of Great Akuecbany Cirɔŋ Kuol of the Redior clan people of Ruaal. Other section people associated with this Kɔŋɔɔr also remained in this area of Jalwau to later become those sections of Pakɔɔr Bäc and Adöör.

There was *Buɔth-Anyaar,* which started as a collection of youth parties, later joined by a number of clans, individuals and families from the rest of Rek. *Buɔth-Anyaar*, later to become a section within Malual Dinka, was originally a group of youth from different sections of the Kuei that went after a buffalo herd that came from the east, running due west past the big cattle camp of Amongpiny. That buffalo herd came from what later became the Nuers' toch" land of Ganyliel. After long pursuit of the buffalo herd those youth groups did not return to the cattle camp. They began to feed on the meat of whatever buffalo they had killed and then proceeded in their pursuit of that buffalo herd further west from Amongpiny. As days went by other youth parties decided to follow, tracing the first groups. They eventually joined them at a distance which also made them decide not to return to Amongpiny society. They thus remained in the area which now became known as Bulic-Mathiang in Adöör land after they crossed the toch called Kol of Adöör that presently separates the Gok and Agaar from the Rek of Tonj East. Here, the groups began to increase as they also attracted hunters from the Lith section who were living at the Karɔm territory in the now Gok land area of Pagor Payam. They were also joined by hunters from very far away Amongpiny and even by the Agars who had to come from what is now Amothnhom land. Others came from what is now the Panyoon territory of Agaar. Luac hunters from Rɛɛlkou to the northeast of them also joined them in this hunters' big forest of *Bulic-Mathiang*.

All traditions existing among Bahr el Ghazal Dinka communities are agreed that a number of girls and women also joined these *Buɔth-Anyaar* parties and were as such able to marry and form a distinct group that continued to stay to be a section of their own. When Rek society later moved altogether from the Amongpiny area and from Karɔm those Buɔth-Anyaar youth parties also decided to move, following this migratory wave as part of the big moving Rek society, but maintaining its distinct entity. On arriving in the area which is current Jalwau in what is now Tonj East, *Buɔth-Anyaar* settled in a separate settlement with Tɔng-Manyangdit, who is Tɔng Anei-Barek, as their spiritual leader. Tɔng Anei later led this *Buɔth-Anyaar* faction of Rek to the Northern Bahr el Ghazal region of Awiel from the Abiem area in northwestern Tonj. *Buɔth-Anyaar* was therefore an offshoot section of the Kuei.

Then there was the Adöör section of the Kuei. The settlement centre for this Adöör was later to become what is now the yik village of Adöör in current Adöör lands of Chief Mabior Dau Garang. Part of the Adöör society settled at the very historic settlement centre of Angääc which continues to be an Adöör land to the present day. Parts of Adöör later went away with the rest of the Rek following the split caused by the wife of Buɔŋlek. They joined Lith and are now the Adöör section in Apuk-Giir in Gogrial East county.

There was also the Lou section of Kuei. This Lou section is

believed to have incorporated and assimilated a lot of later arrivals from Agar land and even from Nuer lands. Many families from the ruaal totem were subsequent breakaway individuals and lineages from the Parum or Redior mainland of Amothnhom in Agaarland. They were welcomed and accommodated by this Lou section of Rek. This accounts for the rampant presence of the Ruaal groups of lineages that came from the Macot Mayen lineage in Agaarland. Many Parum people can now be found among different Lou sections in the Reklands. The Pamuon clan people in Lou Paɣer, for instance, are descendants of Muun Macot, son of Mayen Aweckɔc. They are now an executive chieftaincy in the Gɔny and Matik sections in Lou-Paɣer territory. Sub-chief Deng Chol of the Macuet section in Lou-Paɣer is also a descendant of a Ruaal man by the name of Jiel Aköt Jerbek, brother of Aköök Jerbek who later pioneered Lou-Paher territory. Aköt Jerbek in subsequent decades left Amothnhom in Agaar land to join the Rek society at Angääc in Adöör. Some of the Parum lineage families are among those who led Lou factions that later broke off from these Lou-Paɣer areas and migrated further north to become the pioneers for the present Lou-Ariik in the far end of Tonj North county. They did their migration along the toch and went to the present Lou-Ariik territory before the Patɛk clan people later arrived in the area from Aköök-Teek.

Due to the sudden split which befell Rek society at Angääc following that devastating war caused by the wife of Buɔŋlek, Lou society also split very greatly. The Lou part that settled at Angääc was hard hit at the battle and its remnants ran west with the Buɔth-Anyaar people of Tɔng Anei. They were under a Parum spiritual patriarch, Diing Wol Leek, popularly presented by traditions in the Awiel area as Diing-Keramindïk whose descendants are now known as Paciɛrmeth. Some of the lineages of this Ruaal group who also went with Keramindïk are now the Palɔu and Pakäm clan people in Awiel areas. Others are known as Papuɔl while others are Pakuin or Parum proper. A number of the Ruaal groups later joined Lith following the earthquake incident at Panyang in Luackoth. Those are the Parum clans and lineages that are now in the Apuk of Padoc in Northern Tonj and in the Apuk of Pathuɔn in Eastern Gogrial as well as those in the Juwiir area, but those of Deng Mabuɔc in the Apuks of Thiet and Thɔny are recent arrivals from the Twic area of Akuär. They first went to Jur-Manangɛɛr from Twic. They then came to the Thiet area of Juwiir through the Apuk of Giir Thiik some time during the Turkiyya.

It is this same Ruaal people in Lou who went and maintained the name of Lou in the Abiem area of Lou territory of Chief Aguer Gɛng of the Pakäm clan people of the ruaal tree totem. At the time when the whole Rek society was still in present Jalwau areas, Ruaal groups that later came from the Amothnhom area in Agaar land were more associated with the Lou section of Kuei and with Lith which is Apuk. The presence of Ruaal groups among non-Apuk and non-Lou areas of Rek at present is due to a later social fusion within the Rek.

Beside Kɔŋäär, Buɔth-Anyaar, Adöör and Lɔu, there was a section known as Aliääp. The clans that constituted Aliääp are those which came under the authority of a certain Teek who was a son of Kɔɔk Manyang, son of Awukdiääny Mading, also known as Awukdiääny Ayak Ring. Other clans of this section of Aliääp also became known as Thiik, under a certain Ker Ker whose descendants later became the Paker people who are divine masters of the underground water. One Parum lineage, now of Makɔm Wol, and his brother Arop Wol, later trailed in from Agaarland of Amothnhom at the beginning of the 17th century and settled with the Thiik people of Aliääp. They are the descent line from which came Great Majɔk Makɔm who ruled the Thiik section as sub-chief to Chief Deng Acuil of the Patɛk clan. Chief Deng Acuil is a descendant of Teek, son of Kɔɔk Manyang. This Majɔk Makɔm was appointed as sub-chief for Thiik in 1927. He ruled the Thiik area for more than six decades. The Thiik area thrived under his care until the area was recently promoted to executive chieftaincy level with one from the descendants of former Ker Ker (of the Paker clan) as its chief. The Thiik section of Aliääp is now separate from Chief Deng Acuil's area of Aköök-Teek.

For proper understanding of how one section of Aliääp acquired the name of Teek a brief summary of the family of Teek is necessary in this account. Teek is the name from which came the clan name Patɛk, meaning the family lineage of Teek. This line started with a girl, Ayak Ring AwikjÖk who had a brother by the name of Ayong Ring. They were from the Gajaak Nuer section that now lives on the Sudan-Ethiopian borders on the eastern parts of the Upper Nile state.

One time, according to the Patɛk legends, Ayak went to play with girls in a nearby village stream. When they came out from swimming, her belly began to abnormally distend. Her brother Ayong thought his only sister had been impregnated illegally by somebody. He committed suicide! After this, a god from that nearby stream revealed to someone in a dream that it was he who conceived with the girl, saying that Ayak will bear a male child and he should be called Awukdiääny. The river god also said that Awukdiääny will also bear one son to be called Kɔɔk. The dream ordained that Kɔɔk will bear eight sons.

In the course of time the dream became true and so there was Kɔɔk from Manyang Awukdiääny. Kɔɔk was surnamed as Kɔɔk-Ajök when he grew up. He became a known fighter and he killed a lot of people in battles and in his fights with individuals. As time went by, his family and the Gajaak society became exhausted from paying blood (dia) compensation cattle all the time. They decided that they should get rid of him but his sister let him know what had been secretly resolved about him. He therefore escaped from the Gajaak country to what is today's Borland. In Bor, he became a guest of a certain Anei of the Pahöl clan people of the thigh bone totem. Anei was one of the landed gentry in Bor land and had married a certain

Arek[66], daughter of Longar Ayueel from the Pagong clan. While in Bor, Kɔɔk-Ajök showed his being from a powerful spiritual clan and he made several amazing feats. Traditions are disagreed as to the manner of his being part of the later Jaang migration to Bahr el Ghazal. Some say he was part of the migration still with Anei who became known after the crossing of the Nile as Anei-Barek. Other traditions say he remained in Bor with the Pahöl section people who are present Juor-yol in Bor, but that he later ran into trouble with the Bor community when he again began to kill people following small quarrels, so much that the Bor people also wanted to kill him.[67] According to this version, Kɔɔk-Ajök escaped under hot pursuit and on reaching the Nile bank at the Shambe Shore of Anyɔɔp, a big crocodile came out of the Nile and offered itself to carry him across to the west bank. Kɔɔk accepted and jumped on the crocodile that took him safely to the west bank of the Nile and in this way, Kɔɔk was able to escape from his pursuers, the Bor people. At the west bank, Kɔɔk travelled till he reached Rek society still in the area of present Pagarau in what is now Kiec land. Kɔɔk-Ajök settled with them. Here at Pagarau Kɔɔk married and he had eight sons in the course of his lifetime. This made the dream come true. Some of the eight sons are given as:

1. Awëër-Atunŋor who became the ancestor and founder of the Pawurbuɔk clan people who are now in the Kɔngoor area;
2. Aweerthi, the founding father of some other sections of the

---

66   Arek Loŋaar was the mother of Tong-Manyangdit and his brother Thiek Anei. Tong-Manyangdit became the ancestor from whom came the big Parek clan in the Awiel sub-region. Thiek Anei, his brother, on his part became the father of Ayii Thiek from whom came great Payii clan who now live in Tonj, Gogrial and Twic plus sections that went to live with the Lou in the Mapɛl areas in the Jur land of Western Bahr el Ghazel state.

67   From an interview with elder Parek Bol Machar (Parek Bany-Abuɔk) who married from the Patɛk people. He gave this version he found from the Patɛk and from his own Payii traditions. Interview dated 4.2.1999.

Patɛk clan people found in several places among Rek society;
3. Ajiɛk Kɔɔk, the founding ancestor of the Pajiɛk clan in Ajak-lɛɛr, in Twic and in Kuac-Agör area of Kuajök in Gogrial West;
4. Chuɔl Kɔɔk, who became the ancestor of the Pacol clan people in the Kɔŋöör area.
5. Mabut Kɔɔk, who became the founding ancestor of the Pabut clan in the Pakäm, Nyang and Athoi sections of the Agar Dinka.
6. Then he bore the sixth son whom he named Teek, who became the founding father of the present Patɛk clan in Aköök of Teek, in Lou-Ariik territory, Lou, Aguer Gɛng and many other areas in Gogrial and Awiel. As our focus is on Teek, the narrative will therefore continue with Teek. The remaining two sons and the other five are not the focus of this narrative.

One of the miracles made by Kɔɔk-Ajök while in Bor land is when he organised the Bor people for a revenge expedition to Bɛɛr land. The Bɛɛr, who are the present Murle, a Nilo-Hamitic people to the east of Bor Dinka, have been constantly waging wars against the Bor community and looting their cattle and children. Slightly before Kɔɔk's arrival from Nuer land, there was a fresh attack by the Murle and there was an atmosphere of war in the whole of Bor land. With his host Anei Awutiak who later became Anei-Barek, Kɔɔk made ritual practices and blessed the Bor revenge expedition. He told them they will defeat the Murle this time and will bring loot in cattle and children. In consequence Bor waged an attack on the Murle community. The Murle were disastrously devastated and the victorious Bor expedition returned with large numbers of cattle and children. The Bor society made a feast and acclaimed their newly found Spear Master. Cows were contributed to him. Anei Awutiak became happy with his guest and offered him a bull by the colour of Malɔu and he was proclaimed in the feast which was convened for the purpose. Spear Master Anei Awutiak declared that Kɔɔk was to keep the colour of *Lou* among his herd. Anei, from those who are now called Juör-rɔl in present Bor, told Kɔɔk to keep the colour of Lou for posterity. He told him that he was to later hand this issue of the colour of Lou down to his children and his descent lines to always keep the cow of the colour of Lou.

As willed by Spear Master Anei, Kɔɔk-Ajök kept getting the cow Lou and when he came to stay with Rek society in the Pagarau area and later in the Payii River area and in Amongpiny, his ever getting the cow with the colour of Lou made him name a section of Kuei using the name of Lou with himself as the spiritual patriarch of that faction of the Kuei. When the Rek later came to Angääc, it was his son *Awëër-Bäny Atut* who was in charge of the Lou section which had then divided into Aliääp, that subdivided into Teek and Thiik sections. The clans and families that were directly associated with Teek became known as Teek. In this way Teek and Lou became important historical components of the big Kuei section of Rek.

During the split caused by the battle of the wife of Buoŋlek, Teek society of clans moved to areas of Wunkuel, Midɛɛr and those areas that are now Ngapagɔk and its outlying areas. Thiik society of Aliääp moved to where it is today. The remaining Lou communities went to the areas of Patɛu and to an area now call Diɔɔr but they later converged at Agäwei, Cuum and the rest of the areas that are now Mathiang section of Lou-Paher. Some time later, Lou divided into clans that became Lou-her (the white Lou) and Lou-col (the black Lou). Lou-col went to what is now Lou-Ariik also known as Lou-Mawien territory. Lou-col people went to that area in around the beginning of the 17th century.

Lou-her, which in time became known as Lou-Payer, remained in the territory of the present Marial-Lou areas. Pagak, Pajieng, Parum and Payiĕk, all led by Great Jerbek, were the Lou clans that went to pioneer Lou-Ariik territory. Part of the descendants of Teek later migrated from the Aköök-Teek area and followed their former Lou people in what is now Lou-Paɣer where they later proceeded to the Lou-Ariik territory of today.

There was also the big Awan section of Kuei. It then consisted of six sections of Ariääu, Thöc, Cueitim, Adöör, Duör and Gurwel and as earlier explained, sections which constituted Awan took the western direction when they left Angääc at the time of the split, but they settled in the area of Amoldɔu in what is the present Aköök-Teek. They settled in this Amoldɔu and its adjacent areas of Ngircuk, Yungcuk and Wajabak in what is now the Luackoth area. They also covered the areas of the current Majur cattle camp area. This community of Awan later had a problem of leadership between Ayii Thiek and Gong Loŋaar. Both were from the Spear Master clans. Gong was the elder son of Loŋaar, the leader of Jaang migration to Bahr el Ghazal. His father was known to descend from the Pagong's famous ancestor, Ayueel Jiel, who was widely believed by the Dinka of the Middle Ages to be the source of all the holy Spear Masterhood. Parting from the rest of his father's family members at Angääc he took the route taken by Ayii Thiek's sections of Awan. He came and settled with those of Ayii Thiek at Amoldɔu. The internal struggle for recognition and spiritual supremacy which cropped up led to quarrels among the elderly sons of the various wives of Loŋaar even before the Rek moved out of Amongpiny.

Following the split at Angääc, each headman from Loŋaar's family household within Rek decided to join any section of his choice. This accounts for why Pagong people are found in almost every section and territory in Bahr el Ghazal. However, large parts of the Loŋaar group of families went south where they make the main cream of the communities in the Muɔk and Yar territories. Some of this Pagong later went to the Mading village of the Malony section of Apuk of Juwiir in the Tonj South county of today. Some lineages later went further west with the Kuei sections of Aguɔk, Kuac and other sections that also went west. It was in these areas that

Pagong later began to ramify to the rest of the western Rek lands of Gogrial and Tonj and to as far as Twic in the far north where they are today known as the Payaath clan people of Great Cyer Deng. Some proceeded from Mabior-Pagong in Aguɔk territory and went further to Awiel East and Awiel South. Others later returned from the Kuac-Agor section of Waau to Yäk in Agaar land where they settled among the Nyuɛi-Macar section people. They are the Aneet clan people who are those of Great Malual Arop of the Rumbek East county area of Aköt.

Ayii Thiek, on his part, was the grandson of Anei-Parek who was the initial opponent of Loŋaar. He opposed Longaar right at the time of the making of the decision for Jaang migration to Bahr el Ghazal from present Jonglei areas in south-central Upper Nile. The decision by Loŋaar was that it is the youth groups from all the Jaang sections to first cross the White Nile River to Bahr el Ghazal in order to fight its inhabitants, after which the rest of the Jaang population in the Upper Nile could be called to follow once the conquest and occupation is completed. Loŋaar was both a spiritual authority, a military leader and, indeed, a community leader with a longstanding family tradition of command and leadership of the entire Jaang during the eight hundred years' stay in the Upper Nile region. His great grandfather Ayueel-Akökboong led the Jaang society to the Upper Nile from the Khartoum region between 490 and 500 AD. His family line must have eclipsed other Spear Master families during those times of the Mediaeval or early Middle Ages when the Jaang were in the Upper Nile region.

As there can be no society without two opposing personages of consequence, Loŋaar's opinion and strategy was opposed by Anei Awutiak who, after the exodus to Bahr el Ghazal, came to be popularly known as Anei-Barek and sometimes as Anei-Thöcjang. Anei-Barek argued that the Jaang must all move out of the Upper Nile to the west bank into Bahr el Ghazal in order to escape the then deadly smallpox epidemic that was known as akoi and sometimes as Jong-alei, a name from which present Jonglei state derived its name. Since there was always a concomitant outbreak of measles, whooping cough and an intermittent cholera, the environment of the Upper Nile Basin region was becoming so unhealthy that Anei Awutiak thought it would be wise to make the whole Jaang society move out by exodus to fight while occupying the would be acquired new lands in Bahr el Ghazal to escape those epidemics that were consuming the society. The Jaang community accepted the logic of Anei Awutiak and so, when Loŋar left Pamac rallying point with his youth parties, Anei Awutiak made the rest of the Jaang move from behind him who went ahead with Ric, the youth parties then known as Kiec-Manyiel. He made the whole Rek and all the sections of the Jaang reach the east bank at the White Nile at present Shambe shore where Loŋaar and his youth expedition were resting and consolidating before attempting the marathon act of crossing the big White Nile River to the west bank to meet with Jur-Luɛɛl, the Belle and the Bongo. Anei's powerful propaganda among the Jaang sections made Luac, Twic, Agaar, Gok, Ciec, Aliap, Rek and the whole of the Padang move one after the other. Loŋaar became angry upon seeing the whole Jaang coming yonder towards him on the riverbank, moving in an almost endless column of people consisting of the aged, women, children and the entire livestock of the Nile Basin Jaang society. People were coming while carrying their domestic provisions and driving their entire livestock.

After a serious quarrel between Anei-Barek and Great Loŋaar on the east bank of the White Nile, Loŋaar jumped into the Nile with his youth parties of Kiec-Manyiel.[68] After they successfully crossed the Nile, Loŋaar decided to stand at the shallow part of the Nile about

---

68   Kiec-Manyiel was the Age-set of Loŋaar. It is the Jaang Mediaeval youth group which implemented many migrations and congests of the Bahir el Ghazal region in 1340 AD.

the edge of the Riverbank. With his spears he began to spear people on the heads as they emerged out of the Nile waters. He killed all those who were emerging from the Nile waters one after the other. People were emerging from the deepest parts of the Nile after they dived and walking in the deep of the waters with their noses pinched closed to not to breathe in the water while walking. Loŋaar killed several people in this way!

This unfortunate act by Loŋaar made some people, even whole sections, return from the east bank to their original departure places. Loŋaar killed a lot of people, particularly among the crossing Rek community. Other Jaang sections like Twic, Gok and Aliap decided to find other shores to cross at. However, the Rek community which was later followed by the Agaar society insisted on facing Loŋaar. Today several people within the Rek continue to claim it was their ancestor so and so who forcefully caught Loŋaar and carried him to the riverbank, across to the west bank, thereby making it possible for Rek community, with Agaar behind them, to cross through the very shore of Anyɔɔp which is today's Shambe shore near that large water body called Kadop.

Loŋaar is presented by several accounts as having been a huge and tall giant, a man in his fifties. Some giants like Wol-Adhieu, Wol-Adiangbar, Agɔth-Cithiik and Awuciu are said to have been the ones who caught him and carried him across to the Nile bank where a great quarrel later took place between him and the rest of the leaders of the clans after the Jaang had crossed to the west bank.

Great Loŋaar was particular with Awuciu, his sister's husband. He was also angry at Wol-Adhieu. Awuciu was married to his sister. Loŋaar therefore cursed him for participating in what he called "the conspiracy by Anei Awutiak". Awuciu did not prosper as a result of that curse from Loŋaar. His family lines are currently not found in many parts of Rek lands except for Apuk-Padɔc, Apuk-Giir, Lou-Ariik and Kuac-Akeen where there are thin lines of Pawuciɛu clan people still preserving the name of Awuciu. Wol-Adiangbar apologised to Loŋaar and was spared. Loŋaar avoided the two great Payöl leaders, Agɔth-Cithiik and his elderly uncle, Anei Awutiak. Loŋaar, however, told Anei to be the one to treat those diseases he had allowed to cross the Nile to the west bank with the Jaang society. He said, "You! Anei, you must be the one to heal those diseases once they appear in the society since you were the one who brought those diseases!" This later became true. Descendants of Anei Awutiak are now known to heal those diseases: measles, whooping cough, smallpox and cholera. Those who did not cross went back to become the east bank or Upper Nile Dinka societies of today.

This act by Loŋaar, the migration leader, created negative feelings among the Rek and the entire Jaang society. The act reverberated to the east and west banks and is a story told all over Dinka lands to the present day, even among the Upper Nile Dinka of today! While this act earned long lasting negative sentiments against Loŋaar, the role played by Anei-Barek won the hearts of all Jaang communities, particularly the Rek society to which both Loŋaar and Anei did belong. This explains why the Amoldɔu communities of Awan later decided to elect Ayii Thiek, the grandson of Anei-Barek, to be their leader and to also become their spiritual patriarch. They rejected Gong Loŋaar for his father's deed at the time of the crossing of the Nile to the Bahr el Ghazal areas.

When the Awan community gathered to decide who was to be their leader, one Pakuɔny old man suddenly sprung up in the gathering with a song. To the surprise of Gong Loŋaar the entire community made a thunderous repeat of that song. They rose up in unison and picked up Great Ayii Thiek, whom they carried on their shoulders above them while singing and moving in their uproarious celebration, saying, "Ayii Thiek is our leader". The following stanzaic lines are excerpts from that song, a song in praise of Great Ayii Thiek. That song continues to be sung by the Payii people today and it goes thus:

"Bäny thɔɔ n Bäny amuk Jäŋ
Wä Ayii Thiek muɔr aguaŋnhom,
Bäny thɔɔ n Mayuääl ɛɛ!!
Bäny thɔɔ n Mayuääl kök!
Muɔ rdiit bir piny, Muɔ rdiit birpiny
Wä Ayii Thiek abi tak athɛɛr,
Jam raan kan ɛɛ!!...

Ya raan ci baar ë Loŋaar!
Ya raan ci baar ë Loŋaar!
Tɔ ŋ thok tä moth, Ayii Thiek
Yien e muɔ r wëi tene ʳook ɛɛ!
Bäny dan buk tak athɛɛr,
Agut buk la wël piny,
Bäny dan buk tak athɛɛr.....!"

Translation:
"We choose the leader who cares for his people,
Our father, Ayii Thiek is the man whose horns are sharpened.
God Mayuääl, we have made a choice! Mayuääl, our God,
We have made a choice! Great Ayii Thiek, the man who shakes the ground when speaking to God.
Great Ayii is a man who trembles the ground when invocating for his people! He is the man we have chosen. Ayii Thiek, our father, will be remembered for all time.
That is how a leader speaks!
We have been orphaned by Loŋaar
Who killed our fathers in Shambe at crossing!
We are the people who have been orphaned by Loŋaar!
The tip of the spear (i.e. power) is to Ayii Thiek
Because he is our life giver, our saviour!
He is our leader whom we will always remember for eternity,
We will still remember him till the end of the world!"

This song of the 14th century AD community of the Rek at Amoldɔu tells the whole story of how that part of the Rek community democratically decided to choose Ayii Thiek, a fact which accounts for the importance and primacy of the descendants of this Ayii Thiek wherever they live in Rekland and in other parts of Bahr el Ghazal. Great Anei-Parek of the Nile crossing time and his grandson Ayii Thiek are the most outstanding historical figures in the Mediaeval family saga of the Payii and Parek clans among the Dinka of Bahr el Ghazal. They are the source of their pride and inspiration to the present day. All in all the story did not end up like that. Gong Loŋaar became annoyed at that Pawutweng old man and at those clans that forced him into a showdown in favour of Ayii Thiek. At the time they were carrying their elected leader in praise of him and singing songs Gong Loŋaar, in great anger, uttered a curse on that Pawutweng man and his people. He declared that descendants of that Pakuɛny old man will not exist on the face of the earth for humiliating him.

This in time became true. That Pawutweng old man and his descendants can now be remembered only as a people of Mediaeval existence. If anything, they cannot be counted or they do not matter in any given locality in Rek lands. That curse was also meted against those clans which collaborated with the old man and his Pawutweng people with whom he rejected Gong Loŋaar. Among those clans that rejected Gong Loŋaar were the Pagor clan people of the gourd, Pagɔɔu clan people of the amuöör bird, Pagak clan people of the forest and the palm tree, Pawɛ́ɛ́l, Padɔlmuöt, Patääŋ, Palɛi, Pakëën, Pawiɛctɔɔŋ, a lineage of Parum, Pacueek and a section of Palual clan people.

As Pakuɛny later withered at a place called *Nguɛɛt-Awan* due to the famine of 1583 AD, Pagɔɔu and Pacueek plus Pawɛ́ɛ́l also underwent the same fate, although there are traces of the Pagɔu still to be found or heard in some parts of Rekland today, yet they are almost nonexistent in the Awan territory of today. Great misfortunes that continued to befall the Awan communities on their northward migration from the Amoldɔu area are believed to have been due to the curse from Gong Loŋaar. Family lineages of the Padiaŋbar and Palual who participated in that fateful election at Amoldɔu did not do well either as the curse of Gong Loŋaar was very all-encompassing.

Graced and coronated by the community, Patriarch Ayii Thiek's lines later went on successfully until his descendants became a large and powerful Spear Master clan. They are presently known throughout Rek lands where they are generally noted as great Payii Spear Master clan people of *Kuel Arieec Kuöc*. But they are also known as Paan-Ayii Thiek, Ayii Jök-ŋäär. These are the people from whom comes the author, the Payii, that is, the descendants of Great Ayii. They are better known by their grandmothers. Significant among all the wives of Ayii Thiek are the following three wives.

The first wife of Patriarch Ayii Thiek is given by Payii legends as Aluɛɛl and her descendants are generally known as Paan-Aluɛɛl and are found in many parts of Rekland. The Paan-Aluɛɛl section of Payii is that of the Payii people of Chief Mou Mou Akɛɛn of the big Buoth-Anyith area in Aguok territory and those of Kuel Ayiɔɔk in the Alɛk area in the same Aguok territory. They are those in the areas of Awan Mou Akɛɛn. A large number of them are also found in Awan Chan and Awan Pajok, the area of those of President Salva Kiir Mayardit whose mother also came from Payii clan. Some of the descendants from this grandmother Aluɛɛl went as far as the eastern county area of Northern Bahr el Ghazal state of Awiel. A number of her lineages also went to live in the Twic area of Adiang.

The second wife is presented as Aläi. Her family lines are those Payii clan people found in the Noi area of Great Paramount Chief Ayii Kuot Agiu. Some are those of sub-chief Akɔɔn Akɔɔn who ruled the Mathiang section of Kɔŋgöör territory for so many decades. Other lineage sections from the grandmother Aläi are found in the Aguɔɔk area in Gogrial West county, Warrap state. Other lineages are found in the Kuac-Agör area where chief Mathuc Madut is chief of one of the many chieftaincy areas. Paan–Aläi are also found in the Apuk area of Gogrial East county, among whom are Paan-Maluil Jök in the Nyarmong section. Some of the descendants of Aläi went into the Luo community where they are a big population within the Jur-col community of the Mapɛl and Alur areas, Western Bahr el Ghazal state.

Akuol-Bor is presented as the third and the last wife of the great patriarch. Her lineages constitute more than half the population of Awan-Parek area where comes the author. The big Payii holy shrines established in this Awan-Parek area since late Mediaeval times, to this modern era, are holy shrines of her descendants who became Spear Masters during their different lifetimes. Those shrines can presently be seen immensely at Wunkuel, Tharakön, Panhom-Thöny and in many other areas in the territory. Lineage members from this Akuol – Bor are found in Laŋakut area of Lou-Ariik and others are found in the Kɔŋöör area where they are the Payii people of Great Deng Kuol Dhol. Other lineages of those of Mapaat Ayii are found in the Lɛɛr area as are those in the Jalwau and Thɔny areas.

The big Parek clan in Gömjuɛɛr territory in Aweil-West county of Malual-Buɔth-Anyaar are descendants of Tɔŋ Anei-Barek. Other members of this Parek clan are found in different parts of Northern Bahr el Ghazal state. As described elsewhere in this book, Great Tɔŋ, popularly known as Tɔŋ-Manyaŋdit, was the elder brother of Thiek Anei. Thiek bore Ayii, whose descendants became Payii clan people in the Warrap state of today. Tɔŋ Anei for his part bore all those who are Parek clan people in the Northern Bahr el Ghazal state of today. When the Awan society of Kuei continued in its migration farther westwards certain events occurred to them as they moved out of the Amoldɔu area. From the Amoldɔu the Awan community moved northwest to a place which later became known as Nguɛɛt-Awan. Here in 1453 AD the Awan community of clans was caught by a disastrous famine which decimated the society. That famine was brought about by two years drought. It made Ajiɛk's family lineages depart to the present Kuac-Akëën area. The Padiaŋbar people of Anei-Adiaŋbar also went with them. The rest of the Awan sections and clans later moved further north to a place called Nyuɔpcol where they settled for a number of decades.

Once again disaster befell them in this place. A localised earthquake swallowed a large population that went to a dance place and were dancing on one of the nights. As a result the Awan community broke up again. They took different directions. Lian, Kuööc, Duöör, Manoon, Buɔɔŋ and Adöör went north to areas that are current Awan-Parek with all its sections of today. Those clans and people who later became Awan Chan, Awan Mou and Awan Pajok went northwest of Nyuɔpcol. They continued in a gradual migratory movement until they finally settled in those areas where they are now in the extreme western areas of Gogrial West county. Awan-Gurwël, Thöc, Majur, Matik and Ariääu moved to their present areas of Wunkuel in present Awan-Parek and its outlying territories.

In time things did not go well with these sections of Awan community and so Ayii Thiek once again migrated to what is now the Atok area with sections that are now still Awan-Parek. He settled at a location presently known as *Thɔrgak* where again an outbreak of smallpox made Awan people remigrate further north with their very old Patriarch Ayii Thiek, who settled with them at what is the present Batäi cattle camp spot and its surrounding villages which are currently Miŋ sections of Kɔŋöör. The Awan-Gurwel section remained in the Thɔrgak area, which is present Atok territory to the northeast of present Warrap town. Due to a two year drought Kuot Ayii and a number of his kin returned to Thɔrgak from Batäi and Wun Kuel in present Awan. He was followed by a number of his former clans and sections of Awan-Parek including Thöc, Majur, Cuɛitim and Ariääu, and although the Cuɛitim section later disappeared during the middle part of the 17th century in what is now the Jur-Bol section of Awan, Ariääu, Thöc and Lian with its present sections of Buɔɔŋ, Kuööc and Manoon remained to form the present Awan-Parek area which maintained its former size with the arrival of new clans such as Pawɛt, Pakɛc and Panyon people who trailed in over the centuries from Nuer land, coming to the Awan-Parek territory at different times and from different directions.

The Pakɛc people, whose totem is the kite bird (acuiil), are a people of Nuer origin. They broke away some time towards the beginning of the 17th century from what are the Paan-Wol Athian in the Gak Wol area of the Agaar section of Pakam. The Pawɛt, who are also a people of Nuer origin, came to the Awan-Parek area by way of the Apuk-Juwiir section of Angol where their remnants are today the Pawɛt people of the famous Dhaal Gɔrnhom who ironically mobilised the Jaang sections of Rek of Tonj and Luacjang and led them in an historic expedition to Nuer land in the later part of the Turkiyya. That expedition met a disastrous defeat in which many people did not return, including Dhaal himself and his warrior sons Mathiang and Muɔrwuel.

The Panyon, who are also a people of Nuer origin, came by way of Apuk-Padɔc to Jur-Lian, then to Awan where they are today. They wandered a great deal before they finally settled in the Awan area. These people later developed population-wise and in those early parts of the Anglo-Egyptian condominium period, one of them, Great Noon Akuei from this Panyon clan became the paramount chief of the whole Awan until Chief Parek Machar from the Payii clan took over from him in the 1940s.

Other clans that now inhabit the Awan-Parek areas are later arrivals due to the great fusion and migratory zigzag of the 17th, 18th and early 19th centuries. The Duör section of Awan later became part of what is now Kɔŋöör after migrating to their present savannah plain (Lil) areas in about the early parts of the 17th century. The Adöör section became extinct in the face of constant wars between Awan and Apuk-Padɔc during the last decades of the 17th century and the early parts of the 18th century. The Adöör section of Awan can now be only recalled through the name of its border village with the Ming section of Apuk-Padɔc. That village is presently known as *Majak Adöör*. The Cuɛitim and Matik sections of Awan also disappeared in the course of the 17th and 18th centuries. The story of Cuɛitim section can be best tackled in relation to the story of Awulian people who broke away from this Cuɛitim section of Awan. They went to Luacjang, then to Twic in Northern Bor where they renamed themselves Awulian. They remigrated back to Luacjang and to Bor from the Awan section of Cuɛitim, some time in the early years of the 17th century.

The Pagong clan within Rek are believed to be of four main branches from which all the Pagong in Bahr el Ghazal radiated, even to the point where others use different names but are still keeping awaar grass and the hedgehog as their principal totemic divinities.

There are the Pagong of Yuööt Amakiir whose population is found in the areas of Muɔk, Yar and Juwiir in Tonj South where they are known as the Pagong of Paan-Mayom, the Pagong of Paan-Agau in the Buoweng area where the big wrist bracelet of the ancient Jieldit is still being kept by the Paan-Agau section of the Mediaeval Yuööt Amakiir. Others are also found at the Apuk-Giir and Aguok areas. Others are known as the Dɛmker section in the Macuet area of Muok where there is also a Pagong section known as Paan-Kuot Aleu who are well known for their potent spirituality. There is the Pagong of Ayaar which is comprised of those known as Paan-Yai and the Pagong section of Muordit Dhol in Aguɔk-Cek area in Gogrial West county, also in Twic and Awan Mou areas and in the areas of Buɔncuai in Awiel East. There are the Pagong of Loŋaar Anyuon found in the Pagakdit section of Kuanythi in the Noi area and those in the other Noi area of Kuanygɔi where they are the Pagong of Wol

Loŋaar. The Pagong Amel are those found in the Aguɔk-Bar area in Gogrial West county, in Kuac-Agör and Apuk-Giir areas up to those in Kongöör and the Lou-Ariik territories in Tonj North county.

THE FAMINE OF 1658 AD IN THE AWAN AREA

Panyinlɛm cattle camp with its outlying village area is a spot about two kms north of the present Rualbɛt administrative centre of Rualbɛt Payam in Awan Payam territory, Tonj North county, Warrap state. Here, there occurred the story of the disastrous famine of 1658 AD, a famine caused by a very bad drought which greatly affected Awan and its neighbouring Rek communities. This famine badly reduced the population of the Awan territory as many families deserted the territory to places not affected by the famine for survival. Stories about that great famine are still being told in the area to the present day. According to these stories there was a preceding two years of an all out drought throughout Awan. There was also a concomitant outbreak of rinderpest disease – a very bad cattle disease which the Dinka call Awɛt. That outbreak of Awɛt depopulated the cattle of the Awan territory almost to the finish. At the peak of that famine families used to gather in a luak (the byre) to collectively die as a family and even as a lineage. The Manoon and Cuɛitim sections withered to extinction as a result of that famine. Left to remind Awan of the Cuɛitiim section people is a family of a certain Deng Akol and a certain Athuai Dol. This Athuai Dol is said to have been a latecomer to Awan from Luackoth. Traditions in today's Awan say he came there with Athuai Thial, the ancestor of those of the late Dr John Garang de Mabior.

During this consummate famine, many lineages from the then proud Palual clan people used to gather in the byres. They used to put water into their milk gourds (ajiëp, ajiip when plural) and they then drank from it just to console their hearts that they were drinking milk. They used to keep their noses on the gourds' muzzles to smell the still existing aromatic scent of the previously present milk, refusing to eat tree leaves and roots. Others ate tree leaves to save themselves from dying of starvation that year. Many of the Palual clan people in Awan perished as such. They are now few remnants in the area. They were until recently being ridiculed and called as Patar-Lueɛk, meaning those who died en masse in the byres.

According to old man Mabuɔc Makuɔk, descendant of Makuɔk Athuai DÖl from Luackoth, some time before that historic famine, Athuai Thial left the Panyinlɛm cattle camp village with his family and went to settle with the KuƆk community of Luacjang in the Ciertooc area of Riäm, an area also known as Lian, some full two days walk east of Awan-Parek territory. They settled at a place still known as Agigim, a spot east of Wuncuɛi airstrip in Luacjang.

The late Dr John Garang de Mabior, who is a descendant of this Athuai Thial, affirmed this at Mayom-Abun in Thiet, where he made one of his historic speeches to the people of Bahr el Ghazal region at the May 2003 SPLM First Regional Congress when he announced that, "…Tonj county is also my ancestral home and I am number seven in our family line since my great grandfathers left Tonj at Agigim in the Luacjang area…". Dr John Garang talked of Lian, Kuɔk and Angääc and that they are now "Awulian in Northern Bor", and according to sub-chief Gai Alɛɛng Mayen of the family of those of Dr John, talking to the author during an interview, the genealogy of the founder of the SPLM/A is as follows: John Garang de Mabior Atem Aruai, son of Akur Ayen Dhiööp, who was the son of Alɛɛr Dhiai, who was son of Athuai Thial, the very ancestor who left Awan in Jur-Lian at Panyinlɛm in 1658 AD.

Dhiööp Alɛɛr is the number seven ancestor from Dr. John Garang in the family genealogical descent line, and is the Tonj man who left Lian at Agigim in Luacjang with his people. He recrossed the Nile with his people from the shore of Dhiam-Dhiam back to the Upper

Nile. They went to Akur in the toch area of the Adhiɔɔk section in Twic land in Northern Bor. From Luacjang, DhiÖÖp Alɛɛr and his people left in about 1710. He went with his four sons: Kulang, Nguëët, Ayen and Nuɛr. They are now Patem clan people in the Lith section of Twic and live in the Nyuak area of Wanglei Payam. They are there as the Awulian section of Chief Thɔn Dau Macuur. On their arrival to Adhiɔɔk land they settled at the Pawuei cattle camp area which later became known as Pawuoi of Deng Biar.

Thial, the great ancestor of the two, did belong to a clan family which revered agaany (the alligator or monitor lizard), anyak (the snake which they call atem) and another reddish snake called *biar* in Dinka. They are in effect those who are called Pathian in some parts of Rekland or Pabuɔkcok clan in the KɔŋgÖÖr area, although they are now called Patep in the Awulian area.

Kuac: Besides those sections extensively described above there was the big Kuac section of Kuei. Most of the clans that formed Kuac were the Padiaŋbar people of Anei-Adiaŋbar, Pabiɛl people who revere the Vapuder snake, part of the piöl or cloud-revering people of Piöl Aŋuet, a section of the Paduɔl clan people of Pabɛɛk descent, Payuɔm, Pakɛn, Pathär, Pamäu who are of Paker descent, the Pajiɛk people of Ajiɛk who left Awan from Amoldɔu. A large portion of them later migrated west to become the Pajiɛk people in the present Kuac-Agör area of KuacjÖk and others from this Pajiɛk later proceeded to Twic. They now live in Akoch-Thɔn Payam. The Pabiɛl later formed a branch now known as Paguäär. Splinter sections of the Pawuciɛu clan people who revere the spine bone (pic) as their totem also were part of this Kuac. The Pahɔr clan people of Nuer origin later joined the Kuac section. Some lineage factions of Parum were also there. Pacol later joined Kuac as did other new arrivals from Agaar land such as those people who are presently known as the Paruɔu clan, from which came Chief Chol Chan Manyang and their branch lineage known as the Lombor clan. A branch of Pagong

THE DINKA HISTORY 241

FAMILY GENEALOGICAL DESCENT OF SUB-CHIEF GAI ALEENG AND DR JOHN GARANG

A.

Gai
↓
Alɛɛng
↓
Mayen
↓
Alɛɛng
↓
Deng
↓
Kulang

B.

Dr John Garang
↓
de Mabior
↓
Atem
↓
Aruai
↓
Akuur
↓
Ayen

Dhiööp
↓
Alɛɛr
↓
Dhiai
↓
Athuai
↓
Thial

was also among this Kuac. The Pahol and some Pajök families also came to stay with the Kuac community. Other itinerant lineages later joined this section of the Kuac. They either integrated into the original clans in Kuac or they became clans of their own.

From Angääc, the Kuac section moved to the Luackoth area in what is now BuÖweng, where it later parted into clans and families that went to the present Kuac-Akëën and what is now Ajak-Lɛɛr. Meanwhile a group of Pajiɛk, Pagong and even Pajiëëng and a number of factions from different clans went further west to the areas of Lɔɔc in the Nyang territory, following another dispersal from the Luackoth area due to the earthquake incident of Panyang earlier explained. The Kuac community therefore divided, some went into Kuac that remained to be today's Lɛɛr in Tonj, from which a large territory of several chieftaincies later acquired the name Kuanythi as sections of these clans also went to settle in those areas that are now Noi territory, Nyang, Abiem and Abuɔk. The other Kuac part that went west through Nyang by way of Lɔɔc, later proceeded further west to become Kuac-Agör, that is, Kuac which is littoral to the River Jur between the present Wau town and Gogrial area of Aguɔk. There is an existing belief that this Kuac is Kuanydit. This Kuac-Agör is thus known invariably as Kuac of Ayiɔɔk-Magong or Kuanydit.

Then there was the Nyang section of Kuei consisting of Nyang-Lɔɔc and Nyang-Lɔu. It was and can continue to be mostly composed of the Pareu clan people who are now in the Lɔɔc section, Pakir, Pamankön, Loc, Pagor, part of Pagak and a section of Ariath who are still Pariath in Nyang. There were also those now called Paruɛɛt. There were also lineages of Padiaŋbar who now call themselves Panääk. There were the people of Ajaang who later became Pajieeng. Some of them later became Pamanluöl after they changed from Pakuieth. The people of Agɔu Loi who are now Pagɔɔu were also within this Nyang section. They were not Pagɔɔu then. They were the Paloi people of gau grass and rock stone which they locally call *Ngai*.

Part of the lineage families of Wol-Akuith were also with this Nyang section. They later moved to the Abiem area where they adopted a new clan name. They are now known as the Alɔkyɔu in both Abiem and Abuɔk. Their agnatic kin in Apuk of Juwiir, Kuac-Akeen, Ajak-Lɛɛr, Awan-Parek and Apuk of Padɔc and elsewhere in Tonj areas are known as Pakuiëth. They are Pawuliol in Gokland and Pathɔɔth in Agar land. In Bor land, they are the Juör-Mac clan. There were also those from the Parum lineage who later changed to be known as Paluɛɛc and are now mostly known as people of the Durra. They are mainly found in the Akurbiök area in Abiem of Chief Ariaath Mayar Marɛng after they moved from Abuɔk, where they were among the original pioneers of the area of Abuɔk Ayiɔɔm territory.

The lineage of great Ker Ker, which became the Paker people of the underground water, was also among this Nyang section of Kuei. In later times they changed to become Paliɛm and now live in Abuɔk. A certain Maluil of Nuer descent was also among the Rek migrating waves that later came from the current Agaar land. He came up to Angääc in the present area of Jalwau where he joined Rek society and became one of the people that form the Nyang section of Rek. They were originally people of Agaany, but his descendants later came to acquire a name from an intermediate ancestor who did have a relation with the little rodent known in Rek language as luil. His descendants subsequently became the Paluil clan people. They later settled in Abuɔk territory among the area pioneers. They are still there in a miniature form today. Splinter factions of the people of blood were part of this Nyang section. They now live in AbuƆk as Pamäi clan people, still as the masters of the blood. They are called upon to consecrate, bless and legitimise blood dia compensation cattle as they are the ones required to conduct reconciliation and peace occasions between two parties after an incident of homicide or murder. Other clans that have now come to be in the areas of Nyang and Abuɔk were latecomers from various lands in Bahr el Ghazal.

The Padhieu, who have now become the traditional ruling masters of the Abuɔk and Nyang territories, came from Ngok of Abyei in the early parts of the 18th century. A faction of this Padhieu group went to Lou-Mawien where they are now the Padhieu clan people Them Madut, who is popularly known as Them-Aɣɔijök. The Padhieu, who are descendants of Wol-Adhieu, are known to have made a great transhumant movement within the Upper Nile and Bahr el Ghazal. A large part of them remained in the Abyei area where they are the Padhieu people from whom Great Chief Deng Majök comes. Others call themselves Pajöök. They also have a big legendary story of their ancestor, Wol-Adhieu, who had an historic dispute with Loŋaar- the leader of the Jaang migration from the Upper Nile to Bahr el Ghazal. It is essential at this point to give a brief account of this quarrel as a touch to the story of the Padhieu and the historic dispute between Wol-Adhieu and Loŋaar Ayuueel.

THE DISPUTE BETWEEN WOL-ADHIEU AND LOŊAAR AYUUEEL

According to Padhieu legends supported by sources from other Rek communities, Wol-Adhieu was originally Wol Kuac Ngor from the Pawutweng clan people of the cow and puöt before Jaang migrated to Bahr el Ghazal from between Sobat and Zeraf River in the Upper Nile Basin region. He had no brother and but one sister, Ajak-Kuac. When the Jaang migrating exodus arrived at the Nile threshold, coming from the Jönglei areas, when they arrived at the threshold of the Nile east bank, Ajak decided to speak to the river gods in order to let the water recede to allow her brother Wol and the whole community of Jaang to cross to the west bank without getting drowned. She said she would offer herself to remain in the River Nile for the gods. According to this legend, as told by members of the Padhieu in the Abuɔk and Nyang areas, Ajak threw herself into the River Nile and, as legend has it, the Nile waters began to reduce. People started to get into the Nile to cross and while the Jaang were crossing Loŋaar Ayueel began to spear the heads of people as they emerged from the waters during the crossing process after diving into the deepest parts of the Nile.

This made some of the Jaang section people run back to where they came from and not cross to the west bank any more. Many people and sections, however, insisted and so they crossed the White Nile to become the Bahr el Ghazal Dinka of today. They struggled till they got to the west bank. The Pabuör clan who today are the Pawutweng people in the Apuk area of Juwiir say a certain Akɔɔn, son of Anei-Adiaŋbar, made a plan to rescue the crossing society of Jaang from the big giant called Loŋaar who was finishing off the people on the threshold of the Nile bank. The Pakuec people in Gogrial East say it was their ancestor, Agɔth-Cithiik, who rescued the people from Loŋaar.

A very good oral historian, Mel Manyang from the Pabuör clan in the Apuk-Juwiir area, puts it that Akɔɔn Anei-Adiaŋbar (other versions say it was Anei-Adiaŋbar himself) took what the Dinka people call pic, a wooden rod with one piece of the sacral bone fixed on its tip which Dinka women use for stirring porridge during cooking. Akɔɔn or Anei-Adiaŋbar dived into the Nile and made towards Longaar. On coming nearer to where Loŋaar stood in the shallow of the Nile waters, Anei-Adiaŋbar or Akɔɔn began to shudder the waters, causing waves by using that pic. With that, Loŋaar was made to believe it was yet another person emerging from the waters from that direction where something was stirring the water. He speared at that stirring rod thinking he hit at a person and Akɔɔn or Anei-Adiaŋbar who became very close jumped from within the waters and overwhelmingly caught Loŋaar and struggled with him out from the waters and went with him across to the Nile's bank. In so doing he was able to allow the population of the Jaang to throng into the Nile and cross to the west bank.

After people had crossed to the west bank and had encamped in what has come to be known as the Liɛtpaciruööt area of *Ajäk* and *Pagarau* in the present Yirol East county area, Loŋaar took a bull by the colour of Maŋök-Thɔn, a bull the colour of the sky. He took it from the cattle of his son, Jiel. Loŋaar also made the community bring seven uncastrated bulls to make eight bulls in all. He wanted them sacrificed for ritual cleansing after all the illnesses that befell the Jaang from where they came but Loŋaar was also angry with several persons. Among them was Wol Kuac Ngor, whom he accused to have been the one who planned that act of pic for Akɔɔn or his father to do the act of deceiving him. Many sources, however, agree that it was Anei-Adiaŋbar, not his son Akɔɔn, but Pakuec legends make a strong contention that it was their ancestor, Agɔth-Cithiik, who made that plan.

All the same, Loŋaar called all the people to the sacrificial ground in Liɛtpaciruööt where the eight bulls were tethered on pegs. He then started to make his holy invocations in which he threatened his opponents to die from his curse. At the height of his wrath, Loŋaar speared Wol Kuac's foot through with a fishing spear which transfixed his foot to the ground! While Wol was publicly crying from pain, Lonŋaar also took the whole trunk (Dinka people call it agɔɔu) of the sacrificed bull. He put the trunk together with the neck and the head of the slaughtered bull on Wol's head while he was still standing affixed. Then he commanded him to stand for days with that heavy yoke and with the spear in his foot fixing him to the ground!

Loŋaar's aim was to let Wol die in humiliation, but the act was also a deterrent punishment to frighten his other opponents in the society. The legend says Wol Kuac cried for a number of days but we believe he must have cried for only the whole day while standing with a transfixed foot! The legend says Wol stood with the transfixed spear in his foot and the trunk with all its meat and head over him for a number of days till the flesh of the bull's trunk and head had putrefied on him! Loŋaar, who had been doing his invocations on the bulls day and night, became surprised as to why Wol could not crumble and die. He then decided to free him by taking the putrefied meat and bones from his head and removing the spear from his foot.

The story is a long one, but the long and short of it is that the putrefied trunk and head of Maŋök-Thɔn affected Wol's sense of hearing. He therefore developed otitis media that made him suffer a great deal during the rest of his life. He became deaf! Because of the days crying, he was nicknamed by the Jaang community as Wol-Adhieu, that is, Wol the crying man. Wol kept that humiliation at heart and the thing became a vendetta between the two, however, Loŋaar later called for peace and reconciliation between him and Wol-Adhieu who reluctantly and under public pressure accepted that initiative. Bulls were slaughtered for the occasion after Loŋaar's repentance and apology for the physical affliction and humiliation he did to Wol-Adhieu. In that reconciliation occasion Loŋaar gathered pieces of meat from all the slaughtered bulls, libated upon those meat pieces, gave them to Wol-Adhieu and declared it a propitiation act, saying he had come to terms with him. He also declared that the offspring of Wol-Adhieu shall not be subject to a curse from him or from his descendants and that by the blood and putrefied meat and bones of the trunk of Maŋök-Thɔn of his son, Jiel, he has transferred part of the holy power from him to Wol-Adhieu. He added that the holy investiture will continue to go through Wol-Adhieu's descent lines and from there on Wol-Adhieu would become a Spear Master as a result of that investiture from him.

Loŋaar also took the broom (wĕc) usually made from mon, the sporobolus pyramidalis grass, spat onto it to libate, then blessed and gave it to Wol-Adhieu to be his totem, i.e. to be his totemic emblem, telling him to use that wĕc by immersing it into water and sprinkle the people with it during ritual and religious ceremonies where offerings are being made for community wellbeing. In this way, the broom from mon grass became a totem for Wol-Adhieu and his descendants.

When Wol-Adhieu's sister Ajak Ngor was drowned in the Nile River, she was believed to have been carried to the river gods by the pelican (*jak* in Dinka) and for that reason jak the pelican also became a divinity bird for Wol-Adhieu's descendants all over Dinka lands including their agnatic lineages such as the Padhieu in the Abyei, Nyang and Abuɔk areas. The Padhieu people of Chief Bol Deng, the Pawiëcweng clan people of Chief Deng Nyuɔl in Gok-Machar and of Chief Pio Tem Ngor in the Duluit area, all in Northern Bahr el Ghazal state, revere this pelican bird. In fact this legend can be so varied from one section of Wol-Adhieu to the other, but the fact remains that Aturjöŋ Anyuɔn, chief of the Gok-Machar area in Awiel North county, comes from this Padhieu clan. The Padhieu people of Chief Bol Deng and Chief Aturjöŋ are two lineages from Wol-Adhieu that did not return to Upper Nile as part of those who did to later become the Ruweng people. Their ancestors decided to continue with the Rek society till they went to Northern Bahr el Ghazal.

Wol-Adhieu remained as part of the Kuac section of Kuei at the time of the Jaang stay in the Amongpiny area, but when he did not fare well with the Rek society, in which Loŋaar was still a factor, he left the Kuac community and joined those people who later became the Ruweng. From the mass of information so far collected, Wol-Adhieu, or more correctly his children, decided to join a wave of Ruweng families returning from Rɛɛlkou to the present Kiec land in the Yirol area. Those sections who subsequently became Ruweng were staying with the Luac community. They decided to return to Upper Nile following a quarrel between their Spear Master by the name of Loi Jiel and a noted Spear Master by the name of Guöt Akoi from the Pagut clan who are among the Luacjang people of today.

In Kiec land Loi died and was entombed there. Versions from some Ruweng sections in Upper Nile say he was cursed by Great

Guöt Akoi, who took sand from his footprint and threw it away, an act called *kuanycök* in Dinka. That Ruweng migrating group that returned with Wol-Adhieu's people later left the Yirol area of Adöör and crossed the River Nile by the shore of Dhiam-Dhiam to Kɔŋɔɔr in what is now Northern Bor.[69] They settled briefly at what is now Duk-Padiëët in the present ʀɔL Dinka country. The Ruweng returning people were at this time believed to have been led by a certain Ajilik Jiel who took over leadership of that migrating Ruweng after the death of his brother Loi Jiel.

The people of Wol-Adhieu who joined this society included Acuiil Wol and his son Akɔc. There was Jök, Alɔr, Ajiing, Ngɔr-Cikom, Arop Wol, Aduai de Kur and Aru Jiel. One time Ajilik called on Ngɔr, Jök, Aduai de Kur, Alɔr and Aru. He called them for a meeting, the five who were apparently the heads of the moving Ruweng families. He told them they were to move away from the Ruweng mainland area in what is the Ngɔk Lual Yak and Khor Fulus areas of today to the western Upper Nile. This was accepted and the Ruweng community moved out of the area to once again cross the River Nile westwards. They crossed at the spot of Lake Atar, precisely at Kir-Jac on the foot of the ancient tamarind tree (cuɛi) at Agaääc. They then crossed the main Nile at the Jöŋyɔm shore in the present Paweny Dinka country.

This time those Ruweng sections with their newcomers, the family of Wol-Adhieu, were led by a certain Kur Akuɔng whom they agreed to have lead them following a quarrel between Ngɔr and Ayueel Jiel over who should be the migration leader, however, the Ruweng community finally arrived in the Panriɛng area in the north parts of western Upper Nile, having struggled to recross the big White Nile River. Here in the Panriɛng area they found Funj people who fought them and part of them proceeded up to what

---

69   Ibid.

is now Biemnhom territory. In this area Kuol Arop Biong took his Ngɔk part of the Ruweng section of Jök and went due west. He later settled in what is now the Abyei area of Ngɔk. This was now about 1745 AD[70] and because of their ancestor Jök they became the Pajök clan, now in the Abiör section of Ngɔk. In the Ngok area of Abyei, Wol-Adhieu people began to be known as the Padhieu.

While these Padhieu continue to revere their previous totems as they left Bahr el Ghazal to central Upper Nile, then to the western Upper Nile and to Abyei, then back to Bahr el Ghazal, their agnatic kin, the Pajök in Ngok, they also revere what they call ring yath, a type of small snake, red in colour like the red and thin snake which some Rek Dinka call kuel. They also have a divinity called Achai, the spirit of another girl, Acai Jök, whom they gave over to the river gods at the time of their ancient crossing of the Red Sea, coming from Judaea and led by great Jök-Athurkök. In addition to these totems the Pajök clan also revere the original pelican bird of the Padhieu clan.

Some longer time after their arrival to Ngɔk, families of this Padhieu moved out of the Ngɔk area and gradually migrated up to the western area of Tonj North in present Warrap state through Twic. By gradual movement they arrived in what is now the Abuɔk and Nyang territories towards the end of the 17th century. Ayiɔm's faction chose the Abuɔk territory. They were welcomed by the earlier settlers, the pioneer people who are the Pagɔu, Paluiɛl, Paliɛm, Paruɛɛt, Panääk, Paluɛɛc, Pajiëëng, Pamäi and the Alɔkyɔu clan people of the fire totem. This Padhieu section that remained in Abuɔk now wields both temporal (executive chieftaincy) and spiritual authority over Abuɔk to the present day. The area is now called after him as Abuɔk Ayiɔm.

The other Padhieu faction which became Padhieu of Paan-Akɔch and Paan-Mayɔm proceeded to the Nyang areas where they are the Padhieu in Nyang-Lurcuk of today. The Padhieu of Paan-Mayɔm

---

70   Ibid.

proceeded to Nyang-Lɔu. Other factions of this Padhieu became the Panyɔr clan who are found in the Majök section of Nyang. They, however, found those clans who earlier came as part of the main waves of Rek westward migration in Bahr el Ghazal in the last parts of the 15th century when the Jaang were still making their internal movements from the present Luackoth-Aköök and Apuk-Juwiir mainlands. They were welcomed by Pagak, Pagor and Pariath who are the present Paan-Lual Nhial in Nyang-Lɔu areas. The Pamanköön who are now in the Majök and Lɔɔc sections of Nyang, Pareu and Pakiir found in the Nyang-Lɔɔc areas were also among those who pioneered the area and were among the clans found there by the Padhieu people. Those clans later gave primacy to the Padhieu who now rule the Nyang territory of Kuei. The Nyang community is presently comprised of Nyang-Lɔɔc, Nyang-Lɔu, Nyang-Majök and Nyang-Lurcuk. They all constitute what is now known as the Kuei of great Akɔch Majök.

Such a digression from the main topic, the descriptive account of some of the sections of Kuei in Rek society during the Middle Ages, was necessary to give the reader a wider picture of our Mediaeval Dinka society in Bahr el Ghazal. This digression is also viewed to make proper understanding about a total history of the Dinka nation as we tackle one Dinka tribe after the other. At this juncture, the historical description of the sections of the Kuei of the Rek now resumes.

There was and continues to be the big Abiem society of Kuei, consisting of those sections of Abuɔk which we have just tackled above in relation to the Padhieu and Nyang sections of the Kuei. Beside Abuɔk, Abiem consisted of what was and continues to be known as Liaŋröl. It looks like the main or large factions of Ariääth whose descendants became Pariäth clan people mostly formed this Liaŋröl. There were also the Panguet people of Piöl Anguet. They continue to live mainly in this Liaŋröl area of Akurbiöök in the present Abiem area of Chief Ariääth Mayar Mareng. Many sections and clans that formed this Abiem later proceeded to present the Awiel East county areas where they are the current Abiem sections. Others melted into the Gogrial West county territories of Awan and Aguɔk.

There were also the Pakuieth lineages of the fire totem who are now known as the Alɔkyɔu clan in the present Liaŋröl area of Abiem. The people of the lion and of the wind, known as the Palɛɛt and Payuɔm, were among this community of Abiem that later became domicile to Liaŋröl.

A people earlier belonging to TɔŋAnei, but who choose to call themselves the Parek clan, were part of this Abiem. In fact, what was Buɔth-Anyaar that came to Angääc as a separate section of Rek had at Luackoth, Aköök-Teek and Juwiir areas lost a number of clans and a lineage into other sections during the great social fusion in this Rek heartland area before the westward migration was once again triggered by Jur-Luɛɛl's sudden abdication of the interior of Bahr el Ghazal.

The Parek clan people of Tɔŋ Anei later kept what was the Buɔth-Anyaar community. This became particularly so when large sectors of the Kuei and Lith decided to continue further west from this Liaŋröl area of Abiem in that northern end of the present Tonj region. Liaŋöl or Abiem became another Rek heartland area after Luackoth and Angääc. Here, from the Abiem area of Liaŋröl, the Rek split. The Lith or Apuk took to the north to later settle in its present areas called Apuk-Pathuɔn. Part of the Kuei which is Kuac and Aguɔk went west across what is now River Jur and settled in their present areas in what is now the Gogrial West county. The three Awan were later arrivals from the present Awan-Parek area of Nyuɔp-col in Tonj North. With the Parek clan people leading Buɔth-Anyaar were also a people known as the Pabiöng, who were originally the Panyaar clan.

There was, however, an assortment of clans in this Abiem section. Paduil clan people of the blood, Ruaal lineages, the Palɛu or Paguäär of the anyak snake who are also call Pathian in other places, the Paliɛc who were basically Pawutweng, parts of the Pajiééng people of the big black cobra called piën in Dinka, were part of this moving society of the Rek. The Paluiɛl of the monkey, called Padiaany elsewhere, the Parɛng people of the cow rɛng who are remembered for their legendary story of the bead (guët) swallowed by one of their members, the lineages of the Paduɔltiɔp people called the Pabɛɛk in Agaarland but who later changed to be known as Payum, all were also there. Lineages of the Anei-Adiaŋbar people of the heglig tree (thɔu) who later became the Paciɛny clan in the Awiel areas and those who revere the dog, a people called Pataang, were also there. The Patɛk, Pakur, Paluaal and so many other clan factions were among this great Abiem. Many of these clans later proceeded to form the big Pajök consisting of the Pajok large Abiem and Malual-Giɛrnyaang sections of the Kuei in the Awiel East and Awiel North counties. Others went further west to become Malual-Buɔth-Anyaar and Paliëët in the present Palieupiny area in the Northern Bahr el Ghazal state.

LITH SECTION OF THE REK

The Lith component of the Rek was second to the Kuei by demographic comparison. It was and continues to be comprised of three large sections which are generally known as Apuk since the split at Patɛu, a split which was brought to Apuk not by the earthquake incident of the nearby Panyang village area which caused the third historical dispersal for the Rek in their migratory movement as earlier described, but by the story of the Pabuör clan man, Mel-Agaar. The present sections of Lith (that is Apuk) were a result of the split at Patɛu in present area of Luackoth in Tonj East. While the third split of Rek at Panyang was due to an earthquake calamity, the split of the Lith or Apuk at Patɛu was due to a conflict over pasture in the big forest of Patɛu, an area in present Luackoth in

Tonj East county. Here are excerpts from one of the epic songs by the Abuɔk section of Apuk to Mël-Agaar about the conflict over the pasture of patɛu:

> *"...Këdïït Mël-Agaar ka riam wal Patɛu ee!*
> *Wabuɔk–marɔl ciën kök athöŋ eej ooo!*
> *Raan mël e, awayaa,*
> *Këdïït mël-Agaar ka riam wal patɛu ee!*
> *Ya wal riaam kuba dhuk ee!*
> *Ya wal riaam kuba dhuk ee!*
> *Ya wal riaam kuba dhuk ee!"*

Translation:

> *"Oh! The huge herd of cattle of Mël – the Agaar man,*
> *Is squandering our pasture of Patɛu!*
> *Abuɔk – Marɔl, didn't you have a deadly arem!?*
> *Go in and kill this mël and victoriously loot his cattle for his cattle are finishing the pasture of Patɛu!*
> *My cattle usually graze off the pasture and goes back, my cattle usually grazes off the pasture and goes back, my cattle usually grazes off the pasture and goes back!"*

A sample of clans that constituted the Apuk or Lith society of the Rek can be given as follows: There were Pahöl clan people who remained from those of Agɔth-Cithiik, whose descendants joined the Luac community Right Liɛt Paciruot. These people later remigrated from the Luac community and rejoined Apuk. They later became the Pakuec clan people from which came great Giir Thiik. Among this Apuk were the people known as the Paliɛcmuɔk and Panɛu clans. Pagoor were also there as were Paker people, Pawan people of Pabɛɛk descent, Paduɛt, Pawuciɛu of sand and sacral bone, lineages from Ruaal revering groups, Pakuieth people of Wol-Akuith, the Padiaŋbar people who revere the heglig tree, the group of puöt and cow-related lineages, the Paduɔltiɔp groups revering awan (the fox) and the lineage families from the Pagong of awaar grass, the Paluaal who are a people from the Marbek group of lineages alleged to have fought with God during some remote time, were also among this section of Rek call the Lith.

There were the hippopotamus revering people, the wind and lion related clans, the crocodile revering people, kuɔɔt and aguɔr revering lineages, the viper (i.e. anyak) revering people, the cobra revering lineages (the Pajieng) and a countless number of clans in this Apuk called the Lith before part came to Juwiir while part went to Padɔc and to what is now Apuk of Pathuɔn in Gogrial East county. Some even went to Thɔny and later to what are now the Muɔk of Aköt Wut and Yar Ayiɛi territories.

TERRITORIAL CONFIGURATION OF THE LITH SECTION OF THE REK:

The Lith cultural component of the Rek currently consists of:
- **Apuk of Juwiir territory** in the Tonj South county area, comprised of the Macuët, Aliai, Maŋeŋ, Malony, Aŋol, Tarweŋ and the second Macuët sections.
- **Apuk-Padɔc territory** in the Tonj North county area, bordering the Nuers of the western Upper Nile on the toch. This Apuk consists of the big Agurpiny and Mayuai territorial sections, Adɔkthök and Aduëët territorial sections and Miŋ, Rɛɛŋ and Maguk sections.
- **Apuk-Pathuɔn territory** which is Gogrial East county is comprised of Biöŋ, Nyarmoŋ, Buöyar, Amuuk, Abiöör, Abuɔk, Adöör and Jur Man-Aŋɛɛr.
- **Lith sections** in Awiel East county area consist of the big Lɔu of

Aguer Gɛŋ and Ajuɔŋ Malöŋ Yöör, Ajuɔŋ-Piööth and Ajuɔŋthi territories.

Those are the sections of Rek which constitute the Lith component.

GÏR COMPONENT OF THE REK

Clans that comprise what is the *Gïr* section of Rek were initially those from the households of Pagak and lineages from the Pagoŋ clan. There were, however, Paŋɔk clan people of Piöl who are now Paan-Malok Aluiir, Paan–Aluiir Dhur and Paan–Aŋok Aluiir, all in the Padek and Waat sections in the Thɔny area. The Pagak clan people were led by a certain Akec Akɔl, the husband of the great lady of history, Amou Marɔl, in whose name the whole Rek has come to be called by the Agaar people as Rek Amou. This Pagak people are now in the Padek section of Thɔny where they are currently known as Paan-Gai. Chief Akol Aduɔl, who ruled Thɔny for over fifty years, comes from this lineage section of the Paan-Gai. This Pagak lineage section of Akec Akol, the groups of the Pangɔk people of Piöl Anguet and the Paloi clan people of Makuei Bul in Buɔɔt section were the clans of Gïr that did not even come to Panyang and the areas of Luackoth. They did not witness the earthquake of Panyang. They went to Thɔny at Angääc as a result of that disastrous battle of the Rek caused by the wife of Buɔŋlek. They immediately broke away from Angääc and took a southern route to what is now Thɔny by way of Kolkɔu of Adöör, coming through the present Toch of Aköök-Teek. They came directly treading those areas such as Acuuk to Mading and Lang and finally settled in what is now the Thɔny territory. This is the group that went with the old mother of the Rek, Amou Marol. When the Rek split at Angääc as a result of the disastrous battle caused by the wife of Buɔŋlek, Thɔny, who was the youngest son of Amou, had a special liking for his old mother and he very much attended to her. The Pagak people of Amou settled in the big cattle camp of Payiɔk which is on the border with the Gok people of Malou-Pech Payam in today's Cuɛibɛt county.

Amou Marɔl was married by the Pagak people of Akec Akol Gai at the time when her Paral people of Marɔl Deng Kuc were in the Dɔkland area of present Ganyliel while Rek society was in the present Aliääp area of Amongpiny. Some sources say Amou and her elder sister Acuɛi Marɔl were married while west bank Dinka communities were still in the present Kiec land area of Ajäk. Amou arrived at Payiɔk from Angääc at a real old age. At Payiɔk her six sons went out with their Age-set on one particular day in pursuit of the Bongo people who were found in the area as the original inhabitants of the territory.

Old mother Amou remained unattended in the cattle camp at Payiɔk while her sons went with the Gïr after the Bongo. Among the six it was the youngest son, Thɔny, who later thought of their dear old mother. He came back after the second day of their pursuit of the Bongo, leaving his five brothers to continue with the others against the Bongo. As legend has it, Thɔny found their mother to have been miraculously swarmed by termites which had vertically surrounded her and built an anthill which enveloped her up to the neck. The termites built the hill from where she was sitting, however, life was miraculously still in her and as Thɔny arrived and came to her while crying, Amou uttered a few words before the life went out of her.

According to this legend, rampantly told in the Thɔny area, the great lady made a curse on her five sons. As to Thɔny, she praised him for returning to find her still alive and able to speak few words to him. She gave him a word of blessing, saying he will remain to further her name within the Gïr and within Rek society, adding that the territory which was pioneered by her shall be named after him as Thɔny. She assured her young son that the area shall continue to be known as Thɔny after him and that the territory shall continue to be called so for posterity. She then died and when the community returned with her sons a great festival was made and the anthill that smothered the great mother was turned into a holy shrine that has continued to be a centre for annual holy festivals by the whole Thɔny community to the present day. The anthill became a holy shrine of Amou the Great. All types of bulls, oxen and old female cows used to be sacrificed for her at this Payiɔk cattle camp by the whole Thɔny community. Throughout history the great mother became a saint in the Rek religious annals and in Thɔny territory the spirit of the great mother reveals her wants and wishes by means of a dream through certain people even today. Her dreams when told are instantly complied with.[71]

In recent times up to the present day her words come to the Thɔny community through a deity which, according to local tales, descended on Thɔny territory from heaven. This must be one of the Neptillins described in the Bible[72] that deity called *Monybai*, meaning, *the god of the territory*, used to speak through a prophet called *Gumwel* whose descent line continues to be the family from which the deity Monybai chooses a prophet through whom he speaks the words of the great mother Amou Marɔl. The deity Monybai continues to appear in a person from time to time up to this modern era. By means of the deity Monybai or by means of a dream, Amou Marɔl makes orders for bulls from all the sections of the Thɔny territory to be offered in sacrifice to her, particularly those from the Pagak family

---

71   Information obtained from an interview with Chief Akol Aduɔlof the Padek section of Thɔny territory dated 6.12.2007

72   The Neptillins are angelic beings which fell out of favour or disagreed with God the creator so that they came to have no place in heaven. They thus descended to come and live with humans. They are what the Dinka people call Jak in plural, Jɔk in singular. They are either malignant or benevolent. The Amou Marɔl spirit speaks in one particular person among the Pagak people in Thɔny area, Tonj South county.

line of Akol Aduɔl Gai, from whom her spirit always demands one bull and an old cow to be offered to her at Payiɔk among the many bulls to be brought by the Thɔny sections.

The holy shrine of the great mother of Rek can be conspicuously seen at Payiɔk even today. It is surrounded by special trees of piety such as the giant ficus tree (kuel), the Kigelia Ethiopia or sausage tree (ruaal), a thicket of the African lime tree (akɔch) and a type of sycamore tree which the Dinka call lach. Other forms of trees are also there making a kind of a bush with the palm trees (agɛɛp). Some citrus trees called milat are also there in a bush cluster. The whole vicinity is also dotted by eight medium-sized anthills. The holy spot of Payiɔk is a clear sacred ground which could surprise and fascinate a stranger to stand with timid and sacred awe. It is a primeval holy ground! Having digressed for the useful story of the great mother of Rek, our story of the Gïr will now resume.

Apart from Paŋɔk, Pagak and Pagong clans that went to Thɔny as Gïr from Angääc, a number of other clans later went to Thɔny from Panyang in the Luackoth area and joined the first pioneering clans. They were part of the remnants of Gïr that ran south following the earthquake disaster of Panyang. Those groups went by what is now the Wun-Reel and current Wanh-Alɛl areas. They include the Padiaŋbar family who were led by a certain Angɔu Anei-Adiangbar. His descendants are now known as the Padiaŋbar clan of Paan-Angɔu and with the Paloi clan they became the pioneers of the Waat section of Thɔny. They are known there as Paan-Makiir and a branch of this Paloi people of anyuɔn, the grass, went to what is the present Buɔɔt section. They were the pioneers of that part of Thɔny. They are known there as a very powerful Spear Master clan of special potency. They are the Paloi people of Makuei Bul. A faction of the Pawutweng people of the cow and puÖt also were within the Gïr faction who came from Panyang and went to Thɔny. They now call themselves the Paköt and live in the Buɔɔt section.

A people called Pacakiir also went with this faction to Thɔny. They later became the people of Riɛm Atem, who was the first chief for the Buɔɔt section. Chief Riɛm Atem was killed by the Bashbazuk slaves' soldiers belonging to an Egyptian Coptic Christian by the name of Ghataz Abdel Massieh, who during the slave trade ere made a big slave zariba (stockade) at a place called Manyang-ngɔɔk in the Thɔny area. This Pacakiir chief was among the chiefs and other dignitaries of the Tonj areas who were thrown by the slavers into a bottomless pit (kandak), having in it a fire furnace. Those chiefs included Chief Malek Agai of Apuk-Juwiir, Great Dut Agɔɔk from Aköök-Teek and Great Ayueel Baak from the Malony area in Apuk-Juwiir. They died cremated in that pit of fire in the Manyang-ngɔɔk area in Thɔny.

Those chiefs were the first among our historical martyrs who were made to inhumanly die for the cause of their people. Those chiefs opposed the slavers and mobilised their respective communities against the bashibazouks' slave trade activities. They were, however, caught and brought to Manyangɔɔk where they were killed. The Pacakiir is a branch of the Pakuieth clan people of the fire totem.

A lineage of Loŋaar whose descendants are now known as the Pagong section of Majök Mading also went to this area with the Gïr. Those who later became the Pagoŋ of Paan-Mayom later proceeded from this Thɔny area to Muɔk territory where they are now the lineage section of Chief Aköt Wut and another lineage called Paan–Atäny, which also included those of the renowned Spear Master AkÖrÖu Aleu. Others from these Pagoŋ lineages went to the Yar area in later times to become the Pagoŋ of Paan-Demker. Others from whom came Chief CikÖm Ayiɛi CikÖm are there, known as the Pagoŋ of Paan–Aru Jiel, the direct Jiel Loŋaar. Within this group of Gïr that went to the Thɔny area from Panyang was also a section of AdɔlmuÖt who now became the PadɔlmuÖt clan, people of rain. They are found in the Uyon section in Thɔny where they are known as the Paan–Nai. They seem to have parted from the original lion totem which is the main totem of all the descendants of AdɔlmuÖt Puöt. A breakaway lineage from Teek of the Patɛk joined this Gïr and later went along with the Gïr from the Panyang area to Thɔny. They are now the Pagun clan people of the crocodile totem in Thɔny and can also be found in the Uyon section where they are known as the Paan-Yaang.

A branch of the Pakuieth lineage of Akol Anyaar broke from Lith and joined this Gïr migrating group of Panyang. They went to Uyon where they now continue to be known as the Paan-Anyaar. What are now Paan-Acuil in the Uyon section of Thɔny were originally from the PadɔlmuÖt. They continue to revere the lion as their totem, but call themselves PayuÖm. There were also the people of anyak, the viper. They are called the Paguäär. They now live in the Thɔny section of Padek where they are known as the Paan-Akuɔng. Within the Gïr column that went to Thɔny were also the Pagɔu clan people of the *Amuor* bird, a Dinka bird that moves in huge swarms. They are now the Paan-Dut Madhieu in the Thɔny area. There were also the people of blood who now call themselves Palɛɛt in Thɔny. Pakuɛɛny also went there and they are now called the Paan-Maluil. A small descent line from Ker Ker also went to Thɔny, breaking out of Kuei. The descendants from this line later changed from being masters for the underground water and adopted nyieel the pythɔn as their totem. They are now in the Padek section as the Paker who revere the pythɔn and are known as Paan-Kuol Mayɔm. A branch from the Pagor people of the gourd also went there. Paan-Kuot Kacuɔl in Thɔny is a faction from this line. A family group from Ajaang also became the Pajieng people of the cobra. They are now the Paan-Acuil in the Uyon section of Thɔny.

There are the Papui clan people who came from Agaarland. Their arrival to the Thɔny area was followed by a people called Pawan. They are the Payii clan people who came from the present Awan-

Parek. The PabiörŋÖk clan people of Agaany who were of Nuer origin later came to Thɔny and the Parum of Paan-Aciek in Buɔɔt, Paan-Chol Maköör in Padek section and a Parum lineage called Paan-Deng Mabuɔc in Waat were all later arrivals to Thɔny to become part of the Gïr section of Rek. These Parum people of Paan-Deng Mabuɔc in particular are latecomers of the early 19th century. They came from the Twic section of Akuär through Jur-Manangɛɛr and Apuk-Giir. They settled in the Angol section of the Apuk-Juwiir area of Thiet, then to Thɔny. The historic SANU leader, William Deng Nhial, is a grandson of that Mabuɔc who came from the Twic land of Akuär. The Pawan are descendants of Tuɔl Akɛɛn Kuot, sold from Awan by the Payii to Thɔny to become Spear Master for the Waat section. Waat section people went to purchase this Tuɔl Akeen from Awan around the end of the 18th century. All those people trailed to Thɔny beginning from the 18th century. The Pagɔɔŋ clan people of Arou, the tortoise revering people, were also among the late arrivals to the Thɔny area. A branch of them proceeded to Ajak-Lɛɛr and the Pacien area of Kuac-Akëën to become the Paruɔu and Lombor clans. Yak Arou Diing, the common ancestor of this Pagɔɔŋ, Paruɔu and Lomboor came, migrating from the Mading Bor area in the middle part of the 18th century. They were originally from the Padeng clan people of rain. Here, in Lɛɛr areas of Tonj North county, they adopted the tortoise to be also one of their totems in addition to rain.

CURRENT AREAS OF THE GÏR SECTION OF THE REK

- **Thɔny area** in Tonj South county bordering Gok Dinka in the Western Lakes state and comprised of Waat, Uyön, Buɔɔt and Padek sections.
- **Muɔk area** of Aköt Wut in Tonj South county consisting of the Buöweng and Macuet sections. This Muɔk extends to Tonj town.

- **Yar Ayiɛi Area** in Tonj South county consisting of two sections and lying between the Great Apuk-Juwiir and the Muɔk territory.

THE AGAAR DINKA TRIBE

The Agaar Dinka community at the centre of the Lakes state in the eastern part of Bahr el Ghazal region poses as a distinct cultural entity within the Dinka nationality. They have a dialect peculiar to the Agaar community and it is known to all Dinka people as the Agaar dialect. They call it Thɔng Agaar and although they do not very much differ from the other Dinka societies in Bahr el Ghazal, they still exhibit some form of a peculiar cultural outlook that distinguishes an Agaar Dinka or Agaar community from even their neighbouring Atuöt and Kiec to the east, Luacjang to the north and Gok to the west, let alone the large Rek Dinka beyond Gok and Luacjang in the far northwest.

The Agaar Dinka tribe occupies all those areas extending westwards from Rumbek, the capital city of the Lakes state, to their borders with the Pathiöng sections of Gok Dinka of Cuɛibɛt County in the same Lakes state. To the east of Rumbek town, Agaar extensively expands as Aliamtooc-One and Aliamtooc-Two, covering the areas of Pacong and further on to Aköt, the administrative or county centre for the eastern Agaars of the Yäk territory that ultimately borders the Apaak Dinka in the Agaany and Aluäk-Luäk areas of Great Machar Anyijong at the northwestern parts of the Yirol West county. The Agaar community also extends northeast in the same extensive way as Athoi, Amothnom and Panyaar to as far as Aliääp and Bɛɛr where the Agaar Dinka ultimately border the Western Nuer sections of Ganyliel in the toch. They also inhabit all those areas to the true north of Rumbek where eight sections of Agaar collectively called Rup are found. From this Rup, Agaar continues extensively as far as Pakam, about a hundred kilometres from Rumbek beyond which they border the Luacjang Dinka of the Aguër Aduɛl and Jalwau sections of the Rek Dinka of Tonj East county. Agaar communities also extend southeast of Rumbek where they border the Jur-Belle tribe which inhabits the upland plateau areas that begin towards the Ulu area.

According to one tradition among the Agaars, the name Agaar is derived from Agaar Marɔl Deng Kau Kuc, a man from the Paral clan people. The name is said to have come after the Jaang society had moved from the present Khartoum region in Northern Sudan to the Kurmuk area. The Agaar community is believed to have gone to the Kurmuk area from Khartoum as Duör, not as Agaar. They became Agaar in the southern Upper Nile areas currently inhabited by the Greater Bor Dinka community.

When this Duör left the southern Blue" Nile area of Kurmuk in about the end of the 5th century AD or thereabouts, they came by way of the present Jumjum, Balila and Gufa areas in the southern Blue Nile. Then they joined the rest of the Jaang in southern Upper Nile.

During the Jaang migration away from the Khartoum area some sections of Jaang took the White Nile route while Duör and other Jaang sections took the Blue" Nile route. For those centuries leading to the early Mediaeval era, centuries spent by the entire Jaang society in the Upper Nile Basin region, Duör society is said to have started to be identified as Agaar although some traditions say the name Agaar was later acquired after Duör crossed to Bahr el Ghazal, still as Duör. The version which takes Duör to have only become a section of Agaar in the Upper Nile affirms that Duör became Agaar in the southern Upper Nile before Jaang migration to Bahr el Ghazal. This may be true because among the Bor Dinka of today are a people called Dɔng Duör, the Duör that remained. They are a part of the Angakuei section in Bor. There are Pathuyith, Mothnhom, Aliääp and Thoi in Bor areas to the present day and they have their corresponding names in the Agaar land of today. There is even Panhom Agaar in the Athɔɔc area in Bor South.

During Jaang migration to Bahr el Ghazal in the early part of the Middle Ages (1340 AD) the Agaar Dinka community crossed the River Nile to the west bank as one section of Jaang. They left the southern Upper Nile areas at the big Pamac cattle camp area. Some of them departed from the present Panhom Agaar and those areas that are the present Jale and Maar to the northern end of present Bor South in Jönglei state. After crossing the River Nile at the Shambe shore of Anyɔɔp, precisely at the very foot of that centuries old sycamore tree which the Kiec Dinka call 'Kɔɔr' while Rek Dinka people call it 'Aciër', Agaar first encamped in the Ajäk area. They later proceeded to the Dɔkland areas which is the present Ganyliel territory of the Nuers. The Luac and Gok communities took to Rɛɛkɔu from Ajäk, together with the Twic. The Aliap Dinka community which crossed the River Nile at Patereu, Panhom and Gutthom shores took to the left on the west bank and settled as Ajuööt and its various sections of Lual, Dei, AbÖrɔm and Angɔu. Rek on its part thrusted westward to later settle in the Amongpiny area after spending about a decade or so at the Payii River area in what is now the Yirol East county of Kiec.

According to traditions going back to the Dɔkland period which begin from the last quarter of 1300 AD, Agaar communities settled at what is now Ganyliel and those areas that were Paliŋjiɛr. Paliŋjiɛr is our current Panyijar county area, currently inhabited by the Nuers of Adöör of Kuei. It is said the Agaar departed Ajäk to Dɔkland following a fight brought about by two youth groups who developed a misunderstanding over whether it was the day which was longer than the night or the opposite was the case.

It is said there was an economic boom at the time and the youth were just out to create fuss from a trivial matter. Those youngsters had gone to a cattle camp during a fattening season and were just drinking milk and eating from the meat so abundant from their herd. One day such an argument broke out among those youth in the cattle camp. One group said the day was longer than the night while the other group asserted that it was night which was longer and it became a matter for a big quarrel that elders had to come in and propose that the two groups have two bulls of equal size slaughtered for them so that each group competes with the other in the consumption of their bull's meat.

Those who were to finish first were to be deemed right. The proponents of the night being longer than the day finished their bull at first. Perhaps because nights are cooler than day times the night group was able to eat up their bull to finish first whereas those who were to eat their bull in the day could not succeed to finish eating their bull in time, perhaps because the day is usually warmer than the night. They could not consume their bull under the heat of the day. The story is rather long and is unscientific but it is rampantly told throughout Agaar land until today.

The long and short of the legend is that the two groups entered into a fight that led to the Agaar society deserting the fighting scene of Ajäk. Part of Agaar, like the Böör section, went south to join the Aliap community, while the rest of Agaar, the bigger part, went to the Dɔkland areas.

The importance of this story is that it confirms the fact of the Agaar community having encamped at Ajäk after crossing the Nile with the rest of the Jaang. *"Miith rɛcke Ajäk"*, *"Ajäk got spoiled by food"*, this saying remains to be used in Agaar land to the present day. The saying is a living proof that the Agaar community first settled at Ajäk after the Jaang crossed the Nile River from Shambe during their migration to Bahr el Ghazal.

There is, however, another version of this legend among the same Agaar community. It says a certain man did have a social occasion which was attended by members of the community as a usual Dinka practice, but the host decided to deny food and other services to those people on the argument that they were not invited by him. It is said this led to a quarrel which resulted in a fight which grew so big that the Agar society had to finally split with Böör, moving to join the Aliap community to the left of Ajäk and the rest, the bulk of Agaar, took to Dɔkland. The saying of *Miith rɛcke Ajäk* developed in the course of time and has survived the test of time to the present day. Whichever version is true, the truth is that the Agaar community had first settled and lived in this Ajäk area of the present Kiec Dinka land in the Yirol East area before they went to the Ganyliel or Dɔkland areas.

In Dɔkland another version states that the name Agaar came into usage when a certain warrior by the name of Agaar made great feats in their wars with the Nuers. Youthfolk of this Agaar society used to be led into those wars by him and Agaar was able to win several battles at the expense of the Nuers. As war leader the community was made to identify with him. It started with the youthfolk being called Agaar youthfolk. The Nuers' great pestilence of this period made every society rally behind and around any established warlord and his community used to be called after him. Agaar therefore used to lead his society into wars against the Nuers who, in the course of time, began to know this Jaang section as the Agaars, meaning people of Agaar. Great BuÖi Kuot was the apparent spiritual overlord at this time while Agaar Marɔl was a warlord. There was, however, another leader by the name of Apaac Paraau, a very generous man who used to give preference and opportunity to community cattle to drink from his own well till his own cows died of thirst in the end. In any case, the community became well known as Agaar since the Dɔkland times.

Until quite recently the Agaar communities of Panyoon, Bɛɛr and Aliääp were still being called *Agaar Dɔk* but the real Agaar-Dɔk appears to be those sections of Agaar who live north of the present Rumbek city. Agaar Dɔk means those Agaar people who were in the toch. They are those who live about the toch marshes where the terrain is rather muddy and a lowland area. The Agaar sections, which occupy a bit of raised land areas, are the Aliamtooc and Kuei. They are known as the Agaar-Ruup or Agaar of the sandy soil (liɛtic).

Towards the beginning of 1600 AD the Agaar Dɔk society decided to depart this Dɔkland area. They remigrated west to where the Rek society had vacated further west. On vacating Dɔkland areas, Agar Dɔk divided into three factions, the Amothnhom, Monytiik and Nyang sections of Kuei-ɣernhom of Liɛtic under Great BuÖi Kuot, and others came towards the present Rumbek area to their present locations to face the Jur-Belle community who were the Aboriginals of the territory.

Except for the Amothnhom and Monytiik sections of Kuei, Nyang decided to follow the route earlier taken by Rek society. They later came directly to the present Rumbek area by way of present Matangai, however, the Kuei section of Nyang later decided to drop behind. It moved south as the Rek decided to proceed further west. Those sections to become the Pakam community of Kerwaak took the northwestern direction right from Dɔkland and went straight to their present territory of Pakam where they border the Luacjang Dinka community of Aguër Adɛl and the Nuers to the northeast. They were led by Great Kerwaak of the Paderek (Pawutweng) clan. The third column of Agaar from Dɔkland took to the direction of a territory which later became Yäk. Those were largely a section of Nyuɛi who were basically Pathɔth and Patiɔp clans.

Present Anëët people of Great Chief Malual Arop are subsequent migrants who came back from among the Pagoŋ clan people around Wau in what is the present Western Bahr el Ghazal state. They migrated from the Pagoŋ people who are now called the Waau Dinka of Chief Majɔk Majɔk. One section known as Athoi first made a stopover at Loic which was an open land with good pasture land rich in lick salt, good for their cattle. They then extended later to those places where they are in today, a place a few kms southeast of Rumbek city.

The present eight sections of the Rup, consisting of Aliääp, Bɛr, Ajak, Panyoon, Jöth, Akök, Monytiik and Böör, had, however, decided to remain behind in this Dɔkland. They are a later wave that subsequently came and settled in their present territories in between the Pakam and Nyang sections of Kuei. The Köök and Thiyiith sections of Athoi later penetrated deep into the Jur-Belle areas up to the present area of Kuel-Kuac, the current Malou military garrison area, Marat-Tiit and the Makemele areas.

Earlier, after leaving Ajäk, the Agaar community largely went to Dɔkland in today's Ganyliel area. They did not come into hostile contact with the then expected menace from the Jur-Luɛɛl community who inhabited all those areas that later became Kiec and Aliap and all the territories that are present Aliamtooc-One and Aliamtooc-Two. Before the Jaang was to advance westward from Liɛtpaciruööt in the Ajäk area, it was the Rek that took to the front. This made the Rek community the first Jaang section to enter into war with the Jur-Luɛɛl community. Most of the Jaang sections like Twic and Gok with what later became Kiec and Luacjang made their further migration on the toch marshes along the west bank. Agaar, in contrast to the other Jaang sections, had at this time taken to the east and this did not make them the first section of the Jaang to enter into war with Jur-Luɛɛl.

After the initial engagements between the Rek and Jur-Luɛɛl following the crossing of the Nile, the Jur-Luɛɛl community became alert and became sufficiently prepared against the danger from the invading Jaang. They sought to improve on their war implement the '*daŋga*' and its bow. They then started to be on the offensive against this incoming Jaang.

Up to this point in history, it is said, Jaang war implements did not include the shield which they now call '*köt*'. They were using the ambatch wood called '*rör*', used as a shield to ward off implements against oneself. They also knew of the magueŋ, also called '*makuith*' or '*kuɛ́r*'. This implement is used during battles to wave away weapons from the enemy. Their former Nilotic enemies whom they left in the Upper Nile Basin areas, the Nuers, the Shilluks, Anyuak and the Murle, used spears like them. But this time around on the west bank in Bahr el Ghazal, the Jur-Belle, Jur-Luɛɛl and Bongo peoples used bows and arrows called daŋga which is catapulted and swiftly flown through the air. When a Jaang man finds no time to see and to dodge it, he is hit by the daŋga. The Jaaŋ people were still using those spears of the technology of the previous Khartoum and Meroe periods. Their spears, when darted, go a short distant and need a close range engagement whilst the daŋga, which flies far by catapulsion and could not be seen, was able to catch a Jaaŋ man from very far away! A daŋga used to have and continues to have a poisonous substance on its tip and edge.

This daŋga temporarily halted the Rek's determined plan to invade the Luɛɛl and Belle lands and for those initial decades the daŋga affair kept the Rek at bay. This explains why the Rek spent some time in the Payii River area. For a number of decades while Agaar society stayed in that Dɔkland area of Ganyliel they also found continuous war with the Nuers. Towards the end of 1500 AD the Agaar community under the leadership of a Redior Spear Master, Great BuÖi Kuot, decided to abandon that Dɔkland area of Ganyliel and chose to come and manoeuvre to stay with the Jur-Belle community. Jur-Luɛɛl had at that time gone further west with the advent of the big Rek Dinka from the Payii River area. With the coming of Agaar some social contacts started to develop between the Agaar and Jur-Belle communities. One Agaar man who married from the Belle tribe happened to make a visit to his in-laws in the Jur-Belle country. During his stay with the in-laws he was able to learn of a shield technology simply made from a hide of those animals such as the antelope *thiaŋ*. The Agaar man conceived the art and upon his return he disclosed the art of making the war shield out of animal hide to protect oneself by warding off arrows in combat. He found it useful in contrast to the ambatch wood they had been using.

Once the shield used as a protective coat during combats was discovered it was quickly undertaken by the whole of the western Jaang sections. The Agaars, like the rest of Jaang, speedily improved on that. Instead they used giraffe and buffalo skins that are much thicker and therefore impenetrable by the daŋga. This heightened Jaang's onslaught on those animals that used to be hunted only for meat and for their tassels and it was now easy for the Agaar to cast an air of superior combat.

With the shield now at hand the Agaar community was able to turn the tide against the Jur-Belle and Jur-Luɛɛl danger in the area. While there was social interaction, the Jur-Belle's capability to fight the Agaars was no longer there and the Belle community was now receding gradually, giving way to the Agaar encroachment starting southwards. The Gok Dinka community, now at Rɛɛl Kou to the north of the Agaar community, also benefited from the discovery of this war shield technology and this was to later change the military balance in the Gok-Belle and Gok-Bongo stalemate during the period of late 1500 to 1600 AD.

As the Agaar community came back from the Dɔkland area of Ganyliel, its section called Kuei was able to occupy all those areas that are now Athoi and Amothnhom as well as what is now Panyoon but in the course of their coming from DƆkland, great Spear Master BuÖi Kuot decided to seek peaceful coexistence with the Belle community. Traditions among the Agars say BuÖi Kuot gave his daughter by the name of Akon BuÖi to a paramount Belle leader. Akon was accompanied by a gift of a big black '*Macar*' bull. The bride with a bull was offered to the Belle overlord to normalise relations with the Jur-Belle. What is today's Rumbek and its surrounding areas were given over to Buoi Kuot in return for Akon. The Agaar community that had just come out from the perpetual war with the Nuers was not ready this time to again enter into a fight with the Jur-Belle community. They even gave bulls to the Belle for meat which was greatly lacking in the Belle daily diet as they did not have cattle from then until today. Jur-Belle get their meat only through hunted wild animals.

In consequence the Belle overlord allowed BuÖi Kuot, the peacemaking Spear Master, to let his people interact with them peacefully. The Jur-Belle allowed the Agaar the chance to settle side by side with them. Through that peaceful coexistence Agaar communities were able to gradually pacify the Belle through the assimilation process and superior numbers, which became an effective weapon. In the course of the century this overwhelming presence of the Agaar community ultimately caused the southerly withdrawal of the Belle, whose people started to gradually move away from the Agaar community. They chose to settle in the haematite plateau areas where they live today. This peaceful occupation of the Belle country by the Agaars was effected over the course of a century. It started from the late 15th century and became complete by about the last quarter of the 16th century AD.

As a flashback, one section of the Agaar that sought to maintain the ancient name of Duör is said to have remained in southern Upper Nile during the historic migration of the Jaang community to Bahr el Ghazal. They are a section maintaining that ancient name of Duör to the present day. They currently live in Duk-Padiëët and stay in concert with the ɣöl and Twic Dinka communities who now border the Gawɛɛr Nuers in Jonglei state.

Perhaps simply to continue to remember their former name, a section of the Agaar insisted on maintaining the original name of the tribe. They are the present Duör section in Rumbek East county area where they are a people of the Paramount Chief Malual Arop of Aliamtooc-Two. Part of Duör may be one which went to as far as the Tonj North area where they are now a Rek community in Kɔŋöör territory and border the Lou-Ariik and Jur-Lian sections of Awan.

SOCIAL CONFIGURATION OF THE AGAAR DINKA

Agaar Dinka sections:
1. Aliamtooc-One of Great Chuut Dhuɔl, consisting of:
Athoi territory which is comprised of: Thiyiith section of Chief Majak Agɔɔk.
- Gɔny section of Chief Riech Ater
- Gɔny Jɔŋnyang section of Chief Mayom Dhuɔl
- Dhiëëi section of Chief Makuac Kherasid
- Köök-One section of Chief Majak Malok. Köök-Two section of Chief Maŋar Machiek.

Those are the territories which constitute part of the Rumbek Central county.

2. Aliamtooc-Two of Great Malual Arop, consisting of:
- Duör-bar section of Akorbiil of Chief Mangar Marial Banyook. Duör-Cek or Gɔɔp-Yibek of Chief Mayak Biling
- Nyuɛi-Macar of four sections of: (i) Chief Marial Mamur, (ii) Chief Cholic Malek Malual Arop, (iii) Chief Ariɛr Makoi and (iv) Chief Dhieu Matuet of Panyaar section of Paan-Apiin
- Cieny section of Chief Majök Der-Der
- Riaak section of chief Marial Ater Ugɔl and Amiir section of Chief Akol Yuɔl.

Those are the areas that constitute the Rumbek East county called Aliamtooc-Two.

3. Kuei territories of Great Manyiel Cinduut, consisting of:
- Amothnhom section of Chief Madöl Mathok Agoldɛr
- Tiɛk or Monytiik section of Chief Luɔth Marial Buɔc

- Nyang Area made up of: Yɔm territory of Chief Marial Kumbaai; Dor section of two chiefs: Mangar Dhaal Manyiel and Makuet Thokriel and the Awan section of Chief Marial Kodi.

4. Rup territory of eight sections of Great Manyiel Dut and comprised of: Kuei-Acuääth with Kuei-ɤernhom, the big Panyoon territory of Chief Majök Maper and Chief Dut Maker Mayen of two sections of Köök, Lek and Tiɛk of Chief Kök Malok; Ajak section of Chief Majur Aciɛn Kolok; Akök section of Chief Madol Mading Maguär; Jöth section of Chief Abol Kuyök; Aliääp of two sections of Chief Juöl Macɔk and Chief Matur Warweng Liɛny (Aliääp is the Agar territory where Amongpiny is located); Bɛɛr section of Chief Malok Aguɛt Madol and Böör section of Chief Aliir Cipuounyuc.
- Kuei-Acuääth and Kuei-ɤernhom which are the Rup territory of Great Manyiel Dut and Kuei territory of Great Manyiel Cinduut, all form what is the rest of Rumbek Central county.

5. Pakäm Territory of Great Wol Athian consisting of :-
- The big Gak Wol territory of three chieftaincy areas, Manuɛr of three chieftaincy areas, Niel-Niel of two chieftaincies, Lith which is two chieftancies and the Körkör and Anien sections with two chieftaincies each.

Those areas are the sections which constitute Rumbek North county.

The Agaar Dinka community is therefore made up of the three counties of Rumbek Central, Rumbek East and Rumbek North, which are in fact administrative provinces.

MALUAL DINKA

Malual Dinka, which makes an area of five very big counties in a state known as Northern Bahr el Ghazal state, borders Gogrial West county to its eastern borders of Abiem. It borders Akoch-Thɔn Payam in the Western Twic county of Warrap state, Luo sections of Abat to the southwest towards Wau city and the Fertit community called Kresh to the far west in Western Bahr el Ghazal state. Malual Dinka also borders the Massiriya and Rizzeigat Arab Baggara of Southern Darfur and Southern Kordofan to the true northwest. It is also bordered by the Ngok Dinka people of Abyei to the northeast.

Malual Dinka has a population of nearly two million people spread into those five counties. It is basically part of the Rek as it is purely made up of clans and sections that migrated there from the main body of the Rek communities of Kuei and Lith well after much of the Rek have arrived in the present Kuac-Agor and Abiem Mayar Marɛng areas.

Rek sections and communities which later became Malual left from the Abiem area of Tonj North and the Kuac-Agor area in present Gogrial West county. They gradually made their migration due west up to a place they named 'Apuökjang', meaning where those migrating families and sections parted in different directions. Apuökjang is about the present Kar-Ariääth in the Apuɔth-Yelker area, formerly an area of Chief Kuol Makuac Kuol, but which is currently of Chief Kɔng Ayueel of the Pamiath clan in the Awiel East county area of Abiem.

Here at Apuökjang, including the vicinity of the famous Alok village, a man from the Pabiöng clan section of Panyiɛr killed two people from another section. Panyiɛr were under the paramount authority of Great Tɔng Aköt Tɔng. Payii people in Tonj areas know this Aköt Tɔng as the grandson of Tɔng-Manyangdit who is Tɔng Anei-Parek and who led this part of the community of Rek right from Angääc in the Tonj East area of Jalwau. Tɔng-Manyangdit led those sections further westwards to the toch land area of Lual-Aɤöny. Lual Aɤöny is a legendary man from the Paɤɔl clan who is believed to have continued with his westward migration from Awiel West as far as the central African borders. He did not return with the people who went with him up to the present day!

The existing custom among the Jaang of that Mediaeval time was that people used to pay blood dia compensation of three cows to the relatives of a person killed. It was here at Apuökjang that Great Tɔng Aköt made a ritual occasion in which he buried alive a bull by the colour of 'Malual-Ajiɛrnyang'. He then gave name to that society of the Rek as Malual-Ajiɛrnyang from which the present name of Malual-Giɛrnyaang was evolved.

Pabiöng clan people have been committing murder all the time and their people have been paying so much blood dia cattle that their cows were now finishing. For this particular incident at Apuökjang the Pabiöng people killed two men from the clan of Great Diing Wol Lek, also known as Diing Ker-Amindik, a leader who did have influence over those people of the deceased persons. This time demand was made for the Pabiöng clan people to pay five cows for each of the two men killed.

The Pabiöng family concern was therefore required to pay ten cows as such but they had only eight cows left. It was then difficult for them to pay the ten cows and in the predicament that followed their Banydit Chief Tɔng Aköt decided to commit his section to migrate west to let them escape the payment of blood dia cattle. Over thirty clans followed him. They went as far as the Chel River area after spending some time at what later became Mading Ayueel, which later became known as Mading Awiel. At this Mading Ayueel, Great Tɔng Aköt proceeded to the Chel River area where he and his people found abundant lulu trees from which they prepared lulu oil which they found to be deliciously good for seasoning porridge.

They began to pour it on their porridge and began to fill the calabashes to overflowing with porridge and it was from this that such a community later acquired the name of Palieupiny. People who were with him were as such regarded as the Palieuping section of Malual.

Thus it was from this Apuökjang spot that the famous story of *'Banydit Ku Banykoor'* (the sub-chief) took place when the people of Tɔng Aköt Tɔng killed a person from the section of his Banykoor, Kuac Ngɔr. This is what caused the split which prompted Banydit Tɔng Aköt to depart to the Mading Ayueel area and further on to the Chel River area while the people of Banykoor went further northwest. This was towards the middle of the 16th century AD. There, they later became Palieupiny, while those who went further northwest became the real Malual Giɛrnyaang.

Tɔng Aköt Tɔng went to Chelkɔu with his Parek clan people, with the Pakuur and Paluaal of rock stone and bladed spear, with the Panyiɛr and their branch clan called Pabiöng, with the Patääng who are also Ruaal people, the Padur people of Puöt and the Pakeen of the flamingo bird (aken). He also went with the Kuaween people of Apac who are Paker in Tonj areas and Pajul in Gok land. He went with the Dumai people who are Patɛk and Pawan people who are Patiɔp or Paduɔltiɔp, the Pariath people of Piöl, Pagɛu people of the amuöör bird, Pagut people of the hippo, Golbany clan people of the turtle (nhiëër), GolKak people who are a branch of the Parum, Thuri who are the Pajuɔu of the comet (ciër), Golbiin, Pawɛtnyiëng who are Pagor, Padhuny people of the cuur fish who are Paker, the Pagilo of the nuök bird, Pangueet of piöl the rain cloud, the Paciɛrmeth people of Ruaal, Payuɔm people of tap, the tobacco, Paciɛny who came from West Africa, Pajiëëc who are the original Padhieu as they are the descendants of Ajiëëc who was brother to Dhieu-Anyɔr whose family lineages are now Padhieu. He also went with the Pakuiin who are people of ruaal, Paɏöl people of the thigh bone, Pawarjaak who are Paliëëc. There was also an assortment of small clans in addition to the Pajuadha. The Kuawëën people were found on the Chel River area as remnants of the Luo who were Shilluks that had once lived there before sections of the Luo returned to the Upper Nile after their historic quarrel and split of 1500 AD in Bahr el Ghazal.

This Palieupiny community of Tɔng Aköt de Rɛɛng later divided into Paliëët and Buɔth-Anyaar and across centuries they developed in population that now became the Awiel West and South counties. Dominant among these numerous clans of Palieupiny is the big Parek clan of great Tɔng Aköt from which Great Awutiak and Deng-Ajäklang are among those historical figures of that part of Malual.

THE PAJOK SECTION OF MALUAL DINKA

While Tɔng Aköt and his Palieupiny people migrated westwards as explained above, Great Diing Wol Leek, who was also a paramount Spear Master from the Ruaal group now called Paciɛrmeth, went northwards. A group of people called *Jooki* meaning adoptees according to the local usage, were part of the people who made up this group under Banykoor. They decided to migrate north with about thirty or more clans. Gradually this community of clans settled in those areas that are now the Awiel North county. They cover those areas up to the borders with Massiriya and Rizzeigat Arab Baggara at places like Gok-Macar, the Kiir Adem area, Mile 14 and other border areas with Western Sudan.

With continued use of the word Jooki, this community of Diing Wol-Ker-Amindik was gradually given the name Pajok. Some sections that remained at Apuökjang and its surrounding areas became Abiem, which constitutes the present Awiel East county, bordering the Warrap state areas of Akoch-Thɔn, Awan Chan and Awan Pajok to the east. Those who went further north with Ker-Amindik and their Banykoor became Awiel North county. For what has come to be, this group that went north became the true Malual-Giɛrnyaang.

The clans that constitute the Pajok of Diing Wol Leek consisted of his Ruaal people who later became Paciɛrmeth. They consisted of the Paduil clan people of blood, a people who were originally from the Patiɔp clan. Going with Great Diing Wol also were those who became the Padhieu people of achai and the pelican jak. A section of Pariäth people of piöl, the cloud, also went with him. The Palɛu people of anyak the viper, who are Pathian related people, the Paker and Paliec and Pangüëër people of puöt and agaany, the giant river lizard, the Paluiɛl people of the monkey, Pajiëng people of piën, the cobra, the Panyiɛr and Paluɛtmir people of the hippopotamus, sections of Pagong and Paguäär who are Palɛu, the Pakiir of Kiir River but who were originally Parum, the Paciɛny and Padiangbar people of the heglig tree and pɛɛi the moon were among those who followed Ker-Amindik. The Pakuin and Palou people of ruaal the sausage tree and atany, the winnowing tray, Patääng people of the dog, Payum and Pamiaath people of the dawn who are actually Patiɔp of Pabɛɛk origin, Padëp section people of the fire who are actually Pakuiëth or Alɔkyɔu as they are called in some parts of Rek lands, but who are called Pathööth in Gok and Agar lands. They were all among those who followed Ker-Amindik. Sections of the Patɛk clan people of the crocodile, Pangueeng clan people of the turtle, a branch of Parek clan called Paciɛr, Pagak clan people of the mahogany tree and the forest were also there. Other people called Pawarweeng were also among those clans that went with Great Diing Wol-Ker-amindïk. There were many more other smaller clans in this section called Pajök.

1. Malual-Giɛrnyaang. Those are the Pajok clans that proceeded further north from Apuokjang to become the true Malual-Giɛrnyaang and who now make up the Awiel North county population. Others remained to form the present Abiem in Awiel East county. Those clans that chose to go to the northern areas of Awiel to become Malual-Giɛrnyaang currently inhabit those territories which are the Kɔrɔɔk

areas of Diing Majɔk, an area which is currently of Chief Diing Dhan Diing of the Paciɛr people of agɛɛp, the palm tree. Another is the Kɔrɔɔk area of Aciɛn Yɔɔr, now of Chief Aciɛn Aciɛn Yɔɔr of the Paduil clan people of blood, the Atökthɔu-Diing Wol area, presently of Chief Mathok Diing Wol of the Paciɛrmeth people of Ruaal, the Duluit area of Chief Bol Deng, now of Chief Kuot Nyuol Deng of the Padhieu clan people of achai and the pelican, another Duluit territory in the wooded savannah (Gok) area of Chief Gau Deng Gau of the Palɛu clan people of the viper (anyak), another Duluit area in the toch territory of Chief Deng Barjök Ken, again of the Padhieu people, the Makɛm Aköt Wol area of Chief Aköök Ngor Kuany of the Paliec clan people of puöt and agaany, the Pawiecweng area of Chief Santino Deng Nyuol of the Padhieu; the Ayat-Bar area of Chief Garang Diang Aköök of the Pacieny who are Padiaŋbar and the Ayat-Tueng area of Chief Jiel Matuur of the Pakuin clan people of Ruaal.

Malual-Giɛrnyaang of the Pajok section of Awiel North county up to the time of writing this book is currently made up of twenty four executive chieftaincy areas and of course this is likely to increase with the increase of population.

2. Abiem is that section of Pajök which consists of: The big Lou-Aguer Gɛng area of Chief Atem Gɛng Atem of the Pakäm clan people of Ruaal; Wun-Deng area of Chief Piöth Yai Deng from the Patɛk people of the crocodile; Ajuɔng section area of Chief Malöng Yɔɔr; Agurpiny area of Chief Ariik Maroor Arou of the Panguet people of Piöl and Akɔɔn the elephant; Wun-Anei area of Chief Garang Anei Tɔng of the Pacieny who are Padiaŋbar; Makuac Athian area of Chief Teeng Athian Deng of the Panyiɛr clan people of the hippopotamus; Ajuɔngthi area of Chief Them Tɔng Tɔng of the Patɛk clan; Pingdong area of Chief Makuac Makuac Kuol from Pamiath people of Arɔɔl and who are Paduɔltiɔp or Patiɔp; Kuethcuär area of Chief Kɔng Ayueel Majök of the Pariäth clan; Ɣou-Alueeth area of Chief Deng Dhiil Thiëël from the Padiaany clan people of the arial beek bird; the Akanyjök area of Chief Garang Rual Deng from Parek clan people of the red sycamore or fig tree called kuel, the Manyuaang area of Chief Aköök Gai Ngor of the Paliec clan people of puöt and agaany and who are Pawutweng; the Wun-Diing area of Chief Ngong Deng Ngong of the Paciɛrmeth clan and finally, the Duluit Kuac Ngor area of Chief Pio Tem Kuac Ngor of the Padhieu clan people of achai, the pelican.

THE PALIEUPINY SECTIONS OF MALUAL

Paliëët section of Paliëupiny: (Awiel South county)
The Paliëët section of Paliëupiny consists of the Ajak Akol Atäny area of Chief Akol Wɛk Atany of the Pakuin clan people of ruaal; the Kongdeer Dut Jök area of Chief Deng Dut Jök of the Pariäth clan people of piöl the cloud and akɔɔn the elephant; the Buɔncuai area of Chief Manute Gɛng Ariääth of the same Pariäth clan; the Bar-Mayen area of Chief Mawut Unguac Ajɔŋɔ from the Dumai clan people of Dhur[23] and the Thanybur and Akuliec areas of Chief Piöl Gɛng Ariääth of the Pariath clan. These sections which make up Paliëët were part of Gogrial until recently when the condominium authorities annexed them to Awiel to balance the populations of the districts in Bahr el Ghazal when Gogrial was part of the big Jur River district of Tonj.

Malual Buɔth-Anyaar section of Paliëupiny: (Awiel West county)
This is typically the area of Great Tɔng Aköt Tɔng of the Parek clan, the historical figure who led Buɔth-Anyaar right at Angääc in Adöör land of Jalwau in Tonj East to the Abiem area of Mayar Marɛng at the western end of Tonj North. From Abiem, this Tɔng Aköt proceeded with his Buɔth-Anyaar community to Apuökjang in the Apuöth-Yelker area in Awiel East and finally to Chelkou in

what later became the Buɔth-Anyaar area of Awiel West county. Awiel West is a county whose westwards borders extend to border the Raga areas of the Payaja people who are of Luo from Jur-col background.

Malual-Buɔth-Anyaar consists of the big Gömjuɛɛr territory of Aköt Awutiak, the Gömjuɛɛrthi territory of the Awil Aköt Aru area of chief Garang Tɔng Aru of the Pahöl clan people of the thigh bone; the Cimel area of chief Kuac Kuaac Mayiëldit of the Pagɛu clan people of the crocodile and fire, the Cimeldit area of Chief Yaac Deng Yaac also of the Pagɛu clan; the Cimel Ciɛl (Awiel rice scheme area) territory of Chief Mayen Piöl of the Celkou territory of Chief Wiɛu Aleu Jök of the Pagɛu; the Ayat-Cek area of Chief Riiny Riiny Lual; the Ajuet Mawien Diing area of Chief Mawien Mawien Diing of the Paciɛrmeth clan; the Achana area of Chief Ayaga Ayaga bordering the Payaja people who are a Luo people of Jur-col origin and the Aroyo area of Ajiing Upiɛu, now of Chief Apay Angara from the Golbany clan people of Dhuur totem.

On the whole, the combined Malual Dinka was responsible for the final departure of Jur-Luɛɛl in all the areas that are now Northern Bahr el Ghazal state. The Jur-Luɛɛl are a people believed to have gone away from Bahr el Ghazal to Western Sudan, then to Chad and Nigeria, probably to become the present Fulanis who used to come back into Western Sudan as Falata and Ambororos. Some of them also melted into the Rizziegat Arab Baggara in southern Darfur.

LUACJANG DINKA

The Luacjang Dinka community is otherwise known for its marshal name 'Luac-Magɔɔk'. It is made up of twelve sections. The community acquired its name Luac from the story which says that Luac are a Dinka people who used to be relentlessly persistent in pursuing a matter. They are known to pursue a matter to its logical conclusion.

When the Luac community is on the move they will do it nonstop. They were known to have done this when the Jaang migrated from the Khartoum area to the Upper Nile region in 490 AD and again from Upper Nile to the Bahr el Ghazal region in 1340 AD. The Luac community currently lives in the eastern parts of Tonj East county, some one hundred miles east of Tonj town. They border the western Upper Nile Nuer communities of Mayendit and Ler counties.

In those early Mediaeval times in the Upper Nile Basin region, the Luacjang community is believed to have settled in those areas that are currently inhabited by Nyarweng Dinka after the Jaang came from the northern Upper Nile areas. Luac once comprised of the gone Angääc section when the Jaang was in the central Upper Nile region. Luac Dinka belong to the Ruweng cultural group. When the Luac community left Northern Jonglei state areas as part of the Jaang that migrated to Bahr el Ghazal, Angääc remained where they later got absorbed or assimilated by Lak and Thiöng sections of the Nuer in the vicinity of Pam-Zeraf and were part of the Luac who took off for Bahr el Ghazal.

During that migratory exodus to the Bahr el Ghazal region, the Luac community crossed the River Nile to the west bank of the Nile to the very spot where the big sycamore trees still stand today. The Kiec Dinka calls it 'kɔɔr' while the rest of the western Dinka call it 'aciër'. This aciër tree now stands on the Nile bank shore of Pagarau on the edge of the big Toch of Kadop near Anyɔɔp, near a spot called Rumjöök. Here during the nights sounds of mysterious humans are heard celebrating and dancing. Sounds of children rattling about and sounds of people singing are heard from people not being seen! It was from this shore of Rumjöök that the Luac community crossed to Bahr el Ghazal. The Luac community avoided the shore which was used by Rek and Agaar, a shore where the leader of the Jaang migration, Loŋaar Ayueel, was spearing the heads of people who were crossing the Nile because the community did that migration against his decision that they should not follow him at that time according to his migration plan explained elsewhere in this book.

During the Luac crossing moment, there was a big water beast locally known by then as 'ŋuäl', a kind of a dinosaur that began to swallow a number of people who have dived into the water as people were crossing the River Nile. It is said that this Nile beast used to widely open its mouth inside the deep of the water, and up to about fifty people would just walk into it unknowingly and then it would close its mouth and swallow all of them! The Luac population who were crossing came to learn there was such a river monster which was swallowing people inside the Nile waters. A certain Aduɛr, the ancestor of the Wilfred Ring Aduɛr Ngor, decided to pick a big bladed spear from the hands of a certain man by the name of Gäkgäk who was standing with his spears amidst the Luac people on the riverbank. With that spear Great Aduɛr speared the beast which ran roaring afloat the water.

After a short while the beast was seen throwing itself into an upside down somersault and died in an instant! From then the Luac community was able to cross without fear. The Luac people later gave to Aduɛr the nickname of 'Aduɛr-Anguang Nguäl', meaning Aduɛr who darted and killed the dinosaur. The spear remained in the body of the beast and the owner of the spear is said to have returned to Bor land along with those who did not dare to face those threats in the River Nile at crossing. His son Jiër Gäkgäk, however, proceeded with the Luac society. His descendants are now the chieftaincy rulers of the Ariääu and Baar-Apiök areas in the Nyang-Ruup section of the Rubaar territory of Luacjang.

In that migration into Bahr el Ghazal the Luac Mediaeval community was led by a number of its sections' Spear Masters, among whom was Great Guöt Akoi, whose descendants are now the Pagut clan people of Great Athiɛplek in Luacjang. Like most Jaang who crossed the River Nile the Luac community encamped at Liɛtpaciruööt on the west bank in the present Ajäk area in the Adöör section of Kiec Dinka. All Jaang who succeeded to cross to the west bank of the Nile made a long respite to first make traditional rituals and to properly study the terrain and security of the region. When the Jaang later decided to advance, starting to step into the real areas of Jur-Luɛɛl, Jur-Belle and the Bongo further west, Luac for its part decided to take a marshland route northwards. They moved in the same direction with the rest of those sections which were Gok, Kiec and Twic. Those sections took the same route with the Luac. Except for its section called Duöl, the Agaar community had earlier taken to Dɔkland areas in the present Ganyliel and Panyijar areas of the Nuers. The Rek, for their part, thrust westwards to directly face Jur-Luɛɛl right at the present Payii River area. The Aliap had initially taken southwards to the left of Shambe where they faced the southern parts of the Jur-Belle. They were followed by the Duör section of Agaar.

Although there were respite stopover places on the march the Luac made its usual nonstop movement, wanting to reach Rɛɛl Kou, which its reconnaissance party had reported to be a suitable place for the Luac to settle. In their long and continuous movement Great Guöt Akoi featured over and above the rest. Midway in the course of that long trek said to have been done for three consecutive days along the toch marshes of the present Aliääp territory on the east of Amothnhom section of Agaar, the Luac people found a sycamore tree called ngaap in Dinka language. The tree did have nice shade and it was at ripening time so the ground in its vicinity was full of its fallen fruit berries. Those who were on the forefront started to take rest under that ngaap tree to enjoy the cooling shade and they also began to eat from its fallen berries. When Great Guöt arrived from behind he found the people had eaten all the fallen ngaap berries that were on the ground and had shaken or thrown wicks of trees onto its near branches for the ripened berries to fall and they ate them all. They wanted more but they could not get those berries from its high branches.

Guöt, who was a renowned Spear Master, asked the Luac people if the thing was sweet. He was told by just about everybody that it was quite a delicious ngaap. Then he told the Luac he would have to use his spiritual powers from Nhialic to cause the tree to fall down for all to get its berries. With those words, Great Guöt started doing his Spear Master invocations. He asked the tree to throw itself down for his people to eat from her far off berries. Then he positioned his holy spear binhlöŋ and strongly darted it twice into the tree. In the most miraculous way the tree fell down in a somersault instantly, all of it! As he did this miraculous event to the disbeliever of all, he himself died also on the instant! He conjured this tree in the interest of his Luac community and that is why the Luac people continue to remember him as Great Guöt Aɲuaŋ-Ngaap to the present day. He was buried there on the spot and the Luac continued its march up to Rɛɛlkou where they settled for over half a century. This was in about 1370 AD.

Some time later in this Rɛɛlkou area, the Luac community entered into war with the Kiec community, a war which ended in the famous battle of Rɛɛlkou of 1430.[73] This battle was so disastrous that Rɛɛlkou was to be deserted by the Kiec who went back to the Yirol area where remain to the present day. The Luac, however, remained in Rɛɛlkou for some time. Other sources among the Luacjang people say that Luac also vacated Rɛɛlkou soon after the battle and went to the Madol area and its surroundings. At Rɛɛlkou, before the Luac departure to Madol territory, the section and people who later became Ruweng had a spiritual leader by the name of Loi Jiel. This spiritual leader entered into a quarrel with one of the Luac Spear Masters. In consequence his people broke off from the Luac and went back to the Yirol area, following the Kiec. They later crossed the Nile

---

73 The year of this war of Rɛɛlkou was computed through the genealogical line of victor Bol Duöp Bäp whose ancestor participated in the battle of Rɛɛlkou.

back to the Upper Nile from where they once again recrossed to the present Panrieng area of Pan-Ru in western Upper Nile, crossing from the Adɔk River shore. Sectors that became the Ngok of Lual Yak, Paweny and Nyarweng Dinka communities remained in central Upper Nile. The Wol-Adhieu people and those Ruweng sections of Alor and Jök, which later became the Ngok of Abyei, proceeded to Biemnhom and to the present Abyei areas.

At the Madol area, part of the Luac broke away and went to settle at what is the Lɛɛr area of today. The rest of the Luac regarded them as Luac-Tɛɛt. Those are the Luac community now known as the Luac of Aguer Wiɛu in the Khor Fluth area of Pigi county in Northern Jognlei state. At Madol those Luac people who did not go with Tɛɛt began to see the cranes which Dinka people call '*awet-marial*', always flying west in the afternoons and returning the next morning. Elders used to ask themselves whether it could not be worthwhile to check the place where those birds used to fly to. They wanted to know if there could be a good dry land area (Riaaŋ) for the Luac to relocate to. They said a reconnaissance team should go to find out what the place was. The Luac society wanted a dry land area to settle at as they were fed up with the wet lands of the toch marshes which they have been to since they crossed the great Nile River, some decades or nearly a century ago with the rest of their west bank Jaang.

One particular day, a famous and a very strong community giant, too tall a man called Akäl Wuöt from the Pajung, a branch clan of the current Panai clan in Luac, picked up the matter. He took a trip westward to see for himself the place where those awet-marial used to go. As he arrived at the place he was caught by a group of Twic women whom he found cutting grass for thatching their homes. Those Twic women humiliatingly cut off his testicles and so he died!

His dog ran back to where the Luac community is at Rɛɛlkou or Madol. When the dog came back alone people became worried. They then concluded that something may have happened to Akäl Wuöt.

The Twic people had already settled in that good territory, having come there since they left what is now the Gok land area of Pagor Payam and present Pathiöng areas as described under Gok history.

At the time when Akäl Wuöt went to survey the area, the Twic community had gathered around their old Spear Master by the name of Kuol-Alɛl. The old man was very sick, very old and on the verge of death. The community came to him and confided that Twic women had killed a very big person who they said must be a Luac man. Great Kuol-Alɛl knew what was to happen from his experience with the Luac. He told the Twic that there would be an immediate attack from the Luac people. He said the Luac community cannot hesitate to wage war on the Twic to avenge their person[24] and told them to immediately leave the territory, leaving part of their cattle to avoid the Luac getting them on the way driving the cattle. Kuol-Alɛl also told the Twic to first bury him alive before they rushed away from the territory. At that time the Luac was comparatively bigger than the Twic.

It is to be recalled that a big part of the Twic remained in the Upper Nile area. His viewpoint was accepted and the Twic hurriedly went in to bury their Spear Master while still alive. Burial alive has been Dinka practice since ancient times. They buried him in the usual way Dinka people bury their Spear Masters. His grave was dug many metres deep and wide, to the space of a big Dinka house called ɣöt. After he was laid down with an uncastrated bull and uncastrated ram and a wooden frame made into a bed, a muddied heath cover was placed over him. The grave was then laid with earth. They made a sort of a pyramidal shrine usually built over the remains of Dinka Spear Masters after burial. Dinka people call it 'yik', the holy shrine, but as was also told to them by their buried Spear Master, huge wood logs and wicks were piled up on the shrine's mound and they put fire on it.

Then the entire Twic stampeded the area to the northwest, running along the toch marshes in what is the present Lou-Paher section of Macuët and Gɔny. They ran fast enough till they could no longer see the flakes (rial) of the burning fire on the shrine's pyramid. The big pool created by the construction of that shrine continues to be a big water pool at the vicinity of that shrine even today. This shrine of the middle period of the Mediaeval era still remains to be seen today as an astonishing pyramidal mound pre-eminently standing at a place called Alɛl in Padeet village in the Wun-Thuc area of Rubaar in the Nyang-Wiir territory of Luacjang. The Twic, according to this legend, left the area in the night, leaving some of their cattle in the cattle camps still tethered to their pegs to deceive the Luac that the Twic were still in the area.

The morning after the day of the Twic secret departure from the area a reconnaissance party led by a certain Ajaknɛi came to survey the area. They realised that the society which inhabited that Riaaŋ land had voluntarily deserted the territory, tactfully leaving the cattle and some of their domestic possessions behind.

As such the whole Luac at Rɛɛlkou or Madol decided to evacuate into that Twic vacated territory. When the Luac came there was nobody found in the area. The area was a deserted 'no man's land' except for one old man, a cripple by the name of Cic Ayen Cuɔɔr. According to him his people who left him were from the Padeng clan. They left him because he was lame. He was spared by the reconnaissance team of Ajaknɛi which consisted of someone called Awet Riak who became the ancestor of a people now called Paan–Awet Riak in the current Makuac Adɛl area in the Rubaar section of Wun-Adɛɛl. There was also a certain Bol Guang Yai whose lineage later joined a people called Paan-Lual Tiny jɔk of the Pariath clan people in the same Rubaar area. With Ajaknɛi also was a certain Aduɛr from the lineage of Great Aduɛr-Aŋuaŋ Nguäl of the Paduër clan who are now in the Nyarnhom section of Rubaar. A certain Mabior Acuil of the Palith clan was in that team of Ajaknɛi reconnaissance. His lineage people are now those of Acuil Kolnyin and Mayɔt Cimaan in the same Rubaar area. A certain Thokyiɔk Malusth of the Paɤök-gɛk clan related to Paan-Ajaang Deng Malook was also there in the reconnaissance mission. His lineage family now live in the Rubaar area where they are those of Dot Majak, Athian Deng Jöng, Puöt Deng Jöng and many others. Maŋök Anei of the Panyang clan was in the team. His family lines are currently those of Magok Majök. They now live in the same territory of Rubaar.

Deng Jöng of the Pagak clan people of the crow and puöt was also part of Ajaknɛi team. His family section is now known in Rubaar as Paan-Deng Jöng. Kiir Majök of the Yubek clan, from which came those of Madhang Coth Cuɔl, was also in the team, as was Agɔth Lol of the Pabuldiany (or Padiaany) clan from whom come those of Aleu Lökrɛɛc and Arop Gɛi (the semi-chol MuƆng man in the Luacjang territory). He was in the reconnaissance. His lineage, as partly explained above, is in the same Rubaar area. There was also a certain Mawien-Juatwai Mabuɔc of the Paan-Agɔɔk clan whose lineage has vanished entirely off the face of the Luacjang territory.

Those members of Ajaknéi's reconnaissance team were to later become the first among the pioneers of the Luacjang territory. That Twic remnant by the name of Cic Ayen Cuɔɔr had a family line in Rubaar and people like Majɔk Cuɔɔr, who during the research days in Luacjang was the SPLM/A administrator of Luacjang. He came from this Cic Ayen Cuɔɔr's family line.

The rest of the other ten clans that added to the aforementioned pioneers of Rubaar are those who were later attracted into the Rubaar territory of the Luac by Thokagor, the grandfather of Great Adɛl Makol. Thokagor of the 17th century attracted a large number of people to his Rubaar territory as a result of a good deed he did during one historic famine disaster which befell the Luac community in 1715 AD. A certain Spear Master by the name of Tiit Dimkuac was saved by Thokagor when he gave him milk to rescue him from death by starvation. He then gave him milking cows to sustain himself and his family during that famine year. The Spear Master was so pleased with Thokagor that he made an invocation, calling for people from different lands to join Thokagor to become his people. Several people from outside the Luac later began to flock to the Rubaar areas of Thokagor, thereby making Rubaar and Luacjang increase in population.

From the initial Rubaar society of the Luac and those populations called to come to Rubaar by Spear Master Tiit Dimkuac to become the Luac people of Thokagor, Luac expanded to become Kuɔk of Majök Ruai, Athɔɔr section of Atuɛ́r Tɔng, Ateek section of Köör Jök, Abuöng area of Anyuɔn Madhieu, Lian of Ater Yol, Pariak of Monyyiik Mayen, Kɔnŋɔɔr of Muɔrwel Aɣarwak, Ariääu territory of Deng Bol, Baar section of Athiɛplek Dhalbany, Akarab section of Loi Ayuaal, Akök area of Deng Jöng and the big Rubaar section of Thokagor.

It is to be recalled that part of the Luac community people left from Rɛɛlkou with the Ruweng community which went back to the Upper Nile where some of them recrossed to the western Upper Nile areas up to Abyei. It was those Ruweng sections consisting of Luac elements that recrossed the Nile and settled at the present Pan-Ru where they continued to name some places after Luac names, places such as the Kuɔk area in present Awet territory in Pan-Ru. Others went with Kiec to later become the Luac Adut, also known as Atuöt-Luac. Part of the Luac went to Khor Fluth to become the Luac community of Aguer Wiɛu. A section also broke away to become the present Luackoth community of Great Bol Malek in Tonj East county. Yet one lineage went to join the Apuk community of Jök Tong in the early part of the 18th century. They are today's Pakuec clan people of Great Chief Giir Thiik. Others became Pajök while still others became the Panɛu clan from Anau.

FACTORS THAT KEPT THE LUAC POPULATION IN CHECK

The Luac, the Agaar of Rumbek North county known as Pakäm, Gok, Jalwau and the Nuers of the western Upper Nile in addition to Apuk-Padɔc and Lou-Paher, are communities which live in areas regarded as those with a traditional culture of violence where great wars are an annual phenomenon. Luac in particular has had a very long tradition of big wars so that the society became known as an area of constant wars with all its neighbours in which hundreds of people are killed almost every year. Reciprocally, the Luac deadly afflictions are known by all of its neighbours, be they traditional enemies like the Nuers, the Agaar of Pakam and even the Rek of Jalwau or the entire bordering Rek communities of Anan-Atak sections, with whom they even share the same Tonj East county.

Not to touch the annual wars with their Nuer neighbours of Mayendit county in the western Upper Nile over water and pastures in the toch, the great wars of Pakam with the Luac have been like the European wars which led to the formation of the League of Nations. England and France were known as traditional enemies before the United Nations brought order into Europe. This is the situation between the Luacjang and Agaar of Pakam and between them and the Nuers of Mayendit county. They have been fighting for more than a century to the present day. The Rubaar sections of Wun-Thuc, Wun-Adɛɛl in Luacjang, and Gak Wol in Pakäm are areas where these wars, since Mediaeval times to the present modern era, do not allow two thirds of the members of a generation to see old age. Male members of a family or even whole clan are sometimes wiped out in one single combat so sections get badly reduced in a single year. This particular internecine violent tradition requires regular government in South Sudan to develop ways and means to stop such a phenomenon of population depletion. Plans to stop this constant violence once and for all have to be done to stop this phenomenon. This violent region of Pakäm, Luac, Jalwau, Gok and the western Upper Nile Nuers needs special and urgent security attention with an administrative arrangement to stop the constant population depletion by wars.

TERRITORIAL AND ADMINISTRATIVE CONFIGURATION OF THE LUAC DINKA

The Luac, known today as Luacjang, is martially known as 'Luac-Magɔɔk' and as earlier mentioned, it consists of two territories made up of twelve sections:

A. Rubaar Territory
Consisting of the big Nyang-Wiir and the big Nyang-Ruup which are subdivided into the following sections:
1. Nyang-Wiir, comprised of:-
    i. **Wun-Adɛɛl area** of Chief Madut Aguer Adɛl and consisting of eight sub-chieftaincy sections, some of which have also become executive chieftaincy areas.
    ii. **Wun-Thuc area** of Chief Dongrin Yap Thuc, now under Chief Ajuɔng Mading Ruöp Thuc. This area consists of four large chieftaincy sections.
    iii. **Nyarnhom area** of Chief Mawan Dhuriak Aduɛr is composed of five sub-chieftaincy sections.
    iv. **Aköök-Mathöng area** of Chief Acuil Mabior Cinkɔc consists of three sub-chieftaincy sections.
    v. **Akarab area** of Chief Ukɔk Mayen which is composed of three sub-chieftaincy areas.

The above areas make up what is known as the Nyang-Wiir section of Luacjang. It is called Nyang-Wiir because it is a littoral community as they are near or live about the swampland, the toch beyond, which are the Nuers of Mayendit county.

2. Nyang-Ruup consisting of:
   i. **Kɔŋɔɔr-Awet area** of Chief Ajaang Apiöök. The area is composed of six sub-chieftaincy sections.
   ii. **Ariääu area** of Kɔŋɔɔr and Baar Apiöök territories, both of Chief Kur Akol Deng Bap. The two areas are composed of seven sub-chieftaincy sections.

B. **Riäm territory, consisting of:**
   1. **Ciertooc, which is composed of:-**
   i. **Kuɔk area** of Chief Mading Manyiel Majɔk made up of four sub-chieftaincy sections; and
   ii. **Ateek and Athɔɔr areas** of Chief Bai Mayɔt Kur comprised of six sub-chieftaincy sections.

   2. **Riam proper, consisting of:-**
   i. The large **Abuöng area** of chief Bui Det Madhieu Anyuɔn, made up of eight sub-chieftaincy areas;
   ii. **Pariak area** of Chief Monyyiik Amɛnjang Majök and made up of four sub-chieftaincy areas; and
   iii. **Lian area** of Chief Piot M. Kur made up of three sub-chieftaincy areas.

Those areas are what make the Luacjang Dinka community of twelve very big sections. Luacjang can make a province of its own according to its sheer size and population.

GOK DINKA AND ITS SECTIONS

The origin of the name 'Gok' for which a section of the Dinka made a distinct tribe and a cultural group within Jieng nationality has not been clear even to Gok people themselves. This is because most of the names of Jieng tribes have all been epic in their origin. Gok generations came and went, since time immemorial, knowing their society as Gok.

Then what is Gok? And how did this Dinka section come to exist in their present areas? The answers to these two questions are to go into Jieng history. We find that far back into the middle of the Kush Kingdom period, about the 8th century BC, a certain Ajaang Deng, the grandson of Kuc the Great, is presented by oral traditions to have begotten six sons in an area described by an ancient Greek writer Herodotus, as falling south of Elephantinentine" Island and inhabited by nomadic tribes of Ethiopia[25]. Those were the Dinka ancestors and the Black Sudanese communities of that ancient Northern Sudan area which was Wawat. This was the Wadi Al Allagy valley area that extended from the shore areas of a then existing lake which in our modern time has been submerged by Lake Nasir, artificially created by Jaafar Nimeiri's government in the 1970s.

One of those six sons of Ajaang is presented as Magok, whose descent lines grew into a society of families over the course of centuries. His family line continued to identify with their ancestor before reaching the Khartoum area in the 4th century AD.

It is in Dinka tradition to name one's children after the ancestors who are in the family genealogy. This is what Great Ajaang did when he named his six sons. Hebrew tradition, as portrayed in the Bible, is replete with such names now used by the Dinka people. Magok and Meshiek (Maciek) were among the seven sons of Japeth. Such names as Reuel in the Bible (which is Ruaal in Dinka) was one of the sons of Esau who is our Dinka Mayuaal. Such names as

Mayuaal and Ruaal also exist among the Dinka, particularly among the Redior group of clans who are descendants of Mayuaal. Jiel the Great is the remotest ancestor of the Dinka and the Israelites. He is the very Biblical Jiel, whose other intermediate descendants or lineages later formed the Aroerite clan among the Hebrews or Jews.[74] Abiɛl, Palek and Shaul (our Dinka Cawul), the grandsons of Riɛl in the Bible, were among the breakaway emigrants that were led by Abiɛl from Egypt to the Wawat region at the Biblical Exodus time. Those migrants to become our today's Dinka came with their cattle, goats, sheep and even camels and donkeys, though their descendants later abandoned the donkey and the camel when they migrated to Southern Sudan from Khartoum in 490 AD.

When Ajaang's six sons grew in the Wadi Al Allagy valley in that far Northern Sudan area of Wawat, they married and had children who also married and in the course of a century before the emergence of Kush Kingdom, their social ramification continued in the region of Napata so that after a century or more, his family lines began their distinctive characteristics from the others, although they generally knew they were descendants of one ancestor, Ajaang. Ajaang's family lineages later moved from the Wadi Al Allagy region to Napata. Then in 590 BC the armies from Egypt led by General Petronius destroyed and took Napata city.[75] Like the rest of the Nilotic blacks, Ajaang's society moved to the Meroe region and settled at the confluence of the Astabora[76] area which is the modern Atbara River area.

They lived as part of the Butana steppe societies of the Meroe kingdom until the Romans occupied Egypt and began to wage repeated attacks on Meroe. In the end the armies from the nearby Ethiopian

---

74   Ibid, p.15.

75   Andrew Wheeler, Day of devastation, Day of contentment, The history of the Sudanese church across 2000 years, p. 25

76   William Chancellor, The destruction of blacks civilisation, U.S.A, Chicago (19) p. 120

city of Axum were able to deal a final blow on the kingdom's capital, Meroe, in 350 AD, an attack which sufficed to disperse what historians on ancient Sudan regard as one quarter of the Meroitic population. This dispersal has come to be known as the 'first historical dispersal' of the blacks of the Nile valley.[77]

Here, much of Maciek's lineage faction was driven away to Axum by the Abyssinian forces. They were taken to Axum through the Ford of Kemalke, never to return to the present day. They later melted into the Abyssinian society and their trace could only be discerned from amongst the Oromos in today's Ethiopia. The lineage faction of Wol Ajaang went to West Africa with the rest of the Meroitic population that ran west across the Great Nubian desert. That war between the Axumites and our Kushites, a war which lasted for 23 days, was sufficient to disperse a whole population of the blacks.[78]

The lineage faction of Magok is believed to have been among those other Jaang's lineage groups that withstood the attack and remained in the vicinity of the Butana steppes after the departure of the bulk of the inhabitants, who had either been taken as captives to Axum or had migrated to West Africa or had taken a southerly direction along the River Nile to later come to the Jarjar (present Omdurman) and Sheinab (which is present Khartoum) regions. Those who came to the Khartoum region were the Luo, the Nuers and the Funj.

In subsequent times, about the last part of the 3rd century AD, other factors made the Ajaang society finally abandon the Meroe and Atbara regions. They moved to the direction taken earlier by their Nilotic brethren, the Luo and especially the Nuers. At that time, desertification in the Meroe region had reached its peak as a result of continued absence of rains and the Sahara Desert encroachment.

---

77 Andrew Wheeler's Day of devastation ... p. 23
78 James Wani Igga, The history of South Sudan, 2006, p. 102

This desert effectively hemmed to the Nile banks the pastoral societies which remained or had resumed in Meroe areas. They included Ajaang families. Among them were those lineages from Magok. All were kept to the confines of the River Nile due to lack of pasture for the Paan-Ajaang livestock.

Again there was cattle raiding from the littoral communities, the Bleymmes, who are the ancestors of the present Beja of western Sudan. Those attacks were compounded at times by similar raids and attacks from the non-Nilotic blacks who intermittently kept coming in hordes from the inland region which is now Western Sudan. Those inland people from Western Sudan later migrated to this northern region to become the Nuba that were to later make the Nubian Christian kingdoms of Makuria and subsequently those of Alodi or Alwa.

Those inland Sudanese tribes to be later known as the Nubians were attracted by the Nile valley and its culture, but the final precipitating factor for the Jaang departure from the Meroe region in the last decade of the 3rd century AD was the threat from Ptolemy Egypt. In this area some of the distinctive graves, ceramics and statues of Jaang ancestors in the Napata area and cows made of the terracotta clay can still be seen lying broken in fragments on both banks of the Nile up to the Shendi and Matemma areas.

Once in Sheinab (present Khartoum) the Paan-Ajaang became a big society. Here they developed with relative ease as there was general calm in this period. For about a century or less in the time they spent in the Khartoum region the Jaang further developed into a full tribe with sections that have today become tribes of their own. Here in the Khartoum region the Jaang clearly developed its clan system. Some of the miracles and mysterious happenings that started since Wawat times now began to increase, happenings which are responsible for most of the totemic divinities associated with some Dinka clans and families today.

In this Khartoum region the small Gok family, like other Jaang groups, asserted their distinctive characteristic within Jaang society, and in the early years preceding Jaang's final departure from the Khartoum area, a certain man by the name of Mariik is said to have featured and had come to the fore to become the Goks' reference personality at the time.

When Jaang society left the Khartoum region in the last part of the 4th century AD, the Gok community was led by this Mariik who is believed to have come up to what is now Bor land at his full geriatric age. According to some Gok traditions, he was being carried when the Gok were on the move. From Khartoum, the Gok moved to the Blue Nile region with other sections of the Jaang. After some decades Gok people came to the southern Upper Nile along with those who are our present Bor, who were Athɔɔc, Agaar and Aliap.

In the early part of the Mediaeval period (1000–1300 AD) the Jaang community in the Upper Nile continued to increase and multiply, co-opting and incorporating people from other tribes into its ranks and indeed assimilating them into Jaang society. This was when the Jaang became a serious fighting warrior society in this middle part of the Nile valley. Here in the Upper Nile most Jaang people who are now of Nuer origin either joined voluntarily or were war captives, especially during the Nuers-Jaang great vendetta wars caused by the reminiscences of the story of the cow '*Nyayar*' which tradition presents as having been wrongfully taken by a Jaang ancestor from his ancestor at Napata.

Luo people also contributed to the speedy increase of Jaang society. Several Jaang people and clans of today can have their ancestors traced to the Nuers, the Shilluks, the Anyuak or the Luo groups. Besides, Jaang took much of the livestock of the basin's original settlers, particularly those of the Nuers and of the Burun tribe and with this the Jaang prospered in proportions that meant it overflanked and outweighed its middle Nile Nilotic communities put together. At this period the Jaang became different from what it was when it was in Northern Sudan.

Another historic synonym to the name Gok came up in the Upper Nile region. During the early years when the Jaang started to settle in the acquired territories Mariik's society is presented to have settled in the woodland parts of southern Upper Nile. The type of tree which made much of that woodland forest is the tree most Dinka people call gok. The society of Mariik became adapted to this woodland ecology and was so well known for it that they were regarded by the rest of the Jaang community as 'the woodland people of Mariik'. The combination of their ancestral name of Magok and their later choice to live in the Gok forest land made Jaang society identify this community of Mariik as Gok Dinka.

This is how the name Gok came to be given to this Jaang section now living to the west of the Agaar Dinka community and to the southeast of the Rek of Tonj. The Gok administrative seat, Cuɛibɛt, is found midway, on the main road to Tonj from Rumbek. They are to the true south bordered by the Jur-Belle tribe in the direction of Ngaap Payam and are also bordered by the Bongo to the southwest. When part of the Jaang society migrated from southern Upper Nile to Bahr el Ghazal, crossing the River Nile in the famous and historic Jaang exodus of 1340 AD, the Gok crossed the Nile to Bahr el Ghazal as a distinct Dinka tribe.

Back to the Khartoum region, Mariik is believed to have begotten two sons, Laŋdi and Macar-Anyaar. The two later bore children and from their offspring the nuclear cluster of the future Gok society consequently developed in the course of time. When they came and settled in the southern Upper Nile woodland areas the two agnatic kin developed with Macar-Anyaar forming part of the descendants who later made much of the Kiec and part of the Gok sections which now inhabit those areas northeast of Yirol town and areas of Southern Bor.

In the Yirol area a certain Matöt also featured among the Kiec and Gok, so much so that in time those Gok section people came to be regarded as people of Matöt, that is, Gok of Matöt, and in this way, Kiec and Gok societies are considered as a people from one common ancestor. It is because of this that the two are dubbed as one cultural group although they stayed apart for a number of centuries, making them develop some variations even in their linguistic accent and way of life. Yet the Gok and Kiec still remember themselves as direct agnatic kin within the overall Jieng (Jaang) tribal setup. It is to be recalled that one Gok section decided to remain in what is now Bor, where they are now the Gok section living in those areas of Bor South.

During the Jaang migration to Bahr el Ghazal the Gok and Kiec are known to have crossed at Kɔɔrcök, a shore slightly north of Shambe. After crossing they encamped at the Ajäk areas of Karëër and Jöknhiem, about two to three miles west of Shambe in those areas which is now the present eastern Kiec land of Adöör. Then the Gok moved to places such as Malek and Pathiöng, occupying all of the southern areas from Karëër to areas of the present Gel River. It is this Gel River in Kiec land which the Gok people tried to remember when they later named one of their rivers Gel. The Arabs later came and called it 'Bahr Gel', that is, Gel River. A lineage of a certain Juöl who now make up the Pajul clan in the Kiec land of Adöör remained there when the Gok continued to migrate to the present Gok lands.

Before parting ways the Gok and Kiec societies came northwest and settled at a place known as the Mabior cattle camp area up to what is the present Kuor-Ageer and places such as the Awet and Akɔch cattle camps, following the swampland areas of the toch of Pagarau. They then moved together up to Rɛɛlkou. Here at Rɛɛlkou the Ciec decided to retreat back to its present Kiec land after the big war of Rɛɛlkou with the Luac community, a war which took place around 1420 AD[24]. That war also made Luac move away from Rɛɛlkou to Madol, where part of it went to the present Lɛɛr area while the bulk moved to where they are presently. The Gok section of Matöt decided to go with the Kiec to become the Gok of Anyiɛth

Rɛɛc or Gok of Matöt in present Kiec. For reasons unknown a small faction of Gok broke away in the Upper Nile and joined the Anyuak and are found in the present Anyuak areas.

From Rɛɛlkou the Gok reverted south to Karɔm. At Karɔm the Gok is believed to have decided to organise itself into its present sections. Here Laŋdi and Machar-Anyaar emerged as serious fighting powers against the Jur-Belle and the Bongo. It is probable that it was in this area of Karɔm or Ajiing nearby that a certain Duwäär Aköt Gääk Mathiang Ajuɔng from the Kɔngɔɔr section of Gok married Acuɛi, the youngest sister of the famous Agaar Marɔl. Her elder sisters, Amou Marɔl and the eldest Acuɛi Marɔl, having been earlier married into the Rek and Luac societies probably in the Ajäk area in Kiec land or in the Luɛɛl area of Amongpiny.

Acuɛi, known as Acuɛi the eldest, got married into the Luacjang community. She married a certain Maɣääk Akoi of the Pagut clan in the Baar section of Nyang-Ruup. Maɣääk is believed to be the younger brother of the great historic Spear Master by the name of *Guöt-Aŋuaŋ Ngaap*, noted for his powerful spiritual spell with which he was able to conjure one sycamore (ngaap) tree to fall down for his hungry people of Luac to eat its ripened berries. This was during one midday when the Luacjang community was on its trek from Ajäk to Rɛɛlkou[79] as explained earlier under Luacjang.

Lady Amou, said to be the second daughter of Marɔl Deng after the first Acuɛi, got married to a Pagak man from the Gïr section as explained elsewhere under Rek. At Karɔm the Gok community began their greatest period of wars with the intractable Jur-Belle community and the Bongo inhabitants of the areas to the south of them. The Rek, Twic and Luac were to face Jur-Luɛɛl to the northwest while Agaar and Aliap were to face the Jur-Belle to the southeast of them.

The Goks' original plan to conquer Bongo and Belle country

---

79   From an interview with elder Yool Deng Yool in Luacjang, dated 27.3.2001.

was to first organise itself into fighting sections with Laŋdi to tackle the Belle and the Bongo on the west and southern frontiers, while Macar-Anyaar was to approach the Jur-Belle on the southern frontiers. The overall plan was to dislodge those settled Bantu communities and occupy their land, which was so good and large enough for Gok agro-pastoral settlement. While the Gok Dinka was busy organising itself to attack the two communities the Twic society thrust in, overtaking Gok.

The Twic went against the Jur-Belle and in few years the Twic community was able to make the Jur-Belle abandon large parts of what is now the Pathiöng section of Gok. As a result the Twic moved in and occupied those vacated areas. They lived in that area for only a couple of years then, for mysterious reasons, the entire Twic Dinka decided to evacuate the area and migrated further north as far as what has come to be Luacjang of today. This unprecedented departure by the Twic gave rise to a Belle resumption of their former occupied lands. Places like Rum-Twic, Biling and other village areas in Pathiöng show traces left by the Twic that can still be seen today.

Places like the Tit cattle camp area and Ameth village in the present Ayiɛl area, to mention but a few, were first settled by the Twic before they left those areas for the Luacjang area of today.

There are, however, two legends within Gok society about why the Twic left the area. The first states that the Twic went away in present Gok land to avoid begging, locally called *amuɔja*. The second reason is given as the problem of white ants. There is a saying throughout Gokland to the effect that the Twic believe that those living in areas where anthills grow in numbers usually die before old age. Whether this is an historical concoction or it was a true saying by Twic people, nevertheless it has no scientific basis, but the story of the Twic always preceding the Jaang sections on the front, running from begging, permeates almost the whole of the western Dinka lands so that it becomes difficult to dismiss it offhand. It may have been an historical fact.

In the area of Karɔm the Gok community divided and began to adopt its present names of sections. This was in the middle of 1400 AD. The Laŋdi group became the Ayiɛl, Pagɔɔk, Kɔngɔɔr, Waat, Jɔth and Reruöt sections, while the Machar-Anyaar group of clans became the Pathiöng, Panyaar and Akony sections.

According to old man Deng Giir Mamer, Waat was so named because its people used to roam aimlessly about. The Kɔngɔɔr people used to follow the pelican and were always ahead of the Gok. They led the Gok as the community harbingers and were accordingly named so. The Pagɔɔk people used to walk in stealth to detect information. They used to walk like agɔk, the monkeys, hence their name. They were deemed as good detectives and secret finders who were good at reconnaissance at the time of the Gok great wars with the Jur-Belle and the Bongo. Monkeys are arboreal animals and the Pagɔɔk section was therefore given such a figurative name.

Ayiɛl came to be a designated name for the Makuei, Bubaar and Pandit sections. These sections later to become Ayiɛl are said to have once settled in a place without good food yield. They used to lack food all the time and for that reason they frequently waged attacks on the Jur-Belle villages to get durra. In each fight the Belle people would be pushed back, away from their homes and this Gok section people would collect their durra to the point of even taking the durra husks which Dinka people call *ayiɛl*. The rest of the Gok gave them such a derogatory name of Ayiɛl. The name persisted to be in use until it became a fait accompli name for this section of the Gok.

Then came the Pathiöng, Panyaar and Akony. Those were originally one section called Machar-Anyaar. They used to be good hunters of buffalo. Buffalo, as Dinka people know it, is a very dangerous and daring wild animal to the present time. Buffalo fiercely kills people with its horns. Anyaar (buffalo) is an extreme killing black animal and those sections of the Gok who are fond of hunting buffalo were then designated as Machar-Anyaar, giving a connotation of the bravery inherent in the buffalo. They therefore became the Panyaar section as time went by.

A section of this Panyaar later decided to leave the territory to an area full of Tiangs[26] which Dinka people call Thiaŋ and so they became known as the Pathiöng people. They are the present Gok people living in the Abiriu Payam area of today. There is, however, another version about how the name of Pathiöng came about. It is said by these local traditions that a certain Spear Master by the name of Diɛr Yai from the Redior clan was the one who made this Gok section to be called Pathiöng. Great Diɛr Yai is said to have rescued a Tiang which was being chased from the forest until it came to a sudden stop in the middle of the cattle camp.

When its pursuers wanted to kill it, Diɛr Yai prevented the people from killing it. He asked God to take away the animal by his power. God responded and the Tiang disappeared and could not be seen at all! Diɛr Yai became happy and he gave the name Pathiöng to this Gok section people. Yet other existing tales contend that the Pathiöng section of Machar-Anyaar had existed right before the Jaang migrated from the Upper Nile in 1340 AD. They left Upper Nile at what is current Pakerdit in the present Bor centre. Those were Gok sectional formations at the time when the Gok Dinka was to start its war of occupation in the Jur-Belle and Bongo lands.

At first the Gok was led into toch settlement villages by its Kɔŋɔɔr section. They first stayed there in places such as Maker and its outlying areas of Mabor to the upstream of Rɛɛlkou and in places that are now the Baar area which was rup or savannah woodland, up to Thunyicök in the area of Waat in Pagor and Duɔny Payams. They also settled in those places such as Bäc, Pan-Ruup and places like Acuär village. Significant in those settlement areas was Great Jerek Adöŋ Malou of the Paŋaak clan people of the grass totem. Jerek bore four sons, Yak Jerek, Ayong Jerek and Jalbuor Jerek who became the founding father for the whole of the present Jalbuor clan in Gok land. Lastly there was Dhɔɔl who was the fourth son and who became the founding ancestor of the Padhɔɔl clan people of Paan-Kacuɔl who are currently found in the Ayiɛl area of Cuɛibɛt and who are the Ngaak and Pangaak clans in the same Ayiɛl. The family lineages of this Jerek are known throughout Gok land as Paan-Jerek or Paan Adöŋ Malou. They are found in many parts of Gok land, especially in the areas of Waat and Ayiɛl.

Those Jerek people later grew and multiplied in the Waat area. They became warriors in Gok society but there came a time when the Padör and Pagor people procured a Spear Master by the name of Malek Mäl from the Padeng clan people of Ruaal to conjure them with a dispersing curse which goes with "*Ke ci Waat yiök, le riir!*" "The thing which bothered the Waat community is to disperse!" Spear Master Malek Mäl was an emigrant from the Pathiöng territory.

26 The antelope Tiang in English is Thiaŋ in Dinka, plural Thioŋ. 'Pa' in Dinka denotes people, hence pathiong, meaning the people of Thiaŋs.

This act was done by Padeng and Padör because the Jerek people were accustomed to killing people from within and without and as a result of the curse from Spear Master Malek Mäl, Jerek's family in consequence dispersed at the Karöm cattle camp area. The Waat community was fed up with Paan-Jerek. They therefore scattered into different parts of Gok land. Those few who remained in Waat territory became known as the Bɛr and are now only a sub-chieftaincy community led by a certain Ruöp Aɣeu from the Pangaak clan of Chief Chol Madöl of the Padiaŋbar clan people of thou, the heglig tree.

THE BATTLE OF KURNYUUK

Despite all the initial wars of the Gok with the Jur-Belle and the Bongo, it is the decisive battle fought at Kurnyuuk which turned the tide against the Belle and the Bongo. In that battle the Gok inflicted a long lasting blow that made the original settlers give way for the Gok to occupy the territory.

In that battle of history were those historical figures such as Jalbuor and his brothers, Dhɔɔl, Ayäng and Ngaak. Other Gok warriors of the time like Nɔk KaCuɔl of the Pangaak, Riak Malual Riak of the same Pangaak clan, those of Arial Wulek of the Padhɔɔl clan and a certain Gɛŋ Kuol Gɛŋ of the Pajul, were there as the great men of the battle. The battle started in the morning and by midday the Gok was able to break the stalemate. When the Belle broke up they were chased from the battleground of Kurnyuuk up to what is now called Rak-Adhɛng. At that spot the Bongo and the Belle war parties stood their ground. They regrouped, consolidated and fortified themselves while waiting for the Gok people. Among them was one such Bongo hero by the name of Awanyjak who was so famous for his shrewd shootings at the Gok pursuers using what Gok used to call 'dëw', which in effect was daŋga, a type of arrow enveloped with a poisonous spell known as 'mira'. It was a deadly substance that instantly kills a person once hit with it. All the same, the Belle people were defeated in this battle with great losses on both sides. The Gok people came to nickname that Bongo as 'Machar-Awanyjak' and they were to be later known throughout Gok society with that name.

Then there came many battles and raids fought by the Gok sections of Machar-Anyaar and Jur-Belle on the southern frontiers. The same was concomitantly taking place between the Gok sections of the Laŋdi and the Bongo to the southwest. For about half a century relations between the Gok and the Bongo and between the Jur-Belle and the Gok came into open warfare. Those wars only came to an end towards the close of the 16th century. Bongo-Belle resistance was finally brought to its end by two isolated historically decisive battles which marked the final defeat of those Aboriginal communities.

THE BATTLE OF BARANTÖK

The first of these was the famous battle of Barantök fought in 1662 AD. This battle was fought by the Mathiang Age-set. The Godfather for this Age-set was great Spear Master Akec Manyiel from the Pathiöng section of the Gok. The battle of Barantök is that battle in which famous people like Tɔng Aluät of the Paduguër clan participated. Tɔng Aluät was called Tɔng Dhieu Macar as known in Gok land. For this battle the Gok was encamped at a place called Thönyöny in what is now Kɔŋɔɔr land, about seven miles south of the present Yar-Dɔŋ settlement in Pagor Payam territory. In this battle the Bongo were again defeated along with their Jur-Belle allies.

THE BATTLE OF WÄR-ADEET

The other decisive battle of history fought between the Gok and the Bongo is the Battle of Wär-Adeet. This battle was fought in what is now the Pandit area on the big water pool upstream on the Gel River in Ngaap Payam. This is the battle in which the famous Bongo hero Machar-Awanyjak was killed in action by Gok people from the Ayiɛl section. The battle of War-Adeet was fought by the Maköör and Awet Age-sets.

Machar-Awanyjak was a great Bongo warrior of the time. He was a man with a lot of war tactics. He is known to have been killing a lot of Gok people since the appearance of the Gok community from their right scene at Karɔm as they came from RɛɛlKou. After each battle it is said that Machar-Awanyjak would humiliatingly pull out one canine tooth from each of his Gok victims and would make human teeth into a bead necklace so that people's canine teeth completed long rings of teeth worn on his neck as a necklace and across his chest and shoulders! Machar-Awanyjak used to wear those teeth beads in glaring attire during battles with the Gok. With this, Machar-Awanyjak became very famous as a dangerous killer of the Gok people. It was as if Machar-Awanyjak had a magic spell which he used to kill the Gok people. He was also a great mobiliser. He would raise an expedition from both the Belle and his Bongo people, all carrying stones on their heads during the night. When Machar-Awanyjak and his expedition reached Ayiɛl places in the still quiet of the night, all would stealthily throw their stone loads onto the sleeping Ayiɛl people, be they children, women or the aged, killing very many in each cattle camp or village courtyard and in this way, Machar-Awanyjak would defeat and chase the Ayiɛl people in the night as people would bewilderedly stampede into a run from their places of sleep.

Machar-Awanyjak was so abhorred throughout the Ayiɛl community and children used to be frightened of his name for quite a number of years even after his death. In one unfortunate encounter, Machar-Awanyjak was able to kill over 50 strong men using his poisonous dëw (arrow). This, in effect, was a disaster for the Gok community whose population was not what it is today. War sirens went out and drums were beaten throughout Ayiɛl and the entire Gok reached out for a full scale war on the Bongo and their allies the Belle. Elders swore to the youthfolk to kill Machar-Awanyjak at all costs and to bring his head home for Ayiɛl to have rest and peace and for the Gok to be able to finalise its occupation of the contested territory. The Awet and Maköör Age-sets were publicly admonished not to eat until they had killed the dreaded Machar-Awanyjak and had dislodged the entire Belle and Bongo from the territory. This led to a final devastating war which culminated into the historic Battle of Wär-Adeet.

On the zenith of this battle, the Bongo hero received a fatal jab of a spear, right into his left chest below the breast! Jets of blood gushed out and Machar-Awanyjak fell in a somersault and with a sharp but final yell, the 'beast of Ayiɛl' had been killed in action! When the Bongo people saw Machar-Awanyjak dead the battle came to an abrupt end. Along with Jur-Belle the Bongo stampeded the battleground in a final run, abandoning the territory for Ayiɛl to occupy forever. For a number of days the Gok was on the heels of the Bongo who were chased into the deep interior of the forest jungles towards the Zande great equatorial forest. This defeat at the battle of War-Adeet made long lasting reverberations that the last Bongo and Jur-Belle vestiges which still held on to their areas to the south of Ayiɛl also quit, leaving the area for the Gok section of Pathiöng to peacefully occupy.

At the fall of Machar-Awanyjak, the Ayiɛl made a war song of victory, a song which has outlived the test of time. It persisted across the ages till today. The following are excerpts from this song:

"...Ku näk Machar-Awanyjak!
Abi Dor awɛi wɛi ror col ee!
Dor ee!
Dor aci kat Muɔnyjang,
Ku ngic ɤa!
Ye Dor Kat abi Mänyjak nyäng wei!
Näk Machar-Awanyjak!
Abi Dor awɛi wɛi ror col ee!"
Kën ë luel wä ci ya yic!
Kën ë luel wä ci ya yic!"

Translation:
"....And I killed Machar-Awanyjak!
That the Bongo people had to run into the deep of the forest!
Oh! The Bongo stampeded, ha! ha!

The Bongo ran from Muɔnyjang! (the Dinka)!
And he had known me now!
The Bongo ran with a tongue slip of 'Manyjak',
Instead of Awanyjak!
I have killed Machar-Awanyjak!
That all the Bongo had to squeeze themselves into
The deep Zande forest, oh! What my father said
To kill Machar-Awanyjak became true!
The word which was said by my father
Became true!..."

Then Machar-Awanyjak was beheaded by the Ayiɛl war party and was skin-flayed! His skin was brought home and used to tailor or neat a drum which was named after him as drum 'Machar-Awanyjak'. When drum Machar-Awanyjak was beaten, it is said, it was heard all over Gok as far as Agaar land. The Ayiɛl people therefore continued to enjoy the fame from that victory, from that historic feat and in that manner, Gok society was able to complete the conquest of the Bongo and Belle lands.

From then on the Gok community settled and led their uninterrupted peaceful way of life for the whole of the remaining decades of the 16th century through to the 17th, 18th and 19th centuries, only to be interfered with thereafter by the slave traders who brought the greatest pestilent era on the Dinka and the rest of the Southern Sudanese at the beginning of the modern era, a period known in Sudan history as the 'Turco-Egyptian and Mahdist period', a very long period of over seventy years (1821-1898) which Gok people still recall to the present day as the era of Malualthith, the time 'when the earth was spoiled by the red foreigners'.[80] Notwithstanding their great intermittent wars with the Agaar to the east and at times with the Rek to the

---

80   Marc R. Nikkel, Dinka Christianity, p. 49.

northwest and the more than six decades of the pestilence of Malu-althith, Gok society, like the rest of the Dinka, experienced a long period of harmony starting from about the close of the 16th century through to the present 21st century. Since then, Gok Dinka society has increased from its original progenies and from those who joined them from various lands and who after several centuries, equally became Gok citizens. Some of the Gok who revere agaany, the giant river lizard, and those who revere nyaang, the crocodile, as their totemic divinities were originally of Nuer background. A small fraction of the people who are Gok have come from the Jur-Belle tribe itself, through social interaction as the two societies later came to border themselves and were to inevitably interact socially. But on the whole a large number of emigrants who joined the Gok community as new settlers but who are now Gok by historic and social right, are those who either came from Agaar or those who returned from Rek lands. Dinka tribal groups are generally a mixture of the original progenies and the newcomers. So there are many Agaars and many Rek families who are now Gok. Great social fusion took place inside Bahr el Ghazal during the 16th, 17th, 18th and 19th centuries.

Given that overstretched period of over two millennia, the Gok developed into a society. They started their separate existence from that ancient cradle point, northeast of Napata in the extreme north of the northern region of Sudan. Then the Khartoum-Omdurman-Jeilly period and the whole of the Mediaeval Ages they partly spent in the Upper Nile region and partly in Bahr el Ghazal continuing into this modern era. Gok society has therefore developed into a population occupying about 700 square miles of land area. Its original sections of Laŋdi and Machar-Anyaar developed and were further subdivided into twelve sections which made Gok society an administrative province of its own with its current six districts called payams, previously accounted.

Gok territory is a very fertile, cultivable land area. It is a flat, low savannah woodland section of the Bahr el Ghazal region and is largely made of alluvial and loam soils. To its more southwestern borders where they border the Jur-Belle and the Bongo, the soil becomes slightly haematite in nature as this belt borders the approaching haematite ironstone plateau parts of the Western Equatoria region. Generally, the Gok is thick and open savannah woodland and is watered by several streams, rivers and semi-toch" land marshes. It is generally a rain belt area. Gok land has no surface water problem as its water table is also very near. The Gok soil may be the richest in the whole of the Bahr el Ghazal region and it can be regarded as the bread basket area for the entire region.

TERRITORIAL AND SOCIAL COMPOSITION OF THE GOK DINKA COMMUNITY

Gok Dinka is made up of:

(A) Laŋdi section component consisting of six territorial areas of:
- **Ayiɛl section** comprised of Agotciin or Ayiɛl-Kur section, Bubaar section, Makuei or Monythɛɛr section, Anyiel section and Pandit section.
- **Waat Area** comprised of Awan, Bɛɛr, Ngarjök and Pagor sections.
- **Pagɔɔk Area** comprised of Nyang section, Awan section, Yorbul section and Pan-Dut section.
- **Kɔngɔɔr Area** comprised of Lɔu and Amothnhom sections.
- **Jɔth Area** with its Böör and Ayuith sections.
- **Reruöt Area** comprised of another Böör and Ayuith sections.

(B) Machar-Anyaar Comprised of three territorial sections of:-
- **Pathiöng area** composed of Awan, Pan-Barkou and Ubaar sections.
- **Panyaar Area** composed of Kɔŋɔɔr, Kabek, Amel, Yiep,

Nyan-Ruup, Aliääp and Aräny sections.
- **Akony Area** composed of Akɔrkɔr, Anien and Thiik sections.

KIEC DINKA

Kiec Dinka makes a county of its own. It is made up of seven payams and covers all those areas northeast of the former Yirol District. The Kiec territory lies to the true east of the Lakes state in the Bahr el Ghazal region. It is broadly divided into western and eastern Kiec. Four payams are in Lɔu territory that constitute western Kiec lands. The other three payams make what is Adöör territory that makes the eastern Kiec.

Historically, Kiec Dinka is known to have come up as a distinct entity within the Jieng or Jaang society, not in the Upper Nile region or in ancient Northern Sudan as was the case with the other Jieng tribes. Like Dinka Malual and Atuöt, the Kiec came up in the Bahr el Ghazal region. It started its embryonic development soon after the famous historic Jaang migration to Bahr el Ghazal from the Upper Nile region in the first quarter of the Mediaeval Ages.

Before the Jaang decided to leave the Upper Nile at what is now Nyarweng, Twic, ɣöl, Angääc and Bor Dinka areas, a group of blacksmiths, whom Mediaeval Dinka people used to call '*ajoŋ*', singular '*ajuɔŋ*', and fishermen call '*thany*' in eastern Lakes dialects and who are called '*abuur*' in Rek dialect. Those *Thany* and *Ajoŋ* used to be on the West Nile coastal areas. They used to stay in isolated island areas where they fish and do their ironwork. Such marine Jieng people who had earlier crossed the Nile from the Upper Nile came and lived on those islands in the toch of the west bank of the White Nile. Those people were found in those places when the Jaang crossed to the present Kiec land areas of Adöör to the left and right sides of Shambe shore.

At the time the Jaang people crossed the White Nile, individuals and groups of families who did not want to participate in wars with the Jur-Belle, the Jur-Luɛɛl and the Bongo and those Jaang people who did not want to proceed further, decided to join those blacksmiths and settled fishermen. This happened when the Jaang decided to proceed to the deep interior of what is now the Lakes state area of Amongpiny, to the Dɔkland areas to the north on the toch marshes and to the Padunyiel and Awɛrial areas to the south towards Mundari land.

Before the Jaang took off from the southern Upper Nile areas for Bahr el Ghazal some arrangements were first made. The leader of that migration had to be agreed upon. It was to be Loŋaar Ayueel, the great great grandson of Ayueeldit who earlier led the Jaang to Upper Nile from the Khartoum area, and whose father was the one who sent a reconnaissance mission into Bahr el Ghazal to survey the region as to its suitability and security.

Loŋaar had to call on all the youth parties of the various Jaang sections in Upper Nile. He then named them as *Kiec-Manyiel*. According to the mission's report Bahr el Ghazal was inhabited by the people called Belle, Luɛɛl, Luo and Bongo. It was therefore incumbent upon Loŋaar to organise a large force to fight those communities and to chase them out of the region for his Jaang people to occupy it after the conquest, hence Kiec-Manyiel. Kiec is the Dinka name for the bee. The colour of a bee swarm is manyiel in Dinka language. When a swarm of bees attacks a person, it kills by unspecified stings. Loŋaar had to organise this Kiec-Manyiel into an organic force of invasion. They were united by the purpose of invasion and became a corporate body with Loŋaar as their leader. When people were crossing, Jaang society was badly scarred by the act of the migration leader and so the Jaang decided to decentralise for the remaining internal migration inside Bahr el Ghazal. This was so as to avoid the ruthless dictatorship of Loŋaar who had been spearing the heads of people while in the Nile waters during the crossing of the River Nile.

In this way much of what was Kiec-Manyiel parted ways with their leader and chose to go it alone. A part of Kiec-Manyiel joined up with Thany and Ajoŋ when the Jaang proceeded from Liɛtpaciruööt and the rest of the Ajäk area in current Adöör land. All the same, the Kiec-Manyiel main body took the route taken by the Gok clans and the section that later became Ruwen and Luacjang. The Rek took to the present Payii River area from where they later proceeded to Amongpiny in the present areas of Aliääp before they thrust ahead to their present Rek lands in central and Northern Bahr el Ghazal. Kiec-Manyiel had at this stage ceased to be an Age-set. It became a community of its own. All of them had married and had also been joined by some of their former relatives, brothers, parents and even distant kin. They became a distinct social rite but maintained their name of 'kiec', the bee.

When the Luacjang, Twic, Gok and the would-be Ruweng left the Ajäk area northwards along the toch marshes, the Kiec main body went with them. They went as far as Rɛɛlkou, the present 'no man's land'. Rɛɛlkou is a piece of land between the Agaar of Payam, Luacjang and the Nuers to the east of Rɛɛlkou. Some decades ago at Rɛɛlkou, the Kiec went into war with Luacjang and in the disastrous battle known in history as the *'Battle of Rɛɛlkou'* which took place in about 1420 AD, Kiec lost the battle. It therefore decided to return in a gradual movement back to the present Kiec land on the immediate west bank region of the Nile. They joined up with those who earlier remained behind and who opted to stay with thany and ajoŋ, still using the name Kiec. People who later returned from the Rek, Agaar and particularly from Gok, like the Gok section people of Anyiɛth Rɛɛc that went as Gok people of Matöt, all settled to become Kiec. People who later trailed in from across the east in the Upper Nile either joined this Kiec or went south to join the Aliap Dinka or they proceeded to join Rek, Agaar, Gok, Luac or Twic. Examples of these people are those of Sub-Chief Dhieu Abai Tɔng who now live at Akɛthnhom village in the area of Malek of the Gok Anyiɛth section of Kiec in Adöör land. They are a Nuer faction that later crossed the River Nile, following the Jaang. They are now part of the Adöör people of paramount court president Manyang Jɔɔk. Other Nuers came to settle among the Lɔu section people of Kiec. They are among the Kuacdit people in the Lɔu section of the paramount court president, Mabor Cuöt.

Kiec Dinka were therefore an original amalgam of people from various sections, clans and peoples who came to constitute the Kiec during the middle and the last era of the Mediaeval period with Kiec-Manyiel, thany and ajöŋ as their nucleus which the rest of the newcomers came to build upon. Kiec is therefore one of the Dinka tribes that merged up into a tribe inside Bahr el Gazal.

Like the rest of the Dinka communities, the Kiec community underwent great ups and downs in their history. Some of the ups are represented in the great extension which the Kiec people developed and expanded over the centuries. They absorbed and incorporated other people either through wars with their neighbours, particularly the Nuers or through economic booms and good relations. Although the Gok people of Anyiɛth Rɛɛc continue to exhibit the behaviours of their brethren, the Gok people of Cuɛibɛt, Kiec, is, however, generally a cordial and peaceful community. Their wars are usually provoked. The Kiec community underwent several catastrophes and long periods of great pestilence that sought to reduce the Kiec population from time to time. Although there have been occasional mass famine disasters in Kiec land, the Kiec community is not known to frequently suffer from famine. Their good soil, the Nile and its marshes allow no famine except in the days when locusts used to destroy crops.

The same River Nile which provides a good livelihood for the Kiec community had in the late 19th to 20th centuries brought slave trade pestilence in which the Kiec and Aliap communities were greatly ravaged as Nile littoral communities. They were affected by the slave trade more than the other Dinka communities in the Lakes state areas in Bahr el Ghazal. The Kiec population was also badly reduced by a century old dinosaur that kept killing people in the toch, and except for the famous war of 1948 during the British colonial time, a war known as the war of 'Apukic Alam', fought between the Kiec and the neighbouring Atuöt Dinka, the Kiec have not been at war with their Dinka neighbours until recently during SPLA/M time when the Kiec and the Atuöt revolted into severe violent relations. For much of the time Kiec wars have always been known to come from the Nuers of the western Upper Nile.

SOCIAL ADMINISTRATIVE AND TERRITORIAL COMPOSITION OF KIEC DINKA

As earlier described, the Kiec Dinka tribe is broadly divided into Adöör in the east and Lɔu in the west. Adöör of Great Manyang Jɔɔk and Gok of Anyiɛth Rɛɛc makes the following sections:

Adöör (which is the Ajäk area) of Great Manyang Jɔɔk is made up of Dhiim, Palɛu, Ajut, Angoor, Buɔng and Lok. This is what is called Ajäk or Adöör Payam.

- Gok of the Anyiɛth Rɛɛc area constitute what is Malek Payam with the Ding section that is Gok Matöt Proper. This is the area where Ramciɛl of Kiec, the proposed capital city place for the Republic of South Sudan is located. This is where a kind of forest pygmies know as 'gur' is sometimes found. The Gok people in Southern Bor who very much identify with the Aliap by cultural outlook were basically part of this Gok in Kiec and the Gok of Cuɛibɛt who live west of the Agaar. There is also the Adöör section known as the Ajak-Tooc section where Shambe is.

The Lɔu Area of Kiec consists of the Ajak section, Kuacdit section in Pagarau Payam under the overall court president Mabor Cuöt of Lith section, Kuacthi and Nyang Payams and Ajiɛk sections.

ALIAP DINKA AND ITS SECTIONS

When Jaang society left the Khartoum area, some of them came to northern Upper Nile areas by way of the White Nile but sections consisting of Duör, who are present Agaar Dinka, Gok Adhiɔɔk and Athɔɔc who are present Bor Dinka and Anie who, in later times, melted into Duör and into Bor Dinka, all took the Blue" Nile route. They went as far as the present Kurmuk area where they settled for some decades. During those decades those sections felt their cattle did not fare well with that hilly or rugged region as the area borders the Ethiopian highlands which are so mountainous. The Ethiopian Gala tribes were also raiding their cattle. News of the Jaang sections on the White Nile having met serious resistance from the Luo, Burun and the Funj, Nilotic tribes which preceded the Jaang from the Khartoum region some decades earlier, also added to their decision to move out of the Kurmuk area to the Upper Nile region. However, they did not go to northern Upper Nile where a large part of the Jaang sections of the White Nile route were still fighting with these Nilotic communities. They came directly to the southern Upper Nile areas.

On their move the Anie section which was in front made a temporal respite at a place known as Lol, an area in what is the present Aying desert area. The Murle tribal community near that vicinity came while pursuing a herd of guil (antelope-like) animals. They stumbled upon those Anie newcomers. A fight took place in that instant as the Murle attacked those people. This made the Duör, Athɔɔc and Adhiɔɔk all rush in on the side of the Anie, but the Murle defeated all of them at the battle fought on a water pool site of that Lol stream. This was during the dry season month of March in about 520 AD. As a result of that defeat those Jaang communities pulled away and proceeded to the southern Upper Nile areas instead of going to northern Upper Nile areas where much of the Jaang was. They finally settled at a place now called Pamai in the Abuötdit area in present Jale Payam territory. They remained in this area but the Anie later disappeared as a result of a smallpox epidemic which badly reduced the Nilotic populations on the White Nile Basin. Remnants from this deadly disease melted into the nearby Duör and Athɔɔc communities.

Within the Athɔɔc community were sections known as Aliap and Pathuyith. According to a version from the Bor Dinka the Aliap people were named so because they were a troublesome section people. Presently there is a section of the Aliap in Agaar land where they are a people of Chief Juöl Macɔk. Their overall behaviour is believed to be the same with what were the Aliap section people in Athɔɔc land. Among the Agaar Dinka are also a people known as Thiyiith at Malek-Agɔɔk area of Chief Makuac Kherasid in the Pacong Payam area in Rumbek Central county. They are presently the Pathuyith people in Athɔɔc land in the county area of Bor where they are known as Juor-Mac, the people of the fire totem. In Gok and Agar lands they are Pathɔɔth. They are Pakuiëëth, Pabol and Alɔkyɔu in Rek lands. They use other names in Rekland as well. Among the Agaars is a section still preserving the name of Duör. They are in the Aköt area of Rumbek East county. In South-Central Jonglei state is a Dinka section called Duör and they are a people found at Duk of Deng Malual, also known as Duk-Payueel and bordering Angääc Dinka who are culturally assimilated by the Gawɛɛr Nuers.

When those Jaang people from Kurmuk arrived into present Jonglei areas as described above, the Aliap people within Athɔɔc settled among the Jaang people called Awan, a people who came to the area directly from the northern Upper Nile some decades earlier.

When another Jaang section called Adöl later killed 80 people from there, each of those killed with the name of Lual, the Awan community evacuated the area and crossed the River Nile to Bahrel Ghazal to become part of the later Aliap after crossing.[81] The Awan people distributed themselves among a people called Thany until they later joined Aliap who later settled near them after the famous crossing of the Nile.

The two sections of Adöl and Awan were among the Jaang people who settled in the area now called Bor land. The Adöl section is now encapsulated or absorbed by Athɔɔc as assimilated minorities. Also found at the Nile coast or the shore of the present Manydeng Payam in Bor was a Jaang section then known as 'Pakɔrɔɔu' which was a big section but later dwindled as many of them crossed to the west bank to probably become Pakɔɔr people in the present Rek section of Jalwau in the Tonj East county area. Remnants of this Pakɔrɔɔu were later absorbed by the Angakuei section of Athɔɔc in Manydeng Payam.

Found in the Pada cattle camp area about the present Yomshir in the same Manydeng Payam area was a Jaang section called 'Areem' on the border with the present Jale Payam. They are currently known as the people of Pakak Amou. A section of these people crossed the Nile during Jaang migration to Bahr el Ghazal. Some of them settled among the Kiec in the Pagarau area of Ajak of Great Cuöt Chap where they are still known as Pakak to the present day. A fraction of them went with the Aliap people at crossing. The Areem who did not cross during the Jaang migration are integrated into the Bor Dinka community. The current Aliap Dinka who live southeast of the Yirol sub-region of Lakes state came to their present Awerial county areas at different times during and after the historic Jaang migration to Bahr el Ghazal. They are an amalgam of various Jaang communities.

---

81   From an extensive interview with Chief Duöm Akuei Awan from Bor South county. Interview dated 24.09.2004

There are generally four broad sections that make the present Aliap Dinka: (i) Akuei, (ii) Ror-Apuk, (iii) Aker and (iv) Belöök.

At crossing were the Abörɔɔm people part of whom have remained at a place called Yuai in the Nyarweng Dinka area of Duk-Payueel. Another group was the Thiang who are now the Akuei section. In later times the Thiang integrated with Abörɔɔmz so that they became one society under one regional court and are currently comprised of the Biri, Nyakrar, Acɔɔt and Nhial-Madöl sections.

The second group of Aliap people who came to Aliap land, a long time after the historic crossing of the Nile River to Bahr el Ghazal, are a people in the Ror-Apuk territory which is divided into Bun-Agɔɔk and Alɛl administrative payams. They found earlier groups already settled in Aliap land. They came and stayed with Abörɔɔm, Luɛɛl, Weŋ-Acaak and Aŋon. In time part of Weŋ-Acaak joined the Ciɛr who are the current Mundari people. Part of the Abörööm section also joined the Ciɛr community to the far south east of Aliap. The third group that came to Aliap land and became Aliap people were the Carbɛk and Ajuɔŋ people. They settled in what is currently Aker territory, which they found inhabited by Aliap early pioneers called 'Dei', around what is Ramciɛl of today. There were also people called 'Buoŋrial' and Awan. Those communities later moved to the toch area of the present Gutthom Port on the River Nile but the Ajuɔŋ section returned to this Ramciɛl area where they met a people called 'Paan-Agueŋbaar' who in later times left Aliap and went to Yirol west.[82]

The Aker, Dei and Awan sections were later made to come under one executive chief who is currently Chief Manyiel Akuol. When Chief Kon Anɔk was killed in the early 1920s at Mongalla, killed by the British condominium authorities, the chief of the Aker section,

---

82 Great grandmother of the author by the name of Athieng-Köör came from this family of Agueŋbaar which Rek Dinka people believe to have the nature of changing to lions and that they do eat people. This is an earlier belief among the far away Rek Dinka. It may not be true scientifically today.

Achol Bon Akuöc, became the overall chief of the whole Aliap until the son of Kon Anɔk, Abiar Kon, grew up. He then took over the chieftaincy of the entire Aliap Dinka.

Dei, according to local accounts, was a very big section but extremely troublesome. As such the Akuei and Ror-Apuk sections joined against them and defeated them until they dispersed. Some went to the Mundari land while others went away to Apaak in the present Atuöt area and became Apεεr and Acöök. Dei people who remained in Aliap land are only a sub-chieftaincy population under Executive Chief Mapεt Majök Majuc in the Ramciεl area of Abuyung Payam. The fourth group to come to Aliap was the Belöök community which consisted of the Pabuör, Magaar, Kɔc-Acöök, Biri, Jöbolöök and Kɔc-Dut-Cuεi sections.[83]

Thus, from the vast data obtained from different Aliap informants during the research times, it came to be clear that in the time of the Jaang migration to Bahr el Ghazal, the Aliap Dinka community crossed the River Nile at Patereu, Nyingεr and at Beki. Others crossed at Panhom River shores. Ajuööt and Abörɔɔm who crossed at Anyɔɔp first crossed as part of the Jaang big migration exodus. They first settled at Liεtpaciruöt with the rest of the Jaang, then they went south to Beki. Ajuööt consisted of Lual, Weng-Aciek, Angɔu, Dei and Buöngrial. Abörɔɔm, which was the biggest community, later became the smallest section because they fought many wars with an Agaar section known as the Böör, who first settled in the area after they parted at Liεtpaciruöt with the main body of Duör that became Agaar in subsequent times. Abörɔɔm, like the Dei, also fought with those Aliap sections of Weng-Aciek, Lual and Angɔu. Some Abörɔɔm people returned to Bor land while others went to Mundari land. Those who remained in Aliap are insignificant in numbers compared to when they came from the east Nile.

---

83   Much of this information was obtained from an interview by the author with Isaac Kon Anɔk, the political elder of Aliap Dinka, December 2004

To give a bit of detailed information about these Aliap people a brief account of one Aliap family line may be necessary to shed light on the rest of Aliap history. To begin with a certain Jiköm had three sons, two from one wife and another son from a different wife. Those sons were at the head of the migrating

Aliap community. There was a place called Ka, which was a place immediately on the west bank of the Nile. Rɛɛng Jiköm, the eldest, settled in this area. His descendants later constituted what is now the Ror-Apuk area that makes Bun-Agɔɔk Payam. Abör Jiköm, the second son, sat at the Belöök area which was initially known as Pan-Bang, settling with a certain Awang whose descendants are now a minority in this Belöök territory. Abör's descendants now make much of Belöök territory. Abörthi, the young and the third but of the second wife, settled at an area called Aker. His descendants later came to constitute three Payams of Bun-Agɔɔk, Alɛl and Abuyung.

As for Akuei territory, a certain Nyingɛr Apaac, son of Great Bek Diɛr, was the first to come and settle at what is still called Padunyiel, after first settling at a place known as Beki, named after their great ancestor Beki. Nyingɛr departed to Aliap land in Bahr el Ghazal from the south-central Upper Nile region with his people at Beki cattle camp area in present Nyarweng. Part of the people who left with him are said to be the Adöör or Gok people of Anyiɛth Rɛɛc in Kiec land. Some of them now live as part of the people of Cuöt Chap in the same Kiec land. From Padunyiel, Nyingɛr went with his people to the Döör area in Pacuai in what is now the Akuei land of Aliap. Belöök went to areas of Mingkaman further south of Döör. From Döör some came to Awerial which later became the county administrative centre for the whole Aliap Dinka. From Pan-Ka near Padunyiel the Apuk people went to Anguarkou on the Gel River in the current Bun-Agɔɔk Payam area. The Aker people crossed near Gutthom port on the Nile, furthest south of Shambe shore.

Aliap people have a strong claim that Nyarweng Dinka people

were part of them, while they also admit that they were basically part of the Bor Dinka by way of Athɔɔc. Some traditions among the Aliap also assert that when the Jaang departed what is now Bor and Nyarweng territories in the Upper Nile, they were together with the Kiec and Gok and that most of them chose to cross at the Shambe shore of Anyɔɔp with the Kiec and Gok. Then they later left the Kiec and Gok and trekked south along the west bank of the Nile till they came and settled at Beki. Then they went to the area of Padunyiel. This suggests that the Bor, Nyarweng, Kiec, Gok and Aliap were living in one vicinity in the southern parts of the present Jönglei state when the Jaang migration started.

At the time of the Jaang departure during the long trek to the immediate east bank of the Nile and even after people had crossed to the west bank, there was big fusion between sections, lineages and individuals. This tells of the difficulty in making clear-cut descriptive accounts of the various Dinka communities being handled. Most of the Jaang sections that crossed the Nile to Bahr el Ghazal at Kɔrcök (Shambe) departed the Upper Nile at Jönglei areas in today's Twic-East area, so Kɔrcök is in the Twic area of today. This included the Duör, Twic, sections who are now the Twic community's northern Warrap state, Luac communities section who are today's Ruweng and the whole of what is today's Rek. Those who crossed at the south of Shambe shores left the Upper Nile at what is today's Bor. Many of these people left after the main exodus had left from the Twic and Dukein areas of γöl, Angääc and Nyarweng. Chief Mangar Nhial Kon, one of those interviewed and who gave his oral accounts about Aliap, has a geological descent pedigree which goes beyond his ancestor Nyingɛr who was involved as Aliap leader during the Nile crossing to Bahr el Ghazal. A close look at his descent line compared with that of his close kin Isaac Kon (Abiar) also known as Kon Anɔk may give a near approximation of the year of Jaang migration to Bahr el Ghazal:

Far back from the time of Turkiya, a certain Kacuɔl Aguön Nhial[84] purchased a Jɔk called 'Nhial-Duciëëk', a Kunyjuur with which he destroyed Abörɔɔm, Ajuöt and Dei sections of Aliap. This Jɔk killed a lot of people. It greatly reduced the populations of those sections during the 19th and early 20th centuries. A certain Bol of the same descent line later handed the deity Nhial-Duciëëk to Anɔk Nyingɛr who in turn used it against the family lines of Kacuɔl, thereby erasing the Kacuɔl family line from the face of Aliap land. Remnants from KaCuɔl's family lineage ran to the Tindilo area of Nyanguara in the Rɔkɔn area.[85] This was during the Anglo-Egyptian colonial era in Sudan.

It is worth mentioning that many catastrophes sought to reduce the population of the Aliap community since they migrated to their present Aliap land where they border the Mundari tribe of Central Equatoria state.

Among those natural calamities were the smallpox epidemics that affected the Aliap community during the early decades of the 18th century, a communicable disease which decimated and reduced the population to a mere one quarter. This was followed by the great famine disaster known in Aliap history as the 'Famine of Magɔɔk', locally called '*Cɔk-Magɔɔk*', which was caused by a locust destruction of crops for four consecutive years. This all the more reduced the Aliap population in the 1840s.

This population depletion allowed the Bor Dinka to occupy the eastern parts of Aliap as that famine disaster which followed the smallpox epidemics made the Aliap Dinka abandon the entire east Nile. Foreign intrusion from the slave traders also had its negative bearing on the population of Aliap, especially those who were readily found on both banks of the Nile. By the time of that of Samuel White

---

84 From an interview by the author with elder Isaac Kon Anɔk of Nyingɛr descent line, December 2004.

85 Ibid.

Baker who came using the Nile between Gondokoro and Khartoum in the early 1870s, passing to and from Gondokoro near present Juba in Equatoria, the Bor and Aliap communities were to bear the yoke of both Baker's and the traders' activities along the Nile route. This was because the Nile part of Aliap and Bor provided several ports where their steamers frequently made stopovers. By this time the Bor community had moved to settle up to Jale, north of Bor town. Baker's opening of the White Nile route to foreign comings and goings also made an immediate exposure of the communities on both banks of the White Nile. The Aliap community completely abandoned their east bank settlements, running away from slave traders, and as Bor town was to be a port, Bor society also ran away from the Nile and Aliap fishing communities called '*Thany*' or '*Monythany*' who took the whole burden of slave trade which drastically reduced their population.

Apart from all the above catastrophes that reduced the population of the Aliap community, some Aliap people remigrated back to Bor lands in later times. At the Yomshir area are people called AnƆk, Guale and Angakuei sections in Bor. They are those who later returned from Aliap and were a people earlier called Abutnhiim and Thiang.

In the Twic area is a place called Paliau. It is one of the last places where some of the present Aliap Dinka communities took off to cross to the west bank.

SOCIAL AND TERRITORIAL COMPOSITION OF ALIAP DINKA (ALIAP DINKA AND ITS SECTIONS)

Kɔc-Arek section of Aciek Anyang Buɔngkuac
Buɔngkuac was the cause of the war between Aliap, led by Chief

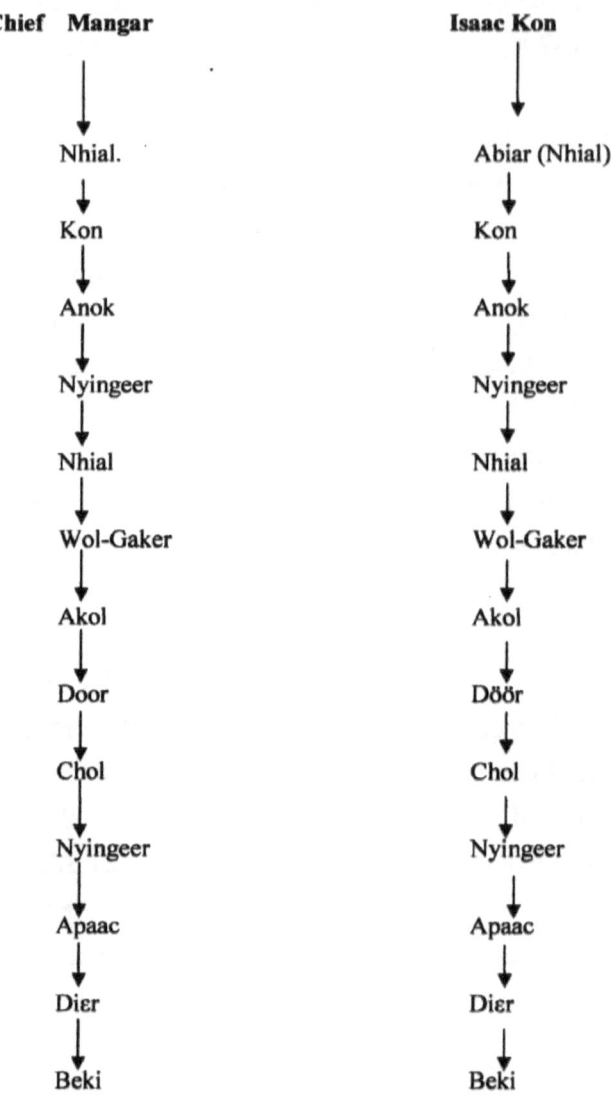

A genealogical pedigree of Chief Mangar Nhial and his uncle Isaac Kon Abiar as proof of the time of the Jaang migration to Bahr el Ghazal

Kon Anɔk, and the British colonialists in Bahr el Ghazal Province in 1924. Buɔngkuac refused to carry a load from one British authority, causing the imperialist to beat him. Chief Kon AnƆk reacted by avenging for his humiliated citizen and he mobilised the Aliap community to wage war against British colonial authorities in his Aliap land. His war is known in history books as *the Aliap revolt*. Although that war ended with Chief Kon Anɔk put to death at the hands of the British authorities in Mongalla in 1924, Chief Kon Anɔk showed himself as a patriotic leader of his people.

- *Akuei section*
- *Ror-Apuk section*
- *Aker section*
- *Belöök section*
- *Nhial-Madöl sections of Chief Wol Athölueth*
- *Second Nhial-Madöl section of Chief Mathith Panthεr*
- *Acɔɔt sections of Chief Malual Apuöt*
- *Second Acɔɔt sections of Chief Panthεr Köro*
- *Biri section of Chief Nyan-Awur Kenjök*
- *Nyakrar section of Chief Maker Apuk Ayiɔk*
- *Ror-Apuk section of Chief Angolic Deng*
- *Buölek sub-section of the same Chief Angolic Deng*
- *Buölekthi section of Chief Ajuping Koot*
- *Mabör section of Chief Chang Jɔngkuc*
- *Weng-Aciek section of Chief Anyak Malith*
- *Lual section of Chief Awur Midεr Achan*
- *Angɔu section of Chief Manyiel Angeth Maat*
- *Aker section of Chief Adhum Kelei Angol*
- *Angöök, Dei and Payar areas of Chief Mapεt Majök*
- *Thany section of Chief John Dut Akol*
- *Patereu section of Chief Aciek Ater Majuc*
- *Belöök section of Chief Acuöth Nhial.*

ATUÖT DINKA

Atuöt, in the southwestern parts of the Yirol sub-region of Lakes state in Bahr el Ghazal, are a particularly distinct Dinka cultural group which speaks two languages: Dinka language, which they call Jieng language and their own Atuöt language, which is largely Nuer. Atuöt people are a composite or amalgam of communities which are partly Jieng, real Dinka by origin, partly Nuers and partly Kakwa people whose origin is traceable to the Yei.

The name *Atuöt* is, however, said to have come from the word *Gatuöt,* meaning Gol-leader or clans' headman. In the late 18th century an emigrant Nuer man by the name of *Rel* came from the Nuer land area of Ganyliel where he was a clan's headman. Rel came with his family and followers. They came to the Kiec area of Adöör where they found the Kiec community around the present Lake Yirol area. Here they were welcomed and accommodated by a certain landed gentry by the name of *Tiök* from the Ajäk section of Adöör.

In time Tiök gave his daughter Nyinɔɔr to this newcomer. Nyinɔɔr and Rel had children who subsequently formed a family tree, which developed into a large social and agnatic cluster that covered a large area in a period of three centuries. It is the descendants of Nyinɔɔr and of those Nuers who came with Rel who now make up the Luac, Aköt, Jiëlek, Kuɛk and Akec sections of Atuöt Dinka. Those are the five sections that form the Rel or the real Atuöt group. They speak Rel, the true Atuöt language not understood by the other Jieng or Dinka sections of the same Atuöt. They speak that language in addition to Dinka or Jieng language.

The other sectors of Atuöt are those people known as Apaak who are pure Jieng (that is, pure Dinka) by origin. The Apaak sector of Atuöt are only connected with Rel groups by geographical and administrative association. The Apaak are made up of the Awan, Apɛɛr, Acöök, Rir, Palual, Aparɛɛr, Gueer and Pakuac sections. These

Apaak people were part of the Kiec until 1943 when the British colonial administration of Lakes District in Rumbek decided to annex them to Atuöt as a result of the famous historic war between the Kiec section of Manyang Cinthok and Awan section people of Apukic Alam of Apaak over a then disputed toch pasture land of Lake Nyibör – a toch territory located northeast of Aluäk-Luäk. It lies to the south of the big gär, water body.

However, the Awan section people in the Apaak land of Atuöt are known as the 17th century emigrants from the Kakwa tribe in the Yei area of Eastern Equatoria. The Apɛɛr section people of Apaak were on their part a breakaway people from Aliap Dinka to the east. The Apɛɛr are a people from whom came Tokmac Miir Bit (who is Ali Abdel Atif), the Sudanese military officer who was the head of the Sudanese '*White flag league*' which implemented the assassination of Sir Lee Stack on the streets of Cairo in 1924. Ali Abdel Atif and his White flag league also staged the famous 1926 *Blacks revolt* in Kassala. Ali Abdel Atif's White flag league was the first Sudanese political party to be formed by the Sudanese.

TWIC DINKA OF BAHR EL GHAZAL

When the Jaang migrated out of the present Khartoum areas in around 490 AD, it was moving as sections. There were the Jaang sections that went along the Blue" Nile to beyond the Kurmuk areas in southern Blue Nile. They included what are now Agaar, migrating there as Duör. That column of the Jaang consisted of people who are our today's Gok, Athɔɔc, Adhiɔɔk and Aliap. The Anie and other smaller sections were part of that column. Those small sections later disappeared in the course of Jaang's stay in the southern Upper Nile areas to which those sections directly migrated in later times, coming from those southern Blue Nile areas of Kurmuk and its surrounding localities.

Sections of the Jaang which opted to take the White Nile route from Khartoum included today's Rek, Luac and the whole of Padang that consisted of clans of the Marbek groups. The present Twic section, found in the Upper Nile and in Bahr el Ghazal, was part of the Padang section of Jieng. The Twic was a section known as Kuac when it came from the Khartoum region. The whole of the Jaang that took the White Nile route was led by Great Ayueel-Akökboong from the Pagong clan people who descended from the historic patriarch Jieldit. Other traditions from his descent line say he was called Ayueel-Paguangli. All in all there was Ayueel the Great who was the overall spiritual leader of the Jaang society at the time the Jaang departed Khartoum and he was the overall leader of the Jaang migration from Khartoum to the Upper Nile region. This Great Ayueel took over the community overall authority from Deng the Great who is believed to have been taken up into heaven by a whirlwind in the present Khartoum city area.

Although Ayueel-Akökboong was the overall leader, there were leaders for each section of Jaang who were also spiritual leaders in their respective sections. According to oral traditions among some Twic people, Kuac was led by Twic-Acuil, Kuac-Ajök and a certain Noi. Noi and Twic-Acuil were from the Pahöl clan people of the thigh bone totem. Those leaders led the Kuac from Khartoum up to what is now Twic land in Northern Bor. Other Jieng or Jaang sections came and settled in that southern part of the Upper Nile. The Kuac specifically settled at the Pamac cattle camp area and its surroundings in between the present Jale and Maar Payams. Their arrival to this area must have been towards the beginning of AD 1000.

The Jaang spent several centuries in the northern Upper Nile areas around and before the present Renk areas of Abialang Dinka. The Blue" Nile faction of the Jaang lingered in between the Khartoum and Kurmuk areas, and between Kurmuk and the southern Upper Nile areas. It was here in this Pamac settlement area that the name

Twic later replaced this name Kuac. The story of how the Twic began involves legends that are rather mythical but there are many communities who have their origins traceable to obscure mythological realms. So be it for the Twic.

THE BEGINNING OF TWIC DINKA

Sometimes towards the 12th century AD or thereabouts, tradition has it that a certain Ariɛm Abuwiir, also presented as Ariɛm Adhuöny, came and joined the Kuac settlement in the present Northern Bor area at a cattle camp place called Patunduur which was inhabited by a certain Yiep Ayueel from the Pagong people of Awaar. There was also a certain landed gentry by the name of Leek in the same place. At a place known as Athöpei cattle camp nearby was another noble by the name of Thiäng. The three big personages were all from the family line of Ayueel-Akökboong the Great. There was also a certain Ariir Ayuel who lived with a section at a nearby coastal village known then as Pacuil, about the toch. Another noble by the name of Adiang also lived at a place called Mayom-Cuɛr and had influence up to what is now the Paliau settlement areas. What is the present Twic area of Kɔŋɔɔr was home to another principal by the name of Ajak-Amot. Also at the Pakɔɔu settlement was one such man by the name of Ajak Kur Ayueel.

The society in that territory was almost one of Ayueel who had come there many years prior from the northern Upper Nile at what is now the Rabek area in the White Nile region, where Great Ayueel who led Jaang from Khartoum first settled with his people since the Jaang arrived in northern Upper Nile areas from the Kosti and Aba Island areas. This society of Ayueel has long been in this southern Upper Nile area of Jonglei before Ariɛm came and joined them at Patunduur. Among this community of Ayueel was a certain kuot, alleged to have come out of a gourd said to have mysteriously fell from the sky at a big cattle camp called Pagɛlgɛ. This kuot or gourd became the founding father for all the gourd and its seeds' revering clans among the Dinka. They are known as Paguɔrkuɔt in some parts of the Rek lands. They carry different names in other parts of the Jaang land.

The legend continues to say that Ariɛm came with a knife (*pal in Dinka*) in his hand and *acuöth*, which is a Dinka name for an old tethering robe. It is *wien* when it is still new and strong. It is *acuöth* when it is overused and can no longer hold the cow to its peg. Ariɛm also came with röl, an old or dried up femoral (or thigh) bone. This suggests he was from the thigh bone revering clan since then known up to now as the Paröl clans.

Ariɛm came to be known to keep the knife with him for operating to remove pus from any swelling, be it of a cow or a person. In time as he stayed in this society Ariɛm married a certain Abuk, daughter of none other than Yiep Ayueel himself. They bore seven sons and one girl. Among his seven sons was Twic, who was the eldest of the seven. The areas where those people lived were ecologically a wet area which used to have consecutive annual flooding more than today. This meant a lot of mosquitoes with the presently known malaria. It also meant many diseases in such an environment. As floods always destroy crops, there must have also been hunger from time to time.

THE EMERGENCE OF THE COMMUNITY NAME TWIC FROM KUAC

One day, Ariɛm called on his seven sons. He told them the land was not good to continue to stay on. The discussion ended in a resolve to leave the area for good but Twic of all the sons had a girl he loved so dearly. The girl lived in a faraway neighbourhood. She was a daughter of a certain Apilik, also from Great Ayueel's lineage. Twic requested his father and brothers allow him to go and spend the night with that girl before they moved away from the area. He was allowed and so he went and slept away. As he was with the girl in what some Dinka sections continue to practise till today called 'Kör-nin', his father left with all his brothers and the sister. Kör–nïn in Dinka is a night which a suitor spends with his fiancé to date her. This is done at the girl's home with permission from the girl's people.

When Twic returned in the morning, he found his father Ariɛm and all his brothers and the sister had gone away with all their domestic provisions and the cattle they did have! Left was their old mother Abuk Yiep Ayueel. When he was seen by his maternal uncles, he was embraced with joy that at least one son had remained with them and his old mother Abuk, who was left by the departed party due to her age. They got hold of him on the fear that he was to also go away in search of his brothers and father. He was persuaded to stay with his maternal uncles. So he accepted and asked his mother's relatives to contribute cows for him as a condition to enable him to stay with them. Cows were readily contributed for him and he was now able to have cattle of his own.

One day in time Twic got up and called upon his maternal uncles and presented to them the need for him to name the territory, saying the area should be named after a person. He went on saying it would not sound well if the area were to be named after Yiep or Leek and that it is good in his ears for the territory to be called Twic. His old grandfather, Yiep, became surprised. He asked why a territory has to be called after a daughter's son.

On hearing those words from his grandfather Twic became angry and retorted that, "if so, then, you shall see with your own eyes what will happen to this land if it cannot be called Twic". Yiep and Leek dismissed his idea all the same. He was told it cannot happen that an area with its owners is called after a newcomer, moreover a daughter's son. Then Twic answered that, "if so, it will not rain here for five years!" With that statement the community told him, "the people and cattle could still get water so abundant in the toch", and so they parted with him.

When the dry season came Yiep and Leek went to the toch with their people and cattle, while Twic and his few cows went to the areas which are now Patäl, Padiët and Ajak where he was able to make his cattle drink from water which used to come out of the dry ground at a water pool or stream after he pulled out the vetiveria nigritana grass (awaar in Dinka). Twic continued doing that while the entire area dried up following a bitter five years of drought. Even the toch dried up and there was no pasture for the cattle. There was no way also for people to cultivate. The community was now in famine as there could not even be fish to fish after all the local ponds and streams had dried up since long ago. Rains from the Ethiopian and East African highlands also failed to bring the usual annual floods.

When things became so bad Yiep himself called on the society and told them, "it is better to succumb to my daughter's son's power". Yiep continued by saying, "it is his curse that has made the area dry up like this just as he said five years ago". The old man continued in his talk to the gathering, saying, "let us allow the area to be called Twic after his name". This was accepted and so people set out in the morning to go to where he was in order to call on him to come and take over the territory and to remove the curse upon the land.

When people left to go to where he was, the power in him showed him that his old grandfather Yiep and his uncle Leek's people were on their way to him. He therefore prayed to Nhialic (God) to assist him by providing the atmosphere with clouds, like it was to rain. This happened! Twic then set out towards his grandfather. When they met midway, he asked them where they were going. His grandfather told him, "the land is spoiled by your drought which made people and cattle die". Old man Yiep outstretched his arms to embrace his daughter's son and pleaded to him, saying, "I myself, Leek and Adiang have accepted to let the area be named after your name and the land can now be called Twic as you want...!" Twic was pleased and so he told his grandfather, Leek and Adiang to call all the people of the land to go to Patunduur with all their cattle where he was to make a ritual festival and call off his curse after the land has come to be called Twic. The next morning all went to Patunduur where Yiep, Leek and Adiang and other heads of families, sections and villages declared their allegiance to Twic, saying before the gathering that they have accepted the area to be named after him, to be called Twic as of that time.

With that, Twic got out his cows *Aker, Mälith-Thɔn* and *Majak-Thɔn*, which he said were to be ritually killed to name the sub-sections of his area which has become Twic. Sections were to be named according to the colours of those cows. The community regathered the next day for the areas to be publicly named by Twic to slaughter the three cows to transfer their colour symbols to the said areas. At the height of the occasion Twic gave the cow *Aker* to a certain Ajak Ayueel, telling him, "the area you live at shall be called *Paker*". He also gave the ox bull *Mälith-thɔn* to Ajak Kur Ayueel of the Paköu and said the area shall be called *Lith*. The people living in that section later became known as *Juör-Lith*. The ox bull *Majak-Thɔn* had disappeared overnight and it was believed to have been stolen by the Adiang people and so Twic said, "Adiang people shall be called *Ajuɔng*," meaning thieves or lions. He cursed them not to grow population-wise.

Twic also declared to the public that he and his offspring shall never eat or break the thigh bone (ɣɔl) and that it is his maternal grandfather Yiep and those of Leek, Thiang, Adiang and Ariir to take the thigh bone in all the publicly ritualled bulls in Twic land. Having done and said all these, Twic turned to the issue of drought. He then made his invocations, and called for rain to fall down for the community and the cattle. He also declared that 'deng', which is rain in Dinka, shall be the yath totem for him and his descendants. *Deng* therefore became the totemic divinity which he declared must be observed by all the sections of Twic. Having said all this, rain started to fall all over Twic and the community rejoiced and believed in Twic as their God-given spiritual leader.

Twic remained paramount during the rest of his lifetime. Other traditions give a belief that he participated in the making of the big holy byre called *luak* for the spirit of Dengdit established in the Rut land village of Bangborou, a holy byre which famously became the rallying religious centre for the whole Jaang, particularly the Padang communities of Ayueel the Great. That luak remained as a religious centre for centuries until it was burnt down in 1993 by the ECS converts when the Twic in Northern Bor took to Christianity in the most fervent way. They considered that *luak* of Dengdit as a relic symbol of superstitious beliefs of the Mediaeval pagan society in the Upper Nile but the legendary story given above which was taken from Twic and Bor lands is how the name of Twic came about. Great Ariεm is believed to have been a descendant of that Pahol man called Twic who came from the Khartoum area as one of those who led the Kuac section of the current Padang Dinka to the northern Upper Nile areas. Then Twic society remained in this southern Upper Nile area as Twic until the Jaang decided to migrate to the Bahr el Ghazal region in the first quarter of 1300 AD.

SEPARATION OF THE TWIC INTO TWO

Shortly before the Jaang decision to migrate to Bahr el Ghazal, two sons of a certain Duääng from the Pahöl clan had a quarrel in this Twic area. These were Noi Duääng and Ajiing Duääng. They were big family heads and Spear Masters at the same time. Their quarrel divided Twic society. The Jaang decision to leave the area for Bahr el Ghazal coincided with this quarrel within Twic society. Quarrels in a ruling family or class always bring division in the society or country. When the Jaang took off for Bahr el Ghazal, Ajiing Duääng and his adherents decided to remain, but Noi Duääng left with those of Kuol-Alɛl as leaders of the sections of Twic who accepted the appeal for the Jaang to abandon the wet and unhealthy ecology of the Upper Nile where cholera, measles, whooping cough and, worst of all, smallpox epidemics were finishing families and sections at the time.

When the Twic sections came and the Jaang migrating communities were now standing on the threshold of the Nile's east bank, Great Noi Duääng took the gourd with milk from his Dengdit's deity cow '*Aluɛl*'. He poured the milk into the River Nile and pleaded to the gods in the river. He appealed to all the unseen beings in the Nile to allow him and his people to cross safely but following the quarrel between Ajiing and his brother Noi, their sister by the name of Adhar decided to leave Twic with Noi. This made Ajiing greatly annoyed and therefore he meted a curse against her. When people went into the Nile water to cross to the west bank Adhar was drowned! This was attributed to the curse from Ajiing Duääng who remained in Twic land. It is said that the family line of Great Noi of the Pahol in the Akuär area of the new Twic land in Bahr el Ghazal continued to marry her to procreate children to further her name till today.

Before crossing the River Nile Great Noi made rituals. He killed a bull 'Malual-Thɔn' on the Nile bank. The bull was an offer to the river gods. All rituals were done in the dawn at between 4 and 5 am, the time when the Twic crossed the River Nile to the west bank. This was in the month of March in the year 1340 AD. After crossing the River Nile, the Twic people of Noi Duääng and Kuol-Alɛl encamped at a place now called Pagarau in present Kiec land. They also went to Karëër and then moved further to the coastal area of Lake Nyibör, and to what is now Amothnhom in the Agaar land area of Paan-Gɔl

Mayen which later became the main homeland area of the Redior or Parum clan people of ruaal, the Kigelia Ethiopia or sausage tree.

At that time Amothnhom sections were still in Dɔkland where they had moved to after the famous Jaang migratory crossing of the Nile to Bahr el Ghazal.

From this Lake Nyibör coastal area, the Twic moved to the present Gok land areas that are now Pathiöng in Abiriu Payam of Cuɛibɛt County in Western Lakes state. But Kuol-Alɛl's group opted to go to an area known as Mabior in the Rɛɛlkou area where Luacjang, Ruweng, Gok and Kiec had gone to. Kiec is pronounced 'Ciec' by Lakes state Dinka societies. After Pathiöng area, where there is a village called Rum-Twic to the present day, the Noi section of Twic went to Karɔm. The two groups later converged at an area now called Yar-Dɔng, which is the current Pagor Payam area of the Gok Dinka, near the toch between the Gok and Jalwau sections of the Rek of Tonj East. At this Yar-Dɔng stopover place the Twic spent the whole of summer. Then they proceeded during the autumn season to a place which is now inhabited by Luacjang in the eastern parts of Tonj, through the great forest area known as *Bulic-Mathiang*.

When the Twic took off from this Yar-Dɔng area of Pagor Payam, northwards to what is now Luacjang, something of significance happened. An old lady by the name of Akuot was too old to walk and could not be carried any further as she has been carried in all the movements from place to place since the time of crossing the Nile. She was to be left behind this time but her daughter Abuk impressed on her husband to appoint one of their children to remain with the old mother. Her husband by the name of Chol Dhiendiör of the Parum clan accepted his wife's point of view. Awël, an adolescent girl, was selected out of the children to remain to care for the old grandmother. The two were left forlorn under a big sycamore tree called abiɛi in the Yar-Dɔng village while the Twic migrating society proceeded in their migratory march.

After the Twic community had gone away due north, old lady Abuk saw the seeds of a gourd kuot, just at the cattle camp presently called Aduuk which is near Pagor village, a small town in Gok land. She collected them and made the small girl Awël to sow them. The seeds sprouted and grew till they produced a good kuott from which they made a solid water gourd called '*kolong*' in Rek dialect. They used it for getting water for themselves. The old lady blessed the small girl with, "you will multiply in this territory". When the Gok community later came to this area, they were found and in the course of time the girl Awël was married and in her lifetime she made a family and a complete clan now known as the Pagor clan people from where originated the name of the current area of Pagor, which is also the name of the payam.

Meanwhile, the Twic communities of Noi Duääng and Kuol-Alɛl went on till they encamped at what has come to be known as *Bulic-Mathiang* in the area which seemed to be an area of the Manuɛr section of Pakäm but which the Adöör section of Jalwau also claim to be their area. Here, two things happened. Great Noi got out an ox bull of the colour of Mathiang and had it slaughtered, partly as a ritual bull for his community and partly for the youth folk who were constructing a road from that spot of Bulic to what is now Luacjang. The road was to carry on it the old Spear Master, Kuol-Alɛl, who was being carried on a locally made stretcher. He was being carried by the youth while the Twic continued with its migratory movement. Bulic is a thicket of palm trees and when Twic killed the ox Mathiang there, the area started to be called Bulic-Mathiang till today.

From Bulic-Mathiang the Twic arrived at a place which the Luac people presently call Pathöbek and they found it good to settle at. The road that was done by this moving Mediaeval Twic is still the route being used now by the Agaars of Pakäm when going to a place called Körthok to Pathöbek in the Wun-Thuc area of Nyang-Wiir in the Rubaar territory of Luacjang. When now in an area that later became Luacjang, the Kuol-Alɛl sections of Twic chose to settle in what is today's Wun-Thuc areas, while Noi's section people covered those areas that are now Wun-Adɛl, and so the Twic settled in the Nyang-Wiir areas of Rubaar of today's Luacjang.

HOW THE TWIC WENT AWAY FROM LUACJANG

While the Twic was now settled comfortably in the current Luacjang area of Rubaar, a certain man from Luacjang came by from Tuur or from what is Madöl of today, an area in the toch marshes. He was called Akäl Wuöt.[86] He came to survey the land for the Luac to move in. The man was very fat, huge and tall. Twic women, who went to a nearby plain towards the toch to cut grass for thatching their home houses, got him there. They made a joint effort to catch him up and they killed him by cutting off his testicles with their knives! This was so that he do not go back to tell his Luac community of the whereabouts of the Twic people and also so that the Luac do not know of the good piece of land the Twic have now settled at.

When Great Kuol-Alɛl heard of this, he was perturbed and so he called on his counterpart, Noi. He told the rest of the Twic community that the person killed will surely be avenged by his people. He said the Twic community must leave the area altogether to avoid war with Luac. He also said that he should be buried first. Old liege Kuol Alɛl told the Twic to quickly dig his grave to be buried alive. There he spoke, asking people to make a big mound on his grave which in effect was a shrine since he was a Spear Master from the Parum clan people.

Kuol-Alɛl instructed the Twic to pile tree wicks and logs onto his grave mound which he said was to be built up. He told them to put

---

86 Luacjang version says this man called Akäl Wuöt came from Madol near Tuur and Ler because Luac left Rɛɛl Kou since their war with Kiec Dinka in 1420 AD. See also other references to this incident in this volume.

fire on to it to burn while the community runs away nonstop until they could not see the flickering flames of fire or any other sign of fire. He said that will indicate the Luac cannot reach them anymore. He also told the Twic to leave some of the cattle behind and on their pegs for this can stop the Luac from pursuing them. All these were done by the Twic. The Twic people stampeded off by way of Macuët in the present Lou-Payer area of Marial-Lɔu to only have a pause at a place called Wun-Kuel in the present Gɔny section of Lɔu-Payer, again on the toch marshes towards the present Meshra River port. The Twic proceeded headlong only to have a brief stop in the areas that are now the Aduëët and Ming sections in Apuk-Padɔc but their real stopover place was later to be an area called Tɔng-Tol, a place continuing to carry that name to the present day. It is now a border village area between Apuk-Padɔc and Lɔu- Mawien.

Then, perhaps, in less than a decade, the Twic proceeded and settled in what is now Lɔu-Mawien, although a part of them now called the Amuöl[87] section in present Twic went to settle along the Wëdho River area in what is now the Warkɔu areas of the Jur-Lian section of Awan-Parek. This was in about the 1530s AD.[88] After a decade or so the Twic proceeded further up to a place they named Tɔng-Tol. They named this place after that Tɔng-Tol village in Apuk-Padɔc where they had a decade before coming to what is Lɔu-Mawien of today. This new Tɔng-Tol is to the south of the toch

---

87   Great Spear Master Kuot Ayii Thiek in Awan area married lady Achol from among the Amuöl Section people of Twic as his first wife. Lady Achol came and bore Great Bol Kuot who is ancestor number six for the author.

88   The genealogical time chart from the author's Mediaeval grandfather Kuot Ayii runs as follows: Anei the author was born 1952; Madut the author's father was born about 1883; Aköök the first grandfather is estimated to have been born around 1823. Gɛngdit the second grandfather must have been born about 1766; Tong-Abuɔɔk the third grandfather of the author must have been born about 1650 AD; Bol Kuot, the son of Achol from Twic may have been born in around 1590. His father Kuot Ayii, the husband of Achol, may have been born in 1532 AD.

of Mading which became the territory where the Twic finally began their settlement as the Twic of Bahr el Ghazal of today. The Twic finally arrived in their current homeland towards the middle of the 16th century AD.

ORIGINAL INHABITANTS OF PRESENT TWIC LAND

On the Twic community's arrival to their present homeland they found it was inhabited by the Jur-Lueɛl community. On the very day of the Twic arrival in Tiit-Cök and another place called Jööng, now renamed as Paduél, the Jur-Lueɛl people were found to have killed a giraffe at that place called Jööng. The two places were the first places to be arrived at by the Twic after Tɔng-Tol. It was late in the afternoon that the Twic arrived at Jööng and Tiit-Cök. The giraffe was left dead on the ground by the Jur-Lueɛl people who were to come and have it flayed (skinned) the next morning in daylight, not knowing that a foreign invading community of Jaang called the Twic will come that same evening. The Twic people who encamped at Jööng went straight in, flayed the dead giraffe and consumed it without asking who killed the animal.

When the Lueɛl people came for their animal the next morning, they found a horde of newcomers to have swarmed the area and they had also skinned and eaten their entire carcass. The Lueɛl people were mesmerised as to the kind of people who just come and eat up such a big animal killed by other people. They knew what will follow would be very bad for them. They decided to quit the area at once, having realised that what was to ensue was none other than a fight. They left quietly without asking who the newcomers were.

Yet the Twic followed them in pursuit through to Tiit-Cök and further on to as far as present borders where the Abiem section of Malual Dinka live today. Then the Twic stopped and encamped at a place to be later called Lɔu, which is the present Lɔu area of Chief Aguer Gɛng in Awiel South county. It was only here that the pursuing Twic turned back, having failed to catch up with the fleeing Jur-Luɛɛl. On their return, they found a place with good but extensive grass. Part of these people decided to remain there. This is the area which later became the Noon Deng Malek section of the Twic and which currently became Akoc-Thɔn Payam of Chief Longar Awic Ayueel.

An old Paɣöl man decided to settle with his people at a place later renamed as Palɛng of ɣɔl where the present Mayen-Abun town is. In time ɣöl became a big section which is now known as Adiang-Mayom of Cyer Deng. The Padiɛɛt, Payaath and Padhieu came to settle this Adiang territory of Twic. From here the Adiang section expanded as far as present Wun Rɔɔk, the payam centre for Adiang which later bordered a Rek section called Aguɔk and the other Rek communities called Awan Mou and Awan Chan Nyäl. The Nyangkuei people of Great Cɔɔm-Aguërkök and Nyang-Aɣɛɛr with another Noon of Great Chol Guöt became the present Akuär of Chief Läng Juuk. The area is now Aweeng Payam in Twic.

As Twic society gradually settled it began to demarcate areas for each section to settle at. There came to be the Anyuɔn area of Great Noi and Maper section of Great Adiɛl, the ancestor of those of Ring Yuöt. There was the Ayiëët of Ming section of Ayiɔk who are known as Awangjök. There was the Abiɛl area of Abiirdit from the Payath clan and Aɣɛɛr of Wac Ajiing, an area which is now the Amuöl section of Twic. The later migrants from the Rek section of Jök Tɔng, ancestor of great Bol Nyuɔl, Nyuɔl Agutbuɔng and his people went and settled at the very Tiit-Cök which later acquired the name of 'Tiit of Bol Nyuɔl' who was a man from the Pajök clan. Here, the Bol Nyuɔl group grew at Turalei in the Amuöl section. This is the very Bol Nyuɔl from the time of the Anglo-Egyptian condominium, who became the overall leader of Twic. The entire Twic area became known since then as Twic of Bol Nyuɔl. The

Twic were known as so throughout the condominium era. But at the time the Twic came from Tɔng-Tol, a certain Makuac from the Payath clan who took to the right direction with a group of his Köök section people, following part of the Jur-Luɛɛl community which ran northwards from the present Akuär area of Aweeng Payam. They later became Kuac-Köök, now known as the Kuac of Chief Madut Ring. Noi remained at Paduél with his direct faction people who later became the Akuär territory of Chief Läng Juuk. Kuac, like the case of Cobok in Adiang, was part of Akuär until 1986 when it became an administrative unit of its own. It is now called Ajak-Kuac Payam in the eastern parts of Twic county.

TERRITORIAL AND ADMINISTRATIVE COMPOSITION OF THE TWIC IN BAHR EL GHAZAL

Twic, the northernmost county of the Warrap state in Bahr el Ghazal, otherwise known traditionally as Twic-Mayardit, is broadly divided into Twic-West and Twic-East. It has six very big payams. Twic-West is made up of the three Payams of Akɔch-Thɔn of Chief Loŋaar Awic Ayueel in the far west, Pan-Nyɔk Payam to the east of Akɔch-Thɔn and Wunrɔɔk Payam of Adiang-Mayomdit to the east of Pan-NyƆk Payam. The eastern Twic consists of Turalei Payam of the Amuöl section of Bol NyuƆl in central Twic, Aweeng Payam of the Akuär section of Chief Lang Juuk and Ajak-Kuac Payam of Chief Wundit Madut Ring in the Far East, bordering Ngok of Abyei to the north and the Nuers to the east.

Turalei town in the Amuöl area is currently the county administrative capital seat for the whole Twic.[89]

---

[89] Much of the information about this Twic Dinka of Bahr el Ghazal was found from an adept historical chronicler, Madit Athuai Deng of the Pakäm

TWIC DINKA SECTIONS BY PAYAMS

Adiang-Mayomdit of Chief Mayen Deng Cyerdit which is comprised of the following sections of Wunrɔɔk Payam: Majök (1), Majök (2), Kak, Hol, Jöbaar section, Awudëng and Gumtɔɔr.

Amuöl territory of Bol Nyuɔl now of Chief Garang Nyuɔl Bol which is Turalei Payam and comprised of: Aɤɛr, Anganya, Abiɛl, Athöön, Kɔryɔm (1), Yar and Kɔryɔm (2) sections.

Akuär area of Chief Lang Juuk which is Aweeng Payam, currently of Chief Madhöl Lang Juuk and consisting of the following: Maper, Ayiëët Matiök, Tɔng, Marial Maper, Anyuɔn Kuel Ring, Noon Chol Guöt, Nyang-Aɤɛr and Nyang-Kuei sections.

Kuac Madut Ring area which is Ajak-Kuac Payam, currently of Chief Wundit Madut Ring and consisting of Guötjör, Atöör, Aɤɛr, Ayuang and Duör sections.

Mabok area which is Paan-Nyɔk Payam of Chief Ayuel Kuol Bol and which is comprised of Goi-Awaak, Goi-Awaak (2), Luit, Aruɛt, Liangröl, Akak, Yɔm and Alueeth sections.

Thɔn area which is Akoch-Thɔn Payam of Chief Loŋaar Awic Ayueel and consists of Noon Deng Malek, Cuär Aguer, Thɔn, Noon (2) and Thɔn Pakuɛk sections.

THE NGOK DINKA OF ABYEI

To discuss this Dinka section called Ngok who inhabit the areas now call Abyei county in the extreme northern end of Bahr el Ghazal region after Twic we must first discuss the entire Padaŋ, a Dinka cultural group to which this Ngok section belongs culturally. The Padaŋ people are a broad sub-cultural group of the Dinka

---

(Palual) clan people in the Akuär section of Twic during an interview with him dated 10.5.2002, later verified by further interviews of other Twic elders.

consisting of the Ngok group, Mediaevally known as Paan-Ajuööt Ajɔng Apiny. They are the Ngok people of Lual Yak and the Paweny people of the Atar district. These Ngok people of Abyei are also known as Ngok Jök people. The Ngok section of Padaŋ also consists of the Pan-Ru people of Panriɛng county and the Alor Kur Kuot people of Biemnhom county. The last two are distinctly known as the true Ruweng people. The second group are what are known as Paan-Maɣën, who consist of Nyarweng Dinka, Duör Dinka, Riec, Rut and Thoi Dinka communities. The third of the Padaŋ are the Dongjol group who are Ageer Dinka, Nyiel Dinka, Dongjol itself and Abialang Dinka. The fourth are the Maɣääk group of the Padaŋ which includes ɣöl of Duk-Padieet and Luac of all sections.

Thus the Padaŋ Dinka cultural group is roughly comprised of four sections within the overall Dinka nationality. The Padaaŋ (pl.) are simply Paan-Ayueel Jiel. Some people say the Padaaŋ are Dinka people from the east bank of the White Nile, particularly those who originally inhabited the east bank of the Zeraf River. Others say the Padaaŋ are Paan-Dengdit, descendants of Deng the Great. This contention from the Padaaŋ people may not be true for all as it is the Jieng in general who are descendants of Dengdit, but these Ngok people of Abyei had a rather authentic claim to Dengdit since there are several Dengs within the Dinka genealogical social and anthropological cobwebs in history. As such, attempt is being made here to delineate this Deng, the ancestor of the Ngok people of Jök, from the other Great Deng of the Wawat region, the father of Ajääŋ and Manuɛr as explained elsewhere in this book. We are not even talking of Deng Abuk of the immediate creation time or Deng Noi of the ecumenical flood time. We are talking of one of the Dinka Deng of the Khartoum period.

Dengdit, the ancestor of the Paan-Jök, is one of the many Dengs who lived as a spiritual headman for the Jääŋ when they lived in the present Khartoum area during the last part of the Iron Age. If we are to depart from the story of those Jääŋ people who came from Egypt, people who were led by Abiɛl the Great, then this Dengdit is that intermediate descendant of the ancient Jök-Athurkök, who is believed to have been the leader of the faction of Jacobites who migrated from Judea in the Middle East to the ancient Nile region of Wadi al Alagi in the far northern end of the present northern region of Northern Sudan. He is that ancestor who came with a faction some decades after the arrival of Jieldit and his group, heading the biggest faction of our today's Jääŋ that came from Judea in 936 BC, after the first group that came from Egypt, Great Jök-Athurkök subsequently came from Judea in 953 BC following in the footsteps of the first group of Jieldit. Like Jieldit and his faction, Jök-Athurkök joined the Jääŋ community in the Wadi al Alagi area.

As was the case with Jieldit and his faction before him Jök-Athurkök did not find it easy to cross the Red Sea (Wär-Pa-kuɛɛk). According to legends from Pajök clan elders in the Ngok area Jök-Athurkök went to the sea threshold on the east bank and while pleading and doing invocations to the gods of the sea to allow him and his people to safely cross to the west bank, a voice is said to have come from the sea, asking him to offer them a beautiful girl from among his daughters in order for him to be allowed to cross with his people.

Jök-Athurkök is said to have shared this with his people and Achai-noŋ, who gladly accepted to be offered, was selected to be given over to the sea gods for her migrating community to cross the sea! She was therefore thrown into the Red Sea in a ritual way. In consequence, the sea waters began to separate. Great Jök was as such able to cross with his people and as a sign of respect to this story, Pajök clan members continue to name their elder daughters with the name of Achai-noŋ in commemoration of that daughter of Jök-Athurkök given over to the sea gods during crossing. The Pajök people also give some gifts to Achai-wär in order for one to safely cross any river. They continue to do this practice to the present day.

When the Jääŋ society came to the Khartoum area about a century after the fall of Meroe in 350 AD at the hands of the armies from the nearby kingdom of Axum, Jök-Athurkök's descendants settled with the lineage families of Jiel the Great at what is today's Jeilly. Among the Athurkök people was a certain Dengdit who came from the primogenitary line of that ancient Jök-Athurkök. This Deng lived to be the overall spiritual leader of the whole Jääŋ society in Khartoum. He is believed to have raised a large family and is the very Dengdit who was taken up by a whirlwind, never to return to this day. Some Dinka people believe he was taken to heaven where Nhialic is. His children, from whom come the Pajök, who the Paröl call Juör-röl clan people, in Bor, include all those who form the thighbone revering group among the Dinka today. Whether this Dengdit of Khartoum is the same descendant of Jök-Athurkök or is a descendant of Ajääng Deng Kuc, son of Abiel, is something further research will ascertain.

In any case, the narrative is to proceed with the story of this Ngok people of Abyei. Towards the beginning of the 5th century AD the Jääŋ decided to leave the Khartoum region all together. They left Khartoum in three migratory columns. After reaching what is the present Asahessa area, one column took the Blue Nile route. The second column took the east bank route of the White Nile after Aba Island. The third column, consisting of the entire Rek, followed the path taken by the Nuers on the west bank of the White Nile. Descendants of Jök-Athurkök took the Blue Nile route. The rest of the Padaaŋ, descendants of Jiel the Great, choose the White Nile route. They came and settled in what is today's Rabek in the White Nile province.

The Jök-Arthurkök community and their current section people migrated along the Blue Nile until they made a stopover at what was Makuar in present Sinar, an area which was inhabited by the Funj at the time. Those descendants of Jök and those who went there with them spent some time in this area, having displaced the Funj, but when they found their cattle had no proper pasture they once again migrated to the Sobat River area. They were, at this time, led by a certain Bulabek, son of another intermediate Jök of the Sinar and Makuar period. Some of the descendants of Bulabek remained at Kuanylual Thuään, the present Nasir area where some of his family members became Nuers. They are the people from whom came the present SPLA chief of general staff, Lieutenant General James Hoath Mai.

Upon their arrival to the southern Upper Nile, the Pajök and their followers settled at what is now Nyarweng of Duk-Payueel. Others settled in the current ɣol Dinka areas of Duk-Padieet. The majority went to those areas that are the present Twic areas of Jonglei. In the ɣol section of Nyiel some Pajök remnants are what are still known as the Paan-Jök section people. When ecological factors and a number of epidemic disease outbreaks became serious in the south and central Upper Nile region the Jaang society decided to migrate to Bahr el Ghazal in search of new lands that could support life for them and their livestock. Like the other sections of the Dinka, the areas that were inhabited by the Padaŋ groups were hard hit by cholera and smallpox. This is why much of the Padaŋ decided to vacate their areas when the Jaaŋ decided to emigrate to Bahr el Ghazal. The Pajök people migrated in association with the Rek community. This explains why Wol Kuac (later to become Wol-Adhieu) and Loŋaar Ayueel featured greatly as part of the Rek during and after the crossing of the Nile at Shambe shore to Bahr el Ghazal, however, Wol-Adhieu and his people later decided to leave the Rek community and rejoin the Padaŋ group, the Luac people, taking to Rɛɛlkou with the Kiec while the Rek proceeded in their westward migration movement.

Following a quarrel between two great Spear Masters, Loi Jiel from Padaŋ and Guot Akoi from the Pagut clan among the Luac people, these Padaŋ people who later became Ruweng remigrated to Adöör land in the Yirol area of today. From Adöör they proceeded to cross the River Nile by the shore of Dhiäm-Dhiäm. They crossed to Kɔŋɔɔr in what is present Twic in Northern Bor. They once again proceeded to the present ɤöl area of Duk-Padiëët and to those areas that are the present Ngok of Lual Yak, where another intermediate Jök, the father of Bulabek, was born in around 1640 AD.

After the death of their spiritual leader, Loi Jiel, the leadership of the group went to the younger brother, Ajilik Jiel. Among the family heads of this remigrating group of Padaŋ was a certain Achuil, the son of Wol-Adhieu, whose eldest son (Akoch Achuil) was a significant personality during the migratory march from the Yirol area of Adöör to the south-central Upper Nile region. There were also those of Arop Wol, Aduai de Kur, Ajiing and Aru Jiel.

RUWENG MIGRATION TO THE WESTERN UPPER NILE

After nearly a century in this central Upper Nile area, those Padaŋ sections that later became known as the Ruweng made a decision to move out of their respective areas to the western Upper Nile area of Panrieŋ. These people came to be called Ruweng because one night while the population was on the move, they assembled their cattle in one place where they conglomerated them untethered. Because there were no prepared wooden pegs to be tethered to, the cows did not sleep! Instead they bellowed for the whole night and from this, the migrating community acquired their new name 'Ruweng' that is, the cattle did not sleep the whole night. Others pronounce it 'Rurweng'.

Those Padaŋ groups who did this migration included the Ngok section of Jök-Athurkök. They were led by Kuol, the son of Dombek

Bulabek Jök. They also consisted of the people who became the true Ru people who are known today as 'Pan-Ru Dinka' and who currently constitute what is called Panrieng county in Unity state, western Upper Nile. They were led by Loi, one of the grandsons of Ayueel Loŋaar. There were also clans and sections led by the ancestor of Great Kur Kuot. These Ruweng section people later settled in those areas that are now Biemnhom county, northwest of Pan-Ru. They temporarily lived in a place now known as Adɔk, Nyandiär and Kuɔk. They arrived in this area around 1710 AD and temporarily settled near the Nuer-Bul section. Here occurred a significant historical event of the time worth recording as part of the migration of the Ngok to their present homeland. The Ngok section of Achaak did have one powerful Spear Master by the name of Kuot-Awet from the Paguor Kuot clan. This old liege did have a very beautiful daughter who attracted many people including the neighbouring Nuer people. Several applicants came to have her hand but Kuot-Awet decided to ask all those applicants for a very impossible bidding. He demanded that the dowry in cattle to be paid by he who would marry his daughter should, as a condition, include a cow by the colour of Rɛɛng which must have two tails (Rɛɛng-Ayɔlrou)! In the process it was a Nuer man from the Bul section who paid the highest number of dowry cattle. The Bul Nuers neighboured the Achaak section people. He was all the same implored by the girl's father to bring Rɛɛng-Ayɔlrou. The Nuer man went out, rummaging around until he got the two-tailed cow of the very colour of Rɛɛng (Rɛɛng-Ayɔlrou). Unfortunately, Great Kuot-Awet declined to give his daughter over to the Nuer-Bul man. He used all intrigues and delaying tactics with empty promises until the Nuer man and his people lost patience. The Bul Nuers launched a surprise attack on Achaak, killing many people including Kuot-Awet himself. War broke out and escalated to involve the whole Ngok and the whole of the Bul sections of the Nuers. As the war raged on the Ngok were put on the run. They were defeated and chased by the Nuers. In the course of that war there was one Ngok strategist by the name of Ayom Ngäc who used to go for reconnaissance to find places the Ngok people could run to the next day. This reconnaissance man came back with a fabricated story, saying there was nowhere to run to any more. He told the Ngok that, 'Piny aci guud', meaning 'I found the land has come to its end, the heaven has touched the ground and there was nowhere to run to any more'. As such, the Ngok community began to ask what they should do. Ayom replied that the only way out was to fight back at the enemy in an attritious way in the hope of beating the Nuers back. The Ngok went in to fiercely fight until they were able to chase the Nuers. They chased the Nuers back to where they came from. This was how the Ngok rescued themselves from that historical episode in the course of their migration to their present Abyei homeland. The Nuers incurred many casualties in that battle, so Achaak was greatly reduced and it is said that this is what reduced it to be the smallest section among the present nine Ngok Dinka chiefdoms of today.

After this war known in Ngok Mediaeval history as the war of Kuot-Awet, the Ngok community continued their onward migration. They came to a place called Ngɔl, where Great Kuol bore Monydhaŋ. This was around 1750 AD. From this area of Ngɔl Monydhaŋ's son, by the name of Alor, later became the one to lead the Ngok community to the present Abyei area. They arrived there around 1785 AD. There, they found people called Begi or Girma in the area. They were a people generally known by the Dinka as Luɛɛl because they were a rather brown people. Part of this Luɛɛl group ran from the area to the west while a small part of them decided to remain in the area to become the present Alei section people in Abyei today.

According to traditions from the Ngok of Abyei, from the Malual Dinka in Northern Bahr El Ghazal state and from the Twic and Rek, Luɛɛl people were a cattle owning tribe of dwarfs who were a brown people with very hairy bodies. They were said to be very small cowards who would run away upon seeing a stranger. The territory north and south of Kiir River was the place where those Luɛɛl people lived and most of this area is inhabited by the Twic community today. As was the case with the Ngok, the Luɛɛl vacated north and westwards upon the arrival of the Twic Dinka.

Ngok Atuŋdiak, also known as Ngok of Deng Kuol or of Abyei, borders Massiriyia Arab Baggara to the northwest. They border the Malual Dinka to the southwest, the Twic Dinka of Warrap state to the southeast and the Alor Kur Kuot and Pan-Ru Dinka communities of Biemnhom and Panriɛng counties to the true east of them. Ngok is an area of nine chiefdoms or sections which are:

1. Abior section from where paramount Chief Kuol Adöl Deng Kuol comes
2. Acuɛɛŋ section
3. Acaak section
4. Bongo section
5. Diil section
6. Anyiel section
7. Man-Nyuar section
8. Marɛɛng section
9. Alei section.

Alei (Alien) are a Dinkanised former Begi or Jur-Luɛɛl. The Malual Dinka people to the southwest of Ngok think that some of the remnants from this Luɛɛl people are what they call the Thuri clan in Northern Bahr el Ghazal. Others were found northwest of the present Nyamlel up to 1933 AD.[90]

---

90 Fr Nebel and Fr Grazzola, SNRXI, 1933

UPPER NILE DINKA COMMUNITIES

1. Abialang Dinka

This large Dinka section lives at the last northern end of Southern Sudan in Upper Nile state. They border the Sabah Arabs of the White Nile in former central Sudan. They are bordered by the Shilluks to the west, by Burun people of Maban to the east and by the Dinka section of Ageer to the south towards Malakal. Abialang Dinka belong to the Padang Dinka cultural group of Ayueel the Great, who they think is the owner of the land they now occupy. However, the Abialang also believe in a certain remote ancestor by the name of Diing the Great. They regard their land as Piny Diing while the people belong to Ayueeldit, that is, people belong to Ayuul and the land belongs to Diing.

Descendants of Diing in the Abialang territory are known as the people of piöl the cloud and they also call themselves the water people of the river. They believe in Diing as the owner of the territory called Abialang and as the father of the whole Jaang or Dinka nation.[91] Their traditions consider Ayueel to have been himself a son of this Diing. They say Diing did have a number of wives, but one of those wives did not have a son. She only had a daughter by the name of Acuɛi. One day, the woman without a son went to the River Nile, which all Dinka people call 'Kiir', and she became pregnant with a child who became Ayueel, who later bore several sons who filled the land and made a number of Dinka sections, among which is Abialang. Ayueel is sometimes called Ayueel-Apiök, Ayueel-Wɛɛr, Ayueel-Loŋaar or Ayueel-Agithbor-Atiöóp. His many sons are presented as being Göc (the beginning), Ayong, Akoi, Loi, Loŋaar, Jiel, Ariir, Aker, Yiep, Kur, Thiang, Adiang, Leek, Akuei,

---

91   From an interview with elders in Pabuny village, Renk county, in December 1990 and later confirmed by General Nyong Deng Nyong from the Abialang Dinka, interviewed 20 August 2003.

Diing, Gol, Yuaar, Deng, Jök, Ayiɔɔk and so on. Ayueel who bore all those sons is believed to have been buried at Duk-Payueel in present Nyarweng territory.

When the Jaang increased, one of Ayueel's sons, Loŋaar Ayueel, crossed to Bahr el Ghazal as part of the Rek in 1340 AD. He went with his family lines and a number of lineage members while most of the descendants of Diing, Akuei, Ker, Göc and Ayiɔɔk returned northward from the present Nyarweng and Bor areas to become the Dongjol, Ageer, Nyiel and Abialang sections of the Jaang. Some of them later came back around the present Malakal area where they are now called Dongjol Dinka. Others proceeded from Nyiel to become Ageer Dinka while others still proceeded further northwards up to the Renk area and as far as Geiger and the areas around the present Jebellein and beyond.

They became the Abialang. They now border the Sabah Arab Baggara at the Khor-Ayueel and Jebellein areas, at Masmum, Garbil then called Agerdit, Roro and Wulu areas on the borders with Chai of Maban region of the Burun people.

They also border Ageer at Bemacuk, Bul, Aturuk and Man-Apiöök up to Thibin where they also border Chai of Maban. Abialang is a name which came from the name of 'Laŋ', called Nabak in Arabic. The Abialang were used to eating so much Laŋ on their way as they were moving back to their present location after much of the Jaang migrated to Bahr el Ghazal. Those groups, sometimes called Dongjol groups, returned back to northern Upper Nile from Bilnyang behind the present Juba city.

Territorial and administrative configuration of Abialang Dinka: Abialang is a very large Dinka community inhabiting the last end of the northern Upper Nile state. Its administrative centre is Renk, which is their county centre, also called Renk. Abialang is made up of 13 territorial sections:

- Akɔɔn section of Chief Adol Akol Wɛk,
- Luääŋwiën and Jai-Kuat sections of the same Chief Adol Akol Wɛk,
- Dhök, Köweng, Nyida and Matjak sections of Chief Aliny Ajal,
- Dɔŋ-Lɔu and Payuer sections of the same chief,
- Giɛl territory of Chief Yusif Ngor Deng Ngor and comprised of:
  i. Aguɛɛm section,
  ii. Banweng section,
  iii. Thɔn-Mac section and
  iv. Kuac section.

As already explained above, almost the whole of the Abialang are descendants of Ayueel and Diing. They are people of the divinity flesh Dengdit and they are known to conjure people even in a trivial quarrel and so it is advisable not to run into a feud with an Abialang man.

2. Ageer Dinka
As explained above, Ageer people also belong to the Padang Dinka cultural group. As described above, Ageer people developed in the present Dukein areas of Nyarweng and Hol in central Upper Nile where they migrated towards the end of 1300 AD after much of the Jaang migrated to Bahr el Ghazal. They border Abialang on their northern ends. They border the Shilluks who are on the west bank of the White Nile. The Burun people of Maban live to the east of them.

3. Nyiel Dinka
These are the Dinka people of the Wunamon oilfields area between the Ageer and Dongjol Dinka, north of Malakal city. They are people of the oilfields of Paloch. The Nyiel and Ageer are people of the Mellut county. In addition to the Dongjol and Abialang, they are what are regarded as the Dongjol group of Padang Dinka. The Nyiel, Ageer and Dongjol live in an area which the Dinka people

call 'Aɣɔlic' and this is generally a rich oil region in the northern parts of the Upper Nile state. The Nyiel Dinka is a territorial area of only three sub-sections.

4. Dongjol Dinka

The Dongjol are Dinka people whose county is Akɔga, north of Malakal city. They cover all those areas beginning from the northern suburb of Malakal, in between the Nyiel Dinka and Malakal. They inhabit the east bank areas of the River Nile with the Shilluks to the west of them across the White Nile. The Dongjol people are actually part of the urban city of Malakal and it is not necessary to describe their administrative setup here.

5. Ngok of Lual Yak

The Ngok of Lual Yak of eleven sections inhabit all those areas along the Sobat River and those areas east of Malakal city. This Ngok is one of the biggest sections of the Padang Dinka. With the Ngok of Abyei and Paweny they make up the Ngok sector of the Dinka Padang. The story of the Padang Dinka has already been given under Ngok of Abyei, Abialang and Ageer. The Ngok of Lual Yak people are generally descendants of Ayueel. Their county administrative centre is Baliet on the Sobat River. Its territorial area consists of the Ajuba, Ding, Baliet, Duut, Abii, Awiɛr, Adöng, Ngaar, Balak, Dhiaak and Acaak areas.

6. Paweny Dinka

Paweny Dinka are people of the Atar former district area. They are part of the Ruweng section of the Padang Dinka and are mostly descendants of Ayueel the Great. They are presently part of Pigi county on the canal mouth in the northeastern part of Jönglei state. The Paweny consists of six territorial sections, the Palei, Jueny, Atung-diak, Aniek, Bugo and Thiony areas of Chief Thɔn Kooc.

7. Nyarweng Dinka

They are the Dinka of the Duk-Payueel area where Great Ayueel is believed to have been buried. Their area has been one of the Mediaeval Jaang centres before a large part of them migrated to Bahr el Ghazal.

The Nyarweng and ɤol Dinka of Duk-Payueel and Duk-Padieet are adjacent to each other and are combined as people of the Dukein county, although Nyarweng people are culturally part of the Padang while Hol people originally belonged to the Gok cultural group. Nyarweng is territorially divided into five chieftaincy areas of the Abuɔk, Aborɔm, Bingkaar, Ajör and Pawai sections.

8. Luac Dinka of Khor Fluth

Luac Aköök Yieu Dinka community of Khor Fluth Area: These are late Mediaeval offshoots who broke away from the main body of the Luac Dinka at about the end of the 16th or the beginning of the 17th century. They broke away from the rest of the Luac community at the present no man's land area of Madol. In the toch marshes they then moved to the current Leer area where they first became known as Luac-Tɛɛt. In their eastward migration led by an Age-set by the name of Magɔl, who decided to migrate after a solitary bull Marɔl-Thɔn of a certain Aguer Ajak, they crossed Bahr el Jebel River and settled in an area then known as Akoch Ke Rɛɛŋ, from where they again moved to Gɔɔr and to what is today's Rut land in the east bank after they crossed Piðu or Acony, which is today's Bahr el Zeraf River. From there they gradually moved to the present Khor Fluth area in around 1919. Here, in the Khor Fluth area, they continued to be the subjects of constant wars since their arrival to the Upper Nile region. These are the people from whom come General George Athor Deng Dut who, using this community, was able to defend the SPLA from Riek Machar's rebellion of 1991 which badly divided those involved in the SPLM/A liberation struggle between 1991 and

2002. George Athor, after peace in the country, himself fell out with his own government in Jonglei Juba in 2010 following his defeat by General Kuol Manyang Juuk. He rebelled and set up a deadly insurgency against the government, an armed movement which ended with him killed by the government forces on 19 December 2011.

This Luac community is made up of six sections of Kuec, Kɔgɔ or Yom-Kuei, Acuil-Lith, Mut, Aliɛr-Gɛng and Ric. The Kuec are the section people who keep the ancient holy spears of the deity Aguër. They are the people from whom the Pakuec clan people in Apuk-Giir Thiik left the Luac society to become the Rek people of Lith, also known today as Apuk, who constitute the Geogrial East county in Warrap state and Luac Adut which forms the Atuöt-Luac section in Yirol West county, Lakes state. A splinter part of them also broke away and joined the big Rek to become the Luackoth people of Great Bol Malek Jök, a people who make up today's Palal Payam in Tonj East county.

9. ɤöl Dinka

As earlier discussed under Nyarweng, ɤol Dinka are an earlier branch of the Gok Dinka. Gok people of Cuɛibɛt county and another Gok people of Matöt, now of Anyiɛth Rɛɛc in Kiec land and the Gok people in Bor South, form one ancient Jaang section called the Gok. Because the ɤol people remained in that part of the Upper Nile and neighbour Nyarweng, they are administratively joined up with Nyarweng to make one administrative district called 'Dukein county'. They are known as the people of Duk-Padieet. ɤol Dinka is made up of five large sections under paramount chief Monykuer Mabuur of the Angääc section of ɤol.

The five areas of ɤol are:
1. **Angääc,** consisting of the Cor, Dukuɛr and Jak sections.

2. **Nyiel** area[92] of ɤol of Paramount Chief Lual Wuor Ajak (Lual-Atungtiir) is comprised of Pan-Jök section, Kangaap section; Pan-Tiök section; Agööt section; Padunyiel section; Patél-One section[93] and Patél-Two of Chief Diɛr Macol Deng Diɛr.
3. **Duör-Ayueel** area of ɤol, consisting of the Durbaai, Ceng-Pajook,[94] Ric and Paan-Pajook sections.
4. **Nyiel people** of ɤol are largely emigrants from the Adöör section of Kiec in the Yirol area.
5. **ɤol Dinka** lies along the Duk-Padieet ridge in Northern Bor, extending from the Nile River to Panyook in the north east, bordering Gawɛɛr Nuers of Ayod district to the north and the Nyarweng Dinka people of Duk-Payueel to the south.

10. Duör Dinka

The Duör Dinka community is basically a remnant of the Agaar Dinka. They live in between the Angääc and ɤol Dinka in central Upper Nile. Some of these Duör are the present Duör section people in the Aliamtooc-Two territory of the Yäk section of Rumbek East county of the Aköt area of Chief Malual Arop. Part of the Duör are presently found also among the Rek section of Kɔŋöör in the Tonj North areas of Akop where they are an executive chieftaincy area called Duör under Chief Kon Aguer Mawien of the Paduɔltiɔp who are the **Marbek Dinka Group: (Thoi, Rut & Alual)** Patiɔp clan in Agaar land. These Duör Dinka in south-central Upper Nile have become culturally assimilated into the Bor Dinka cultural group.

---

92   Pabörköi cattle camp is a spot in the Nyiel area of ɤol Dinka. It is where the oil drilling company is situated in this Dukein county.

93   Patél section is where the home area of those of the late William Nyuon Bäny Machar is. William Nyuon Bäny was one of the founders of the SPLM/A and was SPLA chief of staff number two after Kerubino Kuanyin Bol.

94   Those are emigrants from the Gok Dinka of Cuɛibɛt county in Western Lakes state, Bahr el Ghazal region.

11. Thoi Dinka

Rut, Thoi and Alual belong to the Marbek group of the Padang Dinka. In those early Mediaeval times when the entire Jaang was still in Upper Nile, the people who are now Rut, Thoi and Alual sections were in an area now called 'Amögöök', currently inhabited by the Gawɛɛr Nuers.

When part of the Jaang vacated those south-central areas of the Upper Nile to Bahr el Ghazal, those sections found it difficult to remain in a vacated environment. They went further south to those areas that are now Bilnyang areas, east of Juba. This is because one of the greatest pestilences of the time befell them from the Nuers after those Jaang left for Bahr el Ghazal. In time those Jaang communities remigrated back to their former place when the Luo, who later went to Kenya and Uganda, fought them back.

As time went by, Thoi came to stay in those areas of present Alam. The Luac Aguër Wiɛu people, coming from Bahr el Ghazal, later came and settled in the Khor Fluth areas of Wunlɛm up to Nyinthar-Malual and became neighbours with the Thoi and Paweny as well as the Rut in the west. The Thoi Dinka consists of Lek, Anyaak, Ajerou, Pajimaar, Keeth and Athɔny sections. Thoi Dinka is currently part of a county with Rut, Luac of Aköök Yieu and Paweny. This is a county known as Pigi county. Thoi lies almost to the junction of Bahr el Jebel and the Sobat Rivers between the Rut and Malakal areas.

12. Rut Dinka

The Rut Dinka community, Mediaevally known as Majak Athoi Ayueel, is of cultural and religious significance for the Padang Dinka people or perhaps for the entire Dinka nationality. It is a religious centre where the historic 'luak of Dengdit' is situated. The original Mediaeval luak (shrine) was at Ucung in today's Ayol where it is kept by the Bang people known as Cieng Malai. The second shrine of f ...he was Dengdit was built in about 1817 in the Wundeeng section at a place called Alam, which is today's holy village for the Rut, Padaang and even the neighbouring Nuers.

Before the misbalance created by Jaang migration to Bahr el Ghazal in the 14th century, migration which empowered the Nuers' sections of Lak, Thiong and Gaweer to cause the remaining smaller sections of Jaang (Jieng) to abandon the area, the Rut Dinka community was in those areas that continue to be Amogook.

While still in this Amogook area, the name for this society of Majak Athoi came about. There are two versions from the local traditions about how the society got the name of Rut. The first says that, "one autumn season day a huge hurricanic tropical whirlwind came from the east to the Amogook settlement, causing the community to be greatly worried about the destruction it was to cause. The elders succeeded to calm the people down as the people started stampeding, running for their lives. Elders argued to the running population that the wind was bringing the cool breeze of autumn (rut in Dinka) and will do no harm.....". When the wind suddenly decided to avoid where people were gathered and took a different course due west, people rejoiced and from there, the idea came for the community to be called "Rut" after that cyclonic wind.

The second version states that a community liege, Athoi Ayueel, did have children and a good estate with cows. His elder son, Majak Athoi, used to disappear with all the family cows during autumn. He would always go east, to the same far distant lands, leaving his younger brothers in Amogook with their father and the rest of the family. He would only come back to his father and brothers in Amogook after a year and he left behind the calves that went with him while suckling their mothers. He used to hide them in that unknown place. Because he used to disappear during rut (autumn) his father gave him the surname Rut instead of Majak. He therefore became known as Rut Athoi. In time this Rut became a community leader and his name remained to be used for identifying that community of the Amogook territory.

In time, the Gaweer Nuers who came slowly migrating from the Fangak Island areas began to make continued attacks on the Rut society, whose population was not commensurate with that of the attacking Nuers. As a result the Rut community withdrew from Amogook, firstly to areas that are present Rut land. The Rut Dinka have one paramount court president over five executive chiefs with Korwaac as their Payam. There is Athoor, composed of Was and Panaak sections. There is Bior composed of Cuzi and Jok-Buny sections. The paramount court president is James Kong Machol Goc from the Angooc section of Paan Yokjok in the Waw section of Athoor. The chiefs are: Thon Megaany Akook of Cnei section, Chief Panhom Deel Luol of Jok-Buny section, Chiefs Panhom Puur and Michar Puurof of Pagong and Palual in the same Jok-Bany section, Chief Knol Gaac Akol of the Apaciek section in Wau, Chief Nhomtiop Lual from the Panaak section. Rut, Luac and Thoi make up the Khor Fluth area in Pigi county.

13. Alual Dinka (an extinct Dinka tribe)

Alual Dinka, once the largest section of the Padang, later scattered all over Dinka lands following their alleged fight against Nhialic (God) in what the legend presents as the central Upper Nile area of Athɔɔr and Alam at what is now Rut Dinka territory. The story of this section of Jaang having fought with God at one point in history is so rampantly told by all Jieng people in both the Upper Nile and Bahr el Ghazal regions to the present day. Those who were once Alual section people can now be found among Pan-Ru Dinka in the western Upper Nile. Others are scattered in Lakes state areas where they are sharp-edge or bladed spear and rock stone revering people. They are the Padhɔɔl clan people in the Ayiɛl and Waat sections in Gokland. In Reklands they are the Palual clan, Pakuor, Pamiyiɛi, Pakӧt and so forth. They are the Paral clan and Paan-Ayii Maluɛɛl in Agarland. Others are the Pakir in the Biong section of Apuk in

Gogrial East. They are also found in the Awiel and Ngok areas of Abyei as they are found in many Padang areas in central and northern Upper Nile areas. Alual Dinka is no longer one entity found in one place like the other sections from the Marbek group. Great Lady Luac Akɛɛn Buk, the author's mother, comes from the Palual clan people in the Awan-Parek area. The Palual clan people belong to this Mediaeval section of Alual.

Annexed to Thoi are remnants of families that were Alual in those Mediaeval times. Those families are known in Thoi today as: (i) Paan- Awuol (ii) Paan-Abiel Adiwuoot and (iii) Paan-Deng Akolo. Their executive chief is Gaijang de Lual Deng. They are a section known as Alual in Thoi.

13. Twic Dinka of Jönglei

The Twic people's land in Twic-East county borders the Duk county of Nyarweng and Ɣöl, Wuroor county of Lou Nuers to the north east. It also borders Pibor of the Murle to the east and Bor county to the south. To the west is the White Nile beyond which is Kiec and the Aliap Dinka people of Yirol East and Awɛirial county in Lakes state, Bahr el Ghazal region.

According to the ancient and Mediaeval legends in the area, Twic society came with the rest of the Jaang from Khartoum as Kuac, not as Twic. As earlier explained under the general introduction to Twic, the Kuac section was led by its clans' leaders who included Kuac-Ajök, Twic-Acuil and Noi. The last two were from the thigh bone revering clan, the Paɣöl, now called '*Juör-ɣöl*' in Twic and Bor lands. Legends say the three leaders led Kuac up to the present areas where the Twic are in present Jonglei state with the big Pamac cattle camp and its outlying areas between Jale and Maar as the starting points. The Kuac section that later became Twic and belongs to the Padang Dinka group must have arrived in these areas towards the beginning of AD 1000. It was in this place that the would-be Twic-

East county community started out of Kuac.

As fully described under Twic of Bahr el Ghazal, legends about the beginnings of the Twic Dinka section start with a certain Ariɛm Abuwiir, also called Ariɛm Adhuöny, who came and settled with the Kuac community of Yiep Ayueel at a cattle camp area presently called Patunduur in what is currently Ajuöng Payam, whose administrative town is Paliau. Here at Patunduur Ariɛm married a daughter of that community leader and gave birth to seven sons, the eldest of whom was named by him as Twic. In time, the legend continued, Ariɛm went away with six of his sons while Twic remained with his old mother, Abuk Yiep. Twic continued to stay with his maternal uncles who contributed some cows for him to own. From those cows Twic later married within his maternal uncles' lineage. In those early days there was no incest. He then grew to be a Spear Master of powerful efficacy.

With time it came on Twic to want to let the territory be named after his name. He called on his grandfather, Yiep, and confided to him the need for the territory to be called Twic. When the grandfather disagreed, Twic made a curse of five years of drought that made the community finally yield to his wish. Those of Great Leek Ayueel who lived in the same area and another Thiang Ayueel who lived at what is now the Athopei cattle camp area in current Ajuöng, those of Ariir Ayueel from Pacuil on the Nile coast of Ajuöng, those of Adiang from Mayen-cuɛr and those of Cuɛr Ajak-Amot in today's Kɔŋɔɔr, all were summoned into that community gathering at Patunduur. It was in this gathering that the territory and its people were renamed as Twic, an occasion in which Twic himself named the present sections of Twic after the colours of the cows Aker, Malith-Thɔn and Majak-Thɔn, bulls and cows which he ritualled to name the area sections and mark the end of the drought as he called for rain that fell on the same instant. The area and people therefore remained to be known as Twic, instead of Kuac, although one of the sections that went to

Bahr el Ghazal continued to preserve their ancient name of Kuac. They are the Kuac section of Twic which is presently Ajak-Kuac Payam, known as Kuac of Chief Madut Ring in the eastern part of Twic county.

A century after the community acquired its name part of Twic and much of the Jaang society in the Upper Nile Basin region decided to migrate to Bahr el Ghazal in 1340 AD. During this migration the Twic community broke into two at the present Pakër area. A faction led by a certain Ajiing Duääng, also known as Ajiing-Kuac, decided to remain in the area while a large part under Great Noi Duääng and Kuol-Alɛl took off with the rest of the Jaang sections and crossed the River Nile to Bahr el Ghazal. The story of those Twic sections that went to Bahr el Ghazal is explained in detail under the Twic of Bahr el Ghazal section.

The Twic who remained in the Upper Nile developed into:

1. **Ajuong area** consisting of Abiɔng, Nyapiny, Ayoliel, Kuac and Adiang sections. These sections of Ajuong are those areas which make up Paliau Payam in Bor North county.
2. **Paker area** consisting of Anɔk, Kir-Amou, ɣol, Berë, Akonycɔk sections (this is the area where Jönglei is located near Burthai port) and Ajuluk or Thɔny section. The seven sections make what is Maar Payam in Twic-East county. The two payams, Paliau and Maar, make the former Jönglei Payam.
3. **Lith (One) area** is Nyuak Payam with Wangulei as its Payam. This is historically the Lith territory of Ajak Kur, so known since it was named by Twic Ariɛm at Patunduur in around the 12th century AD. Lith people made the Pakɔu area of Ajak Kur Ayuel their first settlement area. The area now consists of the **Ayuaal section, Awulian** section[95] area of Chief Thɔn Dau

---

95   Awulian people remigrated in the 17th century from the Bahr el Ghazal area of Luacjang. They first left from the Cuɛitiim big cattle camp area called Panyinlɛm in present Jur-Lian territory of the Awan-Parek area in about 1650

Macuur (this is the home area of those of the great leader and founder of the SPLM/A, the late Dr John Garang de Mabior) and the Dai-Acueek section of Chief Lual Garang Lual.

4. **Lith (Two) area** of Chief Ajaang Duot, who in his lifetime was the paramount chief of the whole Lith, with Pawél as its Payam administrative town. This Payam consists of the following areas: the big Kɔŋɔɔr area of Chief Duot Ajaang Duot; the Adhiɔk area of chief Awai de Ajaang Awai and the Abek area of Chief Ayiik de Bol Arɔk. Lith is of three Payams. It is an area of six sections. Lith Two is the Kɔŋɔɔr Payam and with Wangulei and Pawél Payams they constitute the area formerly known as Lith of Ajak Kur Ayueel.

14. Bor Dinka

Bor Dinka territory is bordered to the southwest by non-Dinka tribes called Mundari and Baria of Central Equatoria state and by the Aliap Dinka of Lakes state on the west bank of the white Nile. It is also bordered to the east by the Murle tribe of Pibor county and to the north by Twic Dinka people.

The name 'Bor' is a derivative from the fact of the territory being a low flood land. With heavy monsoon rains and east African floods from the Nile River, Bor land usually gets flooded, especially by about the month of July up to November at which time the River Nile and its swamps become gorged with water, creating a lot of fish and high grass which sprouts and becomes associated with mosquitoes. By about October each year the flood waters recede into the River Nile, its streams (ponds or 'baar') and swamps, and so by around December and January, Bor land is dried up and cattle people begin to move to the swamplands for water and pastures.

In years when there is no annual flooding or in years of drought

---

AD. The Awulian section, in this part of Twic in Jonglei, is the native home area of those of the late Dr John Garang de Mabior.

cattle people can reach the main Nile after those swamps and streams are dried up. This is true of Bor areas. The Twic area usually remains with water nearly all year. This is because Twic is a bit tilted as the land slopes north and westwards and is thus able to stagnate water during the floods. In years of drought the Bor community move with their cattle to the toch" land areas of northern Twic where they sometimes meet with the Nuers.

When the Jaang migrated from the Northern Sudan areas of the present Khartoum state the people who became Bor Dinka were known as the Adhiɔɔk. They took the Blue" Nile route with other Jaang sections, Duör, our present Agaar Dinka. With them were the Gok people who have now broken into Gok of Cuɛibɛt, Gok of Matöt and Gok of Anyiɛth Rɛɛc in Kiec land and the present Gok in Southern Bor. There were Anie and within Adhiɔɔk was a sub-section called Aliap, which later became a distinct entity with its name of Aliap in Bahr el Ghazal. The rest of the Jaang took the White Nile route to Kosti-Rabek-Jebellein as they came to the northern Upper Nile areas of Geiger and Renk.

Those Blue" Nile factions of Jaang went as far as the Kurmuk and Geizan areas where they settled for quite a number of decades, but when their cattle could not fare well in this rather rugged and mountainous area bordering the Ethiopian highlands, those Jaang sections decided to again migrate to the Upper Nile Basin region. The Ethiopian Galla tribes were also posing constant problems as was the case with the White Nile Jaang groups, who were also at war with the Luo tribes that pioneered the area almost half a century before. The Galla tribes are a Kushitic people inhabiting southeastern parts of Ethiopia. They are now known as the Oromo people.

Then the Blue" Nile sections later migrated westwards towards the White Nile part of the Upper Nile region but through the present desert area of Aying. Ahead of this Blue Nile migrating column of Jaang were the Anie section people. These Anie people decided to make a respite stopover at a water pool on a stream during their continuous march. Here, a youth party of the Murle stumbled on them as they ran into them, pursuing a wild herd of *guil* animals that led them into this water pool. The Murle thought this to be strange for in those days it was unacceptable for a strange person or people to tramp into the precinct of others. The Murle instantly attacked the Anie, thereby drawing in the rest of the Jaang sections of Duör, Gok and Athööc which found Anie attacked as they arrived from behind. All the same the Murle defeated all those Jaang who had to pull out and proceed westwards till they arrived in such places as the Pamai cattle camp area of present Abuötdit in present Jale territory. Found in the area were a Jaang people known then as Adöl, Pakɔrɔɔu, Awan and Arëëm. Those pioneers found present Twic and Borlands as areas with only elephants, hippopotamuses and other toch" land game. It was a no man's land.

In time, about a century after their arrival from the Kurmuk area, the Anie melted into Athɔɔc and Duör and the section that was Aliap in Athɔɔc became a distinct community of its own. Adol got encapsulated by the Alian section of Athɔɔc in the Jale area. The Pakɔrɔu, who were fishermen on the Nile coastal areas of present Manydeng, also dwindled as part of them later migrated to Bahr el Ghazal and are believed to be the Pakɔɔr people in the present Rek section of Jalwau in Tonj East county. The Pakɔrɔɔu people who remained were absorbed by the Angakuei section of Athɔɔc in Manydeng Payam. Awan remnants migrated as part of Aliap and the present Awan people in Aliap may be those Mediaeval Awan that were among those Jaang people who pioneered present Borland. The Arëëm people were found settled in the cattle camp area of Pada, about the present Yomshir airstrip area in Manydeng Payam, bordering the Jale Payam areas. They later became the Pakak people of Amou. A section of these Arëëm crossed to the West Nile after the famous Jaang crossing to Bahr el Ghazal. They joined what became the Kiec and can now be found as part of the Jieng within the Ajak section of Great Cuöt Chap in Yirol East county. They are still known there as people of Pakak.

The Bor Dinka community is a very peaceful society except for their relations with the Murle tribe to the east (relations between them and the Murle have been turbulent since Mediaeval times to the present day). For the last ten generations, no war has ever occurred between Bor and Twic, no death cases and therefore no murders or 'tiɛr' between Bor and its neighbouring Dinka communities. They share common threats and make common defence with the Twic, ɤöl and Nyarweng people of Dukein county. Before Turkiya, the Lou Nuer used to wage wars on the Bor Dinka and it used to be an affair of Twic, ɤöl, Nyarweng and Bor itself. However, both the Bor and Twic communities are known for their restraint and they go into war or fight after all other considerations have been tried.

When the Jaang decided to migrate to Bahr el Ghazal in 1340 AD, the Athɔɔc (now Bor) people did not participate. Their plan to move was thwarted by the news from the Jaang people and sections returning from the Nile shore of Shambe that the leader of that migration, Loŋaar Ayueel, was spearing the heads of people in the Nile waters.

Those Jaang people who crossed at Kɔrcök, called Shambe shore, and those who crossed at Rumjöök, are those who departed the Upper Nile region at what is the Twic area of Jönglei and its surrounding extremities up to the ɤol and Nyarweng territories. Those were the Twic sections of Noi and Kuol-Alɛl, Rek, Luac, Duör (Agaar) and Gok plus those who later became Ruweng. Those who crossed at those shores to the left of Shambe departed the Upper Nile Basin region at what is now Borland proper. They are later departees after the main exodus took off from Twic and from the present Dukein areas. They include those who are present Aliap, present Thiyiith in Agaar land, Pakak in Kiec land, Pakɔrɔɔu now in the Rekland area of Jalwau and the Awan people in Aliap. Yet those who left what is Mading Bor of today to cross at Tombek shore have now become part of Atuöt and are part of those known as 'Atuöt-Luac' in Yirol West county. They were Guala people when they crossed from Bor.

When a certain British explorer came to the Nile shore, which later became Mading Bor, he found a fisherman there. He was a certain Ngeth Ango. The explorer tried to have a meeting with the community. He requested the community provide him with a bull to be slaughtered in order to name the place. Ngeth readily offered a bull with the colour of Mading. Among many community leaders who were present at the naming ceremony were old men Deng Athok of the Paleek area of Anyidi and elder Kaang Makuei of the Kuoi section. The bull Mading was slaughtered and the spot was now declared as Mading. Then, the explorer also inquired about the limitless water he saw and he was told, "it was Abooric". Finding it difficult to gutturally pronounce the word 'Abooric', he just told the gathering that the place should better be called 'Mading Bor'. This was accepted and the location became known as Mading Bor from then till today. Mading Bor then grew to later be the capital town for the Bor community and has become the capital town for the Jonglei state. Almost all the people of Bor are either Juor-Mac who are the fire revering clans (Pathɔth /Pakuiëëth) or Juor-ɣöl, who are the thigh bone revering clans (Paɣöl).

Social and administrative configuration of the Bor Dinka:
- **Gok territory of Bor** consisting of Abi, Guala, Abaang, Paleek (Anyidi), Adɔl, Makuac, Lualdit, Wɛrkok, Kon-Beek, Köc, Dɛɛr and Ateer sections.
- **Athɔɔc territory (central Bor)** consisting of the Manydeng Payam which is made up of the Biöng, Angakuei and Pathuyith sections.
- **Jale Payam**, consisting of Alian, Abuötdit and Jueet sections.
- **Gok and Athɔɔc** are the two big sections into which Bor Dinka is divided and the two consist of five payams which make up Bor county.

16. Alor Dinka: (Alor Kur Kuot)

The Alor Dinka community has been largely tackled under the Ruweng section of the Padang Dinka. It is located west of Pan-Ru Dinka in the western Upper Nile region in the Unity state of Bentiu. Alor derived its name from the leader who led the clans and sections to be later named Alor after him. Alor people were part of the Ruweng migration to the Bahr el Ghazal area of Rɛɛlkou, returning to the Upper Nile and again to the western Upper Nile location of Biemnhom where they are presently. Alor Kur Kuot consists of three sections, Thiyier, Amaal and Manteeng.

17. Pan-Ru Dinka (Jaaŋ Bilkuei)

Pan-Ru is a Dinka community or a sub-national group belonging to the Ruweng sub-cultural component of the big Padang Dinka cultural group. Pan-Ru people live in the northern parts of Unity state, northwest of Bentiu in the western Upper Nile region. The Pan-Ru community is made up of two broad sections of Awet and Kuel. Awet is in itself made up of the three sub-sections of Kuɔk, Aniëk and Diäär. Kuël, which is the largest section in Pan-Ru, consists of the nine sub-sections of Kuocgöör, Bibiök where the Bilkuei family is found, Bugo-Angɔu, Bugo-Bol, Ngɛ́ɛ́r, Agaany, Palei, Miɔcigiu and Atungdiak.

The nine territorial sub-sections of Kuël are traditionally administered by a system of five executive chiefs locally called Nazir. Ngɛ́ɛ́r, Bugo-Angɔu and Miɔcigiu are under the authority of one Nazir-Dau Mathiang from the Ngɛ́ɛ́r sub-section. Palei, Atungdiak and Bugo-Bol are under one executive chief or Nazir Lat Kɔcnɔɔr from the Palei sub-section. Bibiök, the largest, is under one Nazir-Maker Dau. The Agaany and Kuöcgöör sub-sections are under one Nazir-Jam Maper from the Agaany sub-section.

Pan-Ru is a county of Ruweng with Panriɛng as its county administrative centre. Pan-Ru is a South Sudan legislative assembly constituency in its own right and is joined up with the Nuers' section of Leek to make one constituency for the national parliament in Juba. Future census counts may qualify Pan-Ru as a constituency to the national parliament without Nuer Leek.

Historically the Ruweng component of Padang had lived in the present area of Adɔk from where Ruweng split. The Luac component left to join the rest of the Jaang at the south-central part of the Upper Nile prior to the historic Jaang migration to the Bahr el Ghazal region in the first quarter of the Middle Ages. The Ngok of the Lual Yak component of this Ruweng went to their present Abuöng and Sobat areas. Paweny people opted to remain with the Ngok people of Lual Yak. Those who regarded themselves as the mainstream section of Ruweng opted to call themselves 'Pan-Ru', meaning Ru family. The community departed the Dɔkland areas of Nyandiar and Kuɔk together with the Alor and present Ngok people of Abyei. Those make up the true Ruweng community among Padang Dinka.

These Ruweng communities went to the present areas that are now the Pan-Ru territory from where the Alor and Ngok people of Kuol Arop Biong proceeded westwards. The Alor community then decided to remain in their present Biemnhom area while the Ngok went ahead to finally settle at their present area of Abyei. They went there in about the early parts of the 17th century AD. The Ru or Pan-Ru people were led out of Adɔk territory by a certain Loi, one of the grandsons of Great Ayueel Loŋaar. When this Ru community chose where they now live the territory was named as the 'land of Loi', a name for which the Pan-Ru territory is also known to the present day.

This Pan-Ru land area was inhabited by a Nuba people called Chat who are part of the Jalwau section of the Nuba today. Chat people later receded back to their present Nuba mountain areas upon the arrival of the Ruweng Dinka communities.

CHAPTER FIVE: DINKA CATTLE

THE DINKA CATTLE COMPLEX

This is an otherwise difficult but very interesting topic about Dinka society. More understanding about the Dinka as a people can be obtained from the critical reading and understanding of this chapter. Much of the rural Dinka daily vocabulary refers to the cattle. The larger the herd the more prestigious the family or the Dinka person. Their religious and social life is centred on the cattle. An outsider spending even a single day among the Dinka in their rural setting can most readily notice the social, economic and religious significance of the cattle to this predominantly pastoral people whose livelihood largely depends on those cattle. Such a person cannot fail to be impressed by their preoccupation with their cattle and the time and labour they devote to looking after them, the large vocabulary they have for cattle, their colours, the great interest and pride they have in the art of making different designs to which their horns are made to grow as explained elsewhere in this book. Dinka people are ethnically divided into twenty five tribal groups that live

Fig 32: Showing a Dinka young man at the cattle camp cleaning his cows while tethered at their pegs. The cows appear to be enjoying this cleaning as part of a massage for them.

in the two vast regions called the Upper Nile and Bahr el Ghazal. Despite some form of heterogeneity in some ways among them they remain united by their physical characteristics, language, pride in being Muonyjang with Dinka and their remarkable cultural homogenity. The most important of their similarities is their love for their cattle. They have numerous myths that explain how they acquired cattle in history, how and why they respect cattle and why they do the kind of devotions they do to their cattle. Cattle provide the

Dinka with much of their worldly needs. Cows provide the Dinka with milk or general dairy products which they consider the best and most noble food on earth. They consider the cow as a sacred domestic animal as will be described in the succeeding paragraphs under this chapter.

During dry season months when there are no rains, Dinka herdsmen suffer the burning heat of the open plains due to herding their cattle away from the tree shade of the woodland areas.

When rains come they then endure the onslaught of mosquitoes which swarm in the nights at the cattle camps, away from homes and villages. They also suffer the impact of the rains of the wet seasons while attending to their cattle. Dinka cattle keeping demands constant attention. They must be found good and sufficient pastures and sufficient water. They must be kept in secure places called cattle camps, sometimes in the *luak*, be herded well and protected day and night from wild animals. While they are in the cattle camp and are tethered to their pegs they must be regularly dusted with dung ash called *arop* to make them appear clean and healthy, as dusting cows with *arop* constantly discourages ticks, which Dinka people call *acaak*. Fresh or undried cattle dung, called *wɛɛr*, *wär* in plural, must be collected and stored away from where the cows are tethered. The place where they sleep or spend the nights is well cleared of dirt and mosquitoes are smoked off using dung fire. Collecting cattle refuse or *wär* is a known daily business for boys and girls. Collection of dung or clearance of the tethering ground is done each morning by them. Women, and everybody who owns cattle, are involved in this cleaning exercise, especially if the cattle are many and the boys cannot do the job alone. Cattle sleeping places must be cleaned thoroughly and regularly.

Part of the dung is, however, spread in the morning in order to dry up during the day. Boys and girls besmirch this fresh dung in a specially cleared place for the sun to bake them dry to be later gathered in at about 5 p.m. It is then piled up to form a dung hearth called a *gɔl* which is usually placed at a place called *biöcök*, that is, 'among the big bulls', also called *yɔk-nhiim*, that is, to the front of the kraal. *Gɔl,* the dung hearth, is also put in the middle of the cows' kraal amidst the female cows. Another one is usually put where the calves *(mith yɔk)* are tethered. The dried up cattle dung is piled up into a dung hearth which is then lit with fire to slowly provide smoke to protect the cattle from mosquitoes and other insects such as flies, *luaŋ* and *thoor.*

Apart from clearing their sleeping ground and cleaning them in addition to the business of herding them at grazing times in the pasture forests, men also sleep in the middle of their cattle during the night. Some of the men sleep alongside or in front of the cattle to reduce the danger from wild animals such as lions and hyenas, two predators that usually take the advantage of the darkness of the nights and begin to attack the tethered cattle. The cows are milked for the use of their owners and are assumed to know this. Cattle and whole rams' sacrifice in ritual or religious occasions is the central tenet in the Dinka religious world view. The cattle (and sheep/goats), whole bulls (called *thɔn*) and whole rams (*thön-amɛl*) in particular are, in the eyes of the Dinka, the perfect sacrificial animals acceptable to Nhialic, to their ancestral spirits and to the spirits of their sainted Spear Masters or high priests.

Sacrifice marks every stage of Dinka life such as birth, initiation, marriage, illness, offerings to Nhialic and to the lesser gods which Dinka people call *Jak,* death and annual seasonal cycles as are done for the first rains following the long dry spell of winter. All are marked with sacrifice involving the use of cows, goats and sheep. Besides this, Dinka people do sacrifice for seeds' blessings, annual rituals that are carried out in late April or early May when the first rains begin to fall and before cultivation. Sacrifices are done with cattle to ensure the fertility of the crops, prosperity and general wellbeing of the community during the wet season period that is about to come. Whole bulls and rams are the ones given as a benediction for the new planting season. For the Dinka the cow is second to humans yet is also the first in their experience and relations.

As will be borne out after completing this chapter, cattle are of supreme importance to the Dinka, both symbolically and practically. They form the basis of Dinka livelihood, religion and the entire social structure and with this, it is true to say that the importance of cattle in the Dinka economy has had great influence in the politics of contact between the Dinka and other pastoral peoples neighbouring them, people such as the Nuers in western Upper Nile and the Murle in the eastern parts of Jonglei state. This contact which was initially based on exchange has long since developed into hostile relations when those cattle herding neighbours started to desire access to Dinka cattle and the grazing areas in the toch lands of Bahr el Ghazal. Dinka cattle have been both directly and indirectly a major cause of the rise of conflicts in that they represent social, cultural and economic security. Cows are part of the family and this can be seen from their physical interaction with their owners. Cows meekly bow their heads and their horns to accept a robe to be looped on to their necks in order to be tethered and pegged to the wooden peg called *löc* that halts them from further movement till the next day.

The relationship between cattle and people in Dinka society cannot be effectively described by an Indigenous scholar writing in a foreign language like this. This is because almost everything in Dinka life revolves around cattle and every conversation, idiomatic, symbolic and figurative talk and singing and the entire folklore are all linguistically imbued with references to the cow which they call *weŋ*, *buɔc* when it is a castrated bull and *thɔn* when it is an uncastrated bull. Any conversation with a Dinka man must eventually have a mention of the cow, particularly their most cherished, the bull.

Issues and things daily tackled by Dinka law courts may be eighty

Fig 33: Showing a boy looping the tethering rope onto the cow to peg it

percent related to cattle. The remaining twenty percent may be about women, work activities, rains or no rains and other pursuits of life. Go to the cattle camp and you will certainly find the ideal kind of life in its fullest essence. The pace of life you will find is one in which the cows and their owners stay together, moving to and from grazing pastures and living in such a close symbolic proximity to each other, enjoying a convivial social life together. Take a night in the Dinka cattle camp and you will certainly see what happens right from dawn. As dawn begins to come the cattle camp becomes astir. Boys and girls begin to move among the still sleeping herds. They move in between the herds to stock the dung fires and to collect away the new fresh dung to where they dry them for the evening when it is then used to fuel the camp. Depending on the availability of pasture cattle are then milked and strolled out into the pastures to graze. As the boys go after them to tend or herd the cows in the forest, young men follow them at some given time during the day. They go and participate in herding them till the sun begins to go down in the west which is when all the cows return to their own tethering pegs in the cattle camps where again they are tethered by the boys who came with them and the girls, women and men who remained in the camp during the day.

DINKA CATTLE VOCABULARY AND METAPHORICAL ASSOCIATION

The Dinka obsession for cattle is expressed by them in many ways. If the Hindus revere the cow as their god, Dinka people view the cow as being part of their life. They perceive the cow as itself a reflection of the human community. Existing in a symbiotic relationship with their cattle, Dinka people believe they cannot survive or flourish without cattle. This is because almost every aspect of their social, religious and material life is derived from the cow. The cycle of their seasonal migration constantly keeps them and the cattle in an unbroken contact.

In the Dinka world each cow is known by its name and according to its sex, colour, markings and the shape of its horns. Cows are known and they also know themselves by their lineages, family clusters and previous owners. Cattle are called like humans by the Dinka herders or owners and they respond to such calls from their owners. Like pets, they know their owners. They know when they are to be milked, when they are to be tethered and when they are supposed to be released for grazing. They even know when they are supposed to be taken to the toch at the beginning of the dry season.

They bellow at certain times of the day to draw the attention of their owners when time to milk them comes, when time to release them for grazing comes and generally when they need some attention or when looking or wanting to have their calves with them. Certain cows become so intimate that they go into demise if one of their offspring is unnecessarily given over in default. Cattle and their names are recalled and often recited during marriage negotiations and in the courts of law. The whole of the Dinka aesthetic universe, traditional story making and community belief system, metaphors of colour, of beauty and power dialectics, idiom making, figures of speech, satiric and sarcastic talks, proverbial talk and sayings, all are largely derived by the Dinka from their cattle literature.

According to the Dinka social complex a Dinka man or woman would always exist with his or her cows in such an intimate relationship that the cattle form part of his or her real life. A given cow may be kept as a permanent family cow and its offspring usually form a cluster of lineages since they are not dispensed with. Payment in marriages is not done from these types of cows and their offspring. They aren't given away for whatever reason. Such cows are sometimes kept and preserved as cows of primal parents. Just like the case between man and his wife and his children, some cows are kept to be intimately known to the family members for generations.

An example to this can be cited as a case in point. This example goes thus: some years towards 1950, a community liege in the Awan-Parek area, Madut-Kuendit, was distributing the dowry cattle of his newly married daughter, Agom Madut. The old man allotted one particular heifer of two years old to his newly married wife, Luac Akɛɛn Buk, who became the mother of the author. That heifer was of the colour of 'Nyanakɔl'. The old liege later accredited that heifer as the spirit-cow (*weŋ-atiëp*) for this wife of his. This made the cow *Nyanakɔl* become a cow of *atiëp* and could not be dispensed with. *Nyanakɔl* grew to become a permanently known family cow for years. It became known as *Akɔl Pan-Luac* that is, Akol of the children of Lady Luac Akeen. Akol was a known lactic, milch and dam cow with characteristic attitude of it having to deliver towards spring every year. As such, *Akɔl* became a milking cow every spring season. *Akol* would refuse to go to the toch with the rest of the cattle when winter season dictate going to the toch. It used to refuse in order to keep staying where the family members are. *Akɔl* was therefore known as a cow which spends the dry season with the author's mother in the village. It used to get water from the village well.

For being a good milking cow which used to be milked every year, almost all the children of Lady Luac Akɛɛn were weaned from the milk of the cow *Akɔl*. The author's elder sister, Madut-Kuendit who was the first to be weaned with the milk of *Akɔl*, was later married into Pacuɛr clan, leaving *Akɔl* still a family cow! The author who was also weaned from the milk of *Akɔl* later married while *Akɔl* was still alive. Its offspring formed a cluster and when the cow *Akɔl* subsequently died from old age, family people mourned her. The children of Lady Luac did not eat from its meat.

Some cows among the Dinka can identify with certain families that they even become part of the family. *Akɔl* was such a cow! Those powers in the Dinka unseen world, powers such as the spirits of their dead relatives and ancestors, the gods and clans' divinities called *yiëth*, actively participate also as part of the Dinka cattle complex. This is because spirits of the ancestors of all the dead relatives, including dead parents, do own cows and cows are kept in their names among the herds. Family and clan gods and totems also have their specific cows among the herds in a kraal. They are kept in their names and offspring from those very cows are also kept in their names. Women spirits also own or are assigned a goat and a cow called *Weŋ-atiëp* is cited above. Such a cow, usually a small heifer or small bull, is bought after the bride has married by her father, brother or guardian soon after her marriage. Her husband

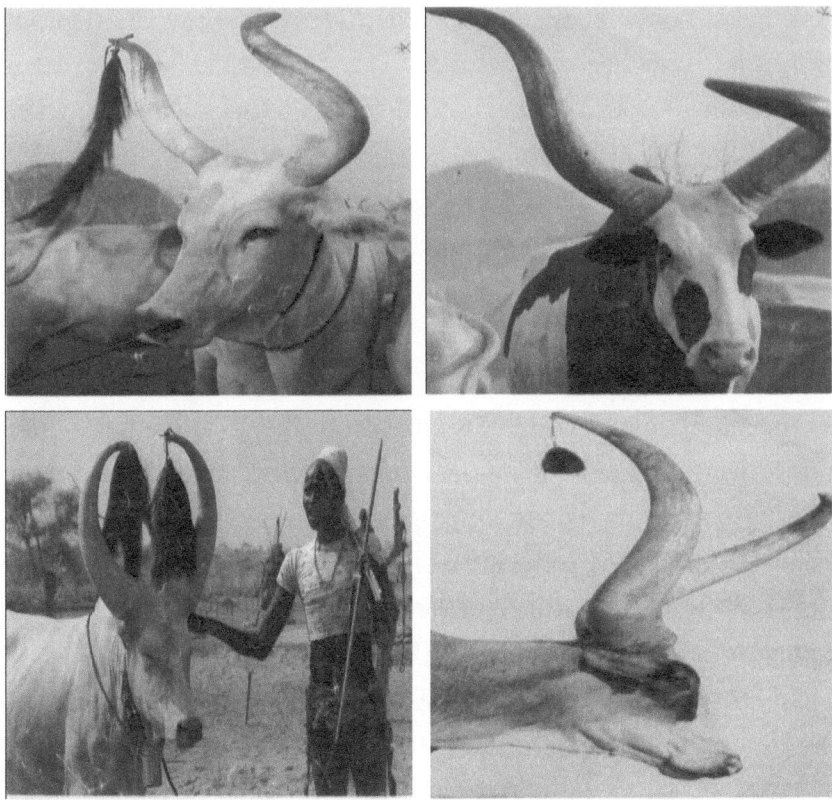

Fig 34: Some selected horns' designs made by Dinka people on their song bulls

also provides her with the same. That cow is kept by her husband as his wife's spirit-cow till it is later taken over by her sons as their mother's spirit-cow. Such a cow and its offspring are not given out except for the marriage of her sons. Even in this case, such a cow and its offspring are not all paid into marriages. One or two from this cow may be paid out into the marriage of her son(s) and the rest remain among the herds to continue the cluster or family line of that spirit-cow.

Should the husband or son dispense with that cow or all of its offspring, the woman's spirit will become angry and she becomes sick and can only recover from that sickness if that cow or offspring from it is restored. When such a cow is reclaimed and brought back a sample of hair from its hump is plucked, libated upon and smeared or rubbed on the sick woman's head. Invocations and pleas to her spirit are then made by the husband, the son or by a *bäny-bith* brought in for this purpose. They make appeals, calling upon the angry spirit to leave the lady now that its cow has been reclaimed and brought back as its cow.

In reality, most of the Dinka people bear names from the colours of their female and male cows and from the style of their cattle horns. During their dancing occasions some of the men hold their arms up above their heads, imitating the curves of the horns of their bulls. Dinka dancing songs are all imbued with rich metaphors about their bulls, cows and girls, great feats and the glorious deeds of their fathers or ancestors in the past.

In his finely groomed song bull of display which he frequently parades before people in the cattle camps and sometimes in the villages, on social, cultural and religious occasions, a Dinka young man can subsume all he knows in his people's traditional lore through singing songs that convey his ability to express and portray the beauty of the bull and of his fiancé. Dinka people make very good linkage between social standing, self esteem, history and the ownership of cattle. Family property is associated with cattle ownership. In the Dinka world any family or person without cows is considered an *abuur,* a person devoid of cattle who can hardly be held with regard or esteem according to the criteria of Dinka society. Political and spiritual importance of a person is backed up and sustained by ownership of cattle, for no Dinka Spear Master or community chief could ascend to such a position if he did not have cattle. A Dinka man needs to own large number of cows to be regarded as a noble man worth respecting.

Apart from these social, ritual and religious uses the prime use of cattle in the Dinka world is for production of milk and perpetuation or continuity of the family through bride price payments in marriages. According to the Dinka the acquisition of cows relates to the setting up of a family large enough to perpetuate one's name after death. This is because in the Dinka concept raising a large family of many wives is also for one's prestige in one's lifetime as more cows and a large family qualify a Dinka person to be among the aristocratic Dinka social class. For the Dinka, wealth in cattle promotes or maintains a person and family to be among this Dinka nobility or upper social class.

To make a successful and conclusive exposition of the Dinka cattle complex is to tackle the very Dinka obsession and interest in their cattle through their vast colour vocabulary. The Dinka obsession and interest in the cow makes them give intense daily focus to the cattle that some people view as them being slaves to the cattle. Others think this obsession and preoccupation with cows should better be described as *'cattle syndrome'*, but, whichever way, this chapter is about Dinka cattle relations.

While Dinka colour vocabulary is about cattle in general, the rich metaphoric vocabulary from cattle is mostly about bulls rather than the milk producing female cows. The metaphorical association between the colour of the cows and some natural features, as well as certain aspects of the Dinka social environment which adds to the Dinka cattle social complex, is the topic of the succeeding paragraphs. Each cow or bull has a colour or a number of colours for which the Dinka formulate a name. That name, be it of a bull or cow, is given to children as birth or personal names when they are born. A Dinka child therefore grows up with that name as a symbol of his or her identification in the family, in the clan and in the society. Cattle colours that are used for Dinka personal names are metaphors which symbolise the actual things in the environment. Those metaphors or symbols try to tell the extent to which Dinka thought is oriented towards the cattle and how each colour represents a given experience.

To describe a cow the Dinka people use certain terms or names preceded by a prefix or suffix. Those prefixes and suffixes identify the sex and status of the cow, that is, whether the cow is a calf, a heifer, a bullock, a grown up cow, a castrated bull or an uncastrated bull, which Dinka educated elites would like to call an ox. Those prefixes and suffixes are added to the kind of colour the cow has. The type of horns, style or lack of horns also play a role in the naming of a particular cow or bull. A bull or ox's name is usually preceded by '**ma**', a prefix used for the male kind, even in humans.

A situation still arises when the Dinka have to differentiate between the castrated and the uncastrated bull. The uncastrated bull or ox for clarity's sake can better be described as a 'whole male'. It takes a Dinka suffix term, *thɔn*. The castrated *bull* takes the prefix term *buɔc*. A bull with no horns on its head is distinguished by the term *macɔɔt*. Heifers take the prefix *nya*, meaning a heifer or young female cow. Indefinite article *a* is used as the prefix for the grown up female cow. Calves are generally preceded by a prefix *manh* from the word *meth*, meaning child. The prefix *manh* is therefore added to the colour names of the calves. The feminine prefix *nya* or the masculine prefix *ma* are also added to the colour of the calf to indicate its gender. *Manh*, used for *manhweŋ*, is neutral and general for both sexes of the calf.

While discussing cattle colours associated with the naming system, mention must be made at first about a very conspicuous parallelism between the prefix '*ma*' used for the bulls and oxen which is also used for men's personal names. Those having the prefix '*ma*' for bulls are likely to be the names for men, and those with the prefix '*a*' for cows are likely to be the names for Dinka human females, girls and women.

Although many Dinka birth or personal names have no connection with the cattle names, the majority of the Dinka personal names or colours are cattle names. Dinka communities from Lakes state and those in the Upper Nile region are particularly fond of using cattle names or colours for naming themselves.

However, all Dinka men and women use cattle names or colours as surnames that they add to their actual names. *Wol,* for example, is a name for a man and when he becomes an adult, an initiated man, he can be given or he can choose a colour name of a bull of his choice to add to his birth name. If he has a bull by the colour of *Madiŋ,* he can become *Wol-Madiŋ*. As he goes into old age he can be called *Wol-Madiŋdit*. That is, the old *Wol-Madiŋ* or *Wol-Madiŋ* the Great.

From this very point, let us try to give examples of the prefixes, suffixes and colour naming for the cows starting with the bulls: The terms for the bull of the colour configuration of *Makuei* comes from two colours, black and white. In this *Makuei* the prefix *ma* indicates the cow is a bull. The word *kuei* in *Makuei* is a name for the fish eagle, a bird of similar black and white colours. The bull in question is wholly black except for its head, which is white.

The author's father, Madut Aköök, also known famously by his ox-name as Madut-Kuëndit, chose to take the colour configuration of this fish eagle in reference to his bull, which was fully black in colour except for the head, which was all white like the fish eagle. He therefore became Madut-Makuei during his youthful age. As he started to grow into old age, his being called Madut-Makuei turned to Madut-Makuendit. This, in his late life, turned to Madut-Kuëndit. Surnames are used by Dinka people mostly to call themselves in an expression of respect and regard.

While a castrated bull is called *Makuei*, a whole bull of the same colour configuration is called *Makuen-Thɔn*. A grown up female cow of the same colour configuration is merely called *Kuei*. A bull-calf of the very colour is also call *Makuei* while a cow-calf or heifer of the same colour configuration is usually regarded as *nya (n) Kuei*. Some Dinka call it *Nanykuei* and a bull of this colour with no horns on its head is called *Makuei acɔɔt*. Adjectively, it becomes *Makuen-acɔɔt.*

Dinka colour vocabulary is largely based on cattle colours. When cloth came from Europe and beads came from the oriental world the Dinka people easily associated the colours of those beads and cloths with the colours of their cattle and those new things easily fitted into their linguistic culture. Therefore, a black or red cloth material (alath) with white spotted colours was easily given the name of *Ma Kuac*, a term for a spotted bull, a colour which was picked from that of the leopard, *Kuac*. Since the colour of the leopard (red, white and black) was taken by the Dinka people to use for spotted cows, it therefore goes without saying that a grown up female cow with those colours could normally go with the name of Akuac, the '*a*' preceding Kuac being a female prefix. The female calf goes with the name of *nya (n) Kuac*, which is a name for a heifer-calf with the colours of a leopard.

A bull with bridling strips of colours like that of a mongoose, *Agoor* in Dinka, and crocodile or *Nyang* is called *Manyang, nyaang* for a cow and *nya (n) nyang* for a heifer. The green colour called *Ngök* is used for bulls or cows of the same colour. For instance, Dinka people call a bull with the tawny colour of the nigritana grass, awaar *Maŋök* and *Ngök* for a cow of such colour. A heifer is therefore *nya* (n) *Ngök*.

The red colour like that of raw meat or pure blood is used by the Dinka to call a bull of that colour *Malual*, *Aluɛɛl* for a grown up female cow and *nya (n) Luel* for a heifer. A heifer is what the Dinka people call *dɔu*, which is the Dinka name for a cow-calf. *Yar-Tuɔŋ* is the Dinka colour for a bright cow, white like an egg. Dinka people use the names *Yar* and *Mayar* for a cow and bull that is pure white in colour. We therefore have whitish cows called *Yar* and a purely white bull *Mabior* (Rek) or *Mabor* (Agaar, Gɔk and eastern Dinka). Rek people also call such a bull *Mayar*. A cow of this colour which is called *Yar*, is *nya (n) Yar* when it is a heifer and *Mabior-Thɔn* when it is a whole bull or ox. People in eastern Bahr el Ghazal also call it *Ayör*. They call it *Mayör* when it is *Buɔc*, a castrated bull. For something black like soot the Dinka call it *Col*. Like is the case with the white colour, the black colour '*Col*' is used only for female cows and not for the bulls or oxen. A female cow carries the prefix *a* before *col* so that it is call *Acol*. A heifer of that black colour is called *nya (n) Cool* with a double *o*. But a bull is called *Macar,* old or young. It is *Macar-Thɔn* if it is not castrated and *Macardit* if it is an old bull.

Dinka children acquire basic vocabulary of names of the various colours of things in the environment as part of language learning. They also learn how to transfer those configurations of colour to the livestock, goats, sheep and cattle, and to all domestic animals including dogs and birds such as chickens. A Dinka child begins to know the colour of their bulls or cows in general before he/she sees the animals or items from which the colour given to the cow or bull was taken. A child is able to know the bull *Makuac* or the cow *Akuac* before he/she encounters a leopard, *Manyang* or *Nyaang* before he/she sees the crocodile.

A Dinka child or person is therefore able to recognise the configuration of a particular colour in nature by reference to what he/she first knows of it in the cow on which his/her attention from childhood was concentrated and focused.

Dinka perceptions of colour, light and shade in the world around them is also connected with their recognition of colour configuration in their cattle. Suppose Dinka society did not have cattle, which gave them such a rich colour vocabulary, it is astonishing how the Dinka would have found a way of describing visual experiences in terms of colour, light and darkness. Some of the Nilotic communities, the Luo for example, do not have such an elaborate colour vocabulary based on cattle colours as is done by the Dinka and the Nuers. This is because they no longer depend on cattle as they lost the importance of cattle in their economy long ago. The Luo therefore do not have poetic images and symbolism based on cattle colours and names.

Like the example given of the author's father above, Dinka boys begin to take colour names of their bulls when they reach manhood or are initiated. They add those new names called surnames to their original traditional personal or family names given at birth. The new name, also called their ox-name or *Miör,* starts to be used by intimate friends, age mates and family members till the young man becomes known and begins to be called by such a name later by the wider community. A young man comes to be identified with the bull whose colour he has taken for his surname. He is then associated with that particular bull which becomes his song bull, the one that he would always proudly parade before girls and before all the people. He will create and develop praise-songs for that bull and will invent ways of referring to its appearance, making such songs with imageries and symbolism fitting to that bull and its colour. Among the Dinka the talent of composing songs with convincing imagery derived from the traditional colour names of cattle is regarded as a mark of intelligence in a young man, and although certain Dinka men are gifted with the art of song making more than others, Dinka society is generally acknowledged for its poetic ingenuity and originality and this is made possible by their cattle culture.

DINKA CATTLE COLOUR IMAGERY

Dinka people are very good at literature and they do great exploits in cattle-related imageries and symbolism. Examples of the Dinka use of imagery in their names are very replete but a few can be cited below:

A man having a dark black display song bull, a bull with the colour of *Macar* will not be pleased to be directly addressed by his age mates as *Macar*, the actual colour of his bull. He would prefer to be addressed using one or more metaphoric names related to the very black colour of his bull. Calling him *Tim Atiep,* 'the tree which provides shade,' would be the best way of referring to the blackness of his bull, *Macar*. He may alternatively choose to be called *Köör-Acɔm*, 'seeks for snails', after the black ibis bird (*agaal*) which is known to seek snails and is a dark black bird. He could also better be called *Bun-Anyiɛr,* 'thicket of the buffalos', which suggests the darkness of the bush in which the buffalos always take rest during those sunny days. He may also call himself *Akiu-yakthok*, 'cries out in the spring's drought'. This is an imagery referring to the small black bird which Dinka people call *ajiëc,* a bird that makes its characteristic cry at this time of the year, that is, during the dawns of late April and early May when rains have started to fall but drought sets in again. This small black bird, *ajiëc,* mostly makes its characteristic cries during the dawn when people are about to wake up or have started travelling.

For a man having a white bull, *Mabior*, as his song bull, he could be addressed thus: *Atït yök Pɛɛi*, 'gives light to the cattle while awaiting moonlight to come up'. This metaphor refers to the brightness of the bull *Mabior* which is compared with the brightness of the moon during the night. He may choose to be called *Tuɔŋ Wut,* 'ostrich egg', suggesting the bull *Mabior* to be as white as the ostrich egg. The mere hearing of the ostrich egg brings to mind the white image of an egg.

A man having a bull with white and black colours which Dinka people call *Majök*, 'marks of the creator', may choose to be called *Buŋ-Aciëk,* meaning 'the colour from the creator'. Alternatively, the man may choose to be known as *Jök-Apiöök*, emphasising the whiteness of the white parts on his bull *Majök* in contrast to the black part on his bull. *Apiöök* would be a metaphoric imagery for the white elephant tusk which is made into *apiöök* and is worn as armlets and wristlets.

One of the men owning this type of a bull in Rekland decided to give to himself a surname of Arumjök, after the black and white markings of this bird called arumjök, the sacred ibis. Another man called himself Arɛc Ruääi, 'spoiler of the marriage'. The metaphor involved in this Arɛc Ruääi is that the bull Majök is always one of the much valued type of bull for its colours. A bride's relatives are not always ready to see that Majök is not among the dowry paid on their girl during marriage if the bridegroom's side did have it. If the bridegroom's side refuses to pay that type of a bull into the marriage, that marriage will surely be spoiled, hence the surname Arɛc Ruää*i*.

A young man having a bull of the colour *Malual*, the red-brown bull, may decide to be call *Ayiëëk'Bud*, meaning, 'shaking the bush', after the behaviour of a lion when it is in a bush. The lion is also known to be of this colour. Another young man may want to be called *Aruël-yɔk*, 'warming the cattle'. This refers to the red rays of sunlight that show as it appears coming up in the morning from the east. Another man may call himself *Akɛr-yɔk Ma'c*, 'throwing the cattle with fire'. The metaphor of fire in this case is that of the red colour configuration of the bull *Malual*.

A man with *Acɔɔt*, a bull with no horns, for example, may call himself *Anhiar Kol* after the hippopotamus that has no horns and is of this red colour of the bull. The hippo is believed to always stay in a cool water pool which the Dinka people call *kol*, the deeper part of the river which is usually very cold.

A man having a grey ox called Malou can be called Ländit, 'the big game', after the elephant which is of this colour. Another may call himself Alor-Giir, 'going towards a cyclone'. A cyclone is known to have the Malou or grey colour configuration. Someone with a bull having very big horns may be called Ayɛɛc-Läi, 'carrying the animal', after the elephant, which has very big and long horns called tusks. Great Chief Giir Thiik, chief of Apuk-Pathuɔn territory in today's Gogrial East county did have such a surname in his lifetime. He was known as Giir-Ayɛɛc Läi. He was Ayɛɛc L*äi* for his bull, which did have long horns figuratively said to symbolise the elephant tusks. A certain *Makuɔk Mawien* from the Lian section of

Awan-Parek in Northern Tonj was called *Adhoŋror*, 'breaks the trees in the forest'. This imagery refers to the elephant which is known to break trees in the forest. *Makuɔk*'s bull must have been a big grey bull of the *Malou* colour of the big elephant. Someone in the eastern parts of Tonj has a surname *Athek Luak*, 'respecting the byre'. This metaphor refers to the fact that elephants in the Dinka world are known to pursue people but would stop if a person it is pursuing runs into a luak. There is a Dinka story and belief that elephants do respect the byre, because a luak is big like itself and carries the same grey (*malou*) colour which is the colour of the elephant.

A bull or ox with spots of the white and black colour configuration which Dinka people call *Maker*, that is, the colour of the soldier ant known by the Dinka as *ajiiŋ*, makes its owner call himself *Majiiŋ*, after the columns of the black ants carrying white particles, which may be grain particles or ants' eggs or termites. A female cow of this colour is called *Ajiiŋ*. Someone may, for instance, surname himself as *Yanh-Nuɛr,* for a bull that resembles the monitor lizard which Dinka people call '*agaany*'. Most Nuers do not eat agaany because it is their community totem, yath or divinity. A bull of this kind is called *Manyang*. It usually has a pattern of rather dotted lines of red-brown and white colours with some shades and light showing black spots like the monitor lizard.

A man having an exceptionally white bull may also call himself *Makuel*, 'star-ox', after the brightness of the stars when they shine during a clear night sky. He may call himself *Baai-Ciɛlic,* 'the courtyard'. This is a metaphor which refers to the cleanness of the courtyard, for Dinka women and girls are known for their serious attention to the cleanliness of the courtyards of their homes. Somebody may be called *Kɛr-Kuei*, referring to a bull with a white head and white-black patches on its body that appears like the fish eagle, like *Majök, Makër, Maŋär* and *Marial*. Such a bull is much admired by the Dinka. Someone with the bull *Majiiŋ* can also be called *Abï-nyieer*, 'bringing rain drizzles'. This refers to the spots of light showers which drizzling rain makes on a person's body.

A bull with the bridling colour configuration of a mongoose rodent, which Dinka people call agoor, is called Manyang because it is likened with the crocodile and the rodent mongoose. This is because it has the strips of lines resembling those of the crocodile and rodent. A man with a bull of such colour configuration would surname himself as Arɛc Mɛɛi, 'spoiler of the fishing occasion or the fish battle'. This metaphor refers to the crocodile, which in many fishing occasions frightens Dinka fishing parties from the river. Referring to the same crocodile, the owner of this type of bull may call himself Ayup-Riäi, 'the striker of the canoe'. Crocodiles are known to sometimes strike at the fishing canoes in rivers they inhabit. The imagery referred to here is of the colour of the crocodile simulated with that of the bull.

A bull with the colour configurations of the chanting goshawk, which the Dinka people call *lith*, is called *Malith*. It is also the colour of the baboon which Dinka people call *agɔɔk*. *Köör-Ajiith*, 'the lion of the chickens', is a surname taken by some men having such grey bulls of the baboon or hawks' colour. They used it in reference to the habit of the chanting goshawks which always hunt the chickens.

Referring to a bull having white and black colours as its main colour configuration called *Majök*, a Dinka man may call himself *Ajökdit*. Great Chief Parek Machar of Awan-Parek was popularly known as *Parek Ajökdit* in his lifetime. Sometimes Dinka people use a combination of colours referring to both the colour of the cow which bore the bull and the colour of the bull itself. Someone having a black bull with a white head but whose mother was a cow with a red colour configuration and white head (*yɔm*) could be called *Makuën- yɔm, Makuei*, the son of *yɔm*'.

The author of this book is popularly known in his rural countryside area as *Anei Maker-Akuac*. His *Maker* bull from which he got the surname was borne by a cow of the soldier ant colour, *Akuac*. Somebody may be called *Marial-Ajak* from his bull *Marial*, which was borne by a cow with the colour configuration of *Ajak*. Ajak is a cow with red colouration on the hind parts, beginning from the lumbar to the hip and down the thighs and legs. The rest of the body is white but another red colouration covers the shoulders, the neck and the front limbs down the hooves. Great paramount chief of Lou-Ariik, also known as Lou-Mawien territory, did have two surnames for which he was famously known in his lifetime. He was known as *Ariik-Alɔmŋaar*, that is, *Ariik*, who has a bull with big patches of white and black colours of *Marial* on his rib sides. He was also known as *Ariik Nganybɛt*. *Nganybɛt* was a bull of the colour of *Marial*, the type of bull with the colours which Dinka people admire more than any other colour. They take this type of bull to be the first rate colour of choice. Dinka people buy it very expensively with up to ten cows at times. It is bought with such a number of cows if one does not have it among his herds. *Nganybɛt* is a metaphor referring to the bull *Marial* which was left eight times by people who failed to succeed in buying it. They left it with the owner for not meeting the number and the types of cows needed by its owner until it was Ariik Mawien who finally came and succeeded in bringing the types and numbers of cows the owner wanted in exchange for his bull. The story around the purchase of this *Marial* bull was heard all over the territory of Lou. It went far and wide, echoing across territories to as far as those distant lands of Apuk of Giir Thiik in Gogrial in the west and to as far as the Luacjäng territory in the east. News of this also went to those areas like Thɔny in the far south, after Apuk-Juwiir in the Thiet area. Great Ariik Mawien was therefore given the second surname of *Nganybɛt* in reference to that hard-won bull *Marial*.

For the exquisite beauty seen in the crane bird, *awet-marial*, those who possess *Marial* of such colour configuration of the crane bird use

*Fig 35: Showing awet-marial,
the crane bird*

its colour as a surname for themselves. Deng-Awet, in the Lou-Ariik area is one such example of a man with the surname *Awet-Marial*. A completely black bull with a line or stripe of white colour on the neck, particularly one in which the white stripes pass by the bull's lap like that of the black cobra, is usually called *Aröl-Jök* and here comes the famous surname of *Agiem-Röljök* from the same Lou-Ariik territory. *Agiem-Röljök* may have got such a surname from great *Agɔth Muɔr* from Apuk of *Pathuɔn* in present Gogrial East county. *Agɔth Muɔr* was popularly known during his famous lifetime as *Agɔth-Röljök*.

Git-beek, 'artisted the crane's way', is a surname mostly used by those who own the bull *Marial*. They always choose such a meta-

*Fig 36: Showing the Marial bull,
the precious bull of the Dinka people*

phoric surname for the similarity in colour configuration between the bull in question and the beek bird.

The importance of the bull *Marial* to the Dinka stems out of the fact that this type of bull increases the chance of winning the bride in a marriage contest over a particular star girl in a given territory. As *Marial* embodies the value of even ten cows, which is mostly its price to purchase, and is the bull colour which represents wealth and pride, a suitor whose dowry cattle has among them this bull *Marial* is sure to win the decision of the bridewealth's side in his favour.

For this reason, *Marial* is a special colour in Dinka cattle keeping. If a lucky man on one morning finds his cow to have delivered among the herds a bullock of the classical *Marial* colour, he will certainly be expected to make a feast in which he will kill a number of ordinary bulls and rams as services to the public in celebration for the birth of the cow with the colour of *Marial*.

In any case, it is difficult to exhaust the entire Dinka ox or bulls' names with their multiple colour symbolisms for it is not practically convenient to present the entire Dinka colour metaphor related to all the cattle in a book like this. The few examples given above may suffice to show the interdependence of the Dinka perception of colour and shading in nature and in cattle. Examples given can show the Dinka effort to link cattle with features of the natural and social environment through perceived similarities of colour and shading. With their vast experience of colour metaphors Dinka people are able to understand a wide range of natural features with cattle as the central theme.

CASTRATION AND NON-CASTRATION OF BULLS

At this point mention has to be made of the Dinka practice of castrating most of the bullocks, the bull-calves. Two crucial reasons dictate whether a bull-calf or bullock is to be castrated or left uncastrated in order to be a future uncastrated ox which Dinka people call *thɔn*. The first reason comes from the Dinka unquenchable thirst for song bulls of display which they use for aesthetic purposes. This makes the Dinka people castrate as many bulls as they can. The issue of castrated (*biöc*) bulls paid in marriages is another factor. A certain number of first class bulls called *adɔŋ*, usually ten and onwards, are always demanded by the bride's side during marriage negotiations and dowry payment. The number of bulls in one's kraal is also used as a measure for knowing the number of one's cows in the society. Cows' pegs are lined up in a row of ten pegs from the calves to where a first class bull is. This is so that the cows of so and so are numerically known by the number of bulls he has. Ten bulls means one hundred cows, for instance. Each kraal or *gɔl* must have among the herds one or two *thɔn*, one of which must be *thɔn cï ŋiiny* and the other as *dhuk* which is *thɔn* being *thɔn*still groomed, soon to take over from the aging *thɔn*. There can, however, be more than the two uncastrated bulls in one kraal or for one person.

Dinka people classify cows into those that can be called dam cows and those that are called stud cows. Dam cows are good milch cows, are likely to produce heifer calves (daau) and are also likely to produce more milk. A cow which produces more milk is called weŋ-ciɛk or miciɛɛk, the stud cow. Where a bullock of a valued colour such as Marial is produced by a good milch or dam cow, it becomes very difficult for the owner to decide whether to castrate it or not! A predicament comes in between castrating it to become a song bull of display and keeping it uncastrated to produce heifers that could also become stud cows. In most cases a Dinka man in this predicament would prefer to castrate the bullock to be his song bull of display, than have it remain as thɔn for stud purposes. He would trust that his same dam cow (midaau) will still produce for stud a bullock of less important colour which he can keep as a whole ox. In many parts of the Dinka land it is very rare to find a much valued bull of the Marial colour kept to be thɔn. However, some people can go against this conventional concept. They can be so brave as to keep a bullock of the valued colour of Marial or Majök so that it becomes thɔn. Again, the underlying purpose is to let it produce more of its kind so that the owner could have the chance to have bulls of the more valued types, Marial, Majök, Makër or Maŋär. Dinka people place value on colour and beauty more than milk production although this may sometimes convey some kind of hypocrisy, for milk as food is also among the reasons why Dinka people rear cattle.

In any case, there are certain criteria followed in choosing not to castrate a bullock in order to remain as *thɔn*. A bullock destined to be *thɔn* usually has certain features detectable from its appearance as soon as it is born or once it begins to show its true features. A small suckling bullock or bull-calf showing a big hump (*duööl*) with a big dew lap (*lɔk*), a rather short but nice looking tail, called *yöl*, big buttocks called *aŋuim* and also the eyes and face peculiar to that of *thɔn,* such a bullock would dictate the owner to leave it uncastrated to become *thɔn* in future. Certain other features such as the kind of hooves (ungulas) it has and the way it stands can also add up to being allowed to grow into a future *thɔn*. The would-be *thɔn* also shows a sturdy or muscularly built neck with a thick face and head. When those features are seen in a bull-calf the chances of allowing it to become *thɔn* are therefore greater.

Other determinants for making a bull-calf become *thɔn* are also of significance to be mentioned here. Most of the bull-calves from what are called sacred cows or cows accredited to family gods (*jak*), to primal parents such as *Garaŋ* and *Deŋ,* to the spirits (*atiip*) of important ancestors and dead fathers, to the spirit (*atiëp*) of one's mother or one's wife and/or to the clan's totem are not castrated. They are allowed to grow to become *thön* because they are the usual objects for ritual and religious sacrifices and offerings to those gods, primal parents, spirits, ancestors, fathers and clan's totems.

Notwithstanding those factors described above, only a few bull-calves end up to become whole bulls. *Thön* are not allowed to be many in one's cattle kraal for reasons of security among the cattle themselves. Uncastrated bulls grow up with fierce attitudes. They are always inclined to go out to look for another *thɔn* to fight with. If there are so many *thön* in one kraal or cattle camp they will be engaged in fighting with each other and killing themselves so that there can be virtually no stability in the cattle camp. There can be no time even for them to cohabit with the cows that are in the productive age and times. This is therefore one of the reasons why Dinka cattlemen do not have many whole bulls among their herds. The issue of a bullock being allowed to grow to become *thɔn* is not a random thing. As earlier explained it is not just any bull-calf that can become *thɔn*. *Thɔn* come from those criteria described above. Bullocks are also castrated as a way to control those with unimpressive colours and types deemed not necessary to multiply among the herd because they are unnecessary or unwanted and cannot be allowed to produce more of their kind. Despite this general practice there are some Dinka communities that do not show seriousness in this and their cows are just cohabitated, even by *thön* from unacceptable types and colours. Those are behaviours of modern times. Conservative Dinka tribes, Luacjang as a case in point, do not allow whole bulls from unknown sources to cohabit with their cows. This is to keep their herd pure and coming from *thön* whose mothers and fathers are known by their owners.

OX-NAMES FOR DINKA CATTLE OWNERS

With all the complexities involved in the Dinka naming system, a man's metaphorical ox-name is not expected to refer directly to anything in his personal appearance, but in songs the same man may be given several metaphorical ox-names as was the case of Chief *Ariik Mawien* who in his lifetime had two ox-names, *Alɔmŋaar* and *Nganybɛt,* as earlier explained. Even those who do not have bulls of such colour configuration may choose to name themselves with ox-names of the colours they admire, colours that in songs become a source of praise and pride. Dinka self esteem and standing in the community are intimately bound up with cattle in this way. In the rural countryside someone with no ox-name may not be found among Dinka men. If there is, then that person may be a sloven. Some women and girls are even given ox-names attached to their birth names just as is the case with men.

DINKA IDIOMS (MAANY) ARE LINKED TO CATTLE

The Dinka daily mode of expressions, speech styles, phraseologies and talk jargon are idiomatically linked to cattle, for it is through cattle that Dinka people, especially men, explicitly conceive their lives and thus the lives of their cattle. Their versatile knowledge in the vocabulary surrounding the cattle is expressed through talking, using all those linguistic devices. In Rek lands, dancing young men at a dance occasion can be found saying their dance-idioms full of cattle names, particularly of their song bulls and oxen. Dancing young men raise their arms up simulating the horns of their song bulls. Even when alone, not in a dance, a young Dinka man can be found or seen posturing to simulate his bull's horns. He does this just for enjoyment as he sings and recites his idioms about his bulls.

Dinka herdsmen are known to spend most of their daytime herding their cattle and because of their continuous stay with the cattle they become intimately associated and so identified with them that they behave like the cattle themselves. Some herdsmen could even be found in the pasture bellowing like their oxen or bulls. Such things as singing for the bull, for an admired girl, idioms making, dancing and the curving of raised arms during the dance are some of the ways Dinka men express *dheeŋ*, which is gentlemanship, handsomeness or beauty. When dancing in a dance occasion or when parading a song bull a young Dinka man makes such bodily postures and attitudes considered by the Dinka people as graceful. A number of admired varieties of movement are introduced during the dance by a young Rek Dinka man as his dance gestures. Examples of these are the lowering and bending of the left arm or of both in imitation of the artificially formed horns of his song bull of display. The kind of dance played by the Rek Dinka of the east and central parts of Rekland is called *magoŋ*. Although the Agaar Dinka do a characteristic leaping up kind of a dance called *dheeŋ nhial*, unlike that of the Rek, they all raise up their arms the same to imitate their bulls. The Agaar girls do the same and even do it more than their Agaar men during the dance. Although Malual Dinka men make their dance using one leg, they also make such bodily postures and mimic their bulls' horns as they raise their arms up with various curves, as do the Rek and Agaar girls.

When gathering momentum for the actual dance to take place, Rek Dinka men run in an organised line, circling the dance ground. This running in a circle demands serious exercise in which people are seen sweating profusely. In this Rek type of dance men advance and retreat, guiding or driving their female partners backwards and forwards. Rek dancing young men could at times be seen stamping the ground and shouting their idioms before the girls and the playground audience. Young men in this way regard themselves as oxen and the girls as the cows. The stamping and idioms making and the shouts they make are stylisations of the sounds and vigorous movements of bulls and oxen. This activity is based upon the themes of the running of the oxen (*thön*) when they run with the cows in the herd, manoeuvring and sensitising in an effort to cohabit them. In Dinka thought, bulls or *thön* are the equivalents of young warriors in the camp.

Thɔn, the whole bull, is the centre and head of all the herds of a given kraal or *wut*. It is seen by all the cattle as the father of the herds and could be simulated with the father in the family and viewed as the senior figure among the herds in the cattle camp. *Thɔn* is the begetter and master of the herd just as much as the husband or father is in the family. When cattle camp people move with their cattle to another camp, it is the castrated bulls that are bedecked with tassels on their horns and bells tied on their necks. Tethering ropes called *wiin* are coiled on every cow, which must also carry its own rope but *thɔn*, the master of the herds, is spared from all this. It has special roles of begetting and protection of the herd from dangerous animals. *Thɔn*, among the herds, is known to play this protection role when it chases away a strange whole bull coming from another herd and when it fights with even the lions which in some cases attack the herds. *Thɔn* in a herd knows all the cows and bulls of its kraal. It knows which cow is ready to be cohabited and which cow is not. *Thɔn* among the herds symbolises the man or husband in a family. Castrated bulls are like ordinary men in the society. Female cows are like women folk, while *thɔn* in the cattle camp is like a hero, a war hero. He is like the chief or head man in a community or family. *Thɔn*, like the husband in a family, is a symbol of procreation and is therefore viewed as the master of the herd. While human beings and cattle are substituted for each other in restitution for homicides and are exchanged out in compensation for some human lost, *thɔn* is usually not handed over in blood dia compensations and in compensations for loss incurred by its owner(s). Whole bulls are very important and are intimately associated with virility and fertility of the cattle and of their human owners.

When discussing Dinka cattle relations like this, mention must be made that sheep and goats are not directly equated with human beings in all the Dinka transactions. It is only the cow that is equated to humans and that is why it is the only accepted medium of exchange in marriages and in blood dia compensations. Even in minor and major injuries it is the cow that is paid to compensate the precious blood lost by the injured person. In minor cases, however, inferior creatures such as goats and sheep can be made to represent the cattle. For larger compensations like bridewealth and homicides, payment is always made in cattle, not with goats or sheep. In the Dinka world, there is a hierarchy of values in relation to man and his domestic animals. On top are human beings, beneath them are the cattle and beneath the cattle are the sheep, then the goats. The rest of the inferior creatures then follow. Goats and sheep may sometimes be substituted for the cattle as cattle can be substituted for humans.

In a cattle camp, a young man who has no display song bull to parade about will sometimes take an ox bell, called *löth*, and begin to walk about with it, singing his songs and ringing the bell to simulate the presence of the ox. Men also shout out their ox-names in an exercise which Dinka people call *muöc* or *Maany*, a poetic saying or phrase shouted out in praise of one's song bull. Dinka men are famously known to do these poetic shouting praises for their bulls at many of their social occasions, such as in dancing occasions, marriage ceremonies, courting, when parading their song bulls and when young men walk together in groups while the girls are milking cows in the cattle camp. They also do this while leading their decorated bulls and singing their songs. In so doing, they draw the attention of the girls to their bulls and to themselves. Both the bulls and those young men please the girls and together they form a unity with the meaning of what cattle camp resilience is.

This enchantment and preoccupation of young Dinka men over their song bulls of special beauty is also found in Dinka girls. This fact is better illustrated by the fact that Dinka girls are always ready to prefer a somewhat ugly young man who has a fine bull in preference to a handsome man having an indifferent bull. Most girls are enchanted by young men who praise them in praise-songs called *këëp, wɛc* or *waak* and can fall in love with them even if they do not own sufficient cows to marry with. This indicates that those who excel in aesthetic practices have a place among girls. This is generally known to be the case with all the girls the world over.

In a Dinka cattle camp a young man who owns a decorated bull, who wears good beads and other fineries, coupled with nice praise-songs, is enough to be accepted and loved by several girls. In most cases, Dinka girls are attracted by whoever owns beautiful bulls and or whoever has cattle. The songs and their inherent praises to girls is another source of attraction to girls.

The following song from one Dinka young man from Kɔŋgöör in Warrap state, also translated into English and interpreted, is given below as an example of the role played by bulls and girls in most of the Dinka songs:

Cɔl Këëër adεp nhom!
Cɔl Këëër adεp nhom,
Ku bi yala riau-riau,
Ku Ayaŋ Agany Akol,
Määth acie Kën alεεŋ
Nyan bäny!

Mänh moc na cï dhiëëth
Aku bï ya kai ë tik,
Ku nεk ariaukeen
Ku pec weŋ, nääk weŋ ala yic mël.

Ala yic mël, Ayaŋ Agaany!
Maŋardiën Ayaŋ Agaany,
Kït aya wur-biöök!

Gem pïu, nyaal ë kɔn cï döu,
Gem pïu, nyaal ë kɔn cï döu
Aku kee kïn miit cɔl aciëk mawargak kou,
Muɔɔr maper!

Ku mijiɛɛk Deŋ Kön ayie rou,
Tök aya yɔɔk ë tuŋ nhial!
Nhial gääric ë kɔɔu acï tir bi nɔk nhiäk
Tö le diɛt ke göör!?

Aku ka ke gɔɔr na wën ayie Deŋ Kön
Wä mahn Ajak, ke yïk ya riɛn kië.
Go yinär, Ngɔth Jiel Marial yɔc
Juɛk dhëëŋ!

Ku Ayaŋ Agaany, nyanë bäny,
Awaa ï yiee ca wut dɔkic
Maper-Lual ë këër nhom ɛɛɛ!"

Translation:
"Let the kraal's front burn!
Let the kraal's front burn!
As to glimmer with blinks.
And you, Ayak, daughter of Agany Akol,
Friendship (love) isn't for a joke,
Daughter of the chief!

When a gentleman is born,
And he came as the first child to the mother,
And rituals are made for his birth,
And a bull is offered to the gods in sacrifice,
For his welomem, it entails an oath,
For sacrificing a bull is oath in itself!

It entails an oath,
Ayak, daughter of Great Agaany!
My bull, Maŋar, is for you, Ayak Agaany!

*Maŋar has large patches covering of white and black colours
parts of his body!
Its colours are like when you go to dish water out at a drying
pool!
Its colour is like you go to dish water at a drying water pool!
And on it is a short, red rainbow colour!
My white and red- coloured bull Maper!*

*And the two bulls of Deŋ Kön are of the
Majak colour of the pelican bird
One has horns pointing high up into the sky!
"When you fierce the sky with such long poles,
Will you not commit murder one day
When birds come to hover above you?"
Well, they hovered on till it was Deŋ Kön,
Son of Ajak who gave my surname!*

*Then, my maternal uncle,
Ngöth Jiel, Marial-yɔc
Increased the beauty of my bulls
By offering me an additional bull!*

*And you, my dear Ayak Agaany,
Daughter of the chief, I have come!
I have come to your Kraal's end with
My red, the Maper bull!"*

SONG INTERPRETATION

The young man, the owner of this song, was a man from Kɔŋgöör territory in the Akɔp sub-region of Tonj North county, Warrap state. His mother, according to the song, came from Lɔu Ariik, a neighbouring territory of Great Ariik Mawien. The young man was in love with the daughter of the son of the chief of Kɔŋgöör territory, Ayak Agaany Akol. The song was sung in the 1960s, about half a century ago. The song in its first stanza of six lines begins with a clear metaphor of colour and love to a daughter of the chief of the territory, Ayak Agany Akol. The six stanzaic lines introduce a young man who came and stood at the last end of the cattle camp (kraal) of those of his loved one, Ayak Agany. Standing with him is his favourite song bull of the most preferable colour, *Maɲar*. In the song, right at the outset, he makes a very powerful metaphor derived from the colours of his bull, *Maɲar*. To him, the shining black and white colours of his bull gave glimmering pied bright lights that blink on and off, thereby making the cattle of those of Ayak's kraal to be clearly seen even if it was now dark, late in the evening. He announces his arrival to the cattle camp of his beloved girl Ayak. To further please the girl, he gives a regard to her as a girl from the nobility, a daughter of a chief, not one from the ordinary folk.

In the second stanza of four lines, he introduces his background. He talks of his importance. He describes himself as a gentleman with primogenitary rights in their family. He introduces himself as the firstborn son of his mother and, of course, of his father and that is why his father slaughtered a bull at his birth to welcome his first child who, praise be to God, was a male child. According to him, a bull was sacrificed as a thanksgiving offer to God. This was in appreciation of what God did for them, the parents. If Ayak is important for being a daughter of the chief, he also is important for being the firstborn son for his parents. In the Dinka world, firstborn sons have limitless rights and opportunities and this is probably what gave him such a bull of the colour of *Maɲar*. He stated his strength to Ayak to please her even more.

Having emphasised his importance in the second stanza, he came to the third stanza of three verses or lines. Here, he declares to Ayak that the bull *Maŋar* that came with him is for her marriage, not for any other girl. He makes Ayak know it is going to be paid on her as a dowry bull and will soon belong to her brother. He goes on explaining to his lover the spaces covered by the colours on his bull *Maŋar*. This is a restatement of the colour symbolism he introduced in the first stanza. Up to this point of his poetic song, it is the bull *Maŋar* which is still the dominant bull.

In the fourth stanza, the colours on *Maŋar* are more explained in that they glitter like those of algae (*nyaal*) in a pool which is drying up. Then he announces to the girl (Ayak) the fact of him having another bull by the colour of *Maper*, the colour of the *bushback* which, according to him, has a short red colour of rainbow crossed on a very white colour (like paper, *mawargakou*).

Beside *Maŋar* and *Maper*, he also tells Ayak in stanza five that he has two other bulls of the colour of the pelican bird called *Majak*. He calls them *Mijiɛɛk* because they are two. To him, one of those two bulls has very tall horns, pointing high up into the sky. Now, at this point, he turns to this tall-horned bull, which he begins to question. As a typical case of personification to the bull, he asks that bull, saying, "will you not commit murder one day when birds begin to hover over you!?" In stanza six, he says the birds hovered on and on till his father therefore gave him the name, his new ox-name.

In the last verse of this stanza, he tells Ayak that his maternal uncle, Ngɔth Jiel, called by his ox-name Marial-yɔc, gave him an additional bull which added to the beauty of his bulls: *Maŋar*, *Maper* and the two *Mijiɛɛk*. He concludes his song by telling Ayak that he had come to their cattle camp, not only with *Maŋar* but with his *Maper* bull, and he therefore announced his presence.

Although this is part of a long song, the author found it necessary to take that part which shows the intimacy in the lives of the Dinka men and their cattle, particularly the bulls. If you know the special circumstances in which a Dinka man or woman composed his or her song, you can be able to clearly understand the essence, meaning and importance of the message being conveyed through this song. The song cited above fully brings the interplay between colour symbolism with love as one of the unceasing values of life. The role of cattle in Dinka life and the social cobweb that brings together Ngɔth Jiel, the maternal uncle, paternal relations as represented by *Deŋ Kön* and the entire two neighbouring territories of Lou and Kɔŋgöör through Ayak Agaany Akol, daughter of the chief of the territory of Kɔŋgöör and Ngɔth Jiel Marial-yɔc from Lou-Ariik. From the song, words of praise for the bulls could be distinguished as are expressed by such descriptions that make the presence of the *Maɲar* bull to cause bright light that lights the cows at the kraal's end in the time which must be after twilight. The rainbow's red colour on the bull Maper makes us see the rainbow in our mind's eye, and we could see the tall horns of one bull, Majak, pointing high into the sky with birds flying in the sky having the possibility of hitting themselves upon those horns and being killed or murdered. See how the man praised himself and how he praised his fiancé through cattle and their colour symbolism. All the praises are metaphorical imageries conveyed through cattle symbolism. Cattle are therefore the media through which Dinka people express most of their wishes and thoughts. Dinka literature is generally beautified by cattle colour imagery, symbolism and metaphor. The use of figures of speech in this song is a vivid indication that Dinka language can use cattle colours as the media through which they express themselves.

DINKA PERSONAL NAMES AND THE CATTLE

That cattle are integrally part of the Dinka social life is clear in many ways. Many of the Dinka personal names given right from birth are basic colour symbolisms from their cattle. Some are names from the colour of the bulls which, for example, have been sacrificed in order to bring about the birth of the very child. The male name *Magɔɔk,* from *Magɔɔk-Thɔn* which, for example, was sacrificed to propitiate God, or one of the gods to allow childbearing which may have been difficult, is given to a male child in appreciation of the success brought about by the sacrifice of that ox. In other words, such a naming is sometimes given in compensation to the bull so sacrificed. Other Dinka people are given personal names from the colour of cows, bulls or oxen paid into the marriage of their mothers. A girl or woman given the name of Ajak, for example, would certainly bring to mind that a cow of the colour configuration of *Ajak* was paid by her father in the marriage of her mother during his wedding. A man with the name of Marial would suggest a bull of the colour *Marial* paid in the marriage of his mother. So is the name *Yar* 'the white cow'. As a feminine colour name, the name Yar is usually given as a name for girls. When that cow is a bull, it is called *Mayar* according to the Rek Dinka. Lakes Dinka communities call it *Mayör*. They call the female type of this cow *Ayör*. The Agaar and Gok Dinka people call the white bull *Mabor* while Rek society calls it *Mabior*, a difference of '*i*' between the letters '*o*' and '*b*'.

Maŋar, Makur, Maker, Makuei, Majök, Magak, Maliap, Marial, etc, are names given to some of the Dinka men from the colours of bulls which have bold pied colours of black and white colourations on their bodies, depending on the design and appearance of the colours on the bull. Those men with the names of Mabior/Mabör, Mayar, Mayör, Matuur (the colour of the Nile perch), Matuɔŋ 'white as an egg,' all are names given to bulls of the white colour.

As a reminder, if the prefix '*a*' precedes the colour name of a person instead of the prefix *ma* then the person is a girl or a woman. If it is used for the cow, it is a female cow.

A bull with red colour configuration is call *Malual*, the red coloured bull. If the name has prefix '*a*', then it is *Aluel* which is also given as a name for a girl, a woman or grown up female cow. If the red colouration in the bull is mauve or purple-red, then the bull is called *Madök*. If it is a female cow, it is called *Adök*. A bull with scarlet-red colour is *Madöl, Adöl* if it is a female cow. If the bull is maroon or dark-brown-red in colour, it is given the colour name of *Maliik* and is called *Aliik* when it is a grown up female cow. If the red colouration in the bull is pale, it is given a colour name of *Mayen, Ayen* for a cow. If the bull's red colour is too minimal to qualify for any of the above colour names, then it is regarded as *Malöök, Alöök* if a cow. If the red colour is even less apparent, dull or faint, then the bull is called *Mameer, Ameer* when it is a female cow.

Furthermore, if a red or semi-red cow or bull has a patch of white colour on its sides, the colour name *Akɔl* or *Makɔl* is therefore given to it. If that cow has a white mark on its head instead of its sides, it is *Mayɔm* if it is a bull or a man, *Yɔm* if it is a cow or a girl or woman.

Malou, on the other hand, is a Dinka colour name given to a man whose father may have paid a bull of the grey colour, *Malou*, in the marriage of his mother. *Malou* is a colour name given to a bull with grey, cloudy or mustard colour of the soil or earth, the colour of an elephant. All the cattle colour names are given to people, depending on whether the person is a male or female.

To better understand the Dinka cattle and colour naming system, it is imperative at this juncture to have a look at some aspects of grammar used in the names of the cattle that are given to some Dinka women and men. In this, we find there are some exceptions to the rule of the prefix 'a' preceding a colour name for a female Dinka person, like in the case of certain colour names such as the grey or *Malou* colour configuration. The prefix 'a' is not put before *Lou*, the grey, to become *Alou*. Whereas there is *Malou* for the male in both cattle and humans, there is no '*Alou*', but '*Lou*' for a female Dinka person or cow.

Cows and bulls with pimples or discreet red and white colours on their bodies are given the colour name of *Diŋ* without the usual prefix '*a*' used for female cows and for girls, but the prefix '*ma*' is used for bulls and men to become *Madiŋ*. When the colour name from this type of a cow or bull is used for people, we then have Madiŋ for men and Diŋ for girls and women. The two examples, *Lou* and *Diŋ* given above indicate that there are exceptions to the use of prefixes in Dinka use of cattle colour names.

Dinka men with the name Makuac derive such a colour name from the bull with the colour of a leopard (*kuac*). It is *Akuac* when it is a cow or a girl/woman. *Marɔl, Majak, Maper* and *Matɛɛm* are those bulls with white and red lines (*Marɔl, Matɛɛm*) on their bodies or those with large patches of red colour on their white bodies. Many Dinka men are given such colour names.

A totally black bull is called Macäär, also written as Machär, Dinka men with the name of Macäär (dark black) acquire their names from such black bulls. A female cow is called *Acol* when it is totally black, so are girls who are called Acol although *Achol*, which is a name given to girls, has a different meaning from that of Acol. The name *Achol* in Dinka is not related to the cattle colour. It is a name given to a female child born after the one before her had died. It is *Chol* when it is a male child. *Achol* or *Chol* therefore means a child who has come as God's compensation for the lost child before it. Achol is given for both human and cattle females.

Aker is a name given to a female cow or female human from the colour of a cow with black and white colours rather made in the pattern of the soldier ant, that insect called *ajiing*, which walks in a line and makes a painful bite on people. Aker is a name so common among Dinka girls and women. For a bull it is called *Maker*. Men are, as such, given the name of Maker, which can also be given as a surname. The author is Anei-Maker-Akuac.

Most of the Dinka bulls' names are given at initiation but personal names related to cattle are given at birth. The bulls' names are not made to coincide with birth or personal names. A man may have a personal or birth name of *Majak*. If so, he cannot also be given a bull name of *Majak* for he cannot possibly augment his social standing by having the same colour configuration of *Majak* which was basically his birth name. Worth mentioning here also is the great reverence a man places on the bull from which he acquired his surname. A Dinka man does not eat from the meat of a bull whose colour was given him as his colour name or a bull which was his song bull if it happens that the bull dies from whatever cause. If, for instance, a man's song bull dies, he will mourn the death of that bull like you mourn the death of your closest person. Such a young man would strip himself of all his beads and ornamentations. He will not take a bath or eat for weeks and will remain forlornly secluded from the rest of his people, crying or mourning for his song bull he has lost. He could even choose to go away from the cattle camp or even from the territory and would return only when a good Samaritan came around to console him (*duudic*) with a bull or cow of some sort. The intimacy between a man and his song bull is like the intimacy of a parent and his or her child. To miss one's song bull is like missing one's child, wife or husband.

In as much as Dinka people are associated with their cows by their colours, Dinka men are also identified with their bulls linguistically, all for aesthetic purposes clothed in the value of love for girls. The ultimate end of all these is intrinsically marriage to this or that girl for one to have a wife or wives, a home, a family and posterity with a descent line that would remain to be perpetuated by one's children after one's death.

In the homes and cattle camps, men sometimes behave and represent themselves as bulls. This concept and behaviour by Dinka men is seen as similar to that of whole bulls among the herds. They take the position of bulls (*thön*) because, like the whole bulls, they are the ones who cause their wives to beget. They are the begetters, protectors and, like the whole bulls among the cattle, they are the ultimate centres, source and leaders of their own homes and families. Bulls (*thön*) stand to symbolise virility in the Dinka concept and this is why it is the uncastrated bulls (*thön*) that are the objects of sacrifice and offerings for ritual and religious purposes. Castrated bulls are not offered to Nhialic in sacrifice because the essential part of their body (testicles) has been removed and they are not considered as being whole as such. Something superior to humans like God, gods, ancestral spirits…. etc, cannot be given as a gift a bull or ram which is not whole, like castrated bulls or rams.

Castrated bulls (*biöc*) are used for social services, not for religious or ritual purposes. Because leadership in the Dinka concept is one of man, men have it as their responsibility to fight in wars to defend or attack. Uncastrated bulls have the same duty to protect the herd from any external danger. *Thɔn* is viewed by the herds as their head and their representative that always come forward to face any challenge to the herds in the absence of man, the owner.

In much the same way women and girls look at man as the source of procreation, strength, aggression, protection and sexual potency also found by female cows in their uncastrated bulls or ox. When cattle are on the move it is the bulls that take the lead. The cows follow. In the case of humans it is the man who leads when walking with his wife or any female one. This is what happens during journeys for, like the bulls or oxen, man must be in front to be the first to encounter whatever danger may be lying ahead. Apart from the moral fortitude, strength and bravery to face any challenge as a leader and source of family existence, *thön* and men are the foundation of the kraal and family respectively.

The following war song, sung by Dinka men when mobilising for war, succinctly explains this bull and man claim to leadership among the herds and women respectively:

"Na liɛu ɛɛ ke Muɔr Wuöt aliu ee
Lɔŋ Wëndït aŋoot wei ɛɛ!
Na liɛu ee ke Muɔr Wuöt aliu.
Na cabɛn, ke Muɔr Wuöt a cï bɛn!..."
Translation
"If I am away, there is no bull in the camp!
The head is still away, the leader has not come!
If I am away, there is no bull in the camp.
When I have come, the bull of the camp has come!..."

In Dinka, a camp means *wut* and *wut* is a composite of people and cattle. It is a basic social grouping. *Wut* also means a cattle camp, a section, an area or tribe. *Wut* generally implies both men and cattle. In the livestock song above, the singer simulates himself to the bull, the uncastrated bull. By Dinka notion, a herd or cattle without a whole bull or *thɔn* is like women without a man among them. Dinka cattle bring and hold the human group together. Generally Dinka society interests go around cattle. All their individual and collective interests meet in the cattle. Family and descent groups share the herd as their common property for generations. Marriage and procreation are possible through cattle. As will be found under marriage, no family or individual can hope to prosper without cattle.

CATTLE AND SACRIFICE MAKING

In the Dinka world, cattle occupy the central position in their religious thoughts. Right at creation, the Dinka first human parent to be created, *Garaŋ*, chose the cow and the sheep as his first rate animals of choice from all the animals which Nhialic created at *Panthou*, the Dinka creation spot. In their oral mythologies, Dinka people believe the cow and sheep to be the cleanest, pure and God chosen animals to be always sacrificed as offerings to Him. They also believe that since God is male in His physical and spiritual nature and His first human creation was male which He created in His own image, He also dictated that man should give Him the male, the undefiled or uncastrated bull and ram as offering. For this reason Dinka people have taken the cows and sheep, particularly the uncastrated oxen and rams, as the perfect sacrificial animals to be given to Nhialic since those primordial times from creation. For this same reason, Dinka people look at the cow as the only animal fitting as the substitute for human beings. Cattle are offered in sacrifice to Nhialic the creator, to the gods (jak), to clans' totems (yieth) and to (atiip) the ancestral spirits and the spirits of the primal parents such as *Garaŋ* who is Adam, *Abuk* the Biblical Eve, *Deŋdit* and other children of *Abuk* and *Garaŋ*. Those aforementioned powers and spirits and primary parents are considered by the Dinka as powers in the unknown or unseen world and are best placated or propitiated by offering them sacrificial bulls and rams to be pleased so as to abandon a person who was sick as a result of their anger.

Except for sacrificial offering and for social occasions, Dinka people see cattle as having rights like humans and are not killed merely for meat. Cattle are known to understand the wishes of their owners and are known to have intelligence, although some types of cows are believed to be more intelligent and more responsive than others. The long-horned type of cows understand better and more quickly than the short-horned type, that have the reputation of being bold, pugnacious, stupid and obstinate. Dinka people look with disgust upon their neighbouring non-Dinka communities who see cattle as merely a source of meat. Although Dinka people do eat the meat of a sacrificed cow or the meat of a cow killed for social reason, they are ashamed to show appetite for meat as a reason for killing a cow. *Weŋ acïe nɔk apath,* '*a cow is not killed for nothing,*' says the Dinka. When a person is regarded as *Acuɛt yɔk,* 'cattle eater,' it is a big insult. Such a person is regarded as not being a Dinka, for that kind of insult implies that the person so insulted does not acknowledge the true value and meaning of the cow, for he should know that cows are part of human beings and cannot be killed just for meat. Dinka people give their lives in defence of cattle.

The society has an established belief that a person who kills a cow for no good and conventionally accepted reason, and without a public ceremony, is usually haunted (*cien*) by the soul or spirit of that very cow. People who kill cattle in an overt way or for the mere purpose of meat are known to have died in consequence, in much the same way a person who kills another person unjustly is haunted (*cien*) by the ghost or spirit soul of the deceased. Those people who kill other humans in a very unjust way and those who do not reveal having killed a person so that cattle are paid to the deceased relatives for his soul or life, are usually killed by the ghost of the person killed. It is because of this fear that the ghost of a killed cow will always return to kill those who killed them for no good reason that Spear Masters often announce to the sacrificial bull or ram the important and compelling reason for which it is being victimised. This is why also the sacrificed bulls and rams are compensated by naming the child born after them in order to preserve their memory in a way similar to their concept of perpetuating the names of their dead relatives. After all, cattle have rights according to their kind within the total setup of the Dinka society.

BULLS AS SACRIFICIAL OBJECTS

To conduct a ceremonial sacrifice of the ox, *thɔn,* the ox is ceremonially brought by a crowd of young men who then tether it on a big sacrificial peg, the kind of wooden peg which Dinka people call *ŋuɛɛk*. The ordinary tethering peg for cattle, goats and sheep is called *löc*. The sacrificial peg is permanently fixed in the centre of the homestead, east of *yoro*. In ritual, religious or ceremonial occasions, the sacrificial ox or bull is then, and always, tethered on the big *ŋuɛɛk* facing the east, and a large crowd of people then gather behind it in such a way that *yoro* comes to be in the middle between the sacrificial ox and the people. Positioned in front of the gathering are the Spear Masters, the invocators. As is the Dinka custom on religious occasions, women and girls are made to sit slightly apart from the gathering, usually on the left side as people sit and stand, all facing the east. Dinka sacrificial ceremonies usually start in the morning and gain momentum at about 10:00 am when youth groups finally bring the bull to the sacrificial ground where it is then tethered. At this very time religious and war songs for the ceremony start to be sung by all in unison and at a high pitch so that the high sound of people singing is heard from far away distances. These singing episodes bring to the sacrificial environ the religious essence of the occasion. Ululations by women, the running and marshal activities done by young men, activities which they do while lauding their idiomatic praises, adds to the varied high singing pitches made by war and religious songs being sung. The war and religious songs plus activities by the youth, and the prayer songs and invocations done by the Spear Masters, marks the ceremony as a religious one.

As the momentum gathers and focus is ascertained, the Spear Masters begin to come up, ushering the stage of sacred religious invocations. One Spear Master, the high priest, says his intense invocational words which are repeated in staccato phrases by the whole congregation in a chorus form. The sororal nephew (*anyaal*) repeats the words of the Spear Master, making another type of sound and rhythm. The priest or Spear Master, in his holy invocation, calls upon Nhialic in the form of a plea to answer his requests and his community wishes, request and wishes that are for the wellbeing of his community. He also tells the ox why it is being sacrificed so that it goes, when killed, with the knowledge of the purpose for which it was killed. Each Spear Master comes up to say his invocational words to Nhialic, to the spirits of the ancestors and to his clan's genii (totems) and to the sacrificial bull. This they do in turns by succession and by seniority and social order existing in that particular community. Invocation by Spear Masters is not done at random. At the climax of these invocations the ox begins to stand relaxed and urinates. At this particular point it is believed that the bull has heard and absorbed the invocational words and messages and that is why it now begins to stand with its head cast towards the ground, apparently affected by the holy words of these invocations. The spirit or power in whose name it is being sacrificed will be deemed to have accepted the bull since it began to urinate. At this stage invocation is instantly stopped and the bull is caught up by the multitude, at which point it is ceremoniously thrown down and tied up with tethering ropes and religiously slaughtered. Then people go into a merry dance and celebrations take the whole day.

Dinka sacrificial occasions differ in size, form and content. The example given above is about one ox and a sacrifice done in the home of an individual owner of the bull. Although it is a communal event, it is more of a clan's or lineage occasion. The entire population of a territory is not expected to attend. Such types of sacrificial occasions in their totality, as are done in annual sacrificial occasions, are done at particular sacred places where ritual occasions are made. Uncastrated rams and uncastrated ox or bulls are sacrificed at the courtyard where *yoro* and *ŋuek* are situated. For sacred families *Yiik* or *Yik*, the holy shrines, are the sanctuaries or holy places where sacrifices are made, sometimes annually.

The cattle are therefore the very religious means by which Dinka people propitiate and communicate with Nhialic and the powers in the unseen world. 'Dinka religion: their belief system', a book published in 2013 by the same author tackles in detail this topic of the role of cattle in Dinka religion. It must be stated clearly that

Dinka cattle relations cannot be exhausted by a single writer and cannot be well treated through one chapter, however, the narrative given about Dinka cattle relations can give a clue of the important role cattle play in Dinka life.

CHAPTER SIX: THE SOCIAL INSTITUTION CALLED MARRIAGE OR THIËËK

INTRODUCTION

Among the Dinka people in the rural countryside, the man's love for the girl does not necessarily determine the decision to marry her however warm their love may be. In Dinka custom, marriage is not simply a union of a man and a woman or a culmination of the love between two people of the opposite sex. It is an alliance between the two families of the spouses in the closest practical sense and is a union between two clans and the entire kinship at its wider scope. The consent between the groom and the bride is subordinate to the consent of their family superiors. However, Dinka young men have these days come to have some kind of freedom in the choice for their brides but their father has to consent to their selection. Marriage in the Dinka world binds the two families or kin, among whom the bride wealth is collected, received or distributed as shares to the family.

A clan's descent line is a fundamental and overriding goal and duty to every man. Dinka society considers marriage the first obligation and duty a man and a woman must strive to do in life. Every Dinka male and female is expected to marry and raise a family. A Dinka man is allowed by custom to marry or be married to as many wives as he can. In Dinka society marriage is not only a fulfilment of the objective of continuity, it is also an obligation, a discharge of one's social duty. To have married, according to Dinka culture, is to have done the main duty required of oneself in the family and in the society. The duty, obligation or the intrinsic urge to marry is strong, felt and is believed by all in that it even tends to outweigh the duty to fetch and rear the cattle. All Dinka young men's preoccupations with cattle and girls are seen as means and methods for getting married in the final analysis. As pointed out by Dr Francis Mading Deng in his book, *Tradition and modernization,* 1970, any Dinka man who has gone beyond marriageable age and does not want to marry is considered by Dinka society as *ayuur*. An *ayuur* is a lowly person with no sense of public opinion and his own future. Most Dinka young men would try their best to afford to have a wife even if he were to remain with nothing thereafter. He would prefer to be in possession of a wife and trusts in Nhialic to answer for his poverty.

In all Dinka marriages cattle are paid as the dowry by the groom's side, which gives that dowry to the bride's relatives. The bride price differs from one Dinka tribe to the other, from a few tens as is the case with the Upper Nile Dinka people to a hundred or more as is the case with many Dinka communities in the Bahr el Ghazal region. In the same way the bride price is raised by the groom's family through consanguinity, customary and legally binding contributions, bride price is distributed reciprocally in the bride's family, that is, the groom's paternal uncle is matched with the bride's paternal uncle, groom's maternal uncle to the bride's maternal uncle, the groom's brother to the bride's brother, and so on and so forth.

For all the Dinka, chiefs' daughters fetch more dowry cattle in the same way their sons are expected to pay more cattle for their wives. As Dinka society is made up of social classes, the chieftain or aristocratic class marry girls from the same social class of the nobles. Some middle class people sometimes strive to marry from the chieftain class provided they pay the required number of cattle. The ruling or aristocratic class of the Dinka nobles does not marry from the lower or commoners' class but if a star girl emerges from the lower class, a member from the ruling family can descend down to pay less dowry than he would have paid if he was marrying from the upper class. A new dimension has recently been introduced into the Dinka marriage system by the educated and urban Dinka. University graduates have now come to fetch more bride price among the Dinka, a factor which is likely to positively promote enrolment of girls into schools. Dinka marriages in towns are nowadays going up, both in money and in cattle. Bahr el Ghazal Dinka people in towns have gone to even three hundred cows while east bank Dinka have resorted to money, owing to the insecurity posed by cattle rustling going on in that region.

Like is the case with homicide, cattle are paid as substitution to replace the girl being married and taken away into another clan from where she will not return for good, unless after a divorce, when the marital union is terminated by both sides to the marriage and through a law court. The girl given in marriage is therefore known to have lost her legal membership to the family where she was born and is given over to the new family and clan of her husband, where she becomes a legal member even after her death. Women are buried where they were married, for they belong to the family to which they are married and which is where they spend the rest of their life after they are married. Moreover, Dinka people take all humans to be a composite of eight important bones or body parts, the two tibial bones, the two femoral bones, the two upper limbs, the vertebral column and the cranial bone. They argue that the eight bones constitute what a human being is and cannot be just taken free. This is besides their contention that the girl is taken away to form a new family with her husband and she goes to procreate children who will all belong to another clan. The cattle they demand and which are handed to them in place of their girl are later paid to bring wives for her brothers and her share-taking relatives in order to bear children into the lineage, thus restoring to them her place which was lost in the family, into the lineage and into the clan through marriage. The children to be brought forth by those wives will be like the children she will bear to her new family, lineage and clan.

A Dinka marriage dowry is called upon and dictated by the deep concern for the continuity of generations in the family genealogical lines and for social continuity in the society. This cannot be assured without cattle paid as dowry, for without cattle involved there will be no public demonstration and validation of paternity. The Dinka *pater* system, the paterlineal order, which is the main purpose for Dinka marriages and existence, cannot be validly guaranteed without cattle payment. It is usually the payment of the bride price in cattle which authorises the Dinka husband to reckon the children to his stock and gives him control over both his wife and children to the exclusion of any claim by the wife's kindred. The family, lineage and clan system therefore gives strong meaning to Dinka social order.

Under the chapter on the Dinka cattle complex we find that a man's wealth in cattle directly affects the likelihood of the remembrance of his name through having cattle, which must be there to ensure his name during his lifetime and during the rest of posterity even after his death. The availability of cattle mostly found through marriages of daughters is bound up with the number of children that a family must have. A man and family must have enough girls to sustain the availability of cattle for the maintenance of paternal continuity. Cattle are the only means Dinka people use to legitimate marital union. In the Dinka way of thinking, when two families have a marriage between them each has provided the means for the continuation of the other. The girl produces children for her new family while dowry cattle paid in exchange for her are used by the girl's people to marry wives who would produce children for them and in this way both sides do not lose but ensure mutual continuity through marriage and the cattle dowry.

In marriage a Dinka man owes a debt of gratitude to his wife's parents. This is so because procreating and bringing her up as well as training and imparting into her the future duties of a wife is worth rewarding. Parents are also respected by their sons-in-law because, through their daughter, the husband is able to bear children to continue his father's lineage and thus guarantees his own family line and continuity. From the Dinka husband's point of view, his wife's parents are the primary source of the continuation of his own agnatic line, hence his serene respect for his wife's parents. It therefore goes without saying that children and cattle are the two ultimate things a Dinka man must strive to have as they guarantee his prosperity and continuity from generation to generation. The two, children and cattle, are ensured through marriage. This ultimately gives value to the man's life and is the only way a man assures himself of the kind of immortality which Dinka men aspire to during their lifetime.

As the family lineage and clan continuity through procreation is founded upon this social institution called marriage, the whole lineage and at times the entire clan is involved in the marriage process, as marriage is not simply a union of a man and a woman. Unlike the western world view, the involvement of almost the entire agnatic social structure transforms Dinka marriage from a personal desire for marriage to that of a social obligation and community duty for continuity. In Dinka society family is the basic institution where society begins. Dinka societal values converge in this institution called marriage. This also makes Dinka marriages a means to all values. Love, respect to the ancestors and the mythical powers in the unknown are deemed as important values in Dinka society. All of these cannot be possible without a home and a home cannot be made without a wife in it through marriage which, to the traditional Dinka, is also not possible without cattle.

In a society like that of the Dinka where there is nothing called a domestic servant to meet the personal needs of a man who could not marry, marriage in itself provides a man with a life partner whose duty it is to primarily serve and care for him. In Dinka society a woman takes a deep and sincere pride when she has shown to the family, the clan and the entire society that she has served and fulfilled the necessary loyalty and feminine faithfulness to her husband. While it is not the principal reason for marriage, young men become desirous when they see married men being affectionately served and tenderly cared for and respected by their wives.

Apart from those principal reasons as well as continuity through procreation, marriage is also conceived by the Dinka society as a collective investment by the family, since a married woman is anticipated to bear female offspring which would fetch more cows to the family and lineage through bride wealth payments or dowries paid upon them during marriage. According to the Dinka custom and social traditions, close relatives and at times clansmen come in to assist in the payment of bride wealth, knowing the marriage will reimburse them with a profit of cattle more than is being paid on the bride herself, a rather more than a decade family economic investment.

At times marriage is brought about or made to take place when the mother of a young man has become of age and cannot prepare and provide services to even her own children. In this case marriage is done as a relief to one's mother. The same accounts for a husband doing another marriage as a relief to his old wife who cannot afford to run the home as she used to when she was young and active. She cannot any longer pound durra for food for the household members. She can no longer fetch or carry water from such distances as is usually the case in the Dinka country. Water in many parts of the Dinka land is known to be collected from far distances, especially during the dry season months. This, though a trivial reason, can suffice to be a strong reason which could compel a young man to marry but for a man whose wife has become older, it is a compelling reason to make him marry again. In Dinka thought, old couples cannot properly care for themselves, for reason of the woman's incapacity. Younger wives do better for their old husbands.

As earlier stated, marriage in its deeper sense is an obligation, a social duty required even by the spirits of one's ancestors. A wife in the home stands to symbolise the existence of familyhood. She symbolises the existence of a lineage and therefore of the pater line. All spirits of the bygone ancestors, family gods and totems associated with the clan, lineage and family must have a home with a woman available in it to serve them. Any male born must marry a wife to cater for those spirits, totems and gods; and since Dinka people are deeply religious in their search for God's favours and for cure, ancestral and God's protection is secured through marriage, for without marriage the relationship between the man and his ancestral spirits, even the clan's totems and gods, will be deemed to have been severed and prospects of one's wellbeing are not assured if there is no wife in a home.

If marriage was not made obligatory and augmented by polygamy, how could Dinka society have succeeded to sustain its marshal nature? Without marriage being institutionalised and made obligatory, Dinka society would not have acquired its present numerical superiority in the Nile valley region. The warlike nature known for the Dinka in South Sudan demands a constant supply of fighting men and this is ascertained only through marriage made into a social contract between a person and Dinka society. It is not up to a girl or young man to tamper with society's demands to marry. This explains why there are no harlots and hermits in Dinka society.

Again, Dinka society takes hospitality seriously as a great value. While they do it perfectly in the cattle camps, there comes a time when a young man would want to marry in order to have a residence separate from that of his parents so that he would be able to impress his age mates and guests with his own family hospitality, which calls for more effort than his old mother can make.

Even though love and the need to secure and own a constant partner through marriage in order to sexually satisfy oneself as a biological need is not made apparent as one of the reasons why Dinka people marry, some young Dinka men find it very difficult to have their sexual urges answered by illegal means. This is because the majority of Dinka girls are schooled by their parents, relatives and customs against pre-marital sex for fear of being devalued by the society when it is discovered, heard or noticed that such a girl has had pre-marital sex. Pre-marital sex is greatly abhorred by Dinka society and its customs and any girl who enters into pre-marital sex ceases to be a girl right from the time it comes into public notice. The practice of pre-marital sex is also known to make a girl run the risk of illegal conception. Pre-marital sex is also responsible for many of the Dinka violent wars and this has a frightening impact on Dinka girls. They therefore choose to love their young men without entering into sex with them. Sex among the Dinka is only for social reproduction and for this reason fornication is prohibited. Adulterers are greatly despised and are heavily fined and the marriage of a woman who commits adultery may be terminated. Sometimes adultery becomes one of the sources of conflict and clan fightings. Incest on the other hand is usually unimaginable and is indeed abhorred. In rare instances, however, young men make up their minds to marry in order to secure a sexual partner but notwithstanding this reality, such urges are mere undertones and are not a strong reason behind young men's intentions to marry.

On the whole, marriage as a social institution is viewed by

Dinka society as a natural duty into which no young Dinka person of marriageable age needs to be compelled. It is an automatic and voluntary duty to marry and to be married, especially when one has come to be mature and one's right to marry has come in the family line. Both Dinka mythical and living worlds dictate and enforce marriage upon everyone. Not wanting to marry deprives a person from all those good things that are used to accrue to a person as a result of marriage. Besides this, young men or girls who are found to be disinterested in marriage are abandoned by their kin and their age mates. They also undergo an ancestral curse for abandoning the duty to continue the lineage and they generally suffer withdrawal of respect from the whole community and so nobody can stay unmarried in Dinka society.

TYPES AND WAYS TO MARRY AMONG THE DINKA

In Dinka society there are several ways through which a person arrives at a marriage. There are also different types of marriages. All of these are legalised by the payment of bride wealth, done in the form of cattle dowry. For the rural Dinka, cattle are the only accepted medium or currency for dowry payments, not through any other means. As earlier discussed under the Dinka cattle complex, it is the cattle and only the cattle which can be paid in human compensations such as in homicides, where cows of sufficient but legally determined number are paid to the family of the deceased as blood dia compensation called *apuk*. Apart from compensations for blood and for complete human loss, cattle are paid in exchange for female members of another clan who are taken or given over to become new but legal members of a different clan, lineage and family to which they are brought by means of marriage. Due to money having now posed as a new alternative economic means for a living, east

Nile Dinka people are nowadays accepting money for dowry in their marriages and this will tend to weaken the Dinka culture if it is allowed to continue or expand to Bahr el Ghazal. Should the government succeed in stopping the ongoing tribal violence and cattle rustling prevalent in Jonglei, Warrap and Lakes states, the Dinka use of cattle as their customary currency for marriages will resume as normal.

DINKA CUSTOMARY MARRIAGE

In counting the ways by which Dinka people arrive at a marriage, it would be in keeping with Dinka norms and custom to begin with the most celebrated customary means to marriage. This, in the eyes of the Dinka and their customary law, is what could be regarded as *customary marriage*, which is a very respectful form of marriage in which the union between the couple comes as a result of the mutual acceptance of each other by the two sides to the marriage, that is, the two families who are the bride wealth and bridegroom, following serious and lengthy marital procedures, including negotiations and bride wealth payment in cattle. In fact, Dinka customary marriage, *ghost marriage* and those other forms of marriage which have no criminal background, usually undergo certain formalities that may be viewed as formal, legal or socially accepted. These types of marriages lead to the conclusion that marriage among the Dinka is not a simple thing that can just finish in a short moment but is a long social happening stretching over not less than two years at times. There are certain formalities, processes and procedures that are usually done in a normal Dinka marriage before the bride is finally handed over to her husband. These processes and procedures include how to choose the girl, which is called *mɛt mɛt nya*. This phase is followed by what Dinka people call *jöt jöt ruääi*, which is the delivery or conveyance of the marriage proposal. This is followed by *kuɛn ruääi*, the marriage negotiation stage. After negotiations comes the dowry payment known as *akak* in some parts of the Rek lands. Many call it *luny luny*, the optioning of the cattle to the bride's side by the suitor's family. This is followed by the division of dowry cattle, which Dinka people call *tëktëk yɔk*. The handing over of the bride, which is called *gɛm nya* comes last.

In this customary means to marriage, it usually starts with the father of the marrying young man initiating to his son the need to marry a wife. At times the initiative could come from the son who would propose to his father and his people a girl he has been in love with for quite a time and whom he has studied, leading him to think she can make him a good housewife. In the case of the proposal coming from the father, he would let his son know of the name of the girl and the background of her parents and family. In so doing the father would begin by asking his wife or wives to prepare social services for a family meeting he would convene to share that choice with his family members who, in this case, are elderly men and those who may be directly concerned. Women are not made to be part of the meeting except in some cases where direct paternal aunts may be allowed to attend such discussions involving the choice of a girl to be married. The maternal aunt capable of being invited to such a crucial meeting must not be a young woman as she must be old enough to be considered prudent for such meetings.

Women are generally known to easily divulge secrets that were used as pros and cons, views which are usually advanced during family discussions over why it should be this family or that, this or that girl and not the other girl or that family. After serious and elaborate discussion the family would then arrive at a decision to choose a girl of a given man in a given family and clan. In most cases the choice usually goes in line with the opinion of the father although his son's view and the views of the family elders are sought in the course of the discussion. After the decision has been made a proposal to marry that girl from that family or clan is then dispatched. A deputation headed by one of the elders is dispatched to deliver that marriage proposal to the father and relatives of the girl for their opinion. Once the girl's father and relatives have welcomed the proposal the marriage process is then set in place.

At times, and as a necessary procedure, the suitor is made to visit the girl for her opinion. He is usually accompanied by a group of his age mates, mostly from among his clansmen. This process is called *thuöt*, officially authorised courting. When the suitor and his party of age mates arrive at the girl's home, they are warmly welcomed by a team of girls who were gathered and prepared for this purpose from the family or village. Relatives of the girl make it possible for the two groups to sit together for the suitor to officially present his request to the bride to have her hand in marriage. The suitor would therefore pose a concern to hear from the bride's own mouth if she has accepted him to marry her or not. In most cases, the girl does not go against the opinion of her family elders, especially if the man does not have any physical defects. She would therefore announce her compliance and her being ready to be a wife to the suitor. At this point the suitor would jump up in jubilation, loudly uttering his most cherished idioms. He does this as a sign of his welcome to the girl's approval of him. His team also go into merriment and the girl's people will know that their daughter did not contravene her people's opinion. At times, women who usually collect and are always around, go into merriment with their usual ululations. The girl's people will now know their daughter will soon be married and the family will have additional cows.

Having obtained the girl's approval the suitor and his party would return to give back their report to the father and people. Once all these preliminaries are done the suitor's relatives would then take the next step. They would decide to pay a collective visit to the home of those of the girl to officially present their intention to marry their daughter and be in-laws. This period is called *jöt ruääi*. Women from the groom's side also go with their men. The suitor's elders are thus welcomed by the girl's relatives and lavish services are rendered. A big bull is usually slaughtered. Food which is seasoned with butter oil is served in big quantities and white stuff beer is brewed for those elders and women. For a day or two discussions or talks and services go on together.

The girl's side presents, in a formally organised gathering attended by members of the community, the number of cattle, bulls and oxen they want to be paid in lieu of their daughter. A heated debate for bargaining is allowed to go on between the two sides until neutral elders from the community are allowed in at a certain stage to try to act as go betweens. They come up with a figure they see fit for the girl's relatives and affordable by the suitor's side. Still, at a certain stage the chief of the territory or his representative is ultimately made to come to give a final ruling, a final number of cows, bulls and oxen. His role is to arbitrate between the two sides. He gives a final word for marriage negotiations to come to a stop and marriage agreement is deemed to have been concluded. If the chief cannot be available, his representative will give that final word with which both sides must comply.

After all this, a song to seal the marriage agreement is introduced by the groom's side as the primary benefactors. That song is sung by the groom's party. The girl's side also introduces their clan song which is also sung by all of the girl's party, who are deemed the secondary benefactors. Then comes the song of the territory, common to all. In between these songs are cheers and ululations from women who have been sitting outside or in the rear, listening. If the discussion was going on in a luak, the women were thus listening carefully to the negotiations.

If marriage discussions are held in the middle of the courtyard, outside the luak, which is sometimes the case, especially when

Fig 37: Showing a Dinka marriage discussion session in earnest

discussions take place late in the afternoon, women sit to the far left of men, saying nothing but waiting to only ululate and provide merriment when the marriage negotiations end in an agreement. In the Dinka world women's role in marriages is relegated to the provision of services to the guests and organisation of the bride when she is about to be taken to her husband after all marital processes have finished. Their presence during marital discussions or negotiations is not a must, for their opinion is not in any way sought in the talks. The decision to allow marriage to take place or not, the determination of the bride price during marriage negotiations and when the bride is to be delivered to her new home, all are prerogatives of the men.

All in all the conclusion of the marriage finally leads to the people of the groom's side inviting the side of the bride to go to their cattle camp for the payment of the agreed bride price. With this the marriage process shifts to the cattle camp from the homes. There in the cattle camp the suitor's relatives who have the issue to

THE DINKA HISTORY 439

Fig 38: Showing bride's relatives being shown the marriage dowry cows, from which good quality cows are finally selected by them.

Fig 39: Showing 150 cows finally chosen by the bride's relatives after serious debate. Inferior and old cows seen in figure 36 have been rejected.

contribute to the marriage are made to bring their cows, which they add to the cows of the suitor and his brothers and father.

If the author is to take that ritual of the Rek Dinka as the standard practice for all the Dinka, then dowry payments are contributed in a customary marriage as follows:

1. Ideally, the father of the marrying son pays ten cows and a bull. They are called *yɔk wun moc,* 'cows of the groom's father'. If the father has more than two wives, junior to the wife whose son is marrying, he can pay more than the ten cows, for each wife has to pay her own share of cows from among the cows allotted to her by her husband.
2. If the suitor has an elder, a sibling brother who by his primogenitary right had earlier married, perhaps twice, which is usually the case among the Dinka, that elderly sibling will be required to pay 10 cows and a bull plus the ox (*thɔn*) of the marriage. If the required bride price figure is high, this elderly sibling brother called *wĕndït* will be required to pay more than ten cows. He may go to 15 or 20 plus two bulls, the big ones called adɔŋ, first class bulls, depending on the required bride price and depending on his cattle status.
3. Each sibling brother, especially the one who is junior to the suitor, is to contribute five cows and a bull to the marriage of his brother. If there is another brother elder to the suitor but second to the first, then that brother will be required to contribute eight cows and a bull.
4. The suitor, in ideal situations, is to himself pay 10 cows or more, depending on what he has. This is plus his song bull which must rank first among all the bulls paid into the marriage. Should the number of bulls required be more, he can go to two bulls from himself alone but if the bride price is high the suitor will still be required to pay more than ten cows if he can afford to.
5. If the father of the marrying man has brothers who are paternal

uncles to the bridegroom the one who is elder to the father will be required to pay 10 cows and a bull if this is the first son of his brother to marry. He may go beyond 10, provided his cows and bulls are striking ones, but if he had earlier contributed to the marriage of his brother's eldest son, he will be required this time to pay only eight cows and a bull or he could even pay less than this. The other paternal uncles, junior or senior to the suitor's father, can contribute five cows each or two of them can join their hands to pay what they can afford.

6. Some other paternal uncles and relatives who have an issue to assist in the marriage can pay a contribution ranging from one to three cows depending on how close that person is and on the existing relations each has with the suitor or the suitor's father. Paternal aunts, sisters to the father of the suitor, are required to contribute to the marriage. Maternal aunts pay one cow each depending on the type of son now marrying. If the sisters to the father are many then their contribution is done, according to the seniority of their brother's son who is marrying.

7. Maternal uncles, brothers to the suitor's mother, are required to pay five cows and a bull. These maternal uncles' cows are called *yɔk naar*. Some landed gentry could pay more than the usual five cows required by custom from maternal uncles. This is always true of the big families. On the mother's side are maternal aunts called *malɛɛn*. They are also required to contribute a cow each. Their cows are called *yɔk malɛɛn*.

8. Friends to the suitor and other distant paternal relatives may contribute voluntarily, depending on the nature of the marriage and especially if they were honoured to be participants in the course of the marriage processes or stages.

9. Worth noting is the fact that the suitor, his sibling brothers, his stepbrothers, the father and direct paternal uncles may contribute more than is required when the bride price is higher

than their supposed contributions could solve. It may even go to more than is contemplated, especially if it so happens that competition is encountered over the girl when, for some good or bad reasons, the relatives of the girl decide to allow another or more applicants, in which case competition arises. Should competition come in the entire lineage or clan will be drawn into the contest as the entire kinship reputation will certainly be put to test whether they can unite to face a challenge from another clan.

When the girl's relatives are satisfied and have accepted the paid dowries, a big ritual bull is then slaughtered before the cows are driven off. In Rek lands this ritual bull is called *muɔr yɔk nhiim*, the bull that is slaughtered for the in-laws before they take away the dowry cattle. After this the girl's relatives, now called in-laws, go in to drive the cows to their cattle camp. They are accompanied by some youngsters from the groom's side up to their cattle camp. The bulls of the marriage are first cleaned and decorated with tassels, collars and bells. At times such cattle are first made to pass through the homes and villages of those of the bride for women, children and the aged to see them. Marriage bulls are made to pass from one homestead to the other and from one village to the other in order to show them to the villagers and kinfolk. The young men who are displaying those bulls sing their bull songs. Sometimes new songs may have been created for the marriage. Family men and women who come to see the dowry cows and bulls also sing in jubilation. They even dance around the bulls. They do this to express joy since their girl brought them cows to add to what their family and clan already has. The father of the girl and family elders are expected to welcome and sprinkle those bulls with *arop,* which is usually kept in the luak in a gourd for such and other occasions. They say blessing words before those bulls are made to pass through the homes and villages on their way to the cattle camp. The entire family, village and community at large becomes happy with the arrival of the bride price cattle. People become joyful in the villages and in the cattle camp(s).

In any case, there is a strong observance to be very carefully followed as the dowry cattle are brought in. The mother and father of the girl are not allowed to partake of the milk from the dowry cows of their daughter and are also not allowed to tread on the dung of the cows from the marriage of their daughter until a customary ritual called *ŋɔu* is done by the bridegroom's side. These two people, the mother-in-law and father-in-law, cannot drink the milk from these cows until the *ŋɔu* ritual is made. This *ŋɔu* could be a big ram or a bull which may be two to three years old. It is not necessarily a very big bull but it must be a fat bull. When *ŋɔu* is brought by two to three people from the groom's side, both the mother and father of the bride are made to go into their main house of the homestead and the ram or bull is let around the house several times. Those letting the bull or ram go around and around the house are saying, '*Ma yïn aca cuɔp! Wa yïn aca cuɔp!*' That is, 'Mother, I have come to your aid! Father, I have come to your aid!' This statement is repeated many times as the ones with the bull or ram are going around the house. 'I have come to your aid,' means, 'I have brought *ŋɔu* and you will no longer die'. The bride's parents inside the house repeat the same words verbatim. The node of the tethering rope, called *wïën cɔɔc*, at the ram's neck or at the bull's neck, is given through the door for the mother and father to catch while they repeat the statement. Done three times or more, the groom's emissaries would then call for help to slaughter the ram or bull almost at the doorstep. The bride's parents are then called out to come and put their feet in the blood which flows upon the ground from the sacrificed or ritually slaughtered bull or ram. With this done, the ritual called *ŋɔu* will be deemed over and the girl's parents can now tramp or tread over the dung of her daughter's dowry cows and drink milk from those cows without any fear of illness coming to them due to the cows of their daughter's marriage. Although this ritual is for all the girl's parents, *ŋɔu* is more serious about the girl's mother. This is because the danger of *ŋɔu* to the girl's father is sometimes weakened by certain simple practices and the bride's father can tread on the dung *(wär)* of his daughter's cattle before the *ŋɔu* ritual is done to them. Since the bride's father is the only parent who attends the last stage of the dowry payment and is in reality the one who gives the final word for the bride's party to take the paid dowry cattle, a special cow for the girl's father is separately shown him. That cow is always a pregnant heifer which is conspicuously beautiful. After all is okay, the girl's father is made to taste the blood from a piece of ear cut from a ram and a metal ring called *til* or *milaŋ* is put on his wrist. This allows him to eat with the rest and the *ŋɔu* ritual later completes the rest of the process of the *wun-nya* rituals.

In any case, the need for a *ŋɔu* ritual sacrifice is triggered by the arrival of the dowry cattle to where the mother-in-law may come in touch with the cows' dung in addition to milk. There is a belief among the Dinka that this ritual called *ŋɔu* is a must if the girl's parents are to live, for they may certainly fall sick in a very severe and sudden way and may die when the *ŋɔu* ritual is not done to make the girl's parents normally drink from the milk of the cows of their daughter. The *ŋɔu* can be done even before the bride is delivered to her new home and even before the dowry is divided between the family and kin. It can, however, be delayed, provided the parents do not come into contact with their daughter's dowry cows, not even one cow. This is because the illness which usually comes onto any of the parents due to the *ŋɔu* ritual not being done has always been fatal and Dinka people always place extra caution for the *ŋɔu* ritual to be done at the appropriate time.

DIVISION OF DOWRY CATTLE AND THE ISSUE OF ARUËTH

In some instances when there is no fear that the girl may cause trouble by secretly going with another man to whom she may have been overtly in love with, or if there is no fear that she may elope with another suitor despite the marriage concluded by her people, dowry cattle can be divided among her relatives while the bride is still a girl in their home. She would even be there to witness how her father and people on both sides are dividing her dowry cows, but, on the whole, it is ideal that dowry cattle are divided after the bride has been given over. Dowry cattle division is one of the significant stages in the Dinka marriage system. It is one of the stages that brings almost the whole kinship together. Quarrels and fights arising from the division of dowry cattle are not infrequent, especially if the girl's father does not want to give rightful shares to his relatives and in-laws, the bride's maternal relatives.

For the dowry cattle to be divided, certain procedures and arrangements have to first be made by the bride's side. People who would likely get a share of from three cows onward are informed by the bride's father to prepare for the provision of services in their homes during the dowry division days. If we are to again take the Rek Dinka way of doing it, then *mony nyandit*, the eldest married daughter and her husband who deserve a share called *ariɛk* are notified to provide a bull to be slaughtered for meat services to the guests when they come. They are also told to prepare beer and food services for the occasion. *Wendït*, the eldest brother of the bride and the son of *wendït*, who have the primogenitary right in the family, these people are asked to avail a big bull each to be slaughtered for meat services during the dowry division. They are also asked to prepare sufficient white stuff beer in their homes. One of those bulls would be called *muɔr akuëth*, also called *muɔr ric*, the bull for young men or youth groups. The bigger bull from the bride's brother or from *wën wëndit* is called *muɔr ruändit*. Any relative who may have the right to eight cows as his share is also asked to provide a bull for services. The father of the bride and his wives, plus the rest of the bride's brothers would, in addition to the bride's mother, do the rest of the services during division days. Paternal and maternal uncles and aunts only prepare white stuff beer. Brothed porridge and the porridge seasoned with butter oil, *diääŋ,* are all served. The rest of the members of the family of the bride are made to participate in the provision of services. Some may provide rams. Others provide beer or food, or do certain things that are required by the marriage as services. It must, however, be mentioned that the east bank Dinka system of dowry division is markedly different from that of Bahr el Ghazal being described. There is no *ariɛk* to the bride's eldest sister like in Bahr el Ghazal where there is also something called *aruɛɛth* or reverse cattle paid to the groom's side by the bride's kin.

With all these preparations and arrangements done, a word or a person is sent, inviting the groom's side to come for the cattle division. A day for their arrival is fixed and community elders are also made to know the dowry cattle of the girl of so and so are going to be divided on a given date. In response to the invitation the groom's people begin to send a team of about three men to come and approve the slaughtering of the first bull called muɔr akuëth, which is usually slaughtered late in the afternoon. They also come to let the in-laws set the service work into motion, knowing the marriage guests are coming the following morning. The next day, after the arrival of those harbingers, the groom's side begin to arrive, coming in big numbers, by columns. The youth folk of the groom's side are expected to come in large numbers. They come in a festive way, singing and doing traditional dances in the courtyard of the bride's mother. The rest come with the women folk. Signs of joy from singing women and old and young men goes on as the groom's parties begin to arrive. Their play shouts alert everybody, even the far off villagers. Everybody becomes aware of the arrival of the guests. The guests are serenely welcomed and distributed to their prepared guest places with the women taken to their own places. The guests are accorded with high respect. What follows would be enjoyment by the groom's side and the attending members of the community. Abundant white stuff beer, meat, food and all the other things of the marriage are now served in earnest.

Meanwhile, serious arrangements and talks leading to going to where the cows are also goes together with these festivities. It is from those talks that the bride's father and the father of the groom are known to separately sit to scheme out how the dowry cattle should be divided. It is from this close talk that actual figures or shares to be given to so and so are made by the two principals. They may be assisted by one or two aides from both sides, particularly the eldest sons to both. This is one of the critical moments involving the use of wit for a bargain. With Bahr el Ghazal Dinka, the apportioning of such types and numbers of cows to be given to so and so must go with the kind and number of reverse cows the groom's side would receive in return. Reverse cows are what Bahr el Ghazal Dinka call *arueeth, aruëth* in plural. In most parts of Rekland, arueeth or aruëth is a serious matter during the division of the dowry cattle. If not well tackled by the bride's side, it could lead to the dissolution of the marriage even before the girl is delivered to her new home. With reverse payments, there are a number of cows that the bride's kin must pay to the bridegroom's relatives whose cows are given to him or her. The bride's wealth side must pay the bridegroom's kin a certain fraction of the total number from their own cattle and not from the cattle given to them by the bridegroom's side, unless there is good reason for the bride's kin to pay from the very cows given to them as their legal share. In some parts of Dinka land, Dinka Agaar and Dinka Ngɔk, for example, reverse payment consists of approximately one third of the total bride wealth paid. It is 40% of the paid dowry among the Rek Dinka of the Tonj region, but some parts of Tonj-like Riaaŋ *nhom* people of Tonj East county do their aruɛɛth system the Agaar way. The east bank Dinka do not pay reverse cows as aruɛɛth like is done by the Bahr el Ghazal Dinka. They only pay what is called *adhuk-wiin*, which is merely one cow given to their daughter's husband, their son-in-law.

What Bahr el Ghazal Dinka communities call aruɛɛth is to the east bank Dinka a mere one cow with its suckling heifer. It is called the *alökthök* cow given to the son-in-law in order for him to be drinking water and eating normally with his in-laws. This alökthök is, however, the same with alökthök done to a son-in-law in some parts of Bahr el Ghazal, although in Bahr el Ghazal it is just one good heifer given by the bride's father to his son-in-law in order for him to be able to drink water and eat from his in-laws.

Alökthök to the son-in-law is, however, a social ritual which is attended by all of the groom's age mates. It is an occasion done separately from the marriage occasion because it demands many services that cannot be done concurrently with marriage which itself requires a lot of services and takes a long time to finish. Some families are, however, able to do ruääi for the marriage and alökthök at the same time, Ideally alökthök is done after the bride has already been delivered to her husband. Alökthök, which the Bahr el Ghazal Dinka confines to the son-in-law, is made by the east bank Dinka to include close uncles of the bride and the groom. The Bor and Twic Dinka, or all of the Dinka communities of Jonglei state, includes the parents, close uncles and the community chiefs on both sides. They give alökthök in the form of a goat, bull or money nowadays. Those are what the Rek Dinka in Bahr el Ghazal call *awulör* which are expenses a suitor gives to his in-laws in the course of *hhuööt* (courting) and in the course of the marriage.

With aruɛɛth there are, however, no set or fixed rules for calculating the amount of reverse cattle to be paid, except for the Bahr el Ghazal Dinka. The variation in this is because Dinka marriage is not commercial in essence. The role of the cattle is but to legalise the new social bond between the two families and clans of the two spouses. It is this non-commercial nature which makes the Dinka call for the bride's side to pay the reverse cattle, which in Bahr el Ghazal is customarily compulsory and legally binding, for it has become a custom and has therefore become a law enshrined into Dinka customary law put into a statutory form in 1976. Dinka customary law, which became one of the sources of the country constitution, adopted this practice and it has become legal in Bahr el Ghazal. However, the purpose of aruɛɛth is not very clear although originally it was initiated to help the groom have some cows with which to find the new basis to start his own cattle after he had given away all or most of his cows into the marriage and has a new home and family now that he has started his independence from his parents. In later times it was found that bride price has very much gone up, unlike how it was during those times before this expensive modern era. This invited a range of family networks to contribute for one single marriage which goes beyond fifty cows, while the aristocrats and cattle tycoons go beyond hundreds. This is what invited the extension of reverse payment from what was only the groom to include all his kin who are also made to pay heavily. Aruëth are therefore paid to the groom and his people according to their contribution. The bride's kin also pay reverse cows according to the shares they received during the distribution of the dowry cattle.

With reverse payment in mind, a man will assist a friend or a relative to increase the amount of dowry cattle for the purpose of making the marriage succeed and also on the understanding that he will be partly refunded through reverse payment. His remaining cows will be later refunded when the daughter of that woman is married. When failure to pay the lawfully prescribed reverse cows comes to be the case on the part of any bride's kin, the groom's relative or kin so affected will go to court with that in-law and the law court will see to it that the right of the groom's kin is upheld and he is given his right. Generally a great deal of litigation concerning failure from the bride's relatives to discharge their obligation to pay reverse cattle preoccupies many of the Dinka law courts in Bahr el Ghazal, particularly among the Rek. It is even more of a problem in Tonj areas where bride price has continued to go up. Failure to fulfil the promised cow or cows to the bride's relative(s) is another source of multiple cases preoccupying Dinka law courts.

According to the Rek Dinka of the Tonj region, four cows are paid back to a suitor's relative or brother who paid ten cows as his contribution to the marriage dowry. This is true if his cows got apportioned to one person who has a right to ten cows. If his ten cows were spread out during the distribution so that he cannot get exactly his four reverse cows, that relative will be entitled to the right to compile a law suit against the groom himself and the court will give him his right from the groom, for it is his marriage and in-laws who disadvantaged his kin or relative. Three reverse cows are paid for every eight cows received by the bride's relative. Unlike their Rek counterparts, the Agaar and Gɔk Dinka pay three reverse cows for every ten dowry cows received by a bride's relative, one for five cows and two for eight cows. Riaanŋhom Dinka in Tonj East county give one reverse cow for every five dowry cows received. In some places one reverse cow is paid for three cows received. Bride's kin or relatives given one or two dowry cows are not required to pay any reverse cow. The east bank people give a special cow called *riɛt* to the bride's father. This cow is called a*kɛc-wär* among the Rek, but it is generally known as *weŋ wun-nya,* a special cow of the bride's father. In the east bank there is also another cow called *puɔt*, given or chosen by the bride's eldest brother. Bahr el Ghazal Dinka people call it *ayup*, a cow of special choice by the girl's eldest brother. In Bahr el Ghazal the husband of the eldest daughter, whose sister-in-law is now being married, is allowed to choose for himself one good cow, one good heifer and one good bull among the dowry cattle. This is done before anybody from his in-laws is apportioned his share or before anybody from the bride's family is allowed to choose any cow. *Mony-nya* is, however, not allowed to choose the cow which was earlier allotted to the bride's father right at the time when the dowry cattle were driven from the groom's cattle camp. A relative who received two first class bulls as his share from the marriage bulls is required to pay one first class bull as a reverse bull. It is given to the groom's relative who gave him those two bulls, but he is not required to pay a reverse bull if the two bulls he received came from different groom's relatives. In a situation where all the first class bulls of the groom himself are given to different relatives of the bride so that the groom cannot get a reverse bull on account of his bulls having gone to different in-laws, the bride's father or brother will be required by law to pay to his son or brother-in-law one first class bull for the bulls taken by his own relatives. The same is true of two or three oxen (*thön*) paid into the marriage by reason of the marriage being a big and expensive one and amounting to more than a hundred and fifty cows. The bride's father will be required to pay one *thɔn* as a reverse ox.

At times the dowry demanded by the bride's side may have not been paid all at once. A certain number of dowry cattle may have been pledged to be paid in due course and by specific relatives. Certain relatives on the bride's side are matched up with those relatives of the groom's side, especially if the legal contribution of that relative is equal to the right allotted to that relative of the bride who must wait to receive his share on a later date. The same is true for the reverse payments. At times a bride's kin may postpone paying his required aruɛɛth to pay it another time. This is accepted by the groom's relative if the reason for postponement is reasonable and convincing. Those are cases which subsequently go to court if the postponer breaches the agreed time or he decides to repudiate his earlier promise. In fact, the problems found in the distribution of the dowry cattle and in reverse payments also form part of what we have chosen to call the *Dinka cattle complex* in the last chapter.

KUETH NYA OR THE TAKING OF THE BRIDE TO HER NEW HOME

After the completion of the division of the dowry cattle, the groom's party would return to their homes, expecting the bride to be brought shortly. The preparation takes days for the girl to be first organised. She would need those ornamentations due to a bride, things like bead necklaces, waist beads and elephant armlets called *apiöök*. Those things such as apiöök are expensively bought, even with a cow in the form of a bull or a heifer. Beads of the types brought to Dinka brides are also bought with a bull or a heifer. Women charged with the duty of taking the bride to her new home are informed to also prepare themselves. Girls of her age are also made to be among the ladies to accompany her. Those girls do include a younger girl to later remain with her as her assistant for at least a year or so. The ladies are chosen among the most credible ones in the family. Their duty is to counsel (*wëët*) the bride about how she should behave and work in her new home, now as a wife, to no longer behave like a girl. They are to coach her about her duties and responsibilities towards her husband and his parents as well as children and the family at large. From them she will learn more about what a husband is and how to hold in balance the relations between the people of her husband and her blood relatives. She is schooled by them about how to pay respect and humility to her husband and people like her husband's parents and other elders. She is even told how to talk, how to eat and how to walk in the courtyard. She should not do this or that. All these should in clear terms include how she should cook, how many times she should cook and how to generally care for the husband.

After the preparations of the bride are over, a word is dispatched to the groom's people about the bride being brought to them. As women take this part of their role very seriously many do go, even those not selected or allowed by their husbands are always known to want to do so on their own. One or two men are there and then made to accompany the women who are taking the bride to her new home. Women who are usually selected to take the bride to her new home are always credible women with a good reputation from the bride's family.

GEM NYA OR THE HANDING OVER OF THE BRIDE

Usually the team moving with the bride always prefers to reach the groom's home in darkness so that the bride is not just seen by everybody. On arrival ululations from both sides become the signal that the bride and her party have arrived. The rest of the arrangements leading to *nya acï gam,* 'the bride has been given over,' or *nya acï päl yöt ke moc,* 'the bride has been allowed into the room with her husband,' may take place the same night of their arrival or postponed to some other date, depending on the opinion from the groom's family or according to the prevailing circumstances. The old ladies who are presumed to have done their work on the bride, one of whom must be the bride's paternal aunt, now retire back to their womenfolk and they now become part of the women guests but at least two very direct old ladies are expected to remain to sleep on the door's threshold outside the bridal house to guard against any inconvenience from within and without that nuptial room. They sleep there to make sure their daughter does not misbehave inside the wedding room as she first comes into contact with her husband, the time of the beginning of their union. Meanwhile the team, as they are being lavishly served with beer, food and meat from slaughtered bull or rams, goes into festivities until their return after two or three days, leaving one or two girls to remain with the bride to assist her for some months. Those women are called *dhioop, dhiɔp* when singular. Finally she is of her husband's family, so that even if she goes back to see her relatives at some given time, she does so as a guest, not as a legal member of the clan any longer.

While all the kin on the bride's side are called *paruäidië* (my in-laws) by the groom, all women who are related to the bride are collectively called *dhioop* from the word *dhiɔp*, which is also used for one in-law woman. The word dhiɔp is also used basically to denote a sister-in-law. All the girls from the bride's clan are also called dhioop. The brother of the bride is called *thu* and when there are more, they are called *thuu*. Thu and Thuu apply to all the agnate young men who are related paternally to one's wife. They include the boys. The wife's father is called *wa*, meaning father. The paternal uncles are also called *wälän,* meaning paternal uncles-in-law. A paternal uncle-in-law older than one's father-in-law is wa, just the way one calls his in-law father. The actual mother of one's wife (*man-nya*) is called *ma,* meaning mother. The wives of one's father-in-law are also called mothers-in-law. This is also used in a wider sense for every woman from the clan of one's wife. All these cordial names are used for in-laws as a sign of respect, for in the Dinka world the highest respect one must make is to the in-laws. The serene respect called *athɛɛk* imposed by the marriage system in Dinka society accounts for the positive social relations found among Dinka people.

Described above is the ideal pattern which is followed by all the Dinka people in a marriage we had called customary marriage, which is the natural and culturally accepted way of arriving at a marital union. Those who respect public tranquillity, norms and customs perform their marriages in the above manner. It carries with it the highest prestige to both the bride and the groom. People who have sufficient number of cattle always do their marriages in this customary way and it is the kind of marriage which strongly keeps the Dinka social cobweb.

MARRIAGE THROUGH BETROTHAL, CALLED 'LUNY KƆU', AND 'MEK' OR CHOICE

Apart from that classical customary marriage so described above, there are two other means to customary marriage. These two also carry more respect and weight in contrast to all other forms of marriage. The two are betrothal, called *luny kɔu* and choice, called *mék*. They can be explained in terms of the capacity to marry or be married. Among the Dinka, capacity to marry or be married is largely determined by age and seniority in the family. Dinka people do not have notions of age by years. The capacity to marry or be married is determined by puberty. But a man may be betrothed to a girl before he is initiated to manhood. Some social dictates may make the family betroth a girl for their son while he is still a boy and is in his adolescent age. The betrothed girl may have reached her puberty age but she has to wait for the boy to grow or to be initiated in order for her marriage to him to be concluded. Betrothal of this kind is rare but it does happen. In this form of betrothal a number of cows, mostly five or ten, and a bull, are paid to the father of the girl after the official formalities of application and acceptance are made first. The cows so paid are considered as cows of luny kɔu, 'betrothal dowry'. Luny kɔu may be done to a girl at puberty and the man is also of age to marry but certain circumstances act as hindrance to the implementation and the marriage has to be delayed for some time while the girl is booked. A grown up man can also book an immature girl. He can pay five or ten cows to the girl's father and wait for her to attain maturity or marriageable age when he would then complete the marriage and the girl becomes his wife.

Mɛk, which is choice, is a slightly different form of the beginning of marriage. In mɛk from the word '*meek*' the choice placed on the girl could be called designation, which is not betrothal in a sense for it does not involve payment of any dowry cattle. It only involves the expression of choice. A ring, called *milaŋ,* which is a metal object from either copper or bronze, is put on the girl's wrist as evidence of the man's choice of her. Mɛk is usually made by the father of the boy. Additional difference between betrothal (luny kɔu) and choice (mɛk) is that mɛk is distinguished from betrothal because betrothal confers certain legal rights upon the girl and is considered to some degree as a marriage, conferring retroactive marital rights to the suitor, even before the marriage is completed. The betrothed girl remains the legal bride to the man or boy while she remains a girl, still awaiting the completion of her marriage. Any person showing interest in the betrothed girl is not allowed by the family, and the man who did the betrothal can raise a legal case against any one tampering with her. In betrothal talks were held between the relatives of the betrothing man and the relatives of the girl and agreement preceded by consent from the girl's father and people was reached. This agreement is usually concreted and legalised by the sacrifice of a bull and there was therefore bloodletting. These crucial things are not done in mɛk.

In both cases such early booking is a source of pride to both the small girl and the family. It enhances the girl's status in contrast to her peers. Both mɛk and luny kɔu ultimately lead to customary marriage. The two express the high esteem with which the parents of the girl are held by the choosing or betrothing family. It underpins a hardened determination on the part of the boy's father to marry from those parents. It also indicates how clean the family background of the parents of the girl is and the betrothing or choosing father wants to share in that positive background and reputation.

MARRIAGE THROUGH ELOPEMENT; JÖTJÖT

This type of marriage comes by compulsion from the groom who decides to agree with the girl he is ardently in love with. He secretly courts the girl of his own accord. The two agree to secretly escape to the place of the groom. Dinka people call this serious act of transgression *jöt nya*, elopement of somebody's daughter with a view to compelling both sides to accept him in marrying her. The groom does this grievous offence to the girl's people when he is either sure his people do not want the girl or the girl's relatives do not want him. Elopement, abduction and impregnation are actions which are judged as wrong by Dinka custom but which certain young men and girls do as measures aimed at influencing marriage to be possible in their favour. In elopement the man takes the girl to the home of the one he knows would be in charge of his marriage. Some young men take the eloping girl straight to the chief's home. By so doing he has shown he wants to marry that girl but, whichever way it takes, elopement is a serious offence which prompts the girl's kin, if they implicitly accept their daughter to marry to such a man, to go armed into the cattle camp of the man's relatives and seize all the cattle they can find. Sometimes a fatal fight takes place as a result of the man's people making resistance to the forceful seizing of their cattle for an elopement to which they were not a part. In the past such fights used to be done using clubs call *thieec*, *thiec* for singular. Injuries incurred used to be mostly head injuries. Although there used to be death cases, they used to be few, only grievous head injuries used to be the case. In the recent past till today Dinka society has become more violent. They abandoned the use of clubs and went with spears in their wars caused by such offences as elopement. With spears many people are killed.

Others sustain grievous wounds. Nowadays, Dinka people have acquired firearms due to the long war of liberation that brought

Fig 40: Showing an armed expedition by Dinka young men angered by the news of a girl from their clan eloping with a young man from another clan. They are angrily rushing to confront the man's relatives unless his relatives pull out from the cattle camp so that they can seize the cattle in reparation of the wrong done to them.

independence to South Sudan. Cases of violence using guns have made elopement feared by the young men of today and their loved ones but generally elopement is still a problem that keeps Dinka rural society in trouble. However, in addressing such cases, some prudent kinsmen of the wrongdoer do not attempt to obstruct the angry people provoked by their son. Instead, if they wanted their son to marry the girl, which would be preferable, they approach the chief to summon the girl's relatives so that marriage can be discussed under the supervision of the court of law. In response the chief does the summons. For determining what is to be paid to the girl's relatives when both families have come to the court, they are made to state their positions. In the case of elopement it is always certain that the man says to his people and the court that he persuaded the girl to elope to be his wife and wants both sides to agree. If both sides agree then the court will fix the day for dowry cattle and the court helps to fix the number of cows and bulls to be paid as down payment. *Wanhalɛl Dinka customary law* in the Bahr el Ghazal region had determined

31 cows, five first class bulls and one *thɔn* to be given by law to the relatives of the eloping girl and the rest of the bride wealth can be demanded later by the girl's people when they call the groom's kin to their home for marriage discussions. Although several cases of elopement had been ending up in separation of the two parties by the court due to strong objection to the union by either side, many marriages start from elopement, and despite its basic lack of respect due to its abruptness and trespass into the rights of others, marriage through elopement has come to be one way some Dinka men make their marriages.

Rek Dinka law courts, particularly those in Tonj areas, make certain arrangements for elopement marriages. If the cattle seized by the angry youth from the eloping girl were less than the amount fixed by Dinka customary law, the difference is compelled to be paid by the groom's side. If more than 31 cows and five big bulls plus one ox, what the law had prescribed, was taken by force, the excess is returned by law. In the case that the girl's side insist against the marriage, not wanting marital union, they are allowed by the court. Their daughter is handed over to them. The girl is given a small heifer called *weŋ buɔŋ*, also called *dan adhoŋ,* 'the cow of the skirt'. It is called so because the girl becomes a woman as in their elopement process she had sexual intercourse with the man. She would no longer be regarded as a virgin. She is no longer called a girl. She must from then wear the bridal dress and continue to dress as a woman, whether married to this man or not. If the girl later appears to have conceived, then a pregnant heifer is taken from the man and that cow is to be taken with her to the new man who becomes her husband after marriage is agreed and done. That pregnant heifer is given over to the man who subsequently married her in order to comfort him because his wife is brought to him while she is not a virgin. The pregnant heifer is given in place of the girl's virginity.

MARRIAGE THROUGH IMPREGNATION

Illegally impregnating an unmarried girl is the worst offence to occur to a Dinka family, lineage or clan. Illegal conception comes to a girl who has accepted illegal sexual intercourse with a man whom she is in love with. They do this for the purpose of love without being aware of the possibility of conception. Sometimes a girl who is in great want for the man she so loves may trap the man to have sex with her at the time conception is very likely. At times it is the man who forces the girl to have sex with him, especially when he has knowledge of the girl's recent menstrual flow. He does this in the hope to conceive with the girl as a shortcut for him to marry her. Many cases of this nature do occur in Dinka society because the young man may have insufficient cows or legal rights to enable him to marry the girl he so desires. He therefore decides to resort to illegal means in the hope to compel both families to allow him to marry her.

Whether it was the man or girl who enticed the other into having sex aimed at illegal conception to compel the two families into accepting the marriage, the whole thing remains to be viewed by Dinka society as being so degrading to the girl's family and her entire kinship. In contrast to elopement, impregnation of an unmarried girl is a bad omen to happen in a Dinka family. It means the girl's people become vulnerable to the decision of the man who had rudely abused their natural right through conceiving with their girl.

Illegally impregnated girls give no good ground for her relatives to go to war with the relatives of the offender, nor do they have grounds to seize the cattle from the relatives of the offender. Their only choice is to go to court so that the offender is made to come with his people in order to tell whether they want to marry the girl or not. When they come to court the girl and the man would first be made to let the court know if it was true that conception came from the very man as claimed by the pregnant girl or not. After intensive cross examination of the two by the court to establish the truth, the opinion of the girl is sought if she intends to be a wife to the man or not. In most cases she is expected to say this is her intent. At this the court would turn to the man for his opinion. If he expresses an objection to marrying her, the court and public at the hearing will first exert some effort to circumvent the man to accept the marriage in the interests of public peace and tranquillity. If he insists upon refusal and his father and people stand in support of his objection, the court will see no basis to compel marriage to take place. A separation verdict is then passed by the court and the man is fined for the offence and asked to pay a pregnant heifer to the girl plus a bull to buy women's dresses for the girl to use since she can no longer be dressing like a girl. The girl is therefore handed back to her people to be later married by someone else.

Should the man say he intends to marry her and his father and people gave consent, then the court will ask the girl's father and relatives to transfer the matter home to start marriage processes provided the groom's side pays the legally authorised number of cattle as a means to soothe the anger of their in-laws. In this case, impregnation becomes a means to marriage although the value of the bride will no longer be the same as that under customary marriage and/or marriage through elopement.

MARRIAGE BY CHOICE FROM THE GIRL'S SIDE

Against Dinka conventional trend whereby it is the groom's side that initiates and chooses the girl and family from which to marry as discussed under Dinka ways to marriage, it also occurs that a girl's father, with the approval of his kin, may decide to choose a man who should marry his daughter. This usually happens when a girl is spoiled, has eloped and was rejected or is impregnated by somebody who could not marry her. It can also happen if a woman is divorced and must remarry to have a new husband and a home, for in the Dinka world no woman can stay without a husband and a home as can be the case with urban women. After elopement or impregnation it may be the girl's side, especially the father, who refuses the marriage to take place. He therefore decides who to relate with by proposing to offer his spoiled daughter to a person of his choice. When such a thing occurs the chosen man and his father will feel honoured. They would readily accept, especially if the chosen is not a young man whose right to marriage makes him ineligible to marry a spoiled girl. A person is chosen by the girl's father and kin for varied reasons. Firstly, it may be because the man is known to be well-mannered and is a good manager in his home. It may be because he has enough cows to pay the needed dowry, or he may be a man from family stock, which is appreciated by the girl's father and kin.

All in all some marriages are arrived at in this way among the Dinka. Apart from this a girl may overtly decide to go to a man she of her own accord has decided to be her husband, a man with whom there never had been any love or an affair. This can also lead to marriage once the man and his people accept the girl for a wife.

MARRIAGE THROUGH ABDUCTION

A man in some circumstances may choose to gather his age mates and make them assist him in secretly going out to apprehend somebody's daughter, who he wants to marry but either has no time to undergo all those processes such as flirtation, courting and so forth, or he may feel inferior to be accepted by the girl while he has enough cattle to pay on her. Such an act is also done if the suitor has discovered that the girl he is so much in love with is about to be married by someone who is prepared to marry her before he or her people are prepared to enter into her marriage negotiations and dowry payments. While abduction may lead to marriage in certain instances, it is more than rape. It is a classical offence and it is not done in many parts of Dinka land. Abduction which is the forceful taking of a girl with the aim to marry her largely against her consent is rampant in some Dinka places. Those who frequently do such acts are those from noble families who do not care about all the marriage processes and public opinion, provided they made their choice of a girl. Objects of this behaviour are usually the star girls in the community.

GHOST MARRIAGE

'Ghost' in Dinka means spirit or the shadow of a dead person, called *atiap*. In the Dinka world all the dead relatives, brothers and parents are considered and accepted as part of the living family. They are not severed off from the family by death. A dead relative is understood and felt to still exist in spirit as a member of the family, lineage and clan and he or she still forms part of the family with rights that are enjoyed by the living brother(s). Dinka people believe in spiritual life after death. It is upon this belief that men, even girls, who die while too young to be married, or who die leaving behind no son, should have married in their name a wife or wives to have a male issue born unto them in order for their line to be maintained for their continuity. If a married woman dies without a son, she is regarded as *thuööm* and it is the duty of her husband to marry for her a wife to procreate children to perpetuate her name and family line. If she was not married it is the duty of her brother(s) to marry a wife to her to keep her line within the family and lineage.

Ghost marriage, which the Dinka people do as part of their culture, is founded upon this very concept of continuity and posterity for every child born to a legally married parents, be it a male or female child, grown up or infant. Except those who die through miscarriage, any infant who dies after birth is considered by the Dinka as already being a created human being after he or she completed the full gestation term in its mother's womb and physically came to the world as a fully created human being. It is his or her full gestation term period which counts. This is what qualifies him or her as a member of the family lineage or clan, for God's divine activity to create it with physical being and a spirit soul was intentionally done fully. There is no way to deny there was somebody created by the creator with an intention to create a human being. The dead infant or child continues to maintain his or her seniority or position within his or her mother's birth order. Those dead infants or children are therefore not deprived of their agnatic right to have their names and line perpetuated just like those who are alive.

Like the Old Testament Jews, the Dinka people do ghost marriages. They marry wives for their dead relatives and procreate children in the dead person's name and through this, the dead person's family line is maintained. While this is done for the males the same is done for dead sisters and daughters, the barren and the impotent. That of the barren and impotent is, however, levirate marriage.

When a decision is made by the family and members of the lineage to marry a wife for the dead man, sister or daughter, the living person to act as the official genitor is always junior brother to the dead man, sister or daughter. The agreed heir to the name of such a dead person must marry a wife for him or her. If the dead person was senior to the heir, even though he or she might have died as a baby, his/her ghost marriage must have priority before anybody junior to him/her is allowed to marry for himself a wife. Nowadays, emphasis has come to be restricted to that of the male ones. Ghost marriage for dead girls or sisters has come to be for those who died at adolescence and maturity age.

Although the impotent and the barren do their marriages themselves, unlike that of the dead for which the word ghost marriage rightly applies, procreation is done by a person of their choice. That person may be a brother, half-brother or any of the paternal kin. That person is not responsible for the woman as long as the impotent husband is physically alive and is able to do for his wife all the needs of the home except for the conjugal role for procreation. This is a bit different from that of the barren wife who, because she is a woman, cannot cohabit with her wife. She is, however, the owner, and children must be called after her as the legal father. She is by essence a woman-husband and is responsible for her wife in terms of upkeep as long as she has been recognised as a member of the family with shares and rights. This is when she is divorced by her husband due to her barrenness and has come back to her people. If she is not divorced the situation becomes different. Her husband marries a wife into her homestead and finds for that woman a person to procreate children for her homestead. Such a person is always one of the sons of her husband. If for some reason this cannot be possible, her husband himself can procreate children for that woman whose children must be children of the homestead of the barren woman and the female children must acquire their names from her name, the barren. The male child that would accrue from that marriage will thus represent the homestead, the mother line of the barren and the problem of continuity for that barren lady is solved.

In some situations ghost marriage may be performed by a wife whose husband has died, leaving her without a son. This is done by a widow already old enough to bear any child through levirate arrangements within the family, or she may be a barren lady and her husband had no close agnates to do the ghost marriage obligation. In this case she is the genitor by name and is fully responsible for the marriage and the woman. She does the marriage herself as *wun ruääi*, head of the marriage. After she secured the bride she would then invite a man of her choice to come and cohabit the woman for her natural sexual needs and the children resulting from that ghost marriage will then belong to her dead husband provided she is their mother in silhouette to the actual mother. If the dead husband did have a son or sons from other wives, the sonless or barren lady would still have a wife to be married for herself and she would choose one of her husband's sons as *ala yöt*, the genitor, to produce children with that woman in order to perpetuate her family line as part of her husband's overall descent line.

In a ghost marriage the girl to be married is chosen by the genitor who must be the one to flirt, date or court her as he would do for his rightful marriage. He does all the procedural aspects of an ordinary customary marriage earlier described. The genitor's relationship with this wife of a dead person is closer, more intense and directly personal, not nominal or impersonal in their stay. Since the woman knows him and only him, they behave and stay as husband and wife. This is because even the idea to marry this woman initially came from him or it was done in his name on behalf of his dead relative, brother or father who is not physically seen by her. The only distinction is that both the mother and children are called after the dead father and their rights and shares within the family come as those of their dead father, not from the genitor's shares and rights.

In contrast to levirate, the genitor's responsibility over the woman is total and complete. He treats her like his wife and the woman also handles him like the actual husband except in situations where the woman and her children come into conflict with him over his tampering with rights and properties of her dead husband, things which are legally her rights within the context of the family. Notwithstanding all these, the relationship between this type of a genitor, called *ala yöt,* and the wife of a ghost person is only psychological and vicarious rather than purely legal. Yet, such a woman cannot commit adultery with another relative, even with any brother of the genitor. The genitor will have a legal right before the court of law for adultery on behalf of the dead husband. This is because he is the legally and socially accredited representative of the dead person. There is a Dinka saying to the effect that, *except in her bedroom, a wife belongs to the whole kinfolk.*

Ghost marriage is nearer to normal customary marriage and is one way by which the power, rights and spiritual existence of the dead are enhanced, although in this modern era the urban Dinka may view both levirate and ghost marriages as having negative undertones that tend to endanger the psychic wellbeing of women. Because of consistent death from diseases and too many wars in which many Dinka young men are killed before they marry and even after they marry, ghost and levirate marriages are very many among the Dinka even today. Death from predatory animals such as buffalos, lions, elephants, snakes and dangerous river animals and creatures such as hippopotamuses and crocodiles adds to several deaths among the Dinka. Ghost and levirate marriages continue to play a major role in the Dinka social setup.

LEVIRATE MARRIAGE

We have earlier explained under customary or legal marriage that this is the normal union between a man and a woman but in polygamy, the man may be married to another woman. This is not the case for the married woman. Under this normal customary or legal marriage, both the wife and her children biologically and legally belong to the husband of the woman. Children trace their line through him. This normal customary or legal type of marriage does not differ to marriages by non-Dinka communities around the globe. It is the other Dinka marriages, ghost, levirate and polygamy that make a bit of difference between the Dinka and other peoples but Dinka customary and ghost marriages give rise to what is call levirate marriage, a kind of procreation arrangement which a family does when the husband or genitor dies. The Dinka marriage does not come to an end upon the death of the husband as is the case with other communities. Marriage can only be terminated by divorce, not by the death of the husband. With the Dinka, a widow is legally inherited by a genitor who is usually the deceased's brother or direct paternal relative as described above. However, the death of a wife before she had three children with her husband or with the genitor can lead to the dissolution of the marriage whereby the Dinka law court gives the husband or genitor the right to recover his dowry cattle from his in-laws so that his kin are able to marry for him a new wife in order for him to continue to procreate children in his name for continuity purposes.

When a husband or the genitor dies, the woman or his wives become *tiŋ* or *diär jɔɔk,* a widow or widows. After the mourning period of about a year or more the widow or widows are made by the family to just transform their marital union into levirate, by which she is or they are given over to live (*rëër*) with the husband's nearest agnate, who may be the eldest son of the husband from another wife elder to her. He may be one of the younger brothers to her late husband. The widow must not be judged too old for the son of her late husband. If she appears rather older than her husband's son and she is still at her childbearing age, it is preferred that her husband's brother be the better genitor although the responsibility lies with her husband's son.

While levirate arrangement is automatic for the son of the dead husband, especially the eldest son, the consent of the widow is sought at first in the choice among the sons of who can be her genitor. Where the husband is survived by a son or a number of sons, it goes without saying that the widow must confine to one of those sons. In case there is no son left by the husband, one of the junior brothers of the dead husband can be the genitor. In some cases the legal heir to the widow can delegate the right of cohabitation to another relative within the family or lineage. In this case he remains to retain his overriding right over the widow. The cohabiter, who is not the legal heir, has no right to interfere with management, properties or entitlements of the dead husband. The legal heir remains to act as the legal guardian and supervisor over the estate of the deceased until such time as the widow's son or sons has reached maturity and is or are able to take charge of their mother's or father's affairs and properties. The cohabiting agent in this case has no right to sue the widow in case of adultery with another man. It is the legal heir who has the legal right to sue the adulterer and the widow.

Although Dinka customary law does not allow divorce after the death of the husband, a widow who decides to commit adultery or who becomes easygoing and a source of disrepute to the family, can be divorced irrespective of whether she has children or not. In the case where she has no children the cattle dowry paid on her are recovered from her relatives. If there are three or more children, the dowry remains unrecovered except for the five cows called *yok töny*, 'the pot's cattle', which must be recovered, leaving the rest of the cows with the in-laws because of the children, to be legal. By all practical measures, levirate is primarily a legal interest of the dead husband and his kin. It is a cultural must as such and the widow has to cohabit with a family man of their choice.

In levirate there are no ceremonies done after the decision is made to choose a family member to be the genitor or cohabiter, except for the silent rite whereby the family or lineage elders gather with a ram, *thɔn amääl*, to announce the decision to the spirit of the dead husband and the dead ancestors so that the genitor or cohabiter called *ala yöt* sleeps with the widow as an officiated person for the purpose of procreation and continuity. The ram is slaughtered with invocational words from those family elders and this rite is done for the wellbeing of the one chosen to step into the shoes of his late brother or relative. The genitor becomes the pro-husband and foster father to the orphans while the dead husband remains as the *pater*. Levirate is not a marriage. It is an internal arrangement done within the family context for marriage and procreation continuity. It is done because the procreative potential of the widow must not be frustrated or severed following her husband's death nor should the dead man's name and participation in the family and society be allowed to come to an end simply by reason of his death.

Levirate arrangement is supported even by the widow's relatives. This is because, in Dinka thought, the woman's procreative rights as well as all those associated with her dead husband including her children are her husband's exclusive prerogatives. Her dead husband's people derive their authority from this. Again the woman, as a legal member of the family clan and society, has the natural right to procreation and continuity in her own right as much as the husband. As such it is not a right for her dead husband's people to deny or refuse her to continue with her own procreation and continuity right.

As earlier explained the Dinka people have a saying that 'the wife belongs to all the people', *tik e kën raam abën*. It is the woman who makes it possible for the society to exist and she is the one who makes the society move ahead. The society and family therefore remain vigilantly concerned with what happens to a woman. As is usually the case the genitor, who also takes the position of a foster father, is obliged to provide the widow with a home and her orphaned children with a father's or paternal care and responsibilities.

While levirate may be viewed in the negative by other cultures, particularly the non-African or western cultures that see it as an aspect of human rights abuse to the widow, levirate in Dinka culture is a stabilising arrangement. It saves the marriage from collapse after the death of the husband. It is therefore compulsory to both the widow and the genitor. Dinka people inherited or brought this practice from the Middle East where the Hebrews still keep it today as part of their heritage as explained in the Bible.⁹⁶ Like any other form of marital union levirate arrangements between the genitor and the widow can be cancelled by the family and sometimes by the court. This is only done on legitimate grounds. If the genitor cannot stay peacefully with the widow and their peaceful stay cannot be assured after all the conciliatory and reconciliatory attempts by the family and/or by the court, the woman can be made to choose another genitor within the family or the family elders can choose an alternative genitor among the family members. However, where the woman has fallen into disrepute through illegal sex as earlier explained, a divorce can be initiated and the entire marriage is dissolved. Notwithstanding this, there is a strong judicial disposition from Dinka customary law against divorce or dissolution of a marriage after the husband's death. To let things remain as the dead man left them seems to be the guiding principle. Even in situations where normal customary marriage could be dissolved, Dinka courts often refuse the dissolution of the levirate.⁹⁷

SORORATE MARRIAGE

In sororate marriage, a dead wife is substituted with another girl who is always her sister or step-sister. In the past, even a paternal uncle's girl used to be given to the widower as replacement for his dead wife. This is done where the deceased wife leaves very small children and their maternal aunt (*mɛlɛɛn*) is viewed as the rightful girl to be substituted into her place to tenderly nurse them the way they could have been brought up by their mother. Sororate marriage is also done when a wife died before she could have a child. If the

---

96   Deuteronomy Ch. 25:5-8, 'Brother must not reject his brother's wife when he dies…..', the Holy Bible.

97   F Mading Deng, Tradition and modernization. A challenge for law among the Dinka of the Sudan, (3rd ed), Kush Inc. Washington D.C. USA (2004), p. 139

relations between the two families into the marriage were so cordial that both sides do not want the marriage to be dissolved, a sibling sister is given over to replace her dead sister as an *adutïc* wife, a consolace wife to her sister's former husband. He becomes husband to his former sister-in-law! In this case, only a few or a nominal bride price of *arop*, cows for the rite of spraying the replaced girl to be a new couple with her former sister's husband, which will be further explained, are paid to the girl's father. It is a blessing rite to survive the marital union after the death of a wife. The few cows may range from five to ten cows paid to the girl's father. This is done to avoid the implication of incest. Fewer cows are paid because the cows for the first marriage are implicitly transferred onto the new one. The dowry cattle earlier paid on the dead sister therefore remain uncollected. A token dowry is only topped up.

This type of marriage implies that the first marriage has been essentially dissolved by death and the relationship with the in-laws could only be maintained by a new marriage through her younger sister. Although the husband may have been consulted for his opinion, the girls need not be consulted as to whether she should accept being given over in replacement for her sister or not. Girls have deep-rooted respect, allegiance and loyalty to their fathers and any decision made by a father, or one in place of the father, is not usually subject to rejection by a daughter. Dinka daughters see their fathers or guardian fathers as the ultimate power on earth to determine who should marry them, for the father or that guardian will be the one to continue to provide her with the necessary paternal role and services after they are married. Sororate marriage is a clear indication that Dinka marriages do not merely come as a result of the purchase of a woman by a man and his kin. It is such a powerful union between the two parties that even the death of a wife or husband does not necessarily break the social bond that was earlier agreed unless the prevailing circumstances cannot allow the marriage to continue even by sororate means.

To further clarify this Dinka type of marriage called sororate marriage, distinction had to be made between it, levirate and ghost marriage. In the levirate, the previous marriage continues to exist while in sororate it is altogether a new marriage, despite that undertone of the first marriage preserved. In sororate marriage the dowry cattle paid on the dead wife becomes the basis for the new marriage. Insofar as dowry is concerned, it is an extension of the first marriage, but it is the physical absence of the first wife that makes her sister a wife in her own right, because even the children that result from her union with the former husband of her sister are biologically and legally hers. The union between the sororate wife and her deceased sister's husband is one between a wife and husband.

With ghost marriage, the union is between the genitor and the bride in the name of a dead man. The entire marriage and the in-laws are of the dead man, whereas in sororal marriage, the death of the woman gives rise to a new marriage by the same husband. The objective of sororate marriage is to perpetuate the name of the living, not of the dead. The children of the dead wife remain as orphans. They belong to their dead mother. They only receive the needed tender care from their maternal aunt who always treats them like her own children. As stated above the children of her dead sister stand a better chance of being taken care of by their own maternal aunt being turned into their stepmother. The tender and affectionate care they get from their maternal aunt who replaced their dead mother is one of the principal reasons for her becoming a wife to their father by sororal means. Among some Dinka societies, sororate marriage is not done if the dead wife was survived by children. The orphaned children are seen as being tangible symbols of the existence of their mother's marriage. Their father can normally marry elsewhere, not necessarily their maternal aunt. However, it is the condition of the children which forces both sides to enter into the sororate marriage.

DISSOLUTION OF MARRIAGE OR DIVORCE

In Dinka society marriage, once arrived at between the two parties, is not easily dissolved except as a result of the death of the wife who leaves no children behind. Barrenness of the wife can cause the marriage to be dissolved. Because of levirate arrangements, death of the husband does not cause marriage dissolution. Dinka society uses all means possible to restrict or discourage marriage dissolution and divorce. Despite this the Dinka law courts are bedevilled by a substantial amount of cases concerned with the consequences of dissolving marriages.

With divorce, the first and obvious reason is always the wife's barrenness, which Dinka people call *ruut*. A barren woman is called *rol*. *Ruut* in the eyes of the Dinka community is a failure to fulfil the fundamental obligation of marriage. The dowry cattle are therefore returned to the man, all except for *weŋ buɔŋ*, 'a cow of the skirt', which is in effect a compensation cow for having in the first place that girl to be made a woman, no longer a girl. Her marriage potential is obviously reduced as her virginity is no longer there after she has been undergoing cohabitation that has put her to the status of a woman. If the wife did have a child before her barrenness, a good number of cows are left to her people to preserve the legitimacy of that child. Five cows are the legal number per child. But if barrenness comes after the birth of two or more children, divorce is not allowed by the court. According to the Dinka thought, barrenness in a wife is the first to be suspected if she does not conceive for about a year since she has been cohabiting with her husband. Sterility in a man is not easily thought of. While a substantial amount of time is allowed to lapse before the woman is declared barren, certain factors are first regarded as being the cause of no conception. Some malign gods or totems may be thought of as being responsible for the problem. A direct relative who was not given a share in the dowry division is always among the reasons for delayed conception by a wife. Maternal uncles who are angry are always the frequent suspects. Certain propitiation and appeasement rites are made in the hope that the woman would become pregnant. This always brings success except in rare cases.

Constant death of the children of one particular wife makes the woman suspected by her husband and all the kin as having some evil which she kept hidden. Such a woman is suspected to have been committing extramarital sex with men other than her legal husband. Dinka people have a strong belief that a woman who secretly makes extramarital sexual intercourse causes social impurity to herself and her children as well as to her husband, and because of this her children usually die very easily. Women whose children die in sequence because they concealed extramarital sex are believed to suffer some supernatural punishment. For this reason the court would grant divorce once such a case is brought before it. Divorce is allowed so that the man recovers his cattle to remarry in fulfilment of his right to procreation and continuity in his family and lineage.

Another reason which usually brings divorce to a wife is theft. A woman who is found to be a thief is believed to have brought serious social disrepute upon the family. This is because theft is an abhorrent public scandal, a crime that greatly reduces the status of the family in the eyes of the community. Children, particularly daughters, of a woman known to be a thief do not usually find suitors to flirt with, court or date them, let alone marry them.

Should a wife prove to be extremely verbose and very abusive to her husband and the entire family in the home, habitually insulting a husband in a grievous and injurious way so that the reputation of the husband, family and lineage cannot be assured, the court can grant divorce. Such women are publicly called *tiŋ rac thok*, 'a woman with a bad mouth'. A wife who continues to nag and grumbles in her notoriety so much that she wearies the husband in an unbearable way is considered as a wife with bad character, a notorious woman who can be divorced if her husband and kin take her to court for this.

In those days until the recent past, adultery used to rank highly among social offences which had far reaching consequences. Adultery in the house is already a bad omen. Dinka people have a strong belief that an adulterous wife makes her husband die owing to the impurity she brought to the husband and even to the household in general. An adulterer is evil and impure and it is for this reason that adulterers are not allowed to come near a sick person. They are not allowed to even pass where the wind may be blowing towards the sick. There is a belief that once a sick person inhales into their nostrils the air with the evil scent from an adulterous person, that person will die. Adultery carries with it the worst social impurity to the family, children and the husband, and it was for this reason that those who committed adultery used to be excommunicated from the territory altogether. Children of adulterous women have no place in Dinka society. Dinka law courts are very well known to accept divorce on the grounds of adultery, especially if the wife is of a young man or suffered no sexual or other social neglects from their husband. However, some husbands take it as normal and prefer to take seven cows for compensation rather than divorce unless the wife is persistently adulterous and fornicatious, unable to confine herself to her husband or her genitor.

Divorce is also allowed if the wife develops a mortal disease that is known to be transmittable to her children, thereby becoming a familial disease to be inherited. Diseases such as pulmonary tuberculosis and leprosy can be cited as those diseases for which the court can readily grant divorce once the husband and his relatives present a case of divorce on those grounds.

Dëjöök is another grounds for which a man is allowed to divorce his wife and recover his cattle dowry. Dëjöök can be described as a word used by the Dinka people for things ranging from carelessness to untidiness, ill-manneredness to being indecent. It also covers being bad at cooking, bringing up the children and upkeep of the home. Dëjöök also includes being uneconomical. It is a general term which cannot be properly delineated or described. It is all of those things so described. A woman can fall into such a description if she is found to have any or more of the above characteristics. Dëjöök is so indefinable that in most cases the court can only rely on the husband's subjective description about his wife. At times dëjöök can be so clear in a woman that it can be objective proof. All in all when a case of dëjöök is taken to court the jury is usually likely to sympathise with the husband and a divorce is quickly granted.

GROSS INDECENCY

While dëjöök is essentially a matter of general character[98], it is also thought to include all those acts, omissions and circumstances which tend to relate to dëjöök. These circumstances can be grouped together as acts of gross indecency. Although it is very wide to describe, acts of gross indecency may include all those acts which, in the opinion of the Dinka court, are too unbecoming for the obligation of respect which a wife owes her husband or which relatives-in-law owe to each other. As is the case with dëjöök, if the husband can give proof to his case without necessarily going into details to justify the cause of his grievance, the court with the help of genuine witnesses may decide to go soft to save both sides from public embarrassment and resolutely grant divorce because the substance upon which marital relations was based appears to no longer exist. This act of gross indecency may not have been committed by the wife herself. Her close relative may have been the one at fault and the wife must account for her relative's mistakes.

---

98   Ibid p. 181

This is what it is in marriage. Gross disrespectful mistakes done by either side to the marriage are labelled onto the wife or husband in marriage, particularly the ones from the wife's side. In some cases, however, if the wife is viewed innocent by both the court and her husband, the court is bound to order for an appeasement cow or cows called *weŋ or yɔk Awëc* and the cows are released to save the marriage from divorce. Conciliatory payments in cows, also called appeasement cow(s), paid to the husband have always been the best mechanism by which the court makes divorce difficult and only done as a last resort.

There is also another factor, but it is one which is very empirically difficult to prove. This is what could be described as wizardry, which Dinka people call *peeth*. If this peeth is discovered in a wife after marriage it could sometimes lead to divorce. A wife discovered to be a wizard will be an immediate source for divorce unless she has already borne children, in which case it becomes useless to divorce her since her children are already going to be part of the family. No matter how difficult it is to prove it, there is an existing conventional belief among the Dinka that certain people or families have eyes which have the extraocular power to look through others and be able to pull out some parts or organs or fix killing objects into people's bodies without being seen as they remove or put them in. A lesser but equally dangerous component of this category of people are what are called *rɔɔth*, weird people. No family which is known to have no peeth and rɔɔth can discover such things in a wife and be comfortable with it. Although Dinka courts are less disposed to granting divorce on such grounds there are several instances in which the court allows divorce, especially when pressure from the husband and his relatives is very strong for divorce for this discovery of rɔɔth or peeth in a wife.

There is also another crucial reason for divorce to be granted by a Dinka Court of law. This is what could be described as 'desertion' or 'escape'. If for any reason the wife after official marriage decides to run or escape from her home with another man it is a clear justification for the marriage to be dissolved. The husband would first have her returned by law. He may then call for divorce which could be granted. He recovers his dowry cattle and the woman goes with her new husband, depending on the position of her people who would later have a right to demand dowry cattle from the new man. In any case, those are cases in which violence with fatal consequences cannot be ruled out. Such instances are very rare although they do occur. Some husbands would prefer to resume their wives in order for the court to exact the seven *aruɔk* or compensation cows out of the man for adultery as a way to gradually get his dowry cows back. This is particularly so if he knows his original cows and their offspring cannot be easily found from his in-laws. If the woman cannot be returned to him after she has escaped or deserted with that illegal man, he will be entitled to a divorce and the court would therefore assist him to recover his cows.

While there are other factors which could prompt divorce or dissolution of the marriage, those cited above are known as the principal reasons for which a particular Dinka law court is compelled to decree divorce or dissolution of the marriage but worth noting here is the fact that although divorce or dissolution come largely as a matter between the husband and the wife, it often involves the whole kinship on both sides. The side of the husband has always been the initiator owing to the many wrongs and ills that seem to mostly come from women. While Dinka society has a very serene respect and regard for women and its economy is largely based on the female gender, they nonetheless consider most of the societal vices to come from women. Disrespect to social norms and values have been known to come from women and girls. Most of the Dinka wars and fights are due to elopement, impregnation of girls, adultery and the like.

Not attributing divorce to come from the husband alone, Dinka society also allows divorce suits to come from the wife if for any reason she can convince her people and the court to accept the termination of the marriage. The grounds for a divorce coming from the wife are few but can always be very strong once they come to court. Women's requests for divorce are always more compelling than those of the husband. Women's cases for divorce are always genuine and not motivated by the opportunity to recover the bride price as is the men's at times. A woman would always find it difficult, almost impossible, to call for a divorce when she very well knows she will have to leave her children and go away, back to her people and later to a new husband and family again without her children.

While it is rare for a woman to call for divorce, she does so when her conscience and wellbeing are so threatened that she cannot afford to stay with that husband or family. Life with her husband has to be terribly hard to be able to win the sympathy of her kin and the court. While her family has much more to lose, *"not only because the cattle of her bride wealth will have multiplied far beyond the number they can possibly hope for in her remarriage, but also because her divorce often works against her chances for a good remarriage"* (F Mading Deng, *Tradition and modernization*, 1971, p. 184). Among the compelling reasons are impotence and wanton beating of the wife by the husband.

Impotence in Dinka is the sexual inability of the man's penis to stay erect and be able to ejaculate semen and sperm into the woman during sexual intercourse in order that her reproductive system does the rest, like fertilisation and gestation. Sterility, on the other hand, is a situation where the man can normally stay erect and ejaculate but has insufficient sperm in his semen to release into the woman, thereby causing the woman to not conceive. A man is rarely suspected of sterility especially if he has only one wife. The case of impotence is obvious. The woman discovers it right from her first encounter as a bride with her husband. She may, however, conceal it in her bosom as is usually the case until such time when even members of the family, on both sides, begin to raise their eyebrows.

Generally there is no way to tell whether the defect for lack of conception is attributable to the husband or wife but in the Dinka world, women are shy and feel embarrassed to openly go to court for divorce with an argument that a husband is impotent or sterile. Moreover, impotence and sterility are not grounds that entitle the wife to ask for divorce. If her primary objective is to procreate and to have children the matter is secretly settled within the family as the husband also needs to have children, since he paid dearly for his wife in order to have children to continue his family line and name. A relative or brother or paternal relative is made to act as a genitor to procreate children for both the brother and the woman. It is only when the husband refuses to allow such a family arrangement that the woman can be entitled to raise a case of divorce. The court can therefore permit divorce if the husband persists to refuse.

The second grounds for a wife to seek divorce is when her husband also cohabits with her sister, half sister or daughter of a close relative. This is a pure case of incest or *akeeth*. It is a gross disrespect on the part of the husband to do so. There is a Dinka conventional belief that a man's incest with his wife's sister or wife's female relative is followed by consequences of incest. This is believed to fall on the wife and her children. Suppose a husband goes in to marry a girl closely related to his wife, then the wife will have good grounds to table a divorce suit before the court. Deciding to court a girl related to one's wife will give the right to the wife to raise a case of divorce, although courtship short of marriage or sexual intercourse may not make the court decree marriage dissolution but in any case it is an indication of the man's disrespect or disregard to his marriage and to his wife. A husband who attempts to do this can be asked by the court to pay an appeasement cow to his in-laws, the father of the sister-in-law in particular. Conciliatory or appeasement performances are made between the woman and her husband after the court has successfully turned down her litigation for divorce.

Failure to establish a home for the wife may also be good grounds for the woman to request divorce. This is especially so if it takes years and is viewed by the wife as being intentional on the part of the husband. If, in addition to failing to provide maintenance, her case can be even more valid the court can intervene to order the apportioning of some of the man's wealth to her. It is her husband's duty to make a home for his wife, cultivate her fields during cultivation season, and provide her with cows, sheep and goats and be found or seen to stay with her. In a situation where the husband insists on not doing these things for the wife, in spite of the court's ruling to do so, the wife can be granted the right to divorce the husband.

Insults and defamatory abuses habitually uttered by the husband to the wife's relatives or parents in particular can give right to the wife to sue her husband for a divorce. His insults to the wife do not give grounds for her to sue her husband, asking for a divorce. This is contrary to that of the husband who is granted the right to divorce his wife who keeps insulting her husband. This is justified by the Dinka concept of a husband not being equal to the wife in terms of social status. In Dinka thought the husband is not an equal partner to the wife. The wife is equated with the status of a boy. The husband is the head of the family and of the household. He brought her to his family as a vehicle to ensuring his continuance and as a personal assistant to helping him found a family. Insults to the husband legally gives right to him to call for divorce because her respect, loyalty and allegiance to the husband as the one who has matrimonial power over her is no longer there for the stability of the home and the marriage itself.

Divorce for the woman may be granted also if her husband decides to disappear and goes to an unknown place and establishes no physical contact with his wife for a substantial period of time so that her wellbeing and procreation comes to be at stake. In this case the woman may go to court which makes her husband's kin need to find her someone within the family to cohabit with her so that children are begotten for the lineage in the name of her husband. This is after the court has at first made the family members seek out the whereabouts of her husband and bring him back to his home. It is the abject failure to find him or bring him that will make the court direct the family to find her a genitor. If this also cannot be done the court can grant her the right to divorce.

A woman may also be granted the right to divorce her husband if her husband has proved to be too cruel for her to live a decent life. Traditionally Dinka men, as for all men in Africa, reserve the right to reprimand and even beat their wives as a means to discipline them and make them behave and comply with the wishes and rules of the family and of the husband in the home. Any interference on the part of her relatives, be it her brother or even the father, is not acceptable by custom, even by the court, but if the husband persistently decides to go beyond the limits for admonition and his relations with the wife become that of mistreatment that she has to be persistently beaten and habitually insulted for no good cause, her relatives may interfere and divorce may be demanded by them and if the court finds proof, termination of the marriage is therefore granted and dowry cattle are returned. However, while husbands find it easy to rally their kin to their sides, women find it more difficult to win the support of their kin in cases of divorce. A woman's chance of convincing her people is always much poorer. This is because her people do not benefit as cattle dowry are returned and children remain with their father. They only receive back their girl whose status has become one of a woman and her chances to remarry and fetch them a good number of cows are always very grim. In some rare situations the wife and her relatives may adamantly insist that divorce be carried out contrary to the opinion of the court and the husband's side. In this case the court could acquiesce its position provided the woman's relatives promptly bring all the bride price cattle by themselves except for 'the cow of the skirt'. If there are children in between, five cows per child are deducted as the children remain with their father or paternal kin.

All in all, the court is always obliged to do the ceremony called *puök arop* to the spouse whose marriage it has accepted to dissolve. *Puök arop*, the spraying of the separated wife and husband, is done by the court members to emancipate the divorced woman from the status of a married woman. In doing this rite, the woman is brought before the jury and her legs sprinkled with the cow dung ash taken from the chief's cattle hearth. She can now be free to be married by somebody else.

When divorce is granted, its complications become multiple as many people are affected. After they are divided the dowry cattle begin to spread to several people and to several territories as people pay some of them and their offspring into their different marriages. Others are paid out for different transactions including debt settlement. As it is a legalised custom to collect back the very cows which were paid into the marriage with all their offspring, it becomes a concern of almost the entire community, as dowry collection touches all those to whom a single or number of cows had gone during the time when the original marriage was valid. All the kinsmen who contributed to the marriage and those who took shares as paternal and maternal relatives are all involved in the process of the bride price being recovered. In the past dowry cattle used to not be sold, at least for the first two years until the bride had a child and had proven she can make a good housewife. Nowadays it is not the case. Dowry cattle are easily dispensed with, especially if the first indications for marriage instability have started to show.

Divorce and dissolution of marriages and the problems encountered during the complicated process of retrieving the dowry cattle is one principal reason why Dinka people make a lookout for such factors which can guarantee future stability in the marriage. Great care is made when choosing the right family, the right parents and the right girl. In most cases, sufficient time is given for the would-be couples to undergo a slow process of flirtation and courtship, then comes marriage itself. This renders mutual opportunity for the young men to study the girls they have in their heart. Sometimes very rich cattle tycoons do not necessarily have to undergo such slow processes. They just decide to make a choice and go into marriage straight away. At times, girls are made by their families to marry old but rich men from the aristocracy. This may be done against their opinion and wishes. Because of their riches in cattle and power many old and important men in the society usually have a large number of wives. Unlike girls in the urban centres, rural girls are mostly predisposed to accepting whoever proposes to marry them as long as the applicant is a Dinka man from her own area or from a nearby territory. They do this unless certain urgent circumstances compel them to reject that suitor. Sometimes Dinka girls put on an attitude of neutrality as long as the decision as to who should marry her does not come from her but from her people. Dinka girls grow to maturity while they do not know who will marry them, a young man or an old man, for the issue is not on how old or young is the husband. It is the dictates of culture and custom that matter. As a member of the society girls are bound to comply with what they found established, as men do for their part when they are required to do certain things which are against their will and even against their own life.

CHAPTER SEVEN: THE ORIGIN OF THE DINKA PEOPLE (AN ETHNOGRAPHICAL SURVEY)

INTRODUCTION

This chapter has a unique standing for all the chapters of this book. This is because it seeks to tackle the Dinka from their very remote historical beginning. It begins from Garang (Garaŋ) and Abuk (Adam and Eve), the first human pair to be created by Nhialic (God) on earth. However, before going into the details of what this study has sieved out of the mass of data obtained from documents containing ancient world mythologies about mankind, documentaries on those inscrutable times after creation, and the data material given by the olden Dinka people in their rural settings, data taken during the three decades of research work done on Dinka society roots of origin, it is crucial and imperative at first to draw the attention of the reader to the point that written history is quite a new thing to the Dinka as it is to all the people of South Sudan, to whom the art of writing is a recent experience.

Nearly every literate Dinka man and woman has never been so well informed about his or her past as it will be after completing this chapter. On the whole it is an unhappy fact that the older generation of the educated Dinka did not have time to write about the early and even the more recent history of their own nationality. This is in spite of the fact that the art of writing started to be acquired by members of the Dinka society as far back as the close of the 20th century. Yet large bodies of historical knowledge about our past have continued to be passed down through oral accounts rather than having it documented! This is sad because this vast fund of knowledge was not hard to collect nor was it difficult to reconstruct. On the contrary, every fact which the reader will find here in this book is and has been available to any Dinka elite for the last fifty years, and although the data information about the primordial, Mediaeval and our ancient past was so taxing to collect using individual initiative and means, it has not been buried or very obscure information which no one has heard or to which none can gain access.

As an introduction to the Dinka concept of their beginning, use has been made of the data obtained from the Bible, from the ancient Middle and Near Eastern histories and from the vast oral accounts given by the Dinka themselves. The data to be found in this book and this chapter in particular are those Dinka oral accounts sieved out from their epic and religious songs, legendary tales, creation mythologies and deeds of their antediluvian and ancient ancestors who lived as part of that human population which inhabited the face of the earth before and after the world flood of Noi (Noah)'s time.

With material data blended from all those sources, our discussion of the origin of the Dinka people will now begin from their very beginning, from the first human pair, Garaŋ and Abuk, who came to physically live on earth in our present human form at the time of creation, calculated by one Irish archbishop, James Ussher, to have taken place some 4004 years before the flood of Noah[1.] To substantiate this postulation a Jewish first century historian, Flavius Josephus, went in to use manuscripts available during his time to calculate and came out with a postulation that Noah's worldwide flood occurred 1556 years after the creation of Adam. Well, although there is an apparently wide gap between Ussher and Flavius, several scholars on creation and flood stories roughly came up with similar timings suggesting a difference of a few thousand years below or above to the actual dating of the creation time.

A straightforward and exhaustive reading of the Bible, of the ancient texts on creation and flood stories by early Mesopotamian or Babylonian society of the Babel tower times, stories written down by Sumerians, by Akkadians and by the Assyrians, all when read together present a panorama with some features of people, places and events similarly found among Dinka ancient myths and tales. The still remembered Dinka antediluvian and post-diluvian personages who lived between the creation and the flood times and in the post-flood eras present great similarities to those Biblical personages.

Some of the similarities and parallels that Dinka ancient tales and myths present made this study conclude that Dinka primordial forebears must have been part of that ancient Middle and Near East or at a given period of time were a part of the Hebrew culture before their later descendants migrated to ancient Egypt, then to ancient Sudans' northern region, some centuries BC, specifically a century before the establishment of the Kush Kingdom in ancient Sudan.

As the Bible Genesis presents an antediluvian family genealogy of ten generations of patriarchs from Adam to Noah of the flood time, Dinka's own antediluvian genealogy also does the same. There is for the Dinka a genealogical line of ten generations of very significant figures, beginning from Garaŋ of the creation time to the Dinka Noi of the same world flood.

Although the Bible's book of Genesis portrays 30 sons and 33 daughters borne by Adam and Eve during their lifetime of 930 years, emphasis is only made for the line of Cain and the son of Abel who is Seth, down to Noah of the flood time. The line of Cain is portrayed on a secular plane while that of Seth is introduced on a religious and moral view, traceable down to Noah, the righteous man who survived the worldwide flood. The same is found in the Dinka antediluvian genealogy of the sons of Garaŋ and Abuk. Dinka people place great emphasis on one son, Deng-Mayuääl. Dinka custodians of history and genealogists adopted the primogenitary system all the way from Garaŋ down to Noi, who is the same Jewish Noah of the flood.

From Deng-Mayuääl, the eldest son of Garaŋ, remembered popularly among the Rek Dinka as Deng Abuk, come all the Spear Master clans who now wield religious authority among the Dinka. Other sons of Garaŋ are less emphasised by Dinka mythology as are other sons of the Biblical Adam, and while the Bible tells of rivers at Aden, the Jewish creation spot, Dinka creation myths also talk of rivers at Panthou, their creation spot. This explains why some of Garaŋ's daughters, Nyanwiir and Nyankiir, for example, were to bear the names of those rivers. Both the Dinka and Biblical rivers can be understood to have been located in the ancient Middle East, and while the Biblical creation story, which is revealed in the book of Genesis, talks of God's prohibited tree of the knowledge of good and bad, the Dinka creation story also talks of a God forbidden tree, which they call 'aŋo'.

Dinka people still remember the name of that tree to the present day, and like the Hebrews, they know that man did not come into existence by evolution, but by God's creation and divine activity. The Dinka flood story is just the same with that of the Hebrew's Bible. They know the old world of those of the descendants of Abuk and Garaŋ was brought to an end by a worldwide flood caused by the creator who became disgusted when man perverted from His ways and became wicked. The Hebrew book of Genesis in the Bible talks of murder between two of the sons of Adam (Cain killed Abel), of course following a disagreement between them over something. Dinka mythologies also talk of Garaŋ's sons having quarrelled so that one of them (Akol) deserted the family to a much mythologised abode.

Again, mythologies like these are found in the Bible Genesis (Gen. 5 &11) and in the ancient Near Eastern tales. Dinka people consider the society that was from Abuk and Garaŋ (the first antediluvians) as a race of people who were very long-lived persons, and while the Biblical story of the fall of man chased out of the Garden of Eden by God (Gen. 3) was due to the woman (Eve), the Dinka version which can be predicated with this story is that it was the woman who caused the withdrawal of God away from *manhacuuk*, mankind, and went to stay up in the void, never to visibly interact with man to the present day except only through dreams and miraculous acts. A lot of similarities and parallels from the Biblical world and from the ancient Near East can be cited endlessly when comparing those in the Dinka mythical and ancient stories. Most of these will be found in the course of our narrative on the origin of the Dinka which now follows.

THE BEGINNING OF THINGS

According to the Dinka they began from *Garaŋ* who is, with all probability, the very Biblical Adam. Garaŋ's mate at creation is Abuk, who may be the Biblical Eve. Abuk and Garaŋ are therefore the Dinka first grandparents to be created by Nhialic during His creation time. To the Dinka, mankind descended from Abuk and Garaŋ. They are the first couple of mankind but they were not only the grandparents to the Dinka. They are grandparents to the whole of *manhacuuk*, the entire human race. The two are widely believed by the Dinka to have been created in the east by Nhialic, the Dinka name for God.

They were created under a tamarind tree which is *cuɛi* in Dinka.

He created the two at a place which Dinka people still remember as *Panthou*, a home ecology of the heglig tree in an area believed to have been between two rivers, suggesting the Biblical Pishon and Gihon Rivers. Dinka traditions still talk of this area of *Panthou* as an area of great happiness, also pictured so by the Bible which calls it a paradise. Except for the Pajiɛk clan people who do their religious occasions facing the west, all the Dinka to this date continue to do their ritual occasions, holy practices and festivals facing the east from where their ancestors are believed to have come.

DINKA CREATION MYTHS

There are two mythical versions which Dinka oral traditions present about how Nhialic created Garaŋ and Abuk in a location they call *Panthou*. The first version states that Garaŋ and Abuk were created through a divinely inspired intent and purpose and that Garaŋ was the first to be created, formed or moulded from the clay just as a potter moulds and fashions the clay. This version says that Nhialic created the earth and other things before He thought of creating Garaŋ to take charge and manage them, that, from the formed, moulded or sculpted clay the spirit or life soul was breathed or imparted by Nhialic into his nostrils and Garaŋ rose up in a human form with the physical image of Nhialic Himself, the very physical image we see in ourselves today, then he took Garaŋ to where there were many good things including the cows and all forms of animals and birds. There, Garaŋ was given the responsibility to give names to all those things according to their nature immediately after creation. This place which the Dinka call *Panthou* was an extraordinarily beautiful place. Nhialic started to teach Garaŋ the language, much of which the Dinka people still speak today.

Panthou did have one conspicuous but fateful tree called *aŋo* standing in the midst of a heglig thicket. There, Nhialic thought of

Fig 41: Showing the animals and birds in the days of creation

a companion for Garaŋ and making him sleep Nhialic took one rib out of Garaŋ's left chest and from that rib Nhialic made Abuk in the same human form but as a female and she became Garaŋ's wife. According to this version, Nhialic commanded them not to eat from that tree as it was a special tree whose berries are believed to be very deliciously sweet. To this day the Dinka people still remember that tree as a special tree of Nhialic, a tree which they believe to have been very sweet. To date, Dinka people liken anything very sweet to that aŋo, 'ci ja bi dɛny abi ciët aŋo,' says the Dinka, meaning, 'it has became so sweet as if it is aŋo!'

The other version says Nhialic created the first human parents in the east, again at a place called *Panthou* and that *Nhialic* shaped the clay into two human forms and put them into a pot and covered it. When *Nhialic* later uncovered the pot, Abuk and Garaŋ had grown up. At dawn, Garaŋ was full grown and the breasts of Abuk were already large and so they married. The two became the first couple of the future mankind which Dinka people call *manhacuuk*.

Garaŋ and Abuk are therefore the first grandparents of the Dinka race and it is because of this that both Garaŋ and Abuk are adored by all Dinka to the present day. They are worshipped with venerating songs during holy or ritual occasions in which offerings and sacrifices are made to them, occasions in which they are invoked and propitiated for mercy and help when one or any of the Dinka community is in difficulty. Their names continue to permeate the whole Dinka society to the present day. They are worshipped throughout the Dinka world and many female born are given the name of the great mother. The same is true of Garaŋ, the great father at creation. The author, for example, has two daughters with the name of Abuk.

Both versions appear to be mythically akin to the Biblical account of the creation of man and the universe which according to the ancient Hebrew began in the Middle Eastern region of today, precisely in the mountainous area of present Armenia which is today the valley to the east of Tabriz. Ancient Persians used to call it in their historical times, the *Meydan el Shah* (the king), the garden of the Shah. If in such historical times this location was considered to be suitable for the Shah of prehistoric eras before Neolithic times, it must have been an extremely beautiful and fruitful place. Besides documented ancient evidence from the Middle East which portrays this area as having other advantages, the area was known for all sorts of wild grasses from which our current wheat and barley were isolated. Other wild grasses found useful for food were also discovered in later times in this area. They included corn which was then known as einkorn or emmer.

According to agricultural historians this area is where a hunter-gatherer society of the first antediluvians used to collect in 10 to15 days sufficient quantities of grain to last them a whole year and if paradise is measured by the effort one has to put in to work for his living, then this area was paradise indeed.

On the whole there are endless similarities in the Jewish and

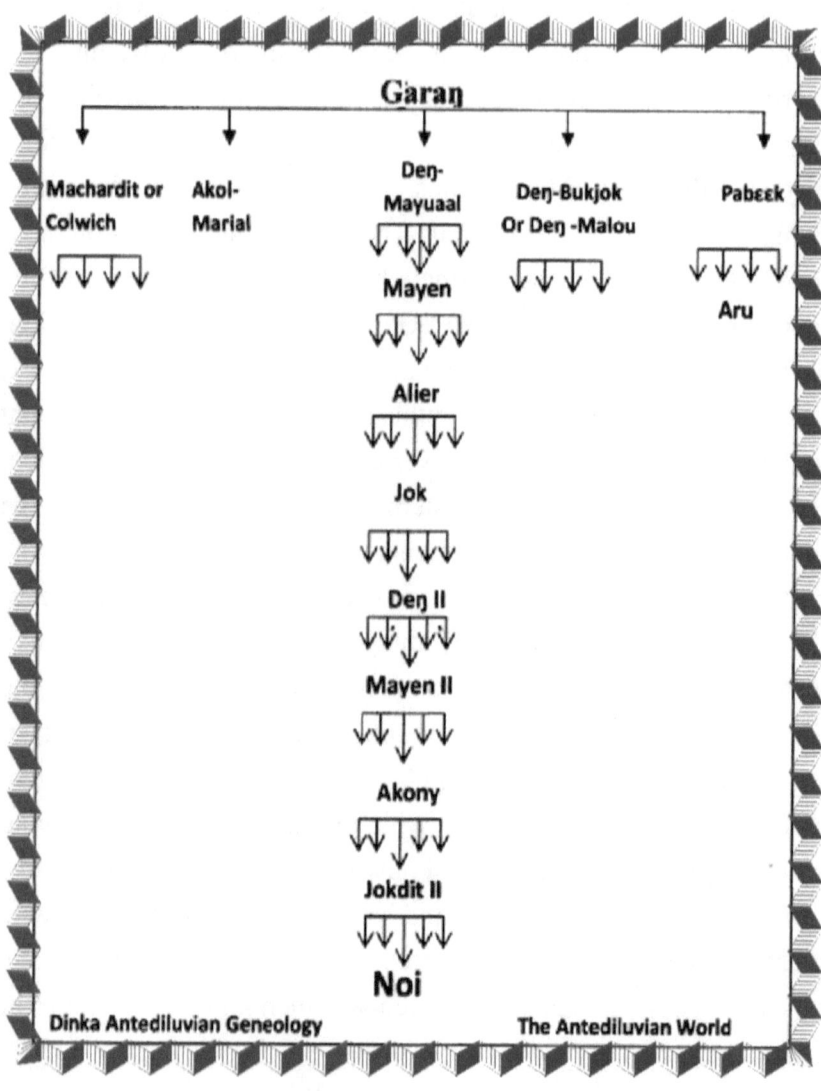

Fig 42: Showing Dinka genealogical descent from the first man (Garaŋ) at creation to Noi of the flood time

Dinka accounts of the beginning of things. As can be seen above the Jewish Adam and Eve are the first human beings to be created by God and are the first couple of the human race. The Dinka Garaŋ and Abuk in contrast are also the first human beings to be created by Nhialic and are the first human parents from whom mankind began and refined. Like the Jews, Dinka ancient traditions point to the east, that is, to the Middle East as their cradle land.

Dinka Garaŋ and Abuk bore sons who quarrelled just like the Biblical sons of Adam and Eve. Garaŋ and Abuk had sons and daughters just like the Jewish or Biblical Adam and Eve. While Jewish genealogists put Adam's children at 63 (30 sons and 33 daughters), Dinka genealogists succeeded to only remember eight children, five sons and three daughters. It is clear that in this modern time of ours such an extended memory going too far into such prehistoric vistas of time as to know all the children of the first parents at creation, all by their number and names cannot be very much blamed on the Dinka, a society still largely illiterate up to this 21st century.

At creation, according to Dinka mythological traditions, Nhialic created all forms of animals and birds, plants and other creatures and things and He made Garaŋ to name them and choose the best he could from them. Some Dinka traditions go further to say that Garaŋ was taught language by Nhialic Himself when Aköök-Mariel taught Garaŋ how to speak right at the time of his creation. In order to master the task of managing the earth and its ecosystem Garaŋ had to be instructed. Part of this instruction was studying and naming the animals and plants. We do not know how long this took. It might have been days, months or even years. They say Garaŋ was created as a fully grown adult male. He had not had the usual childhood, adolescence and boyhood. At *Panthou*, Garaŋ received instructions from Nhialic about a great body of information in his daily interaction with Him (Aciek), information about the animals, about nature and even the stars, the ability to think and reason and choose. He learnt about blood sacrifice and what was pleasing to Nhialic as well as what was not. Dinka use of the cow and sheep as domestic animals for rites making must have started from that moment. The creator gave him details about how he himself was created, how his mate Abuk was created and it was from his creator that Garaŋ made his offspring to know how Abuk came into being. This useful information was presented to the Dinka through oral transmission all from epoch to epoch from one generation to the next until today when it has to be documented like this for the first time.

After naming all creatures including trees, grasses and herbs, Garaŋ took the cow and the sheep as his first rate animals of choice from all the living things around him in the vicinity of *Panthou*. They then lived in perfect harmony with Nhialic and a state of complete innocence prevailed at *Panthou*.

THE FIRST DISPUTE WITH NHIALIC

While in that lap of luxury, says one Dinka myth, a snake came up and confided to Abuk the importance of the aŋo and the need for them to eat the fruits of that tree forbidden by their creator. Abuk yielded. She succumbed to the serpent's powerful persuasion. Timidly, Abuk is said to have gone out of their stay place to the site of the forbidden tree and there she plucked the fruit from the aŋo and ate it. On finding it delicious Abuk decided to persuade her husband Garaŋ who also succumbed to his wife. He also ate from it. Soon after they all ate from the aŋo, their creator appeared to them from nowhere and after vehement blame, they were punished by being turned out from that beautiful and plentiful home of sufficiency and the innocent luxury of life. Well, we do not know whether the snake worked his subtle deception for minutes, hours, days or months before Abuk yielded to its persuasion. It is unfortunate that evil could enter into such a pure and innocent atmosphere and spoil it!

In His extreme disgust, Nhialic decreed to Garaŋ that he and his descendants will have to undergo death at any given time in life, never to return from the dust, and that Garaŋ was to toil to get food. This was to be for posterity. As for Abuk herself, the one who enticed her husband, Nhialic declared a more direct, personal and immediate punishment that was to be extra severe compared to that of Garaŋ. Abuk and her female seeds were to undergo perpetual serfdom to man as man symbolises Nhialic Himself, that she herself and all the like of her shall for eternity suffer during childbearing. Man will often subject her to harsh, overbearing, insensitive and domineering lordship. The snake that was created with four legs and used to have upright posture, like Garaŋ and Abuk, was cursed to lose all its four legs and since then has been made to crawl on its belly forever. As the myth has it, the serpent became angry with Abuk and Garaŋ for what it called 'the extreme punishment meted out to it', that it is to crawl on its belly while they were left to walk on foot. The serpent therefore promised Abuk and Garaŋ that it will for all times take revenge by biting on the foot of their offspring and this is believed to explain why snakes always bite the feet of people. They are always found to have hidden on either side of any village lane where they are known to bite people, especially during night walks. For this myth, see below a picture of the serpent and our two initial parents being chased from their first place of abode, drawn by one of the Biblical scholars, Lambert Dolphin, in his 'Adam's diary of creation and the fall.'[99]

---

[99] Lambert Dolphin, Adam's diary of the creation and the fall

Fig 43: Showing Garaŋ and Abuk being chased from their luxury abode by their creator following their disobedience to the creator. They ate the forbidden fruit of the aŋo!

THE DINKA FIRST PARENTS AFTER THEIR QUARREL WITH NHIALIC

This initial disobedience to the creator resolutely led to the first schism between Nhialic and the first Dinka grandparents. They were turned out of the luxury spot of *Panthou* and according to this legend, Abuk and Garaŋ re-established themselves and made a home in a cave in some other place within the *Panthou* region where they lived the rest of their lives by regeneration. There, the legend continues, they grew to a final old age after living for almost a millennium. According to the Dinka, people used to not die in the beginning, but Garaŋ told the creator that to make people there would be no place for people if there was no death.

The Bible put the age of Adam at 930 years. Dinka people do not know precisely the years led on earth by Garaŋ. They just say Garaŋ and Abuk grew into old age and began to be young again! The estimate of nearly a millennium years by Garaŋ came as a result of calculation contrasted with those of the Biblical patriarchs from Adam to Noah of the flood. The author has taken labour to work out the genealogy line, with life ages for each of the historical figures along the descent line from Garaŋ down to Noi of the flood. The panels, symposiums and workshops held at various Dinka towns on the research material approved those calculations that gave roughly 10 000 years from Garaŋ to Noi as expounded by some Bible scholars for Adam's genealogical time ages to Noah.

THE CHILDREN OF ABUK AND GARAŊ

Long after a century or so, Garaŋ and Abuk are said to have begotten a child for the first time. That child was a son. Dinka traditions present him as Deŋ (Deng), meaning special, holy or sacred and in the course of the millennium, Garaŋ and Abuk bore several tens of children, but Dinka oral traditions provide only eight among whom were three daughters. Names of the other girls and sons are unknown.

These children of Abuk and Garaŋ presented by epic traditions are: Deŋ the eldest, and who is popularly known throughout the Dinka world up to the present day, as Deŋ Abuk, although he is invariably known also or heard in many of the divinity or religious songs as Deŋ Garaŋ. He is mostly called Deŋ Mayuääl[100] and at times as Deŋ-Marial. He did not die to be buried on earth. He is believed to have ascended up to where Nhialic is. He went up late in life and his children remained to perpetuate his line among man.

---

100   Mayuääl means something hairy and is a male being.

The second son is believed to be another Deng who is distinctly known as Deŋ-Malou. He is also known as Deŋ–Bukjök. The third son is said to be Akol-Marial, the hot-hearted. The fourth son was Pabɛɛk, meaning dawn or daybreak. This is the father of Aru, who is an important early antediluvian figure very much associated with creation stories by the Patiɔp clan people among the Agaars to the present day.

The fifth or the last of Garaŋ's sons still being remembered is presented as Colwic or Macardit, Macar the Great. The still remembered three daughters are believed to be *Nyankiir*, so named after our present Nile (Kiir) that kept watering Panthou, *Nyandeeŋ*, the sacred gift from the creator and, finally *Nyanwiir* or the river girl.

Except for Akol-Marial, the other sons took their own sisters to wife them or more correctly, the sisters took their brothers to husband them and for the remaining nine millennia the society up to Noi of the flood time developed from them.

In the course of the century at the Panthou region, the creation area, those of the five sons of Garaŋ had a quarrel over a colourfully beautiful bull, Marial.[101] Right from creation, the cow started with man and continued to interact with man and the Dinka people know the cow as an animal chosen by their ancestor at creation. *"Weŋe cak ke Jaŋ wathéér ciɛ́k Kɔc"*, say the Dinka. Ownership for cows is not a joke for the Dinka, even for a university professor.

Deŋ-Mayuääl, the eldest, wanted to own the bull Marial so that he gives to himself the surname by the colour of the bull, Marial. He wanted to be called Deŋ-Mariääl instead of Deŋ Mayuääl, a name he had wished to be consecrated for him only to be used during ritual or religious purposes for his father's creator. He was surnamed as Deŋ-Mayuääl because he was very hairy and looked like the creator

---

101 Marial is a bull with peculiar beautiful colours which are made up of large patches of white and black hairs on its body. It is a bull of special preference to the Dinka even today.

himself. Nhialic the creator was seen as a very immense old male being in complete human form, but full of long hair on the head to the face, the mouth, the head and on his macho-built arms.

Except for the youngest brother Macardit, also called Colwich, and the third brother Pabɛɛk, the other two brothers, Deŋ-Malou or Deŋ-BukYök, and the hot-hearted Akol-Marial, were also in dire want of this very bull. Each wanted the bull for his own pride. Traditions says it was difficult for the father to make discretion as to who of the three sons was to own the bull.

When the scramble for the bull went into a quarrel and then into a rift, it is said that Garaŋ secretly took the bull in dispute out of the herd to a distance where he mysteriously dug a pit which he covered with earth and then heaped up to look like an anthill. After that Garaŋ made a pretence by telling his three sons who were in dispute that he had decided to intercede and adjudicate into their quarrel over the bull. He called on all his family members, including Pabɛɛk and Macardit, the sisters who were in effect their wives, and their old mother Abuk. His grandchildren were there, too. All gathered before him.

As the myth has it, Garaŋ is said to have stated that if any one of the three was to locate the whereabouts of the contested bull, the bull was to belong to him who was to locate it. Akol, the hot-hearted, could not wait to allow the eldest brothers to take the first chance as it should be. He could not wait for the order of things. His impatience made him take precedence over the two elder brothers who were also posing for the first opportunity in the search for the bull Marial. Akol was grudgingly allowed to try his luck first. He therefore stepped out in search for the bull in the whole of the vicinity of Panthou and its outlying areas, Unfortunately Akol could not see even a trace of the bull, not even a footprint. At long last Akol opted to plead for God's help. He knelt down in supplication, praying that God of his father should come to his aid by causing the sun to shine intensely in the hope that the bull might feel the heat and begin to appear in search of either tree shade or water from the nearby two rivers of Panthou. For a whole day the sun fiercely shone in vain. At sunset Akol had failed to locate the bull and he had to give up as such.

The next day it was the turn of Deŋ-Malou who, like Akol, tried his luck but to no avail. Deŋ-Malou, like his younger brother before him, therefore turned to God and also supplicated for divine help. He pleaded that God bring a very cloudy gale in the hope of frightening the bull off from where it might be. God responded on the instant. A huge cloudy hurricane cycloned over the whole of *Panthou* and the adjacent outlying territory. The hurricanic gale swept upon the earth in a near catastrophic manner. Deŋ-Malou (also called Deŋ-BukYök) hoped the gale would uncover the bull. Still there was no sign of the bull Marial.

Nevertheless, Deŋ-Malou made yet another supplicatory attempt. He prayed and appealed to his father's creator to do yet another divine act to reveal the dear bull for him. A big cloud gathered into rain from nowhere. In no time it rained with an ear-deafening series of elephantine lightning with thunder that shook the whole of *Panthou*. The small human family of Garaŋ and Abuk were terrified. Garaŋ was even made to think that the bull might be extruded out of the pit by the vibrating force resultant from the earth shaking. Yet, there was no sign of the bull at all and in the end Deŋ-Malou had to give up in a silent disgust.

Then, and at long last, came the turn of the eldest son, Deŋ-Mayuääl, who for the last two days had accepted to remain in patient waiting while his younger brothers tried their luck.

Deŋ-Mayuääl started by invoking his primogenitary right of being the firstborn son. In an intensely sacred supplication Deŋ-Mayuääl called upon his father's creator to cause a heavy rain to fall over *Panthou* and in that instant his request was answered. A big torrential downpour fell over the land from morning to dusk, thereby dissolving the anthill and the bull became clear in the pit. Deŋ-Mayuääl, who went out in search of the bull, was able to see the bull in the pit and he made it come out. When he was seen coming with the bull Marial no further argument was made by the rest of the claimants who had to acquiesce and allow the bull to go to him. Henceforth Deŋ-Mayuääl came to own the bull and he was from there and then surnamed Deŋ-Marial. He was therefore known and called with such a surname of Deng-Marial across ages and generations of the first millennium after creation. To date, the bull with the colour of Marial is a usual prerogative of the firstborn son in any Dinka family as a result of that mythical story from creation time.

At that point Akol the hot-hearted considered himself as the loser. He instantly parted *Panthou* in a grudge. According to this myth he went up into the void, in the heights where he is believed to put up with the light and heat giving planet, the sun. Some traditions, however, say Akol went forlornly off to a forest region in the east of Panthou where he established himself a family outside that of his brothers and father. Some Dinka chroniclers say he went away with his cows, sheep and goats and became a cattle herder. The other brothers remained at Panthou where their descendants became well known hunter gatherers. This version about Akol-Marial reminds us about the Biblical Cain who quarrelled with his brother Abel whom he killed. Cain then went to the east, in the land of Nod (Gen. 4:13-15) where he established himself. That antediluvian region of Nod is modern Ardabil in present Iran.[102] Nod in Hebrew means a wandering place. Cain, who may be this Akol of the Dinka, settled in this region as its pioneer and his descendants later founded one of the first antediluvian cities with the name of his son, Enoch.[103]

---

102 'From the Garden of Eden to the flood', in The patriarchs, by EG Ban (2000), p. 8 of 17

103 David Rohl, 'Genesis and the flowers of Horus', transcript of a lecture given on Sept. 3rd 1997, at Millstadt forum; 'What is truth? Man between fantasy

Akol is said to have taken one of his sisters as his wife, with whom he founded his line of antediluvians.

Going back to the first version of the myth about Akol, according to this legend or myth the sun, which the Dinka call the Akol, acquired its name from the name of this discontented son of Abuk and Garaŋ. Because Akol was believed to have gone up into the void with such a hot heart, the remaining members of Garaŋ's family saw it as appropriate to liken the hot shining planet in the sky with that hot-hearted Akol.

If Akol had not gone in fact into the sky but to the Biblical land of Nod to the east, then it can also be true that Garaŋ's household at Panthou could still liken the heat and light giving planet, the sun, with the name of that departed hot-hearted brother of theirs.

GARAŊ'S DIVISION OF ROLES TO HIS SONS

The quarrel between the sons over the bull Marial, which resulted in Akol departing *Panthou*, precipitated Garaŋ's decision to assign roles to his remaining four sons, an act which can be regarded as division of labour among his remaining sons. As is the case among the Dinka of even today, the myth made no mention of the role of the three daughters. Right from the creation of Garaŋ and the division of labour, emphasis was placed on the male gender. Deŋ-Mayuääl was to be supreme and heir to his father. He was to be managerially responsible for all the affairs of his father. Garaŋ vested him with spiritual and sacred domains and he was to have first and the last word in everything and every situation. He was to be responsible for the natural forces such as rain, drought and water, apart from the people's wellbeing, as he was also to be the channel through which Nhialic (God) was to listen and speak to man, a thing which later

---

and reality' p. 5/24.

went down in descent across the Ages even to the present day. Dinka people widely believe that Spear Masters who are holy men of God had in them blood or holy flesh from Deŋ-Mayuääl. Such members from the holy lineages among the Dinka even today perform all those functions and roles assigned to Deŋ-Mayuääl by Garaŋ.

Deŋ-BukYök, also called Deŋ-Malou, on the other hand, was to care for health and heal the sick. He was to see and communicate to people the reasons for the illness. He was also to say what was needed to placate or propitiate the spirit or evil believed to be the cause of the illness. Deŋ-BukYök and his descendants are believed to have played this role during his lifetime and his spirit continued to speak in some people who are regarded among the Dinka today as *aciek or kunyjur* in Arabic, such people known to have extraocular power that makes them see the invisible and things that are opaque to the ordinary eye.

Pabéék, who was *Wënciél*, was to be responsible for matters to do with the earth and its utility. He was also to be responsible for matters related to day and night. The last son, Macardit, was assigned to problems related to the mother and the mother's affairs. The last son is called *Kun* by the Dinka. In as far as Deŋ-Mayuääl was to his father, Macardit on par was to his mother. As the one associated with the mother, that is, with the female gender, he was, and his spirit continues to be, associated with women's procreation.

If a woman failed to conceive, this would be seen to be due to the procreation spirit of Macardit or his mother Abuk, who may be angry and must be propitiated. The anger of Macardit is usually placated with a black bull, sacrificed for him and a female cow, sheep or goat, preferably an old cow, is slaughtered for Abuk, the great mother. Macar, the last born son of Abuk and Garaŋ, is presented as black in his complexion, hence his name Macar, meaning black man. This explains why Dinka people offer or sacrifice a black bull or black ram to the spirit of Macardit. Because Macardit is assigned to women's affairs, uncastrated bulls or rams are not offered or sacrificed to his spirit, and because Deŋ-Mayuääl is considered sacred and holy and has the primogenitary right and is the one given the investiture as the head of the family and heir to Garaŋ, a white bull, uncastrated, is always sacrificed to him, not just a bull of any colour. Something white is associated with grace, purity and sacredness and Deŋ-Mayuääl is just that. This explains why Dinka Spear Masters, the spiritual high priests, are usually those who are elder sons in a holy clan.

THE PANTHOU CREATION AREA: ITS EXTENT AND ECOLOGY

The early antediluvian area referred to by the Dinka ancient people as *Panthou*, where the creator sat or stood to create the universe and all the living and non-living things plus the first two human parents of mankind, Abuk and Garaŋ, must have been a large region, not just a spot or a narrow area. Despite this, Dinka primordial traditions emphasise Panthou as a spot. In Dinka language *pan* either means home or family lineage. *Thou* means heglig tree. This means Abuk and Garaŋ were truly created at a place or spot consisting of a number of heglig trees and in a wider geographic sense, *Panthou* as an area should be understood as being conjectural. Our only means of identifying this creation spot and its region must be based on the Bible and on the striking clues from our Dinka mythological tales on creation.

Dinka ancient traditions strongly assert that Abuk and Garaŋ were created under a tamarind tree at *Panthou* in the east. They say our people, that is, our forefathers, came to Sudan from the east. They point to what is now the Middle Eastern region of today. They also talk of rivers about *Panthou*. Two of Garaŋ's daughters, Nyankiir (the Nile's daughter) and Nyanwiir (the river girl) had their names associated with water courses, suggesting rivers about or passing through *Panthou*.

Gen. 2:10-14 gives striking proof to this Dinka contention. It talks of a river 'issuing out of Eden' and which thereafter divides into four heads, producing the rivers that are Euphrates and Pishon which go through the whole length of Havilah, Gihon which passes around the whole land of Cush and the Hiddekel which is the present Tigris in Iraq, flowing east of Assyria.

From the above two sources, this work was made to look at the vast ancient documentaries on creation and the beginning of man. The vast wealth of information so far acquired from those masterpieces helped as scholarly contributions to the reconstruction of this thesis on the Dinka creation area of *Panthou*. However, it must be clearly stated from the outset that the *Panthou* region or creation spot we are discussing does not any longer exist as a physical geographical land area at present. We are discussing what it was and the area or region where it was prior to the flood time. The almost worldwide catastrophe of the flood which cleared away the old world in Noi's time undoubtedly altered considerably the topographical features of the earth, filling in the courses of some rivers and creating others. This is especially true of the Middle East, the Mediterranean region, Europe and the whole of the oriental world. The land configuration of those parts of the world has changed considerably. This is a fact we should know and remember from the outset.

By all probabilities *Panthou* which must be the Biblical Garden of Eden had been situated in that mountainous region in the present valley of Tabriz where is situated today's capital of the Iranian Azerbaijan. In prehistoric times this place was called by the Persians as the *Meydan el Shah*, the garden of the Shah. Ancient Near East traditions think this *Meydan el Shah* was such a beautiful place, having all sorts of flowering plants of varied colours and a variety of edible fruit producing trees as well as abundant wild grasses from which our modern forms of grain were identified in those ancient times.

One of the researchers on creation and the Garden of Eden, David Rohl,[104] in his masterpiece lecture on the Genesis delivered in 1997, found the garden of Shah, the Rivers Gihon and Pison, the mountain of Cush and the gold mines of Havilah. He found them when he went to do his archaeological surveys in the valley of Tabriz. He was doing his research work following what the Bible keeps telling us about the creation area, the Garden of Eden and the land of Nod to which Cain was exiled. From the valley of Tabriz, Rohl continued his search eastwards until he reached Ardabil with villages bearing the names of Nod such as *Lower and Upper Nod*. People living in those villages as well as the town of Ardabil attested that they are people of the *Land of Nod*. In Hebrew nod means wanderer and it may be from that name that the story came that Cain became a wanderer and could not remain at one particular place because of his sin of killing his brother Abel. To confirm his findings Rohl went to the mapping centre of the Iranian government to look up the official maps. He found those names on the map. This confirmed the Biblical story about the Garden of Eden, the land of Nod and the entire region with those rivers.

At long last Rohl succeeded in locating the original Garden of Eden (the Dinka *Panthou*) through the use of the clues from the Old Testament. The creation area is precisely in the east of the valley of Tabriz, near the head waters of the Tigris, Euphrates, and the Aras which is the river Gihon. North of Tabriz, there is a mountain pass known as Cushedag or the mountain of Cush and east of Tabriz, there is the *Meydan el Shah*, the garden of the King, watered by the river Pishon which is the land of Havilah with the ancient gold mines. It is now a heavily industrialised area and its ancient orchards, the

---

104 David Rohl, 'Genesis and flowers of Horus', transcript of a lecture given on Sept. 3rd 1997 at the Millstadt forum: 'What is truth, man between fantasy and reality'.

cedars and oaks can be found there even today. In those primordial times before this present industrial grime this place must have been a paradise, the Garden of Eden (the Dinka Panthou) or the Meydan el Shah.

CLIMATIC CONDITIONS AFTER CREATION TO THE TIME OF NOI'S FLOOD

To best tackle this otherwise difficult part of the study, it is imperative to divide the pre-flood period into phases according to the revelations found from the vast Dinka ancient accounts and from the Biblical and extra-Biblical sources. Phase one will attempt to describe the conditions of life immediately after creation and the then existing climatic situation at the time of creation or the time during the first millennium years after the creation of those of Abuk and Garaŋ. This will be followed by a description of life conditions for the other two millennia that followed (phase two) while man led a wretched type of life. The third phase would be treated as the time when those antediluvians settled into an organised agricultural and husbandry period of life. The fourth period will try to portray the era when the antediluvian man became organised and civilisations arose with some forms of governments, nations or kingdoms. The fifth period is the time of catastrophes and chaos, violence and wickedness that preceded the time of prolonged droughts, plagues and suffering, which ended in the catastrophic flood that wiped out that human population which descended from Abuk and Garaŋ. Life conditions have been determined and shaped by the prevailing climatic conditions in each of those phases.

Phase one – This period began with the time when Garaŋ and Abuk came into being, the time when the two only knew of Nhialic, their creator, who physically interacted with them on a regular basis.

The two were in a complete state of wholeness and harmony such as existed between them and their creator, between them and the nature around them. They were in perfect harmony and a state of innocence prevailed before they were put into dispute with their creator by the snake over the forbidden tree called the aŋo. The climatic conditions of this antediluvian period were very different from our world of today. Global climatic conditions did not vary very significantly as it is today. In the first two or three millennia after creation it is possible to assert that a water vapour canopy encircled the earth planet and this accounts for why there were stable temperatures throughout much of the antediluvian world. This water vapour canopy acted as a radiation filter, thus filtering out the harmful effects of ultraviolet and cosmic radiation. The earth planet was still one major continent. The barometric pressure may have been much greater than it later came to be in the times leading to the flood of Noi. Combined results of these conditions could have been one of the reasons why antediluvians lived such long life spans of nearly a millennium in contrast to our less than a century lifespan of today.[105] Because the prevailing weather was colder people of this time had hairy bodies. They were naked because they had not learnt how to make clothes. Dinka people say their primordial forebears used to stay naked. Some wore treated tree leaves, barks or leaf bunches.

PEOPLE OF THE FIRST MILLENNIUM AFTER CREATION

Garaŋ, Abuk and their children lived for a number of centuries, except for Deŋ-Mayuääl, who is presented to have been taken up alive in a whirlwind never to return. The rest of the first generations of Abuk's and Garaŋ's direct

---

105   E G Ban, 'The patriarchs' (in) From the Garden of Eden to the flood, (2002), PP 8-17.

descendants appear to have died in the Panthou region. The first cluster of this human family at Panthou could be regarded as those humans of the early old Stone Age period. After they lost favour from the creator about a century earlier, they lived in stone caves and rock shelters in that Panthou region. They used to also sleep in tree trunks for security purposes, a means to protect themselves from wild animals.

Deŋ-Mayuääl, otherwise called Deŋdit, that is, Deŋ the Great, who was taken up alive into the void, is believed by the Dinka to stay in the sky where he obtains rains from the creator for *manhacuuk*, that is, for humans or mankind from below. The spirit of Abuk, the great mother, continues to be invoked by the Dinka even today when they ask for rain. Abuk is believed to speak to *manhacuuk* through thunder. For want of rain, village children of even our modern times would call out with:

'Deŋ ee lɔc tuɛny!
'Deŋ Abuk Lɔc tuɛny!

Translation:
'Oh, rain! Rain quickly!
'Rain, son of Abuk, rain quickly!'

As is the usual practice in the Dinka rural world, children would do this call for rain during those days when the rains of late April make people greatly expectant to have rain. Children go about in their home singing this song rhythmically while playing throughout the village or villages, appealing to Deŋ-Mayuääl, son of Abuk, up in the sky, to give them rain quickly. Their call is usually answered. If at certain times a Dinka man or woman is faced by an abject situation, he or she would in solemn supplication call on the great grandparents or on Deŋ Abuk to assist or alleviate the suffering or answer their desperate wishes and wants.

Those first human parents, their children and their grandchildren, formed the first human society and in addition to their later descending generations and those of the dead ancestors, they make up what Dinka people regard as their primordial mythical world of Abuk and Garaŋ's times. The spirits of those dead ancestors of the early pre-flood world and other entities known by the Dinka as yieth or totems which are protecting spirits, do combine to constitute an intermediate divine world which the Dinka traditional community consider a ladder to the one single creator Nhialic, who is best translated as the English God.

These early antediluvian humans, Abuk, Garaŋ, Deŋdit, Deŋ-Malou or Deŋ-Bukyök, Macardit, Pabɛɛk and other children of Abuk and Garaŋ, their immediate sons and daughters and the later ancestral spirits which became divinities, all still manifest themselves today through human experience. Some of these spirits are known to inflict specific types of pain or illnesses on the Dinka people. Some are known to have certain likes and dislikes. When they fall upon a person and possess him or her, they can be identified by the peculiar aberrational behaviour which they induce in a person. They make a person quiver and make extraordinary movements and some incongruent talk.

Although this early human society of about the first quarter of the first millennium after creation lived in a kind of luxury life it is to be noted that they used to stay naked because they had not learnt how to make clothes. They did not know how to build houses. They slept in caves, in trees and between tree trunks to avoid attacks from wild animals. They ate raw meat because they had not discovered the art of making fire by then. They ate from some tree fruits, leaves and roots. From them the knowledge about edible fruits and tubers and edible insects, vegetables, tree leaves and so on may have been handed down to our post-flood humans and to our ancient world peoples who handed that practice over to our modern man, our Dinka of today.

Phase two – This is the time when man in the early antediluvian society began to settle in groups and spread to many parts of the Middle and the Far East and to Africa by way of Egypt and the Horn of Africa as they have multiplied. During this period conditions in the two regions and North Africa were generally favourable up to the time of the last Ice Age. We are not speaking about Europe which was not by then habitable by those early antediluvians, due to glaciers which covered Europe as far as the Alpine region. The deserts of today, the Sahara Desert, the Libyan Desert, the Arabian Desert, the Syrian and the Thar Desert in western India had not yet formed at this phase. They were grasslands and forests, suitable for hunter-gatherer people. The mountains of the Sahara were thickly forested, large lakes filled the depressions and a number of rivers may have existed at this time and were flowing.

Among them were the present dry riverbeds of Arabia which some scholars think made up one of the rivers of the Garden of Eden.[106] Man at this phase in history led a very wild existence although there are indications that he had started to learn how to use materials around him to suit his needs. Those materials included stones, which played a very important role in life. The people learnt by experience which stones were most efficient for making tools. They were able to chip scrapers, choppers or hand axes in addition to spearheads and arrows out of those stones. They used those implements for digging up roots, skinning animals, and cutting and scraping animal skins. Their hunting methods included chasing wild animals. Hunting in later times started to be a group activity. Stone boulders were thrown in unison at an entangled prey to prevent its escape. For big game, pits were dug in a path through which animals went to drink water. Delicate sticks were placed on those pits and covered with grass. The animals would step on those sticks and fall into the pit and the

---

106   Colbourn Rushton, The origin of civilized societies, Princeton university press, (1968), pp. 81-96

hunters would then kill the animal using stones and other weapons. They also chased and herded the animals over steep cliffs, forcing them to fall over and break their limbs. At times they used to drive animals into muddy or swampy lakes or rivers in which they would get stuck, and as time went by man developed yet another technique whereby they trapped and caught wild animals around water points. After succeeding in killing the animal the hunters would skin the carcass and eat the meat raw.

Women were known to remain behind, collecting wild fruits and berries. Life of this kind needed very strong people. People of this period had thick bones with stout huge bodies and were very hairy and slightly taller than peoples of subsequent times who had shifted from eating raw meat. Animals of this period largely escaped from the Middle East, either going north or south of this region to avoid those many hunting methods from man.

This Middle East and the Far East early man, however, continued getting meat from smaller animals like tiangs (thiäŋ in Dinka), all forms of antelopes and gazelle plus rodents and vegetables after the bigger game escaped to Africa and European regions. The discovery of fire in later times also led to these people abandoning eating raw meat. The size of the human skeleton therefore began to shrink from this time onward.

At this stage man decided to adopt a settled life with a husbandry or pastoral kind of livelihood. From some of the Dinka primordial epic and religious songs which outlived the effects of time, we begin to know of the names of villages and peoples of this antediluvian society descended from Abuk and Garaŋ.

The Dinka genealogical descent list (see Fig 42 above) of the calculated ten generations from their first parent at creation, Garaŋ to Noi of the flood time, includes two of those antediluvian figures. There is the first Mayen, son of Deŋ-Mayuääl (Deŋ Garaŋ or Deŋ Abuk) and another Mayen of the seventh generation who is the son of

Deŋ Jök the first. The following extracts from some of the Dinka epic songs dating far back to that antediluvian era are likely to have been from songs of the time of this Mayen the 2nd. The excerpt goes thus:

(1)
'Tä cieŋ Mayen Deŋ
Ake tä mec mec mec,
Ke raan anin kueer wayaa!
Mayen ee täc roor εε!
Ke Ɣɛn amat akol ke wεεr!"

(2)
Ru Deŋ nyieer,
Deŋ atueny Panthou εε!,
Deŋ atueny pan e Garaŋ,
Madhɔl wa kɔŋ Ɣa muɔc!,
Wa Abuk ee!
Kɔŋ Ɣa muɔɔc,
Yin Wä Garaŋ
Kɔŋ a muɔɔc!."

(3)
"Mathɔn la nhiaan aci la yi gur ke Nhialic ee !
Jɔt Mälɔu ku jɔt ariëël!
Mathɔn la nhiaan aci la yigur ke Nhialic εε!
Nhialic ee ke lan Jäŋ
Ɣɛn bi Wä kony ee!"

Translation:
(1)
"The abode of Mayen Deŋ
Is a very, very far place,

That a person walks till he sleeps on the way!
Oh, Mayen! Do I have to sleep in the forest!?
No, I must walk a whole day and night!"

(2)
"The rain is drizzling throughout the night,
It is raining at Panthou!
It is raining at the home of Garaŋ,
God! Our father, give us rain at first!
Oh, mother Abuk; give us rain at first!
Oh, Garaŋ; Our father, give us rain at first!"

(3)
"Oh, the uncastrated bull is struggling with God!
Oh, it has already raised cumulus rain clouds of the dawn!
The bull is struggling with God!
The creator is for the whole mankind.
Oh! Our father, the creator will help us!"

Among the Rek Dinka in Bahr el Ghazal, those three separate songs are sung in one succession. As can be understood in the three songs, they are songs which must have a remote origin going far back to those epochs of the antediluvian community given the names of Panthou village and names of popular early historical figures such as Garaŋ, Abuk and Mayen. The three songs must have begun to be sung during a community gathering in which a plea was being made to the creator to give rain to their settlement. It appears from the song that there was drought in the territory and the community had to get a bull to be sacrificed to the creator as an offering to propitiate Him to give them rain.

Dinka oral tradition is rich with the names of the villages or settlements of those earliest members of the human race, those who lived during the interval between creation and the flood. Among these are Pay*ä*ny, Pan-Nhial, Panthou and many others.

Panthou in the Edenic region is given in this song as the home of Garaŋ. It is also said to be the home of those of Mayen Deŋ. It is said to be a very, very faraway place. The line about distance suggests that the gathering was in a different settlement which was quite a distance away from Panthou. It could be Pan-Nhial, Pay*ä*ny or some other village. These societies depicted by the three songs are those before man decided to organise and make towns and governments. Our classification of the pre-flood world considers these antediluvians as those of the third millennium which must be the time when man abandoned his cave and hunter-gatherer practices and became a settled farmer and herdsman. This is the time when man was not yet organised into governing systems that later resulted into nation states and kingdoms, organised systems usually referred to as 'civilisations'. It is that time when man started to organise himself into hamlets, a bit away from his earlier wild existence.

MANHACUUK IN THE 3RD TO 4TH MILLENNIUM AFTER CREATION

Although we have just moved out of that apparently mythical era, the era which appears to be the last quarter of the glaciation period and the beginning eras of what geologists call the *Holocene period*, this part of our work on Dinka origin will try to throw light on man's nomadic condition and his spread prior to the ecumenical flood of Noi.

This is the era when some features such as names of people, places and events become discernibly visible and the human population is seen to have clearly spread outside the Edenic region of Panthou. While the later Mesopotamian written sources appears to have mythologised many of the historical figures of this period, persons whom they largely presented in the form of gods, the Biblical accounts of the Old Testament of the Hebrew people makes the people of this time appears as real humans. Dinka traditions on par make the events and people of this time to be real humans and real events despite their oral traditions not being capable of clearly tracing proper Dinka descent lines to this period.

During the pre-flood time, as we have come to know, the tempo of life was much slower. We all know that people of this period still lived longer than the post-flood, or more specifically the pre-Abrahamic, peoples. There were fewer pressures of information and events than is the case today. The human inhabitable world was smaller in scope compared to our today's human inhabitable world. Those pre-flood peoples, the antediluvians, also did have methods of preserving memories, something which man of today does not have in the same degree. One of the methods of conserving memories was the *storyteller* who told tales through many generations without losing anything from those stories. Probably all the major epic tales of the pre-ancient world, including those of creation and the flood eras as contained in the Old Testament and kept by Dinka chroniclers and bards, were transmitted orally before they were finally written down to script. Since our ancient ancestors were part of that human society of the time referred to as prehistory, it is not surprising that they were able to use that ancient method of handing information down orally. Apart from *storytelling* there were other methods of saving ancient memories. Our ancient forebears, ancestors of this period, had developed their way of relating to their creator who had at this time decided to part with *manhacuuk* and went to stay up in the void. For religious purposes much of our ancient memories were incorporated into religious songs, annual festivals and annual rituals as was also the case with the Hebrews and other peoples. In this way we became connected with them and those before them.

According to written sources on prehistory which also agree with ancient Dinka traditions, mankind at this period started to occupy that Endenic or Panthou region assumed to cover those areas which are now Lake Urmia and the Caspian Sea region and those territories of today's Ararat, the mythical home territory where Sumerian civilisation later emerged. According to geologists this area is known for its complex geological structure. Today's Lake Urmia is a dead and salty lake with a volcanic island at the centre of it. The entire area is an earthquake prone territory, then and now. Geologists think that those earthquakes of the prehistoric times made it difficult to obtain any archaeological proof for this pre-flood population.

Man at this time had spread to the whole of the Middle East, Asia Minor, the Pontain region, the Punt and the Nile valley as far as East Africa and as far as Mongolian areas and westward to Keympt which the ancient Dinkas knew as Rip land (now Egypt). Some millennia later man spread further west to Carthage. One of the villages or settlements of this period which, like Panthou, permeates the epic songs and tales or legends emanating from this era, is Pan-Nhial, a territory which in all probability points at the southwest Asian region which may have been located at present Yemen or Saudi Arabia of the today Dinka. Ancient tales of this period tend to blame one woman as the cause of God's withdrawal up into the sky where He decided to live, far from mankind! This tale attributes the state of unhappiness which characterised this period to the mistake done by the woman of this village and of this period. It is the pestle story which will be told in the next sub-heading.

Miseries of life are said to have always been caused by the woman gender. The first was by the great mother at Panthou although her name, Abuk, is not usually mentioned, apparently for the respect of the great mother. Her offence of Nhialic is differently told. In one legend it was curiosity that made her eat the fruit from the forbidden tree of the aŋo. In another it was sheer disobedience to Nhialic as most women do to their husbands even at present. The Dinka relegation of women gender away from leadership and decision making appears to emanate from these mistakes by women of this and the previous eras. During this epoch, long after those of Abuk's era, it is said that the creator was still very near and used to hang about with *manhacuuk*. According to those legends heaven was very low up in the sky and God used to visibly hover over people. He used to even visit *manhacuuk* and appear to them directly and physically. It is said God was such a gigantically huge, tall and immense being in human form. He was very hairy, immeasurable with immutable charm and graceful appearance.

They say Nhialic used to appear as an old male being covered to the shoulders by long grey hair with a moustache that covered even the mouth. His body used to reveal pied colours, mostly blue, white and red, especially when standing. His arms and hands are described as being powerfully built and to the present day, Dinka people say God is left-handed and that He used to hold a holy sceptre, which they call *wai rial*, on his left hand, a sceptre with which he struck things into fire when He intended to destroy or punish. His voice used to be such a sonorous, lofty and at times elephantinic one. Some sources say He mostly used to appear by the head in a cloud and He sometimes appeared on a mountain, a hill or on big trees, sometimes on a luak. They believe in Him as the final judge.

THE PESTLE STORY AND GOD'S WITHDRAWAL TO THE SKY

At this time, conditions of life became so bad to those inhabiting the south eastern regions of the Mediterranean following the retreat of the glaciers. The life of those who moved to live in the north of the Mediterranean became much more comfortable. Weather became milder and animals that trekked there from the Middle East and from North Africa became more numerous because the mild weather improved their pastures. The Middle East and North Africa were already desiccating due to hot weather. Contrary to Europe, life in the Middle East and North Africa started to be grim due to climatic catastrophes which they began to experience. The population in the Middle East continued moving north. Part went to the Far East up to the Mongolian region. Others chose to move to the wet jungle swamps of the various river valleys and the Mediterranean shores and coasts. Part, however, remained to face that grim life of the rugged Middle East!

It must have been a terrible time for those who lived in the previously bountiful Middle East and who became gradually impoverished.[107] The above community depicted by the epic song must have been the antediluvians of the 4th millennium after creation. As mentioned earlier, Dinka ancient tales attribute the difficulties of this terrible era to the woman. Perhaps for lack of respect and against an incessant warning, a woman of this period is said to have used a too long pestle when she was pounding grain and by so doing, she touched or pricked God's firmament in an overhanging low sky!

In disgust for that act, the creator is said to have decided to withdraw up into the heights, far away from the people, and the physical contact between the creator and *manhacuuk* ceased from that time till people of another epoch thought of making a long rope aisle, mysteriously anchored to the sky, a rope which people began to climb up from the earth to heaven, which Nhialic had chosen as his place of abode. As the ancient tales have it this mythical rope was used for centuries by *manhacuuk* as the route to and from heaven till the time when the sparrow cut that rope between the earth and heaven, thereby severing contact between man and his creator. The sparrow is that little bird that the Rek Dinka call atoc-toc or atoc-maguɛn.

The withdrawal of that creation deity called Nhialic up into the

---

107 Ibid. p. 5

sky prompted *manhacuuk* to name him as *Nhialic*, meaning 'in the sky'. The word 'nhial' which the Dinka of today still keep for the words 'up', 'above' and 'sky,' is an Edenic (or Panthou) word which originated from Nhialic himself. The language the Dinka speak now is that very language imparted to Garaŋ by the creator at Panthou. It is that pure language, the holy language from Nhialic which continued as the pre-Babel or Edenic language (Gen. 11:1) until Nhialic later introduced different languages at the time He destroyed the tower that was being constructed at Babel in Babylonia to enable man to go to Him in his abode up in heaven. The present Dinka language is surprisingly that very language which was the mother of all world languages of today. Cultures as diverse and far apart as the Chinese and the Maya have ancient traditions about a single, global language and an instant diversification by the creator.[108]

After Nhialic could not be reached any more and could not have any physical contact with man on earth, the society decided to instantly complain as all avenues for human contact with their creator were closed but, in the days when man used to go to God's abode in heaven using that rope aisle, a group of super or angelic beings began to descend from heaven and interacted with man on earth. Those super humans consisted of renegade angels who rebelled against God in heaven. They mingled with those pre-flood people. Those beings came to tell of the mysteries and powers of God and were able to know and interpret God's secrets among man. They began to act like the creator Himself, so much so that *manhacuuk* turned to them instead of to Nhialic, whom they could not see any more except through dreams and through imaginations. Some of these beings decided to be benevolent in their interaction with man. Others were highly malevolent. They acquired the names of the spirits of the dead ancestors and were as such considered

---

[108] Henry M Morris, 'The confusion of tongues' (in) The tower of Babel by James Montgomery in his voice on Nimrod and Babel, (2004), p. 16.

divine beings. Man became disposed to them instead of to his creator. Dinka forebears took them as jak, jɔk in singular. Until today Dinka society still interacts with those invisible beings that may be described as jak or lesser gods. They are properly explained in the book by the same author entitled 'Dinka religion: their belief system'.

This antediluvian community from the 4th to the 7th generation since creation, is the one being portrayed by Dinka ancestral traditions, people of the very millennium leading to the time of the flood of the Great Noi. Man at this time entered into so many wars against each other. The society began to break into groups and families. All sorts of crime-making permeated this period. This also coincided with climatic changes in the Middle and Far East as well as Punt and North Africa. Except for the domesticated animals like goats, sheep and the cow, most of the wild game had deserted northward to Europe. The climatic change must have been a very long and drawn out process. Dinka ancient stories attribute this to what they call God's wrath as the primary cause. In those early times up to now everything which was unusual was connected or attributed to God, especially the unexpected natural catastrophes.

From deep historical reading and analysis of those pre-ancient Dinka stories, the society to which Noi did belong must have moved out of Pan-Nhial in southwest Asia and lived near the southeastern corner of the Euxine Lake, our present Black Sea area in search for water and good pasture. Many communities did the same. The Mediterranean Sea coastal areas, those of the Euxine Lake and the Bosporus region, now the Balkans, and those areas covering northwestern Anatolia which was hitherto rich with rivers leading to and from those primeval seas, were full of those antediluvian peoples of the times leading to the flood catastrophe. This partly explains why the story of the flood of Noi is known by almost all the world communities, not because they copied from one another but because the tales about that flood came from people who had similar experiences from that same flood.

In the days before the people of Noi must have moved to that southeastern corner of the Euxine Lake which was to some extent near to the Ararat mountain region, Noi's society had a belief that their creator decided to move up into the void not only due to the pestle story done by the woman, but because he wanted to separate himself from *manhacuuk* which had at the time become sinful, wicked, corrupt and violent and no longer in respect of their creator. It is said He withdrew to avoid his providential secrets and workings being known by mankind who had been spoiled by renegade angels (Gen. 6:1-4) who revealed to man the eternal mysteries that were not to be known to mankind.[109]

In the course of the last millennium prior to the flood of Noi, the antediluvian society made one occasion after another, calling on Nhialic and making sacrifices and offerings to propitiate Him to reduce their suffering. They made pleas for the ills in the society.

According to those traditions Nhialic heard their prayers and solemn appeals during one occasion and word is said to have come from Nhialic in which He promised to be in contact with manhacuuk only when they requested Him, and that he was to be requested through some righteous people from the descendants of Deŋ-Mayuääl, who was given holy investiture and God's wisdom at the time of the distribution of labour by his father Garaŋ. According to this tradition Nhialic confirmed that the male offspring or male descendants of Deŋ-Mayuääl were to be His spokesmen and representatives within the society of mankind on earth and that He was to be present and listen to people when members from the family line of this chosen people made offerings in a sanctified place, especially dedicated to Him, or when He was invoked by those members of

---

[109] The antediluvians The Genesis File, http:///www.genesisfiles.com/antediluvians.htm

Deŋ's bloodline. This explains why Dinka people from the mundane clans call on Spear Masters to offer their sacrificial animals to God rather than they themselves doing it alone. Since then the millennial society descended from Abuk and Garaŋ accepted they would have to relate to Nhialic the creator through these holy men, who continued to be known up to the present day as *bäny-bith* or Spear Masters. In some places like the Middle East they are spiritual patriarchs or prophets.

THE DINKA VERSION OF THE HUMAN SUFFERING BEFORE THE FLOOD OF NOI

From those ancient Dinka stories, those from the Hebrews, Mesopotamians and the ancient tales of the Far East, tales which have been partly explained above, a picture of human population, events and climatic changes is seen as we fix on the millennia between that creation time and the eras leading to the flood time when human presence on earth was almost wiped out all together. By about the end of the 1st millennium after creation, the time Garaŋ must have died, historians on the pre-flood world suggest a population of about 120 000 people living on the confines of what is now the Middle East.[110]

By the time of the flood man had reached several billion according to population growth since creation. In those centuries leading to the flood time man's knowledge about *Nhialic* became irreparably wicked. Everywhere was vendetta and warlordism with raid after each raid all across the inhabitable land. This must have been the time when those renegade angels called super humans or devils (jak) descended from heaven and chose to live with man. They demanded

---

[110] Lambert Dolphin, On the great flood of Noah (1983), Revised 1991, 2001 & 2004

man worship them as gods, gods rampantly found in Greek and Roman mythological tales as well as those found in the Sumerians, Akkadians and Assyrian tales. Those tales seek to parallel those of the Dinka. During this era, man had invented a lot of war implements. They discovered building and agricultural technology as well as those of art and even music. This is why there are stories about antediluvian towns, villages and cities.

When violence and all forms of crimes filled the earth and all forms of God's warnings could not find ground, God became frustrated and in time gave up on His own creation. Accordingly, God started His punishments by first causing a prolonged drought of many centuries, a long period within which environmental change from temperature alterations resulted in the emergence of deserts and a lot of changes in the surface water, thereby causing pasture and water problems almost in the whole of what was the Middle East of today, the Far East, the Punt and North Africa. Many people died of famine owing to lack of food as cultivation became difficult. This explains why populations of this epoch had to live along the then existing rivers and around the lakes and along the Mediterranean coasts. It was this overstretched and long-lived drought which dropped the wild game off the Middle East to central Europe and to the Alpine areas and the interior of Africa.

Yet this did not bring man closer to his creator, who for ages has not been seen by them after His withdrawal from mankind into the sky or heaven. According to those ancient tales *Nhialic* decided to use fire with which He destroyed selected points in the hope that mankind would correct himself from those bad ways. Towns and settlement villages were put on fire on several occasions and fire came from upwards as rain. Nevertheless, such miraculous events and happenings made no change in the attitude of man. Thus, after centuries of continued evil, God decided to wipe those antediluvians off the face of the earth as He did to the people before Abuk and

Garaŋ. There is an unconfirmed belief among the Dinka which talks of the world having humans on it before the world of those of Abuk and Garaŋ. All in all, Dinka ancient myths are so replete with legends and tales about this period leading to the flood's time.

THE WORLD FLOOD OF NOI ACCORDING TO THE DINKA (ITS POINT OF ERUPTION, EXTENT AND TIME)

In tackling this topic of historical importance, a topic marking the end of the old world of those of Abuk and Garaŋ and the beginning of today's world, we will use the data acquired from written sources on ancient Middle East flood stories and the Biblical version on the world flood. Emphasis will be put on the Dinka version and the modern scientific discoveries about this very ecumenical flood.

In the first place, let us begin with the Dinka historical figure called Noi who must be the Biblical Noah in the ancient Hebrews' account of the very flood. A tight reading of the genealogy using the Masoretic text of the Bible Genesis suggests the flood to have taken place 2 256 years after the creation of Adam. This periodisation grossly differs with our scheming of the time between this flood and the time of our Dinka first man at creation. This Biblical time length cannot be overtly disputed because 2 256 years could be a sufficient time for large parts of the earth to be filled up with people.[111] A conservative population growth calculation would place the population at 120 000 persons at the time of the death of Adam, who is our Garaŋ. It is not surprising to therefore put human population at 7 billion during the time of the flood.[112] Despite the violence and catastrophes of the era preceding the flood the death rate was

---

111 Barry Satterfield, Creation and catastrophe chronology, (1983), p. 9
112 Population growth since creation

low during this antediluvian time compared to the death rate in our present world.

In Dinka, the word *noi* is a name used for people, places and territories. There are territories or areas in Dinka lands with the name *Noi*. For instance, there is Noi territory under the suzerainty of Chief Ayii Kuot Agiu with its current Warrap town as its administrative centre, a town which is also the administrative capital for Tonj North county. Warrap state acquired its name from this former village of Noi territory. *Noi*, like Garaŋ and Deŋ, Abuk and other Dinka universal names, is commonly found among all the Dinka sections in both Upper Nile and Bahr el Ghazal. However, some Dinka families tend to arrogate themselves as the owners of the true and actual family lineage of Noi but these are intermediate Noi whose descendants continue to perpetuate the name Noi as a commemoration of that world ancestor. Perpetuation of the names of ancestors by the descent lines is a well known practice among the Dinka, although Agaar Dinka have come to be generally known to use the names of colours of their bulls and female cows in addition to names of things, events, times and places. Yet, there is *Paan-Noi* or Noi's family lineage in Agaar land. This family of those of Cawul Lom had a claim to being the actual descendants of that Great Noi of the flood. This is not true because Noi is a universal ancestor for all mankind of today. Among the Twic Dinka of Bahr el Ghazal was one such Noi who was one of the two great men who led the Twic section of Bahr el Ghazal during the historic migratory exodus which took the Dinka to Bahr el Ghazal from the Upper Nile region during the Middle Ages.[113]

Thou nyieŋ Noi nhial is a famous and popular saying among the Agaar Dinka. This saying succinctly explains Dinka traditional knowledge about the flood and that world figure called Noi. 'Thou'

---

113 From an interview dated 27.5.2002 with a group of Twic elders led by old man Madit Athuai Deng of the Pakam clan.

in Dinka means death. 'Nyieŋ' means leave or left. 'Nhial' means up. Thus, the saying can be translated to mean '*death can still leave a single person like Noi, even if death were to come in a massive way*'.

The saying refers to that worldwide flood which wiped out almost the entire human population from the face of the earth. Yet Noi survived that catastrophic disaster as to be the fountain seed from whom the present mankind developed. The Dinka story of the flood is very similar with the Biblical version and this is one of the points that support the genealogical association between the Israelites and the Dinka. According to Dinka ancient tales, mankind or *manhacuuk* increased on earth but they all stem from one man, Noi of the flood. Man used to speak one language since the time of Abuk and Garaŋ. They talk of an ancient or early pre-flood plenty and prosperity, an era when *manhacuuk* had grouped into settlement hamlets and had learnt of animal husbandry and cultivation. They talk of man of this period having acquired some advancement in metallurgy, in the lyre and even in building houses. They affirm that at this very epoch man became so proud and his previous knowledge about Nhialic became irreparably perverted.

As stated earlier, the whole earth was filled with vendetta and warlordism and people began to worship divinities that were not their Nhialic, the creator of their primordial ancestors. The tales say Nhialic decided to give warning to *manhacuuk* by physically coming down and speaking to them or through some signs or miracles and when all those warnings were to no avail Nhialic resorted to direct punishments by firstly bringing a plague of diseases that killed man en masse. He also brought prolonged droughts of several years, making many people die of famine due to lack of food throughout the then inhabitable world which was largely the Middle East and North Africa.

Like tales from other communities and nations, Nhialic became frustrated that He had to finally use fire with which he burnt homes, villages and fields. Yet *manhacuuk* was still non-conforming. Some

Dinka societies still call this era **"kek aka yie ke piny bɛn rac acin!"**, that is, *'those are things which make the creator completely destroy the world like He had once done'*. This statement, usually used against wrong deeds, indicates the Dinka knowledge of the pre-flood society that was wiped out by a punishment from Nhialic, the creator.

After such a long time of continued evil the creator in the sky finally decided to cause a flood with which he wiped out man from the entire face of the earth. The flood came as a result of several days of heavy rain day and night. "Na Cɔk a Deŋ Noi!", that is, *"as if it is that rain of Noi!"* Dinka people of today still contrast heavy torrential rains with that ecumenical rain of Noi. They still describe that flood to have submerged everything, many metres below the water, yet one single man with his three sons survived the catastrophe. That man they present as Noi. The tales talk of *riai*, a boat or a big canoe in or on which Noi floated on the flood water with a sample of the animals of today. Dinka traditions do not however agree with the Hebrews on the names of Noi's three sons. Some Dinka sections are completely blank about the names of the three sons, but they all agree that Noi did survive with his wives and three sons.

Other Dinka sources talk of Deŋ, Jiel and Ajääŋ. The author is sketchy about this but all Dinka traditions give a belief of one black son. They say the eldest son was white in colour, the middle son was black in complexion while the last son was neither white nor black. He was red-brown. The eldest and the last sons were very hairy. This could be accepted by science if we are to consider the effects of solar radiation on the pre-flood man of the Middle East in those days when prolonged droughts created deserts and melted glaciers. The human gene pool is likely to have started to have a tint of black pigment that was to appear in the person of Jiel. Blacks may have been likely among those families and sections of man later blotted from the earth's surface by that flood of Noi. From our scheme of genealogical family tree tracing we rest upon Jiel to have been that middle son of Noi who was black in colour. The three must, in all probability, be the Biblical Shem, Ham, and Japheth.

The Dinka version goes on to say that the flood's rain went on for something like two months, day and night, nonstop! The world under heaven was all water and all that was on the earth surface died except for Noi, his family and all those animals with him in the boat. The boat must have not been an ordinary boat. It must have been quite a huge thing of the steamer type. According to Lambert Dolphin in his '*On the great flood of Noah*', the boat was a barge-like structure and was probably built of cypress or cedar timber known as gopher wood according to the Middle East forestry authorities on ancient vegetation. Lambert says it was a boat of about 450 feet long by 75 feet beam and 45 feet high. The boat is believed to have had three decks with one door and an 18 inches window on the top of the roof. In it were a pair of each of the 17 600 species of animals that are presently known to our man of today.[114]

According to Dr. John Morris of the *Institute of Creation Research*, the boat also contained food provisions for a complete year's subsistence. The same source also assumes that two third of the species originally created by God must have perished in that world flood.

THE HISTORIC ARK OF NOI

This flood of Noi was not a mere local flood. It was not a local catastrophe and although Dinka ancient tales do not tell us of the time length for the construction of that boat, Jewish flood legends say it took 120 years for Noah to complete its construction! Then, if the flood were a local one, there would not have been a reason to take the trouble to build such a huge boat called the ark for 120 years. Migrating onto the high mountain ranges of the Himalaya

---

114 Lambert Dolphin: On the great flood of Noah

Fig 45: Showing the Ark of Noah (our Noi) according to Dr Mace Baker and artist Joshua Auke (Dinobooks.com)

region, the Ararat and the Alps in the west would have been far easier or more feasible. The boat must have been constructed on dry land far from water and when Noi sought to persuade his immediate society to go into the boat with him in order to be saved from God pronounced impending flood, none responded and so they perished along with those who did not have the opportunity to reach the ark on the flood days.

According to the Dinka the flood was started by a heavy and continuous torrential downpour of rain and the earth's bowels concomitantly erupted, also causing deep underground waters to burst forth and the windows of heaven to open asunder. In about one week the entire earth's surface was water, labelled up with seas and oceans. The boat with Noi and his family floated on the water until mountain peaks were not to be seen any more. The boat finally rested, however, on one mountain peak after several months. This is the mountain which the Bible calls Ararat mountain, and by gradual recession the flood waters began to disappear off the face of the

Fig 46: Showing samples of animals assembled by Noi ready to go into the ark

earth and Noi began to once again view the world from inside the ark. There was no life left, even the trees had been uprooted from their places and had largely rotted. Landscape was noticeable only through the mountains after a year or so. In time vegetation began to reappear and a bird from the boat began to alert Noi of the land becoming receptive for any form of life again.

This catastrophic event is dated to 2 657 BC according to those scientists who made an emeritus research and came out with *creation and catastrophe chronology*.[115] Prior to this flood of Noi, there occurred some centuries back a flood event which nearly caused universal destruction, but not to the proportion of this worldwide flood of Noi.

During the last years of the Ice Age, the last part of the Pliocene epoch, there appeared a tremendous glacier melting which caused the melted waters to move about in torrential sheets, thereby raising the level of the seas by hundreds of feet. Because of its primordial time length that catastrophe went out of human collective memory, although it could correctly be asserted that this event may be one such catastrophe which Dinka ancient tales refer to as the disaster that wiped out the first world humans before that of our Abuk and Garaŋ.[116]

---

115   Barry Satterfield, Creation and catastrophe chronology, Sept (1999) pp. 8-10

116   EG Ban, 'The Patriarch' (in) From the Garden of Eden to the flood, (2007), p. 9 of 17.

Apart from the Dinka and Hebrew versions of this worldwide flood, the world has about 500 legends on this flood that nearly halted the existence of man on earth, having left only a few individuals to restart humanity. Most of those legends have a common pattern. They have a theme of man's guilt of transgression against God (or gods). The legends also agree that God or one of the many gods of the time sent a flood to punish man and they also say that before the flood instructions were sent to a selected individual to build an ark. The Dinka individual is Noi. The Hebrew individual is Noah. The Chaldeans talk of Ziu Sudra. The Assyrian's figure is Utnapishtim. The Sumerian flood figure is Atrahasis. The Indians talk of Manu. The Greeks' figures who survived the flood are Deucalion, Perseus, Megaros, Alakos and many others. Those names were lost in the memory of many millennia. This gives proof that it was not only Noi of the Dinka or Noah of the Hebrews who survived that worldwide flood alone.

This forces us to also view this flood in the perspective of science, and to do this we must accept that floods are natural disasters, happening in every part of the world and in any epoch in human history. Although we now have the *tsunamis* in our time, that one of Noi's time was exceptionally out of proportion and the people of Noi's time must be right to attribute God's wrath as the cause of that flood. With all our acknowledgement to the traditions coming from our ancestors and our allegiance to Biblical accounts of the past, modern man and his science tells us to use empirical methods to prove given information scientifically, and to this end we have been forced to consult all aspects of the then existing physical conditions at the time of this particular world flood.

THE FLOOD'S POINT OF ERUPTION, EXTENT AND TIME

One classical Greek writer, Diodorus Siculus. who wrote, among other writers, about the history of the Greek island of Samothrace, an island lying at the western entrance of the Dardanelles, made us understand that there came at the time so much water into the Euxine Lake due to glaciers melting (Euxine Lake is our today's Black Sea) and this led to the flood occurring. EG Ban later affirmed this argument. Both agree that the voluminous waters resultant from the melting of all the glaciers and ice caps on mountains in that region caused the Euxine Lake to burst out through the Bosporus and the Dardanelles, thereby inundating the west coast of Asia minor and the low-lying parts of the island of Samothrace.

Looking at the topography of the Black Sea region (see the map of the Black Sea) it has a low shoreline in the Balkans to the north and west of the sea, and a mountainous shore in the east and south towards Russia and the mountains of Anatolia and the Caucus. It means that the waters of the flood covered larger territory in the northwest where the seabed is up to 500 metres in depth each day on the north and west, and less in the south and east. The southern shore of the Euxine Lake has a big sea mount that can be clearly seen as a finger pointing from the southeast to the northwest. That sea mount is a long string of hills forming a peninsula in the lake. It must have acted as a death trap to the people who lived there 100 metres above the lake, or people may have succeeded in escaping there at the time of the flood thinking themselves secure, but were trapped when the water reached the top and they found that instead of being on a secure hill they were unfortunately on a shrinking island, cut off from the mainland!

Scientists are agreed that the basic cause of the Euxine Lake outburst was that the level of the lake and other seas then around rose because of the melting of the glaciers. The level of the seas became much higher than the level of the Euxine Lake as it was a landlocked water body. Eventually either the pressure of the water from the Mediterranean or an earthquake caused the water to gush out at the Bosporus. Geologists say that northwestern areas of Anatolia (present Turkey) are prone to earthquakes. It is therefore possible that it was an earthquake that cleared the earth's crust out of the Bosporus but prior to the event there was that long drought which brought many people around the lake and around the oases of that lake. Undoubtedly all of those people must have perished there.

According to a more recent newspaper article by Barry Wigmore entitled, *'The hunt for Noah's ark'*, an article he wrote after an expedition which went to explore the old shores of the then Euxine Lake to find the natural and geological conditions that may have precipitated that terrible flood, the heavy rain was caused by the way the Euxine basin was filled with rushing water that went in with a force and quantity that the expedition report puts at about 100 times that of Niagara Falls in East Africa.[117]

That article goes on to say that the noise of the rushing water must have been heard in a 100 mile radius and that the spray of water that rose into the atmosphere from the Euxine basin must have formed smoke that enveloped a roaring snow and made an atmospheric canopy that resulted in a torrential rain which went on for forty days and nights. There is presently a big waterfall in Africa, much bigger than even the Niagara Falls. It is the Victoria Falls. It is between Zambia and Zimbabwe. The name of that waterfall in the local African language is *Mosi-O-Tunya*, which means *'the smoke that roars'*. The spray of water, which is the 'smoke', can be seen from miles away and the roar of water can be heard from about 15 miles. No doubt the flood that started to fill the Euxine Lake must

---

117   19 Barry Wigmore, 'The hunt for Noah's ark' (in) The Times (London), (2000), p. 15

have been an extremely frightening experience which definitely left its signs in the tales of the flood of Noi. The question which poses itself is that, would the people of that time be wrong to attribute such a frightening disaster as a sign of heavenly wrath? Would people of today take it differently?

Now, what can we say of the survivors in the context of these new scientific findings? According to the Dinka it was only one family of Noi who survived that catastrophe. Dinka knowledge of Noi, the Hebrew Noah, is one proof of the Dinka being part of the Semitic race but it is scientifically not true that there was one human family that survived the flood. It is discernible that there were survivors other than Noi or Noah alone and his three sons and their wives plus his wife. Many people succeeded in escaping the deluge. Man spread out to all directions, to the region which later became Egypt, to those areas which became Sumer, an area which later became Mesopotamia. Some people succeeded in escaping to the steppe lands north of the Euxine Lake and from there to Europe. Others went to those areas in central Asia. Those are people who escaped southeast. Some went to those lands that are now India and to the Turkestan region of the Caucus from where others may have proceeded to China and the Mongolian region of today. This accounts for the over 500 tales about the same flood. All flood tales around the globe originated from those survivors, not from our Noi or the Hebrew's Noah alone, although different communities give a version of their own according to their historical development and language. There are, however, similarities, not coming from each having copied from the other in the course of time, but because those similarities came from people who did have the same experiences.

The Dinka and the Old Testament talk about a rain of forty days and nights, but science tells us that the flood was due to a waterfall coming from the melted glaciers and from an earthquake that simultaneously poured water into the Euxine Lake and this gradually took two years to become a complete flood disaster when the level of the lake was raised to the level of the Mediterranean. Two years must have been a sufficient time for Noi to build such a huge maritime boat call the ark that housed such a large number of animals, birds and family members. But many animals must have run or walked away to far lands before the flood came to a disaster level. There is certainty that animals could save themselves better than humans. This is because animals do not have the considerations of humans about family, property, farming, implements, domestic items, etc. Animals have instincts and they can just flee. Many of the animals must have escaped before the flood reached its catastrophic proportions, as long as the flood took time to build up until the earthquake from the lake's bed at the Bosporus and rain from the atmospheric canopy set in to cause the torrential onrush that became a disaster.

Escaping by boats could have been an option for those who lived on the sea mount or those who were engaged in fishing and had boats. Those people may have used the boats to reach the mainland and safe places.

As we read this scientific analysis let us resort to the map of the Black Sea topography. It is certain that we can conclude that in the north where the Black Sea (the then Euxine Lake) advances very fast because of low shore lines boats were not probably feasible. People living in this part of the Euxine Lake needed fast decisions but then the flood was an extraordinary experience so that even in modern circumstances it would be difficult to predict how people would react. However, those who must have been living in such areas like present Pompeii must have recognised the danger in time and had opportunity to escape. Moreover, they lived near an area of a very active volcano and must have known the possible dangers.

It could rightly be postulated that people in such places must have escaped (check the map of the Black Sea region). According to the map, if there were people living on the northern shore lines of the lake, which must have been the case, then those people had a long distance to travel before reaching safety, but those who lived near the current south shore of the lake had a short distance to travel to safe places. So, if Noi/Noah and his family lived near the southeastern corner of the lake, which was nearest to the former ancestral home of those of Abuk and Garaŋ, the valley of present Tabriz, then there was certainty to reach the Ararat mountain area, which was a safe place.

Thus, there were people other than our Noi/Noah who escaped the flood although the rains caused by the flood were spread in a very wide radius. It left the earth wetter for a very long period as it also transformed the earth's topography and the Euxine Lake became the Black Sea thereafter. The increased moisture in the air, due to evaporation from sheet flooding of that region of the Middle East, central Europe and the Mediterranean to as far as Anatolia and the Caucus region and North Africa, resulted in such inundation and rains never experienced for a number of millennia.

Despite this scientific presentation, the Dinka and Biblical story about the flood must be seen to have been essentially correct. This is because if the flood had the speed and intensity so described by many writers, then not many people could have survived the event, neither in the shallow water in the north nor in the deeper water in the west and near the south shore. The Mediterranean region must have remained as an ocean for maybe a century. The flood and its effect certainly took a long period of recuperation until the remaining people could organise their lives again. Yet there is an Iranian myth that says their ancestors escaped the flood and went to a place where a long dense atmospheric canopy period of snow from the sky created snow and ice which forced them to build a var, an underground city. Archaeologists had discovered this place, a complex underground city near the area of Lake Van in historic Cappadocia in the vicinity of the modern city of Derinkuyu,[118] but after the flood, the world was desolate and this leads us to the Dinka version of the world after the flood.

AFTER THE FLOOD AS THE DINKA KNOW IT (THE DINKA PARENT STEM)

INTRODUCTION

In this part of our historical handling of the Dinka roots of origin one is forced to be using several methods at once, moving to the time when the immediate post-flood humans had to form the genesis of man and the world we are in today without interruption, as was the case with the antediluvian world that was populated by the descendants of Abuk and Garang (Garaŋ) of the creation time.

This tremendous middle phase in world history, the time between us and the antediluvian people of before the flood of Noi, dictated such methods as the moving forwards and backwards in order to successfully blend and neaten together those information fragments gathered here and there from Dinka ancient and primordial traditions, and have them agree with what the twentieth and twenty first centuries had discovered of how man lived and developed after that flood of Noi prior to the rise of the first world civilisations, Sumer, behind Biblical Mesopotamia and the pre-dynastic Egypt of the pharaohs.

Our analysis of this terrible length of time must be data intensive. This rather obscure and primordial period as it appears must be tackled in phases: The first would be the Palaeozoic or Pre-Paleek period of more than half a millennium and which commences from the time Noi stepped out of the boat after the flood waters had faded,

---

118 20 Turkish Tourist Bureau, Cave towns and gorges of Cappadocia, (1997), Andrew Collins, op.cit. Ch III ,pp. 3-13

and we are to sequence it with the time when another world event took place, the time of major geological change which divided the earth planet into its present continents.

The second phase would be the Mesozoic period which covers that era after the continental division, the time when Paleek was born and the fifth generation began after the flood of Noi. This moved through to the time when man made a gigantic lift from just a simple primitive farmer, living in grass or leaves-thatched huts with mud walls to that of a civilised and organised life where kingdoms arose with such historical kings as Nimrod in whose time man decided to build a tower aimed at reaching heaven where Nhialic could be accessed by man, an act which made Nhialic destroy that tower at Babylon and disperse humanity to different directions of the world with man's original Adenic language confused so that each group or clan could not hear or understand the other.

The third phase would be the time when the existing Dinka tales and Biblical similarities in peoples' names, places and events begin to chart a clear pathway that enabled us to discern and tackle with some form of clarity those who became the ancient ancestors of our present Dinka people as we find them beginning to migrate from western Asia to the Mongolian region and back to the Sumer area of Ur as part of the great transhumant movements that took people to and from in the era after the Babel tower catastrophe.

Our fourth and the last phase of this primordial antiquity will cover those times when the great Chaldean patriarch became the direct and clear ancestor of the later Dinka and their kin, the Nuers, Israeli and Arab peoples, migrated to Palestine from Ur in Babylon and whose descendants later moved to Egypt, where part of them who became Dinka and Nuers migrated to ancient Sudan's northern region of Wawat at the time when the bulk of those Israelites, also called Jacobites, returned to Palestine in what the Bible calls the exodus (Gen.: 12:37-18:27) from Egypt. The rest of the story of the Dinka from within ancient Northern Sudan and their migration to Khartoum and to the Upper Nile region in Southern Sudan shall constitute the next chapter.

DINKA KNOWLEDGE OF THE POST-FLOOD PERIOD

Dinka bygone generations of the 18th, 19th and 20th centuries left the Jaang version of the immediate post-flood period for our present 21st century generation. Dinka rural societies from whom this rich data material was obtained got it from those generations. They later gave it over during the research for the benefit of our present generation, our general readership the world over and for our future generations to come. They left this great wealth of knowledge about that great length of the primordial, the antiquity, the ancient and the Mediaeval periods for us to put it to script like this.

What they told gives much evidence that the survivors of Noi's ecumenical flood were real historical figures, and although there may have been other communities or people not covered by the flood or who may have escaped that universal catastrophe, our Dinka traditions only know of those eight people who were in the boat: Noi, his wife, his three sons and their three wives. That Dinka ancient accounts of this post-flood period are rather similar with those expressed in the Bible is another proof of the Dinka Middle Eastern ancestry.

"Noi stepped out of *riai*, the boat, with all the animals and creatures that were with him in the boat, his wife as well as his three sons, Deng, Jiel and Jök, and their wives. Some people say it was Ajaang, not Jok", the Dinka story proceeds with, "and they started present *manhacuuk* or mankind by repopulating the earth through the children that were born to them after the flood". This Dinka version entirely agrees with the Hebrew rendering of the same as it came in the Bible. "These are the three sons of Noah and of them was the whole earth overspread" (Gen. 9:19 KJV), says the Bible.

Where was Noi stepping to from *riai*, with his family and all the animals and creatures that were with him? Our ancestors were also good at geography. They point to the east, not south, west or north. They point to the east and give descriptions indicating present Turkey, in total agreement with the Hebrews' description that points to the same Turkey where Ararat mountain can be located even today. This area called Turkey was until antiquity known as Galatia or Gaul but before that it was called Gomoria after the descendants of Gomer, who was one of the sons of the last sons of Noi who the Hebrews call Japheth. Some of these people from Galatia or Gaul later migrated westward to what are now France and Spain. For many centuries France was known as Gaul, after the descendants of Gomer and in the northwestern parts of present Spain is a region called Galatia up to this day.[119]

Then Noi and his family started to live an altogether new life by starting a home in this Anatolian region which is present Turkey. Perhaps during this time it is said the black son ridiculed his father Noi so while he was soundly asleep after his wife gave him a strong beer, Noi meted a curse upon that son and Dinka people had a belief that the problems of the black race stemmed from that filial curse. The Hebrew version says it was Ham and Canaan was cursed for his father's sin (Gen. 9:25). Israel's later invasion of the land of Canaan which is Palestine may be understood as a divine implementation of that curse.

Dinka ancient tales continue to say that both the three sons of Noi and their father lived to be very old. Some of them even outlived their children, their grandchildren and great grandchildren and this made them to be seen as special among their descendants. As is

---

119   Information obtained from internet article on Eber

the case among today's Dinka they became heads of their families which began to be clans in their names. They lived surrounded by large populations in the respective areas they chose to settle at. Their descendants began to name themselves by the name of the man who was their common ancestor.

Some went straight in to claim their long living ancestors as their gods and here began the Dinka taking of Dengdit as their divinity rather than an ancestor. Garang and many significant ancestors in Dinka history are deified as family, clan or national divinities to the present day. Others are sainted and big pyramidal shrines are made as their holy tombs to house their spirits and/or their physical remains. Uncastrated bulls and rams are ritually slaughtered for those ancestors in annual celebrations up to today. This is done throughout the Dinka lands.

Noi started the practice of cultivation for food and the rearing of domestic animals selected from among those animals that came with him in the ark after the flood. Human population started in that way according to the Dinka oral traditions. Man started after the flood in the eastern parts of the Anatolian region of today's Turkey and like their antediluvian predecessors, they multiplied by means of brother marrying sister and by means of their long lifespan. Descendants of Dengdit remained in this Anatolian region while the people of Jiel migrated to what were to be Jericho in Shinnar which later became Sumer, then to Babylon in Nimrod's time. Paan-Jök went northwest into what later became Gaul (France) and into the Ashkenazi region, which later became Germany. Others went to an area which became Medes, then Persia, where they finally became Iranians. Others went as far as those lands that are present India and to the Caucus region.

In all those areas, man settled as a collection of small farming villages and hamlets. Those in Shinar spread out around the lower Tigris and Euphrate Rivers. This was in the Palaeozoic era, a period of about five centuries between the flood of Noi and the time of the division of the earth into its present continents when Paleek was born. This Paleek, son of Great Abiɛl Wulek, is presented by some Dinka traditions as having a brother by the name of Jöktɛm.[120] Paleek, Jöktɛm, Jök and Abiɛl are common names among the Dinka to the present day.

By genealogical calculation and comparison with the Hebrew's Peleg whose brother is also presented in the Bible as *Jöktan*, it is probable that he is the same Dinka Paleek. The Bible says he was born during the first half of the first millennium after the great flood of Noi. About him the Bible says, *'and unto Eber were born two sons: the name of one (was) Peleg; for in his days was the earth divided, and his brother's name (was) Jöktan'* (Gen. 10:25 KJV and 1 chronicles 1:19 KJV). Those are some of the striking similarities with the Jews.

If man at that period in time can still live up to 600 years as is the case of Shem (Deŋdit) in the Bible, then it is likely that the division of the earth took place in the Dinka Paleek's time. The following Dinka pedigree indicates where Paleek comes in the Dinka genealogical descent line from Noi of the flood to Jiel of the Chaldeans at Ur in Southern Mesopotamia.

'Deŋ' was the name of the eldest son of Garaŋ at the beginning of the antediluvian world. Deŋ also became the name of the eldest son of Noi of the flood time. If this Deŋ is the very Shem of the Bible, then he lived to be 600 years. His firstborn son Wulek, whose subsequent rendering made him also known as Wol, must be the Biblical Elam, the first son of Shem who is our Dinka Deŋ. If Deŋ lived to be 600 years old then those of his descendants have a right to deify him as their god or divinity figure. Whether it is this Deŋ Noi or the first Deŋ Garaŋ, it is a sainted name associated with holiness, purity

---

120   Information obtained from an interview by the author with old man Jɔk Daau Kacuɔl in Cuɛibɛt town dated 8.5.2002, repeating what Santino Deng Tëëng said in 1993 in Wau.

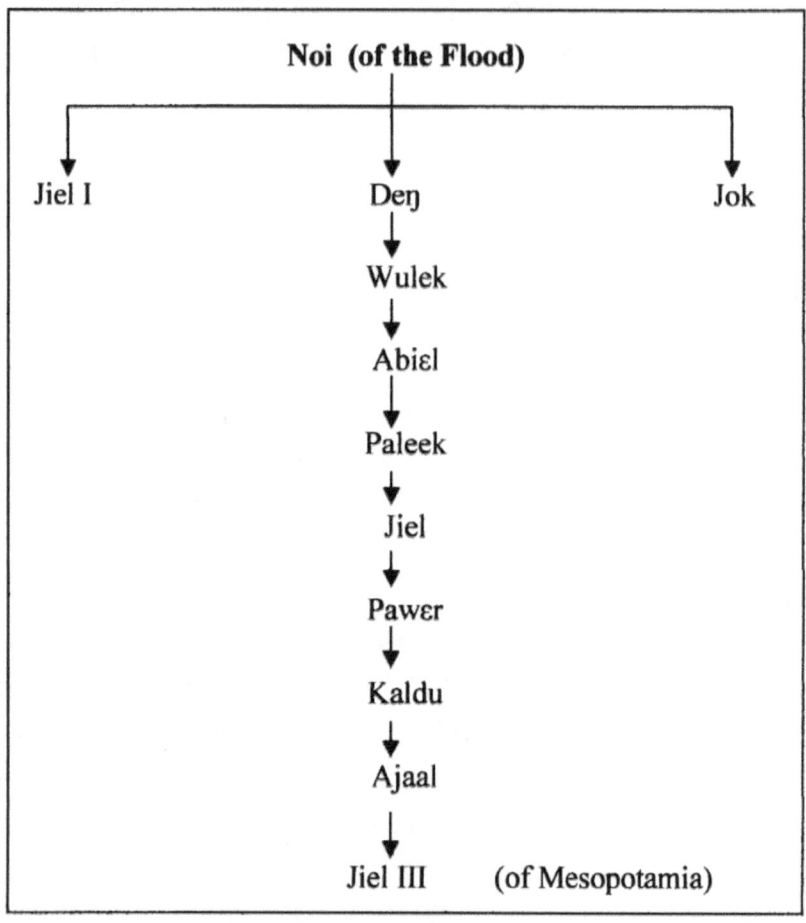

Fig 47: Showing Dinka Primordial pedigree from Noi to Jiel of Mesopotamia

and sacredness. Until recent times the name Deŋ used to be given to the firstborn son in every Dinka family.

Since Deng lived to be the one to kill Nimrod, the first world king in Babylon after the flood, the son of Cush, according to extra-Biblical sources, Deng must truly have every reason to be deified if he lived for 600 years and he was the heir to Noi for being the eldest son of the founder of mankind after the flood.[121] There is also a

---

121 From an interview with old man Agɔɔk Baŋocooth, section of Duɔny

Dinka tradition which says that one of their ancestors of the Babel tower's time refused to let his people help in the building of the tower of Babel and so his language was not confused when God intervened and destroyed the tower, scattered the population and confused people to talk and hear different but new languages. Jewish tradition says this ancestor who did not participate in the building of the tower of Babel was Eber, the great grandson of Shem. In this way some Dinka oral historians think that it was from their ancestor that the original human language, the 'Adamic language' or the *'lingua humana'*, remained with them to the present day. Linguists are required to prove this Dinka contention.

THE TOWER OF BABEL AND THE DINKA

Then came a call from a man called Nhomŋɛk, the Biblical Nimrod, for all the people to gather and live in one place to be able to plan how to gain access to the creator in the sky. 'Nimrod' in Dinka means 'nhom-ngɛk', meaning the obstinate minded person who does not listen to the views of others. Until the time of Nimrod, mankind spoke few words and one language, Garaŋ's language from Panthou. The vocabulary of man had not at that time reached what it is today.

Perhaps in response to the call, or due to the land being receptive as we still call it *the fertile crescent* today, those who went to the west, north and southeast after the flood several centuries back all remigrated to Babylon and found it a nice plain in the land of Shinar. They all settled there in hamlets and villages as hunters and gatherers of food from the wild in addition to tilling the land and making animal husbandry, and although Nimrod later ended like Julius Caesar (101-44 BC) he was able to organise that primitive

---

Payam in Cuɛibɛt County, Interview dated 10.5.2002.

early society. He made out of them the first post-flood government in human history and committed them to build Babylon as his kingdom's city. His population later extended from Babylonia (present Iraq) to Assyria where he also made the people build other cities including Nineveh. Nimrod made many towns and cities in his lifetime. It must have taken him many years to organise people into an urban life when he built those cities and towns.

While doing all this Nimrod (Nhom-Ngɛk) was also a terrible tyrant, a dictator and killer of people. His ambition and ego for grandeur fit the following words from none other than Julius Caesar himself. *"When the gods wish to take vengeance on a man for his crimes, they usually grant him considerable success and a period of impunity, so that when fortune is reversed he will feel it all the more bitterly".* So was it for both Nimrod and Julius Caesar. Nimrod decided to commit his Babylonian society to build a tower reaching into heaven, perhaps as a means to restart direct communication with Nhialic and maintain contact with Him.

The crux of the matter is unveiled clearly by these words from Nimrod himself, "Let us make a name for ourselves, lest we be scattered abroad upon the face of the whole earth". In analysing this fundamental phrase those people of his time could be understood to have fear haunting them, fear of a force that was pushing them apart in order not to live closely together, a force which could ultimately scatter them and have them live as isolated communities where they could be exposed to some great danger like happened in the time of Noi when that force destroyed man in a universal flood.

Nimrod's goal must have been to resist any further scattering of the people over the face of the whole earth, and instead he opted to create a city where the achievements of a united and integrated people would be centralised but it was not fear alone which made them think like that. There must also have been the normal human fundamental urge for man's glory and greatness. "Let us make a name for ourselves" is another statement from Nimrod, a statement which is self explanatory. It underpins the inner motive on the part of Nimrod. The phrase reveals one of the basic philosophies of man and that is glory to mankind. If that tower at Babel was a religious tower and yet it was built to make a name for man, then this is where God had to intervene. The statement revealed Nimrod's master motive behind the call to maintain communication and contact with the creator. It became a rebellion to God and a means to share in the glory of God. The tower was a grandiose structure aimed also at compelling God to be available to mankind whether He liked it or not! God saw this Babylon under Nimrod as an affront to Him in that it sought to do things against or without God.

It was also an affront to the society as Nimrod used peoples' energies for his own purposes. He also ruled his people tyrannously. Most of all Nimrod wanted a house so high up in the sky to escape to if a flood ever came back again like it did in the time of Noi. Nimrod was also a warrior, not a hunter of wild game as it is alleged in the Bible, although hunting wild game was at that time a big matter which used to involve kings for their huge manpower and for being seen as gods themselves according to ancient beliefs. It was through his ability to fight and kill and rule ruthlessly that in his kingdom of Euphrates valley city states were all brought under him and consolidated and so he ruled Babylonia by compulsion.

That lofty tower of unequalled grandeur stood immense in the plain of Shinar, a few kms north of today's Baghdad city with the top almost reaching to the heavens, showing man's puny extravagance in thinking. Man of that time saw that tower or had participated in the construction of that tower as a means to revive the previous contacts with their creator and for this reason very few saw it as an affront to the creator, and that is why almost all were involved in its architecture, its masonry work and in bringing its building materials from as far as the mountain region of the Caucus in the east and the

Fig 48: Showing the tower of Babel

Anatolian region of Ararat ridge to the north. This is why its story is told by almost all the world communities today, Dinka people being one of them. The Babel tower was not our mere engineering work. It involved energy from those giants of our prehistoric world when man used to live for centuries, not today's humans. Any normal building couldn't have drawn the attention of the creator. The tower's top used to disappear into the space and it was extremely immense down and up.

So what happened? The answer is that Babel's tower story is a popularly known one among the Dinka. As Nhialic could not tolerate that rebellion by man and cannot also wipe out humanity against His earlier assurance to Noi, never to destroy mankind in totality as he did to the antediluvians by means of that devastating flood, God himself descended from up in the sky and made very lasting mighty acts. Striking the tower down with a thunderbolt, God dismantled the Babel tower! That colossal structure, "He brought it to nothingness!", say the Dinka people. Furthermore God dispersed the Babylonian population and confused people not to hear or understand each other. Man therefore took to different directions the world over. They scattered while speaking different languages. People did not come together and live in one communion any more, nor did mankind have one language to this day anymore! The Babel tower event was a mighty incident in human history which God associated with another mighty act. He divided the earth planet into five continents by a colossal earthquake aimed at completing His dispersal of people and making them not come together again like they did in Babylon to behave like they did in the days before the flood.

At some given moments in world history, God does perform certain wonders called miracles or mighty acts. He does these acts Himself or through some of his righteous people such as, in the case of the Dinka, the Spear Masters. According to the Dinka miracles are supernatural interventions that God makes against the natural order of things. He does these interventions in a way that accomplishes his purpose, brings glory to Him and threatens man to be aware of God's presence all times. "Every act of God is a miracle", say the Dinka. Nhialic usually seems to allow nature to operate according to the principles or laws which He originally created for it. Thus, for example at Wär-Pakuɛɛk, the Red Sea, the normal course for the water was to obey the laws of gravity and remained unparted and moving according to the current and gravity but, as the Bible tells us, God's sovereignty overrules natural laws and causes matter to operate in ways that go beyond the ordinary. He made the waters of the Red Sea separate into two and stopped them from flowing, allowing the running Israelites to pass on a gap of dry land created by the parted waters. We, the Abrahamic children of Jiel the Patriarch, are the only people God had chosen to enjoy such help through such a powerful act when we are in great need. See Dinka Jiel IV, the founding ancestor of the Pagong clan at his crossing of the Red Sea at Bab el Mandeb.

THE CONFUSION OF LANGUAGES

Originally, after the great flood, "the whole earth was still of one language and one speech" (Gen. 11:1). The Dinka ascribe to this scriptural statement. Because of man's united rebellion against God, refusing to scatter throughout the world as God had commanded, and concentrating instead in the vicinity of Babylon, God confounded their one original language that was used since creation. Dinka people perfectly know of this human dispersal at Babylon and its attending diversification of language and they strongly assert the claim that their ancestor made his lineage family not participate in the construction of the tower and they were the only family spared by God to speak that original language of creation which they now continue to speak.

Although the exact location of that ancient tower of Babel is still a matter of uncertainty because of the many remnants of ancient ruins in the present Baghdad city and its outlying suburbs, some Jewish and Arab traditions locate the tower ruins at a town called Borsippa (the tongue; tower) which is a distance of about 11 miles southwest of the northern portion of Babylon, a site which was formerly a suburb of the city.[122]

Then, where did the ancestors of the would-be Dinka people go, following the Babel tower dispersal? This question leads us into a

---

122 Lambert Dolphin, The Tower of Babel and the confusion of languages, p. 16 of 28 Internet http:///www.idolphin.org/babel.html

very crucial phase in our long search for the Dinka roots of origin. In the genealogical descent lines above we find that Dinka people descended from Deŋ, the eldest son of Great Noi of the flood. We also realise that there were two ancestors between this deified Deŋ and his great grandson, Paleek, in whose time the events of the Babel tower and continental division of the earth took place. We also found Deŋ to have lived much longer as to be the one to kill Nimrod who was the king and leader of the rebellion against God at Babylon; we therefore have every reason to suppose that his son Wulek and his grandson Abiɛl must have also lived to be witnesses to the events. Both migrated away from Babylon as part of the human onrush to different directions following the Babel tower destruction by Nhialic.

DINKA PRE-ANCIENT FOREBEARS WENT TO MONGOLIA, CHINA AND SOUTHWEST ASIA

At the wake of those devastating events Deŋdit's family community migrated to southwest Asia where they settled for a much longer period. Here they developed into astrologers, those who worshipped the stars and still believed in their deified great grandfather Deŋdit. Some of today's Dinka clans who believe in the celestial bodies such as the moon and a host of planetary items as their classificatory or totemic symbols had their beginnings from that formative stage in southwest Asia. In this region they developed into something like a tribe. In their concept of the cosmic world they knew there was something much higher, over and around, existing within and coming from without, a superior or creative deity from whom came the primordial gene that made man, with their ancestor Deŋdit as the primogenitary output of that creative being. They revered those celestial bodies as conveyors of their wishes to that one existing by itself.

Within that society of Deŋdit came up a patriarch by the name of Kaldu who was son to Pawɛr Jiel.

According to traditions going to the times of this southwest Asia, this Kaldu grew to be performing divine acts. He lived to be very old and made a name and a family tree which in time grew into a clan and a tribe. But this Kaldu and his society is presented to have reemigrated from this southwestern area (now Arabia) wanting to go back to Babylon, the very area where Nhialic spared their ancestor Deŋdit and his father Noi, but they settled midway in Ur, an area their fathers left at the time of the Babel tower crisis.

In Ur, descendants and society of this Kaldu became known as the Chaldean tribe or community, but one person by the name of Jiel later migrated to Palestine, an area then inhabited by a race known as the Canaanites, descendants of Canaan. According to our time chart computation this must have been around 2095 BC. Other scholars on prehistory also agree with this dating. In Palestine Jiel married AƔok, his half sister! They bore a son by the name of Juöl, meaning single born. Some traditions say they bore four sons who are referred to as *Paan-AƔok* as it appears in one of the Dinka epic songs usually sung by diviners when attending the sick. The following excerpts from this song tend to confirm this AƔok as an ancient grandmother of the Dinka of this period:

> "Wa Aliɛr e dɔm piny ɛɛ,
> Këdiit Paan-AƔok ɛɛ!
> Wa Aliɛr e dɔm piny ɛɛ...!"

Translation:
> "Oh! Our father Aliɛr, hold the land,
> Great descendant of AƔok's lineage,
> Oh, hold the land...!"

This song is usually sung repeatedly by a diviner and is loudly recited by a group of people in a circle clapping their hands in unison to stir aciek or a god in the diviner to speak to let people know the cause of the sickness in a person.

Some traditions among the Gok Dinka, while accepting the name of Juöl, the single born, give him another name of 'Dhuök', 'Dhuökciën' or 'Dhuökwut', all connoting return and in this case it implies Jiel should return to Mesopotamia or Babylon from where he came.

Whether *Jiel* and *Aγok* bore four or one son or not, we are concerned with *Juöl* whose descent line makes the Dinka and the Nuers. We are tracing him because he was the single son of our Great Jiel who is Abraham of the Jews. Juöl grew and married Abuk-Aniɔɔk and they bore two sons. Machiek or Esau was the eldest and he later became the ancestor of the legendary Mayuääl-Cuërköök, who himself became the founding father of the Ruaal revering family tree among the Dinka of today. Maciek is presented by some traditions to have quarrelled with his father and decided to separate. He is said to have gone to the region towards Egypt, where one of his miracle performing descendants, Mayuääl-cuärköök, later joined an emigrant faction of another intermediate Jiel who was crossing the Red Sea at Bab el Mandeb to Wawat in ancient Sudan. They came from Judea to join their kin who came from Egypt to Wawat in ancient Northern Sudan prior to the emergence of the Kush Kingdom. Jiel and his society were migrating from Judea as a breakaway group of Judah, Reuben and Samson. They left following the Egyptian destruction of Jerusalem in 936 BC, that war which was led by Thutmose III and which was in the time of Rehoboam (II chronicles 12: 2-4, 9).

The second son was Riɛl, the Hebrew or Biblical Jacob. Riɛl married and had several sons who later migrated to Rip land (Egypt) following a period of great famine in the region of Canaan. Rip is the Dinka name for the country which in pre-ancient times was called Keymt but which subsequently became our today's Egypt.

ARE DINKA AND NUERS DESCENDANTS OF JACOB OR ARE THEY NOT?

Hebrews (the Jews) are descendants of Eber who was son of Shelah, the son of Arpachshad who was the third son of Shem (Gen. Ch. 10:22-25). This Eber, also called Heber in the Septuagint Bible, is the Dinka Aliɛr. The following comparative Biblical and Dinka genealogical descent lines only indicate variation or difference in the names for the same historical figures.

Descendants of Jacob (Israel) who were emancipated by God from Egyptian bondage, who accepted His word through Moses and went back to their promised land of Canaan were many, in contrast to a small handful of about 500 members of the same Jacob's household who branched off from the main body of the Jacobites at exodus and came southward to the Nile region where they first settled at Elephantinentine" Island opposite Aswan. They then proceeded to the Wawat area in ancient Northern Sudan. Those Jacobites who followed Moses were able to conquer their promised land from the Philistines and quickly made a nation called Israel there. The Jacobites who were led by Abiɛl to Sudan became the Dinka and Nuers of today. A century later they gave the impetus for the rise of the Kush Kingdom in Sudan. Their written records containing their history died with the rest of the Meroitic culture after Meroe city was destroyed by Axum in 350 AD. Dinka people with Jewish brothers are kin because they are descendants of Deŋdit, who is Deng Noi, who is Shem, they are kin except that they are geographically well apart with a gulf of several millennia between them, as the Dinka and Nuers came to be Sudanese and Africans while the Jews or Hebrews have remained to be people of the Middle East.

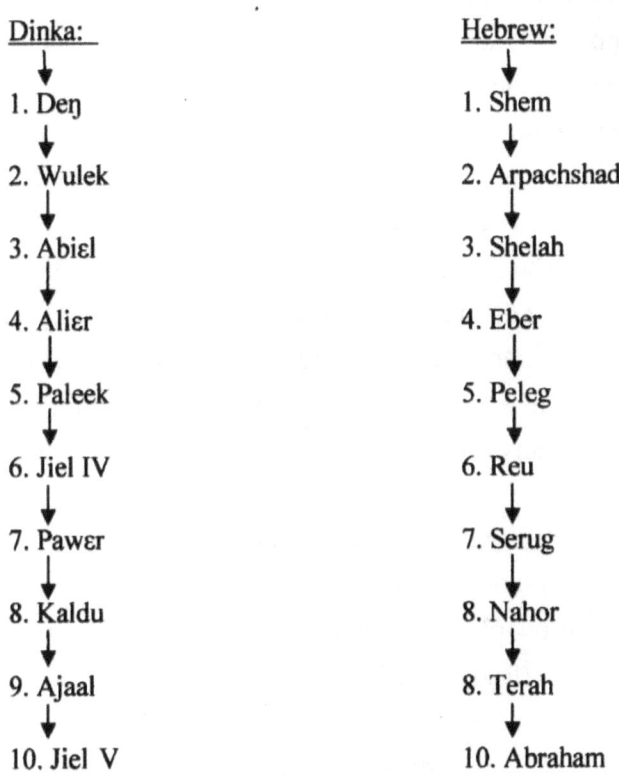

Fig 49: A genealogical descent chart showing Dinka and Hebrew historical figures with difference only in their names

FROM JIEL IN CANAAN TO AJAANG IN ANCIENT WAWAT

Like the Hebrews and the Arabs, Dinka people are direct descendants of Jiel who is the very Abraham of the Jews. The Arabs call him Ibrahim but, from Juöl,[123] the Jewish Isaac, the Dinka people belong to the two descent lines of Mayuaal (who is Esau) and Riɛl (who is

---

123 Juöl in Dinka means a single born son, also meaning the only one like God. In Hebrew, Isaac means Yahweh or God. Isaac and Juöl mean the same person.

Jacob), also called Israel. The thigh bone revering clans, the PaƦöl, Payii, Pajök and many others among the Dinka derived their thigh bone totemic observance (Yath) from this Jacob, who during his wrestle with God became disjointed right at the sinew of his thigh or femur bone (Gen. 32:24-32). Descendants of Reuben among the Jews venerate this Ʀöl to the present day. Reuben, being the eldest son of Jacob who is the Dinka Riɛl, was accredited with the duty of having to take Ʀöl as his nagualistic item of respect by primogenitary obligation, and Reuben handed Ʀöl to the rest of his descent lines whether they be Jews, Dinka or Nuers. The author comes from one of those clans revering the thigh bone. Dinka people are therefore from the two sons of the Biblical Isaac, Riel and Mayuääl, and are therefore descendants of Abraham.

Let us begin with Mayuääl or Esau's descent house among the Dinka. These people are known and they know themselves as the Mayuaal, Ruaal (Reuel), Redior or Wundior group of clans. The story of the family of Mayuaal is well explained in the Bible in Gen. 36 or Deuteronomy 36, from verses 1 to 40. They are the ones referred to in the Bible as the Edomites and our Dinka Redior people come from the clan of Reuel among those Edomites. One of the descendants of (Mayuääl) in subsequent times joined a migrating faction of Reubenites, Judah, who were coming from Judea in the year 936 BC. They were coming under another intermediate Jiel who was Jiel VIII, the founder of the House of the Pagong people among the Dinka. Jiel VI is that Jiel who was the chief of the tribes of Reuben and founder of the Gideon family in Judea (I Chron. 5:7). There is also another Jiel who was the ancestor of King Saul (I Chron. 9:35). There are several other Jiels in Jewish tradition but they are of no significance for our account of Dinka history. Our interest lies with Jiel VIII who became the founding ancestor of the Pagong clan in South Sudan.

Mayuaal celestially crossed the Red Sea when the waters closed him off with a group of people who were to cross the Red Sea to Sudan, when some of these people of Jiɛl VIII violated the promise which he made when he pleaded with God to cause the waters of the Red Sea to part into two to enable him to cross with his people on the dry sea floor and not to tamper with any of its marine creatures such as fish.[124] That very Mayuääl is the historical figure who miraculously entered a big sausage tree called ruaal, the Kegelia Ethiopia tree, where he was found after he crossed the Red Sea by air. It is that Mayuääl known as Bänyköök, the Agaar Dinka know him as Cuarköök, the founder of the house of the entire Redior group among the Dinka. He was an Edomite, a descendant of Esau, who is Machiek or Mayuääl in Dinka, and belongs to the clan of Reuel in the mountainous land of Seir, also called Edom (Deutr. 2:4).

EGYPT AND THE DINKA FOREBEARS

As it is described in the Bible all the descendants of Esau, our Machiek who is also called Mayuääl, did not go to Egypt with the people of Jacob, that is, the people of Riɛl when famine made Jacob move to Egypt with all his family, following his son Joseph who was sold by his brothers to some Arabians, who were in fact Ismaeli traders coming from the region of Gilead and going to Egypt (Gen. 37:17-28). We will shelve the rest of the story of Mayuääl and how his descendants came to Sudan. It is fully discussed in chapter four under Dinka routes of entry to ancient Sudan.

The rest of the Dinka clans are descendants of the different sons of Jacob. The Pagong and PaXɔl group of clans are, for instance, children of Reuben. They are Reubenites. The Patiɔp or fox revering group of clans are descendants of Samson who is himself a descendant of the Manaoh line of Dan (Gen. 15:4-17). They are Samsonites.

---

124 A miraculous phenomenon involving the cessation of the flow of the Red Sea waters similar to the miraculous phenomenon that occurred earlier at the Red Sea part of Succoth when the Israelites were fleeing from Egypt.

Cawul is the ancestor from whom descended the Paral group of clans including the people of the rock stone and the bladed spear. They are descendants of Simeon and Levi as are the fire revering clans and so on.

The stories of most of the sons of this Jacob, which Dinka oral traditions had handed down across the ages, used to be told in the most vivid way by some Mayuääl Dinka bards or traditional chroniclers as if they read the Bible.[125] While the Biblical eldest son of Jacob, Reuben, lost his birthright from his father for committing adultery with one of his father's wives, Dinka tradition does not give to an elder son of the same historical figure such a story. However, in Dinka, a father's wrath makes his elder son forfeit his birthright to the father, especially if the problem involves adultery with a father's wife. In this case the father gives the redeemed wealth, usually cattle, over to the estate of the sons of his favourite wife.

Dinka traditions are so replete with stories of women's jealousies and women's scramble for favours from their husbands, jealousies which usually determine the space and position of their children, particularly of their sons. While a black son is told to have made a mockery of, or had made ridicule to, his father Noi, this story is believed to have occurred soon after the flood, inviting a wrath and a curse on his progeny instead of himself! There is a Dinka tradition which says an elder son of the pre-Egypt period was punished to lose his cattle, goats and sheep for abusing his father's couch. It is not clear if this son may be this elder son of Riɛl. In Dinka literature, there are a lot of epic deeds attributed to the ancient times that go back to this period when a sojourner, an itinerant figure, comes from a distant land with an estate of flocks, cattle and people and quickly becomes a landed gentry with godly connections that shape

---

125 Aköök-Mariël from the Pabuɔkcok clan in the KɔŋgÖÖr area in Tonj North county area of Akɔp is one such bard who described the above story with a precision as if he was literate and had read the Bible.

the history of that period. The story of the children of the elder wives conspiring against the children of a woman favoured by their father is rampant among the Dinka and is told without going directly to Jacob as it is told in the Bible. However, the Dinka tell it as a story of an ancestor of that period.

Today's Dinka people talk of their ancestors having migrated to Rip land which is Egypt. Their oral traditions do not tell when those ancestors really came to Egypt from Canaan, but some sources suggest the end of the old kingdom period as the time of Jacob's migration to Egypt. Our understanding of Egyptology tells us this was the time when Egypt's old kingdom with its glory was coming to an end and Egypt's growing instability was causing signs of decline although, at this time, Egyptian agricultural production was expanding due to new irrigation projects which were put in place. This is why there was surplus for people from distant lands who were flocking to Egypt to buy food as clearly explained in the Bible (Gen. 42:47). When Jacob's people had famine in Canaan, they came to Egypt.

Since Dinka ancestors went to Egypt as Jacobites there will be no difficulty in telling the story of their stay in Egypt. For 450 years Jacobites remained in Egypt and were the builders of some of those impressive monuments called pyramids. Because of their long stay in Egypt they knew of many things about Egypt. The Dinka people of today can even tell you the country was ruled by an authority called *Muɔr-ŋaknhom* which is the Dinka word for a king, the crown head. This is also the title they use for the pharaoh and for the emperor.

Those Dinka ancient ancestors participated in every aspect of life in Egypt so that Egypt continues to be remembered even in our people's lore today. Several songs with reference to Egypt as Ripland are rampant among many of the Upper Nile Dinka, north of Malakal. Their stay in Egypt is confirmed by so many things. For instance, they know the Mediterranean Sea in their Dinka language.

They know it as 'Baau of Adɛkdiɛt', meaning a limitless water body that birds fail to successfully fly across.

This is true because the Mediterranean Sea is such a large intercontinental sea, covering an area of about 970 000 square miles (2 512 000 sq. km). That is why birds fly until they fall into its water when they become exhausted. A few birds like aweer the pigeon or the yellow-chested dove can, however, fly it. The sea is situated between Europe to the northwest, Africa to the south and Asia to the east. It gets its waters from the continuous inflow of the Atlantic Ocean in the west and the Nile River in the south[29].

According to Professor Abdel A'al Abdalla Osman, former vice chancellor of the University of Juba, some of the Egyptian pharaonic temples of antiquity are found to have portraits of the Nilotes with v-shaped scars on their foreheads, drawn while giving offerings to the pharaohs[30]. Among the Nilotes, it is the Dinka who do v-shaped scars on the face, a practice still with the Bor Dinka of today.

In the time they were in Egypt our people know they lived in Lower Egypt, in the border region of Goshen which is the very region of Rameses, southeast of the delta region. They came as shepherds (Gen. 47: 1-10) but in the course of their stay in Egypt they learnt many crafts. They stayed until the time they started to be persecuted by the Egyptians. The Dinka genealogical descent from the different tribes of Jacob becomes discrete here in Egypt until the time of the exodus when we begin to know of Abiɛl, who appears as the leader of that small faction that migrated to Wawat in the ancient far northern region of Sudan.

This is the time when we can only be certain of the Paɣol who are Reubenites, the Patiɔp who are Samsonites, a clan belonging to Jiel Juöl, a descendant of Reuben from whom came the subsequent Jiel who migrated from Judea and crossed to ancient Northern Sudan by way of Bab el Mandeb. In Dinka abiɛl means something holy. It is one of the Dinka many names for God. In Hebrew the connotation of God as father is defined in Peoples of the Bible in the Reference Bible of King James' version of the holy Bible, Page 1386.

THE ERA OF OPPRESSION

Persecution of our people in Egypt came up during the last dynastic period of the old Egyptian kingdom. This is one of the times when Egypt reached its highest pinnacles as a power in the Mediterranean region. It was the time when Egypt was ruled by pharaohs who have no memory of Joseph. All the sons and grandsons of our ancestor (Riɛl) have all died during this time. In fact, persecution started slightly before the beginning of the four hundred years of our peoples' stay in Egypt. This is a very important period in the annals of our history. It is a period which demands more and more exploration to dig out the true facts of that epoch which is so much imbued with those amazing stories as told in the Exodus. As a people whose ancestors were being persecuted to the degree which invited God's sympathy to intervene on their behalf, Dinka people have every right to uncover more facts about this period in their long history.

The flood of Noi was a world disaster covering perhaps the whole human race. The events at Babel, the confusion of languages and the earthquake which divided the earth into continents, all were done by God to the entire mankind, but this later event in Egypt, the plagues and the exodus, were particular with only our ancestors who are today's Dinka, and their branch the Nuers and their other kin, the Israelites. It was a catastrophe confined to Egypt, so Exodus is a story of the Egyptians, the Dinka, the Nuers and the Jews. It did not concern other nations surrounding Egypt and that is why no nation made record of the exodus except for those who were involved, the Jews and the Egyptians. Dinka documented records about this event have gone with Meroitic writings, but Dinka ancestors of the ancient eras kept some scattered versions of it in their oral memory.

In going about this very topic of oppression or persecution in Egypt, some questions rightly pose themselves. Yes, it is crucial to first know why the Egyptians persecuted our ancestors. What did they do that caused the Egyptians to persecute them? And what was the nature and degree of persecution?

From the start Joseph's personality and deeds were known to have impressed the Egyptians, particularly the pharaohs so that he was even made at one point the minister in charge of Egyptian finance and the whole Egyptian economy. Relations between our ancestors and the different pharaohs at the time were so good in the days when Joseph was alive. This explains why our ancestors were officially received and allotted that border region rich in pasture and good for agricultural activities. Rameses or Goshen was since Joseph's time the granary city for Egypt. The official ceremonies done to Jacob by Egypt at his death very well explain that our ancestors once enjoyed rights and respect in the eyes of the Egyptians. The Bible's Genesis 50 tells us Egypt mourned Jacob's death for seventy days and his body was returned to his home village in Canaan by an elaborate and official Egyptian delegation involving a huge army of chariots and cavalry in addition to ministers, senior members of the pharaoh's palace and members of the Egyptian nobility and other national dignitaries. This very large government retinue even amazed the inhabitants of Machpelah in Canaan, where Jacob was given a state burial by the Egyptians who entombed him near his father Isaac and his grandfather Abraham (Gen.23:7-20).

As Joseph died and the generation which came with Jacob died, there came times when those exploits of Joseph were forgotten. Our ancestors had at this time increased in population and had begun to fill the land of Egypt, taking almost every field of work. An Egyptian pharaoh of this time began to feel threatened by the ever increasing numbers of our forefathers. He was also threatened by their strength and achievements. The pharaoh declared his fears in a royal edict that alerted all the Egyptians that our people were aiming at overthrow the crown. A general mobilisation against our forebears was stepped up by this pharaoh with a call to afflict and oppress them. They were as such made to do the work of the Egyptian peasantry, to do the masonic brick and huge mortar work and other activities which demanded hard labour. They made roads and built towns and cities with free labour. They built Rameses and its huge granary stores. They built Pithom city and all the fields required hard work. They were treated harshly and abused. Egyptian midwives were instructed to kill every one of our women's male babies during deliveries. Other male infants were thrown into the Nile. Female babies were spared, however. The case of baby Moses placed by his mother in a basket made of bulrushes and laid at the brink of the River Nile when she was tired of hiding him from the Egyptians, is a classic example of the degree of persecution (Exodus 2:10). There was a real suffering, sorrow and a general wish to leave Egypt by our ancestors but who was this oppressing pharaoh, persecuting our people? The Bible does not give us his name.

THE PHARAOH OF OPPRESSION

The Bible does not provide the name of this very intriguing historical figure, but modern research efforts have lately given us conclusive evidence that the pharaoh who persecuted our ancestors was Phiops II, who is historically known also as Pepi II. This was one of the pharaohs who reigned for quite a long time. Egyptian ancient records present him to have reigned for more than ninety years.[126] His pharaonic period, and that of Pharaoh Merenre Antyemsaf II who succeeded him as the pharaoh of the exodus, covers the last

---

126   Mark, 'Last update', (in) Biblical chronology, Org, November 20,(2000) p. 1

part of the old kingdom which was known for its two hundred years of chaos, instability, poverty and despair. It was this Pepi II who was the pharaoh whose daughter found Moses as a baby in the bulrushes at the brink of the River Nile.

Having now known why and when our ancestors were oppressed and persecuted and by which pharaoh we can now proceed to discuss the exodus, that amazing event in world history, an event in which a family of 70 emigrants who came from Canaan grew into a people who in their totality were subjected to slavery but who suddenly threw away the shackles of generations of slavery and moved en masse, in their entirety, away from that country to the country where their ancestors came from more than four centuries ago. There, they made a completely new life and made a nation of their own. We will also discuss how a small group of these people succeeded to branch south from the main exodus into another country called ancient Sudan to become the future Jääng, who in today's Southern Sudan are the Dinka with their progenies, the Nuers.

THE BIBLICAL EXODUS ACCORDING TO THE DINKA

Our starting point for this topic is designed to make a flashback into a bit of the history of Egypt to give a synoptic overview of the country from its pre-dynastic era to the time of the pharaohs as a necessary prelude to understanding this historical event called the exodus with involvement of a supernatural power on the side of our ancestors.

Egypt's recorded history is about 5000 years old. It started to be a civilisation about 3000 years BC, beginning with the first pharaoh, Menses.[127] The country started to be called Tawy, meaning a country

---

127   Alenyo George William, The Luo: The black Jews of Africa, (2nd ed),

of two lands, Upper (Southern) and Lower (Northern) Egypt. Its first primitive settlers are believed to have been descendants of a certain Mizraim, one of the sons of Ham, who became the ancestor of a group of families from whom the first Egyptians descended. Those primitive peasants were fairly short by modern standards, tanned in their skins with stiff brown hair. They were Caucasian. Darker-skinned peoples called Luo and the Bantus from the south of Egypt later migrated down the River Nile into Lower Egypt.

Continued interaction and social fusion between those two physical stocks produced what tempted historians to believe that Egyptians were initially negroid. Mizraimites developed into communities of simple farmers with villages or settlements made of huts and farmhouses and dwelt more to the Nile, the delta and the Mediterranean Sea littoral areas with the primary task of growing food only for their subsistence. By about the end of the 4th millennium after the flood came the sudden lift to urbanisation from that primitive simple farm life. Simple tools used for cultivation were now replaced by wheel and ox-plough, temple furniture, weapons, jewellery, wheel-made pots and other manufactures. All these produced large scale and skilled artisans. People went to big monumental tombs instead of graves for rulers, temples, palaces and workshops. Into those urban centres came regularly imported exotic substances of trade, things used in everyday life, particularly from the oriental world and from Africa to the south.

From those small urban centres arose small principalities which in time became kingdoms in both the north and southern parts of Egypt, which started to be known as Tawy, and up to 3400 BC, a certain Menes emerged from the southern part of the country and united the two kingdoms into one country called Keympt. Mense became the first king to establish the pharaonic system and in time entered the

Shalom Books Ltd, Nairobi, Kenya, (2009), p. 2

blacks from Kerma in ancient Northern Sudan. Those blacks soon became the Luo and the Funj. All were primordial descendants of Ham through Canaan. They found their way to the interior region of the Nile and back to ancient Northern Sudan where they vacillated between Upper Egypt and Northern Sudan. These people went ahead as rulers of Keympt and pharaonic Egypt is known for its long lists of Luo kings.

The entry of the negroid blood made a tincture in the racial composition of the country. Then entered people called Ishmaelites, descendants of Ishmael, son of our Patriarch Abraham, who is the Dinka Jiel. According to Gen. 21:8, Abraham sent his son Ishmael into the desert region of Paran towards Keympt. For jealousies known in co-wives, an Egyptian mother of Ishmael, Hagar, and her children, were unwanted by AƔok, the elder wife of Jiel. God blessed Ishmael to be a nation in the future. In Paran territory Ishmael therefore developed into a large family and his descendants became Ishmaelites. These Ishmaelites later came to Egypt and displaced the Luo back to ancient Northern Sudan where they once came from. They took over the reign of power in Egypt and established regular commerce over the whole of the Middle East. The Bible records in Genesis 37:25 says that Ishmaeli traders reached out to the east for oriental goods and on their way to Egypt through Canaan they bought Joseph from his stepbrothers into slavery in Egypt.

From between the era of Pharaoh Menes and Pharaoh Pepi II was the old kingdom period in which extensive irrigation and ploughing were introduced and the famous pyramids were built at this time. Rulers of this time were called pharaohs and were believed to exercise divine authority. This is the long era when art, especially painting, sculpture and architecture, greatly flourished. Towards the middle phase of this era is the time when Abraham came to Egypt and returned to Canaan. A century later came those Ishmaelites and Jacob probably came during the last half of that millennium BC.

With the close of the old kingdom came a chaotic period when Egypt entered into a devastating experience at the time of the exodus as we will now see in the coming pages.

THE PLAGUES OR DISASTERS

As earlier explained, Phiops or Pepi II ruled Egypt for more than ninety years and is the pharaoh in whose time Moses was born. He is the pharaoh who wished to kill Moses and he did not die until Moses himself became 80 years old. It was his daughter who found Moses in the bulrushes and took him back to his mother to rear him for her.

When Pepi II died, having persecuted our ancestors all his life, he was succeeded by yet another persecuting pharaoh, Merenre Antyemsaf II, who reigned for only one year when he also died, drowned in the Red Sea at Pi-Khiroth while chasing the Israelites during the exodus. Merenre Antyemsaf II followed in the footsteps of his predecessor in their policy of persecution of our ancestors.

The plagues and the exodus that followed, when read carefully, constitute one of the most stupefying events in the historical annals of the human race! It is one of the miraculous acts of God which sets back those who attempt to teach that the world came to its existence by itself through evolution and not by God who, according to us, the people of the book, created the universe and all that is in it. The plagues and the exodus are no ordinary or everyday happenings!

The Biblical account of this most amazing event gives us the whole picture of what happened. Let us begin from Sinai, or precisely Mt. Horreb, where in Exodus 3, an angel of God appeared to Moses in a flame of fire from the middle of a bush. In the discourse that followed God of our ancestors announced to Moses His intention to deliver our ancestors from Egyptian bondage. He said he heard their sorrows, sufferings and their cries and had decided to come down "to deliver them out from the hands and power of the Egyptians and bring them out of that land to a land good and large..."

The second important thing in Moses' encounter with God is His sending of Moses to Pharaoh Merenre Antyemsaf II to allow our people to leave Egypt. He also authorised Moses to go and gather our ancestral elders, sections or tribal leaders and teachers to announce to them His intervention to deliver them out of Egyptian slavery.

With this, God promised Moses to assist him, saying He would stretch out his hand and smite Egypt with all His wonders, aimed at making the Egyptians allow them to leave Egypt. Moses was given a rod to perform wonders, convincing the Pharaoh and our ancestors that he was indeed sent by God. Aaron (our Dinka Arɔɔl) was to take the role of an adumbrator in assisting Moses in his mission.

At the palace Merenre Antyemsaf rejected Moses' message of God and instead increased the labour upon our ancestors. The stalemate went on between the pharaoh, Moses and God till God decided to let our people depart Egypt under His direct power, supervision and guidance. He made them start off during the early morning hours of the month of Abib (April). They all gathered at Rameses where the exodus started (Ex. 12:37). Here, from Rameses, our moving 3-5 million people came to Succoth with all their flocks and cattle. They even took some of the Egyptians with them who may have been sympathetic. Before the moving multitude crossed at Pi-Khiroth on the Red Sea, there was a disagreement at Succoth as to the route to be taken. A group of elders proposed the direct route to Canaan by way of Philistine for being shorter but Moses, the leader of the exodus, insisted on the long desert route to the country of his in-laws, arguing he had been directed by God to use that long and meandering route full of hostile tribal societies which delayed their arrival to the Promised Land for forty years!

At this point, a small faction of Reubenites, those from Samson and from the other clans, broke off and branched south during the confusion. Dinka ancient traditions going to those Napatan and Meroitic periods say this faction of our ancestors was led by a certain Abiɛl. The faction was a few hundred people that did not draw the attention of the main body of the exodus, nor of the Egyptians. Moreover, the chaos and darkness were such that a small number could slip off from the main column unnoticed. When news of the departure of the Israelites reached Heliopolis, the capital city of Egypt by the time of the exodus, the pharaoh decided to pursue the Israelites. A huge army on chariots was quickly assembled and the pharaoh himself took command and led the pursuing force.

At this very point in time Egypt was plunged into chaos when the king (pharaoh) and the whole of his pursuing army were drowned in the raging waters of the Red Sea during their attempt to cross to coax the escaping Israelites. It was a catastrophe, a holocaust such as seldom happens in the history of an entire nation. Earth, sea and sky participated in the event. Those plagues so described in the Bible were not merely localised phenomena. They included tectonic upheavals, volcanic eruptions and turgid atmospheres of dark smoke, dark ashes, cyclonic windstorms and total darkness. An entire nation's agriculture was laid to waste. Cattle were destroyed by the millions. The earth's largest standing army of that time was destroyed and overwhelmed in one fateful night of terror and 60 000 more were swallowed by the sea with all their chariot-pulling horses!

But did this colossal event cover the whole country of Egypt? Or were there regions and places spared? Notice the amazing description by the Bible: *"And Mount Sinai was altogether on a smoke... and the smoke thereof ascended as the smoke of a furnace, and the whole mount quaked greatly"* (Exod. 19: 16, 18). This is a vivid description of Mount Sinai in the throes of a volcanic eruption, accompanied by a severe earthquake!

The exodus was a time of tectonic violence seldom witnessed by man except during Palek's time when God used a colossal earthquake to divide the earth into continents. The Bible says, *"the hills melted like wax at the presence of the Lord"* (Psalms 97:5). In the book of Judges we also read, *"Lord, when thou wentest out of Seir... the earth trembled, and the heavens dropped, the clouds also dropped water. The mountains melted from before the Lord, even that Sinai from before the Lord God of Israel"* (Judges 5:4-5). Upheaval went as far as the mountain region of Seir after Sinai.

Incredible as it may sound, such a calamity as the Bible describes in vivid detail was also recorded in ancient Egyptian documents. An Egyptian eyewitness attested to the plagues that God sent upon ancient Egypt, an old wise man by the name of Ipuwer who lived more than ten years after the exodus. He wrote his eyewitness accounts of the events on a papyrus which was only found in 1828 by the research team who came from the Netherlands Museum of Leiden. That text is now folded into a book of 17 pages and written in hieratic signs. Alan H Gardiner later translated it in 1909, and from the translation he made into a book he had called Admonitions and the amazing dramatic catastrophes that God sent upon ancient Egypt came to be known. According to Gardiner, commenting on Ipuwer's papyrus, "it is not a mere local disturbance which is being described here, but a great and overwhelming national disaster" (Gardiner, Admonitions).

Now, see the astonishing parallels between the eyewitness written observations in that ancient papyrus and the record of the Biblical book of Exodus:

AN EYEWITNESS TO THE DISASTER

The old wise man, Ipuwer, describes unbelievably the story of lamentation, ruin and horror. He gives an Egyptian version of that national calamity. He writes:

"Forsooth, the land turns round as does a potter's wheel. The towns are destroyed. Upper Egypt has become a dry waste. All is ruin! All the residences were overturned in a minute. Years of noise! There is no end to the noise. Oh, will the earth cease from noise!? And tumult (uproar)? Be it no more!?" The use of the word 'noise' here means 'earthquake'. We are all aware that earthquakes are often accompanied by loud ominous sounds from the bowels of the earth. According to those lines of Ipuwer there was an earthquake with a lot of noise throughout Egypt.

THE DISASTER BY BLOOD

Also notice the following amazing similarities between our Biblical account of the plagues of blood in Egypt and the Ipuwer's description of the very event as an eyewitness: "…there was blood throughout the land of Egypt. Disaster is throughout the land. Blood is everywhere. Men shrink from tasting human beings and thirst after water… that is our water! That is our happiness! What shall we do in respect thereof? All is ruin!" The Bible in Exodus 7:20-24 describes the same thus: "… *all the waters that were in the river were turned to blood…. and all the Egyptians dug round about the river for water to drink, for they could not drink of the water of the river*". Both versions give a picture of blood everywhere, even rivers.

THE DISASTER ON DOMESTIC ANIMALS

For the destruction to the livestock, the Egyptian eyewitness uses few words in just a sentence. He writes: "*All animals, their hearts weep. Cattle moan*". Compare it with the Bible description in Exodus 9:3. "*…the hand of the Lord is upon thy cattle which are in the field, upon the horses, upon the asses, upon the camels, upon the sheep. There shall be very grievous murrain*". Cattle and other animals died in their millions throughout Egypt.

DESTRUCTION BY STORM

After the calamity by frogs, lice, flies and murrain on the animals, God brought on Egypt the destruction of a massive hailstorm which destroyed crops everywhere. The Egyptian eyewitness also recorded this thing by saying, *"...and the hail smote every herb of every tree of the field... the flax and the barley was smitten, for the barley was in the ear, and the flax was boiled. Trees are destroyed; neither fruit nor herbs are found. Forsooth, gates, columns and walls are consumed by fire. Lower Egypt weeps... The entire palace is without its revenues. To it belong (by right) wheat and barley, geese and fish. Forsooth, grain has perished which yesterday was seen. The land is left over to its weariness like the cutting of flax."* Exodus 10:15 describes this crop and vegetation destruction thus *"...there remained not any green thing in the trees, or in the herbs of the fields, through all the land of Egypt"*.

The two statements above show clearly that the disaster that came on Egypt's crops and vegetation was not the consequence of a long lasting drought. Rather, this was a sudden onslaught of disaster, virtually overnight! What was visible yesterday was perished today! The produce of Egypt was cut down, like the cutting of flax, a sudden, incisive event!

DESTRUCTION BY LOCUSTS

Compare how the scripture describes this destruction and how this Egyptian eyewitness puts it as he saw it: (Exodus 10:4-5), *"...tomorrow will I bring the locusts into thy coast, and they shall cover the face of the earth... and they shall eat the residue of that which is escaped, which remains unto you from the hail, and shall eat every tree which groweth for you out of the field"*. Ipuwer says, "No fruit or herbs are found............ hunger".

DESTRUCTION THROUGH DARKNESS

On the darkness which God brought upon Egypt, Exodus 10:22-23 says, *"...and there was a thick darkness in all the land of Egypt, three days, they saw not one another, neither rose any from his place for three days.* Ipuwer just says, *"...the land is out of light".*

This darkness which came upon Egypt as described by Ipuwer and the Bible is further described in another ancient Egyptian document, a black granite monolith or shrine at the border of Egypt, inscribed with hieroglyphics all over its surface. The message on that granite monolith declares about the town of El-Arish:

"The land was in great affliction. Evil fell on this earth.... It was a great upheaval in all the residences.... Nobody left the palace during nine days of upheaval, there was such a tempest that neither the men nor the gods could see the faces of their next..." That calamity is thought to have taken nine days to stop!

With the swarms of locusts covering the skies and earth for three days, Egyptian counts nine days as the total length of time of impaired vision and light, but the Jewish Midrash book explains that the total darkness lasted seven days. According to the old Dinka bard in Kɔŋgöör, Aköök-Mariëël, he declared it took ten days for sunshine to come to Egypt due to the hailstorm and locusts. During the first three days one could still change his position, but during the next three (the three of the Bible), one could not move from his place! And so, Egyptians did not correctly know how many days darkness took the land. They thought it was nine days.

THE FINAL NIGHT OF DEATH

The final plague of the last night before the Israelites left Egypt is also described by this Ipuwer thus: *"Forsooth, the children of princes are dashed against the walls, cast out into the streets.*

Prison is ruined and he who places his brother in the ground is everywhere. It is groaning that is throughout the land, mingled with lamentations..."

What Ipuwer is describing as *"children of princes dashed against the wall"* was a big happening. A death angel was sent in the middle of the night to every Egyptian house, killing every firstborn including those of the cattle. This caused great wailing in every house across the whole length of Egypt, even in the palace as Merenre's firstborn son was also killed. Can you imagine every household of a whole nation undergoing the simultaneous death of their firstborn son!? This may be why the Midrashi's legends say that, *"As many as nine tenths of the inhabitants of Egypt perished that day!"* There was also a massive earthquake in that last night and a darkening hailstorm so that those who fled from the earthquake were killed by the storm, and those who found shelter against the storm were destroyed by the earthquake! All the houses and temples tumbled.

The massiveness of this last night's earthquake in Egypt is more fully explained by another legend in what is called Haggada. This ancient legend says, *"in the last night, when Egypt was smitten, the coffin of Joseph was found lying on the ground, lifted out of the grave"*. This may be true as earthquakes in our modern times are known to have similar effects, causing coffins to protrude from their graves, especially in hillside cemeteries. When the entire nation rose to cry in that fateful night before our ancestors actually departed, even the pharaoh rose up in the night with all his servants and joined in that great national cry! Imagine a head of a nation wailing!

THE PHARAOH OF THE EXODUS AND HIS FATE IN DINKA MYTHOLOGY

In the end, in those catastrophic upheavals, what happened to the pharaoh, Merenre himself? That granite temple shrine at El-Arish is found written on, saying: "...*His Majesty......assembled his forces and ordered them to follow him after the Israelites but the king (pharaoh) and his army never returned...*" The El-Arish shrine continues in its last lines with, "*...the king was thrown by a great force at Pi-Kharoti. He was thrown by the whirlpool high up into the air. He departed to heaven. He departed this life*". Where is this Pi-Kharoti? Exodus 14:19 describes this Pi-Kharoti. It says, "*but the Egyptians pursued them, all the horses and chariots of the pharaoh.....and overtook them encamping by the sea, beside Pi-ha-Hiroth (Khiroth).*

Pi-Kharoti is the Pi-Khiroth, the place where the Pharaoh and all his forces came upon the fleeing Israelites as they were camped. This is the same place where the Pharaoh met his fate in the raging maelstrom of the Red Sea, the place of the 'whirlpool'. El-Arish legend says, '*He went to heaven!*' This is a fine way of saying he perished and never returned!

The final thing in the episode is that invaders called Amalekites, who were Hyksos from the southeastern region bordering Egypt, a people from the eastern mountains immediately came in, exploited that wretched condition of the country and captured Egypt without any resistance. Prince Geb, the son of the gone pharaoh, did not have opportunity to even take up the throne and regather Egypt for a resistance against the invaders. He therefore fled before the invaders could reach the capital. He went to one of the provinces in the west of Egypt and did not return to Heliopolis. The Amalekites or Hyksos marched to Heliopolis with ease and then ruled Egypt for the next 400 years.

During this period, the liberated descendants of Jacob had succeeded to continue with their march away from Egypt. They went from Egypt till their occupation of Palestine. Jacob's families divided their newly occupied lands according to their grouping. They ruled the territory as a council called Judges but by the time the Hyksos were expelled out of Egypt Israel became a monarchy. It became a United Kingdom under King Saul who was then succeeded by his son David and on to his grandson, King Solomon.

THE ABIEL FACTION COMES TO THE WAWAT REGION IN ANCIENT NORTHERN SUDAN (THE COMING OF THE DINKA ANCESTORS TO ANCIENT NORTHERN SUDAN)

We now know what the exodus was, how our ancestors were delivered out of the hands of the Egyptians. In the confusion, in the early morning of the month of 15 April in the year 1230 BC, the day of the exodus, an assortment of Jacob's families left the main body of the exodus at Succoth. They branched out and took the southern direction with their cattle and flocks and under the leadership of Abiɛl from Reuben's household or clan, the group ultimately succeeded to filter to Upper Egypt. They joined a small colony of the Jacobites who had earlier come and settled at what came to be called Elephantinentine" Island opposite what is present Aswan.[128]

The symposium held on the Rumbek Secondary School premises in December 2003 to evaluate the research data material on this Dinka history determined that those ancestors who came with Abiɛl to Elephantinentine" Island on the Southern borders at the time of the exodus may be put at 500 people, men and women, young and old. The years spent in the wilderness by the main population of the exodus have been the same years spent by this Abiɛl group before the entire colony moved to the Wawat area that is the present Wadi Al Allagi Valley area in the Derr-Toshka region, in the far end of Northern Sudan.

---

128   R. Werner and colleagues, Day of Devastation, Day of Contentment ,the history of the Sudanese Church Across 2000 years, Paulines Publications Africa, Kolbe Press, Nairobi , Kenya, (2000), p. 100.

The following genealogical descent line of six generations of the PaƔɔl Dinka forebears from the first Abiɛl, who is Reuben, to this Abiɛl of the exodus time, may help in imagining the time length when this faction arrived in the ancient Northern Sudan region of Wawat.

From behind, while the Israelites went to Palestine and their faction led by Abiɛl went to Wawat at the far end of ancient Northern Sudan, Egypt continued under Hyksos' rule. These foreigners ruled Egypt for about 400 years but in the year 1050 BC Egyptians were able to throw off the yoke of those Hyksos and Egypt's greatest dynasty of the new kingdom period was now ushered in. This was the famous 18th Dynasty whose era corresponded with those of King Saul, King David and King Solomon in Israel. This is the great 18th Dynastic era of those of the great pharaohs such as Queen Hatshepsut and her son Thutmose III, the Napoleon of ancient Egypt and his son Amenhotep II, who succeeded him. Thutmose III, the son of Queen Hatshepsut, whose other name was Shishak the great conqueror, is the Egyptian pharaoh who in 936 BC conquered the whole of Palestine, the entire kingdom of Judea and Israel up to Jerusalem in the time of King Rehoboam, King Solomon's son (II Chronicles 12:2 V 4, 9).

The destruction of Judea in 936 BC and the final capture of Jerusalem by Thutmose III led to the dispersal of the population. It was from here that another faction of Reubenites who are now the Pagong people among the Dinka migrated to Northern Sudan and joined the Abiel group. Those Reubenites did consist of elements who were Samsonites (now Patiɔp clans among the Dinka) led by Jiel the Great. From Judea they came to Arabia then to Yemen, from where they came to cross Wär Pakuɛɛk (the Red Sea) at Bab el Mandeb to ancient Northern Sudan. They were then able to join their previous brethren here in the Derr-Toshka area in the valley of Wadi el Allagi as earlier described. This group of Jiel was later followed by another

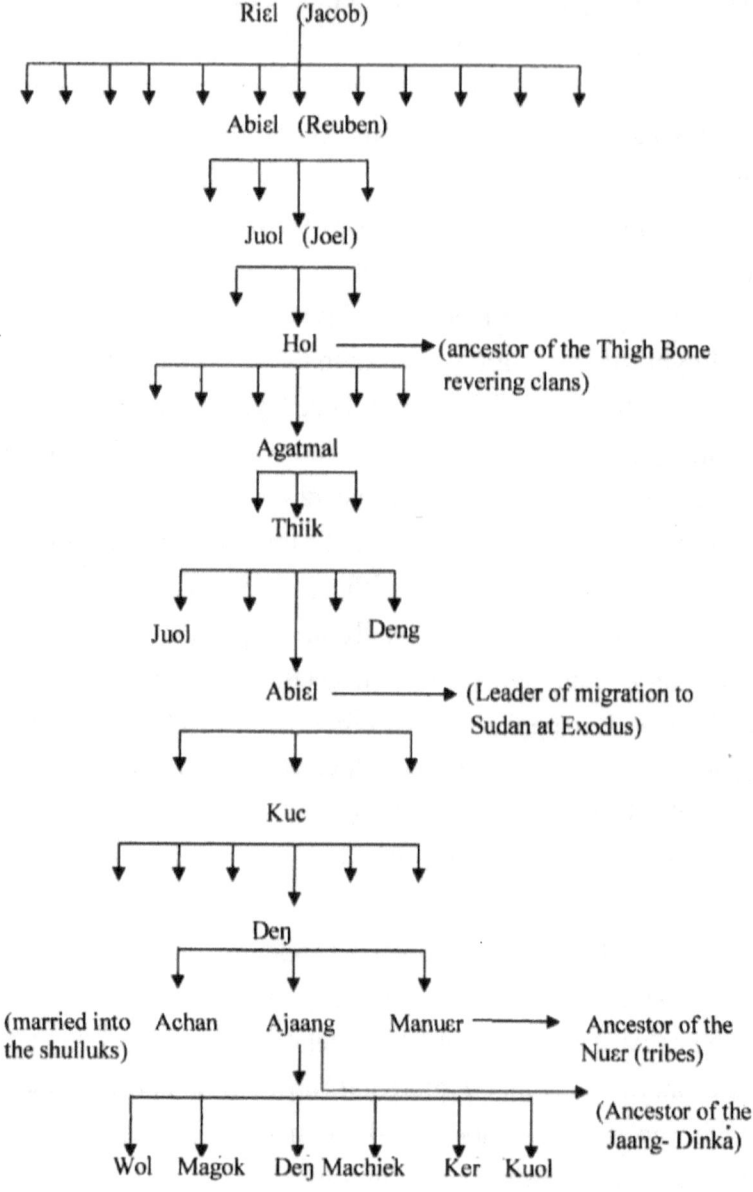

Fig 50: A genealogical chart showing the Dinka descent line from Riεl (who is Jacob) to Jääng, the founder of the Jääng nationality, later to become the Dinka in South Sudan

emigrant group of Jacobites led by great Jök-Athurkök who also crossed the Red Sea. They also joined the rest in between Dongola and the second cataract area. These are the people who later became Ngok Dinka of Abyei.

CHAPTER EIGHT: A LINEAGE FROM PRIMORDIAL CHALDEANS BECOMES JÄÄNG AND NUERS IN SUDAN, DONGOLA REGION

In chapter seven, we tried to trace the Dinka from the very beginning of man at creation and with the rest of mankind and we found they are the children of Abuk and Garaŋ through Deŋ-Mayuääl, Deŋ-BukYök who is Deŋ-Malou, Pabɛɛk and Colwich or Macardit. We discussed them through the whole length of the antediluvian period until the Great Noi of the world flood. We also traced the Dinka into their parent stem during that primordial post-flood era called the Palaeozoic or pre-Palek period. We tackled Dinka racial origin from the three sons of Noi through another Deŋm, who is the Hebrew's Shem. We waded through those very obscure and difficult prehistoric times until they first appeared as Chaldean in lower Mesopotamia and through Jiel II, some of them became Edomites in the land of Canaan while others became Jacobites who came and lived in Egypt for well over four centuries, and from both Egypt and

Edom some of them came to ancient Sudan in the 7th century BC, after which they developed to be known as Jääng while their kin became the Nuers. They later became Muonyjäng and Jieng before they became today's Dinka.

In this chapter we will discuss the Dinka as a Sudanese national community along with those ancient Sudanese peoples which they found in that region before the emergence of the blacks' kingdom of Kush in the 8th century BC.

DINKA FOREBEARS AND THEIR ROUTES OF ENTRY INTO ANCIENT NORTHERN SUDAN

Egypt-Nile Route

Dinka ancestors came to the ancient Sudan region of Wawat through two very important routes. The first group to come to Wawat by way of Egypt were those Jacobites from Reuben's family lines. They were led by a certain Abiɛl the Great. This faction came out of the main body of the exodus at Succoth. They went south from Succoth until they reached Elephantinentine" Island on the Nile at the southern borders of Egypt, where they joined a small group of Jacobites who came there from Egypt some years back. As discussed in the last chapter under the exodus they came to this Elephantine Island at the beginning of the Egyptian New Kingdom period, about 1230 BC. From that Egyptian border area both the former colony and that splinter group from the exodus joined up and moved to ancient Wawat in the present Wadi el Alagi area in Northern Sudan.

They settled in between the first and second cataracts, a fertile valley or plain area then known as Dakka on the east of the Nile, an area on the mouth of the present Wadi el Allagi in the Derr-Toshka region. They settled in that fertile land as far as the present Abu Simbel areas across the Nile on the west bank. Here, those Dinka ancient forebears stayed much longer until they were joined more than a century later by the group of Jieldit, Mayuääl's people and the Patiɔp people of Samson who came from Judea through the Eastern Sudan region of Halaif after crossing Wär-Pakuɛk (the Red Sea) in what has come to be known as Bab el Mandeb of today. These groups broke from Judea following the destruction of Jerusalem and the occupation of Judea by Egypt under Thutmose III in 936 BC.

Found in this ancient cataracts' region of Wawat were present Nilotic black communities who had inhabited the region since Kerma culture times.[129] Those communities were the Mazoi who covered those areas from the first and the second cataracts. They are probably the present Mahas section of the Nuba. To the west of those Mazoi were a people called Yam. Between Yam and Mazoi to the south and Wawat to the north were several smaller tribes, the most significant of which were people called Irthet and Sethut. Those were actually Luo tribal groups. There was the Funj south west of Yam. Some of those tribes, particularly the Funj and the Luo, had trailed out from Egypt at different times. Some came shortly before the exodus in the pharaonic era of Phiops or Pepi II while others came at the time when their settlement in the west bank area of Upper Egypt was submerged by floods caused by the digging of a canal in Upper Egypt in the sixth dynastic period. The Luo on their part came to this region after their displacement from Egypt by the Ishmaelites during the middle era of the old Egyptian kingdom period. Those were the Nilotic communities who must have been the heirs of what historians had called Kerma culture in ancient Northern Sudan.[130]

---

129   Rodney R Baird, Nubia: Geography, (2000), pp.1-3

130   Roland Werner & colleagues, Day of devastation, day of contentment, The history of the Sudanese church across 2000 years, Paulines Publications, Kolbe Press, Nairobi , Kenya, (2000),pp. 64-68.

Bab el Mandeb Route

When Egypt came under Amalekites, which we already know to be the Hyksos, the country came to be full of foreigners who entered Egypt under the veil of those Hyksos. But when Egyptian nationalism came to the fore once again those Hyksos were eventually driven out and a true national government was put in place under the new and Indigenous pharaoh and here came the era of those great rulers of the 18th Dynasty which we explained earlier. Thutmose III rose to be a great conqueror and he made Egypt to be once again the mightiest monarchy in the Mediterranean world. In 934 BC Thutmose (also called Shishak) raised an army with which he made an expedition into Palestine. He captured cities on his way to Jerusalem which he also ransacked two years later. At this time the century old mightiness of Israel which was started by King Saul and reached its magnificent glory in the times of King David and of King Solomon was brought to naught. That mightiness of Israel was no longer there after Israel became two but it was a weak kingdom with Solomon's weakening as the King of Judea.

Few figures in history are as venerated as Alexander the Great, the young Macedonian king who entered the world with the belief that ability, focus and determination in a leader would enable him to conquer the whole world. The Romans were the first to append the title of *Alexander the Great* to his name, and history and popular perception have kept his legend intact for centuries.[131] And so was it for Thutmose III. The Egyptians gave him the titles of *Thutmose the conqueror* and later *The Napoleon of Egypt*. As Alexander later captured the entire eastern half of the ancient world, Thutmose III before him brought the whole ancient Mediterranean world under Egypt, including former Solomon's Byzantium or the former Babylonian world. When Thutmose led his armies into Palestine and

---

131 Steve Forbes and John Prevas, Power, ambition and glory, Grown Business, NY, USA (2000), p. 100

defeated all those on his way to Jerusalem, up to Megiddo, he was able to conquer 118 cities and towns, one after the other, including Jerusalem, then known also as Kadesh.

At this time Solomon's temple in Jerusalem had no match in the ancient world. It was built and furnished from treasures brought from all over the world when, in the time of King Solomon, Israel was a world power. The temple was now envied by peoples of the surrounding nations. Does the Bible talk about this time of Egyptian invasion and humiliation for the Jews when in Rehoboam's time Jerusalem was ransacked and all its treasures looted to Egypt?

Yes, the scripture says, *"and it came to pass, in the fifth year of King Rehoboam, Shishak, king of Egypt, came up against Jerusalem... with 1200 chariots and 60 000 horsemen and people without numbers that came with him out of Egypt, the Lubim (Libyans), the Sukkiims and the Ethiopians (Sudanese). And he took the fenced cities which pertained to Judah and came to Jerusalem"* (II Chron. 12:2-4).

As can be seen vividly described by the Bible, Jerusalem fell to Thutmose without proper resistance. Shishak (Thutmose III) *"took away the treasures of the house of the Lord, (the temple), and the treasures of the king's house (the palace); he took all; he also carried away the shields of gold which Solomon had made"* (II Chron. 12:9). Thutmose's motive may have been to repay for the disaster which the Israelites and their God inflicted on Egypt during the exodus time.[132]

This great invasion confounded the already existing state of warfare between Judah and Israel under Rehoboam and Jeroboam, two kings of the divided kingdom of Solomon, of David and of Saul before them. Within that violent pestilence, communities and families decided to migrate away from the two kingdoms and it came to pass that a faction of Reuben, Judah and some family members

---

132   Immanuel Velikovsky, Ages in chaos, (2000), p. 212

from Samson who belonged to the Manoah line of Dan, (Judges 15:4-17) departed Judah for the Nile region, where they have since been hearing of their brothers who parted ways with them in Egypt at the exodus.

Their Jacob lineage of Reuben who had come to Wawat since exodus times were living in peace with the local inhabitants and were not at that time the attention of the great pharaonic Egypt. On the way a few of the Edomites also joined them. Those Edomites were from the Reuel household of Esau. Among them was Mayuääl, from whom later came the founding ancestors of the Redior households among the Dinka today.

An old patriarch by the name of Jieldit, who in our Dinka ancient descent line is Jiel III, led this migrating group to ancient Northern Sudan through Eastern Sudan. They were not running fugitives, however, but a slowly moving emigrant faction, for they departed with all of their provisions, their cattle and flock. In tracing their movements, it was found they passed through the region which was periodically contested by members of the Judah household with those of Edom, and passing through the Arabian Desert of Edom, they only had a stopover sometimes at what has now become Wadi al Gauf in Northern Yemen. There was water and good pasture for them to make a respite over there. Then they proceeded, crossing the big Adana valley from Sirwa to what are now Damar and Yarim through to modern Taizz. When they reached Barim's threshold on the east bank of the Red Sea, Jieldit encamped to first offer to the gods of the Red Sea his ox bull (thɔn) by the colour of Malou to let his people cross the sea without any harm. Traditions from these Jiel and Mayuääl clans say their ancestors came to ancient Northern Sudan after crossing *Wär-Pakuɛɛk*, 'the sea of all peoples', our today's Red Sea.

On the east bank threshold of the Red Sea on the spot then known as Barim, and during his moment of ritual sacrifice to the gods of the sea, Jieldit made intense meditative invocation, pleading to God of his grandfathers to cause the sea waters to separate for a dry gap for him and his people to pass through, as was once done for Moses when the waters of the Red Sea at Pi-Khiroth parted and he crossed with his people. Jieldit commanded the waters of the sea to cease moving. He made assurance to the sea gods that he and his people shall not touch any fish or sea creature they may see on the dry sea bed while crossing. Jieldit had this famous invocational statement that survived all ages and is still being told throughout Dinka land to this day:

"*Eyin Wär–PaKuɛɛk!,*
Yin Kën Alëëk!,
Kën Wä!, Kën Ajaal!,
Kën Wadit Jiel!, Nhialic Wä!,
ŋany yï yic ba tem Ke Kackië!,
Cä rɛcdu jak, Cä Ken Yänydu jak!".

Translation:
"*You, the sea of all peoples*[133]
You of the ebb, god of the sea wave,[134]
That of my father!
That of Ajaal!
You of my grandfather Jiel (i.e. Abraham)
God of my father!
Open your bowel
To let me cross with my people!
I shall not touch your fish
Nor any creature in your bowel!"

---

133   The Red Sea is 'Wär-PaKuɛɛk' in Dinka, meaning 'sea of all people'.

134   'Alëëk' is the Dinka name for the sea or river ebb/river wave. It is also a name of one of the grandmothers of the speaking or invocating Jieldit and, therefore, is the grandmother of all the Pagoŋ clan people.

With those pleading invocational words of appeal to the gods of the Red Sea, gods of the Sea waves, to God of his fathers, with those words while standing amidst his people, Jieldit raised his arms up, skywards into the air with his holy sceptre (*wai rial*) and the holy spears (*biith*) with a final command to the sea to separate its waters for a dry path for him and his people to cross. Miraculously enough, the Red Sea waters separated on the instant, just like it happened to Moses at the Egyptian Red Sea point at Pi-Khiroth. Jieldit immediately marched in for about a day's walk to cross to the west bank with his people, but unfortunately some of his people from behind could not tolerate seeing fish on the naked ground of the sea bed without killing some for themselves. A number of them began to kill those fish of their choice while parts of the people were still waiting on the east bank at *Barim* (Bab el Mandeb), waiting to squeeze into that miraculous sea path to cross.

Upon that violation of the promise made by Jieldit to the gods of the sea, the sea waters which had parted immediately came together and resumed their usual course, thereby drowning those then still inside the sea bed and preventing those who were still on the east bank from crossing! The event was partly a victory and partly a disaster! The people who first crossed with Jieldit to the west bank of the Red Sea later proceeded after thanksgiving rituals. As the legend has it, those who did not cross the Red Sea decided to return to their former areas in Judea and Edom where they came from.

Besides that miraculous crossing of the Red Sea, another wonder occurred soon after Jieldit had crossed with a good number of people. Mayuääl the Edomite was one of the people who did not cross. He remained on the east bank of Barim at the vicinity of the strait of Deire which the Arabs later renamed as *Bab el Mandeb*. He did not return to Edom when those few cut off from crossing returned. Instead Mayuääl prayed to Nhialic and was lifted up into the space that he walked in the air till he crossed the Red Sea to the west bank.

After his celestial crossing of the Red Sea, Mayuääl did not join the community of Jieldit straight away.

According to legends from his descendants and from other Dinka sections, Mayuääl came and entered a big sausage tree through its hollow and began to stay there. We are not told how long he remained in the sausage tree hollow. The legend just proceeds, saying Mayuääl was later found in the sausage tree by one of the daughters of Jieldit, a girl whose name is presented as 'Alëëk'. Other Redior clan people among the Agaar Dinka give a different version about this girl. They say she was called Nyimuööth and that she was a daughter of Agaar Marol. This version seems to hold no water, in that Agaar Marol is a recent Mediaeval figure who physically appeared in the events of Bahr el Ghazal after crossing the White Nile River to Bahr el Ghazal from the Upper Nile.

The Patiɔp clan people of Pabɛɛk origin in the same Agaar land also claim this Nyimuööth to have been a daughter of Aru Pabɛɛk, not of Agar Marol. Yet, we find this Aru Pabɛɛk as an antediluvian man. If there were not another intermediate Aru Pabɛɛk then this girl in the legend is an ancient lady. This makes the version of the Pagong in Rekland to be of historical substance. The girl who found Mayuääl in the hollow of the sausage tree was therefore a daughter of Jieldit and this leads us to tell the story of Mayuääl-Bänyköök in the perspective of Alëëk, the daughter of Jieldit.

THE STORY OF MAYUÄÄL

Alëëk Jiel, an already mature girl, used to go out into the pasture to herd the cattle, a usual Dinka practice even today. It is normal among the Dinka to see girls herding cattle in the forest pastures. There, one particular day in the forest, in the pasture place, Alëëk saw a lonely being sitting under ruääl, the *Kigelia Ethiopia* or sausage tree, known in Dinka as Ruaal. She therefore made for him as she realised him to be a human being from far but, as Alëëk was approaching, Mayuääl suddenly disappeared into the tree in quite a mysterious way. The tree was an old primeval sausage tree immensely standing alone in the pasture plain. It provided a good shade for cattle herders in that part of the pasture forest. With that, Alëëk gave up and went back for her cattle and did not mind about what she saw.

Another day, Alëëk saw the man again when she came to the very place with her cattle. For the second time, Mayuääl went into the tree's hollow upon seeing the girl from far. This time Alëëk decided to come up to the foot of the tree ground. She was inquisitive to know of a person who stays in such a place for days and would not want to go to where people are. Under the tree the girl called on that being to come out of the tree and be able to talk to her, to tell his story of having to stay in a tree hole. Mayuääl is said to have responded by coming out of the tree and the two began to talk. For several days, the two became acquainted. For weeks and months, they developed a relationship which ended in an affair that resulted in Alëëk becoming pregnant. This made Alëëk later confide to her father Jieldit that she had a relationship with a certain man who forlornly stays in a tree hole in her pasture forest and she did not know what he eats and where he came from.

Jieldit took interest in the story, for in that part of the land there were no people except for the *Ichthyophagis*, the *Creophagis* and the *Colobis*, a very short nomadic ancient black people of that area and whose existence is not known today. They lived on fish and hunted elephants and were more coastal than Jieldit and his people, who had temporarily settled on their way to Wadi al Allagi valley. That valley was where it was planned to join Abiel's people, who have at this time started to be Paan-Ajääng. The description of Mayuääl given by Alëëk did not fit those black and shorter people. On the whole Jieldit appointed his sons and others to go and be shown of such a person reported to stay in a tree hole (kɔ̈k) in the pasture forest. He told the people not to kill him but to bring him over to him in the cattle camp.

Ahead of the party Alëëk arrived first to the vicinity of that sausage tree, having first hidden the people who came with her. Mayuääl therefore came out of the tree for his usual affair and conversation with Alëëk, but he was soon overtaken and apprehended, gripped and firmly held by Alëëk's people. Despite attempts to escape through changing himself into different non-human forms, Alëëk's brothers never let him go. He changed to a vulture, again into a crow (gak), a chameleon (ŋany kudɔt) and into a hedgehog. Yet, they kept holding him until he finally changed to human form as before. When Mayuääl could not change any more, they took him to Jieldit, although against his will. While with Jieldit at the camp Mayuääl revealed that he was an Edomite from the Reuel household in the region of Seir and that he had joined the Jieldit group on the way and had come with them all the way until Wär-Pakuɛɛk where he was barred from crossing with Jieldit by the event of the sea so he later decided to cross the Red Sea by air and he chose to live in the tree which he called reuel (now ruaal) after the name of his great grandfather and clan.

Strange as the story may be, Jieldit made him stay as a guest and in the course of his stay he was found to have superhuman qualities. Mayuääl was able to heal the sick and could raise the dead! People began to come to him for blessing and for healing and to make the dead come back to life! People knew he came from the sky, that is, from heaven. They saw him as probably the spiritual incarnation of the earlier Deŋ-Mayuääl, that primogenitary son of Abuk and Garaŋ, if not Deŋ Noi whom their ancestors had since long deified as their god. Mayuääl is said to have been telling people he came from heaven and would return to heaven one day. One particular day a child of the patriarch Jieldit died in the camp and was buried. Mayuääl is said to have gone in and raised the child from the grave, but from thither he decided to announce his intention to leave the people for heaven.

However, Jieldit intimated him of his concern about his daughter Alëëk, who was about to deliver. Responding to this Mayuääl said he is leaving her to the care of her father and brothers but still as his wife. In place of a dowry payment Mayuääl gave to Jieldit the power of tapping underground water, done by pulling the nigritana vetiveria grass awaar from its place so water just comes out in torrents for people and cattle to drink from. That divine power was the dowry he was to pay for Alëëk. After saying this Mayuääl made Jieldit and his sons follow him into Alëëk's pasture forest to show them how to do it when they get underground water after pulling up awaar grass. They went up to the vicinity of his big tree, ruaal. There, Mayuääl made a stop and with a few words of invocation, he pulled that vetiveria nigritana grass out of its place and water gushed out in torrents. He then told Jieldit that *"....this divine power is the dowry I have paid to you for your daughter"*. Jieldit is said to have accepted this power transferred to him and since then the power of getting water from the underground by pulling awaar became a power in Jieldit. This power continued with his descendants for quite a long time up to the end of the Middle Ages or until the beginning of the present modern time. Descendants of Jieldit had continued to be known throughout Dinka land as the people of Awaar with the divine capacity to tap water from the dry ground of the awaar grass.

Besides this Mayuääl also made another divine transfer of the hedgehog, which Dinka people call *goŋ*. He made his divine transfer of *goŋ* to Jieldit to become his nagualistic creature, a totemic divinity for him and his descent lines. It is from this *goŋ* that the descendants of Jieldit became the Pagong clan since then to the present day.

Having given the divine power for underground water and *goŋ* to be the totem for Jieldit in exchange for Alëëk, Mayuääl now proceeded with his in-laws to the sausage tree place. There he stood meditating for a while, after which he told the in-laws he was going into the hole of the tree but was coming back to them. On his return he brought out with him a bundle of durra which Dinka People now know as rap, the present sorghum type called durra in Sudan.

The one used as a staple food by the Dinka until that time, Dinka ancestors did not know the durra crop according to this legend. He also came out with the winnowing tray which the Dinka people call *atac* or *atäny*, a locally woven design from the porbolus grass (mon) and leaves from the raffia palm tree or Bengal cane which Dinka people call *akarab*. Atäny is used by women for isolating grain powder *(abik)* from its grain or durra particles they call *ŋeei*. He also came out with *adiany*, a cradle frame used for carrying babies and children by their mothers when on a journey. The Jääng people later introduced it to the rest of the Nilotics in the Nile valley region. The durra and winnowing tray were symbolic metaphors for people to be concerned about production to avail food for the Jääng community. Descendants of Mayuääl have continued to be known as people of the durra (kɔc rap) and are called upon to cause someone to have good durra yield, as they also use their divine power in them to ward away those birds that eat the durra while in the fields. They also spell away insects that seek to spoil the durra from healthy ripening. *Adiany* did connote Mayuääl's ability to make women to procreate and to this end, members of Mayuääl's lineages are called upon to perform divine blessing to make a woman beget if for any reason a woman happens not to conceive. They are also called upon to bless a couple for assured procreation and for the wellbeing of their children. The power to make a woman conceive for procreation is a known divine power in almost all the members of the Manyuääl clan all over Dinka lands, even today. Mayuääl lineage members earn income from this power to make women conceive.

After all these performances Mayuaal is said to have returned with Jieldit to the camp where he thereafter called on the people for his last words. Before his departure he is said to have talked to Jieldit, telling him he was ascending back to heaven where he said he came from and that he was leaving his wife Alëëk to the care of her father, adding she was to later give birth to triplets, three sons who were to be called Rum, Wol and Akuiɛn.

Rum was to be the first, Wol was to be the second while Akuiɛn was to be the last son. Having said this, Mayuääl was said to have looked up into the sky and raised up all of his arms and called on the creator to throw him three holy invocation spears, which he was to leave behind for his would-be born three sons. Heaven is said to have responded on the instant. Three big spears, the unbarbed spears, the sacred or holy spears, the type which Dinka Spear Masters use as *binh-löŋ*, the invocation spears fell down just before him! Mayuääl is said to have picked them up and gave them over to Jieldit for his three sons when they are born and had grown up.

Finally, in the midst of a gathering, Mayuääl is said to have looked up again and called for heaven to take him up into heaven. A whirlwind just came from nowhere and the gathered people of Jieldit saw Mayuääl lifted up by this sudden wind, never to return to the present day. He went up to the glare of the whole gathering! This miraculous happening is said to have occurred before Jieldit joined the rest of the Jaang society in the Wawat region. If so, then it may have taken place midway between the present Asoteriba Hills' area in the Halaif region and the Red Sea area.

The legend continued as Alëëk later gave birth to three sons who were named accordingly. They grew to become Spear Masters in their lifetime, each with a spear that was ordained to him by their gone father. The three are also believed to be the founding fathers of all the Mayuääl or Redior clans among the Dinka of today. From the lineage of Rum came the clan name of *Parum* while Akuiɛn lineage became the source from which came the clan name *Pakuin*. Wol later bore Aŋok whose name was derived from ruaal the sausage tree for its green colour. From this Aŋok came the branch name of the clan *Paŋɔk*. The different clans descended from these three sons of Mayuääl all revere the sausage tree as their primary totem wherever they are in Dinka land. They call themselves '*wundior*' or '*redior*' for their connection with the power to do with women's procreation and because their ancestor once changed into those things such as vulture called *gon* and *gak*, the crow. They venerate those creatures as their nagualistic creatures that had divine association with their ancestor Mayuääl. These are venerational creatures handed down to them since their ancestor Mayuääl. They are also called the people of *Atäny*, the winnowing tray which relates to durra and women folk.

Through Jieldit who is also the founder of the Pagong clan, the Pagong clan people are maternal kin to all the Redior people of Ruaal, and while Pagong people have their own version about how their ancestor got that divine power for obtaining water by pulling awaar, this story of Mayuääl makes the Pagong to have got the holy investiture for the acquisition of water through the pulling of the nigritana grass from Mayuaal. The Pagong and Redior people are inter-related as such, and although this was a big and lengthy digression, it was necessary to bring the story of the Redior and Pagong people and how they came to Sudan as important sections of the Dinka.

JIELDIT AND HIS FACTION JOINS THE JÄÄNG IN WAWAT

Long after Mayuääl had gone up into the sky as explained above, Jieldit and his people proceeded from the Asoteriba Hills region of Halaif. He gradually arrived at the Wadi al Allagi area in Wawat. The two factions of the would-be Jääng society had now come together once again after a long break of nearly two centuries since they parted at the day of the exodus in Egypt. In this Wadi Al Allagi area the society developed and adopted the name of Jääng, later modified as Jieng. Those who came from Egypt to become the group of Abiɛl and Dengdit included the thigh bone revering people, the Paχol, the cloud or piöl revering people of the rain, the cow or pawutweng (paderek) revering people, the fire (pakuieth) and forest revering groups of people called Pagak and perhaps many others. Those who came through Bab el Mandeb included the Pagong people of Awaar and the Ruaal people of Mayuääl. With them in this route were those ancestors of the Pabɛɛk who are the Patiɔp clan in Agaar land and who are Paduoltiop in Rek lands, all the water related groups called Paker in Rek lands, Pajul in Gok and Agaar lands, the bladed spear and rock stone revering people came through Bab el Mandeb.

In time that little fertile land of Wadi al Allagi became too small for the Jaang community and they had to extend or move to the Dongola area between the third and fourth cataracts. There was a large basin that held enough flood waters during the wet season to allow crops to be grown. From here to below the present town of Debba, where the Nile flows southwest for about 100 kms below the fourth cataract, was a broad silty floodplain area suitable for their agricultural activities. Until that time Jääng people were purely cattle keepers, hunters and fishermen and were of a nomadic nature after those many years of their transhumant movements. Their farming activities were based on the annual flooding of the Nile and they had one harvest per year. They knew of millet and wheat, but with the coming of the group of Jieldit from the east, durra which was brought by Mayuääl began to replace wheat. The Jaang then adopted the durra which they called *rap-jang*. They continue with it to the present day. They kept adding new crops including beans, pumpkins and other edible crops, cucumbers and tubers, depending on the type of soil and climate. This group of Jieldit also brought the practice of putting or fastening the bells on a bull's neck, a practice they copied from the Abyssinian Megabarae tribe through whose region they passed.

Elephant tusks for ivory was another source of income in this region, as was timber. Acacia trees, call pëny in Rek dialect, which used to grow on the edges of the many existing valleys was greatly utilised. Dinka ancestors used it for timber for trade with the Egyptians and they also used it as firewood in the homes. They also made much of the art of pottery. Their domestic articles of the homes consisted of pots called *töny* and jars called *alɛi*, all made of the terracotta clay so abundant in the vicinity's soil. They grew *gourd* which they call *kuot* and from it they made so many utensils including calabashes and spoons in addition to big and small water containers and milk gourds. Their beautiful decoration practice has continued to this time although modern pots from metal have begun to appear as new domestic home articles. The calabash, called *aduök* and *kec* or *rök* for various use in the home, had particularly beautiful designs, yet up to the time of writing this book, the *tony* and *alɛi* from baked clay plus those domestic utensils from the gourd still form much of the rural home articles for the Dinka today.

From copper, which they call *bäu* in their language and bronze, which they call *milaŋ* they were able to make various wristlets and anklets also called *milaŋ*, plural *milɔɔŋ*, worn for decoration and beauty. They made the bronze into the very precious expensive wristlets and anklets called *anhomriaak*. They also mined *abeer* (iron ore) which was made into different forms and shapes of iron called *lung* (plural *luun)*, from which they manufactured so many things including hoes for cultivation, knives for cutting meat, axes and adzes or carpenter's axes which they called *akɔrcɔɔk*, all for cutting trees and other hard objects such as bones. From *luuŋ* they made many articles of war such as various types of spears, indented wristlets called *nyuiny* and a heavy wristlet which they call *gur*. Animal tassels called *dhuɔr* were made and worn on the arms. They also made armlets and wristlets from cattlehide, which was also used for sleeping mats.

The flora and fauna of the region was not what it is today. There were trees of all sorts including the ebony (called rit) tree from which the Jaang used to make a very strong club they call *atuel*, *thieec* or *loc* for fighting. There was a kind of palm tree which in particular was in abundance and produced very sweet dates and this made the palm tree nationalised by the kingdom in later times so that it became identified with the kings and state trade. Ancient Jääng people called it *thön-bäny,* literally *the heglig tree of the authorities or the tree of the nobility*. The elephants of a very huge type were in abundance as were the giraffes. Jääng men used to be very tall and gigantic and were very handsome. They used to live longer than the other peoples in the same region. Many of them used to live 120 years or more.

The men wore leopard skins. This was more so with the nobility. Women wore sheep and goats' skins stripped of wool and made into a very practical and beautiful apron that almost covers the whole waist down the buttocks and to beyond the knees. *See that Dinka girl in traditional dress on page 45.* Most of the women wore copper rings on the upper lips and ears and men wore the same copper rings on the ears. Some wore girdles called *awäät* in Rek dialect. Others wore girdles of fine wool hair from the wild cat which they called *dhök.* They wore these on their loins. They particularly used it when they went into battle and into communal dance plays. They painted their bodies with white and red ash from the cow dung and had ostrich feathers on their heads. They wore bead necklaces and waist beads.

They ate boiled or roasted meat from their cows, goats and sheep as well as from the then abundant wildlife and from the domestic birds like chickens and various types of Nile birds but principal for their meals was the milk from their cows and flocks. Milk was on equal par with fish, which was a daily or hourly diet as fish was in abundance from the Nile and its streams and many valley pools and ponds. It is the abundance of those high quality protein foods which made the Jääng ancestors very healthy and very tall, huge and handsome with smooth nice looking skin as described by one Greek historian, Herodotus, who visited the region in 430 BC. Jääng people used small wooden rafts which they called *riäi* to navigate to and from the Nile and to fish in.

From available iron ore they manufactured fishing spears and harpoons which they called *agɔɔr*. They also knew of gold which they used to obtain in great quantity. To the east of them declining towards the rising sun was a country called Endera (modern Eretria), an area or country inhabited also by a naked people then called the *Gymnetae* who were expert hunters of wild animals, especially elephants, and for that reason, they were known by the Greeks as the elephantophagi (or elephant-eaters). They also knew of the gold and were involved in its trade, as with ivory. Those many items of trade were actually the ancient reason for much of the Egyptian busy trade caravans that traversed Wawat to and from the east.

Then, in time, the black tribes began to organise themselves into small chiefdoms with the Luo providing leadership while the Jääng and the Mazoi offered to do the military aspect of the society. Several Jääng patriarchs like Dengdit, Ajääng and many others became spiritual lords and provided the priest class, worshipping their Dengdit and celestial gods, Amon-Re of the Egyptians being one of those gods. This is the time when the third group arrived from Judea, a group led by great Jök-Athurkök.

KUSH KINGDOM AND THE DINKA ANCESTORS

The society of Jääng developed along the Nile in the course of those centuries after they came from Egypt and Judea through Eastern Sudan, crossing Bab el Mandeb. They interacted with all those black communities found in the region, especially the Luo and Funj groups. A lot of intermarriage between the Luo and those Jääng ancestors led to closer relations between the two communities. For example, the Shilluks who married the daughters of Dengdit-Achan began to be known as the people of *Achan* while the Luo conversely called the Jääng people Kuadeeng, people of Adeeng.

When Egypt had gone into decline at the close of the new kingdom, those Nilotic blacks, with the impetus from the Jääng, agreed to have a unified monarchy under the name of Kush. This was the work of the hereditary ruling families.

The different sections of the Luo and the Funj had since then recognised the military valour with which these Jääng communities were known in that part of the Nile valley. In the days when the Egyptians had to fight for their liberation from the Hyksos, many Jääng young men accepted the Egyptian call on the blacks to the south of them to assist them in fighting the Hyksos. The Jaang people went back to Egypt in large numbers and participated in the uprisings that led to the overthrow of the Hyksos' rule in Egypt. Many of them therefore became part of the later Egyptian army. Those soldiers began to return to their people and the Jaang people were now seen by the rest of their Nilotic blacks as being capable of providing an army for a new kingdom.

However, some time prior to these developments, in the course of the 11th century BC or thereabouts, a new wave of immigrants entered the region between the 3rd and 4th cataracts. They came from Libya in the west, a region where increasing desiccation of the Sahara desertification process was dropping them to settle along the Nile as farmers. Branches of these people later proceeded to the Red Sea hills region in the east while others pushed south along both banks of the Nile. Some of them went west as far as those areas of Wadai and Darfur. Those who chose to remain on the Nile became part of the Nilotic communities although these people, known as factions of the Bantus, later returned to West Africa at the wake of the destruction of Meroe by Axum in 350 AD, while the original blacks, the real Nilotics, took to the Khartoum region, still keeping to the Nile.

At this very time, in the early parts of the 8th century BC, about 780 BC, the different tribal chiefs considered the Luo for their tradition to kingship when they were in Egypt. All the tribal chiefs and the aristocracy of the Nilotic blacks' heartland people saw the need for a coming together to form a kingdom of their own. They all agreed for one of the Luo chiefs by the name of Alara to become the first king of the new kingdom which they called 'Kush' in commemoration of their great, great ancestor Kuc, the son of their Biblical Ham. Kuc was also the name of the Jääng ancestor, son of Abiɛl, the leader of the Jääng people from Egypt at the exodus. Alara is universally regarded as the first and founding King of Kush Kingdom. They also made Napata their kingdom's capital. Nabda in Jaang language later became Napata. It rose from a village inhabited by the Irthets and the Jaang people. Jaang sections closed in during the last decades (of 790 BC) and their nobility and Spear Master families and clans had come and settled as far as Kurru, about present Dongola, a few kms north of this Napata, the capital. Influenced by none other than their strong Indigenous African culture that flourished since Kerma culture time far before the era of pre-dynastic Egypt, those Nilotics developed a unifying language when they later shifted from Napata to *Muɔrwĕi*, a Jaang name later corrupted to read as Meroë.

King Alara reigned as King of Kush until 755 BC when he was succeeded by Kashta and then Tharyakua, who extended Kush rule up to Egypt's southernmost region of Aswan as far as Thebes, but it was Tharyakua's successor, Piɛŋ of Jääng ancestry, who made Kush Kingdom reach its climax. It is this Piɛŋ or Piɛngke which historians usually write as King Piye or Pienke. Pieng used his Jääng marshal population to conquer the whole of Egypt in his 20th year as king. He established the 25th Dynasty in Egypt, ushering the period regarded in Egypt's history as the period of the black pharaohs which came to last in 653 BC when the last native Egyptian dynasty, the 26th Dynasty, called the Saite Dynasty, rose to power under Pharaoh Psamtek I.

In 722-721 BC, in the time of King Hezekiah of Judah and of King Hosea of Israel, it was a Jääng king, Tharyakua, who was king of Egypt and Kush. Tharyakua in Dinka means *fight for our cattle*.

He is the Egyptian pharaoh of the two worlds, Egypt and Kush, usually written as Tirhaqa by historians on ancient Sudan including the Bible. Tharyakua from Thebes, the capital for both Egypt and Kush, led a huge army of 10 000 men on chariots to Israel as a reinforcement to King Hosea and King Hezekiah who were being devastated by King Sennacherib of Assyria. It was blood and filial ties between the Jääng Nilotic community and the Israelites that dropped King Tharyakua to Palestine from Egypt to reinforce their kin (II Kings 17:4-7).

Unfortunately that reinforcement became a disaster to Kush, particularly to the Jaang whose people made up much of that force. Of the 10 000 men only about 5000 or less returned home with Tharyakua. Sennacherib victorious armies laid to waste the whole of Israel and captured Samaria, the capital of Israel, and took its citizenry and the army, which surrendered to them as fugitives to the country. Some of our people went to Assyria as part of that army which surrendered. It is this defeat of Israel along with the Kush-Egyptian forces of Tharkakua in 722 BC which made Assyrian King Sennacherib dispatch a great army led by his kingdom's high officials to King Hezekiah of Judah with a threatening letter, asking him not to rely on or have trust in the chariots from Egypt (II Kings 18:21-24). Although Judah was not captured by Sennacherib in the final analysis, the disaster which befell Tharyakua's reinforcement greatly affected the Kush Kingdom.

The kingdom was later not able to withstand Assyrian military invasions which ended with the capture of Egypt in 671 BC. Tharyakua, who became the last black pharaoh of Egypt and Kush, withdrew from Egypt altogether in 654 BC and our people then contended with Kush instead of the unified two worlds of Kush and

Egypt under them. They came to the safety of their capital, Napata. Although denied Egypt that had made it a great world power, Kush under Jaang, Luo, Funj, Yam and Mazoi continued as a kingdom on the middle Nile between the 2nd and the 6th cataracts. It endured for the next one thousand years. Egypt remained to be later colonised by the Assyrians and by a succession of the Mediterranean powers and Persia.

The last attempt to regain the control of Egypt by these Nilotics was in the time of King Tatunkamon (Tutankhamun), a Funj figure by origin. Tatunkamon's defeat by the Assyrians in Egypt in the year 664 BC brought an end to our people's thoughts about ruling Egypt any more but, about six decades later, the dreams about Egypt resurfaced. This made King Aspelta start preparations aimed at reconquering Egypt, but Egypt was at this time (591 BC) under Psamtik I who vigorously reunited Egypt after the filth from the Assyrians and founded the Egyptian 26th Dynasty called the Saite Dynasty. Under Psamtik II who succeeded him, Egypt attacked Kush to preempt the preparations that were being made by King Aspelta of Kush. That invasion sufficed to cause a shift of the capital from Napata to Meroe, a town to later grow into a big ancient city located 200 miles south of Napata and about 100 miles north of present Khartoum. Psamtik's Egypt effectively ransacked and burnt Napata in 591 BC.

THE SHIFT FROM NAPATA TO MEROE

There are two principal reasons given as to why our Nilotic rulers of the Kush Kingdom shifted their capital city from Napata to Meroë near present Shendi. One version believes it was the attraction of ironworking that dropped the kingdom to its southern parts around Meroë. Unlike Napata there were large forests that could provide wood to fire the blast furnaces for iron smelting. At that time also there came a lot of Greek merchants into the kingdom and Kush was not able to any longer depend on the Nile as the only route for trade. Greek merchants had also based themselves along the Red Sea coasts up to Egypt and Arabian and Kush goods could now get exported to the outside world through the Red Sea instead of only through the Nile to Egypt as it used to be before. Meroë was nearer to those sea coastal ports than was Napata so there was the economic reason as Kush was to now prosper even more than it was in the times of Napata city.

The second reason for choosing Meroë was purely a security one. In their furious delta region battles in the 660s with the Assyrians, the Assyrians had fought them with weapons of a new kind, weapons of tempered iron instead of those made of bronze and hard stones. The use of iron weapons as guns had later began to spread even to Sainte Egypt from nearby Asia and Kush was now to pose no match for this iron-based warfare. Napata was too close to Thebes to resist a well organised attack from Egypt when possessing modern weapons. Moreover the great wars for the control of Egypt and those wars with the Assyrian Empire over Egypt and Israel had exhausted Kush of its fighting manpower and it then needed to turn to its internal consolidation and economic development as a kingdom. The remaining population needed a respite from all those wars.

Whatever the precise reasons for the shift to Meroë may have been, those reasons were accompanied by a then growing anti-Egyptian sentiment among the Nilotic aristocracy in the towns. At Meroe the kingdom became more African, self-consciously and deliberately Nilotic or Kushitic than in Napata. In Meroe our people developed real cultural vigour and renaissance. Their rituals and gods became Indigenous, Meroitic in content and form.

Here, in the Meroe region, we begin to see some of the Jääng people settled around one of their landed gentries. One of them by the name of Chandit became that Iron Age Jääng figure from whose name the present Shendi town later developed.

ANCIENT GEOGRAPHY OF MEROE

Although the island of Meroe was also a mountainous area like the region of Napata to the north, it did have extensive forest areas full of all forms of wildlife, among which were elephants, giraffe, buffalo, lions, leopards, all forms of antelopes and gazelles in addition to all sorts of rodents, hyenas and the fox. Animal stories which now permeate Dinka lands and Dinka lore may have their origins from this Meroitic era of from the 4th century BC to the 3rd century AD. The ordinary rural populations of the Kush Kingdom in this Meroë period were partly hunters and partly farmers but they were greatly involved in ironwork and were also mining gold, copper and various precious stones. The Jääng and Nuer components of those Nilotes were cattle herders. The area was bound by great hills of sands to the west towards Libya and by continuous precipices towards Arabia and the Red Sea hills region in the east. It was bounded at the higher parts to the south by the rivers Astaboras (modern Atbara), Astapus (the White Nile) and Astasobas (the Blue" Nile).

The type of houses that were dwellings for our people, the rural folk, were mudded wall houses supported by a frame of wattle, circular in shape and thatched with grass quite abundant in the steppes or plains of the region. Jaang present house structures are an improvement on those ancient huts and are more of a permanent nature. The ancient or Meroitic huts were dictated by their owners' nomadic characters, as they were on the move almost every decade or century. Their use of the existing metals for body adornment was more than they do today. The bronze and copper were particular metals used to make various rings such as ear and mouth rings, wristlets, armlets and anklets. The Jaang of this period up to the end of the Mediaeval era used beads very extensively. More prized was that ancient bead called *guén-jäng*, the bead of the Jääng people. As earlier described, they used animal skins for cloth, particularly of the goats, sheep, antelopes and gazelles. They used ostrich feathers and wild cats' fine woollen skins applied or worn on or slightly above the buttocks.

The houses in the Meroitic cities were either formed by woven split pieces of palm wood or of bricks and rock cemented by fossil or rock salt. The ebony and carob trees, known for their hard makeup, were used for erecting the houses. According to King Ezana of Axum, writing about our Meroitic people, Meroitic cities and towns were built of masonry and straw.

In the course of the intervening centuries before the Kush Kingdom was banished by the regional forces in 350 AD, the kingdom became more originally African than it was in Napata, and because they believed in some form of life after death they built huge tombs, although not as immense as Egypt's famous pyramids to the north. They were built as royal tombs. About fifty of these ancient pyramidal tombs can still be seen rising out of the desert sands at Meroe today (see Fig 51).

Our people developed the art of writing and were able to record their daily activities and events but it is unfortunate for our people to find their ancient language (called *Meroitic language*) is not possible for linguists to decipher even up until today, although about 20-30 words are now being understood. As to whether that difficult language is relative to the Nubia or Bantu language group or to the Luo, Jaang or Hamitic language is not yet decided, although all indications point to the Jaang language of today. However, it is our cherished belief that once successfully deciphered, it will be Jääng and this will prove to have continued to be so up to the end of this language kingdom. This is because the beginning of the kingdom was Luo and Jaang.

There was no clear Nubian presence at the time. The arena of the kingdom in Napata and Meroe was dominated by Jääng, Luo and Funj peoples.

Fig 51: Showing ruins of Nilotic kings' pyramids at the northern cemetery in Meroe, built from the 3rd century BC to the 2nd century AD

THE BEGINNING OF THE DECLINE OF KUSH KINGDOM

Although our Nilotic Blacks no longer ruled Egypt, Kush rulers in Meroe continued to use the title of pharaohs, but unlike the Napatan pharaohs, Meroeitic kings developed their own art of writing, distinct from that of Egypt as was formerly used in the Napatan times, and because of the long term political stability, Meroe was better developed than Napata. This may also be due to the development of iron and regular commerce which greatly flourished with its various neighbours, especially the eastern world as far as India and the maritime Greece in central Europe.

Just like the rest of the ancient world powers, the Kush Kingdom was not to last forever. Although Axum would give a lasting blow to the kingdom later in 350 AD, conditions leading to weakness and decay started much earlier, especially in the time of Queen Candace when things suddenly changed in both Egypt and Kush. Egypt to the north of them came under Roman rule at the time Kush was ruled by a one-eyed woman, Candace, who in the late 23rd BC decided to wage war on Roman Egypt. At the head of 30 000 men she invaded Southern Egypt as far as Thebes, having already overrun all those places such as Aswan, Syene, Elephantinentine" Island and Philae. She ransacked those towns, captured their inhabitants and even razed down the huge statue of the Roman emperor Augustus Caesar, which was built at Thebes, the capital.

In reaction to this Kushite invasion by a queen the Roman governor of Egypt by the name of Cassius Petronius went out, leading an army of 10 000 infantrymen and 800 horsemen against Candace's 30 000 blacks brought all the way from Meroe. As history has it, those 30 000 soldiers from Kush were not well armed nor well commanded. They carried large and heavy shields made of rawhide and had but only hatchets. Some had pikes while others had swords. Petronius broke our people and defeated them with great losses, although they fought with great valour for three days. Roman Egypt did have guns quite superior to the traditional weapons used by Candace's army. That powerful Egypt was earlier made to give itself up to these Romans owing to this element of the gun.

All in all, Petronius pushed our people back as far as Napata, the religious and still commercial city of Kush at the time. The destruction of Napata in the early months of the year 22 BC led to one of the greatest dispersals of the Nilotic societies of Kush. Part of the Napatan population was taken captive to Egypt. Others ran west towards Libya and eventually went to the different West African hinterland regions. Those were the Bantus who had originally come from West Africa in the days before the emergence of Kush as a kingdom. The rest who were original Nilotics, the Indigenous peoples, ran to the Meroe region to join the rest of the Nilotic blacks.

But much of the priesthood of the kingdom were decimated here in Napata. This became the beginning of the destruction of our blacks' civilisation through that dispersal and it is from here that William Chancellor acquired the title of his second to none masterpiece, "*The Destruction of the blacks' civilisation*". The destruction of Napata is regarded as the first historical diaspora of the blacks from the black heartland. Despite this occupation of Napata Petronius and his Egyptian armies later withdrew from Napata, Egypt occupied much of the northern Kush region of Wawat, leaving Napata desolately a razed city in a waste, never to come up again to the present day! Candace's subsequent attempts against Roman Egypt were, however, repulsed back to Meroë.

THE FALL OF MEROE AND THE FINAL DISPERSAL OF THE BLACKS

After our Nilotic people withdrew to the southern parts of the kingdom following the sacking of Napata by Roman Egypt, the region was later repopulated by two groups of people: The Blemmyse who are the present Beja from eastern Sudan and the Nobataen people who came from Western Sudan. These people came to the region by gradual infiltration when the Romans had decided to abandon the area, apparently for them. The Nobataens came from the west and became the later Nuba who in subsequent times formed the Christian kingdoms of Nobatea, Makuria and Alodia. Before the fall, Meroitic authority in Meroe region had begun to shrink during its terminal years of decay. This is because of the expansion of another powerful Abyssinian kingdom based at Axum to the east. For some decades the Kush Kingdom nearby and in Meroe eked on until 350 AD when King Ezana from present Eritrea led his forces from Axum, the capital of the Abyssinian kingdom, and defeated our Nilotic forces in a series of battles that ended with the destruction of Meroe city itself. That inglorious defeat and the fall of Meroe marked the end of an African monarchy which existed in the African Nile valley region for more than a thousand years! Our people were greatly dispersed. They ran in many directions. Historians regard this as the second historical dispersal of the blacks in that heartland region of the Nilotics.

BURIAL SYSTEM OF THE MEROITES AND TODAY'S DINKA BURIALS

Like our Dinka Spear Masters, who used to be buried alive since Mediaeval times until the practice was stopped by the British colonial authorities in the early 1930s, the latest Meroitic kings appear to have been buried alive with a number of sacrificed beings, which for our today's Dinka Spear Masters has come down to rams or ox bulls, and although the Dinka of today don't use bricks to make pyramidal tombs (which they call *yik*, the holy shrines), they do use piled up mud pyramids. Like a Meroitic royal burial, Dinka people bury their Spear Masters in separate but huge graves from which the heath is taken and placed aside to create a large deeply dug pit upon which a huge pyramidal structure made of mud is piled during each festival. That pyramidal shrine becomes his enduring home from where his soul or spirit is addressed by his descendants. Here, offerings are given to his spirit annually in festivals made by his descendants and the community.

That holy pyramidal shrine becomes a rallying religious centre for the clan and the community. Notables are either buried in their byres or in the cattle camp mounds. This was the practice for the Meroitic nobles who were not kings. Present Dinka Spear Masters are laid on a bed in a room-like structure which is dug deep and overlaid with an apartment that prevents the heath or earth from touching the body from below. Ordinary members of the community are buried at the edge of the courtyard or in their huts. Dinka people lay their dead into the grave lying straight with their heads to the west and their legs facing the east. There is therefore a noted similarity between the burial of the present Dinka Spear Masters and the burial system of the Meroitic kings. The holy shrines made by the Dinka people of today for their sainted Spear Masters are replicas of the ancient pyramids used for the kings of Kush Kingdom. The Payii holy shrines in Tharakon, Wunkuel and Panhom Thɔny, those of the Patɛk at Pankɔɔr in Lɔu-Ariik and the shrine of Paan–Adɛl in Luacjang, plus many of the Payii shrines in Apuk-Giir and the Aguɔɔk areas, continue to remind people of the Jääng ancient religion centred around a shrine.

JÄÄNG AFTER THE FALL OF MEROE

First of all, the name Jaang (though tackled earlier) has two sources: it came from the ancient Jääng word 'Jang' which linguistically means people. It was also a derivative from the name of Ajääng, the elder son of Dengdit IV, Deng, the brother of Manuɛr and Achan, Ajääng being a descendant from Reuben's line of Abiɛl that led his Jacobite faction of clans from Egypt at the exodus to the ancient northern Sudan region of Wawat. Ajaang became the common ancestor for most of the Jaang population that developed in the areas of Wawat to the north of the later Kush Kingdom and during the great years of the rise of the Kush Kingdom in the Dongola region at Kurru near Napata, the capital. Ajääng is represented by various Dinka oral traditions to have married a woman by the name of Agäär, with whom he bore six sons who are presented as (i) Deŋ, (ii) Machiek, (iii) Magɔk, (iv) Kër, (v) Kuɔl and (vi) Wol.

While there were other sections of Jääng society like other clans or families who came with Abiɛl from Egypt, and the other big factions that later came with Jieldit and Jök-Athurkök, all from Judah through Bab el Mandeb, Ajääng's primogenitary right of descent from the main line of Abiɛl gave him the upper hand for all of the emigrant families of Jacob in that ancient Sudan to take their name from him for easy identification within the region of the Nilotic blacks with whom they have come to stay. Accordingly, all the factions became known as Jaang after this Ajääng Deŋ.

Ajääng's six sons married and formed several nuclear households, from which developed Ajääng's family tree. When his grandsons and great, great grandsons' children married and the sequence and extension of procreation continued in the Napatan region as it was in the Wawat area of Wadi al Allagi, a society descended from Ajääng began to know themselves as 'Paan-Ajääng', meaning the Ajääng lineage group of families. They seemed to have imposed an accepted presence and leadership that overshadowed the other parallel lineages from Ajääng's direct and distant kin. This population of Ajääng and those of his agnatic kin reached the proportions of a tribe large enough to provide the Nilotic societies with a warring community which became a basis for establishing an independent kingdom, different from that of the nearby Pharaonic Egypt which had been casting dominance on the region for centuries.

As explained above, the Jääng as a tribe provided the impetus for forming the Kush Kingdom and although the kingdom started with a Luo king, the subsequent kings who even conquered Egypt, like Piɛŋ and Tharyakua, came to be from Jääng society. The history of the black pharaohs in Egypt is actually a history of the Jääng people with their Nilotic peoples such as the Luo and Funj. Except for the Mazoi and Yam who seemed to have been joined in later times by West African inland tribes to form Nubia that became heir to Kush, the entire history of what was the Kush Kingdom was that of the present Dinka ancestors and the Luo plus Funj.

As came above, it was this Jaang aspect of the Nilotics that took an army of 10 000 blacks with Tharyakua to Israel to fight against the Assyrians in 722 BC. A recent archaeological discovery in Meroe had shown a huge Jaang king's mummy in an excavated overlaid royal house. The mummy has the present Dinka tattoo scarification marks on his cranium, a lot of gold decorations and a bull and two rams with several valuable items such as gold buried with him. Dinka knowledge of *Muɔrnaknhom* the king and the rampant stories which go beyond the Khartoum region are indications of Dinka awareness of a onetime ancestral presence in that pre-Khartoum ancient Sudan kingdom of Kush.

That the Jääng stayed in this northern region of ancient Takkaze (Atbara) and the river Seda (main Nile) areas after the fall of their kingdom of Kasu (Meroe) in 350 AD is well illustrated by their many stories and names of places they still remember to the present day. After Meroe was sacked, more than a quarter of the kingdom's population dispersed in disarray. Here, some sectors of the Jääng population such as those of Wol Ajääng's lineage groups went west with a group of blacks of Bantu origin. They ran or migrated across the Nubian Desert to Chad and Libya where the lineage families of Wol Ajääng proceeded as far as west coast countries such as Mauritania and Senegal. There, in Senegal, those breakaway Jääng sections of Wol Ajääng finally settled and are now known as the Wolf tribe, from whom comes former Senegalese president Abdu Diof, a tall and huge personality who visited Juba, Southern Sudan, in 1973 and declared his Dinka or Jääng origin before South Sudan parliament.

LUO AND NUER MIGRATION TO KHARTOUM AFTER THE FALL OF MEROE

The Luo group of tribes are known from the ancient Jääng stories to have left the Meroe region headlong to the Khartoum area after the devastation and fall of Meroe. They came to Khartoum along the main Nile River. They then settled in the present *Halfa al Muluk* area where they established a number of tribal chiefdoms headed by independent kings with Halfa al Muluk as their common meeting headquarters where they used to settle their common tribal disputes annually. Halfa al Muluk is an Arabic phrase for '*halfa of the kings*'. It is those Luo chiefs or kings from which the Arabs came and named the valley as they found it and so called it the area of kings.

The Nuers, who have also developed into a parallel tribe alongside Jääng society since Napata, later followed the Luo on the same route. They came from the Butana steppes region of Meroe and Atbara and settled in the present Khartoum North areas which are now renamed *Bahry* by the Arabs. The Nuers came and inhabited all those areas of Khartoum North including Tuti Island.

Some of the Nilotic tribesmen were captured by Ezana forces and were taken to Axum along the Atbara River to Kassala. Among them were some of the Jääng people who later melted into different parts of Ethiopia, notably among the Oromos where, like those Jääng who are among the Karaŋkaŋ community in southern Blue Nile and those went to West Africa, they lost their Jaang origin and culture altogether.

However, the main bulk of Jääng society remained in this Meroë area together with tribes then known as Dhɔng and who are our present Nuba who now inhabit the mountain areas in central Sudan. They briefly remained with the Jaang in the Meroë area to continue to resist the foreign incursions from Roman Egypt and from the Blemmyes, who kept attacking the Jääng for their cattle. The Danagla, the Mahas and those who later became the Alfawiin branch of the Nuba ran west, wishing to cross the Great Sahara Desert. They were following the traces of those who left earlier, only to return later to find the Jääng and Dhɔng had moved only a little distance due south.

By about AD 370 the Jääng community had moved southwards to those areas that are now Matemma and Shendi, not in a real migratory movement but they moved slowly, covering a relatively short distance, still keeping to the Nile on both banks. According to Jääng ancient stories Matemma was later coined by the Arabs when that place was originally called Matɛm after an old Jääng landed gentry who had settled there even before the destruction of Meroe. The area was known as Matɛm village much before those migrations. Then the Jääng people moved further south to those areas that are the present Al Banaga and later to the Jeily and Khartoum-Omdurman areas.

Present Khartoum was known as *Tenasehu* while Omdurman was known as *Jarjar*. Tenasehu was a name given to what is the present Khartoum area by ancient peoples known by historians as *Shehinab culture people*. Jarjar was a name given by the Jääng people at the time they arrived in the Khartoum area. Present Al Banaga was a settlement village of a *Duör* man by the name of *Banɔk*. Jieldit, the father of Ayueeldit, settled with his estate at a location which became identified with him and from him the village acquired the name Jieldit after him. When the Jaaliin Arabs came later and settled this home area of Jieldit they changed the name to be the Jeily of today. The same was the case with Chandit, another Jääng gentry who settled with his people in that area. The Arabs later changed it to Shendi from the name of that Chandit.

By this time, while the Jaang was now in these Khartoum-Omdurman–Jeily areas, the Nuers had largely moved to as far as the present *Jereib Shark* township on the east bank of the Blue" Nile in present Khartoum. They also settled those areas that are *Jereib Garb*, that is, Jereib west. The Nuers in Khartoum settled on both banks along the Blue Nile River and the Jääng developed into a large tribe of sub-sections over the centuries on the main Nile region between Khartoum and southern Egypt. The family of Ajääng's younger brother, Manuɛr Deng, also developed into a tribe which in time dropped its original *Paan-Manuɛr* into *Nuɛr* without the prefix 'Ma' in Manuɛr.

Here in the Shehinab (Khartuom) area the Jaang gave a name to this place. They called it *Kartoum*, a name which replaced Shehinab as time went by. *Kartoum* is a Jääng compound noun, meaning the meeting of the two rivers. 'Kar' in Dinka means stream or a river branch. 'Tuom' means meet. It actually means the confluence of the two rivers, the Blue and the White Nile rivers. It is this Jääng name of *Kartoum* that the Arabs later transformed to read Khartuom, taking it to mean the elephant tusk in their Arabic language, the elephant tusk called *Kharthum*.

Omdurman is also a Jaang name given to that settlement they first called Jarjar when they first arrived from the Shendi–Matemma region. They called it Jarjar because it is rocky and all deserts. There were no trees in the locale. The Jääng section people, who are now the Pawutweng group of Dinka clans, settled in this area with other Jääng people. One time a great woman of the locality died and perhaps she was so dear a mother that a man who was her son cried for so many days that his wailing cry drew the attention of those who used to pass by. When they paused to ask why a grown man should be crying aloud like that, the villagers told the passersby that, *"he is a man crying for his mother who died days back"*. In Jääng or Dinka they used to say *"E mony dhur man"*. This word *monydhurman* was made to replace *Jarjar* as the name of that locality and it continued to become our present day Omdurman. Other places such as the present *Buri* township in Khartoum was also named by the Jääng people. The place was a fishing settlement where fishermen used to stay on the riverbank. Jääng people called it the *buric* fishing camp. The name remained to undergo later usage till it became Buri. The same was the case with *Tiaptiap* which in later times became that big township called Fatihap in the Omdurman province of today's Khartoum state.

A Nuɛr man by the name of *Tut* settled on the island between the confluences of the two Niles. The place started to be called the home of Tut and from him the island in later times became known as *Tuti Island* to the present day. This Nuer name tut means thɔn in Dinka. Thɔn is a name for uncastrated bull.

REASONS FOR THE JÄÄNG MOVE TO THE KHARTOUM REGION FROM A TBARAI SHENDI AREAS

When the Jääng finally moved out of the Matemma and Shendi areas and came to the area of Khartoum *Omdurman-Jeilly,* following the footsteps of the Nuers, Luo and Funj who came to the Khartoum area before them, it was because of two main reasons: (i) the incursions from the Blemmyes and Barya tribes. These tribes and the inland tribal communities, who kept coming by columns towards the vacated main Nile region, were all vying for Jääng cattle. The Jääng in these areas were now faced by an all out menace coming from the north, east and west. The only safe corridor was to move further south to this Khartoum region which was but a toch" land lived in only by fishermen after its former ancient people of Sheinab had either disappeared or gone elsewhere. In Sheinan culture people went to an unknown place. The Khartoum region was a no man's land, pioneered only by the Luo and the Funj who did not, however, settle in the main land areas of Khartoum and its mountainous area of Omdurman. They settled far off, north east of present Khartoum North as described earlier.

The second reason for the Jääng move to the Khartoum region was due to the climate. The Great Nubian or Sahara Desert that had cleared off the patchy vegetation of the pre-dynastic era and which became complete during the whole of the Kush Kingdom period had cremated the region and became so bare and hot at this time. The desert encroachment hemmed in the remaining populations and their livestock to the immediate confines west and east of the main Nile River, and pasture areas became scarce or insufficient for the livestock. The environment was extremely hot in a desert region with virtually no trees or grass. Loneliness was another factor, since all the Nilotic communities which were with them had all gone away from the region. They were already east of Khartoum.

Those were the reasons which made the Jaang abandon that area between Atbara and the sixth cataract. They therefore came to the Khartoum area in their totality and settled almost the whole of what are the present Khartoum state areas of today as earlier explained.

CHAPTER NINE:
THE JÄÄNG MIGRATION FROM THE KHARTOUM REGION TO BLUE AND UPPER NILES

INTRODUCTION

In the last chapter, we tried to tackle the Dinka by having to trace their ancestors since their arrival from Egypt, following that clamorous year of the exodus, to the Wawat area in ancient Northern Sudan. We also tried to surface how another group led by Jieldit later came from Judea by way of the Red Sea through Bab el Mandeb and joined the main Jääng community in the area of Wawat in that northernmost part of ancient Sudan. A group led by Jök-Athurkök that came after Jieldit was also discussed in that chapter. We then tackled the Dinka forebears, covering how they became the Jaang tribe and their role and place in the formation of that more than a millennium old kingdom of Kush. We thoroughly discussed them through that ancient period up to how they came to the Khartoum region during the late Iron Age times prior to the Mediaeval Ages.

This chapter will tackle our Dinka ancestors as they migrated out from the Khartoum region to both the Blue and Upper Nile areas and how they became Southern Sudanese along with their former Nilotic communities. It will cover the Middle Ages, which is also called the Mediaeval Ages, that time when Dinka ancestors were in the Nile Basin region called the Upper Nile. This chapter in history, the Middle Ages, will begin to reveal the Jääng people in a more detailed way. There will be more and more Mediaeval figures than the last chapter, when we only knew of the names of patriarchs, kings and common ancestors. Sections, which are today's national communities of the Dinka as are clans, will begin to vividly appear in this Mediaeval period.

Some of the Dinka readers will also begin to acknowledge their Mediaeval ancestors as this historical narrative on Jaang society will appear a bit clearer. This phase in our descending account on the origin of the Dinka will also shed light on the violent relations which came up between the Jaang and their former Nilotic communities, violent relations which characterised this Mediaeval era, especially between the Nuers and the Jaang, and between the Jaang and the Murle. This was also the era of those epidemic diseases that sought to bring to extinction some of the Jaang sections, prompting large parts of the society to vacate Upper Nile ecology to Bahr el Ghazal, also following part of the Luo people who went there at the beginning of the Mediaeval era. With this synoptic summary of what chapter nine will give us about the Jaang and their Nilotic peoples, we shall now begin our narrative on the Jaang migration to the Upper and Blue Nile areas from the Khartoum region.

JÄÄNG FIRST CONTACT WITH THE ARABS (THE STORY OF AWALAD ABBAS)

Long before the fall of Meroe small bands of Arab tribesmen like the Juhiena Arabs had started to infiltrate into the middle Nile region, an area lying between what is present Abu Hamad and the Sabaloqa areas near Khartoum. They trailed into this Nilotic heartland region through southern Egypt by way of what was known as the Atamiir Desert which descends to cover the present Abu Hamad areas. They used to come as traders and mingled with our Nilotic peoples who were in this Napata-Dongola Great Nile bend region. As traders they moved up and down the Nile in between the 3rd and 6th cataracts, selling the articles they used to bring from Egypt or Arabia through the Sinai route. Other itinerants also trekked into this middle Nile region through the Bëja country in Eastern Sudan. Some of these traders settled among the Jaang people in the Butana steppes areas. From the 4th cataract southwards the land was a green flora with patchy fauna. The land was still good for the Jääng society and their livestock. Nomadic and sedentary life was simultaneously practised by the Jääng in this area and for those decades before they moved to the Khartoum region, peaceful infiltrant parties trailed in and gradually settled, intermixed by some form of social contact with our Jääng forebears, and this did not cause any concern in the area.

During this time a certain *Abbas* is presented by Jaang traditions to have been one of those emigrant Arabs who had earlier come and settled with an old Jaang patriarch, Deŋgdit. After a nice stay with him, Deŋgdit is said to have given him one of his daughters by the name of Acol, a girl with whom Abbas bore a number of children, who became the first among the founding fathers of the present Ja'alyin Arabs in Northern Sudan.

The Arab Ja'ali tribe seemed to include all those riverine dwellers between Dongola and Khartoum, but the Ja'alyin proper are those who live between Atbara and Khartoum, particularly those in the present Jeilly areas. Ja'ali people say they are descendants of Abbas, who was one of the uncles of Prophet Mohammed. This is through an eponymous ancestor, Ibrahim Ja'al. However, on the strength of some Mediaeval Arab sources, it was the lineage of Umeyya, Omar and Abu Baker, groups of the Quraysh Arab tribe of the prophet Mohammed, who entered Sudan well before the official entry of the Arabs into Sudan in 642 AD. There has not been a clear mention of an Abbasi migration into Sudan, nevertheless, there were individual trading itinerants from Abbas descent and who came and settled among the Jääng in that Matemma-Atbara area and later in the Khartoum region. Among them was this Abbas who subsequently became a son-in-law to the Jääng patriarch Deŋgdit.

In support of this, and tracing from all the Arabs' traditions, one tradition says that descendants of Ibrahim Ja'al migrated from the oasis region in Western Egypt because of the war between them and the people of Umeyya, and from that part of Egypt they trailed to Dongola and to Berber and further south to the Matemma and Shendi areas. Here, some sources attest they found the Jaang still in those areas long after the fall of Meroe and before the Jääng came to the Khartoum area.

However, Dinkas' own traditions suggest that shortly after their arrival to the Matemma areas small groups of Arab stock began to radiate out from the country of the Blemmyes and settle on the east of the Nile region between Khartoum and Meroe, in the Al Banaga plains where they later moved to the Jeilly area which was then settled by the Pagong people of Jieldit. Some of those Arabs later settled in Khartoum among the family of Deŋgdit. Here, Dinka traditions continue to say that Abbas came as a single-handed young man and settled with this Deŋgdit who was then the overlord Spear Master and *bäny* of all Jaang people in the Khartoum region. This Deŋgdit was a man from the Payol clan. Other traditions say he was from the Pajök clan, the people of Jök-Athurkök. Whichever is the truth, Deŋgdit was the Jääng fait accompli spiritual leader in this Khartoum area. According to this source Abbas proved a faithful cowboy of Deŋgdit, making the great liege pleased with him. Deŋgdit in time decided to give him his daughter Acol and when he died after good old age, he is said to have willed his authority, his family and his Jääng society to this Abbas, who temporarily became patron over the Jääng people in the whole of the Khartoum region. In those decades the Jääng began to witness more groups of Arab traders joining this Abbas. Together with the children of Acol, those Arabs of Abbas were regarded by Deŋgdit's family and, indeed, by the entire Jääng society, as *'Paan-Acol'*, that is, 'the people of Acol'. On their part, those Arab trading settlers of Abbas regarded the Jääng people of Deŋgdit as *Awalad Abbas*, meaning *people of Abbas.*

It was from this social interaction that the Ja'alyin Arabs in Sudan later began to convolute history by continuously calling the Dinka Awalad Abbas, as if the Jääng people were themselves descendants of Abbas! Rather, it is the Ja'alyin who are of Jääng blood through Acol, daughter of Deŋgdit. If so, there is no denying that some particular sections of the Dinka which directly descended from Deŋgdit have some maternal blood relationship with the Ja'alyin section of Abbas by way of those children of Acol. Perhaps to overemphasise the whole process, the Dinka people can be regarded as being the maternal uncles of the Ja'alyin, particularly the Payol people. By maternal blood from Acol and by that social and historical association, Dinka people are, however, related to the Ja'alyin, but the Ja'alyin historical claim which takes the whole Dinka nation as Awalad Abbas is not grounded on a patrilineal truth and is therefore an exaggerated popular tradition which has unnecessarily persisted from Sudanese traditions for over a century now.

From what happened in Meroë in 350 AD, Jääng society must have spent nearly a century to arrive in this Khartoum region where they stayed for almost another century. They arrived in Khartoum at about the beginning of the 4th century AD and by about 450 AD or a bit towards the end of that century they again moved out of the Khartoum region in a final migration that took them away entirely from Northern Sudan. Our discussion of the Jääng migration to Southern

Sudan will also tackle the migration of the other Nilotic tribes to the Blue and White" Nile regions and we will discuss how those Nilotics came to be in Upper Nile and Bahr el Ghazal while others, like the Funj and the Uduk, remained to be people of the southern Blue Nile areas to the present day. Firstly let us discuss how the Jääng settled in the Khartoum region.

JAANG SETTLEMENT AREAS IN KHARTOUM

When the Jääng people came to the Khartoum region from Matemma and from Al Banaga-Shendi-Atbara areas north of Khartoum, they settled in this Khartoum region for more than half a century. The group of families that are now the Padang cultural group settled around their patriarch Jieldit, who chose to settle north of Khartoum, an area which is now known as Jeilly, so named after him. This is the area where the entire Padang would later depart the Khartoum area for the present Rabek-Jebellein areas in the White Nile areas of the northern Upper Nile.

The Jääng sections of Abiɛl that initially came from Egypt and which included the whole of what is now Rek society settled in all those areas that are Omdurman and Khartoum as far as Jebel Aulia, and those Omdurman areas that are now the Sudan military college area which the Arabs later renamed *Wadi Saidna*, the valley of our master.

The cattle revering clans (Pawutweng, Paderek etc.) settled into all those areas which the Dinka had called *Tiäptiäp*, south of Omdurman. This is where much from the Jaang cattle used to be kept during rainy seasons. Layers of cow dung piled many metres high underlay the present Fatihap township. Construction activities in this part of Omdurman city had always shown *arop*, the cow dung, dug out metres deep from the ground. Those who settled in those areas that are the present Buri township area where the Sudan police college is situated on the Blue" Nile River, a few kms to the centre of Khartoum city, were a Jääng people called Kuac and who are our present Twic Dinka people. There were among them a number of the Payol clan lineages, however. This is the area where Kuac departed Khartoum at the time of the Jääng migration away to the Upper Nile.

The Duör section people of Mayuääl, including the Paral clan people of rock stone and of the bladed spear, as well as the people of Great Mariik who are our present Gok Dinka, all settled those areas which are now the east and west townships of Duem. Those places are currently called *Duem el Shargia* and *Duem el Garbia*. The Athɔɔc and Adhiɔɔk, now Bor Dinka, covered those areas of Jebel Aulia, Bager and those as far as the Soba vicinity where they converged with the Nuers at the present area called Masit.

The Nuers had extended up to the present Juneid sugar factory area. Deŋgdit, who, as legend tells it, was later taken up perhaps to heaven by a whirlwind and disappeared into the sky, had settled with his Payol clan people at what is now Khartoum centre, including present Sudan republican palace headquarters' vicinity and up to what is the present Khartoum hospital area, the railways quarter area and the whole of the military general headquarters area as far as Khartoum international airport. Part of the Jaang also settled in those places that are present *Umbada* where it is said a sort of concubinage later started to be practised between the first Arab trading settlers and the Jääng girls, thereby producing offspring believed to have then formed a society which the Arabs of recent times regarded as the first national beginning point, hence the name Umbada, the nation's beginning, which is currently one of the Khartoum city townships, west of Omdurman.

Although the Luo, the Funj and Burun tribes settled a bit far off from the main Khartoum city and its Omduman areas, and were staying in those areas which later became known as Halfa el Muluk up through *Um Dom* to Soba, the Shulluk component of the Luo had split up to what later became Khartoum North, which present Khartoumers have come to call *Khartoum Bahri*, so named after a certain Bari of Mamluk descent. Bari came there as a running figurative from Mohammed Ali Pasha's onslaught on the Mamluk in Egypt some time around the 1840s.

The Shilluks covered all those places such as the Kobar prison area and its outlying suburbs that included the present industrial area of Khartoum North township where they met with the Jääng sections of Padang who extended from Jeilly up to the present Shambat area. The Shilluks even settled those areas now called *Dor-Shaab* and *Hela Kuku* townships as well as the whole of what is now Haj Yusif on the east bank of the Blue" Nile part of Khartoum. The Funj in fact settled in the present Soba area before the Jääng could extend there.

All the Nilotic tribes who had lived with the Jääng since Kush Kingdom times and up to this Khartoum area knew the present Dinka people as Jääng, the original ancient name for the tribe.

LUO-FUNJ AND BURUN MIGRATION AWAY FROM THE KHARTOUM REGION

While all the Nilotic communities have came to the Khartoum region, the former Heartland region of the black race (Matemma-Atbara-Meroe-Napata and Dongola areas) continued to be the corridor of insecurity from the desert-tested hordes called Blemmyes. The threat also came from the cattle seeking inland tribes from Western Sudan and with increased infiltration by Arab trading itinerants, trailing in from Egypt to the north and from Arabia across the Red Sea in the east, the Shilluk community with the rest of Luo tribes, including the Funj and Burum communities, all decided to vacate their settlement areas in the Khartoum region. They migrated further southwards along both banks of the two Niles. The Shilluks who took the White Nile direction first settled at what became known in subsequent times as the *Aba Island* area. Until late 18th century AD this island was still being inhabited by the Shilluks before the Arabs later came in and occupied it and the name continued to resist all the Arab racial attempts to Arabise every piece of land in Sudan Jääng and the Nuers later got them in the current *Pakan* village which was settled by a Shilluk landed gentry by the name of *Abuor*. The Luo covered those areas of Jebellein up to the Tunga-Fashoda and Kodok areas. This Shilluk, Funj and Burun migration away from the Khartoum areas took place during the first decade of the 4th century AD. The Nuers made their migration another decade later.

Until the beginning of the 4th century AD the rest of the Nile valley region south of Khartoum was but a vast stretch of unsettled, uninhabitable wasteland up to the confluence area of the Blue and White Niles. It was a terrible and inscrutable swampland of what is geographically called *sudd*, probably the largest swampland in the world. Such an inscrutable destiny of swampland appeared at that time to have not been lived in by any human. No society could exist in the sudd since it is 90% water with an endless mass of rotting vegetation from interwoven tree-like vines with steaming heat coming out of a massive expand of papyrus reed filled from the underneath with all forms of man-killing mosquitoes, primeval crocodiles and hippopotamuses. This is in addition to other tropical and marine creatures, including remnants of an extinct race of dinosaurs that continued to threaten any human existence in the Upper Nile and parts of Bahr el Ghazal for centuries. There also existed all forms of fish, primeval turtles called ayuomlual and all types of snakes and pythons called *nyieel*.

It was this type of ecology of primeval swamp, vast expanses of tropical rainforests and a virtually unknown wasteland which Nilotic communities were forced to come to through conditions in Northern Sudan. That inscrutable environment was what our Nilotic communities set themselves against! The ever increasing insecurity coming from Egypt and from the barbaric desert tribesmen posed a continued threat. The menace posed by the Sahara Desert encroachment coming from the north west and from the east, combined to pressure our Nilotic ancestors out of the Khartoum region where they were hemmed in from all directions and confined within the narrower and narrower limits of the River Nile ecology that caused great conglomeration in those limited survival areas. This only resulted in a phenomenon of great migrations characteristic to not only the Niloties but the whole of the black race which happened to live in the Napata Meroe region, the then known concentration heartland of the black race.

While the Shilluks and the other components of the Luo community left their settlement areas in Khartoum North and took due south using the White Nile route, the Funj and Burum took the southeastern direction, going along the Blue" Nile River. The Funj later settled in those areas that are present Makwar up to Sennar where they and the Shilluks later founded another blacks' kingdom, the sultanate of Sennar history called the *Funj kingdom* of Sennar.

NUERS' MIGRATION FROM THE KHARTOUM REGION TO WESTERN UPPER NILE IN SOUTHERN SUDAN

As explained earlier the Nuers were the first to follow the first Nilotic communities, taking the footsteps of the Luo. They, however, took to the west bank route of the White Nile right from Aba Island in the present Kosti and Rabek areas. According to some Nuer traditions, the Nuer community made a long trek until they came to settle in the area which is the present Bentiu locality in western Upper Nile. They succeeded in avoiding the true sudd, called toch" land. Here, in this Nuers' springboard area, they later moved to an area called

Koat-Liec, west of Bahr el Jebel. Then, in this area which became the first Nuers' homeland in Southern Sudan, the Nuers divided into what became 'Gee' and 'A'ak groups, which in effect became the Western and Eastern Nuεrs of today. The present Gaijook, Gaijaak, Gaguaang and the Gawεεr Nuεrs later crossed the White Nile from this Koat-Liec early Mediaeval homeland to areas of the present day Nasir region in eastern Upper Nile. The Gawεεr Nuers, however, branched to the eastern areas of Zeray.

JÄÄNG MIGRATION FROM THE KHARTOUM AREA TO NORTHERN UPPER NILE IN SOUTHERN SUDAN

From what we have read above, the Jääng was the last Nilotic community to depart Northern Sudan at Khartoum. As the biggest sector of the Nilotics and a community with known marshal tradition since the Napata and Meroitic eras, they were not very much threatened by the insecurity which set the blacks into a migratory flight that compelled them to aimlessly move into that inscrutable destiny called sudd. But some decades after all the Nilotics had gone away from that volatile Northern Sudan and the issue of pastures became acute as desertification impact was now more intense than ever before, the Jaang community considered moving out of the Khartoum region all together. This was after sufficient surveys were made by different section leaders. Differences arose, however, over whether to go to the Blue" Nile to follow the Funj and Burun people or to follow the Nuers and the Luo. Differences also arose over the leadership of that migratory move.

Great Spear Master Kur Deng of the Redior House of the Mayuääl people was proposed by Duör and other Jääng sections to lead the migration. But Ayueel the Great has had a family tradition which made him seen by many as the supposed overall leader of that migration. This was on account of the successful migration earlier led by his ancestor Jieldit in the 7th century BC, migration which involved his miraculous crossing of the Red Sea. Ayueel and his family had a convincing claim that Padang, Pabɛɛk, Redior and other sections were the making of his great grandfather, Jieldit, who led those tribal sections of the future Jääng to Northern Sudan from Judea.

The third group led by Great Jök of the Payöl had organised the largest sector of Jaang under him and was regarded as the overall patriarch of Jääng society in the Khartoum region. His father, Deŋgdit, until his miraculous departure by whirlwind up into the sky or heaven, had been the paramount bäny of the entire Jaang in this Khartoum region. Coming from the traditional descent line of Great Abiɛl who led those sections of Jacobites to later become Jaang in ancient Sudan, Jökdit did have overall claim over the entire Jaang and so he was also seen as the paramount patriarch to lead the society into that hazardous region of unknown destiny.

With these claims and disagreements the Jääng, however decided to migrate out of Khartoum using three different routes, with three different overall spiritual leaders. The first column to depart was the faction of clans and sections which decided to go to the Blue" Nile region. This column was under the overall lordship of Great Kur Deng and the Redior clan people. The second was the faction headed by Ayueel the Great and his faction and consisted of the entire Padang. The third was that of Rek and its associated sections of Jääng which came from Egypt with great Abiɛl. It was led by the Pahöl great Spear Master Jök Deng Tɔng. This faction took the west bank route of the White Nile, the route earlier taken by the Nuɛrs. As they were direct descendants of Ajääng they were more related to the Nuers. This explains why they wanted to take the path trod by the Nuers.

With all these matters sorted out the Jaang finally decided to vacate all the areas of Khartoum-Omdurman-Jeilly. The Jääng went away from the Khartoum areas in its entirety. The departure took place during the autumn season in the year 490 AD. But the whole Jääng society first went out and encamped at what is now Hassahessa from where the three routes were now undertaken.

THE BLUE NILE ROUTE COLUMN

Here, the Redior elder Kur Deng on the head of this column first performed the usual rituals for the sections which chose to go under this leadership. This group included the Paral clan who were under Great Marol Deng, and the whole of Duör that later became Agaar Dinka. They included those sections which later became Aliap, the Adhiɔɔk and Athɔɔc section people later to become Bor Dinka, the Gok people of Mariik, the Anie section people and a splinter faction of Rek which later remained in the southern Blue" Nile area of Karŋkaraŋ where they adopted a new name, Regarik. Like the Dinka of today they still say 'piu' for water among other similarities in their language.

While the Funj had gone up to Fazzugli, now called *Wadi Said* in the eastern Blue" Nile area, those Jääng people who went to the Blue Nile areas first settled in those places that are now *Sinja Abdalla, Masmum Adali, Bakori, Hudur, Nibelo* and the *Belagola* areas where the Regariks remain to the present day. The Duör and Gok sections went as far as those areas which are now Kurmuk and present Ingessana Hills' territory. They even went as far as the Lake Tana areas.

This Jääng column had little resistance from the Funj who first settled those areas in between the northern Upper Nile and Blue" Nile Rivers, places such as the present Geiger and Jalhak areas including Jebellein and Rabek. The Uduk, who are a pre-Nilotic matrilineal people, had settled in those areas that are the present

Shalifil, Khor-Yabus and Maiwut. The Burun settled in their present areas of Maban and Dago. The Luo had covered that strip of land all the way from Aba Island to Banjang and parts of the Jebellein areas as well as those parts west of Kodok and the areas of present Fashoda and Kaka up to Lela. Part of the Luo covered those areas of present Anakdiar, Abuöng and the areas of Yakuac. They also settled in what is now the Wau, Ayod and Dukein areas currently inhabited by the Nyarweng and ɣöl Dinka sections. The Luo had also covered all those areas that are present Amuogöök.

The Pere, the present Lokoro tribe, the Luo people who later became Kalenjiin, the Karmoyöng, Dedos and the Lango, all were later made by Jääng arrival to proceed to beyond the present Bahr el Jebel section of the White Nile, the region which historians had always described as the *Kapoeta-Lake Turkana- ImaTɔng Mountains triangle Area* where they formed a Nilotic society who were later joined by Nilo-Hamites from the Ethiopian highlands and before the complete coming of the Jaang tribes from the northern Upper Nile after having come from the Khartoum region.

The Bɛɛr group of tribes such as Paköt, the Murle, Taposa and the Turkana had covered all those areas that are present Waat, Walgak, Jönglei as well as the areas as far as Pibor and the present Kashipo Hills, extending up to the present Taposa areas. The Boya and Didinga also settled within those places. This was the state of the Upper Nile Basin region before the Jääng came from Khartoum and later from the northern Upper Nile region. The Upper Nile Basin area was therefore pioneered by the aforementioned Nilotic societies who have been the Nilotic communities in the '*black heartland of the race*' and who left the Jaang in the Khartoum area several decades back. This part of the Nile valley, the Upper Nile region, including the southern Blue" Nile areas or all those areas from Khartoum southwards to Kapoeta, appears to have not been inhabited or tramped upon by any human as there were no apparent migrants who had ever preceded those Nilotic communities except for the bushmen who may have extended up to this area from beyond the Great Lakes region but who later retreated backwards. Prior to the coming of the bushmen the region is believed to have been home for prehistoric man as there can be no denying that prehistoric man in the East African region had been roaming those areas before and after the geological changes that created the Nile, the great East African Rift Valley, the Plateaus and the great East African Mountains, including the various lakes of the East African region. It can be admitted that there must have been humans up to this part of the Nile valley before man proceeded northwards to North Africa, Europe and the Middle East or Asia, but that was in those primordial times.

THE WHITE NILE ROUTE COLUMN

The second route taken by the Jääng after leaving Hassahessa was the White Nile route. Those sections of the Jääng which came to the northern Upper Nile areas by the White Nile route were the biggest column in contrast to the group that went to the Blue" Nile areas. Without going into those minute details of clans, tribes and sections which used this route, the column was composed of the societies led by the two main patriarchs, Great Jök and Great Ayueel.[135]

Upon their departure at Hassahessa each section made the necessary rituals as was done by the Blue Nile column of Kur Deng.[136] As

---

[135] CA Willis, The cult of Deng, SNR, Vol. xi(1928), Pp.196-208; I Bedri, Notes on Dinka religious beliefs in their hereditary chiefs and rain makers, SNR, Vol. xxii, (1939), pp. 25-31; More notes on the Padang Dinka, SNR, Vol. xxix, (1948), pp. 40-48 and G Lienhardt, op cit , pp. 171-218.

[136] Kenneth Okeny, 'Political structures and institutions in Southern Sudan', (1820-1885) (in) The role of Southern Sudanese in the building of modern Sudan, K.U.P. (1989), p. 35 and L Leek Mawut, Introduction to Dinka resistance to condominium rule 1902 -1932, Unpublished Monograph No. 3 , (1983), U of K, p. 4.

was the case in those days of great Nilotic migrations there was an expectation of violent resistance from those who pioneered or inhabited the Upper Nile Basin region. Generally this column consisted of the big Rek and its sections and the groups that later became Padang consisting of Kuac, later to become Twic. The column also consisted of Angääc and all those sections that later became Ruweng, Nyarweng and all the Marbek group of clans including Palual or the entire rock stone and bladed spear revering groups. The column also consisted of those sections of Adöör, Adol, Areem, Awan, Pakaak, the fire and cattle revering groups of clans and many others. As was the case with the Blue" Nile groups the whole migration was a planned, pre-meditated arrangement. All the provisions were taken and livestock driven, and despite the division into three routes as part of the moving column took the west bank route earlier taken by the Nuers while another part used the east bank route, they were able to group themselves by sections, by clans and families, each headed by a Spear Master or a culture hero, but all under the overall guidance of the paramount Spear Master of their time. In the case of this White Nile column the overall leadership was finally conceded to Ayueeldit with Great Jök as the second in command. Although the Jääng went to either the Blue or White Nile, they were all the same, moving as Jaang. The White Nile column followed in the footsteps of their preceding Nilotes, the Luo and the Nuers.

LUO RESISTANCE TO JAANG MIGRATION INTO NORTHERN UPPER NILE

Slightly after the Aba Island area, the Jaang column of the east bank of the White Nile met a stiff resistance and this made the west bank column of Great Jök cross to the east bank to join the attacked column of Ayueeldit. The two columns now combined into a morning to evening moving long and endless column, fighting one battle after the other. The column succeeded in forcing its way through those areas up to present Jebellein, Jalhak and the areas that are present Geiger. The final decisive battle of history, the battle in which the Jääng was to now continue as a victoriously marshal community on the White Nile, was the battle which was fought at Ärän in around 491 AD. Ärän came from the Jääng word *Rén* which is the plural of *ran,* meaning grave in Dinka.

This historic battle of Ärän is important for the Jääng community for three important reasons. Firstly, it showed great Jaang marshal exploit and ingenuity with which it broke the resistance and penetrated further into the Upper Nile Basin's interior, displacing much of the Upper Nile Basin's original inhabitants. Secondly, that success was a result of the coming together of the two columns of the White Nile route. It permanently sowed the seeds of unity to face any future threat from any community within the region, and the third reason for its importance was that the battle of Ärän legitimised the Renk area as a permanent territory of the Jaang society to the present day.

Present Renk town evolved its name from that Jaang word Ärän. Some sources in the localities have different versions of the name Renk. The area is presently inhabited by the Abialang Dinka community. It has not been inhabited by any community other than Jääng since that battle of 491 AD to the present day.

After the historic battle of Ärän, the Luo, Funj and Burun's resistance faltered. The entire Funj vacated the northern Upper Nile areas and went to the southern Blue" Nile. Those of Burun went to what are the present Maban areas where they continue to live today. The Luo communities broke up. A section of them crossed to the west bank of the White Nile where they settled in those areas that are present Wadakona before they further migrated to what is now Bahr el Ghazal by way of the present Biemnhom corridor. Part of the Luo which later proceeded to Eastern Equatoria and on to Uganda became the Ateker speaking peoples who are the Karamoyöng, Itesyo, Jie and others.[137] Part of this wave later went west but came back to the Nile areas in the 16th century. They became the ancestors of the present Bari, Pojulu, Lotuho or Latuka and the Kwakwa.[138]

After Funj, Burun and Luo vacated this area presently called northern Upper Nile state, Jääng sections of the White Nile column began to settle in it. They settled by fanning to the surrounding areas of the present Bewum territory of Abialang Dinka to the north west of Renk. Large parts settled further north up to those areas such as Kurwiir which is present Jebellein and those areas where the holy shrine of Great Ayueeldit is now situated. The area became identified with Ayueeldit so that it acquired a name from him. It is called Khor-Ayueel to the present day. The Dinka people call this holy shrine *Luak of Ayueeldit*. The Arab Baggara tribe known as *Sabaah* who now inhabit that territory still call it Khor-Ayueel to the present day. This holy shrine area is about 40 kms north of Jebellein towards Rabek in Northern Sudan's White Nile state.

From Renk town and its outlying areas to the north as far as Kurwiir (Jebellein) and southeast to those areas of Bur-Acol which is the modern Malakal city area and its outlying territory east of the White Nile River, all this land space on the Nile after Rabek became the first Jääng settlement area, from where they were able to sustain their forwards and sideways expansion. From here they were able to displace the original pioneers to beyond the present Bor land in southern Upper Nile. Except for the Luo parts which later became the Shilluk, Anyuak, Acholi and Jur-col, Luo sections that went to the Bahr el Ghazal region, the rest of the Luo tribes and the Nilo-Hamites who lived in this Basin region were effectively pushed to the Lake Turkana–Kapoeta–Imatong Mountain triangle region which is now Eastern Equatoria state.

---

137   Ibid, p. 35.
138   John Ryle, The Dinka: Warriors of the Nile, (1978), p. 36

All those Nilotic and Nilo-Hamitic societies who were to migrate away from this Upper Nile Basin region knew it was the Jaang Nilotic community that had fought them out of the region. Except for the Murle, the Jaang did not come into any hostile contact with all those Nilotes any longer, as many of them later proceeded headlong to other countries such as Kenya and Uganda. When the Jaang later migrated to Bahr el Ghazal many centuries later, large parts of the Luo abandoned Bahr el Ghazal and came back to the Upper Nile Basin region where they became Shilluks who went to the northern Upper Nile areas where they are today. A part of them became Anyuak, which went to the Sudan-Ethiopia border region where they are to the present day, while the Luo part, which became Acholi, followed the greater Luo southern migrating communities only to settle in the Eastern Equatoria area of Torit. The Jur-col and Chat, however, decided to remain in Bahr el Ghazal where they continued to maintain peaceful relations with the Jääng. They know the Jääng people as *Ujango* still, from the name Jaang. A small faction of the Luo which later became the present *Jur-Mananer* also remained in Bahr el Ghazal where they were assimilated into the Dinka. Some of them now live in Apuk-Giir in the eastern parts of Gogrial and some live in Luo-Ariik as people of Tonj North. They lived in the most fertile area of the toch between the Bul section of the Nuers and the Lou-Ariik community. Except for the Nuers and the very tenacious Murle, the Jaang became the only master race in the Upper Nile region and it was from this that Jaang society acquired its description as the 'warriors of the White Nile.'[139]

By about the 8th century AD, the time of Abbasid Caliphate in the Arab world including Egypt,[140] the Jääng departed all the areas north of Renk and moved further south along the east bank of the

---

139   Ibid.

140   Ibid.

White Nile. They moved with their livestock because the northern Upper Nile began to lack proper pasture for their cattle which had started to increase after they took much of the cattle of the Nilotic tribes who they defeated in the region. The hitherto desert climate of Northern Sudan had at this time arrived to the northern Upper Nile areas and the environment was no longer conducive for the Jääng and their huge livestock.

Up to about 1000 AD all sectors of the Jääng had come into the Upper Nile Basin areas, still fighting with several of the Nilotic societies, especially the Murle to the east and the Nuers to the west across the White Nile. By this time the Nuer community was still in the western Upper Nile areas of Bentiu and Koat-Liec and were waging raids from there for Jääng cattle. Even the Blue" Nile faction of the Jääng had at this time come from the southern Blue Nile areas of Kurmuk and had joined the rest of the Jaang in those areas that are now central and southern Upper Nile, including the present Pangak Peninsula and Jonglei areas.

First to arrive and settle in those central and southern Upper Nile areas were those Dinka sections called Arëëm, Adöl, Awan, Pakaak, and this later became the Marbek group. These sections came to the present Twic and Bor areas. The Rek, Luac and sections called Padang Dinka occupied the central Upper Nile areas including those areas presently inhabited by the Nyarweng, Hol and Duör.

JÄÄNG MIGRATION FROM KURMUK TO SOUTHERN UPPER NILE

By about the end of the 5th century AD, the Jääng sections that went to the southern Blue" Nile appeared to have all moved to the White Nile Basin region. According to versions from the various Dinka tribes whose ancestral sections had once been to the southern Blue

Nile, this Jääng faction decided to remigrate to join the rest of their brethren on the White Nile owing to a number of reasons. Firstly, the region was so rugged a country that their cattle did not do well in such a mountainous area. The Ethiopian highland communities, the Galla tribes in particular, had also bothered them with raids for their cattle. Besides, there were many of the Nilotic communities having vacated southern the Upper Nile areas to Eastern Equatoria who also encouraged their decision to move so as to fill the vacuum.

All these reasons made the Blue Nile faction of Jääng come to the Upper Nile but they used the route that brought them to those areas that are now the Bor, Dukein and present Twic-East areas. They left the Kurmuk and Lake Tana areas and came through places which are now Jumjum, Balila, and Gufa and then to the desert area now called the desert of Aying. Here they met the Murle with whom they instantly entered into war for stepping into their territory. Then, they proceeded till they reached those areas that are present Jale Payam in the present Jonglei region.

By AD 1000 the entire Jääng was now in the Upper Nile Basin area and here arose the perpetual issue of the Nuers and the Murle, two communities which made the Jääng be at war almost throughout those centuries of the early Mediaeval era prior to the migration of some of them to the Bahr el Ghazal region during the first quarter of 1300 AD. This leads us to the history of the Jääng-Nuer traditional vendetta.

NUER-JÄÄNG MYTH OF ORIGIN

According to Dinka oral accounts, there was Deŋgdit, Deng the Great, who was an ancient man of the Napatan period. This Deŋgdit is believed to be from the primogenitary descent line of patriarch Abiɛl who led a faction that later became the Jääng and the Nuers in Sudan. Deŋgdit was a man of pre-Kush Kingdom time in the northern part of Northern Sudan. He is said to have given birth to two sons, Ajääng the eldest and Manuɛr the youngest. Ajääng later became the founding ancestor of the Jääng, whose descendants are the present Dinka, while Manuɛr became the founding father of the present Nuɛr society. The two had a sister by the name of Achan Deng. She was called so because she was a twin, Angɛɛr having perished at birth. Their mother, it is said, was a certain Agäär.[141]

When Deŋgdit became too old, at the verge of death he decided to give over his only two personal cows to his two sons. The two cows were *Acol*, a black cow by colour, and its heifer *Nyayar*, a whitish colour. Deŋgdit is said to have called on his two sons and declared to them that the old cow Acol had to go to the elder son while its heifer Nyayar was to belong to the younger son, Manuɛr. This was a will from their old father. They were to take them to their herds in their kraals later in the evening when the cattle had returned from grazing.

In the evening, and before Manuɛr could come to his father for his lot, Ajääng did what Jacob did to his elder brother Esau when by pretence, Jacob deceived his blind old father Isaac to give him the special blessing that was due to Esau.[142] Ajääng preempted his younger brother and came to his father much earlier because he did not appreciate the old cow apportioned to him. Deŋgdit was like the Jewish Isaac. He was so old that his eyesight had failed him and he could not see. Ajääng requested him to let him take his apportioned cow, *Nyayar*, and tried to mimic the accent and voice of Manuɛr in order to take the heifer. Not knowing it was Ajääng, who had disapproved of his old cow Acol, Ajääng went away with Nyayar, having been blessed for him by his father.

---

141   From an interview with a group of Gok Dinka elders in Abiriu Payam, Cuɛibɛt county, May 18, 2002. These elders were; (i) Riààk Majak from the Pajul clan, (ii) Mathèèt Nguɛnjang of the Pateny clan, (iii) Agot Anyuon Mabior of the Paduguɛr clan and (iv) Adɛkwut Dhuok of the Pathoth clan.

142   The Amplified Bible (Gen-27, vs 1-46), Lockman Foundation, Zonder vary, (1987), pp. 43-44.

When Manuɛr came afterward and called on his father to take his heifer, the old liege became surprised when he realised it was Ajääng and not Manuɛr who came first and took the heifer. Deŋgdit noted anger in Manuɛr but, he advised his younger son to contend with the old cow, saying Ajaang was after all the firstborn and that there was no way of recovering Nyayar from the elder son. All the same, Manuɛr was so furious he began to weep. At this point Deŋgdit told Manuɛr to go and find his own way of getting his heifer from Ajääng. Manuɛr therefore went away with the old cow Acol with a bitter disappointment. He subsequently tried all avenues to recover the heifer when their father had died. Manuɛr staged one fight after another against Ajääng but Ajääng and his children kept defeating him all the time. As the elder brother Ajääng did have the opportunity to marry twice before Manuɛr, and his children grew up before those of Manuɛr.

In this way Manuɛr could not match Ajääng. All his attempts to recover Nyayar failed and so Manuɛr and his children later declared separation with Ajääng. He moved away with his family and settled further away to the south in the region of the present Matemma locality where he stayed for several decades.

Ajääng and his family remained in the Dongola area of Napata. The two brothers and their offspring had therefore started to live separately. As years went by, decade after decade, the two began to be separate families with the first calling themselves Paan-Ajääng, descendants or family lineage of Ajääng, and the latter as Paan-Manuɛr, the descendants or family of Manuɛr.

In time, this people of Ajaang became known as the Jääng from where the name *Jääng* or Jieng was later evolved.

The people of Manuɛr later became known as Nuɛr. The 'M' and 'A' letters before Nuɛr and Ajääng were dropped in the course of time as both societies of Ajääng and Manuɛr grew separately as cattle rearing people in the region between the 3rd cataract and Shendi and even during their stay in Khartoum.

THE DINKA HISTORY 643

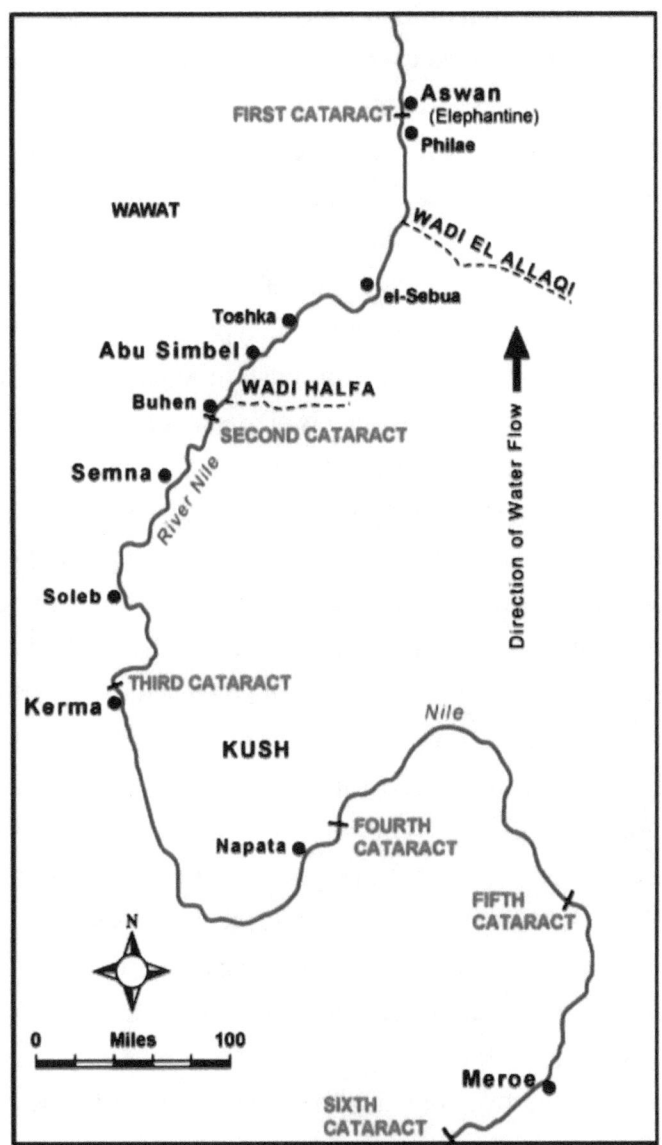

Fig 52: Showing Wadi el Allagi, the birthplace of Ajääng and Manuɛr in ancient Northern Sudan

.With the destruction of Meroë city by the Abyssinian forces from Axum, the Nuers stepped away from the Matemma–Shendi areas and came to settle at Khartoum North.

The Jääng society, however, remained behind. They came to the Matemma, Shendi and Al-Banaqa areas where the Nuers left for Khartoum North some decades earlier. The Jaang appears to have spent the rest of the 3rd century there between present Khartoum and Meroe with subsequent incursions from a people then known as the Blemmyes who used to come from Eastern Sudan, others Western Sudan. The inland tribes immediately started to come in after the fall of Meroe and Ajääng people subsequently decided to follow suit.

They slowly migrated along the west and east banks of the main Nile till they came to settle in the Jarjar[143] (that is present Omdurman) area as far as the whole of what is the present Khartoum city area and its outlying suburbs. Splinter parts of the Jääng, however, remained behind. These were the Pagong people of Jieldit, the Paral people of the bladed spear and the Ruaal people of Mayuaal. They settled in the areas south of Al-Matemma and as far as Shendi up to what is today's Jeily area. This was in about 430 AD. Those clans and sections of Jääng, later Arabs, joined the rest of the bulk of the Jääng in the Khartoum area. By the time the whole Jääng was in this Khartoum vicinity,[144] Jieldit with his Pagong clan people settled what is now Jeily. As earlier stated, the word Jeily is a later derivative from the name of Jieldit.

In this way, the two societies lived separately in this region for

---

143 From Santino Deng Teeng's taped oral accounts now kept by the University of African and Asian studies.

144 One of the proofs that the Jääng and the Nuers once lived in this Khartoum area is the archaeological results found from the excavations done in the Khartoum area, results which established that the inhabitants of early Khartoum were negroes who resembled the Dinkas' and the Nuers' features and some of their ways of life. For this, see A J Arkell, Early Khartoum, (Oxford 1949) p.p. 107-8.

about three centuries until they fully acquired the status of two separate tribes, the Nuers calling Jieng as Jaang, and for the reasons best known to the people of that ancient period, the Jaang invariably knew the Nuers as Naath. The word Naath is an archaic nomenclature, for which the Dinka people in the Upper Nile still know the Nuers. Its origin in ancient or Mediaeval times is known to the Nuers.

When the reasons for the Nilotic southbound migrations became acute again in this Khartoum region, it was the Nuers who again started off due south in search of a permanent abode where land and water could support life and security could assure a chance for survival.

The Nuers this time decided to cross to the west bank of the White Nile to become the first Nilotic people to pioneer the present western parts of the Upper Nile. They slowly moved on the west bank of the White Nile until they reached the present Bentiu area in about 480 AD.[145]

The Nuer came as major sections of Jikany consisting of the Jagei, Dok, Leek and Bul. Nyuong, Lak, Thiang, Gawɛɛr and Lou are said to be a later formation within the western Upper Nile.[146] A century later, after the Jaang had come and settled on the east bank areas of the Upper Nile Basin region and displaced its original settlers, the Nuers started stealing Jääng cattle. This led to an internecine vendetta and a state of constant warfare between the two became the case from the first quarter of the Middle Ages. By the time the entire Jaang was still in Upper Nile their stolen, raided and looted cattle are believed to have formed much of the present Nuer cattle.

The Bul and Leek sections of the Nuer used to rear a type of cow that was an admixture of the original Jaang cattle and those of the

---

145   G P Mardock, Africa: its people and their cultural history, (New York 1959), p. 246

146   Douglas H Johnson, Nuer prophets: A history of prophecy from the Upper Nile in the nineteenth and twentieth centuries, (New York, 1994, p.361)

nomadic Arab Baggara tribes which later came to border them to the northwest. The Jagei, Adok, Jikany, Nyuong and Adöör sections of the Nuers now keep cattle which are purely of Jääng stock. The Jääng on their part also keep much of the earlier Luo cattle plus that of the Funj which they took in the 5th century. This is in addition to almost the whole cattle of Jur-Luɛɛl whom they later displaced in Bahr el Ghazal. The Jääng of today have many Nuers who have been incorporated and assimilated into them across the ages. The same is true of some Jääng assimilated into the Nuer community. The cattle which Jääng keep also has much of the Nuers' stock. The Nuers–Jääng vendetta which has persevered to the present era is believed to have its origin in that paternal and primogenitary injustice from Dengdit and his elder son over the cow Acol and its Nyayar, a story already given above under the Nuer Dinka myth of origin.

In the last part of the 14th century AD, after a large part of the Jaang had already vacated the Upper Nile Basin region to Bahr el Ghazal, a big part of Jikany Nuers decided to cross the White Nile eastwards, perhaps as a result of overpopulation and overgrazing. The Jikany migrating community crossed between present Mellut and Bur-Acol (which is present Malakal). They took to the River Sobat area through Akɔgɔ in the present Dɔngjɔl Dinka country until they reached the Kuanylual Thuään area which is present Nasir. The Dɔngjɔl Dinka sections of Ageer, Nyiel and the whole of Abialang Dinka had by then gone to the southern Upper Nile as far as the Bilnyang area east of present Juba town in Central Equatoria. They were among the Jääng sections which returned to Jääng departure localities in the now Jonglei region because of the act done by Loŋaar Ayueel, the leader of Jääng migratory exodus to Bahr el Ghazal.

As explained elsewhere in chapter four, Loŋaar was spearing the heads of people during the time when the Jääng society was crossing at the Shambe shore of Anyɔɔp in the month of March, 1340 AD.[147] These Dɔngjɔl groups later returned to their present areas in northern Upper Nile by about the end of the 15th century AD.

This was following the arrival of a returning wave of the Nilo-Hamites and the Luo societies which were coming back from the West Nile areas of Western Equatoria region due to tsetse fly problems. Those were the Bari, the Pojulu and the Lotuho tribes already explained elsewhere in the book.

The absence of Jaang society in the Mellut–Malakal corridor was used by part of the Jikany Nuers to cross through to the east. Becoming the eastern Jikany they later distributed themselves up to the Ethiopian borders where they became the eastern Upper Nile Jikany Nuεrs, presently inhabiting the four counties of Ulang, Longechuk, Nasir and Maiwut. Part of this Jikany later cut into Ethiopia to become the Jikany Nuers of the Gambella region. The eastern Upper Nile Jikany divided into what are the Gajöök and the Gajaak. The Gajaak are those Jikany in the Maiwut and Longechuk counties. The Gajook are those who live in Nasir county. In their migration the Gajook section of Jikany decided to remain in Kuanylual Thuään (Nasir) territory while the Lou-Nuεr crossed the River Sobat from Ulang through Nyanding to the Akobo areas.

Those Lou-Nuεrs settled in what are now the Watt and Nyirol and Akobo areas. Parts of the Gajaak and the Gaguaang went further south, east of Nasir to the Ethiopian borders. They settled into the Thiajaak, Jekou, Maiwut and Bilpam areas. The Nuεrs who remained in the western Upper Nile region regard those Nuεrs who went to the Eastern Upper Nile as *Jikany Dɔɔr*, meaning those who went astray or who went to unknown forest lands. The western Nuεrs are known as the *Jikany Cieng,* meaning those who remained in the mainstream Nuer homeland.

---

147   This is a very widely known story among all the Dinka tribes and sections in both the Upper Nile and Bahr el Ghazal regions.

The Gawɛɛr, Lak and Thiang sections of the Nuers started as families which in time decided to cross the River Nile to the east bank from the Adɔk Nuer section on the west bank. They settled in the Pangak Peninsula areas. The Gawɛɛr Nuers later migrated to the areas of Ayod, Amuögöök and Wau, places which were earlier inhabited by the Thoi Dinka community who vacated that area northwards because of the pressures from the Luac Aguer Wiɛu warrior community that broke away from the mainstream Luac of Tonj East when all Luac was still at what is Madol of today.

They went to temporarily live in the present Leer area where they started to be known as Luac-Tɛɛt prior to their crossing to the east bank in between the late 17th and early 18th centuries. The Gawɛɛr Nuers are in fact a mutated admixture of the two Dinka sections of Thoi and Rut and the original Gawɛɛr elements.

As explained above, the war between the Jaang and the Nuers was a traditional one, originating from the story of the cow Acol and its Nyanyar, and although some political figures would want to give political meaning to this at some given time in recent history, the two peoples were of one origin, of one father and one mother.

Nonetheless, the long isolation of the Nuers from the Jääng for maybe more than two millennia since their separation from each other was bound to have a far reaching effect. The Nuers developed a separate language and a peculiar culture and due to that long gap of time, the Nuers in their centuries of development had been exposed to a constant war situation that had tended to shape their outlook and quick acting emotionality with a cultural outlook which seems to make them seen as a more violent Nilotic community than are other Nilotics.

Jääng society apparently spent many centuries in the Upper Nile Basin region since they came there towards the end of the Iron Age, at the beginning of the 5th century AD. Since that time their population increased and their livestock redoubled as a result of the many wars of that part of the Iron Age and the beginning of the Middle Ages, wars they fought against their former brethren, the Nilotic communities, particularly the Murle and the Nuers and to a lesser extent the Luo tribes, the Funj and Burun. Cattle raiding and internecine warfare with the Nuers and the Murle characterised that long period of several centuries in the Upper Nile region, and although this was a period in which Jaang society developed population-wise through absorbing and incorporating other peoples as whole sections, groups and individuals as they acquired much of their present cattle from the Nilotic communities in addition to their present invincible and superiority complex attitude in Southern Sudan, an attitude which they acquired from their many war victories over the centuries.

Despite this apparent prosperity the Jaang also suffered from the very unhealthy environment of the Upper Nile Basin region. The combination of the wet season diseases and mosquitoes affected them greatly. There were dry season diseases also, as there was the seasonal heat of the dry winter season that was coupled by problems of cattle increase and overgrazing. Concomitant with all these was the problem of the periodic outbreak of epidemic diseases such as smallpox, cholera and other communicable diseases. All these made the Jääng community once again think of abandoning the Upper Nile Basin region. Another Great Ayueel of this period who was the overall Spear Master for the entire Jääng society in the Upper Nile decided to send a reconnaissance mission across the White Nile to Bahr el Ghazal in search of suitable land for healthy and permanent settlement. Different from that big Ayueel sainted at Baŋborou in Rutland, this Ayueel is buried at the head of the cattle camp on the toch of former Rut land and the other Ayueel who is buried and sainted at Pam-Zeraf, a place also called Pam Ayueel. This is discussed in the next chapter.

BASIN ECOLOGY OF THE JÄÄNG SETTLEMENT AREAS BEFORE THEY MIGRATED TO BAHR EL GHAZAL

Since their arrival from the Khartoum region at the beginning of the 5th century AD, the Jääng had lived in this Upper Nile Basin area up to the time when some of them migrated to Bahr el Ghazal, some time in the 14th century AD. Those who did not move outside the Upper Nile region must have by now spent almost two millennia in this region.

Jääng population increased and their livestock redoubled as a result of the many wars they fought since their arrival from Northern Sudan. After their initial wars with the Funj and their Nilotic tribes which covered the last part of the 4th century and the first half of the 5th century AD, the Jaang wars remained to be those between them and the Nuers on the one hand and those between them and the Murle on the other. Although cattle raiding and internecine warfare with the Nuers and the Murle characterised that long period in this Upper Nile Basin region, there were times of respite and the Jääng were settled for quite a time so that what were sections had to develop into sub-tribes while others subdivided into further sub-tribes. This is despite bad times of epidemic outbreaks which wiped out or reduced some families and sections.

During all those centuries the Jääng covered all those areas presently inhabited by those Dinka tribes north of Malakal including the present Nasir region now inhabited by the eastern Jikany Nuers. They also covered the entire central and southern Upper Nile region and all those areas now inhabited by the Lou Nuers of Waatt and Ayod.

UPPER NILE GEOGRAPHY IN MEDIAEVAL TIMES

Ecologically the region was an extra wet environment with consecutive annual flooding due to the Nile. Moreover the region was and continues to be a low basin area and rains from the East African highlands used to bring water into its areas in torrents. The region used to be wet for most parts of the year except for those areas that were arid or desert such as Aying and the arid areas of northern Upper Nile. As vast areas of land were wet or covered by water, very tall elephant grass grew extensively and this was associated with abundant man-killing mosquitoes. And as the basin was such an extensive primeval swampland of toch, the region was full of man-killing creatures such as snakes, crocodiles, hippopotamuses and elephants which lived in some deeper parts of the toch that were also known to house the now extinct dinosaurs.

Forest lands were scarce and the climate provided steaming heat from the sun and from a generally humid environment. This was the condition into which our forefathers were forced and they had to adapt to it at a very high risk. The combination of all these seasonal extremes accounts for periodic outbreaks of epidemic diseases. All these made the Jääng society again think of abandoning this Upper Nile Basin ecology in search of a suitable land which can provide healthy and permanent settlement and was also good for their huge livestock. This accounts for Ayueldit's later decision to send a reconnaissance mission across the Nile westward into Bahr el Ghazal to explore its suitability as will be described in the next chapter.

CHAPTER TEN:
THE JÄÄNG MIGRATION TO BAHR EL GHAZAL

INTRODUCTION

In this chapter we will discuss how, when and why the Jääng decided to migrate from the Upper Nile to Bahr el Ghazal across the White Nile to the west, unlike their usual southbound migrations which were confined to the Nile. This chapter will give an exhaustive survey of how this particular migration was effected. It will cover issues of leadership, problems encountered during their crossing of the Nile, sections which migrated and those which remained in the Upper Nile region and why. It will also cover Jaang distribution to those areas they conquered and which they now inhabit in Bahr el Ghazal, and how they displaced the original inhabitants of the region, in other words that lengthy period from the 14th to the end of 19th century, after which chapter eleven will lead to our conclusion of the book as it will cover the Turco-Egyptian, Mahdist and Condominium eras with its heinous slavery and slave trade pestilence, and its final abolition by the British colonialists in 1898.

EXPLORATION SURVEYS INTO BAHR EL GHAZAL

Owing to the ecological and epidemic problems explained in the last part of chapter nine, the Jääng society felt the need to look for new lands which could support life for them and their livestock. It was because of this that Great Ayueel of the Pagong Spear Master clan dispatched a mission of three men to an area which they had heard was so large, rich and good for them and their livestock. This is the area which later became the Bahr el Ghazal region. Jääng people in the two regions are agreed about this exploration mission by a Pagong Spear Master. Some oral sources say the mission took three years for the three men to come back after exploring the whole of Bahr el Ghazal as far as the toch of Lual-AXöny in the far west of Bahr el Ghazal where the sun goes down in the evenings. This would probably be that primeval forest region beyond which is the Central Africa Republic.

Upon a favourable report from that exploration mission, much of the Jääng decided to make that huge and historic migratory exodus into Bahr el Ghazal. It was an exodus because the Upper Nile Basin region was at that particular moment bedevilled by several epidemic diseases that were finishing families and sections.

The society had just emerged out of a very bad summer and autumn when all forms of epidemics had brought great gloom to the society. Measles, whooping cough, smallpox and cholera had all come upon the community and the Jaang was now waiting for the dry season to desert the region.

Whole sections and families were wiped out by a combination of all those epidemic diseases and this is the time when the Anie, Arëëm and Adol sections disappeared. The Spear Masters, the holy men, tried to use their invocations and ritual offerings to their Nhialic to stop those misfortunes, but to no avail. It was from this that the Jääng people gave names to cholera epidemics, names such as 'Jöng-alei' from which the present name of Jönglei was derived. For smallpox, they called it *malekdit* or *akoi*. It was called malekdit because of the blistering rashes it makes on the body and akoi for exterminating whole families.

This migration to Bahr el Ghazal was done under the leadership of a Pagong personality from the traditional line of Jieldit who led the Jacobites section to ancient Sudan from Judea in the 7th century BC through Bab el Mandeb. This is the very ancestor whose other intermediate descendant, Ayueel Jiel of Jeilly, led much of Jääng to Upper Nile towards the end of the 4th century AD. Loŋaar, the great grandson of Ayueeldit who is buried at Bangborou in Rut land and who is the direct grandson of that Ayueel buried at Pam-Zeraf, became the leader of this migration. This migratory event took place in the first quarter of 1300, precisely in 1340 AD.

During the dry winter month of March in the year 1340, the Jääng departed the central and southern Upper Nile areas to Bahrel Ghazal. Some began from the big Pamac cattle camp and its outlying areas and those areas that are present Jale and Maar payams, areas which lay at the northern end of what is now Bor. Here, the Agars and Gok sections departed the Upper Nile. Some of the Rek sections left those areas that are present Thiöbek, Aluɛl, Agɛro and those areas which now constitute Abi, Guala, Paleek in Anyidi area and Angakuei areas in present Manydeeng Payam in Bor, but generally the bulk of Rek and those who crossed at the Shambe shore of Anyɔɔp departed the Upper Nile region at the present Northern Twic and Nyarweng areas or from all the areas that are the present Jönglei areas.

Some of today's Dinka in Bahr el Ghazal still remember their ancestors' points of departure in south-central Upper Nile, places such as Patunduur and Athopei cattle camps as well as the Pacuil village area in the toch and the whole of what is now the Kɔŋgɔɔr area of present chief Duöt Ajäng Duöt. Some people in Bahr el

Ghazal say that their ancestors left at places called Gueer, Manyaang, Adhiɔɔk, Abek, Paköu and those areas of present Akur in the toch of the Twic-East county. Others say they left at the Pagelge cattle camp area, at Patäl and at Padiët as well as the present Nyuak Payam areas of Ayuääl, Awulian and Dai-Acueek. Some of the Aliap Dinka left at Yuai village in the present Nyuak area where the Luac community also departed the Upper Nile but largely at the present areas of Bingkaar, Aborööm, Abuök, Ajör and those territories which are now inhabited by Nyarweng Dinka, currently the whole area now called Duk-Payueel.

THE DEPARTURE PLAN AND THE DEBATE BEFORE THE TAKEOFF TO BAHR EL GHAZAL

Before the entire society took off from south-central Upper Nile there was a serious debate made by the community elders. Disagreement came over whether it was to be the conquest that was to be done first as advanced by Loŋaar, the leader of the migration plan, or if the entire society was to depart the region simultaneously to do the fighting with any resisting inhabitants while moving in one single migratory movement with youth parties fighting the region's inhabitants in the front and the rear. This was the view held by Anei Awutiak who later became Anei-Parek, known also as Anei-Thöcjang, the founding ancestor of the present Payii and Parek clans in the Tonj, Gogrial, Twic and Awiel areas. Anei Awutiak's argument was that Jaang society had to better move out of that unhealthy environment, arguing that it might take time for the youth to effect the conquest of Bahr el Ghazal, by which time those diseases would have further reduced the society.

This view of Anei Awutiak (Anei-Parek) was popularly welcomed by the masses but Loŋaar insisted on his viewpoint. He therefore organised the youth of all sections into the Kiec-Manyiel Age-set and moved with them towards the Nile. According to traditions from the Pagong clan people in Bahr el Ghazal it was a very big expedition estimated at several thousand, organised into three large columns, all under the overall command of Loŋaar who was in his fifties. He is described as having been a macho-built giant of the ancient stock. He was a great fighter and a Spear Master as well. While Loŋaar's invasion youth parties had moved and were on their way to the Nile riverbank, Anei Awutiak from behind succeeded in mobilising the Jaang society of all sections so that the whole thing became an exodus, a massive migration of just about everybody. The Jaang society trekked out in long series of columns by tribes, sections and families, following Loŋaar and his youth parties. The Jääng society left their places with all of their domestic provisions and their entire livestock.

When Loŋaar arrived on the east bank of the Nile, and while he was making a ritual offering of bulls to the gods of the river as was done previously by his ancestor Jieldit when he was crossing at Wär-Pakuɛɛk, Loŋaar saw the Jääng from yonder, moving with all of its livestock and domestic provisions, children and the aged, even the sick and the womenfolk. This infuriated him and he was disposed to confronting Anei, who he knew must have been the one who had insisted on his opinion to let the Jaang move in one big migratory move, much against his own plan.

LEADERSHIP QUARRELS AND RITES ON THE RIVERBANK BEFORE CROSSING THE NILE

When the Jaang committee had all arrived the east bank, Loŋaar had a quarrel with Anei Awutiak, who had the support and backing from all the community leaders. Those of great Tɔng Lerbek, Ajiɛk, Anei-Adiaŋbar, Awuciu, Wol Kuac Ngor who later became Wol-Adhieu and Agɔth-Cithiik of the Pahol all stood with Anei

Awutiak. Those great figures were leaders of clans within the Rek community where Loŋaar also belonged. The rest of the tribal and section leaders stood in support of Anei Awutiak.

Yet Loŋaar insisted on making a ruling. He ordered the Jaang to go back and jumped into the Nile after he called on his Kiec-Manyiel which followed him; and after he had crossed to the west bank at Shambe, at the spot known as Kɔrcok shore of Anyɔɔp, those clans' leaders had a meeting and resolved to make the Rek society get into the Nile waters to cross in total defiance of Loŋaar's authority. They went about selling their decision to the rest of the Jaang sections including the Twic, Agaar, Gok, Luac, those to later become Ruweng, Aliap and those other sections which later returned following Loŋaar's spearing of the people's heads in the Nile waters. All the society leaders agreed to let their people cross to the west bank and it was agreed that the Rek community was to take the lead as the man belonged to their section.

PROBLEMS ENCOUNTERED DURING THE CROSSING MOMENTS

With the resolve made by all Jaang sections to cross the Nile to the west bank against Loŋaar's ruling, the Rek community started the marathon crossing process. People just walked into the Nile only to pinch or close their noses not to breathe as they reached the deeper part of the Nile River. They did so while crossing in several lines which they did by families, clans and sections. Unfortunately, Loŋaar on the western part of the River Nile was so angry for having been opposed. He stationed himself at the shallow point close to the riverbank of Anyɔɔp where he fixed what the Dinka people call apiir, which are dry stalks from the river straw. He fixed those straws to the river bed near the riverbank threshold. When those straws were shaken by a person emerging from the deep waters, Loŋaar would spear his head with a type of fishing spear and the person would die after serious cadaveric wailing and struggling. With this method Loŋaar killed several people among the crossing Rek community.[148]

The act made the Rek run back to the east bank and the entire Jaang was mesmerised into a very serious predicament of what was to be done! Some sections decided to return to their departure points while others like the Luac, Gok, Twic and Ruweng decided to use other shores away from the Shambe shore of Anyɔɔp where Loŋaar was killing people. Those sections went north along the east bank and crossed at Rumjöök shore on the mouth of the big water body of Kadop where they found another peril, the big dinosaur which the Dinka called nguäl. The Aliap people later took to the left, southwards till they crossed at Gutthom shore then they proceeded to Beki from where they gradually went further to the Awεirial county areas where Aliap Dinka is today.

The big Rek of Loŋaar, which later became the Rek of Anei-Parek, with the Duör which became Agaar, insisted and crossed through that Shambe shore of Anyɔɔp. They decided to resolutely face Loŋaar. The Rek society leaders decided on a plan to forcefully get hold of Loŋaar and had him manhandled overboard to the west bank. To do this a number of strong giants had to be selected to make that effort of seizing Loŋaar. Some people among the Rek say a sacral bone, called *pic*, from a then slaughtered ox was prepared[149] and fixed or fastened at the end of a long pole of wood to be stirred in the water to cause him to spear it in the belief that it was a person trying to come out of the water. Then he was to be caught by those giants.

Great Giir Thiik, also known as Giir Kero, in his interview with Godfrey Lienhardt in the 1940s vividly recounted this story of Loŋaar spearing the heads of people at crossing. He explained how his great

---

148 G. Lienhardt, Divinity and experience: The religion of the Dinka, Oxford University Press, London (1961), pp. 171-180

149 Ibid, p. 174

great grandfather Agɔth-Cithiik participated or planned the seizure of Loŋaar[150] during that historic crossing of the Nile to Bahr el Ghazal.

This story of pic used in order to trick Loŋaar is so popular that it is told among the Agaar in eastern Bahr el Ghazal as it is also told among the Malwal Dinka in the far northwest of Bahr el Ghazal. East bank Dinka people in the Upper Nile also describe this event. There is, however, another version among the same Rek Dinka. This version states that it was 'dɛrdɛr' which was made to trick Loŋaar[151] and that it was Anei-Adiaŋbar and Awuciu who made that dɛrdɛr. Whichever was used, Loŋaar was anyway caught by a number of people from the Rek community and was forcefully carried out of the Nile to the other side of the riverbank after a big wrestle with him. In these two legends or versions, Agɔth-Cithiik, Anei-Adiaŋbar and Awuciu feature as the planners and giants who strenuously made Loŋaar make way for the Jaang to cross to the west bank and therefore become the west bank people of Bahr el Ghazal to this day. The following paragraph from Chief Giir Thiik summarises this story of Loŋaar at crossing:

> *"The people were thus finished altogether, and a man named Agɔth-Cithiik called the people together to make a plan to save them from the fishing spear of Loŋaar. His plan was that his friend should take the sacrum of an ox which he had fastened to a long pole, and should move through the water before him, holding out the sacral bone so that it would move the reeds. They carried out this plan, and Loŋaar's fishing spear, darted at the sacrum which he mistook for a human head, was held fast there. Meanwhile, Agɔth-Cithiik left the*

---

150 'Dɛrdɛr' is a Dinka name for a slenderly wrapped up bundle of dry grass usually made and lit with fire to burn a bee hole or a bee colony. This is when people want to obtain honey during bee hunting.

151 Ibid, p. 174, Godfrey Liewhardt.

water and seized Loŋaar from behind and held him. There they remained for a long time locked together until Loŋaar was tired with wrestling".

Whatever versions of this story are available among the Dinka, the seizing and wrestling with Loŋaar as well as his spearing people on the head are told in those versions. Awuciu was married to Loŋaar's sister before the Jaang migrated. His chief opponent, Anei Awutiak, had also married his own daughter, Arek Loŋaar, who became mother of Tɔng-Manyangdit and Thiek Anei, who is popularly known among his descendants, the Payii clan people, as Thiek Arek. Worth mentioning here is that in most of the Rek leaders did have some kind of relations with the Pagong clan. When Loŋaar was forcefully pulled to the west bank by Agɔth-Cithiik, Anei-Adiaŋbar, Awuciu and Wol Kuac Ngor Rek society then made an onrush into the River Nile and crossed to the west bank. Agaar then followed. They crossed from the same shore but, according to the existing oral accounts found among all sections of the Dinka of both Upper Nile and Bahr el Ghazal, the Rek found another problem while crossing. It is said a big River monster called *nguäl* stationed itself at some deeper parts of the Nile where it opened its big mouth and about fifty people would just walk into its mouth unseeing or unknowingly, then it would close its mouth and devour all those people!

The beast was one among the primordial remnants of the then extinct dinosaurs. The dinosaurs were still living in the big sudd region of the White Nile until quite recently when the Kiec Dinka people killed the last of the disappeared race of African dinosaurs. This last dinosaur was killed in about the beginning of the 20th century. The bony remains of that dinosaur can still be found in the toch of Kiec today. It remains made a mount just seen when people go to the toch of Kiec during the dry season. Its vicinity is surrounded by big trees that have arisen from it. The story of the pestilence of that dinosaur is still being told by almost all the Kiec Dinka people to the present day.¹⁵² Like the story of the beast of Rhodes' Island and the beast of the shore of Mabit in the toch of Apuk-Giir which Apuk people called *Nyang Mabiɛt*, nguäl devoured so many people not only at this shore of Anyɔɔp but also at the shore of Rumjöök, where the Luac people faced another nguäl which they managed to kill during crossing. A certain Aduɛr from the Luac crossing community was brave enough to spear it with a big edge-cutting spear known as a tɔŋ, so much that the beast was seen throwing itself up in a somersault, roaring above the water and it then died in that instant. This made it possible for the Luac community to cross to the west bank, followed by the Twic and by those who became the Ruweng and Gok.

The threat posed by this Nguäl the dinosaur also made many sections of the Jaang return to their departure areas. Among those sections which returned were the present sections that are now the Dongjol group of tribes, the Ageer, Nyiel Dongjol and Abialang, present Ruweng people, Adhiɔɔk and Athɔɔc people who are the present Bor Dinka. Nyarweng, Paweny and Ngok of Lual Yak later returned as part of the returning Ruweng from Rɛɛlkou. In fact, all those Jaang communities which are presently in the Upper Nile returned to be the east bank Dinka of today due to this act of Loŋaar and the big river monster. Those of Duör who now live in the Upper Nile broke out of the main body of Duor and so was it for the Marbek groups who later became Thoi, Rut and Alual.

Angääc broke off from the Luac community and returned to central Upper Nile. Some families from among the Twic also returned. Several hundreds of people found it difficult to swim the big White Nile with their children, the aged and the disadvantaged members of the society such as the lame, the blind and the sick and

---

152   From an interview with John Cawuop in 2003.

so they turned right at the east bank under the pretext of Loŋaar's threat and the river monster.

However, despite those perils ranging from that of Loŋaar to that of Nguäl and the sheer difficulty to cross for lack of swimming experience, as was the case with others, all the same a bulk of Jaang crossed to the west bank. It was a marathon five days' exercise for the Jaang to finish crossing to the west bank with all its cattle, flock, the disadvantaged groups and their domestic provisions.

That migratory movement and its famous crossing which took five full days was news across the whole length of the Great Nile Basin as far as Roman Egypt where a medical journal of the time reported on the causes of that extraordinary exodus of Jaang riverine society on the White Nile in 1340 AD.[153] Rumbek secondary school, Cuɛibɛt and Thiet symposiums which were conducted in 2003 to discuss research data material for this book, made a tentative estimation of about 50 000 Jaang people who succeeded in crossing to the west bank after that marathon five days crossing activity in which some people used yachts, barges and rafts made of reeds to ferry their people and provisions across to the west bank. Others even made canoes, especially those who had to cross during the last days.

EVENTS AFTER CROSSING TO THE WEST BANK (ENCAMPMENT LOCATIONS)

After they succeeded to cross to the west bank of the Nile from the aforementioned shores the Jaang did not just proceed ahead. They settled to first regroup, make ritual sacrifices and make proper survey of the actual environmental situation of the region ahead of them. They also settled to first know the fighting capability of

---

153 For a full account of this story, check Luacjang at their crossing day in chapter four of this book.

the people who inhabited the region and paused to wait for those sections which were to still come from behind. Examples of this were sections like Carbɛk and Ajuɔng, both of which later joined the Aborööm, Luɛɛl, Weng-Acaak and Angon of Aliap Dinka of today. The Duör community encamped at Ajäk with the big Rek which covered all those areas that make up the present Liɛtpaciruööt. Twic, Ruweng, Luac and Gok sections also encamped in this Liɛtpaciruoot, Karëër, Jöknhiem, Malek and Pathiöng up to the present Gel River area. The Jaang covered all those areas that are the present eastern Kiec land of Adöör. Aliap people, however, encamped at those places such as Ka, Beki, Aker and Belöök before they proceeded to such areas like Padunyiel and other areas to the south of Shambe. A section of Duör known as the Böör went along with the Aliap people and settled with the Aborɔɔm sections.

They came back in subsequent years to rejoin the Duör who at that time had already become the Agaar community.

From the stories which are found among the Agaar and Rek Dinka communities, it appears the Jaang spent a decade in this Ajäk area of Adöör. The Agaar people left the Ajäk area following a quarrel among themselves. That quarrel is illustrated by a saying which has survived the test of time among the Agar from that time of Ajäk to the present day. "*Miith rɛckë Ajäk*" is a saying which testifies to the fact of the Agaar community having settled in this Ajäk area after crossing. One version from the Agaar community says there was an occasion in which the owner of the occasion decided to deny services to uninvited people who came to share with him for his occasion. This act led to a quarrel which became a big fight that made Agaar vacate Ajäk to Dök land of Ganyliel of today. As for the Rek society, the events were so dramatic with Loŋaar still featuring as the overbearing figure in this Ajäk area.

Here in the Ajäk area, Loŋaar convened a gathering of the whole Rek to lay blame for the opposition done to him by Anei-Parek who mobilised the Jaang to move after him. It was a gathering to blame and punish those of Agɔth-Cithiik, Awuciu, Anei-Adiaŋbar and Wol-Adhieu, the people who planned to trick him with the sacral bone or with dɛrdɛr and who actually seized him and manhandled him overboard to the riverbank till he surrendered to them, thereby making the Jaang cross against his original plan. Loŋaar took one of his bulls by the colour of the sky, Maŋok-thɔn. The Dinka call that type of a bull as 'Mangök-Thɔn'. Some traditions say he took it from the kraal of one of his sons, Jiel Loŋaar. Loŋaar ordered seven more bulls from leaders of the different clans and sections.

With those eight bulls ready on pegs Loŋaar began to express his anger during his invocations. He questioned as to whom the act of pic did, and Wol Kuac, of all the people came out to say it was him. With this the great Loŋaar became furious with him and in a very unprecedented reaction he swiftly speared his foot and transfixed it with that fishing spear, which badly pierced the foot to the ground!

To confound Wol's humiliation and agony, Loŋaar also took the whole trunk, neck and head of the slaughtered bull 'Mangök-Thɔn' and hung them all on Wol's head down to his shoulders. He placed it with all the blood still oozing from the flesh. While he made Wol Kuac stand with such heavy flesh and bones of the big ox on his head and with his foot painfully transfixed to the ground, Loŋaar continued with his invocations, calling on his spiritual power to let Wol die under such public humiliation and agony! He commanded Wol to stand up for days! Loŋaar's aim was perhaps to let Wol die through that deterrent punishment used as a means to frighten the rest of his opponents within the Rek society.

Wol Kuac cried for a whole day and the night that followed and by the second day the flesh of the head and trunk of 'Mangök-Thɔn' had already putrefied so much that the moths and putrefaction fluids had already started to drizzle deep into his ears, causing him to have otitis media! Meanwhile Longar, who has been busy making his invocations on the rest of the bulls became surprised as to why Wol did not die.[154] He therefore freed him from the place where the spear held him. He removed both the spear and the putrefied meat and bones from his head and shoulders.

The story of the humiliation done to Wol Kuac by Loŋaar is known all over Dinka lands for not only was he humiliated but he was also given the surname of 'Wol-Adhieu' by the Jaang people who witnessed him crying for days when his foot was transfixed to the ground and a heavy weight of the head and trunk of the big ox was placed on his head. The new surname became popular for him throughout the whole of that Mediaeval era, so much so that his descendants later adopted that name for which they became known as their clan's name, Padhieu.

As for Awuciu, Loŋaar uttered him a curse, blaming him that he should not have participated in the conspiracy against him when he knows he married his sister and when he very well knew he come from the mundane background. For all this Loŋaar cursed him not to prosper. He told his sister Alëëk that she was to die on the instant for failing to dissuade her husband from the conspiracy. Alëëk died as such and her children remained to maintain a very thin line to the present day among the Rek communities. If any, there are only a few areas like Apuk -Padoc, Kɔŋöör Lɛɛr and Apuk-Pathuɔn where some few households continue to preserve the name of Awuciu. Those people are called the Pawuciɛu clan people in those areas.

As for Wol-Adiaŋbar, who like Adɔlmuöt was a sororal nephew of Loŋaar, he was told he and his descendants would continue to adumbrate invocations from the Spear Masters during ritual offerings or sacrifice making occasions as an 'Agamlöng', the *adumbrator*, and that he and his family line shall also be the ones to bury the holy men, the Spear Masters, and cannot be Spear Masters of their own. This rather

---

154   Godfrey Lienhardt, Divinity and experience: the religion of the Dinka, Oxford University Press, London (1961), p. 180

mild curse on Anei-Adiaŋbar is believed by some sources to have been dictated by Wol-Adiaŋbar's previous good relations with Loŋaar.

Wol-Adhieu, who initially was from the cow revering clan, the '*Pawutweŋ*' people of the cow, was later befriended by Loŋaar who called on Wol-Adhieu to make peace and reconciliation with him. Wol-Adhieu is said to have accepted that reconciliation on persuasion. Bulls were slaughtered for that occasion after Loŋaar's repentance for the physical afflictions and humiliation he did to Wol-Adhieu who had in fact developed otitis media which ultimately made him deaf for the rest of his lifetime.

In that public occasion of peace and reconciliation, Loŋaar took a piece of meat from each of the slaughtered bulls, libated them and gave them over to Wol-Adhieu and declared it as a propitiation act, saying he had come to terms with Wol-Adhieu and so he publicly declared that the offspring of Wol-Adhieu shall not be subject to a curse from him or from any of his descendants in future. He added by saying that, "by the blood and putrefied meat of the bull *Mangök-Thɔn* of his son Jiel, he had transferred part of the holy power and its potency from him to Wol-Adhieu and his descent lines". Loŋaar went on by saying that, "by this investiture from me, Wol-Adhieu is to become a Spear Master". Loŋaar also took 'wëc', a broom from mon grass, the sporobolus pyramidalis grass and he spat on it to bless it. He then gave it over to Wol-Adhieu to be his nagualistic totem, the emblem for his descendants. He told him to immerse it in water and then sprinkle people with it during ritual occasions where sacrifices and offerings are being made to Nhialic (God) for the wellbeing of the community. In this way, mon grass became a divine totem for Wol-Adhieu and his descendants to the present day. In addition to the pelican, mon is the nagualistic totemic divinity or 'yath' to all the Padhieu clan people wherever they are in Dinka lands.[155]

---

155 From an interview by the author with a group of Padhieu elders in Nyang-Akoch, among whom were elder Luka Arou Ayiɔm and others. Interview

As for Agɔth-Cithiik and Anei-Parek, Loŋaar was ambivalent about them. Those were two great figures who came from the Pahol clan and who were themselves Spear Masters and had the public opinion of the Rek with them. They needed a positive approach. Loŋar lifted Agɔth-Cithiik up before the crowd and said, "You, Agɔth-cithiik, will carry the spear in war in this country". He spat on *'binh lääk'* and on a war spear, gave them to Agɔth and sang a song in praise of Agɔth's bravery.[156]

As for Anei-Parek, Loŋaar told him, "you will from now on be called upon to stop such epidemic diseases, such as malekdit or akoi (smallpox), abaric (cholera), measles (tuɔrtuɔr) or kuŋkuŋ and toŋgol (whooping cough) and you will generally invocate for the wellbeing of the community in much the same way as I do since you were so kin as to bring the Jaang out of that unhealthy place". He sang a song in praise of Anei-Parek whom he declared to the crowd as a community manager, but Loŋaar added by to this telling Anei-Parek that, "you and your descendants will not invocate in a ritual and religious occasion in which I or my descendants are the principal invocators, and I and my descendants shall not invocate in a ritual and religious occasion in which you or your descendants are the principal invocators."

This statement from Loŋaar is strictly being observed by both clans descended from Loŋaar and from Anei-Parek to the present day. Descendants of Anei-Parek later desisted from being called Paγol as they opted to follow the agnatic name of their later intermediate ancestors, Ayii Thiek and Parek.

Those of his descendants who live in Tonj, Gogrial and Twic lands are called Payii after their ancestor Ayii Thiek, the second son of Anei-Parek, while those whose ancestor is Tɔng Anei-Parek and who

---

was dated 26.6.2002.

156   G Lienhardt, 'The myth of the Spear Masters', (in) Divinity and experience: the religion of the Dinka, Oxford University Press, London, (1961), p. 176

went to live in the Northern Bahr el Ghazal areas of Awiel adopted a clan name of Parek after that surname of Anei-Parek. Those were some of the events which took place in this Ajäk area and it looks like the Jaang stayed for a decade before they advanced to the interior of Bahr el Ghazal. In the course of their stay Wol-Adhieu left the Rek community and went to live with those people who later became Ruweng. His brother Mël Kuac Ngor left the Rek and went to live with the Duör community where their agnatic kin later became the Paderek clan people. Mël became integrated into Duör and his descendants later became part of the Agar community. One of his descendants by the same name of Mël later migrated from Agaar land to join the Apuk section of the Rek at the time when the Rek was already in what is the present Patɛu village in the present Luackoth area of Tonj East. In Patɛu he became known as Mël-Agaar.

Mël-Agaar came from Agaarland with three sons and a good following from his Paderek clan people. Traditions from the Apuk of Juwiir present the three sons as having been Bol Mël, Pathuɔn Mël and Padɔc Mël. The three sons later made an historic impact among the Apuk section of the Rek.

The story of Mël-Agaar is well tackled under the Lith section of the Rek in chapter four but the long and short of the story of Mël-Agaar is that there occurred a situation at this Patɛu village whereby the three sons of Mël-Agaar divided themselves, with the elder son Bol Mël going to live with those clans of Lith which later became the Apuk-Juwiir of today.

Bol Mël later gained such prominence among the Juwiir people that he became the proprietor of that Apuk community. The area became identified with him so that it started to be known as Apuk of Bol Mël up to the time towards the end of the Turkiyya when a new Parum man by the name of Mathok Malek became the overall suzerain authority over Apuk-Juwiir, at which time Apuk of Bol Mël became Apuk of Mathok Malek to the present day.

The second son, Pathuɔn Mël, went with the Apuk sections of the Jök Tɔng Lerbek of the Payol, later to become Pajök. In subsequent times Pathuɔn was able to have Apuk called after him as Apuk-Pathuɔn. This Apuk, which migrated from Patɛu westwards to settle in their present areas in Gogrial East, continued to be known as Apuk-Pathuɔn until great Giir Thiik of the Payol, now Pakuec, emerged during the Anglo-Egyptian condominium era as the overall chief for the whole Apuk that came to have eight sections, and the name of the area changed to become Apuk of great Giir Thiik.

The third, who was the last born son of Mël-Agaar, Padɔc Mël, went northwards from Patɛu with a faction of Apuk clans. They later settled along the toch of the present Meshra or Akop sub-region of Tonj North and the territory became identified with him as Apuk-Padɔc to the present day.

THE JAANG MIGRATORY WAVES INTO THE BAHR EL GHAZAL INTERIOR FROM THE AJÄK AREA OF TODAY'S YIROL WEST COUNTY

By about 1350 AD those west bank Jaang communities at the Ajäk land of Adöör in today's Kiec territory had explored the situation of the whole Bahr el Ghazal. The issue of Loŋaar's dictatorial leadership was also discussed and the different tribes and sections of Jaang opted for a decentralised leadership. Each tribe and section was to have its own tribal and section leader. The Kiec-Manyiel Age-set was also dissolved. Some of the members of Kiec-Manyiel opted to be a section rather than an Age-set. The Rek had its own Age-sets such as Kuei, Lith and Gïr. Other Jaang sections had their own Age-sets. Those who chose to remain as Kiec became the section which later followed Luac, Gok, the would be Ruweng and the Twic. They went to Rɛɛlkou right from Ajäk.

The Aborööm community of the Aliap and Böör sections of Duör decided to follow those sections of Aliap which earlier crossed at Gutthom shore and settled to the south of Shambe. Except for the Böör section, the Duör in its entirety decided to move northeast to an area they later called the Dɔk land region, which is present Ganyliel territory, where they became known as the Agaar-Dɔk. Before the Jaang advanced out of Ajäk areas, however, it was the Agar community which went first.

This made the Agaar the first Jaang society to enter into war with the Jur-Belle community. After the initial engagements the Jur-Belle became alerted and they sufficiently prepared with their daŋga (arrows) and the bow. The Jur-Belle went on the offensive as such. This effectively deflected the Agaar to the northeast to Dɔk land while the Belle community took some steps back, creating a buffer zone between Ajäk and those areas that are the Payii River area of today. The Rek community later stepped in and settled in this area of the Payii River.

The Luacjang, Gok, Twic, Ruweng and elements of Kiec-Manyiel decided to depart the Ajäk area and went northwest, doing their migration along the toch marshes and, moving slowly, they settled at Rɛɛlkou, northeast of the present Maper area in Rumbek North county. Those who later became the Ruweng decided to return. They followed the previous route and footsteps earlier taken by the Kiec till they recrossed the Nile back to the Upper Nile. Rɛɛlkou departed and Kiec later did the same after their famous war with Luacjang community in 1430 AD.

The Rek came to the Payii River area and Ajäk was now fully vacated except for a few people called *Abuur* or *Thany* who remained as fishermen living along the Nile bank. Aliap and Böör were at this time south of Shambe. Here, in this Payii River area, the Rek spent some time before proceeding to settle at the Amongpiny area presently inhabited by the Agaar sections of Aliääp and Böör. At this

Payii area the Rek organised itself into three big sections of Kuei, Lith and Giir. The Kuei became the Rek sections of Great Spear Master Ayii Thiek.

The Lith, which was entirely Apuk section, was apportioned to the Great Payol Spear Master Tɔng Lerbek, while Giir became a section of a Parum Spear Master Akuiɛndit.[157]

After the famous battle of Ayuɔmlual[158] between the Kuei and Lith on the upstream of River Payii, the Rek proceeded in its westward migration. They came and settled in the Amongpiny area for a number of decades before the incident of Ukɔkdit from the Palual clan.[159] Ukɔk's incident made the Rek vacate this Amongpiny area of today's Luɛɛl Agaar and continue further west to Karɔm in the present Gokland area of Pagor Payam. From the Pagor area they proceeded in a long migratory march up to the present area in the eastern parts of Tonj, areas now called Jalwau, where they settled in what is now the Adöör area. They found a very big cattle camp which they renamed Angääc after that Angääc they left in the Upper Nile.

Here, in the Jalwau area, Rek society uprooted Jur-Luɛɛl which had been retreating since the times of Amongpiny. Jur-Luɛɛl withdrew further west to present areas that are Luackoth and Juwiir to the west. Part of Jur-Luɛɛl withdrew northwest to those areas that are the present areas of Lɛɛr, Awan and Lou-Paher. After occupying

---

157   Information about the Godfather or head of Giir was found from an interview with a group of Parum clan elders in Thiet in 2002. They included old man Nguenweidt and Ruall Akuiɛn Aköröu of the Mayom-Abun area

158   For the battle of Ayuɔmlual and the battle caused by the wife of Buɔŋlek, see the story of Rek in chapter four of this book.

159   Ukɔkdit was a big community liege at the time the Jaang was in the Amongpiny area. He was discovered to be the one who used to turn into a lion and go to the pastures where he would eat gentlemen herding the cattle. At twilight times he would mingle with the cattle, returning to the cattle compound stealing to eat the girls that are outstanding when he was discovered one day, a conspiracy was organised and he was killed during a day dancing occasion in the Amongpiny Rek community.

the whole of what is now the Jalwau areas of Adöör, Pakɔɔr, Bäc and the Kɔyɔɔr section of Akuecbäny Cirong Kuol, the Rek then settled in all its sections, including its hybrid section called Buɔth-Anyaar which later became the genesis of our present Malual Dinka in the far northern part of the Bahr el Ghazal region.

As for further migration of the Rek society to cover the entire interior of the Bahr el Ghazal region and all those areas from the southern parts of Tonj, to eastern and northern areas of Tonj up to the Gogrial sub-region and to the far north and northwestern areas of Bahr el Ghazal, see chapter four where each of the Dinka tribes in Bahr el Ghazal is explained in detail. Chapter four tackles the details of how Bahr el Ghazal tribes made their internal migratory movement inside Bahr el Ghazal. This includes how the Jaang acquired a new name, *Muonyjang*, and how they dislodged the Jur-Belle, Bongo and Jur-Luɛɛl. Chapter four explains how the Agar came back from Dɔk land and came to its present areas in central Lakes state. It also explains how the Gok Dinka succeeded to conquer its present territories from the Jur-Belle and the Bongo and also describes the long migration by the Twic, Rek and Malual. As it tells about the Dinka in the Upper Nile and the entire social dimension of the Dinka nation in this modern time this brings us to the end of chapter ten which will lead us to chapter eleven to conclude our history of the Dinka people.

CHAPTER ELEVEN: SLAVERY, SLAVE TRADE AND THE DINKA PEOPLE

INTRODUCTION

This concluding chapter will specifically discuss albeit in brief those succeeding eras which constitute the transition from the Mediaeval period to our present modern era. This is the time when the Dinka community faced a very long pestilence period of slavery and slave trade which started with the coming into Sudan of the Turco-Egyptian colonialism that lasted for more than six decades from 1821 to 1885. This includes the Mahdist period which was from 1885 to the time of Anglo-Egyptian reconquest of the Sudan that took place in 1889.

The Anglo-Egyptians abolished that infamous slavery and the slave trade in Sudan. We will discuss this slave trade and its abolition in relation to the Dinka people in both the Upper Nile and Bahr el Ghazal, although this slavery and slave trade, as a vast topic, will touch some of the many tribes in Sudan in general and the tribes in Southern Sudan in particular. This chapter is crucial because it gives an in-depth survey to the slave trade era and its importances, a topic without which this book about Dinka history will have no meaningful conclusion. The horror stories and suffering which characterised this Turkiya period from 1821 to the fall of Mahdia in 1898 could make volumes of books if the sum total of what the Turks, the Arabs and the Egyptians did on Southern Sudan was to be exhaustively researched into.

TURCO-EGYPTIAN COLONISATION OF SUDAN

SLAVE TRADE AND THE DINKA

The previously known Jaang decided to rename itself as Muɔnyjang during that early part of the 14th century and continued to make itself known by this name throughout the succeeding six centuries. Then there came a time when, from the late 19th century to the early part of the 20th century, the then invincible Muɔnyjang or Jaang came into a rude shock. For the first time since they left Khartoum at the close of the Iron Age, Jaang society in Bahr el Ghazal and Upper Nile found itself faced for the first time by a destructive phenomenon called *slavery and slave trade* in Sudan, a business in humans ushered into Sudan by the Turco-Egyptian colonialists who invaded Sudan and colonised the country and its people for more than sixty years (1821-1885). Although an Indigenous political and religious movement called *Mahdism* from Northern Sudan was able to defeat that Turco-Egyptian colonial regime and established what was called *Mahdist state*, slavery and the slave trade, which should have gone with the Egyptians and the Turks, became more intense as Northern Sudanese who supported Mahdism became the ones to practise it on the Southern Sudanese even to the degree never reached by past foreign nationals.

Along with the rest of the African communities in Southern Sudan, Dinka people faced that prolonged impact of slavery and slave trade at the hands of the Mahdists, their Northern Sudanese Arabs, the Egyptians with their Turks who came from Turkey, the Europeans as well as Asians. For more than sixty years Jaang (Dinka) and the rest of Southern Sudanese underwent that obnoxious trade that came from Northern Sudan, with the Northern Sudanese doing it themselves and as agents to foreign business entrepreneurs.

While the government or academic institutions in South Sudan may one day prepare a unified narrative of what the north and their usual allies have done to Southern Sudan, each community or nationality is for now bound to tell their own ordeal for the benefit of those generations that do not know the genesis of the strained north-south relations which have continued to be that of violence since those early parts of the 1820s and since the north took over the banner of colonialism from foreigners in 1956 to 9 July 2011.

To begin, Jaang, Jieng or Muɔnyjang began to be called strange and derogatory names by Northern Sudanese who flocked to Dinka lands and the entire Southern Sudan during that part of the 19th and 20th centuries. Names such as Jenge (single man) and Zenge were used when calling a Jaang person. The Fertit tribesmen in western Bahr el Ghazal are communities which were easily decimated in the early years of the slave trade. They easily succumbed to the situation and were recruited against the Dinka in that slave trade business of the Jalaba which became more and more about Muɔnyjang at the beginning of the 1830s onwards. The Fertit also called the Jaang derogatory names. Fertit people have slightly bigger tongues than are the Nilotics and other Sudanese because they are Bantus. It is this tongue problem which makes inflection difficult for the Fertits. They have the letter 'Z' for 'J'. This explains why they called Jaang or Jieng as 'Zenge'. Of course, members of the Jaang or Jieng communities did not like being called that as it reminded them of that infamous slavery and slave trade done to them by outsiders.

During that long period of nearly seven decades, Muɔnyjang was being called Zenge and Jenge by the Northern Sudanese and those tribes from the south which submitted to them for both the spread of Islam and trade in humans. This is the period collectively known in Sudanese history as the *slave trade era,* a period which the Rek Dinka of Tonj and Gogrial up to the Malual Dinka in yje Awiel areas still recall in their popular history as *Riäŋ Turuk,* that is, the pestilence of the Turks. Lakes state Dinka communities in eastern Bahr el Ghazal recall that pestilence period as *Riäŋ Malualthith.*[160] East bank Dinka communities in the Upper Nile region also call it so. During this great pestilence age of slave trade, the Dinkas' greatest pestilence time in modern history, is the age at which time the Dinka superiority complex of the Middle Ages was rudely checked by guns and the foreign slavers with some Fertit tribesmen in Bahr el Ghazal doing the job for those outsiders.[161]

BACKGROUND TO SLAVERY

Admittedly, slavery existed in Africa since earliest times. But the nature of African slavery was somewhat different from that of the Middle East and the western world. Nowhere in Africa were domestic servants used in plantations as was the case in the west. It was also rare in Africa for anyone to use someone as a slave except for the kings who used other humans as domestic servants. Slaves in the African concept, however, existed as persons who were

---

160 'Malualthith' is a term used by Lakes state Dinka communities to mean the light skinned foreigners, the Turks, Egyptians and the Arabs, those Middle Eastern Muslim and even Christian people who "were there in the times when the earth was spoiled", quoted from Marc Nikkel's Dinka Christianity (2001), Paulines Publications Africa, Nairobi, Kenya p. 49.

161 Serafino Wani Swaka, A troubled history of Southern Sudan struggles 1821-2011, Juba, Sudan, (2009), p. 7.

severed from their kinsmen, either because they were war captives or because they were excommunicated or had been sold into slavery as a punishment for their crimes.

Both the masters and domestic servants in Africa were blacks. There was no sense of racism in that kind of practice. A servant usually worked in his master's household and was treated much as a member of the household. In many places in Africa, it was considered an insult both to the master and the servant to refer to a person's status as a slave. Some African communities did not even know of slavery up to the coming of foreign intrusions. The Dinka people in the Upper Nile and Bahr el Ghazal were such communities who did not clearly know of slavery up to the advent of the Turco-Egyptian colonialism in Sudan.

However, from the early days before those foreign intrusions, Arab slave traders were being heard by the far border Dinka people to be buying or capturing the blacks from the Nuba Mountains and from Ethiopia. They used to hear distant stories that some blacks from the Nuba mountain areas in Central Sudan, Uduk land and Burun used to be sold to North Africa and to the Middle Eastern countries. Some were sold to southern Europe.

The slave trade of the Arabs in East Africa lasted for many years after the European slave trade in West Africa had come to an end but the Nile valley slavery persisted for much longer, thereby making Sudan become a serious world attention in the late 19th and early 20th centuries.

In the first quarter of the Middle Ages, the whole Dinka community was still in the Upper Nile Basin region before part of them migrated to Bahr el Ghazal. At that time European traders started to move to the west coast of Africa for slaves. When the two Americas were discovered the need arose for cheap and sufficient labour. As a result the African domestic servitude was turned into an internationally profitable business in human beings. European trading communities from Portugal, Holland, France and Britain took part in that slave trade. They came on ships to West Africa carrying guns with which they captured African blacks from the west coastal countries.

In all, as many as ten million African blacks are believed to have been carried to South and North America and to other parts of the world by those slave merchants. Aboard the ships on the Atlantic Ocean the slave captives lived for weeks in filth and horror. Many were chained hand and foot and packed together in the holds so tightly that they could hardly move. Thousands died in the slave ships from brutal treatment and diseases as well as lack of ventilation while en route to the two Americas across the Atlantic Ocean! Some committed suicide on the way, preferring death instead of their ordeal.[162]

In the case of the Nile valley slavery, specifically that of Sudan, a country in the middle of the Nile valley, that most ignoble form of humanity abuse had started in the times of the Pharaonic Egypt. We do not know for certain what form that slavery took but it is generally known that blacks from the Nile valley heartland of the black race, before the Kush Kingdom came into being in 950 BC, were being taken for Egypt's military and for construction of those enduring wonders of Egypt, the pyramids. The Nilotic ancient communities also knew of this slavery of the time when they lived in the main Nile region in ancient Northern Sudan. Dinka ancient forebears who lived as part of those Nilotes during the Napatan and Meroitic periods must have known of this practice which came from Egypt. This is because some of the Dinka tales dating back to that ancient period speak about *Luɛk*, which can be translated to mean servitude.

Olden Dinka people of the pre-Turkiya period used to tell such stories handed to them through generational succession by their

---

162   The world book encyclopaedia, (N-O), Vol. 14, USA, (1973), pp. 106-112.

ancestors as stories from the ancient past. Those ancient Dinka forebears who may have experienced that ancient slavery in the Meroe region were believed to have shown their military worth like the Mazoi who lived with them in the same region since the times of the Kush Kingdom. Those forebears were famous for their great military wars. According to those stories they were known for their valour, courage and perseverance in the face of trying situations and for this reason, Egypt conceived a long lasting tradition which, although it was about all the blacks, was particular with the Jaang people who are our today's Dinka.

During the era of the black pharaohs to the final destruction of the remaining blacks' civilisation in Meroe, that is, from 730 BC to the 3rd century AD, Jaang ancestors had proved their military might as a power on the Nile valley. They indeed supplied the Nile valley blacks' kingdom with a line of ruling kings and military generals with which the Kush was able to give reinforcements to their brethren in Judah and Israel against Assyrian attacks in 689 BC. King Hezekiah of Judah requested that support from King TharYakua of Kush. A force of ten thousand blacks was sent that year from Meroe to Judah in Israel against King Sennacherib's invasion from Assyria. That force was largely made up of Jaang men and the decisive battle that took place in Judah was one of the proofs of Jaang military capability. For detail of this reinforcement from Meroe to Israel, see chapter eight of this book.

THE BEGINNING OF THE SLAVERY OF THE TURKIYA IN SUDAN

The tradition for moving strong people into Egypt's Army from Sudan was based on the history summarised above and was one of Mohammed Ali's later strong motives for his conquest of the Sudan in 1821. Mohammed Ali, an Albanian Muslim officer from the Ottoman Empire, was mandated by the Ottoman Emperor to conquer Egypt from the Mameluks in 1805. Once in power in Egypt, Mohammed Ali turned Nile valley slavery into international commerce. Having taken much of Northern Sudan into the imperial realm of the Ottoman Empire from 1820-1821, Mohammed Ali immediately instructed his Turco-Egyptian colonial authorities in Sudan to embark on capturing the Sudanese as slaves for Egypt. In response to those directives, Ibrahim, the elder son of Mohammed Ali, set out southwards from Sennar, the initial Turco-Egyptian capital of Sudan, seeking more and more slaves to capture and send to Egypt. The Turco-Egyptian garrison commander at Dongola was ordered by Ibrahim to build boats and distribute them along the reaches of the navigable parts of the main Nile between the Nile's cataracts. Mohammed Ali had timber and nails sent from Cairo for the construction of those boats in Berber for carrying slaves to Egypt.

When Ibrahim[163] made a request for reinforcements from Egypt to properly administer the then occupied areas of Northern Sudan, his father replied that he would send 1000 troops for every 3000 fit male negroes received from him, especially from among the Dinka. He strongly directed that Ismail (more to follow on him) should hurry to open and direct urgent armed raids into the Dinka country south of the Gezira area. He also directed Ibrahim to capture only young negroes, including women and girls of good standing, and send them via Suakin port on the Red Sea for sale in the markets of Jeda to purchase rice needed for the Turco-Egyptian army garrisons in Northern Sudan. He also directed that his Turco-Egyptian soldiers in Sudan be paid with slaves as their monthly salaries. A strong slave in his youthhood was valued at fifteen dollars. Three strong slaves were sufficient salary for an Egyptian officer per month.

This act by Mohammed Ali led to a big scramble for slaves in

---

163   Ibid, p. 122

Sudan. The need to open into the inscrutable swamplands of the sudd in the Upper Nile began to be considered by the Turco-Egyptian authorities as a case for study. The race for slaves in Sudan had begun as such. Sudan slavery was thus raised to beyond international slave trade status compared to that which was on the east and West African coasts.

Although former Northern Sudanese domestic slavery exorbitantly turned profitable, Mohammed Ali wanted blacks from Southern Sudan, particularly from the Dinka, to be the backbone of his Egyptian military establishment for his great wars of conquests in southwestern Asia and in South America. This was so because by then the Egyptian peasantry, the fellahin, were to till the land to sustain the growing Egyptian economy.

Mohammed Ali also did that in fulfilment of the hitherto growing tradition about the blacks and more so about the Dinka. The plans to move to the negro south for the reported large reservoirs of vulnerable blacks continued to be underway. Some time back in 66 AD, during the reign of the Roman Emperor Nero, a Roman expeditionary force had attempted to cross beyond the Upper Nile, but was forced to retreat by the obstacle of the sudd.[164]

The areas south of the Gezira were until then considered mysteriously impenetrable swamp and jungle lands. Ancient thought about Southern Sudan from Northern Sudan and beyond has been that the territory was sealed off by a terribly huge swamp of the Nile and its network of streams and rivers that formed the sudd and which in its full extent was believed to be as big as England. It is probably the largest swampland in the world.

---

164 brahim was Mohammed Ali's eldest son and brother of Ismail who implemented the military conquest and occupation of Sudan up to Sennar. Ibrahim was later sent by his father to Sennar to assist Ismail as a consult and commander of the Turco-Egyptian forces in Sudan. He was a war-tried Pasha who annexed a number of Arab countries before the conquest of Sudan

The then existing concept about this sudd was that no any society, civilised or savage, ever existed there. This naturally protected the African man or society who lived in this region or further south of it. The lust for blacks of Southern Sudan that would later force Mohammed Ali to go against that inscrutable destiny was postponed for the time being when the Jaalyin people of Mek Nimr in Shendi assassinated Ismail Pasha, late in October 1822.[165]

Ismail, the conqueror of the riverine Sudan up to Sennar suddenly decided to leave Medani for Egypt, leaving his elder brother Ibrahim to administer the occupied areas of Sudan. Arriving in Shendi from Medani on boats, Ismail demanded an outrageous contribution of 30 000 dollars and 6000 slaves to be paid to him by the Jaalyin within two days. The Jaalyin and their king, Mek Nimr, could simply not afford that unusual request in an unusually specified time. Losing his temper, Ismail angrily hit Mek on his nose with his big tobacco pipe. Blood jetted out of the old man's nostrils. In a communal resolve to retaliate the Jaalyin decided to pile up grass for an ostensible fence built for Ismail to spend his night there with his retinue. In the night the Jaalyin set that fence on fire. Ismail and all his staff were therefore murdered within the burning blaze. The disturbing news of the death of Ismail went to Egypt and westwards to Dafterdar in El Obeid. Mohammed Ali in Cairo and Dafterdar in El Obeid were enraged and therefore became engaged in the retributive reprisals against the Northern Sudanese communities along the Nile up to Medani and the outlying Northern Sudanese areas of the White Nile, avenging the killing of his son, Ismail. By November and December of 1822 Dafterdar, who became commander-in-chief of all the occupational forces in Sudan had brutally killed 40 000 Northern Sudanese. Northern Sudanese tribes either fled east to the Abyssinian borders or surrendered finally to the Turco-Egyptian forces. The

---

165 Marc R Nikkel, Dinka Christianity, (2001), p. 49

whole of what is now Northern Sudan except Darfur was made to lay down prostrate before Dafterdar.

Then the Turco-Egyptian colonial government sought to firmly root itself after those punitive retribution campaigns across the whole length of the Northern Sudan part of the Nile. Northern Sudanese communities therefore decided to submit and embraced the Turco-Egyptian colonialists. After all, they were fellow Muslims. The Danagla and the Jaalyin in particular found they could benefit from the new colonial regime by participating in the government *ghazwazes* (armed raids) which began to be launched on the Shilluks and on the Dinka communities bordering the Gezira region to the south. They therefore went out in their thousands to form the Turco-Egyptian colonial slavery armed units called *Jihadiya*, Bashbazuk in Turkish language. The cattle owning Arab Baggara, the Masiriya in Kordofan and the Rizzeigat in Darfur, were later pulled in to accompany government expeditions against the cattle owning Dinka, with whom they had long competed for grazing lands.

By 1827 a huge Turco-Egyptian military expedition led by none other than Aga Pasha Khurshid, the Turco-Egyptian governor-general then called *Hakimdar*, was launched from Khartoum against the Abialang Dinka community of Renk. About 500 strong Dinka men and girls were captured in a surprise raid and taken to Khartoum, bound for Egypt.[166] Other loot was taken with those captives, especially cattle, goats and sheep. Thereafter a number of armed raids continued to be launched against the Ngok Dinka people of Abyei and against the Abialang Ageer, Nyiel and Dongjol Dinka communities, not to mention the Shilluks.[167]

This launching of armed raids from Khartoum continued until the Turco-Egyptian authorities decided to establish two military regi-

---

166 Mohamed Faud Shukry, The Khedive Ismail in Sudan, (1938), p. 132

167 PM Holt, A modern history of the Sudan, 3rd ed., 2nd impression, (London)

ments to the borders of the Abialang Dinka and Shilluks in 1837.[168] Since then the annual slaving expeditions into Dinka country in the Northern and western Upper Nile areas inhabited by the Ruweng Dinka of Chief Bilkuei, Alor Dinka areas of Chief Kur Kuot and into the Ngok Dinka territories of Chief Kuol Arop Biong characterised those initial years of the Turkiya, and with the opening of the White Nile to free trade after 1849,[169] the Dinka, with the rest of the southern tribes, witnessed an escalation of violence, sparked off by the increased slave trade activities. Savage slave traders of different nationalities, French, Syrian, Lebanese, Egyptian and Northern Sudanese, appeared for the first time in Dinka country. Among these was a French man named de Mälzac who was reported to have greatly enjoyed surrounding his slave trading stations called Zaribas with the skulls of his human victims.[170] Two Syrian traders, Ibrahim Bass and a certain Habib, became notorious around the Bor Dinka areas. In one single raid they killed over a hundred people among the Bor Dinka and looted many cattle.[171]

In consequence, Egypt was now filled up with slaves from Southern Sudan. Cairo and other Egyptian cities and towns established slave markets supplied through a network of slave routes from Sudan and East Africa. Those routes included the great caravan routes coming from Sennar, carrying the Uduk, Burun and Shilluks as well as the Dinka from those bordering areas of the White Nile. There was later the biggest slave caravan route from Darfur, taking the hinterland West African Blacks from Chad, south and eastern

---

168   R Collins, Land beyond the rivers: The Southern Sudan, 1898-1918, (Yale 1971), p. 280

169   Mohammed Faud Shukry, Khedive Ismail and slavery in the Sudan, Cairo, Egypt, (1938), p. 147

170   PM Holt, A modern history of the Sudan, 3rd edition, 2nd impression, (London) (1972), p. 53

171   Ibid.

Nigeria, Deim Zubayr in the Fertit lands, in Western Bahr el Ghazal from the areas of the Jur of Chat, the Jur-col around Wau and the large Malual Dinka of Northern Bahr el Ghazal.

The Ngok Dinka slaves were taken to Kordofan where they were made to either join that route otherwise known as *Sharia Arbiin*, the forty days route to Egypt, or they were driven directly to Khartoum. Bornu town in West Africa also acted as the slave emanation centre, like Sennar and Deim Zubayr. Wadai in West Africa was another big slave centre. The East African slaves and those from the Ethiopian highland regions were carried through the Red Sea and the Indian Ocean. The sultans of the kingdom of Sennar had, since 1500 through to the 17th century, extracted war captives from the Nuba Hills region and from western Ethiopia and by the close of the 18th century, Sennar began sending military expeditions into the northeastern territories of the Dinka.[172]

THE COMING OF THE SLAVE TRADE TO THE BAHR EL GHAZAL DINKA AREAS

At the time the Dinka border communities of northern and western Upper Nile and the Ngok suffered the initial slave incursions of the first two decades of the Turkiya, the hinterland Dinka communities were yet to experience those initial impunities. Prior to 1830 the hinterland Dinka of Bahr el Ghazal and the central as well as the southern Upper Nile Dinka people did not experience that commercial and militarised slave trade. The menace was being heard of from afar as distant land stories. Slave traders from all over the world were soon to flock to the entire Southern Sudan during the middle of 1830s after they had wreaked havoc on the Nuba, the

---

172   Serafino Wani Swaka, A troubled history of Southern Sudan struggles 1821-2002, Juba, Sudan, (2009), p. 6

Shilluks and the north-south border Dinka.

Kaka in Shilluk land even became the main centre and springboard of the slave armed raids then known as ghazwazes, and although many slave traders came to the Upper Nile region through the White Nile most of them came there by land as the north and west Upper Nile areas are very adjacent to Northern Sudan, especially the White Nile areas of Kosti and Rabek in central Sudan, places which were among the springboards and routes for slave traders coming to Southern Sudan from Khartoum, which had at this time become the capital seat of the Turkiya and Mahdiya. Khartoum was where slave merchants used to obtain concessionary rights licences for slave trade business in Southern Sudan.

By the close of the 1830s slavery and the slave trade had started to arrive in the interior of the entire Dinka lands, both in Bahr el Ghazal and in the Upper Nile. In a big way they came through Western Sudan by way of Nyala to the Fertit areas in Western Bahr el Ghazal and settled at what became Deim Zubayr, where Zubayr Wad Rahma Mansur and his son Suleiman established the biggest slave kingdom for the whole of Bahr el Ghazal.

Zubayr was a Jaali Arab trader from Jeilly. Here in the Ndogo land he raised an army known as Bashbazuk with which he decimated much of the Fertit population. He extended to the Jur-Chat areas, from where slave trade reached the large Dinka community of Malual in the present Northern Bahr el Ghazal state. It was this Fertit Army of slaves which Zubayr later used in capturing the Fur Kingdom of Darfur in October 1874.[173]

---

173   Mohamed Faud Shukry, The Khadive Ismail and slavery in the Sudan, Cairo, Egypt, (1938), p. 172.

SLAVE TRADE ROUTES AND THEIR NETWORK IN DINKA LANDS

From Deim Zubayr the slavers brought the Ndogo, Balanda-Bor, Bandas, Zande, Kresh, Binga, Bai, Yulu, Indiri and the other Fertit tribal communities into near extinction. The Chat community readily welcomed Zubayr and immediately embraced Islam. As slave traders also wanted ivory Zubayr also brought a big type of bladed spear to which the Chat people gave the name *uthuro*. This was a spear with which they used to kill the elephants and rhinos. As Luo, the Chat people did have skill in iron smelting. Their area was rich in iron ore. They manufactured a lot of uthuro on the slavers' demand. A poisonous substance locally known as *mataba* used to be smeared on the blades and tip of that uthuro to quickly kill the elephant once it was speared with it. Needed from the dead elephant or rhino was its tusks and horns, not the meat.

Here, from Deim Zubayr were two routes, the route from Darfur to Id el Ganam through the copper mine areas now called Hofurat Al Nahas. That route used to pass through the tribal lands of Kresh, Yulu and Binga up to Kata and finally to Raja. It then passed by way of Mangaya through Banda land and finally to Deim Zubayr, the slaves kingdom city of Zubayr. From Deim Zubayr the route continued eastwards, passing through Nyabulu to what is now Khor Gana, then to Wau. This was the route used by the slavers to come to the present Tonj areas. Slaves who came to Tonj territories were led by another famous Coptic Egyptian by the name of Girgis Ghataz Abdel Massieh,[174] then to Gondokoro in Eastern Equatoria through Cuɛibɛt, Rumbek and the present Yirol town, then to Terkeka and to Gondokoro. The second route to the Awiel areas was that which

---

174 Girgis or George Ghataz was an Egyptian Coptic Christian who came from Alexandria during that slave trade era.

started at Deim Zubayr through to the Abiem area of the big Malual Dinka where it was met by the route from Dhɛɛn and Adila in Southern Kordofan. That route proceeded up to Twic land in what is now Northern Warrap state.[175]

Apart from those big routes to and from Deim Zubayr there was also the big White Nile route via its tributary, the Bahr el Ghazal River, that meanders through and traverses the whole of the Gogrial areas to Kuajök, after which it finally becomes River Wau, initially entering Liɛtnhom in the area of the Apuk section of Nyarmong to the present Gogrial town and through to what is now Kuajök city. There was another river that branches upstream to become the Lol River, which also traverses much of the Twic Dinka in Northern Warrap and goes to the Giɛrnyaang areas of Awiel. The third route was the main river, on which sits Meshra port, about eight miles east of the present Akɔp Payam headquarters town in the Tonj North county area of Apuk-Padɔc.

Steamboats that were also driven by cloth flown by the winds, used to bring slave traders to the interior of Twic, Gogrial and Tonj during the months of autumn and winter when the swamps' waters of the Bahr el Ghazal marshes have receded back into those rivers and their network of streams and ponds.

Slave traders also came to Twic lands through Ngok of Abyei and from Twic by way of Wunrɔɔk to Gogrial, although the Nyin-Acuil river calling station on the Jur River used to be very famous as the entry point for the slavers to Liɛtnhom in the Apuk-Giir areas of the present Gogrial East county.

Slave traders also came to the interior of Tonj territories through the river port of Meshra in the northeastern parts of Tonj. They also came to the eastern parts of Bahr el Ghazal by way of the two ports of Shambe and Gutthom in Yirol. Other slave traders came to the Bahr

---

175 Santandrea S, A tribal history of the Western Bahr el Ghazal, Nigrizia, Boulogne, Italy, (1964), p.28.

el Ghazal Dinka areas of Agar, Kiec, Aliap and Atuöt from as far as Gondokoro, east of the present Juba city. Gondokoro was then the seat of the Turco-Egyptian colonial government in Southern Sudan.

For the whole of this Turco-Egyptian and Mahdist Period (1821-1898) the Dinka people, though briefly touched on above, came into seriously rude contact with those Turco-Egyptians and a horde of European and Middle Eastern business entrepreneurs with the Northern Sudanese acting either as their agents or as slave traders of their own. After 1849 up to about 100 000 slave merchants, their soldiers and retinues were already in the Dinka areas in Southern Sudan, ravaging the population in an area of about 350 000 square miles.

The Turco-Egyptian Government in Khartoum, under the policy of dividing southern territories into commercial zones as a quick means to earn huge revenues for the development of Egypt, opened South Sudan asunder!

A particular merchant, or a group of traders or companies that paid for a particular zone in Southern Sudan, was made responsible for all the humans and animals of trade in that area. Each merchant or company was given a licence, then known as concessionary rights, from Khartoum.

There was, for example, a joint venture trading enterprise known as the *Aqqad And Company*. That slave trading enterprise of several merchants with trading houses in Khartoum and Cairo was given a concessionary right and control of an area of 90 000 square miles from Bahr el Ghazal to the White Nile and southern Upper Nile areas to beyond Gondokoro.[176]

On the White Nile the Dinka and Baria were badly decimated by the presence of three notorious slave traders. One of these was Alexander Vauder, a Sardinian pro-consul to Sudan who decided to engage in the slave and ivory business on the White Nile. He was

---

176 Santandrea S, A tribal history of the Western Bahr el Ghazal, Nigrizia, Boulogne, Italy, (1964), p. 39.

later killed with his nephew and a crew of 15 men by a party of 4000 Baria in 1867. There was E Kurt Binder and Lafargue from France. To the north of the White Nile was Mohd Khair, who was in control of the Shilluk and Dinka lands of the Dongjol, Abialang and Ruweng areas of Pan-Ru and Alor Kur Kuot in western Upper Nile. His slave empire was based at Kaka in Shilluk land. Then there was Wed Ibrahim, another notorious slave merchant who depopulated the Nyiel and Ageer Dinka communities in northern Upper Nile. The two, Mohd Khair and Wad Ibrahim, even asked the Turco-Egyptian Hakimdar in Khartoum if they could administer the Upper Nile on his behalf.

With the assassination of Ghataz by the Rek Dinka at Athowei in the Lɛɛr area in 1854, Mohammed al Buseili took over his Zeribas and the concessionary right licence for his zone. By 1855 a certain Habashi, commanding one of John Petherick's boats, pioneered the discovery of the main channels of the Bahr el Ghazal River. He sailed up to Nyin-Acuil on the Kɔngɔɔr-Apuk of Giir Thiik borders to the toch, then to Liɛtnhom, the present administrative headquarters town of Gogrial East county. Nyin-Acuil at the time became the calling station for big boats and slave ships that brought many slave merchants to the hinterland areas of the Rek Dinka. These channels brought to Rekland the famous two French traders, one being Savoyard the merchant. He was such an aggressive cattle and slave business man among the Lakes Dinka. There was in later times an Italian merchant by the name of Antonio Brun-Rollet. He was another notorious slave merchant who committed into his employ a number of the Jallaba.

John Petherick had a big trading house in Khartoum and was known for boat making, which he used to sell to a horde of slave traders to use for bringing guns and business items like salt, cloth, beads and so on, all for chiefs who were ready to facilitate them in their slave trade activities among their people. Merchants from central Europe also participated. There was among them the slave hunter of the worst type. He was a certain Heuglin who was working in concert with a certain Lejean. JA Vayssiere on his part was widely known for ivory buying on both the White Nile and the areas of central Bahr el Ghazal.

By 1882, Lup ton Bey, the Turco-Egyptian governor of Bahr el Ghazal, was faced with a delicate security situation. Government stations were threatened by a concentration of hostile Dinka from Kuac, Apuk-Giir and Abiem. In the east of Bahr el Ghazal, the Kiec, Aliap and Atuöt Dinka community attacked the Turco-Egyptian Army garrison at Shambe. This resulted in the deaths of one hundred and fifty Egyptian solders. Seventy five more soldiers were intercepted and exterminated by the Agar Dinka that year and the administrative headquarters in Agar country, Rumbek, was destroyed in 1883 and four hundred Turco-Egyptian soldiers killed.[177]

Involved in that inhuman business, beside the Turks, Europeans and the Egyptians, were the Arabs from Yemen, Syria and Lebanon. There were the Armenians, the Maltese and many others from the Mediterranean world. There were the Arabised Northern Sudanese such as the Beja and the Danagla and, most of all, the actual Arab tribesmen from Northern Sudan such as the Baggara, the Jallyiin from around Khartoum and beyond and the Kababish from central Sudan. All these multitudes of slave and ivory traders rushed to the Dinka areas as to the rest of the south. They galvanised the entire Southern Sudan from the 1830s to the advent of the Anglo-Egyptian colonial rule of 1898-1956.

Among the Ghataz network of slave centres in the Tonj district areas was one famous Zariba at Manyang-Ngɔɔk in Thɔny area,

---

177   R Gray, OP Cit, pp. 157, G. Casati, Ten years in Equatoria and the return with Emin Pasha, (London 1891), Vol.I, p. 76; R.O Collins, 'The Southern Sudan, 1883-1889' (Yale 1962), p.45, G. Schweitzer, The life and work of Emin Pasha, Westminster 1898, vol.I, p. 147

about 12 kms east of present Tonj town. Here, a number of chiefs who refused to aid the slavers in the capture of their subjects were caught, handcuffed and thrown into the furnace of a fathomless pit of fire dug by the slavers for dealing with recalcitrants. Among them was Chief Riɛm Atem of the Pacakiir clan in the Buɔɔt section of Thɔny. At Cuɛi-Ajai, about 18 miles west of Tonj town, was one of the Ghataz Zaribas from where his Bashbazuk slave armies depopulated the surrounding Luo, the Jur-col and the Dinka sections of Yar, Muɔk and Apuk of Juwiir and Nyang.

Because of the river Tonj, Ghataz later transferred Cuɛi-Ajai Zariba to the location that is now Tonj town. From Tonj, slavers would organise armed raids into the interior of Apuk of Juwiir and along the river Tonj to the eastern communities of Luackoth, Aköök-Teek, Jalwau and the big Luacjang in the far eastern end of the Tonj sub-region. At Pawɛng in the Thiik area on the present road to Luacjang was another of Ghataz's slave stockade (Zariba) from where the captured slaves were assembled en route to Meshra port for waiting steamers and ships to hurry them to Khartoum for Egypt slave markets.

Ismailiya the ship was known for carrying slaves from Meshra, Shambe, Gutthom and Gondɔkoro. The Luac and Rek Dinka communities of Anan-Atak (present Tonj East county) had Pawɛng in the Thiik area as their fateful assembly point. The local community leader at the time was cooperating or was indeed an agent of Ghataz's slave trading enterprise against his community.

Other slave centres of Ghataz in the Tonj area included a location by the name of *Athowei* in the Lɛɛr section of Kuac, about 23 miles north of the present town of Thiet. Yonder from Athowei was another spot by the name of *Langkab*, two kms from the northern suburb of the traditional holy village of *Tharakon* in the Jur-Bol section of Awan territory. Langkap was a stopover stockade on the main route to Apuk-Padɔc where there was also another big slave centre at the present Bundiir settlement camp area. Slaves from different directions were assembled at this *Bundiir* slave centre before they were finally chained and driven to the port of Meshra for *Ismailiya* and other waiting river vessels such as *Tawafikia*, which hauled the slaves to Khartoum, never to return again! Other captives from Luacc" jang were driven along the swamp route to the Lou-Paher areas of Wunkuel, then to Meshra port and off on *Ismailiya* and *Tawafikia*. They would be taken to Khartoum and to Egypt, also never to return!

To the east of present Warrap town was a location by the name of *Jaden*, later renamed as *Awuul*. Jaden was a very big stopover slave trading centre where captured slaves from Jur-col or the Luo community east of present Wau town were all joined up with captives from the Rek Dinka areas of Nyang, Abuɔk, Abiem, Noi and those from the nearby areas of Kɔŋgöör. Here in Jaden slaves were finally taken off on the march to Meshra port. Steamers and ships would carry them off to Khartoum via Bahr el Ghazal River which joins the Nile River at its confluence with the Bahr el Jebel part of the White Nile, somewhere upstream before Yoynyang in Bentiu in the western Upper Nile region.

GREAT LUAL NGOR SLAVE KINGDOM AT AƔERDIT IN THE APUK-GIIR AREA OF NYARMONG

As mentioned earlier the same Girgis Ghataz Abdel Massieh had extended his slave trade business to the Rek Dinka county of Tonj and Gogrial up to Twic. One of his biggest slave centres in Gogrial areas was based at a spot now known as AƔɛrdit within the present Lietnhom, the county headquarters for the Apuk-Giir territory of the Rek Dinka of Gogrial East. Here a great Dinka slave agent by the name of Lual Ngor established his slave kingdom in 1868. Lual

Ngor, a trained Bashbazuk soldier, wreaked considerable havoc on all the Rek Dinka areas of Kɔŋgöör, Lou-Mawien, invariably known also as Lou-Ariik, Abiem, Noi, Abuɔɔk, Nyang and the whole of Apuk of Giir Thiik, plus areas of Adiang and Akuär in Twic, as well as areas of Aguɔk, Awan Mou and Awan Chan plus Awan Pajok, all to the west.

While working very well for his slave trade master, Lual Ngor was also able to build for himself a terribly commanding dynasty at this AYɛrdit. Through innumerable armed raidings he was able to loot many cows as well as beautiful young women and girls for himself and his forces. The stories of Lual Ngor's pestilence are still fresh in the whole of the Rekland areas of Gogrial and Northern Tonj to the present day. Like his master Ghataz, he was killed by a communal attack organised by the nearby Kɔŋgoor and Apuk-Giir people at the close of the Mahdists' era, that is, during the few years preceding the Anglo-Egyptian reconquest of Sudan in 1898.

In the Twic Dinka area to the north of Gogrial, *Wunrɔɔk* in Adiang land was the most conspicuous slave centre. Wunrɔɔk on the Lol River acquired its name from the slave's palisaded fences, the stockade or zariba in Arabic. In Dinka, a fence made of wood, sometimes of thorn wood, is called *rɔk*. Rɔɔk with double 'ɔ' is a plural of Rɔk. There were therefore many stockades at Wunrɔɔk from the root word Wun-rɔɔk. Dhaŋrial at Wut-nhom and Apadaaŋ zaribas were parts of the Wunrɔɔk cluster of stockades.

Between Tonj and Rumbek was also a big slave trade network of zariba centres. Notable of these were those at, say, Laŋdit in the Ayiɛl section of the Gok Dinka and another on a location north of Gul-Maar River, that is, north of the present Kubur William Deng's spot. Those centres were so big as to terrorise the entire Gok community.

Pendit, in the northern suburbs of the present city of Rumbek, was one such slave trading centre of far reaching effect among the Agaar

Dinka communities. There are a lot of local stories about this Pendit and its slave traders. The Agaars, however, planned to attack the slave traders at Pendit on one remarkable occasion which continues to give very vivid stories of the *Age of Malualthith* period in Dinka land. There was a large road from Pendit through the eastern section of Agaar through to Atuöt and the Kiec Dinka areas in Yirol where Dinka slave captives were hauled off to Khartoum by steamers at Shambe port and also at Gutthom port in Kiec and Aliap lands.

The big Aqad slave company from Gondokoro, Lado, Rejaf and Juba also used to reach out with its equatorial network into Pendit in Rumbek. Hordes of slave trading merchants had long been in Equatoria. Slave traders like Abu Baker (killed at the battle in Nimule in 1894), Omar Salih (later killed in the battle of 2 February 1897 at Rejaf, Urabi Abdalla), Haj Abu Garja and a horde of the Mahdist slave soldiers went to Equatoria through the Nile River after the Nile's mystery was removed by the British explorers, Spakes and Grant, besides Samuel White Baker who was later followed by General Charles George Gordon, all at the employ of the Khedive Ismail of Egypt.

Prior to the fall of the Turco-Egyptian colonial regime, Southern Sudanese tribes, particularly the Dinka, Baria and the Zande, were now fed up and were on the offensive. In Equatoria, for example, the Turco-Egyptian station near Mongalla came under fierce attack from the Dinka Bor. One hundred and seventy Egyptian soldiers were killed in an ambush by a combined Bor-Nuer native force in 1884. Dinka tribesmen even joined the Baria Chief Befe in 1885 in a concerted attack on the Turco-Egyptian stations at Lado and Rejaf.[178]

Those European explorers had helped to rend the south asunder. Tens of thousands of slave traders and their armies swarmed the south and Juba with Lado, Rejaf and Gondokoro acting as the biggest

---

178 Richard Gray, op cit, p.61

springboards and centres where slavers radiated to the Dinka eastern areas of Bahr el Ghazal and Bor.

Shiekh Ahmed Al Aqqad, a partner in the firm of Al Aqqad Trading Company and who held a government ivory concessionary licence, was so powerful among the Baria people inside and around present Juba. With him was another strong slave merchant by the name of Abu Al Sa'ud. Those Arab slave traders were able to defeat Samuel Baker, who had to abandon the Khedive Ismail's mission of suppressing slave trade in Southern Sudan, especially in today's Juba county areas.

Samuel White Baker handed the administration of Equatoria province to Mohammed Rauf Bey. He also left the command of the Turco-Egyptian forces to Abdel Gadir Hilmi. The two later became governor-generals of the Sudan. Considered to have failed, Baker was replaced with General Charles George Gordon, whose plans and activities as a military man sufficed to dislodge those slave traders in Equatoria in 1874. Gordon's anti-slavery campaigns in Equatoria made most of the slave traders run to the Bahr el Ghazal region. Bahr el Ghazal Dinka people were to bear the combined effect of all the slave traders who had come to the south before Gordon's appointment in 1873.

MAHDIA AND SLAVE TRADE IN DINKA LANDS

Different from the slave trade in the rest of the south, slavery and slave trade among the Ngok Dinka of Abyei and that in the Dinka areas of Malual in Northern Bahr el Ghazal did have a special dimension, especially during the Mahdiyya period. Perhaps due to their close proximity with Northern Sudan, their slave trade came to be politically associated with the Madhists movement in the first instance. They supported the Mahdists' movement against the Turco-Egyptian colonial regime in Sudan. The two areas of the Dinka including Twic gave their lot in support of the Mahdists' revolution, only to discover after the overthrow of the Turco-Egyptian colonial regime that they were giving support to the worst slave traders.

NGOK DINKA SUPPORT TO THE MAHDISTS' MOVEMENT

Great Arop Biong and his Ngok Dinka community suffered the main brunt of what was the slavery of the Turkiyya. From 1826 to the time of the rise of the Mahdists' movement in Sudan (1881), Ngok people, like the other communities bordering Northern Sudan, especially those to the northern parts of Upper Nile region, witnessed unbearable armed ghazwazes. Later on his great son, Chief Kuol Arop, saw what the slavery of the Mahdiya was. The Twic to the south of Ngok also suffered along with the Ngok and this explains why Great Bol Nyuol also committed the Twic in support of the Mahdists alongside Ngok Dinka.

During Turkiyya Mitrɔk, now casually called Miro, in the Abior section of Ngok, was the biggest slave centre of the Turkiyya where slave captives from all over Ngok, from Twic, from the eastern parts of Malual Dinka of the Awiel region, from the far away northern area of Tonj, even the Fertits and the Nuer-Bul people of Monytuiil, were gathered here for their final march to Northern Sudan. Abin-Thöny, the home of Kuol Biong which up to the present time is the traditional rites centre of the Pajök clan people, was another slave centre. Abin-Thöny is the present town of Abyei. A certain Ali Jula, a Massiri from the Mazareni section of the Baggara Arabs was the Turco-Egyptian agent doing almost the whole of the slave trade work for the government in Khartoum. He had a well armed detachment with which he was able to wreak havoc on the Ngok Dinka. He established several stockades throughout their nine territories. Ali Jula raided the cattle of the Ngok in much the same way he took Ngok people for Khartoum and Egypt.

Believing that Mahdiya was a national political liberation movement to rid the country from the infamous Turco-Egyptian colonial rule and its pestilence of slave trade, Chief Kuol Arop gave support to the Mahdi against what he thought was a foreign exploitation of the country. Chief Kuol Arop committed the Ngok Dinka society to join the Mahdist movement in a bid to rid them of the slave trade. The Ngok people therefore fought shoulder to shoulder with the Mahdists forces as part of the Ansars, that is, followers of the Mahdi and his revolution. The Mahdists' appeal was well received by the Dinka as far back as the Agaar Dinka in the eastern region of Bahr el Ghazal, where leaders such as Mayen Dut were mobilising the Agaar Dinka to revolt against the Turco-Egyptian authorities and their zoriba stations. But the very slave traders of the Turkiya, the Jalaba, turned and jumped overboard to embrace the Mahdist call so that most of them became the commanders of the different legions of the Mahdist revolutionary armed movement.

MALUAL DINKA SUPPORT FOR THE MAHDISTS' MOVEMENT

Like the Ngok and Twic, the slave trade in the areas of Malual Dinka in Northern Bahr El Ghazal was very different from the rest of the slave trade in the region. In the middle of the Turkiyya, slave trade on the Malual Dinka people initially came through Deim Zubayr by way of the Jur-Chat areas and from Dhɛɛn to the north. The Chat people in northwestern Bahr el Ghazal were used by the slave traders against their neighbouring Dinka communities, as were the Fertits.

In the course of the devastations by Zubayr in the western parts of Awiel, one spiritual overlord for the Buɔth-Anyaar section of Malual Dinka, a community leader by the name of Dengdit, reached out for arms from the slavers as a collaborator. He is said by traditions from the area to have acquired up to 200 rifles as Zubayr's agent in the territory. This local lord later visited central Africa up to Zulu land in South Africa, taking ivory there for sale as was done by the Baria, who flocked to Ethiopia carrying ivory in exchange for guns.[179] He came back with the name Shak-Shak, the Zulu word for king. Slave trade flourished mostly among the Buɔth- Anyaar and was based in the Gomjuɛɛr area.

The Abiem and Paliëët sections of Malual also got slave trade through Deim Zubayr by the same way of Chat. The large Abiem community was even the route for slavers to Twic and to Mitrɔk slave centres in Ngok. Paliëët and Malual-Giɛrnyaang proper, however, bore the full brunt of the slave trade through Dhɛɛn in the north, but more during the Mahdia. Despite this picture, some sources in the area of Malual, as in the whole of Southern Sudan, consider the slave trade of the Turkiyya to have been far less than the slave trade of the Mahdia, especially among the Malual Dinka people in the west and the northern areas that are Twic and Ngok. Some Giɛrnyaang[180] people paradoxically attribute this to the role played by their paramount Spear Master Dengdit, otherwise known also as Shak-shak. He is presented as being Deng Kuel from the Parek clan people. Shak-Shak must have been the corruption of the name Atiak-tiak or Awutiak, one of the family names of the Payii and Parek clans among the Dinka.[181]

---

179   Serafina Wani Swaka, OPCIT

180   'Giɛrnyanng' is the name of a specific section of Malual Dinka that forms the Aweil North County of today. However, the name is sometimes used invariably by their neighbouring Rek to mean the whole of the Malual Dinka. Giɛrnyang proper are the sections of Kɔrɔɔk of Chief Aciɛn Yɔɔr, Duluit area of Chief Bol Deng, Atokthɔu area of Chief Mathok Diing and those many other sections that makes Awiel North country.

181   The author himself comes from the Payii clan people of Ayii Thiek in the Awan-Parek area in Tonj North county. Parek and Ayii were parallel ancestors

With the Mahdia, slave trade became more intensive on the Giɛrnyaang people. It took the status of warfare between the slavers, or more correctly the Massiriya, and the Giɛrnyaang but, with the news of the rise of a movement in the north, Giɛnyaang rose to embrace the new movement, wanting to avenge and avoid the slave trade brutality of Zubayr of the Turkiyya. The whole of the Malual Dinka in all its sections rose up to support the Mahdist movement against the Turco-Egyptian colonial regime and their ignoble slave trade. Malual Dinka society became part of the Ansars against the Turco-Egyptian colonialists, mistaking the movement as a national liberation programme to rid the country of the foreign ills of the Turco-Egyptian rule.

During the early days of the rise of the Mahdists' movement, Dengdit, a grandson of Awutiak (i.e. Atiak-Tiak) gave his brother's daughter, Awit Duang Kuel Mohamed Ahmed to Al-Mhadi in order to cement and concretise the alliance between the Mahdi and the Malual Dinka community. That girl from the Akeuic village was taken to Aba Island in the Gezira region where Mahdi was encamped. Mohammed Ahmed Al-Mahdi accepted her and gave her a new Arabic name *Magbul*, meaning accepted. This Magbul became the mother of Abdel Rahman Al-Mahdi, the grandfather of the first Sudanese prime minister, Sadig Al-Mahdi, who had also long been the leader of the UMMA (United Muslim migrants association) party in Sudan.

Large parties from the Malual community moved from their areas and sections and joined the Mahdists movement in El Obeid. Those who joined the Mahdists movement specifically included the Padhieu clan people of Great Aturjöng Anyuon of the Makem Aköt Wol area of Gok-Machar in Awiel West, the Pariath clan people of those of

---

from one family line of the remote Anei-Parek who participated in the Jaang crossing of the Nile to Bahr el Ghazal in 1340 AD from the Upper Nile Basin region.

Deng Deng Aköt, the Payom clan people of Cimiir-Adöŋbeek from the area of Aric-thieec, the big Parek clan people of Dengdit from Gömjuɛɛr in the Palieupiny section and the Pagɛu clan people of great Kuac Kuac Mayieldit from the Cimel area of Abiem Great Rɛɛc (Dincol). Rɛɛc Lual of the Paciɛrmeth also took part with his people as did other great warriors like famous Wol Rɛɛc (Wol-Rialkuei), Nyuol (Makuei) of Aturjöng and Aköök Rɛɛc, otherwise known popularly as Aköök-Mayath. Wol-Rialkuei was also known as Wol-Agutlöth and Wol-Arumjök.

In large numbers the Malual Dinka people greatly reinforced the Ansars' fighting front in Kordofan. Like the Ngok Dinka of Kuol Arop Biong, the Malual fought shoulder to shoulder with the Mahdists Ansars and were responsible for the change of tide against the Turco-Egyptian forces in Kordofan. Sons of Giɛrnyaang, Twic and Ngok Dinka were among the fallen in those pitch battles of history between the Ansars and the Turco-Egyptian colonial forces. With the siege and final fall of Khartoum, it was a Giɛrnyaang combatant man who slew General Charles George Gordon at what is now Gordon's Rampart on the Army General HQ's Road in Khartoum. That famous and fateful moment of the day of the fall of Khartoum, a victorious moment of history which marked the beginning of the Mahdist state, was given meaning by Ngor-Makuel who himself slew Gordon.[182]

The beheading of the fallen governor-general was but a later act of the whole of the Ansars. The Giɛrnyaang wing of the Ansars was organised to launch attack on the governor-general Palace, the present republican palace through the military general headquarters, only to find Gordon fortified there, and after the fateful dislodging of that last stronghold of the Turco-Egyptian Army in Sudan, Gordon

---

182 Information obtained from an interview with Captain Mengisto Thiɛp Thiɛp of the SPLA Air Defence Unit in Yei. This interview was dated 22.11.2004. It was later confirmed by a number of Awiel community chiefs, among whom was Chief Aciɛn-Maluɛɛc and Karlo Ken Ken.

was swarmed and overcome by a fervent throng of Ansars with Ngor-Makuel Kuac on the pitch. Ngor powerfully lanced him in the chest.[183]

26 January 1885 was the day! Giɛrnyaang and Ngok were part of the Mahdist's *Black Flag Division* under direct command of Khalifa Abdullah. This division was largely manned by the Baggara, Dinka from the Malual, Ngok, Twic and most of the former slave traders of the Turkiyya were also conspicuously among its various units as commanders.

With the sudden death of the Mahdi on 22 June 1885, Khalifa Abdullah became the successor of the Mahdi as head of the Mahdist state. Under Khalifa Abdullah, slavery and slave trade was vigorously resumed in Southern Sudan and more so in the very Dinka lands from where the support had come. The Dinka Malual and Ngok support to the Mahdists revolution was immediately disowned by the Baggara. As such, large numbers of the Mahdists' followers from Giɛrnyaang and from Ngok therefore returned home from Omdurman and Khartoum to protect their people from Mahdists' slavery. The Dinka-Mahdists alliance therefore faltered and the Dinka country as well as the whole south revolted into a renewed pestilence of the century with the Masiriyya and the Rizzeigat Arab Baggara tribes of Southern Kordofan and southern Darfur now taking the lead. The Jaalyin, the Danagla, the Kababish and the Rufa'a Arab tribes rushed to the south in their multitudes!

Unquenchable stories of the great slave trader by the name of Abu-Mariam and many others in the Giɛrnyaang territory continue to be fresh to the present day. Giɛrnyaang wars with the Baggara slave traders were among the greatest feats for which the Giɛrnyaang Dinka people were very renowned in Bahr el Ghazal.

Famous still in the Awiel area of Giɛrnyaang are the *Battles of*

---

183   Ibid.

Adila on the Dhɛɛn road and the *Battle of Gelma* on the Kiir River area of Majök Anei Yɔɔr, now renamed by the Massiriya as Kuba. Great Wol Rɛɛc one day decided to mobilise Giɛrnyaang for an expedition into the Massiriya area of Adila in order to capture Zenuba, the dear wife of the dreaded Bushara's father who devastated the territory for so long. Lady Zenuba used to bear three triplets at once. A huge Giɛrnyaang expedition went against the Massiriya country at Adila. After the big devastation of Adila and its surrounding settlements, Zenuba was captured at the cost of a big death toll in an attempt to protect her from being taken as a war captive. Bushara himself was killed in that battle by Great Wol Rɛɛc. The woman was found pregnant and when she was killed and her stomach slit open, she was again found to be pregnant with three foetuses in the womb.

When Burma Nasir of the Baggara heard of this from Adhan Umar and from Dar Afat, he immediately set out to organise the Massiriyya, with whom he waged a retaliation expedition against the Giɛrnyaang territory of Gok-Machgar. Four days after the battle of Adila, Wol Rɛɛc and his party started to retreat. On the way Burma Nasir's forces attacked them. Wol Rɛɛc himself was caught, but Great Nyuol (Makuei), that is Nyuol Aturjöng, rescued him by stabbing that Massiri to death in the stomach. During the battle, Wol Rɛɛc's brother, Aköök-Mayäth, who was commanding the rear force of Giɛrnyaang, came under attack. In the ensuing battle Burma came face to face with Aköök-Mayäth and as they darted towards each other, Burma Nasir was caught by Aköök-Mayäth's spear! Taken to Egypt, Burma later died at Aswan hospital from Aköök-Mayäth's spear wound. The attacking force of the Massiriya was annihilated as such. Aköök-Mayäth's song marking this battle is still being sung in the areas of Awiel to the present day. It goes:

"Tɔŋ muk Aköök-Mayäth
Acie kɔl agumo!
Na wɛɛc Ajäwäk
Ke raan adɔŋpiny!
Atɛrda Ɣok Burma!
Adhɛŋ wäär jɔt taŋdië
Aŋot rac puöu!"

Translation:
"The spear possessed by Aköök-Mayäth
Is not dodged by just bending-head down
The way Burma did!
If it misses the horse,
Its rider will fall down!
Oh! My vendetta with Burma!
The man who carried my spear away,
Is still angry!"

Another decisive battle of history between Giɛrnyaang and the Baggara slave traders was the *Battle at Burual*, near Wanh-Aciɛɛn. It is also known locally as the *Battle of Abu-Mariam*. This Abu-Mariam was one of the strong men in the Zubayr's slave trade empire of Deim Zubayr. He was in fact the third man in power. Abu-Mariam in one of his slave raiding expeditions into Gömjuɛɛr territory in Awiel West made a surprise attack on Ricthieec village at dawn. He got hold of a village headman by the name of Wal-Adorjök Wal Aciɛn Anei and demanded that he be given 200 boys, 200 girls and 500 cows. Humiliatingly, Abu-Mariam had Wal-Adorjök tied to the tamarind tree which stood in the middle of the village while his force was on the rampage against the fleeing villagers. When Gomjuɛɛr regained momentum, Wal-Adorjök was rescued. Great Wol Rɛɛc who personally untied him from the tree was able to kill Abu-Mariam in a duel and the Giɛrnyaang people annihilated Abu-Mariam's force of slavers. 300 men who came with him were all liquidated.[184]

Another battle of historical significance between the Giɛrnyaang people of Wol Rɛɛc and the slavers from the Baggara Arabs was what Giɛrnyaang people regard as the *Revenge Battle of Bushara*, locally called *Tɔɔ Machar*. This was a combined Massiriyya and Bashbazuk revenge expedition to avenge the killing of Abu-Mariam and the annihilation of his slave force of Bashbazuk. When this all out expedition arrived in the village of Malou-Noon they were welcomed as if they were conquerors. Hero Wol Rɛɛc had gone to the eastern areas to mobilise the Abiem sections up to the Apuöth areas of Chief Makuac Kuol. Then Bushara and his expeditionary campaign proceeded to cover the whole of the Körɔɔk areas of Chief Aciɛn Yɔɔr to as far as Duluit and Atokthɔu.

On reaching Matuic village Bushara started his devastation. He plundered and ransacked Matuic and all of its surrounding villages and captured Nyibol Ayɔɔm, the old mother of Wol Rɛɛc. When Wol Rɛɛc returned from Abiem, he found his old mother taken into slavery with all his sisters and relatives. Wol therefore committed the area for a siren. He mobilised the Giɛrnyaang communities which he used in attacking Bushara's positions at the location which is present Kuba. Then Bushara and his Baggara forces of slave traders retreated to Adila, their native home.

By the time of Giɛrnyaang's arrival Adila was in a thicket of millet still un-harvested. Bushara's Massiriya went into the millet fields to hide but Wol Rɛɛc's people decided to set all the fields of Adila on fire to let them see themselves with the Massiriya fighters. In the engagement that followed the Massiriya were badly defeated, uprooted and Bushara was killed in action.

While greatly embittered by the Baggara Arabs since the

---

184   Ibid.

Turco-Egyptian time of Zubayr to this Mahdist Ansars' slavery, the Malual Giɛrnyaang Dinka stood their ground. Like the rest of the Dinka communities the Malual Dinka were so skilled, determined and united in defending themselves, although much of its populace was taken into slavery over the course of the sixty years of slave trade in the Dinka lands.

As can be seen from the above examples from Giɛrnyaang, the Dinka people in defence of their lands and properties were so retaliative and violent when they could not retreat into inaccessible forests or swamplands. Where slavers established zaribas or centres the Dinka would try to avoid being in contact with them, yet the entire Dinka land was ravaged, traversed and spoiled. The whole region of Bahr el Ghazal was in effect occupied by the slave traders. They exploited the territory for its ivory, rhino horns and humans in addition to cattle.

By 1860 Jaafar Mazhar, the Turco-Egyptian Hakimdar of Sudan in Khartoum, in a bid to commit the territories of Bahr el Ghazal to the Turco-Egyptian regular administration, decided to dispatch a small force and appointed a certain Nazir, Al Haj Mohammed al Hillali to come to rule Bahr el Ghazal on behalf of Khartoum. Al Hillali landed at Meshra port in the Northern Tonj area of Lou-Paher and Apuk-Padɔc, sailing all the way from Khartoum. However, he soon ran into a misunderstanding with Zubayr Wad Rahma Mansur, the most influential of all the slave traders who had a huge army in the area. In a battle in 1872 around present Wau town, Al Hillali's contingent was defeated by Zubayr's strong men under a certain Rabih. Al Hillali ran back to Khartoum through Meshra. Zubayr and the slave merchants with their armies therefore became fait accompli sovereigns over the entire Bahr el Ghazal. By 1873 Khedive Ismail, the viceroy of Egypt, announced a viceroyal firman, creating Bahr el Ghazal as a separate governorate out of Equitoria. That act by Egypt effectively confirmed the region as the slave traders' zone of their official influence where they could do all that they wanted.

During this slave trade era of more than six decades of abject pestilous turmoil over the Dinka lands, the slave trade merchants brought in guns in large quantities with which they trained an army known as the Bashbazuk which roamed and traversed almost all the corners of the Dinka lands, hunting for people to capture as slaves and for ivory and other valuable items of trade like rhinoceros horns and leopard skins. In time, as their activities intensified while more and more slave traders continued to come in their hundreds, some Dinka individuals and community leaders succumbed to the new foreign powers. The slavers locally recruited a network of collaborators whom they trained and finally posted as their agents. Those slavers' agents greatly deepened the communal ordeal. They amassed wealth and made names throughout that collaboration with slavers.

While the Turks came to Sudan initially as colonial authorities and later as slavers, they inhumanly opened asunder the traditionally invincible Dinka community, exposing them to a mad race of armed traders coming from the usual gateway of danger, the northern Sudan, through that collaboration with slavers.

Faced by the gun, a deadly weapon unmatched by their local traditional weapons of war (spears, clubs, shields), Dinka people for the first time in more than half a millennium were now made to falter at some corners, at least for the time being. The whole of the Dinka land was ravaged and the entire population made to stampede into inaccessible forests and bushes where families and kin made stockades for themselves and their livestock.

Dogs were not allowed to bark in the night! Rather, they were pegged along the slave traders' pathways, routes and interforest lanes during the night. Their work was to alert people in their hideout stockades about approaching slavers. For decades many did not cultivate as the entire society was on the run and villages were abandoned, especially those villages and areas along or near the slavers' routes. The stories of the slave trade era are still fresh among the Dinka communities to the present day.

Almost every family in Dinka land can talk of its persons killed or taken into slavery during that slave trade era. The family line of the author was almost brought to extinction had slave trade abolition policy not come with the Anglo-Egyptian condominium of 1898. The writer's grandfather (Aköök Gɛng), whose brothers were taken to slavery for good, was also captured into slavery during the latest years of the Mahdiya. He was one of the lucky slave captives to be emancipated by the coming of the Anglo-Egyptian reconquest of 1898. After emancipation he came back to restart the family line, which has now become a section after a century of social development.

In Bahr el Ghazal the Fertit tribesmen had been the most affected almost to extinction in contrast to the large Dinka communities in the region. As sedentary communities solely dependent on very little subsistence agriculture, they had no livestock to run with into the bushes like the Dinka. As such the Fertits easily broke up and yielded to the slavers. They were readily recruited and trained into the slavers' Bashbazuk armed units. Like the Burun and the Uduk in the Upper Nile, the Fertit tribal communities in western Bahr el Ghazal suffered near extinction. Strangely enough, they were moved against the Dinka to shoot, capture and loot. Some of them got associated as agents of those slavers in the Dinka lands. Acting as soldiers, their Arab commanders would march them with the word 'Dor!' meaning marsh or go. Unfortunate Dinka victims who were captured by them as slaves were chained in lines by their hands and feet. Two weighty long poles of wood were then placed on both shoulders, connecting a number of them in a single line. The Bashbazuk soldiers, carrying guns in front and behind would march them with the same word 'dor'. The Dinka people later associated the Fertits with this word and it was from there that the Dinka took the Fertit tribal communities as being Dor. The Fertits therefore came to be known throughout the Bahr el Ghazal Dinka lands as Dor and to the present day Dinka people also extended this name to all the non-Nilotic peoples in South Sudan.

SOME DINKA CHIEFS ARE DESCENDANTS OF SLAVE TRADERS' AGENTS

By the middle of the slave trade era some selfish individuals, even from among the landed gentries, joined this infamous business against their own community members, acting as agents for the slave merchants or as pointers, showing their people from their hideouts and at times leading the Bashbazuk forces or giving sanctuary to the slave traders in return for payments in ivory and looted cattle. Such people were given guns to protect themselves with and to use in the capture of their own people, and they therefore became partners in the trade. Several of them made wealth and names as they were also trained to be soldiers of the trade, and through their association with the slavers many of them learnt pidgin Arabic which in later years of the Anglo-Egyptian condominium period became an added incentive for them as they readily became translators between their respective communities and the new Anglo-Egyptian colonial authorities. The Egyptians would hear their pidgin Arabic and conveyed it to the English administrators. In this way communication was possible between the Dinka society and the condominium authorities. Arabic speaking Dinka former slave traders' agents also lent themselves as the best choice for positions of authority since they acted as the channels through which the condominium authorities were able to rule the Dinka.

Like the returning slave soldiers who came back from places such as Cairo and Khartoum after the emancipation of the slaves at the wake of the Anglo-Egyptian condominium period, most of those Dinka collaborators of the slave trade era are now the most prestigious and wealthy families and rulers in most of the Dinka lands. They acquired that wealth and the attending prestige or authority from that unpatriotic background. Dinka lands and history know them. All Southern Sudanese communities in Sudan know the role played by the collaborators during that slave trade era of Southern Sudan's greatest pestilence of the century. However, some Nilotic communities, especially the Dinka and the Nuers, who are cattle owning societies, were greatly supported by their cattle throughout the pestilent years, and as this was not the case with the Fertits, who could not run anywhere and who did not have livestock to support them, they became easy prey to the slavers. Fertit land was badly depopulated from the Wau area up to Raga in the far west.

Some of the Fertits who were not bound off to the slave markets in Egypt and to West African coastal cities headed for South and North America had either escaped to Zande lands to the south or had found themselves in the Dinka lands as Bashbazuk slave soldiers. Some of them were in the Zubayr army, fighting for the capture of Darfur. Until the early 1960s Dinka people in Bahr el Ghazal continued to harbour negative feelings against the Fertits due to that role they played during the slave trade era. Bahr el Ghazal Dinka people used to greatly abhor being called Jenge or Zenge but the Jallaba continued to call the Dinka people with those names until the Anglo-Egyptian reconquest of the Sudan in 1898, which came and stopped slavery and slave trade in the whole of the Nile valley for good. The new colonial masters who replaced the Turks and the Mahdists introduced yet another new name, Dinka, for Jaang society.

While the Mahdists in central and Northern Bahr el Ghazal, including Ngok, were in their full scale war with the Dinka, the eastern Bahr el Ghazal Dinka up to the Bor areas in the southern Upper Nile were also in a state of warfare with the Mahdists as was the case with the Baria in Central Equatoria. Among the Bor Dinka community were those Mahdist slavers such as Omar Salih and Urabi Dafallah who were stationed in the area and were raiding the Bor Dinka for their cattle and grain. Their activities enraged the Bor Dinka who rose and annihilated an Ansar party that was engaged in looting the community. In retaliation the Ansars made a counter raid into Bor villages and captured the chiefs, whom they killed. They, however, brought some to their station in Bor for interrogation before they were to be also killed. One chief, Riak Wai, survived this disaster because he pretended to be a Muslim. He requested to be allowed to pray before he was killed. When he was allowed he began to recite the name of *Allah*. Chief Riak had a friend among the Ansars. That friend is given as Jad al-Rab who, seeing his friend facing imminent death, approached him secretly to inform Riak that he had no way to physically intervene on his behalf but promised to work behind the scenes for his release. Jad al-Rab secretly taught his friend the elementary forms of Islamic worship. He asked him to recite '*Allahu Akbar*' and to make ablutions before praying to Allah while facing the east. He gave him a sibah (rosary) to pray with. If he did as he was told, Jad al-Rab told his friend, there would be a chance for his release. Chief Riak promised to do his best without revealing the source from which he received that religious tuition.

When the turn for him to be killed came he was led to the guillotine where the other chiefs were executed before him. Chief Loc Deng of the Thɔny section and Chief Deng Athou of the Palek section were among the already executed chiefs. Riak's turn came as the last chief to be led to the guillotine, but at that very critical moment Chief Riak requested a prayer mat and water to wash his hands, face and feet. When those things were brought Riak washed and then stood up facing the east, his hands raised heavenwards and loudly shouted '*Allahu Akbar*'. The Ansars, amazed, asked him where he learnt that way of worship. He replied that it was God who told him. The Ansars thus took him for a Muslim and they freed him. He became the only chief who escaped death. Riak and his people later attributed that luck to '*Allahu Akbar*', which they took as their luck divinity, *yath* in Dinka.[185]

---

185 Lazarrus Leek Mawut, 'Dinka resistance to the condominium rule 1902-1932', Unpublished Monograph No.3, Graduate College, K.U.P (1983), p.8.

In a separate development, the Dinka people in Northern Tonj and Apuk people of Eastern Gogrial waged a concerted attack on the Bundiir slave traders' centre in 1896. They succeeded in uprooting the last of the Ansars' stronghold in the area, but that attack was done at a heavy cost of lives, especially to the non-Apuk-Padɔc people like the Kɔngöör, Lou-Ariik, Awan-Parek and Apuk-pathuɔn people. The Ansars at Bundiir were massacred although a number of them escaped to Meshra port where they caught up with the last slaves' ship, *Tawafikia*, which rushed them off for Khartoum never to return. The slave captives at this Bundiir stockade were freed as were those at the Ahɛrdit slave headquarters of Lual Ngor, two years earlier.

The Dinka tirade of uprising against the Mahdists in Bahr el Ghazal, as it was in Equatoria and Bor lands in the Upper Nile, was now on its highest peak at the time when the Anglo-Egyptians and the world anti-slavery movement from Britain and the rest of the western world were pressuring for the collapse of the Mahdists state in Sudan.

It was a relief to the Dinka when in 1898 the Mahdists state collapsed, following Kitchener's last battles at Kareri, the fall of Omdurman and Khartoum and the final killing of Khalifa Abdullah, the Mahdists head of state, and the whole of his cabinet and the rest of the system's dignitaries at Um-Dubeycrat in El Obeid. The fall of the Mahdist state marked the end of the slave traders' menace, confiscation of properties and all the brutalities that ravaged Dinka land for more than six decades. The nearly two centuries (1821-2011) of strained north-south relations in Sudan had its roots from that slave trade era. The Southern Sudanese call for a separate nationhood was not for nothing.

THE ANGLO-EGYPTIAN ERA AND THE DINKA (1898-1956)

The Anglo-Egyptian authorities later substituted the names Jenge and Zenge with a new name, Dinka, although Northern Sudanese continued to use the name Jenge for Jaang people. This continued into the 1960s. Their use of these names carried a derogatory connotation as an apparent reminder of the infamous slave trade era. The Dinka people, who for ages were not used to abuse by other communities, did not like being reminded of that obnoxious era, the era during which time their superiority complex nature of the ancient and Middle Ages was rudely checked by guns and the people of the brown race in unison with the whites and the Fertits in Bahr el Ghazal doing the job for the outsiders.

In spite of the use of such abhorrent names for the then invincible Dinka by the slavers and the Baria people in Equatoria, the Nilotic communities in Upper Nile and in Bahr el Ghazal continued to know and call the Dinka, not as Jenge or Zenge, but as Jaang. The Luo of Bahr el Ghazal call them Jur-col and even know the Jaang as *Ujango*. Those are the names by which they have continued to know the Jaang from ancient times to the present day. How the name Dinka came about has been discussed under the 'Evolution of the Dinka names across the ages' in chapter two above.

ABOLITION OF THE SLAVE TRADE IN DINKA LANDS

The Anglo-Egyptian condominium era, though it was yet another colonial extension with all its exploitation, was viewed by many Dinka people as the era that abolished slavery and slave trade and drove the Arabs away from Southern Sudan until 1956 when Egypt, in support of its Muslim north, compelled Great Britain to hand over the south to the Arabs of Sudan, who continued up to 2011 with their political and cultural colonialism and exploitation. Although the Dinka were at variance with the British, the British laid the first rudiment of infrastructure in Southern Sudan. The present worn out roads throughout the south were done during the British 'closed districts' policy period when the British found the south had real historical grievances against the Islamic north and, above all, when they found Southern Sudanese people as being purely non-Arabs and non-Muslims. They also found the two parts of Sudan naturally divided geographically, the north being arid and desert while the south is naturally imbued with vegetation and sure annual rainfall as well as rich and abundant wildlife.

Besides stopping slavery and the slave trade the British introduced regular administration in the south and stopped many epidemic diseases like cholera and smallpox as well as cattle diseases. The British colonial time witnessed the introduction of Christianity and education into the south, and although there were pockets of British excesses during their pacification period which led to what appears to have been the Dinka natives' resistance to the condominium rule, there was generally a long period of peace, of recuperation and stability in the three southern provinces that the condominium created, until 1956 when the British handed Southern Sudan over to the Arabs and violence started to come back in the most usual way, violence which led to the first seventeen years war of 1955–1972 and again from 1983–2005. Although the Dinka are generally repellent to foreign rule, they did not welcome British departure that ushered Arab internal colonialism that lasted from 1956 to 8 July 2011.

BIBLIOGRAPHY

Several hundreds of the elderly Dinka and other Nilotic peoples in South Sudan were interviewed in the course of my two decades of research work across South Sudan. Those people were in their seventies, eighties and above. Apart from those elders interviewed in their rural countryside settings, several Dinka and other South Sudanese educated elites were either interviewed or made to give their written accounts through research questionnaires. A lot of reference books on the ancient history of Sudan, Southern Sudan, Africa and the rest of the ancient world were consulted in the course of the research. An exhaustive reading of the Biblical sources was also undertaken.

For the purpose of space, it was found convenient to select a sample of elders interviewed across the Dinka lands and a sample of very relevant books and internet materials consulted. I have also found it convenient to divide all my sources into (1) interviews and taped records about the Dinka, (2) published and (3) unpublished sources, and (4) journals and periodicals.

(1) INTERVIEWS

Jök Dau Kacuol, paramount elder and Gok County judge. Interviewed dated 8.5.2002 in Cuɛibɛt town

Awad Kueeth, a Ngok Dinka elder interviewed dated 5.12.2001

General Mark Nyipuoc, a Luo educated elder, interviewed dated 8.9.2001 in Rumbek

Chief Aciɛn Aciɛn Yoor (Aciɛn-Maluɛɛc) and Sub-chief Deng Ngueel, both from Malual Dinka. They were interviewed dated 12.12.2004

Lt. Col. P. Omuot, an Anyuak Luo intellectual interviewed 24.8.2003

A/Cdr NyongDeng Nyong, an elderly intellectual from Abialang Dinka in Renk. Interviewed dated 20.8.2003

Chief Chol Akol Aduol from the Thɔny area in Tonj South county. Interviewed dated 6.12.2007

Chief Chol Chan Manyang, chief of the Ajak Lɛɛr area in Tonj North county. Interviewed dated 4.2.1999

Old man Mabuoc Makuok Majok, an elderly man who was in his nineties at the time of interview. He is from the Jur-Lian area of Awan in Tonj North. Interviewed dated 22.9.1999

Chief Malek Mathok Malek of Apuk-Juwiir, Tonj South county. Interviewed dated 5.12.2001 in Thiet

Chief Akot Makuac Akot, chief of the Apuk-Juwiir section of Mangeng. Interviewed dated 6.12.2001 in Thiet

Lual Liai Maduot, an elderly man from the Jur-Bol section of Awan, a noted chronicler, interviewed at Tharakon village dated 8.2.1999

Old man Akook Madut Akook, an adept chronicler and a Spear Master from the Jur-Bol section of Awan interviewed dated 2.2.1999. He was in his nineties at the time of interview

Old man Kuot Maduot Machar, an old paramount Spear Master from Awan and who at the time of interview was over a hundred years in December 1999. Interviewed dated 3.2.1999

Chief Malek Akuiɛn Luɛth of the Aliai section of Apuk-Juwiir in Tonj South. Interviewed dated 6.12.2001 in Thiet

Elder Anyuc Madut Dhaal from Apuk -Padoc in Tonj North county. Interviewed at Rual village dated 15.1.2000

Elder Dok Akook Macok, a paramount Spear Master and deputy executive chief of the Apuk-Liil section of Padoc. Interviewed dated 15.1.2000

Chief Dut Paduol Mayen of the Adueet and Adokthök sections of Apuk -Padoc. Interviewed dated 20.1.2000

Rual Akuiɛn Akorou, an elderly man from the Ruaal group in the Apuk-Juwiir area of Aliai in Thiet. Interviewed dated 16.2.2002 in his home of Mayom-Abun

Elder Gotbai Mayik Wiɛk, an old man who at the time of interview was in his nineties. He is from the Ruaal group in the Apuk-Jur Wiir area of Aliai. Interviewed dated 16.6.2002 at his home, Mayom-Abun

Machar Madut Mayen, member of Apuk -Padoc Regional court. Interviewed at Akop dated 17.2.2003

Jok Aweer Jok, an old man from the Parum (Ruaal) group from Apuk-Juwiir. Interviewed dated 18.6.2002 in Thiet

Deng Mading Mijak, a Ngok Dinka intellectual from Abyei. Interviewed 2004

Cdr John Lat Zakaria, interviewed in Cuɛibɛt while he was the commissioner of his Cuɛibɛt county in 2003

Elder Madit Athuai Deng from the Twic Dinka of Warrap. Interviewed dated 10.5.2002

Sub-chief Gai Alɛɛng Mayen from the Aulian section in Northern Bor. Interviewed dated 27.12.2003

Elder Luka Ngor Arou Ayiom from the Padhieu clan in the Nyang area, Tonj North county. Interviewed with a group of Padhieu elders dated 9.6.2002

Paramount chief John Gaijang Awuol from the Paweny Dinka of Atar in Upper Nile-Jonglei state. Interviewed dated 27.11.2004

Mayiik Jau Kuol, an SPLA officer from Pan-Ru Dinka. Interviewed dated 27.11.2004

Elder Yool Deng Yool, interviewed among many other old men in Luacjang in Tonj East, dated 27.3.2004

Victor Bol Duop Bap, an intellectual from Luacjang community. Interviewed dated 13.12.2004

Chief Duom Akuei Awan from Bor South interviewed dated 24.9.2004

Elderly intellectual Isaac Kon Anok from the Aliap Dinka. Interviewed dated 10.12.2004

Chief Yusuf Ngor Deng Ngor of the Abialang Dinka. Interviewed with other chiefs of Abialang in Renk in December 1990

Old man Anyuon Gol Mayen of the Redior clan. He was over a hundred years at the time of the interview in Rumbek. He was interviewed in the presence of elderly members of his Paan-Macot family

Elder Santino Deng Teeng, interviewed in Wau, December 1993. He was a former federal minister in the Aboud regime. He was in his eighties at the time of interview. He was an adept oral historian. His tape records about the origin of the Dinka people are kept by Sudan National Archives in Khartoum to the present day

Elder Agook Bangocooth Gaak, from the Gok Dinka. Interviewed dated 10.5.2002

Elderly bard Akook Mariël from the Kongoor area, Tonj North county. Interviewed dated 5.2.1999. This old man contributed greatly to the story of the Jaang migration from the Upper Nile to Bahr el Ghazal in 1340 AD and he made a great feat in recalling Jaang genealogies from Garang to Noi

Gok Dinka elders: Riak Majak from the Pajul Clan, Matheet Nguɛnjang from the Pateny clan, Agot Anyuon Mabor from the

Pathoth clan were interviewed collectively at Abiriu rural town dated 18.5.2002

John Cawuop, a Ciec Dinka intellectual, interviewed dated 18.9.2003

Old man Manyang Jook, paramount leader (Spear Master and court president) of the Adoor section of the Ciec Dinka. Interviewed dated 20.12. 2003

Chief Kon Arou of Abuok. Interviewed at his home in Abuok 18.1.1996

Charles Kuek Wek, Akop Payam court president. He told the story of Ukokdit, who was a cannibal from the Palual clan where he comes from. He also contributed on Jaang genealogy

Captain Mengisto Thiɛp Thiɛp of the SPLA, a native from the Malual Dinka. Interviewed dated 22.11.2004 in Yei

Chief Nyal Chan Nyal, chief of the Awan Chan area in Gogrial West county. Interviewed with many elders from both Awan Pajok and Awan Chan. Interviewed dated 17.3.2010 at Akon town

Chief Amɛt Kuol Amɛt, chief of the Kuac-Agor area in Gogrial West county. Interviewed with a group of chiefs and elders of Kuac dated 30.2.2005

Chief Mou-Ageer Mou Akɛɛn, chief of the Buoth-Anyith section of the Aguok community. Interviewed with his community elders at his village dated 26.9.2008

Kook Ring Ariik, an SPLA officer who is adept on the story of the Patɛk

Elder Moses Majok Manyiel, old man Nekamia Ater Toric, old man Ezikiel Macuɛi Kodi, old man Marial Buoot, all interviewed in Rumbek December 2003

Sultan Dut Malual Arop, community leader of the Agar Dinka. Interviewed in Rumbek, December 2003

Arop Dau Goc, elder from the Pan-Ru Dinka. Interviewed dated 20.6.2010

Nazir Lat Kecnaar of the Palei section of Pan-Ru. Interviewed dated 6.3.2007

Chief Manyiel Lieny Wol of the Gak section of Pakam. Interviewed dated 8.12.2002

Chief Magon Dalkoc of the Manuɛr section of Pakam. Interviewed dated 10.12.2002

Chief Madol Mathok Agoldɛr and Chief Der Makuer Gol, both of the Amothnhom area of the Kuei section of Agar. Interviewed in Rumbek dated 15.7.2004

Old man Tong Mayai, interviewed in Rumbek dated 12.6.2004

Chief Maker Abol Kuyiok of the Joth area of the Rup section of Agar. Interviewed dated 17.7.2004

Chief Marol Majok Dɛrdɛr of the Ciɛny section of Aliamtooc(2). Interviewed dated 22.10.2004

Chief Mangar Marial Banyook of the Duor-Bar section of Aliamtooc(2). Interviewed 22.10.2004

Chief Mayak Biling of the Duor-Cek section of Aliamtooc(2). Interviewed dated 22.10.2004

Chief Mataba Yoro of the Jur-Belle tribe. Interviewed in Ulu town dated 18.12.2003

Chief Cholic Malual Arop of the Nyuɛi-machar section of the Duor area. Interviewed dated 22.10.2004

Paramount Chief Cikom Ayiɛi Cikom of the Yar area in Tonj South. Interviewed in Mabior-Yar dated 12.11.1999

Old man Akorou Aleu, Spear Master and member of Thiet regional court. Interviewed at Yinhgiir in the Muok Akot Wut area, dated 15.11.1999

Chief Maker Nginypiu Machar of the Buot section of the Thɔny area in Tonj South county. Interviewed in Tonj town dated 16.3.2009

Chief Kuel Bangnyang Madhok of the Waat section of Thɔny. Interviewed dated 16.3.2009 at Ayigak village

Gaudensio Madoor Maluac Dut, payam judge for Thiet Payam. Interviewed dated 7.12.2000 in Thiet town

Chief Yoor Lual of Ajuong Malong Yoor in Awiel East. Interviewed dated 18.2.2000

Old Sub-chief Ayueel Makɛɛc of the Malony section of Apuk-Jur Wiir. Interviewed dated 7.12.1996

Deng Cok Arop Dok, Patɛk man from the Paliepiny section of Lou-Ariik. Interviewed in Lou dated 10.1.2003

Elderly Karlo Ken Ken of the Duluit area in the Abiem territory of Aweil East county. Interviewed dated 12.12.2004

Paramount court president Acuil-Gerdit from the Nyang-Akoch area and of Padhieu clan. Interviewed dated 9/6/2002

Mel Manyang of the Pabuor clan Apuk-Juwiir, interviewed 6 July 2002

(74)   *Chief Mangar Nhial Kon from the Aliap Dinka. Interviewed 12.9.2004*

(75)   *Makuok Akot Majok of the Padolmuot clan in the Jur-Lian section of the Awan area. He took his accounts from his uncle Makuok-Awendit who was a known chronicler in the area.*

(2) PUBLISHED SOURCES

G. Lienhardt, 'Divinity and experience: The religion of the Dinka', (Oxford 1960).

Abdel Rahim, M. 'Imperialism and nationalism in the Sudan', (Oxford 1966).

Ali, A.I.M, 'The British, the slave trade and slavery in the Sudan', 1820-1887, (Khartoum 1972).

Arkell, A.J, 'Early Khartoum', (Oxford 1949).

Arkell, A.J, 'A history of the Sudan up to 1821', (London 1961).

Collins, R.O, 'The Southern Sudan', 1883-1898 (Yale 1962).

Collins, R.O, (ed.), 'Problems in African history', (New Jersey 1968).

Collins, R.O, 'Land beyond the rivers: the Southern Sudan 1898-1918', (Yale 1971).

Evans Pritchard, E.E , 'The Nuer', (Oxford 1940).

Holt, P.M, 'A modern history of the Sudan', 3rd edn, 2nd impression, (London 1972).

Jackson, H.C, 'Behind the modern Sudan', (New York 1955).

Murdock, G.P., 'Africa: Its peoples and their culture history', (New York 1959).

Ogot, B.A., 'History of the southern Luo, Vol. 1: migration and settlement', 1500-1900 (Nairobi 1967).

Seligman, C G, 'Pagan tribes of the Nilotic Sudan', (London 1932).

Seligman C G, 'Races of Africa', 4th edn. (London 1966).

Wingate, F R, 'Mahdism and the Egyptian Sudan', 2nd edn., (London 1968).

Deng F M, 'Dynamics of identification', (Khartoum 1973).

Crazzolora, J P, 'The Lwoo: Part I, Lwoo migrations', Verona 1950).

Basil Davidson. 'The growth of African civilisations, east and central Africa to the late 19th century', (Longman Groups Ltd.).

JA Kapiyo & A. Owino, 'The evolving world, a history and government course', Form I secondary, (O.U.P) (Kenya 1996).

David Crystal, 'The geological time scale', (in) 'The Cambridge Encyclopaedia', 4th edn., C.U.P (London 2000).

Y. Fadl Hassan; 'The Arabs and the Sudan', Edinburgh University press, (London 1967).

K. Okeny, 'The political history of Southern Sudan', (in) 'The role of Southern Sudanese people in the development of modern Sudan', K.U.P (1986).

Stanley Burstein, (ed.) by Markus Wiener, 'Kush and Axum, ancient African civilisations', (1998).

FM Deng, 'Africans of the two worlds, the Dinka in Afro-Arab Sudan', (London) Ithica press, (1978).

Hamilton ,JA, 'The Anglo-Egyptian Sudan from within', (London 1935).

Marc R. Nikkel, 'Dinka Christianity', (2001).

FM Deng, ' Tradition and modernization: a challenge for law among the Dinka of the Sudan', 3rd edn., (Michigan 2004).

Derek A. Welsby, 'The kingdom of Kush: Napata and Meroitic empires', ed. by Markus Weiner, (1998).

Walter A. Elwell, 'Evangelical commentary on the Bible', Baker books, (USA 1989).

Helen C.M., 'Sudan: A country study', Washington DC, Federal Research Division of the Library of Congress,(1991).

R. Werner & colleagues, 'Day of devastation, Day of contentment, the history of the Sudanese church across 2000 years', Paulines Publications Africa, Kolbe Press, Nairobi, Kenya, (2000).

S. Wilson, 'The Ethiopian valley. The history of the people called the Dinka', (1908).

Herodotus, 'The histories', Vol. III C.450 BC (in) ancient history source book: Accounts of Meroe, Kush and Axum, (430-550 BC).

Steve Forbes & John Prevas, 'Power, ambition, glory', Crown Business, (USA 2009).

A.J. Achile, 'The history of the Nile valley to the lakes', Edinburgh,(London.1936).

Yusuf Fadl Hassan 'Southern Sudanese and their neighbours before the colonial era', (in) 'The role of Southern Sudanese in the building of modern Sudan', K.U.P,(1989).

Andrew Nam Odero,'Sudan, livelihood characterisation of Southern Sudan: the use of physiographic and agro climatic layers',(2007).

The holy Bible: Deut. Ch.2:4 for the description of Esau's descendants in the region of Mt Seir.

Dr. FM Deng, 'Abyei: the ambivalent north-south border', (Washington DC. 1999).

Douglas H. Johnson: 'Conflict area: Abyei', a summary and elaboration of points raised in the presentation and discussion on Abyei, KCB Management Centre, (Karen 2003).

William Chancellor, 'The destruction of black civilisation', USA, (Chicago 1997).

Equatorial epidemics, (in) 'The medical journal', Vol. III, Egypt, (Cairo 1340).

Creation tips, answers on evolution, creation science, genesis and the Bible (internet).

R.H. Charles, 'Life of Adam and Eve', from the Apocrypha and Pseudepigrapha of the Old Testament: Claredon Press, (London 1913).

EG Ban, 'From the Garden of Eden to the flood', (in) 'The patriarchs', (2000).

David Rohl, 'Genesis and the flowers of Horus'. A transcript of a lecture given on 3 September 1997 at Millstadt Forum under 'What is truth? Man between fantasy and reality'.

Colbourn Rushton, 'The origin of civilised societies', Princeton University Press, (1968).

Henry M. Morris, 'The confusion of tongues', (in) 'The Tower of Babel', by James Montgomery's 'Voice on Nimrod and the Babel', (2004).

'The antediluvians', (in) The genesis file.

http://thegenesisfiles.com/category/antediluvian-world/

Lambert Dolphin, 'On the great flood of Noah', revised edn, (2004).

Barry Satterfield, 'Creation and catastrophe chronology', (1993).

'Population growth since creation' (internet).

Barry Wigmore, The hunt for Noah's Ark, (in) 'The Times', (London 2000).

Andrew Collins, 'Turkish tourist bureau', Cave towns & gorges of Cappadocia, (1997).

'Creation Magazines', (Sept. 1998).

Lambert Dolphin, 'The Tower of Babel and the confusion of languages', internet http//www.idol;hin.org/babel.html.

Abdel A'al A. Osman, 'Some misconceptions about Southern Sudanese', (in) The role of Southern Sudanese in the building of modern Sudan', K.U.P., (1989).

'Mediterranean sea geography' (in) Christmas 2006 www.1yachtua.com.

60. Aardsma Mark, 'Last update', (in) http://www.biblicalchronology.org/ ,

(20 November 2000).

Alenyo George William, 'The Luo: The black Jews of Africa', 2nd edn., Shalom Books Ltd., Nairobi, Kenya, (2009).

Basil Davidson, 'The blameless Ethiopians', (in) Africans in history, revised & expanded edition., Simon & Schuster Paperbacks, Rockefeller Centre, (New York 1991).

Rodney R. Baird, 'Nubia: geography', (2000).

Immanuel Velikovsky, 'Ages in chaos', (2006).

Paul Halsall, 'Ancient history source book: accounts of Meroe, Kush and Axum', 439-550 BC (1980).

Collin McEvedy, 'The Penguin atlas of African history revised edn, Penguin Books Ltd, (1995).

'Kush Kingdom at Napata', (in) 'New world encyclopaedia' http://www.newworldencyclopedia.org entry/Kingdom of Kush.

C.A. Willis, 'The cult of Deng', SNR, Vol XI (1928).

Ibrahim Bedri, 'Notes on Dinka religious beliefs in their hereditary chiefs and rain makers', SNR, Vol. XXII, (1939).

Ibrahim Bedri, 'More notes on the Padong Dinka', SNR, Vol. XXIX, (1948).

Kenneth Okeny, 'Political structures and institutions in Southern Sudan', (1820-1885), (in) 'the role of Southern Sudanese in the building of modern Sudan', K.U.P., (1989).

John Ryle, Warriors of the White Nile: The Dinka peoples of the wild series. Time–Life Book (Amsterdam), (1982).

The Amplified Bible (Gen. 27:V 1-46), Lockman Foundation, Zondervay, (1987).

G. Lienhardt, 'The myths of the Spear Master', (in) 'Divinity and experience: The religion of the Dinka', Oxford University press, (London 1961).

Serafino Wani Swaka, 'A troubled history of Southern Sudan struggle 1821-2011', (Juba 2009).

'The world book encyclopedia', (N-O) Vol. 14, USA (1973).

Mohd Fuad Shukry, 'The Khedive Ismail and slavery in the Sudan', Egypt, (Cairo 1938).

Richard Gray, 'A history of Southern Sudan 1838-1889', (Oxford 1961).

Santandrea S. 'A tribal history of the Western Bahr el Ghazal', Nigrizia, Boulogna, (1964).

G. Casati, 'Ten years in Equatoria and the return with Emin Pasha', (London 1891).

G. Scweitzer, 'The life and work of Emin Pasha', (West Minister 1898), Vol. I.

Adams Smith, 'Nubia: the corridor to Africa', USA, (1969).

W.H. Shea, 'Adam in Ancient Mesopotamian traditions', (1977).

Gordon Childe, 'Man makes himself', (NewYork 1983).

'The royal anthropological survey of the Nilotic peoples of the Sudan and Uganda', (1936).

G. Lienhardt, 'The Dinka of the Nile Basin', (1963).

Fr. Nebel, 'Dinka grammar', (1948).

Henderson, 'The Sudan', (1965).

Evans Pritchard, 'The Nuer', (1940).

Henderson, 'The making of modern Sudan', (1953).

Seligman, 'The Pagan tribes of the Nilotic Sudan', (1932).

Fabunni, 'The Sudan in Anglo-Egyptian relations', (1960).

Stubbs & Morrison, 'Land and agriculture of the western Dinka', (1938).

(3) UNPUBLISHED SOURCES

Lazarus Leek Mawut, 'Dinka resistance to condominium rule' 1902-1932, Monograph (3), Graduate College publications, K.U.P., (1983).

UNP, Upper Nile provincial files. These are Anglo-Egyptian colonial documents which are very informative on issues such as the Dinka-Nuer conflicts.

UNP, 1/6/41, 'Telegrams, Nuer raiding, 1928'.

UNP, 1/7/46, 'Nuer raiding reports, 1928'.

UNP, 1/44/328, 'Upper Nile annals, 1898-1948'.

Intel. 2/26/208, 'History of Eastern Bahr el Ghazal', undated.

(4) JOURNALS AND PERIODICALS

Arkell, A.J., 'Funj origins', SNR, Vol. XV, 1932.

Bedri J. 'Notes on Dinka religious beliefs in their hereditary chiefs and rain makers', SNR, Vol XXII, 1939.

Bedri J. More notes on the Padang Dinka, SNR, Vol. XXIX, (1948).

Casson, A.H, 'The Southern Sudan: then and now', Sudan Pamphlets, Vol. V.

Fergusson, V.H., 'The holy lake of the Dinka', SNR Vol. V. (1922).

Equatorial epidemics', (in) 'The medical journal', Vol. III, Egypt, (Cairo 1340).

'The Bahr el Ghazal Province', SNR, Vol. 10, (1927).

Henderson, 'Notes on the migration of the Missiriya tribe into south west Kordofan', Vol. 22, SNR, (1938).

O'Sullivan, 'Dinka law', Vol. 40, (in) 'Journal of the Royal anthropological institute', (1910).

www.ingramcontent.com/pod-product-compliance
Lightning Source LLC
Chambersburg PA
CBHW020829020526
44118CB00032B/254